D0083484

adopted broad themes so as to cast a wide net about a wide variety of scholars working within each of several major fields. Within these broad fields, however, the seminar chairmen have focused upon specific problems recommended either because they have received the greatest attention of Japanese specialists or because they seem most likely to contribute to a fuller understanding of the modernization of Japan. We trust, as a consequence, that the five volumes taken together will prove both representative of the current scholarship on Japan and comprehensive in their coverage of one of the most fascinating stories of national development in modern history.

Volume two of our series results from a seminar which took place at Estes Park, Colorado, in June of 1963. Present at the seminar were all of the authors whose papers appear in this volume except Martin S. Bronfenbrenner and Saburo Ōkita. A number of other scholars took part helpfully in the seminar, serving as discussants or discussion leaders. These were Wm. G. Beasley, School of Oriental and African Studies, University of London; Jerome B. Cohen, City University of New York; Ronald P. Dore, London School of Economics and Political Science; Leon Hollerman, Claremont Men's College; Marius B. Jansen, Princeton University; Hiroshi Mannari, Kansai Gakuin University; Donald H. Shively, Harvard University. Special thanks are due to Seymour Broadbridge of the School of Oriental and African Studies, University of London, who served as rapporteur of the seminar. The ultimate credit for a remarkably successful seminar and its resulting publication is due to William Lockwood for the care with which he selected and integrated the papers presented in this volume and for the perceptive introduction which he has written for this volume of proceedings.

John Whitney Hall

Contents

CONTENTS

The State
and Economic Enterprise
in Japan

ESSAYS IN THE POLITICAL
ECONOMY OF GROWTH

Edited by William W. Lockwood

CONTRIBUTORS

M. BRONFENBRENNER
E. SYDNEY CRAWCOUR
ALAN H. GLEASON
J. HIRSCHMEIER, S.V.D.
YASUZŌ HORIE
DAVID S. LANDES
SOLOMON B. LEVINE
W. W. LOCKWOOD

JAMES I. NAKAMURA
KAZUSHI OHKAWA
SABURO ŌKITA
HARRY T. OSHIMA
HUGH T. PATRICK
HENRY ROSOVSKY
ROBERT A. SCALAPINO
SHŪJIRŌ SAWADA

PRINCETON UNIVERSITY PRESS

PRINCETON, NEW JERSEY

ALBRIGHT COLLEGE LIBRARY

Copyright © 1965 by Princeton University Press

All rights reserved

L.C. Card 65-15386

ISBN 0-691-02162-7

First Princeton Paperback Printing, 1969

Second Princeton Paperback Printing, 1970

This book is sold subject to the condition that it shall not, by way of trade, be lent, resold, hired out, or otherwise disposed of without the publisher's consent, in any form of binding or cover other than that in which it is published.

Printed in the United States of America

by Princeton University Press, Princeton, New Jersey

330.952

L817s

173352

Foreword

Scholarly studies of Japan have had a remarkable growth in the United States and other English speaking countries since the end of World War II. To some extent this has been the natural result of the popular boom of interest in Japan stimulated by the war and its aftermath and by the increased opportunities which Westerners had to come in contact with the Japanese people. But it is more directly the result of the spread of academic programs devoted to Japan and particularly the growing number of specialists trained to handle the Japanese language.

In the fall of 1958 a group of scholars gathered at the University of Michigan to seek some means of bringing together in more systematic fashion the results of the widely scattered studies of Japan which had appeared in the years since the end of the war. The Conference on Modern Japan which resulted from this meeting was dedicated both to the pooling of recent scholarly findings and to the possibility of stimulating new ideas and approaches to the study of Japan. Subsequently the Conference received a generous grant from the Ford Foundation for the support of a series of five annual seminars devoted to as many aspects of the problem of Japan's modern development.

The Conference on Modern Japan exists as a special project of the Association for Asian Studies. The Conference is guided by an executive committee consisting of: Ronald P. Dore, Marius B. Jansen, William W. Lockwood, Donald H. Shively, Robert E.

Ward, and John W. Hall (chairman). Each member of the executive committee is responsible for the organization of a separate seminar devoted to his particular field of specialization and for the publication of the proceedings of his seminar.

Although the subject of modernization *in the abstract* is not of primary concern to the Conference, conceptual problems are inevitably of interest to the entire series of seminars. Because of this, two less formal discussions on the theory of modernization have also been planned as part of the Conference's program. The first of these was held in Japan during the summer of 1960 and has been reported on as part of the first volume of published proceedings. The second will seek at the conclusion of our series to review whatever contributions to the realm of theory the five substantive seminars may have made.

The present volume edited by William W. Lockwood is the second in a series of five to be published by the Princeton University Press for the Conference on Modern Japan. The other four volumes, of which the first has already been published, are:

Changing Japanese Attitudes Toward Modernization, edited by Marius B. Jansen.

Social Change in Modern Japan, edited by Ronald P. Dore.

Political Development in Modern Japan, edited by Robert E. Ward.

Tradition and Modernization in Japanese Culture, edited by Donald H. Shively.

As their titles suggest, the annual seminars have

THE STATE
AND ECONOMIC ENTERPRISE
IN JAPAN

This is the second in a series of five volumes to be published by Princeton University Press for The Conference on Modern Japan of the Association for Asian Studies. The others in the series are:

Changing Japanese Attitudes Toward Modernization, edited by Marius B. Jansen

Aspects of Social Change in Modern Japan, edited by R. P. Dore

Political Development in Modern Japan, edited by Robert E. Ward

Tradition and Modernization in Japanese Culture, edited by Donald H. Shively (*in preparation*)

Dilemmas of Growth in Prewar Japan, edited by James Morley (*in preparation*)

THE STATE
AND ECONOMIC ENTERPRISE
IN JAPAN

Prospectus and Summary

WILLIAM W. LOCKWOOD

IN THIS VOLUME sixteen students of modern Japan take a fresh look at her rapid economic modernization since 1868. Particularly they address themselves to the question how and why the Japanese have developed over the past century what *The Economist* calls "the world's most extraordinary growth economy."

To search out the secrets of Japan's growth is to inquire, above all, into her patterns of economic enterprise, public and private. It is a study of historical opportunities on the one hand and of human responses on the other. Japan has not lacked opportunity since she entered the modern world, but her uniqueness lies in the vigor of her response, i.e., in the interplay of initiatives that have energized her industrialization from the beginning. The essays published here reveal these initiatives at work in various sectors of growth and in response to emerging national needs and personal opportunities over four or five generations.

The first half of the volume centers in the Meiji Era, 1868-1911, when the foundations of modern industrial society and the modern state were being laid. The second half concentrates on Japan since World War II, when once more the forces of growth have reappeared in such explosive strength as to suggest a second industrial revolution. The era that lay in between—Taishō and early Shōwa—comes into view where its developments grow out of earlier events or where they form the background of the postwar scene. But Japan between the wars really deserves a second volume to explore more adequately those complex interactions of rising industrialism and emergent imperialism that culminated in the disaster of the Pacific War.

From this book spanning a century of modern Japanese history one gains a sense of the essential continuity in the process by which Japan has transformed herself from a remote agrarian kingdom into the world's third or fourth largest industrial power. Persisting goals of national development and personal advance evoke recurrent patterns of thought and action amid changing circumstance. The sustained momentum of growth is striking, even more than the bursts of speed. A pragmatic instrumentalism in leadership and a resilient, cohesive response from the people are evident in the initial decades after 1868, and no less in today's resurgence from war and defeat.

The approaching centenary of the Meiji Restoration seems an appropriate time thus to take stock, backward and forward. Japan's modern history offers clues to her own future and also to the future of other nations now entering the path of modernization.

On the Eve of Modernization

Looking back to pre-Meiji Japan first of all, one sees latent impulses and capacities for the transformation that was soon to set in. By pre-industrial norms, Japan's economy was already fairly productive by the mid-nineteenth century, and slowly expanding. Other potentials for modern economic growth lay in particular institutional characteristics: a high level of education, much of it practical in bent; an economy already rather commercialized and responsive to market stimuli; a low propensity to consume among the common people; and a tradition of government participation in industry, directed primarily toward growth of output and not merely the control of a rising merchant class.

Such factors as these, argues Sydney Crawcour in his opening essay on "The Tokugawa Heritage," made Japan respond vigorously to the new stimuli and opportunities that followed the arrival of Commodore Perry. Meanwhile, cohesion and stability amid far-reaching change were assisted by still other factors of social inheritance: strong national consciousness, peasant industry, and hierarchical structures of social solidarity carried over from feudalism. When a new forward-looking elite seized power after 1868, they were able to join these

4

capacities for change and for order in a sustained drive to modernization.

Phases of Modern Economic Growth

Like most modernizing nations, Japan first had to pass through a transitional era in which political authority was consolidated to provide the architectural framework for national development. This period of administrative experiment (and financial disorder) ended with fiscal-monetary reforms of the eighties. Now commenced that sustained growth in output accompanied by changes in industrial technology and economic structure that we know as the Industrial Revolution.

Successive phases of this historic process are sketched broadly by Ohkawa Kazushi[1] and Henry Rosovsky in "Century of Economic Growth" (Ch. II). They are related to spurts and retardations in the growth of national product as follows:

First Phase: In the early decades national economic growth was achieved mainly within the traditional sectors, notably agriculture. The momentum attained here by modest but pervasive innovations in technique during the early decades provided in turn the resources and stimuli to sustain the rise of industrial, trading and financial enterprise in the modern sectors on an increasing scale.

Second Phase: Beginning about 1905, the forces of expansion came to center more and more in the modern enclave that meanwhile had been building its capabilities in home and foreign markets. Complex structural problems now appear in the differential progress of the traditional and modern sectors; in particular, a widening gap appears in technical advance, productivity, and wages. It contributed to the economic dislocations of the twenties and thirties and perhaps also to the political disorders that eventuated in World War II.

Third Phase: With the wreckage of war cleared away by 1952, Japan broke into a new surge of growth, powered by

[1] Except in the Table of Contents, chapter headings, and List of Contributors all Japanese names are given in the Japanese manner with surname first.

extraordinarily high levels of investment and productivity gains. Her progress in the next decade, steadily diminishing the dualism of traditionalism and modernity, took her another long step down the road to economic maturity. A world economic power of upper middle rank today, she looks forward to continued expansion in the sixties, though perhaps at a less headlong pace.

Parallels with Europe

In its transitional stages Japan's Industrial Revolution offers absorbing analogies and contrasts with the experience of other nations, East and West. Its relevance for non-Western societies embarking on modernization is of particular interest. In many respects, however, it links most closely with the earlier history of Europe, especially Germany. A specialist in European history, David Landes surveys these relations with fresh perspective in "Japan and Europe: Contrasts in Industrialization" (Ch. III). He finds major differences, of course; yet the resemblances to Germany particularly are striking—e.g., the long period of gestation, the role of defensive nationalism, the step-by-step reforms of conservative leaders in pursuit of limited objectives, and the paternalism of the State in its close relationship with a rising business class. By implication these European parallels only heighten many contrasts between Japan's development patterns and those of most modernizing societies today.

Sources of Business Entrepreneurship

The drive toward industrialization required vigorous and pragmatic initiatives across a broad front in order to pioneer new modes of technology and mobilize increasing resources for the tasks of development. Initially Japan drew on capital, skills, and values already present in Japanese society—not inconsiderable as noted earlier. Then as time went on new resources were generated in the development process itself. Political initiatives dominated at first, as the Meiji reformers set about to consolidate the authority of the new regime at home and to fend off threats from abroad. From the outset, however, the means to political strength were seen to be economic in considerable degree. The State itself did not hesitate to pioneer new systems of banking and factory production and modern transport. Equally it lost no time in turning to the private sector for participation and support, extending various aids and encouragements to the formation of a modern business class.

While much has been written about the State's industrial pioneering, less is known about the origin and development of private entrepreneurship in the modern sector. Hesitantly but with gathering force new clusters of capitalists began to emerge in modern banks and industries. Horie Yasuzō describes their appearance in textiles, electrical apparatus, shipbuilding, foreign trade, and other sectors (Ch. IV). Mostly these men came from modest economic backgrounds; wealth, talent and position did not form a single pyramid. All had a good deal of education, however. In family origin many were ex-samurai, while others were commoners, mainly townsmen and farmers of the wealthier class.

Most striking of all was Shibusawa Eiichi, the great Meiji business leader who is the subject of Johannes Hirschmeier's portrait (Ch. V). He bridged the old and new. Of commoner birth, he entered Tokugawa service as a young man and was made a samurai. Originally anti-Western, he became an ardent modernizer. First an official, he soon left the government to become Japan's foremost business enterpriser. With his pragmatic bent, his public ardor, his faith in education, and his genius as a promoter, he campaigned tirelessly to legitimate the new business order. More than any other single person, Shibusawa made the modern business man respectable, through his moralistic Confucian stress on public responsibility.

Role of Agriculture

The Ohkawa-Rosovsky framework of historical sequences (Ch. II), with its stress on agriculture as the primary sector of growth before 1905, poses complex questions of analysis. For one thing it rests on estimates of farm production hitherto widely accepted but now questioned by James Nakamura in his essay on "The Growth of Japanese Agriculture 1875-1920" (Ch. VI). After close scrutiny of data on yields and acreage Nakamura concludes that such estimates as those of Professor Ohkawa in *The Growth Rate of the Japanese Economy* (Tokyo, 1957) greatly exaggerate the growth of agriculture by understating output levels in the early Meiji years. His own corrections lower his estimated range of growth rates to 0.8-1.2 percent a year from 1875 to 1920—hardly half the rate employed in the Ohkawa-Rosovsky analysis. On this fundamental point, therefore, Nakamura calls for modification of prevailing views, and to add to uncertainty Harry Oshima reminds us (p. 355) how scanty is the evidence in support of production estimates for manufacturing and the service trades as well during the early decades.

The non-specialist can only reserve judgment on these historical issues until the experts reach some consensus. He will be impressed with the need for more fundamental research as he follows the debate over the evidence or lack of evidence that lies back of existing estimates. Some revision may well be in order, as Professors Ohkawa and Rosovsky themselves recognize (p. 69). Yet it may not be of such magnitude as to invalidate substantially most of the historical interpretations offered in various chapters of this volume. Some of them it will even reinforce; for example, if Japan's income and wealth are found to be larger in 1868 than hitherto believed, this will only underscore her potentials for modern economic growth as set forth by Crawcour, Landes, and others. Moreover, a modest downward revision of growth rates in agriculture before 1920 would hardly impair the argument that sustained progress in farming and other indigenous trades accounted for much of the scale of Japan's development during the Meiji era.

If such agricultural progress was indeed a decisive force in the early decades of modernization, whence came the stimuli and resources for this achievement? In particular, how could it have been possible without more drastic changes in the small family farm, or the structure of village authority, or the industrial bias of the government? No other aspect of the Japanese record deserves closer study by statesmen and planners anxious to develop other non-Western nations today and seeking non-revolutionary means to move the tradition-bound village off dead center.

Sawada Shūjirō and Harry Oshima discuss this process of agricultural modernization in Chapters VII and VIII. Technical innovation, says the former, was closely geared to the availability of cheap labor and the persistence of the small peasant proprietor. On the initiative of the more substantial farmers, aided by the government, productivity advanced steadily over two generations. Various economic and institutional factors became increasingly restrictive after 1910, however, and breakthroughs to a new level were delayed until the reforms that followed World War II.

The contribution of the State to Japanese agricultural progress has long been a matter of controversy. New light is thrown on its fiscal aspects by Harry Oshima's painstaking tabulation of Meiji government expenditures, central and local. Clearly the direct flow of funds into agricultural improvements was comparatively slight, while tax policy also hardly favored the farmer. Few will dissent from the conclusion that other Asian governments in pursuit of development and welfare today would do well to spend more on agriculture; in particular, Oshima stresses the contradiction between military spending and agricultural progress in Japan. On the other hand, many administrative and developmental activities of Meiji governments benefited the farmer indirectly if not directly, e.g., education, highways, public order. This could be said even of the pursuit of industrialization as ultimately the road to national power and well-being.

Fruits of Economic Progress

Another essential aspect of Japan's economic progress has been the rise in consumption per capita. Nothing has been more important for the expansion of home markets and diffusion of entrepreneurial incentives on the one hand or the political stabilization of a new order on the other. Yet this rise has been little documented in statistical terms. Alan H. Gleason's essay on "Economic Growth and Consumption in

Japan" (Ch. IX) is a pioneering effort. Consumer gains per capita, he finds, just about kept pace with GNP per capita from 1887 to 1925, despite military spending and investment. This seems to have held true for the countryside as well as for the city; consumption rises with productivity. During the interwar period, further gains were interrupted by the Great Depression, the military spending of the thirties, and finally the deprivations of World War II. Recovery since 1952, however, has once again raised the material level of life in Japan to a point 50 percent above the prewar level, or perhaps one-fifth of the present American standard.

Japan's experience thus verifies that the Industrial Revolution can transform the life of the common man, East as well as West, and raise him from abject poverty to at least the lower reaches of the Affluent Society. Equally it is plain that the achievement took three quarters of a century—a long, long time in the impatient perspectives of today—and was attended by grievous miscalculations and setbacks.

Political Economy of Japan's "New Capitalism"

The remarkable surge of practical energies that marks Japan's comeback since World War II has earned for this era the title of "the second Industrial Revolution." It deserves close examination, not only for its transformation of Japanese society but for its testing of policies and attitudes in the political economy of growth which have wide relevance elsewhere.

The springs of high-pitched growth, doubling national income per capita in the years 1954-63, are outlined by William W. Lockwood and others in the concluding section of this volume (Chs. X-XV) as follows:

1. a political framework of security and optimism at home, and of opportunity abroad;
2. a massive infusion of new industrial technology from the West, correcting Japan's lag of the previous twenty years;
3. a rapid rise in the number of industrial workers and

their productivity, outdistancing wage increases despite large advances there as well;

4. a crescendo of investment, public and private, reaching 32 percent of GNP during 1956-60 and matched by non-inflationary savings of like proportions; and

5. a threefold growth of exports, as Japanese goods re-entered markets all over the world

—all this under the aegis of a postwar political and business elite once again blending state and private initiative in an explosive burst of economic enterprise.

More technically, Martin Bronfenbrenner identifies the path of postwar growth as conforming to the Harrod-Domar model—an unstable upward equilibrium, in which increasing supply capacities created by high-level investment on the one hand are balanced by increasing demands generated on the other (Ch. XI). Short cycles of three or four years' duration have marked the course of expansion but without any prolonged period of retrenchment as yet. Hugh Patrick expertly surveys these short swings over the decade 1952-61 in his analysis of "Cyclical Instability and Fiscal-Monetary Policy" (Ch. XII). He concludes that the upper turning points are set by bottlenecks in industry and foreign trade, while the lower turning points appear with declines in inventories, correctives to monetary policy and the drain of foreign reserves, and the revival of business optimism fortified by the government's buoyant forecasts.

Will the Boom Continue?

The question arises, then, whether this postwar boom will subside after fourteen years or more, in the manner of prewar booms, or whether it can sustain its momentum through the sixties.

Several constraints need to be borne in mind:

1. *Foreign Trade.* One major area of policy initiatives is overseas trade, where the government's Long Range Economic Plan for 1961-70 requires that imports and exports grow at 9-10 percent a year. Through 1964 Japan met little

difficulty in financing her import needs, now much reduced in proportion to national income by comparison with pre-war days. Clearly she has a special stake in close relations with the high-growth areas of the developed world. Her liberalization of trade controls and her efforts to consolidate ties with Europe and the Americas are a recognition of this fact. (See below, pp. 475-87.)

2. *Labor and Wages.* A second potential constraint on future growth lies in the labor market. The wage-productivity gap of the fifties began closing in the sixties. Moreover, the decline in population growth will soon begin to whittle away yearly gains in the labor force. As sketched by Solomon B. Levine (ch. XIV), Japan's labor market has long been compartmentalized by political, social, and technical forces, and dominated by the seniority principle in job security and wage differentials. Various "escape hatches" have thus far permitted these practices to survive without undue damage to productivity or incentives. If growth is to continue, however, it imposes requirements of rising labor efficiency that may force a change in these long-standing conventions of the job market and trade union practice.

3. *Regional Disparities.* Rising levels of output and welfare also require more positive efforts to reduce income and opportunity differentials among major regions of Japan and to effect a more mobile pooling of resources on a national basis. In particular the tremendous congestion of metropolitan areas, notably Tokyo, and the lagging progress of the more remote rural prefectures are grossly inefficient, as well as inequitable. Ōkita Saburo presents in Chapter XIII a brief sketch of the government's first steps at planned regional development, in which he has himself been a pioneer. Evidently a larger effort will be required to arrest Japan's historic drift to industrial concentration.

4. *Business Organization and Behavior.* A fourth cluster of policy issues concerns industrial structure and market behavior. Lockwood's account of business enterprise and public policy ("Sponsored Capitalism: Postwar Model," pp.

487ff.) sketches the debate precipitated by import liberaliza-tion over the structure of Japan's new industrial order, with its blend of sharp business rivalries on the one hand and pervasive collusion (often government-sponsored) on the other. One problem is the excessive fragmentation of indus-tries into competing units, in contrast with the great com-bines of an earlier day. Another is the constant threat of over-capacity growing out of the competitive scramble for position, inviting a cumulative downturn in the whole econ-omy if consumption, investment, and exports no longer sustain profits at an attractive level.

Looking to the future, Bronfenbrenner voices optimism, seeing escape from these constraints in various policies of "guidance" open to the ministries. Patrick likewise sees no necessary halt to the upward climb, though he identifies the balance of payments as a restraining factor that will continue to bring on periodic setbacks. Ohkawa and Rosovsky con-cede, too, that these avenues to high-pitched growth remain open; but they doubt that the average pace of expansion will continue at 9 percent even if it remains well above the 4 per-cent average of prewar decades. A secular advance of 6-7 percent annually might well be preferable, in any event, for it would lessen the social costs of rapid change and permit badly needed investments in amenities such as public parks and housing.

Economic Enterprise and Political Democracy

Ultimately, Japan's postwar social order can endure only as success validates her experiment in constitutional democ-racy. Reestablished under the Occupation, parliamentary gov-ernment has operated with considerable stability, thanks in good measure to unprecedented economic progress. Expand-ing economic opportunity in a new atmosphere of social equal-ity is building popular stakes in its survival. Industrial prog-ress is also creating more pluralistic, competitive structures of power through which people can better express their choices in political life.

Still on trial no doubt, Japan's parliamentary order seems slowly to be legitimating itself through its identification with prosperity and peace. On the Right, where political power still resides, one sees a steady advance toward the norms of the welfare state (pp. 510ff.). On the Left, too, is a drift to the center, as portrayed by Robert A. Scalapino in his essay on "Labor and Politics" (Ch. XV). Labor's aim has been turning slowly away from class revolution toward the pursuit of power through parliamentary action. As these trends continue, they gradually create a society that is post-capitalist and post-Marxist, markedly liberal in its values, and Japanized only as a reaction against mechanical imports from the West.

In this political realm, no less than in continued economic growth, the world environment remains crucial.

PART ONE

The Eve of Modernization

CHAPTER I

The Tokugawa Heritage

E. SYDNEY CRAWCOUR

JAPAN'S modern economic growth was long regarded as almost a miracle. The development of a backward, feudal Asian country into a modern industrial nation within a few decades seemed to defy rational explanation. If it no longer seems so miraculous, this is partly because we have now come to understand that Japan a century ago was less backward and less feudal than was once thought. Moreover, many aspects of present-day Japan—her value systems, intellectual activity, human relationships, even material aspects of life—often have more in common with Japan of a century ago than with the advanced industrial countries of today. The process of Japan's modern economic growth has now been analyzed in considerable detail; we can follow it almost year by year. In short we now know a great deal about what happened. We know far less about why it happened.

Why did Japan become one of the first follower countries in modern economic growth? Why was her reaction to outside pressures different from that of other Asian countries? Why did the Meiji Restoration take place? Why did the output of agriculture and traditional industry expand so rapidly after the Restoration? There were differences in exogenous factors which might help to explain the success of Japan's modern economic growth; for example, the particular time at which she was introduced to Western industrial capitalism may have been significant. It seems very likely, however, that much of the explanation must be sought in the nature of her traditional economy—the soil in which economic growth took place.

Considering the amount of study that has been devoted to the economy of pre-modern Japan, and considering that modernization began less than a century ago, it is remarkable how little agreement there is about the nature of her traditional economy. Argument persists, for example, as to whether agriculture a century ago was predominantly semi-serf subsistence agriculture or commercial farming. This may be due partly to wide regional differences and the absence of national data. More fundamentally, however, it stems from Japanese preoccupation with a variety of theoretical constructs of what the traditional economy should have been like rather than what it really was, and to a tendency among scholars to pay more attention to form than to content.

The political system of late Tokugawa Japan did not provide a very promising background for economic development. The Tokugawa government (*bakufu*), while ultimately responsible for the government of the whole nation, had direct access to only about a quarter of its sources of tax revenue. The remainder of the country was divided into nearly three hundred semi-autonomous units (*han*) administered by lords known as *daimyō*. The finances of the central government, which had long been rather precarious, were clearly inadequate for the defense of Japan against threats from overseas. By 1850 the need for political change was generally appreciated. The initiative, however, came not from the rather rigid central government, but from its opponents among the larger south-western daimiates, and the revolutionary flavor thus imparted to the movement for reform gave it more momentum than it would otherwise have had. There was agreement on the need to strengthen the country militarily and economically, and in particular to strengthen the fiscal base of administration, but no unanimity on how this was to be achieved.

The traditional attitude toward economic, especially commercial, development was to restrict it within channels where it could be prevented from upsetting the political and social status quo. It is quite clear that economic developments were pressing against these restrictions and that the need for some changes of economic policy was becoming more and more clearly appreciated. Nevertheless, no distinctive new policies emerged until after the Restoration; perhaps no such decisions were possible until after the changes which the Restoration brought. Thus the development of the traditional economy did not lead directly into modern economic growth. But it did make it possible to implement the decision to modernize once that decision was made.

This essay does not give a full picture of the traditional economy as it was, nor does it discuss its evolutionary trends or its response to particular events such as the opening of foreign trade. Attention is directed mainly to such aspects as seem relevant to the broad process of modernization and especially to the role of the State. The 1860's are taken as a period in which the traditional economy was very little influenced by modern economic forces. For many purposes it would be adequate to select the 1870's or even the 1880's as still representing the traditional economy. Moreover the choice of the 1860's could be objected to on the grounds that this was a decade of political and social dislocation in which the traditional economy was not functioning normally. A period before the Restoration is chosen, however, because the Restoration and the changes which followed modified the traditional society and economy to such an extent that these changes might mask important aspects of the traditional system. While the 1860's may not have been "normal," it is neither practicable nor desirable to go back further. Information—scanty enough in any case—becomes harder to find as we go back in time, and the rate of change even in the traditional economy seemed significant enough to make it advisable to take a period as near the end of the Tokugawa era as possible.

First we shall attempt rough estimates of certain quantitative aspects of the economy. It would be a mistake to regard these as anything better than informed guesses. They will nevertheless be usable for certain purposes, especially as they give some bearings on the productive levels already achieved by the Japanese. Since economic development begins with the response of a traditional society to certain stimuli, we may go on to some aspects of the pre-modern Japanese society that made it particularly responsive in this way.

Aspects of National Income in the 1860's

PRODUCTION AND INCOME

Although scarcely a century has elapsed since the traditional Japanese economy first began to be modified by the impact of the Western industrial system, it is not easy to reconstruct in quantitative terms what it was really like. Some idea of the level and structure of production in pre-modern Japan, however, is essential. This not only gives a point of departure for the measurement of later economic development, it also provides data for the study of the relationship between initial income levels and the process of economic growth in general. Very likely initial income levels are not as important a determinant of economic progress as was once thought, but this can only be judged on the basis of more facts than we now have. Such data are particularly needed for Japan, as it has appeared to be an exception to the general observation that initial income levels in the countries which have achieved significant economic growth were considerably higher than levels in most underdeveloped countries today.

The earliest national income figures available for Japan are those for 1878 in the series computed with great skill and care by Professor Ohkawa Kazushi and his colleagues at the Institute of Economic Research of Hitotsubashi University. (See below, Ch. II.) On the reasonable assumption that modern economic development did not begin in Japan before 1878, figures for the years 1878 to 1880 should provide a satisfactory base for the measurement of economic growth. The changes in the two decades before 1878 were, however, at least significant enough to have had a substantial bearing on the subsequent process of growth, even though not themselves "modern" economic development.

Data for the 1860's are quite inadequate to make a computation of national income at all comparable in accuracy with Ohkawa's post-1878 figures. Even the early years of Ohkawa's series (Table 1) show annual growth rates which seem rather implausible; there appears to be a *prima facie* case for raising his 1878 figures. This does not mean, how-

TABLE 1

Net National Income Produced, 1878-1880
(millions of current yen)

	Primary	Secondary	Tertiary	Total
1878	248 (100)	34 (100)	119 (100)	401 (100)
1879	397 (139)	60 (153)	154 (112)	611 (132)
1880	536 (157)	72 (153)	191 (117)	799 (144)
1878-80	av. 394 (132)	55 (135)	155 (110)	605 (125)
	65%	9%	26%	100%

Source: Ohkawa Kazushi, et al., *The Growth Rate of the Japanese Economy since 1878* (Tokyo, 1957). Figures in brackets are index numbers of income produced in constant 1928-32 prices.

ever, that we must remain completely in the dark, and in Table 2 are assembled certain income estimates that prove informative.

TABLE 2

National Income Produced in the 1860's
(1878-80 average prices)

		Million Yen	Percent of Total
Primary industry		236–259	60–64
Agriculture	210–230		
Forestry	18–20		
Fisheries	8–9		
Secondary industry		40–45	10–12
Tertiary industry		107–114	26–29
Total		383–418	100

A brief description of how these figures were derived will serve to emphasize how rough and ready they are.

Agriculture. Production figures for four major crops were estimated for the 1860's and valued at 1878-80 prices as follows:

		Output at 1878-80 prices (mill. yen)
Rice	(21 million *koku** at ¥7.6 per *koku*)	160.0
Soybeans	(1.8 million *koku* at ¥ 4.27 per *koku*)	7.7
Coarse Grains	(About 20% more than soybeans)	9.2
Raw Cotton	(70 million catties at ¥ 0.1 per catty)	7.0
Total Gross Value of Production of four crops		184.0

* 1 *koku* = 4.96 bushels; 1 catty = 1.32 lbs.

These four crops make up 73 percent of the gross value of agricultural production according to the 1874 *Bussanhyō*.[1] If we assume that their rate of growth was a little lower than the average for all crops, they might have been about 75 percent of the total in the 1860's. This would make the gross value of agricultural production about 245 million yen at average 1878-80 prices. The net income ratio was probably higher in the 1860's than in the 1880's, let us say about 90 percent. The net value of agricultural output would then be about 220 million yen. A fairly realistic range might be 210-230 million yen.

Forestry. The gross value of forestry production from the 1874 *Bussanhyō* was converted to 1878-80 prices using inflators derived from the *Kahei seido chōsakai* Tokyo price series.[2]

	Value of Output 1874 (mill. yen)	Price Ratio 1878-80/1874	1874 Output at 1878-80 prices (mill. yen)
Lumber	2.362	1.231	2.908
Firewood	6.042	1.567	9.468
Charcoal	2.273	1.503	3.416
Other	3.889	1.500 approx.	5.834
Total Forestry	14.566		21.626

This does not include forest products used locally as fertilizer; nor does the coverage in general seem as complete for

[1] "Meiji 7-nen fuken bussanhyō" [Prefectural Production Tables for 1874], in *Meiji zenki sangyō hattatsu shi shiryō* [Materials on the Development of Industry in the Early Meiji Period] (Tokyo, 1959), I.

[2] Tōyō keizai shimpō sha [Oriental Economist], ed., *Meiji Taishō kokusei sōran* [Compendium of Economic Statistics of the Meiji and Taishō Periods] (Tokyo, 1927), pp. 347-51.

1874 as in estimates for 1878-80. Perhaps the figure should be raised to about 25 million yen. If we assume a very high net income ratio of about 90 percent, income produced would be about 22 million yen in 1874. As some increase probably occurred between the 1860's and 1874, income produced in the 1860's might have been around 20 million yen. This is about one-tenth of agricultural production, a proportion which is very stable for the decade after 1878.

Fisheries. The 1874 *Bussanhyō* figure for gross fisheries output is raised by a factor of 1.1 (derived from the *Kahei seido chōsakai* series) to convert values to 1878-80 prices. This gives 7.7 million yen for gross production value, a sum that seems far too low in comparison with Ohkawa's figures for 1878-80. Perhaps it should be nearer 10 million yen. Since the amount is relatively small anyway, it is probably safe to conclude that fisheries income produced in the 1860's was about 8-9 million yen at 1878-80 prices.

Secondary industry. The gross value of industrial production for 1874 came to about 130 million yen at 1878-80 prices according to the *Bussanhyō*. A net income ratio of about one-third seems to be constant in many countries at various stages of development. The reason for this may be that in countries more advanced industrially the greater degree of processing is offset by a higher proportion of intermediate products. In late Tokugawa Japan raw material and fuel costs represented about 73 percent of gross output value in the brewing industry;[3] about 65 percent in the Ashikaga silk-weaving industry;[4] 70 percent in the Hachiōji silk-weaving industry;[5] 45 percent in the Nagano silk-reeling industry;[6] and perhaps about 55-60

---

[3] Nagakura Tamotsu, "Nada no sake" [The Rice Wine of Nada] in Chihō shi kenkyū kyōgikai, ed., *Nihon sangyō shi taikei* [Industrial History of Japan Series] (Tokyo, 1959-60), VI, 199.

[4] Waseda daigaku keizai shi gakkai, ed., *Ashikaga orimono shi* [History of the Textiles of Ashikaga] (Ashikaga, 1960), I, 266, 628.

[5] Shōda Kenichirō, "Hachiōji shūhen no orimono, seishi" [Weaving and Silk-reeling in the Hachiōji District], *Nihon sangyō shi taikei*, cited, IV, 145.

[6] About 4 *kamme* (1 kamme = 8.27 lbs.) of cocoons yielded 1 *kamme* of raw silk. Nagano prices are taken from the 1874 *Bussanhyō*.

23

173352

ALBRIGHT COLLEGE LIBRARY

percent in the cotton-weaving industry. These products account for about 75 percent of the *Bussanhyō* total value of industrial production. The remainder (ceramics, lacquer-ware, etc.) probably had a lower raw material content. On the average, fuel and raw materials may have absorbed about 60 percent of total cost, giving a net income ratio of about 40 percent. Using this ratio (Y. Yamada's ratio[7] of 60 percent for domestic industry seems quite unrealistic) we get a figure of 52 million yen for output produced in 1874. This does not include mining, for which the *Bussanhyō* indicates a gross value of about 3.2 million yen, or about 2.8 million yen in terms of net output. The net output of all secondary industry in 1874 might thus be around 55 million yen at 1878-80 prices. This is the same in real terms as Ohkawa's 1878-80 average.

It should be noted that the coverage of intermediate industrial products in the *Bussanhyō* is indeterminate, and is certainly not complete, so that both the average net income ratio and the net income produced are equally uncertain. About all we can say of industrial net output in the 1860's is that it was probably a good deal less than 55 million yen, perhaps around 40-45 million yen, or about 10-12 percent of the national income produced. This is the ratio of net value added in secondary industry to national income produced (at 1878-80) prices. It in no way conflicts with the statement by Rosovsky and Ohkawa (below, p. 55) that gross value of manufacturing output amounted to about 30 percent of the gross value of commodity production according to the 1874 *Bussanhyō*. "Commodity production" as used by them does not include the output of tertiary industry which is included in "national income produced." Moreover, since the net income ratio is

[7] Yamada, Y., *Nihon kokumin shotoku suikei shiryō* [A Comprehensive Survey of National Income Data in Japan] (Tokyo, 1951), p. 48. Yamada bases his figure on the 1930 Cabinet Bureau of Statistics survey of household industries which yielded a net value ratio of 55%. By 1930, however, most of the industries in which raw materials were a large part of the total cost had passed out of household industry into factory industry, leaving the sort of handicrafts in which raw material cost is unusually low.

lower in secondary industry than in primary, the choice of a gross or net basis also affects the percentages.

Tertiary industry. The sectoral distribution of the population in the 1860's is said to have been something like the following:

Primary industry	80%
Secondary industry	4%
Tertiary industry	9%
Samurai	7%

The division between population engaged in primary and secondary industry is certainly unrealistic, since very many farmers devoted some part of their time to industrial pursuits; but the proportion in tertiary industry may be near enough. Since incomes in tertiary industry seem to have been well above the average, we might allow about 15-18 percent of national income for producers classified here. To this something must be added for tertiary output produced by persons classified as being in the primary or secondary sectors. This might bring the proportion up to say 23-26 percent. Some credit must also be given to the samurai class for contributing to tertiary production. We might therefore raise the percentage of national income contributed by the tertiary sector to, say, 26-29 percent. The proportion is a little higher than in 1878-80.

Even the wide range of 383-418 million yen for national income produced in the sixties (Table 2) may not be wide enough to cover the enormous possibilities for error. Nevertheless, if used with circumspection these figures can still form the basis for some general statements.

National income per head (at 1878-80 prices) was about 13-14 yen in the 1860's, taking Japan's population as about 30 millions. This is considerably lower than the corresponding figure of 17 yen per head for 1878-80. When it comes to comparing these levels with those of underdeveloped countries today, or with pre-industrial income levels in the older industrial countries, the task is practically hopeless. It is not even possible to express such figures in present-day prices. One estimate would put 1860's national income per head at about 16,000 yen in 1952 prices. If we use the price of rice as an index, we get about 1.6 *koku* per head, or about 25,500 yen at the 1952 price. But the index problem over so long a period seems insuperable. In the currency of the 1860's, income per head was about 1.8 *ryō*, and one has the impression that this was quite a respectable amount in those days. Observations made by European visitors to Japan in these early days are of some interest. Sir Rutherford Alcock had this to say about standards of living in Kanagawa in 1859, before the Restoration: "The evidence of plenty, or a sufficiency at least, everywhere meets the eye; cottages and farm-houses are rarely seen out of repair—in pleasant contrast to China where everything is going to decay. . . . The men and women, now they take to their clothing, are well and comfortably clad —even the children. . . . There is no sign of starvation or penury in the midst of the population—if little room for the indulgence of luxury or the display of wealth."[8] At Mishima he observed, ". . . the impression is irresistibly borne in upon the mind, that Europe cannot show a happier or better-fed peasantry."[9]

Conditions were not quite so good in Hakodate, and in Kyūshū even worse, though Alcock observed, "If the villages looked poor, and the peasant's home (bare of furniture at all times) more than usually void of comfort, yet all the people looked as if they had not only a roof to cover them, but rice to eat, which is more than can always be said of our populations in Europe."[10]

Townsend Harris in 1857 observed of the people of Kawasaki, "They are all fat, well clad and happy looking, but there is an equal absence of any appearance of wealth or of poverty."[11] And of the population of Edo he remarked, "The

[8] Sir Rutherford Alcock, *The Capital of the Tycoon* (London, 1863), I, 300.

[9] *Ibid.*, I, 432.

[10] *Ibid.*, II, 73.

[11] Townsend Harris, *The Complete Journal of Townsend Harris* (New York, 1930), 428.

people all appeared clean, well clad and well fed; indeed I have never seen a case of squalid misery since I have been in Japan."[12]

W. E. Griffis, on the other hand, who spent much of his time in Fukui some years later, was impressed with "the utter poverty and wretchedness of the people and the country of Japan."[13] He was "amazed at the utter poverty of the people, the contemptible houses, and the tumble-down look of the city as compared with the trim dwellings of an American town."[14]

Could the Restoration really have brought such a reduction of living standards? Or were these regional differences? Or is the divergence of opinion due to different expectations or temperaments of the observers, or to the fact that the Japanese took more care to make a favorable impression on diplomats than on school teachers? On the whole one suspects that attempts to compare income per head in the 1860's in Japan with that in England in 1700 or in Latin American countries today are probably futile. Other indicators, such as savings ratios and Engel coefficients would be more comparable and possibly more relevant, could they be computed.

Although our national income figures involve some assumptions about rates of growth, it still seems legitimate to compare them with figures for 1878-80. The estimate of Table 2 is an average for the decade 1860-70. All we can say about the rate of growth within this decade is that it was probably positive, and we will assume that the average falls about 1865. There is a considerable gap between this total of about 400 million yen (in 1878-80 prices) and Ohkawa's 1878-80 average of about 600 million yen (Table 1). Even making generous allowance for error, a rather substantial growth of output evidently occurred over the intervening decade or so. It would be going too far to guess what the annual rate of growth may have been between 1865 and 1878-80, but it is safe to say that, although lower than the rates achieved in

---

[12] *Ibid.*, 441.
[13] W. E. Griffis, *The Mikado's Empire* (New York, 1876), p. 415.
[14] *Ibid.*, 430.

the decades after 1880, it was substantially higher than the average annual rate for the two preceding centuries. We can hardly assume that output per head rose by much more than 150 percent during the Tokugawa period, since anything more would imply levels of income in the early part of the period so low as to be implausible. This means that average annual growth during the Tokugawa era could scarcely have been much more than a half of 1 percent. Compared to this the growth between the 1860's and 1878 appears striking. Since the modern sector was negligible at this time, this means a substantial rise in the output of the traditional economy, particularly of agriculture.

Conceivably the low figures for the 1860's represent a fall from a higher level in the 1850's, for the 1860's were characterized by bad agricultural seasons, natural calamities, and the general dislocation that attended the Restoration and its stormy prélude. On the other hand, the growth of foreign trade did provide some new stimulus. What the quantitative effect of all this was is indeterminate. The rate of growth in the 1860's cannot have been so very low, however, since this would imply progress from 1869 to 1878 too fast to be credible. The quickening of growth in the 1860's should certainly not be regarded as a "take-off"; even the growth of traditional production after the Restoration was "pre-modern" in that it involved no radical innovations in technology. But the traditional economy was stirring in the 1860's; it was pressing against official restriction; and it responded quickly to opportunities for increased production once those restrictions were removed. Such developments were vital because they supported the construction of a modern industrial sector when modern economic growth did get under way.

Economic development before 1878 thus seems to have been indigenous in the sense that the potential for it lay within the traditional economy. At the same time it came largely as a response to political changes and the stimulus of foreign trade. This *responsiveness* of the traditional economy is of some importance and we shall return to it later.

SAVINGS AND CONSUMPTION

If national income estimates for the 1860's are dubious, any attempt to estimate capital formation or capital/income ratios would be foolhardy. Again, however, we can get some idea of at least the potential margin for saving. One indicator of this is the proportion of production taken in taxes and other government revenue.

Taxation is the best documented aspect of the pre-modern Japanese economy. Since the bulk of tax revenue is recorded in terms of rice, we can value this at the 1878-80 average price of 7.6 yen per *koku* to get a figure comparable to our national income figures, assuming changes in rice prices roughly paralleled changes in the general price level.

TABLE 3

ANNUAL FEUDAL REVENUES AT THE END OF THE TOKUGAWA PERIOD

	(million *koku* of rice)
Han (1865-70 av.)	10.39
Hatamoto (1857)	1.27
Bakufu (ordinary, 1857-59 av.)	1.06
Bakufu (extraordinary, 1857-59 av.)	0.70
Imperial court, shrines and temples (1867)	0.19
	13.61
Less contributions by *han* to *bakufu*	0.1
Total feudal revenue	13.51

At 7.6 yen per *koku* the total revenue = 103 million yen.

These figures were derived in the following way:

Han. The revenue for the 280 *han* (feudal domains) included in *Hansei ichiran*[15] were totaled by each of nine regions. (The Shizuoka *han* was omitted as it was part of the *bakufu* domain for most of the 1860's and is included in the figures for the *bakufu*.) Each of these regional totals was then

[15] *Hansei ichiran* [Compendium of the Daimiates] (Tokyo: Nihon shiseki kyōkai series, 1928), 2 vols.

adjusted upwards by a factor consisting of total *omote-daka* (official ratable holdings) for the region divided by *omote-daka* for the region given in *Hansei ichiran*. This gave total revenue for all *han* in the region. The regional figures were then added. *Hansei ichiran* reports the bulk of revenues in *koku* of rice, and cash revenues are converted to rice in this source usually at the rate of 8 *ryō* = 1 *koku*. This seems a high price for rice, but the proportion of revenues converted in this way is not large, so no attempt is made here to vary the conversion factor.[16] Total revenues amount to 40 percent of total *kusadaka* (actual ratable holdings), which seems to be a reasonable proportion.

Hatamoto. Nihon zaisei keizai shiryō gives the income of *hatamoto* (direct Tokugawa vassals) "and below" for 1857 as 1,665,000 *koku* (X, 443). The same volume (501-670) indicates a figure for *hatamoto* of 1,266,000 *koku* for about the 1850's, assuming revenue was 40 percent of *rokudaka*.[17] On the same assumption another source[18] gives 1,338,000 *koku* for 1801. Although the 1857 figure specifically excludes salaries attached to particular offices (*kanroku*), it is taken here to include some 400,000 *koku* of stipends (*kirimai*) paid to retainers of the *bakufu* out of *bakufu* revenue. Therefore *hatamoto* incomes, from their sub-fiefs (*chigyōsho*) are put at 1.27 million *koku*.

Bakufu. Various figures are available for the revenue of the *bakufu* in the nineteenth century,[19] and all seem to be

16 The actual computations were done by Mr. Sasaki Yōtaro of the Institute of Industrial Economics of Keio University.

17 Ministry of Finance, ed., *Nihon zaisei keizai shiryō* [Historical Materials on Japanese Finance and Economics] X (Tokyo, 1923), 443, 501-670 (hereafter referred to as NZKS).

Retainers' stipends (*roku*) were expressed as *rokudaka* or the rated output of land on which the grantee was entitled to levy taxes. These taxes, usually about 40% of the rated output, became the grantee's income. In practice the grantee often simply received his stipend out of consolidated revenue in proportion to his *rokudaka*.

18 *Shoka nayori chō* [Roll of Hatamoto] in the possession of Keio University.

19 NZKS, X, 477-501; "Kahei hiroku" [A Secret Record of the Currency] in *Nihon keizai taiten* [Collected Japanese Economic Writ-

mutually inconsistent. The figures for 1857-59,[20] although lower than earlier series, seem reasonably complete. They are itemized and can be split into ordinary and extraordinary revenue. Converted at 1 *ryō* = 0.59 *koku* (the 1857-59 average price), they come to 1.06 million *koku* of ordinary revenue and 0.55 million *koku* of extraordinary revenue including profit on coinage. In the 1860's ordinary revenue was probably about the same, since attempts to raise the rate of agricultural taxes were generally unsuccessful.[21] Extraordinary revenue was probably greater, at least 0.7 million *koku*.

Imperial court, shrines, and temples. The *taka* (ratable holdings) of these institutions in 1864 is given at 473,113 *koku*.[22] Revenue estimated as 40 percent of this would be around 190,000 *koku*.

Converted to yen at the 1878-80 average rice price of 7.6 yen = 1 *koku*, total revenues thus amount to 103 million yen (Table 3), or about 25-27 percent of the national income in Table 2. This compares with total central and local government revenue in 1880 of 93 million yen,[23] which is only about 12 percent of Ohkawa's national income figure for that year. Making all allowances for the inaccuracy of the estimates, it seems safe to say that the proportion of national income made available to government bodies was considerably higher in the 1860's than it was in 1878-80, and a high proportion by any standards. Alcock surmised great regional variation in the weight of taxation in 1860. Of the Tōkai area he wrote, "It is impossible to traverse these well-cultivated valleys, and mark the happy, contented, and well-to-do looking popula-

---

ings] (Tokyo, 1928-30), XLV 169-70; NZKS, X, 436-53, 454-55, 457; *Suijin roku* [Dusty Tomes from the Past] in *Kaishū zenshū* [The Complete Works of Katsu Kaishū] (Tokyo, 1927), III-IV.

[20] NZKS, X, 454-55, 457.

[21] Ōyama Shikitarō, "Tenryō ni okeru bakumatsuki no denso zōchō" [Increases in agricultural taxes in the shogunal domain at the end of the Tokugawa period], *Keizai shi kenkyū*, xxxvii (1932), 85-107.

[22] NZKS, X, 456.

[23] *Meiji Taishō kokusei sōran*, 654, 657.

tions which have their home amidst so much plenty, and believe we see a land entirely tyrant-ridden, and impoverished by exactions."[24] In Kyūshū, on the other hand, "Whatever surplus there may be in the produce must be absorbed by the Daimios and their thousands of hungry retainers. . . . Judging by the general aspect of poverty, nothing but a bare sustenance of rice and vegetables can be left to the cultivators, with just enough over to buy the very homely and scanty vestments they habitually wear."[25] But he concluded, "Whatever may be the experience of the Japanese population in the way of taxation, I adhere to the idea that it is not of a very onerous or grinding character upon the whole."[26]

Assuming that production was not significantly dependent on expenditure by government bodies, the fact that such a high proportion of national income could be appropriated as feudal revenue, and most of it in agriculture, indicates a fairly productive economy with a high potential for saving. Moreover, in addition to taxation, large loans were raised by the *han* during the 1860's, and between 1868 and 1872 averaged at least 2-3 million yen a year.[27] Such a high proportion of national product available to government through taxation and other means in the traditional economy has an important bearing on the prominent role of government investment in modern Japan. The existence of a well-developed system of taxation in traditional Japan, through which the government had access to very large sources of funds not easily available to others, is an important reason for this high level of investment after 1868.

It might be thought that such heavy taxation would leave little possibility for private capital formation. However, this was clearly not the case. Even in agriculture, the most heavily taxed sector of the economy, improvements were being made

[24] Alcock, I, 432.

[25] *Ibid.*, II, 86.

[26] *Ibid.*, I, 450.

[27] *"Hansai shūroku"* [Collected Records of Han Debts] in *Meiji zenki zaisei keizai shiryō shūsei* [Collection of Early Meiji Financial and Economic Materials] edited by H. Ōuchi and T. Tsuchiya (Tokyo, 1931), IX, 139.

in the 1860's which involved new outlays of capital. The phenomenon of land being abandoned because of the insupportable burden of taxation seems to be more typical of an earlier period than of the 1860's. Individual farmers were accumulating substantial sums which they invested in industry and commerce as well as in agriculture. Prosperous landlords and rural entrepreneurs, as well as city businessmen, were a substantial source of private savings. This was recognized by the authorities at the end of the Tokugawa period, and attempts were made to tap such savings through forced loans (*goyōkin*). Some idea of how large these private savings were thought to be can be gained from the record of an 1868 discussion in the Kōgisho on whether or not such levies should be replaced by the issue of government bonds.[28] After considerable discussion it was decided that they should be so replaced, and bonds to the extent of almost five million yen were issued in the following couple of years.

There is little point in trying to measure saving in the 1860's. No doubt saving in some quarters was offset by dissaving in others. It seems safe to say nevertheless that the traditional Japanese economy had a high saving potential, owing to institutional factors like the tax system,[29] as well as a low marginal propensity to consume built into the traditional culture. One indication of this is that even under the strains of the 1860's inflation never really got out of control and prices settled down very quickly after 1869.

Responsiveness of the Traditional Economy

While certain levels of income and saving may be necessary for successful economic development, they do not themselves guarantee success. Unless the traditional economy is somehow responsive to economic stimuli, opportunities for devel-

[28] Hara Denzō, "Meiji shonen ni okeru fugōzei" [Super-tax in the First Years of the Meiji Period], *Rekishi chiri*, XXXIV, No. 2, (1919), 64-69.

[29] It has not been possible to estimate the amount of savings through savings clubs (*mujin, tanamoshi-kō*), but they may have been quite important in the aggregate.

opment will not be grasped and decisions to develop will not be implemented, at least in a free enterprise context. Under this heading of responsiveness fall many factors which do not readily lend themselves to economic analysis, such as the social framework, the value system, the level of education, and all circumstances influencing the supply of entrepreneurs. Over the last few years these social and cultural factors have deservedly been receiving a good deal of attention. But responsiveness is also influenced by other factors which are more strictly economic, such as the degree of commercialization of the traditional economy (particularly of agriculture which forms the bulk of traditional economic activity), the effectiveness of markets, and the traditional role of the state in economic life.

EDUCATION AND ECONOMIC ATTITUDES

Tokugawa Japan had a comparatively high rate of literacy for a pre-modern society, and its relevance to economic development is apparent. R. P. Dore has observed that a population which has received some education is more responsive to further training, has an awareness of and a desire for self-improvement, and is responsive to written directives.[30] The rate of literacy in Japan was probably approaching 30 percent in the 1860's, if we define literacy as ability to read and write at a fairly elementary level. When conscription was introduced in 1873 it was found that 30-40 percent of the conscripts had some education,[31] which they would have received in the 1860's. This figure applies to the young male population; the literacy rate among women and older people was probably lower. Dore estimates that at the time of the Restoration 40-50 percent of boys and perhaps some 15 percent of girls were getting some formal schooling outside their homes.[32]

[30] "The Legacy of Tokugawa Education" in Marius B. Jansen, *Changing Japanese Attitudes Toward Modernization* (Princeton, 1964).

[31] Richard K. Beardsley et al., *Twelve Doors to Japan* (Ann Arbor, 1961), 494.

[32] Dore, "The Legacy of Tokugawa Education," in Marius B. Jan-

At the time of the Restoration there were between 7,500 and 11,000 *terakoya* (village schools) and perhaps a thousand or more other educational institutions of various kinds. The volume of popular literature published at the end of the Tokugawa period is another sign of widespread literacy.

Whereas the samurai class generally received a classical education, that provided for the common people was of a more practical nature. Apart from some elementary classical texts, instruction in reading and writing emphasized the kinds of texts and correspondence with which the pupils would later be mainly concerned. Mathematics was presented in the form of practical problems of measurement, accounting, and so on. In all but the lowest ranks of the merchant and farmer classes the head of a household was expected to have a reasonable standard of literacy and to be able to keep accounts. Furushima writes, "Even peasants of the Edo period had a much more advanced understanding as economic men than have salary earners like us. Through actual experience rather than by formal study of accountancy, they had worked out for themselves, however clumsily, methods of preparing financial statements and profit and loss accounts."[33]

This is true for peasants, but merchants and businessmen received considerable formal commercial education. Surviving records show a high level of accounting technique, and the uniformity of accounting procedures suggests widespread formal teaching. Larger businesses ran schools for their apprentices; private commercial schools seem also to have been common in the larger cities. On the practical side participation at one level or another in the operations of the marketing boards (*bussan kaisho, sembai shihō*) of the various *han* gave large numbers of people some experience of working in the context of large-scale commercial enterprise.

---

sen, ed., *Changing Japanese Attitudes Toward Modernization,* Princeton, 1964.

[33] Furushima Toshio, "Nōka chōbo no riyō" [The Use of Farm Accounts], K. Hōgetsu, M. Tokoro and K. Kodama, eds., *Gutai rei ni yoru rekishi kenkyū hō* [Historical Research on the Basis of Concrete Examples] (Tokyo, 1960), p. 209.

The information which these accounting techniques were designed to provide was, moreover, of much the same kind that a modern businessman in a capitalist economy would want. Even quite detailed calculations of the relative profitability of alternative courses of action, and examples of simple cost accounting can be found in the commercial records of the late Tokugawa period. This suggests that the traditional Japanese businessman's attitude towards economic activity was not very different from modern attitudes, and this impression is strongly confirmed by all the available evidence. Nor was rational calculation of economic advantage a new development in the late Tokugawa period; it can be seen clearly among big city merchants as early as the seventeenth century. But it became far more widespread with the extension of business opportunities to the countryside in the nineteenth century. We should not be surprised, therefore, at the apparent ease with which rural businessmen adjusted to a modern capitalist economy.

The failure typically of the old-established business houses of the cities to make this adjustment requires a little more explanation. Partly it was because they were too closely involved with the *bakufu-han* system and had got into something of a rut. Long experience of mutual collaboration and official protection was not good training for a world of competition and innovation. Also, events of the Restoration period dealt them a series of blows which proved fatal to all but the most self-reliant.[34]

COMMERCIALIZATION OF AGRICULTURE

The degree of commercialization is also of great relevance to the responsiveness of the economy. If economic activity is basically directed toward the subsistence of the producers and their families, such usual economic stimuli as the price mechanism will have very limited effect. It is in agriculture that this problem is most likely to arise. The frequently observed lag of agriculture in programs of economic development

[34] For further discussion of this point see Chs. IV and V.

is probably due more basically to a low degree of commercial-ization than to low initial levels of productivity or technique. Where only a small proportion of output is for a market, incentives which depend on market forces are likely to produce little response. Attempts to use other more direct stimuli may provoke quite unwelcome reactions, as the recent ex-perience of China would seem to indicate.

In Japan, agriculture responded unusually well to the demands of economic development. The annual growth rate of net agricultural output from 1878 to 1917 averaged about 2.3 percent, according to Ohkawa's data cited earlier. Agri-cultural labor productivity increased at annual rates of 2.6 percent, and land productivity rose by 80 percent over the same period. To quote Henry Rosovsky, "This was a tre-mendous record of achievement, even by international stand-ards."[35] It remains impressive even if one concedes some exaggeration in prevailing estimates, as argued below by James Nakamura (Ch. VI). And since Nakamura's revision of the Meiji record consists in raising substantially the esti-mates of output already attained by the 1870's it supports the argument here as to the earlier growth and productivity of Japanese agriculture before 1868.

Clearly commercialization cannot have been the only factor behind Meiji advances in Japanese agriculture; yet these could hardly have proceeded so readily from a mere subsistence base. Japanese economic historians, it is true, have frequently in-sisted otherwise.

"From the economic standpoint, the economy as a whole was still predominantly subsistence."[36]

"In East and West alike, the village in a feudal society is characterized by natural economy and a wide fusion of agri-culture and handicrafts. Since the society of the Tokugawa

[35] *Capital Formation in Japan* (New York, 1961), p. 80.

[36] Endō Masao, *Nihon kinsei shōgyō shihon hattatsu shi ron* [The Development of Commercial Capital in Tokugawa Japan] (Tokyo, 1936), 1.

period was a feudal society, subsistence economy predominated in the agricultural villages of the time."[37]

"Even in 1887-90, agriculture was still at a stage where subsistence production predominated."[38]

Fujita and Hattori[39] persistently put "commercial" in inverted commas when referring to the Tokugawa period. The train of thought of such writers seems to be that every feudal society is based on subsistence economy; pre-Restoration Japan was a feudal society; therefore pre-Restoration Japan was based on a subsistence economy. Every part of this syllogism is doubtful and has been subjected to critical reexamination in the last decade or so. It is possible to measure the degree of commercialization by the ratio of products sold to total production. Despite accumulating evidence that this ratio was not low, there has been considerable reluctance on the part of the more doctrinaire Marxists to revise their syllogism, and this reluctance has resulted in the invention of such confusing terms as "semi-feudal production," "pre-modern capital," and "semi-pre-modern commercial capital."

Rough measurements of the degree of commercialization of traditional Japanese agriculture have in fact been attempted. Yamaguchi's estimate may be cited here for the years immediately after the Restoration, when taxes were still paid predominantly in kind as they were in the 1860's.[40] For the gross value of agricultural production he used average figures for 1874, 1876, and 1877 in current prices. To obtain the quantity of rice sold in 1872-73, he subtracted tax rice and

[37] Tsuchiya Takao, *Kinsei nihon hōken shakai no shiteki bunseki* [An Historical Analysis of the Feudal Society of Tokugawa Japan] (Tokyo, 1949), 243.

[38] Hara Masaji, "Nōgyō tōkei no seiritsu to sono hatten" [The Establishment and Development of Agricultural Statistics], *Nōgyō hattatsu shi chōsakai* [Society for the Study of the History of Agricultural Development] ed., *Nihon nōgyō hattatsu shi* [A History of Japanese Agricultural Development] (Tokyo, 1956), IX, 706.

[39] Fujita Gorō and Hattori Takuya, *Kinsei hōken shakai no kōzō* [The Structure of Tokugawa Feudal Society] (Tokyo, 1951).

[40] Yamaguchi Kazuo, *Meiji zenki keizai no bunseki* [An Analysis of the Early Meiji Economy] (Tokyo, 1956), 37-43.

estimated farm consumption for 1872-73 from average rice output in 1874, 1876, and 1877. (The difference in the periods used probably does not seriously affect the result.) He also made an adjustment for the fact that some farmers bought rice for consumption, though no allowance seems to have been made for seed rice which was about 4-5 percent of the crop.[41] His estimates are given in Table 4.

TABLE 4

PROPORTION OF CROPS MARKETED IN EARLY 1870's
(Excluding Tax Payments in Kind)

	Percent
Rice	15–20
Coarse grains, beans and potatoes	5–10
Industrial crops	80–90
Vegetables	20–30
Fruit	20–30
Total (All crops)	25–31

SOURCE: Yamaguchi Kazuo, *Meiji zenki keizai no bunseki* [An Analysis of the Early Meiji Economy] (Tokyo, 1956), p. 42.

These figures do not include products paid as tax in the proportion marketed. Even so, the figure for rice seems too low. Even in the 1790's it seems to have been not unusual for farmers in the shogunal domains to sell the bulk of the rice left after tax.[42] In the Mito *han* from 1813 to 1837, farmers

[41] Near Edo in 1855 seed rice was 5% of the crop. See Ōkubo Jinsai, *Fukoku kyōhei mondō* [A Dialogue on Enriching the Country and Strengthening the Armed Forces] in Takimoto Seiichi, ed., *Nihon keizai sōsho* [Library of Japanese Economics] (Tokyo, 1914-17), XXXIV. In Kumamoto about 1810 the proportion was around 4.3%. See Kodama Kōta, *Kinsei nōmin seikatsu shi* [Peasant Life in the Tokugawa Period] (Tokyo, 1958), 280. Furushima Toshio, *Kinsei nihon nōgyō no kōzō* [The Structure of Japanese Agriculture in the Tokugawa Period] (Tokyo, 1943), 431-32, quotes figures ranging from 2 to 7%.

[42] Shibano Ritsuzan, "Shibano ritsuzan jōsho" [Memorial presented by Shibano Ritsuzan], quoted in Kodama, cited, 283.

on good land sold a little over half of the rice produced, and those with inferior land between a quarter and a third.[43] Near Edo in 1855 fairly prosperous farmers sold about one third of their rice crop.[44] On balance it seems reasonable to raise Yamaguchi's figure to 20-25 percent, even after making an allowance for seed rice.

Since rice paid in tax is not subsistence production, and since a large part of these taxes were eventually marketed, it seems proper to include this in the proportion marketed. The volume of tax rice paid in the 1860's to the *han* was estimated by taking the amounts of regular and miscellaneous tax rice from *Hansei ichiran* and totaling them by region, using the factors employed earlier in computing total taxes. This gives 9.08 million *koku,* to which is added the *bakufu* figure of 0.59 million *koku* and another 0.3 million *koku* for *hatamoto.* The tax total then reaches 10 million *koku,* which compares with 10.75 million *koku* for 1872-73 when taxes were still paid in kind.[45] We may now try to estimate the proportion of agricultural output self-consumed in the 1860's. For crops other than rice, Yamaguchi's estimates have been retained.

TABLE 5

PROPORTION OF AGRICULTURAL PRODUCTION SELF-CONSUMED (1860's)

	Percent
Rice	20-30
Coarse grains, beans and potatoes	90-95
Industrial crops	10-20
Vegetables	70-80
Fruit	70-80
Total (all crops)	31-42

These figures conceal wide regional variation. In the more advanced areas, which would tend to be more involved in the

[43] Kodama, 284.

[44] *Fukoku kyōhei mondō*, cited.

[45] Ministry of Finance, Bureau of Taxation, "Chiso kankei shorui isan" [Classified Documents on the Land Tax], reprinted in *Meiji zenki zaisei keizai shiryō shūsei*, VII, 441-42.

process of economic development, the proportion of agricultural output marketed was as high as 80 percent, while in some remote areas the proportion may have been as low as 10 percent. It seems safe to say that in Japanese agriculture as a whole over half and probably nearer two-thirds of output was marketed in one form or another. This is far from subsistence agriculture in the usual sense of the term. The commercial flavor of rural Japan appears even stronger when we recall that very many farmers engaged in industrial as well as in agricultural production and that almost all of their industrial activity was for a market.

The judgment that sales were nearer two-thirds of output is supported by what we know of rural cash expenditure. In Okayama *han*, an economically advanced area, as early as 1813 a shopkeeper in Ōi village was selling the following impressive list of commodities: ink, paper, writing brushes, *herasaki*, cauldrons, cutlery, needles, smoking pipes, tobacco, tobacco pouches, teapots, casserole dishes, rice-wine bottles, oil containers, vinegar, soy sauce, bean paste, salt, matting, noodles, kelp, hair oil, hair strings, hairpins, cotton cloth, socks, towels, bamboo trellis, carrying baskets, *zōri*, straw sandals [*waraji*], wooden clogs, tea, teacups, lucifers, wicks, incense, fire pots, lanterns, oil, candles, rice wine, timber, hot water bottles, cakes, *sembei*, trays, funeral requisites, grain, *and other everyday necessities.*[46]

The inference is that the items of this list were regarded as everyday necessities. Other dealers sold agricultural implements, fertilizer, *tōfu*, dried fish, fruit, vegetables, and many other things. By 1864 such luxuries as silk fabrics, imported goods, Echigo linen, sugar from other *han*, indigo balls, medicines from Etchū, Toyama and elsewhere, and high class furniture from Noto were on sale in village shops of Okayama *han*.[47] These items are typical of merchandise sold in villages —and therefore bought by farmers—in the more advanced

---

[46] Andō Seiichi, *Kinsei zaikata shōgyō no kenkyū* [A Study of Rural Commerce in the Tokugawa Period] (Tokyo, 1958), 95.

[47] Andō, 95.

areas of Japan. In remoter areas such as Tōhoku and Kyūshū the list would be considerably shorter.

Role of the State

The leading role of the State in modern Japanese economic development is well known, and derives to a large extent from its role in the pre-modern economy. We have already noted the well developed system of taxation which placed in the hands of the State the means of playing a major part in investment. This alone would not be a sufficient explanation for the activity of Meiji governments, but in fact government played an active part in the traditional economy including some degree of control over almost every aspect of economic life. Because of this, Meiji governments were fortunate in being able to guide the economy through the use of established and accepted controls without having to introduce new ones. In fact they could afford a degree of liberalization.

Economic controls were fairly stringent throughout the Tokugawa period and were tending, if anything, to become increasingly detailed in the 1860's. They were also becoming increasingly ineffective, though they never broke down entirely, largely because of the decentralized nature of the *bakufu-han* system. Control was also shifting in emphasis from control of occupations and consumption to control of markets, prices, and production.

The shogunate had the major financial and commodity markets of Osaka under its direct administration. The regulation of these markets through chartered trade associations (*kabunakama*) which had been abandoned in 1841 was partially restored in 1851 and, after some backing and filling, efforts were being made to strengthen it in the 1860's. At the same time, abortive moves were made by the shogunate toward direct government operation of markets on a national basis,[48] but they came to nothing because of widespread opposition and financial weakness. During the inflation of the 1860's, the

[48] Kitajima Masamoto, "Bakumatsu ni okeru Tokugawa bakufu no sangyō tōsei," [Industrial Control by the Tokugawa Shogunate at the End of the Tokugawa Period], *Jimbun gakuhō*, xvii (Feb. 1958), 55-83.

shogunate issued a spate of decrees to control the price of rice,[49] oil,[50] timber,[51] copper,[52] fuel,[53] manure,[54] and commodity prices in general.[55] It ordered increased consignments of essential goods to Kyoto, where the population was swollen by an influx of both loyalists and Tokugawa supporters.[56] In the field of transport the shogunate controlled all the main highways and set freight rates.[57] It supervised foreign trade and interest rates.[58] It regulated wages within its domains.[59] It encouraged land reclamation and took the lead in the settlement of Hokkaidō.[60] In agriculture it placed restrictions, which were increasingly evaded, on the sale and subdivision of land. It encouraged production of wax, lacquer, paper, and tea,[61] but when export demand for silk led to expansion of the industry it prohibited the planting of mulberries on ricefields (*honden*).[62] In industry, it set quotas for the brewing industry,[63] regulated salmon fishing, the building trades, coopering, shipbuilding, and the production of lime and saltpeter.[64] The shogunate and the three great Tokugawa lords owned and operated or controlled all major mines and forests. Within the

[49] Ishii Ryōsuke, ed., *Tokugawa kinrei kō* [Tokugawa Law] (Tokyo, 1959) (hereafter cited as TKK), I, 146; NZKS, III, 371, VII, 604; Osaka Municipal Government ed., *Ōsaka shishi* [History of Osaka] (Osaka, 1927), vol. IV, part II (hereafter cited as OS), 2325.

[50] NZKS, VII, 430-34; OS, 2477.

[51] NZKS, VII, 854-56.

[52] NZKS, VI, 775, III, 498.

[53] NZKS, III, 499, 542.

[54] OS, 2345.

[55] TKK, I, 146; NZKS, III, 496; OS, 2322, 2329, 2332-33, 2433, 2447.

[56] OS, 2448, 2459, 2522.

[57] TKK, I, 106, 107; NZKS, IV, 933, 983, IX, 827-30.

[58] On foreign trade see NZKS, III, 657, 661, VII, 1332. On interest rates see TKK, I, 218, II, 243-44; NZKS, II, 136.

[59] TKK, II, 443; NZKS, III, 495; OS, 2517.

[60] Takakura Shinichirō, "The Ainu of Northern Japan" (trans. John A. Harrison), *Transactions of the American Philosophical Society*, New Series, L, part 4 (April 1960).

[61] NZKS, III, 512.

[62] NZKS, III, 512, VI, 911.

[63] NZKS, II, 1351, 1385.

[64] NZKS, X, 162, III, 459; OS, 2319, 2496, 2470.

shogunal domains practically no major enterprise or innovation could be undertaken without the approval of the government.

While the shogunate was unable to carry through plans for direct participation in production and marketing on a national scale, some *han* succeeded on the smaller scale of their own fiefs. The trend toward more direct participation by *han* governments in economic activity grew stronger in the 1850's. In some *han*, of which Chōshū is a good example, almost all commerce in the more important products was handled from producer to final sale by official marketing boards. Many of these organizations, or sections of them, carried on into the Meiji period as private companies.

The existence of established channels of economic control made the Japanese economy far more amenable than most to official direction and technical guidance. The close organizational and personal links between the Meiji government and business were forged in the 1860's.

Conclusion

This picture of the Japanese economy on the eve of modernization focuses on aspects which may help to explain Japan's later growth, which seems in some ways unique in modern economic history. Some parts of the picture may have become distorted by this selective emphasis, but the main outlines seem clear enough.

The Japanese economy of the 1860's was reasonably, but not outstandingly productive for a traditional economy. It had a high potential for saving and was already showing signs of quickening economic growth. At the same time, a number of other features made it more responsive than most traditional economies to economic stimuli. It was basically commercial with a well-developed system of national markets. The population was comparatively well educated and economically motivated. Because of efficient and productive taxation systems and its tradition of economic activity and control, government was well placed to play an important role in the process of economic modernization.

PART TWO

The Transition to Industrial Society

CHAPTER II

A Century of Japanese Economic Growth

KAZUSHI OHKAWA and HENRY ROSOVSKY

Introduction

IN ANY ANALYSIS of Japanese modernization it is useful to remember that within a few years we will be celebrating the one-hundredth anniversary of the Meiji Restoration. Almost a century ago there began a series of epochal changes which were to transform Japan from a backward, isolated, and unknown kingdom in remotest Asia into one of the major powers of the mid-twentieth century. Obviously we are not dealing with an ordinary century of Japanese history. By almost any standards this was an extremely eventful period, and perhaps it was more eventful in the sphere of economic development than in any other.

A century of rapid development is, even for the economic historian, a bit too long for analytical comfort. It must be almost intuitively clear that during this period trends changed from time to time forming identifiable and relatively unified *phases of growth*. The dating, identification, and explanation of these phases are the major tasks which we will attempt in this paper. Our hope is that the suggested phases provide a useful framework within which one can examine the entire experience of modern Japanese economic development.

A growth phase is not an arbitrarily selected period of years; it must conform to certain analytical principles. The following principles have been adopted :[1]

[1] This is an adaptation of what Simon Kuznets has called minimum requirements for a "stage theory." See his "Notes on the Take-Off," a paper presented at the September 1960 Meeting of the International Economic Association (mimeographed). All quotations in the next few pages are from Kuznets. When the term "phase" appears in brackets, the word "stages" appeared in the original text.

1. The duration of a phase must be long enough to be distinguished from short-term economic movements. By definition it must be of longer duration than the ordinary business cycle, because the distinctive properties of a phase (see below) will transcend the temporary ups and downs of the cycle. In practice, the minimum length of a phase will probably coincide with the Kuznets Long Swing.

2. The characteristics of a given phase must be distinctive in that, not necessarily singly but in combination, they· are unique to that phase. "[Phases] are presumably something more than successive ordinates in the steadily climbing curve of growth. They are segments of that curve, with properties so distinct that separate study of each segment seems warranted."

3. The characteristics of a particular phase must bear an analytical and historical relationship to the preceding and succeeding phases. This involves more than saying that the preceding phase is one of preparation for the given. It involves something less than the claim of an inevitable historical order of phases. In other words, certain properties of one phase will exert influences which bring about the next phase. "We need identification of the major processes in the preceding [phase] that complete it and, with the usual qualifications for exogenous factors, make the next [phase] highly probable." It also means "specifying the minimum that must happen in the preceding [phase] to allow the given phase to emerge."

4. A phase of modern economic growth must possess certain common and distinctive characteristics within the general analytical scheme. But these characteristics may differ among important groups of units undergoing modern economic growth, and therefore we also need "a clear indication of the universe for which the generality of common and distinctive characteristics is claimed; and for which the analytical relations of a given [phase] with a preceding and succeeding [phase] are being formulated."

5. Finally, a given phase must display empirically testable characteristics. This does not necessarily confine the analysis to quantification. Quantitative phenomena, such as changes

in inputs and output are, of course, most easily measured and lend themselves readily to empirical verification. At the same time, changes in institutions and organization are also observable, and to a certain extent the same applies to technological change and human behavior. Carefully defined, the range of empirical verification can be quite broad.

Having stated the analytical principles of phasing, something must be said about the relationship—or *lack* of relationship—between phases and the much better known stage analysis. The differences may appear superficial; in fact, they are basic. This is not the place to criticize *in extenso* the use of stages, but the differences between the two methods of historical analysis must be made clear. Invented by the German Historical School and recently resurrected by Rostow, stage analysis attempts to formulate a "law of economic development" applicable to the world at large, or at the very least to units the size of "Western Civilization." This requires the law of stages—and there are a great many competing schemes from which to choose—to have wide international and intercultural validity. In effect, stage theory must claim that the process of economic development in all countries is more or less identical. There may be slight variations in timing or other details, but fundamentally the law must hold. Stages follow each other in necessary sequence, and they cannot be skipped. The prime mover of industrialization was the same in England, Russia, France, Japan, or anywhere else—all depending on which particular stage scheme is adopted. Whether it is possible to discover a universal law of economic development need not concern us at the moment. All that must be stated clearly is that we are not in search of such a law. Our ambitions are much more limited. The entire purpose of our work is to comprehend Japanese economic development, and our phases are presented as an analytical convenience for the study of Japan alone. We would not claim that the motor forces of Japanese industrialization are *necessarily* found in other cases of development, either in the past or in the future. Some of the factors may be general and some may be idiosyncratic, and the unambiguous recognition of this fact already serves to differentiate the phase and stage approach. But the differences go deeper. We have not even attempted to formulate a *law* of Japanese economic development, if that term is used to describe an inexorable path of growth. We have attempted to describe what happened, and why and how it happened, recognizing at all times that a series of alternative paths was open to the economy at almost any time. One of the alternatives, which stage theory can never bring itself to consider, is the lack of economic progress once it has begun, while we explicitly recognize this possibility at various points in Japanese economic history. Self-sustained growth, at least in the case of Japan, appears to be a mirage.

We have stated what phases are and what they are not, but how they can be identified has not yet been made clear. The concern throughout is, of course, with modern economic growth, but this is still a trifle vague. By its very nature, a phase is a dynamic concept—according to the dictionary, a transitory state between changes in appearance, structure, character, etc. To put it another way, the emphasis must be on the *change* of certain indicators relevant to modern economic growth, which at the same time meet the previously outlined criteria.

Phases can be discussed in terms of three broad indicators: (1) changes in endogenous relations, (2) changes in the growth pattern, and (3) changes in the economic structure; a brief definition of these concepts may clarify our aims. The term *endogenous relations* refers to the broad picture of sectoral interdependence within the Japanese economy, and an exposition of the change in these relations will be set forth in what follows. Changes in the growth pattern and economic structure are intended to provide a statistical test for the phases derived largely from an interpretation of Japanese economic history. By the term *growth pattern*, we mean the behavior of gross national product, its growth rate, and its major components and their growth rates. The problem will be to determine the congruence of the variations in this indicator and the phasing scheme. By *economic structure* is meant

the classification of the economy into agricultural, manufacturing, and service sectors, and also the more specific area of
industrial structure—i.e. a sub-division of manufacturing.
The problem to be analyzed remains the same. Due to limitations of space, growth pattern and economic structure cannot
be dealt with in this paper. Interested parties are referred to
our forthcoming volume, also entitled *A Century of Growth*,
which contains a much more extensive analysis.

Before turning to an exposition of the phases, it may be
useful to remind the reader of ten key characteristics which
prevailed during the entire century under consideration. These
are:

1. A relatively high rate of over-all growth in terms of output and per capita income, with some spurts and some retardations;

2. A pattern of population growth which, in terms of rates
of natural increase, is reminiscent of the historical experience
of Europe rather than that of currently underdeveloped areas,
and which did not contain substantial emigration or immigration while retaining a highly flexible labor supply;

3. For the given level of per capita income, a relatively high
proportion of domestic investment (and saving) accompanied
by several upward movements of the investment (savings)
ratio;

4. For the given level of per capita income, a relatively low
proportion of personal consumption, accompanied by several
downward movements of the consumption ratio;

5. A sustained low capital-output ratio, showing, however,
an upward drift in the postwar period;

6. Modern economic growth taking place, in general, in an
inflationary setting, the only exception to this being the
1920's;

7. Recurring balance of payments crises such that one may
almost speak of a chronic deficit of foreign payments;

8. The general co-existence of traditional and modern economic sectors, this being partly reflected in the bi-modal
(large-scale/small-scale) distribution of enterprises;

9. The important role played by government in furthering economic modernization, especially in mobilizing and spending investment funds;

10. A specifically created group of financial institutions which greatly enhanced the supply of capital.

We consider these characteristics to be empirically verified,[2] and will expand on them only as becomes necessary in following the argument concerning the phases. One further point can be made. The enumerated characteristics are not necessarily peculiar to Japan; in large measure they seem to apply also to what are generally referred to as "follower countries" or "industrial latecomers."[3]

The Phases: Short and Long

A. The First Phase of Modern Economic Growth, 1868-1905
    I. Transition, 1868-1885
    II. Initial Modern Economic Growth, 1886-1905
B. The Second Phase of Modern Economic Growth, 1906-1952
    III. Differential Structure: Creation, 1906-1930

[2] Consult the following of our joint papers: "The Role of Agriculture in Modern Japanese Economic Development," *Economic Development and Cultural Change*, IX, 1, Part II (October 1960); "The Indigenous Components in the Modern Japanese Economy," *Ibid.*, IX, 3 (April 1961); and "Economic Fluctuations in Prewar Japan: A Preliminary Analysis of Cycles and Long Swings," *Hitotsubashi Journal of Economics*, III, 1 (October 1962). See also Ohkawa Kazushi and others, *The Growth Rate of the Japanese Economy Since 1878* (Tokyo, 1957); Henry Rosovsky, *Capital Formation in Japan, 1868-1940* (New York, 1961); and Irene Taeuber, *The Population of Japan* (Princeton, 1958). The reader may also wish to refer to the statistical appendix in the present paper.

In the list of key characteristics, terms such as "relatively high" or "relatively low" refer to average international experience as assembled in recent years by Simon Kuznets in his articles in *Economic Development and Cultural Change*.

[3] See Alexander Gerschenkron, "The Approach to European Industrialization: A Postscript," in *Economic Backwardness in Historical Perspective* (Cambridge, Mass., 1962). Our characteristics 1, 2, 3, 4, 6, 8, 9, and 10 are also identified for the European follower countries by Gerschenkron.

IV. Differential Structure: Economic and Political
Consequences, 1931-1952
C. The Third Phase of Modern Economic Growth, 1953-
present
V. Postwar Growth, 1953-present

Transition, 1868-1885

THE ATTRIBUTES OF MODERN ECONOMIC GROWTH

The years between 1868 and 1885 form the transition between the time when modern economic growth (hereafter
MEG) became the *national* objective and its actual beginnings
in 1886. It seems to us that with the Meiji Restoration of
1868 MEG became a national objective for the first time, and
we will argue that this type of growth could not really begin
in any meaningful sense until the Matsukata deflation had
run its full course. Thus, transition examines the lag between
the adoption of a national objective and the beginning of its
achievement—in Japan, a short period of slightly less than
twenty years. An understanding of transition requires two
major ways of looking at the data. First, we must examine the
given conditions, i.e., the state of economy and society at the
point where MEG became a national objective. Second, we
must see how the given conditions were shaped or changed—
by public or private action—to bring about the beginning of
MEG.

What is MEG? We define it in terms of the generally accepted Kuznets criteria: (1) the application of modern scientific thought and technology to industry, transport, and agriculture; (2) sustained and rapid rise in real product per
capita combined with high rates of population growth; (3)
high rates of transformation of the industrial structure; and
(4) the presence of international contacts. MEG means the
presence to a greater or lesser degree of *all* of these attributes,
and we will try to show that one cannot find all of them in
Japan until roughly 1886.

We may well begin by asking the following questions: can
any of the attributes of MEG be identified in Japan at the

precise moment of the Restoration? What were the givens? The data for making accurate judgments are not exactly plentiful, but the questions are broad enough to permit tolerably accurate answers.

To begin with, there is no real evidence to indicate that real product per capita was rising in a rapid or sustained manner in the 1860's. Furthermore, there is no reason to believe that population was increasing rapidly at that time. Let us examine some of the available information. In the late 1870's, 75 to 80 percent of the gainfully occupied population was engaged in agriculture; this proportion may have been slightly higher in the 1860's. When the national income figures begin in the 1870's, the agricultural sector produced about 65 percent of the national product. Per capita product— taking into account all sectors—stood at around ¥ 20.00 in current prices, or very roughly U.S. $65, using the postwar rate of exchange. This figure could not have been appreciably higher in the 1860's. Whatever one may believe about the level of wealth in pre-industrial Japan, or about the distribution of income, it is pretty clear that the country in 1868 was strongly typified by the small peasant cultivator working only slightly above subsistence levels. And this is an important (if obvious) point, because it implies that raising the growth rate of national per capita product required significant increases in *average national* agricultural practice and the introduction of new industries. In significant amounts all this came only after 1868.

Our knowledge about the demographic aspects of early modern Japan is a bit more detailed and reaches back further in time. (For this we are all in the debt of Irene Taeuber and Messrs. Morita and Tachi.) According to Mrs. Taeuber, in 1852 the total population of Japan was roughly between 29.4 and 32 million. A report for 1872 suggests a level of 34.8 million. "Thus the increase of population in these two decades of transition from seclusion to the modern era may have amounted to less than 10 per cent; it certainly did not reach 20 per cent."[4] In the 1870's, therefore, rates of increase were

[4] Taeuber, 44.

of the order of ¾ of 1 percent per year, and no one would be disposed to call this a high rate of population growth. At this time, also, the vital rates were in keeping with those of a backward country. Death rates, suggests Mrs. Taeuber, must have been very high, requiring fertility rates in the neighborhood of 40/1000 to produce slow increases of population.

Let us turn next to the rate of transformation of the industrial structure at the time of the Restoration. In the context of detecting modern economic growth, this must be taken to mean the rapid relative shift from agriculture to manufacturing and perhaps services. Perhaps the best information for rendering a judgment on the situation in early modern Japan is contained in the *Meiji 7-nen fuken bussanhyō* (1874).[5] According to this source, the value of manufacturing output amounted to about 30 percent of commodity production. Its structure was as follows:

Value (%)		Value (%)	
1. Textiles	27.7	5. Utensils	7.7
2. Food Products	41.9	6. Paper Products	5.2
3. House Accessories	1.7	7. Capital Equipment	5.9
4. Lamp Oil & Candles	6.3	8. Medicines & Cosmetics	3.6

These figures are subject to a variety of criticisms;[6] nevertheless they clearly reveal certain features of the Japanese economy shortly after the Restoration. We have here a fairly typical pre-modern manufacturing pattern. Textiles and food together account for over 70 percent of the value of all manufacturing output, while what is called "capital equipment" is extremely small. The two most important items manufactured were cloth (15 percent of all manufactures) and the brewing or distillation of alcoholic beverages—mostly sake (16.8 percent of all manufactures). The kinds of cloth which were produced in 1874 are also known. Cotton led by a

[5] *Prefectural Production Tables for 1874* as cited in Yamaguchi Kazuo, *Meiji zenki keizai no bunseki* [An Analysis of the Early Meiji Economy] (Tokyo, 1956), ch. 1. The table of manufacturing output is to be found on p. 14.

[6] There are serious questions about geographical and industrial coverage.

wide margin (63.3 percent), followed by silk (26.7 percent), mixed cottons and silks (8.0 percent), and linen and others (2.0 percent). However, cotton's dominance does not indicate the presence of the modern factory cotton industry; this did not really begin until the 1880's. In 1874 we are still dealing with the old cotton industry largely processing native raw materials.

In general, it should be obvious that very little of this manufacturing took place in "factories" or even in fairly large-scale enterprises. The typical enterprise was small and worked by domestic methods using little wage labor. Much of the manufacturing took the form of rural by-employments. There exist no solid quantitative sources to prove or disprove these propositions, and there may have been some exceptions, but we feel that most students of the subject will agree with this assessment. There is some indirect proof in support of our view in the geographical distribution of manufacturing for the two leading products. Both cloth weaving and sake-brewing were widely distributed throughout the entire country, implying small units of production. The leading six prefectures (out of a total of 63) produced only 29 percent of all alcoholic beverages; the leading 11 prefectures wove 58 percent of all cloth—admittedly a somewhat higher level of concentration.[7]

It would thus be possible to draw a picture of Japan as a fairly typical underdeveloped country: an economy which tended towards being dominated by rice (63 percent of the value of agricultural output), and whose industries were largely of the handicraft type catering to local needs. This need not mean that the industrial structure was static in the 1860's, but it does mean that the pace of progress was slow and the impact of changes was limited. Many students of Japanese economic history may be disposed to object to these characterizations, and there has been much attention paid to the economic changes especially in the first half of the nineteenth century. Although their vocabulary is usually different,

[7] Lack of concentration as an indicator of industrial backwardness was used by Paul Mantoux in his classic study of England. See *The Industrial Revolution in the Eighteenth Century* (London, 1955), 49.

a number of factors are commonly cited as evidence for significant changes in the industrial structure: growth of output in agriculture, commercialization of agriculture, diffusion of traditional industries, and the establishment by certain *han* (clans) of some Western industries. We cannot analyze all of these in detail, and instead will simply comment on some of these contentions.

1. First, the growth of output and commercialization of agriculture. Research has demonstrated that agriculture in certain regions became more productive during the late Tokugawa era. It has not—and cannot—show that there were significant increases in the average level of performance. This confusion between regions and aggregate averages is also important in assessments of the degree of commercialization. The statement that Japanese agriculture by the 1860's had become basically commercial is not rare, but it is almost certainly wrong. *At present* (1963) slightly over 60 percent of agricultural output reaches the market. In the 1860's, before the land tax, the ratio probably stood at a level of about 20 percent.[8] There were, it is true, regions where commercial agriculture was dominant (such as the Kinai and Tōsan), but these were more than counterbalanced by areas where the peasant still practiced subsistence farming, as in most of Kyūshū, Shikoku, and Hokuriku.

2. The diffusion of industry during the first half of the nineteenth century—essentially its spread to the towns and villages—is analogous to the undermining of guilds in the West and the rise of cottage industry and the putting-out system. It is evidence of some changes of the industrial structure, mainly in that it must have increased rural by-employments, but it is not a rapid rate of transformation characteristic of MEG.

3. Many scholars have attributed considerable importance

[8] This can be inferred from the figures presented by Yamaguchi, *Meiji zenki keizai no bunseki*, p. 42. In our assessment of agricultural output reaching the market we exclude tax rice sold by the *bushi* class, because the real point is the extent to which the farmer was practicing commercial agriculture.

to the establishment of certain modern Western industries by a few *han* during the first half of the nineteenth century. Since these were frequently connected with a desire to produce armaments, E. H. Norman[9] went so far as to suggest that the "normal" pattern for an industrial revolution was reversed in Japan, with heavy industry preceding the development of light industry. This is, we believe, a misunderstanding of the implication of an industrial revolution and MEG. One could argue that some of these establishments were useful investments. More to the point, one could stress the technical and managerial experience acquired by a few people. Yet none of this should be exaggerated. Isolated islands of modernity existed and exist in most backward countries, and these should not be confused with the genuine beginnings of an industrial revolution. A few spinning mills and iron foundries cannot be said to change the industrial structure of a country with a population of some 30 million people.

There now remain two other attributes of MEG: the application of modern scientific thought to technology and industry, and the presence of international contacts. Once again we can restrict ourselves to a few brief comments:

1. There existed, in the 1860's, virtually no modern technology or industry, and consequently modern scientific thought could not possibly have been involved in the productive process—except in highly unusual cases. Whatever scientific and technological knowledge was available in pre-modern Japan—and some scholars focusing on *rangaku* (Dutch studies) and the activities of large *han* would conclude that the amounts were not insignificant—must be regarded at this stage as a useful potential for industrialization. If the subject of potentials is to be introduced, there existed one other of much greater eventual importance, and also intimately related to the economic application of science and technology. This was, of course, the stock of education in Japan at the time of the Restoration. As Dore has recently remarked: "Japan, we

[9] *Japan's Emergence as a Modern State* (New York, 1940), 125-26.

are frequently told in these days of growing punditry on the course and causes of economic development, is 'different.' And there is by now a growing awareness that one of the ways it differs from most other late-developing countries is in starting its career of forced-pace modernization with a wide-spread and well-developed tradition of formal institutional education."[10] Briefly, this meant that by the time of the Restoration approximately 50 percent of all Japanese males and 15 percent of all Japanese females were getting some formal education outside of their homes; that total school attendance was over 1,100,000 pupils, mostly in *terakoya* (private elementary schools, primarily for commoners) ; that the *bushi* (Samurai) class may have been completely literate, and that a large number of merchants and farmers also could read and write; that, in view of all this, the concept of universal elementary education was speedily acceptable. No doubt all of these assets helped in the eventual achievement of MEG. In 1868, however, these were merely potential forces for the most part.

2. The reestablishment of diplomatic and trade relations in the 1850's brought a period of considerable confusion to Japan. To gauge the net effect of these influences at the time of the Restoration is difficult. The amount of foreign trade was still very small, and the situation one of considerable flux. There can be no doubt about the impact of renewed contact with the West—intellectual and economic. Certain segments of the economy benefited, others were hurt. The possibility of economic modernization was uniquely tied up with the expansion of imports and exports. Normalization of foreign political and economic relations, following over 200 years of seclusion, was one of the main tasks of the new government. This much can be said: of all the four criteria of MEG, this was the only one in clear evidence at the time of the Restoration; and it was certainly one of the most important forces pushing Japan in the direction of rapid economic change.

[10] "The Legacy of Tokugawa Education," in Marius B. Jansen, ed., *Changing Japanese Attitudes Toward Modernization* (Princeton, 1964).

How the givens were changed to bring about the beginnings of MEG is a story which includes a great many diverse factors. We cannot even list them all, and will have to content ourselves with a highly selective presentation. It seems to us that the government played an especially crucial role in transition, and many of its activities can be subsumed under the general heading of "unification." In this context, unification requires a broad interpretation. It means, for example, the spread of more advanced indigenous agricultural techniques from wealthier to poorer parts of the country, as well as the encouragement of improvements in these techniques. Unification also increased the economic incentives of large groups in the working population. (These aspects will be treated in more detail when we take up Initial Modern Economic Growth, 1886-1905.) It can also include some of the major socio-economic institutional changes initiated by the Meiji government: the abolition of the Tokugawa class structure, the freeing of internal and external travel and commercial communications, and the abolition and commutation of *bushi* privileges. Even the most important reform of all—the Meiji land tax—had significant unifying features, in that agricultural taxes were made uniform nationally and farmers were more closely drawn into the national economy. Most of these institutional reforms were accomplished by 1880, and they did much to further the cause of MEG. But by themselves they were not sufficient. MEG also required a new financial base, and since less is known about this episode we will go into somewhat greater detail.

FINANCIAL ASPECTS OF TRANSITION

Let us cast the problems faced by the new Meiji government in the language currently employed in the analysis of economic planning.

1. The long-run objective of the new government was MEG, and the short-run objective was to achieve the conditions which made MEG a realistic possibility. Negatively,

this required the abolition of certain pre-modern institutions. Positively, it implied establishing the minimum conditions which would permit MEG to begin.

2. The financial targets of the new government were the creation of a modern public budget system, and a modern currency and banking system.

3. Certain financial and physical resources were available to the government in order to achieve these targets. These were: inherited assets from the pre-Restoration period which could be made available through domestic borrowing (although one must recall that there were also considerable inherited liabilities); foreign borrowing; increases in domestic output; and redistribution of income flows and capital stock. All of these resources were limited.

4. Means of implementation were also limited for the new government because it had to economize its available resources, and also because the range of feasible implementation methods was narrow. In the Meiji period, and thereafter, Japan was never a controlled or planned economy. Consequently, governmental targets had to be achieved by means of an economic, rather than an outright political, mechanism. As a result, implementation brought a variety of economic shocks—such as inflation and deflation.

5. Those factors which limit the ability of a new government to act are called boundary factors, and this necessarily includes factors which are not exclusively economic. The following appear especially relevant to the financial targets of the transition period. First, the time element was crucial for the new government, because delays in reaching its targets would have magnified internal and external threats. Second, and closely related, was the problem of the power balance between government and anti-government forces. Policies of the Meiji government had to take into account their possible effect on mobilizing forces interested in its overthrow. Third, relations with foreign powers also limited the actions of the new government. These not only restricted foreign borrowing but also gave a set frame to external trade conditions which the government, at that stage, could not change. For example,

throughout the period of transition, Japan did not have tariff autonomy, and most exports and imports were in the hands of foreign merchants.

The actual years of transition divide themselves very naturally into two sub-periods. From 1868 to 1876 we find a strangely stable economy in spite of chaotic political and social conditions. The years from 1876 to 1885 produced great shocks, inflation followed by deflation, and were a needed catharsis for the Japanese economy. These events deserve closer examination.

The new central government came into power in September 1868 without a systematic financial program, while carrying heavy inherited burdens from the feudal period. Funds had to be found for vanquishing anti-government forces, for continuing the stipends of the *bushi*, and for assuming the debts of the former *daimyō*. Available budgetary records give a clear quantitative dimension of the difficulties: from September 1868 through December 1872, total public expenditures amounted to ¥ 148.3 million as against revenues of only ¥ 50.4 million. This was possible because the government exploited three sources of funds: first and foremost, the issue of inconvertible paper notes, and to a lesser extent loans from big merchants and foreign borrowing. In part, the consequences of these policies were predictable; they also contained some highly unpredictable aspects. Government notes depreciated quickly vis-à-vis specie, but in spite of the considerable increases of money in circulation—from ¥ 65.4 million in 1868 to ¥ 102.7 million in 1872—no substantial inflation is observable. What can be the reasons? We are not at all sure, but the following suggestions may be relevant. During the entire period in question Japan had a large deficit in her international accounts, and this no doubt created anti-inflationary pressure. Furthermore, our speculation is that the velocity of circulation must have been low. At the same time, the transactions demand for money was probably rising as large segments of the population were, for the first time, forced into the money economy. In these terms, the Japanese economy may not have been sufficiently monetized to register the effects of increased note issue. It may have been too early for inflation.

Between 1873 and 1876 the government followed a somewhat more active policy. The land tax was instituted in 1874, national banks were authorized in 1872, inconvertible notes were being retired, and the increases in circulation abated. Governmental fiscal problems, however, remained very serious. The revenue side of the account had been somewhat regularized by means of the land tax, but the expenditure side was still plagued by the size of transfer payments (usually well over 30 percent of expenditures) largely used to meet feudal obligations. These years were not inflationary, and some prices even showed slight declines.

In sum, from 1868 to 1876, from a financial point of view the economic situation was relatively stable. As far as resource utilization and means of implementation were concerned, the government depended heavily on inherited assets and machinery. The issuance of inconvertible notes without the creation of disorder, loans from merchants, the continuing outflow of gold and silver, all depended on pre-Restoration assets— largely the capital stock taken over from the Tokugawa. Foreign borrowing and increases of domestic output cannot, of course, be dismissed even at this time. These too played an important role in resource utilization.

The period of great shocks, 1876-1885, must also be divided: the years of inflation from 1876 to 1881, and the years of deflation from 1881 to 1885. Two historical events are central for an understanding of this period. One was the Seinan Civil War, or Satsuma Rebellion of 1877, which was the last major challenge to the new regime and led directly to an additional note issue of ¥ 27 million. The other was the compulsory commutation of *bushi* stipends through the issue of bonds amounting to ¥ 172.9 million. The latter action, especially, led to major changes in the Japanese economy.

To understand the sequence of events connected with compulsory commutation, one must begin by noting that in August 1876, one month before the final action, the government amended the national bank regulations. Accordingly, the recently instituted specie reserve for note issue was abolished, and banks were allowed to issue notes against bonds deposited with the Treasury up to 80 percent of their capital. Relations between bank-note issue regulations and the pension bonds illustrate well the working of boundary conditions. Both schemes were due to a necessary political compromise. On the one hand, the government had to get rid of the heavy transfer payments before it could institute modern budgetary procedures. And it was certainly not powerful enough simply to repudiate the *bushi* stipends; indeed, the government could not afford to antagonize this group too much. On the other hand, the *bushi* did not at all like the pension bonds. When they had been offered on a voluntary basis, only very few takers were found, in part at least because their interest rate was well below market rates. Compulsory commutation was the government stick; amended bank regulations were the carrot. They opened a road for pension bond holders to invest their funds in newly created national banks. In fact, the number of national banks rose between 1876 and 1880 from about 4 to 148, and in the latter year their note issue reached ¥ 34 million—the legal maximum.

This compromise nearly had disastrous consequences for the Meiji government. It precipitated a rather sharp inflation at a time when the government was least prepared to cope with this type of situation. Total note issue rose from ¥ 106.9 million in 1876 to ¥ 164.4 million in 1879, and this time, in contrast to earlier years, the price level responded. It would be interesting to speculate why an injection of money in 1876-1880 created an inflation when it did not have this effect in 1868-1872, but the crucial point is of a quite different nature. The inflation led to distortions in the economy which affected the government—at that time the main agent attempting to initiate MEG—most adversely.

To begin with, the rice price nearly doubled and, taken together with the fixed land tax, created enormous windfalls for the landowners. There is some evidence that these windfalls were not always used productively. For example, *Kōgyō*

64

iken (Survey of Industries, 1884) reported the following concerning the rural industries founded at that time: ". . . most of these (80-90 percent) are luxuries, imitating foreign products and mostly made of imported raw materials. The manufacture of these contributed little to increase the national power." At the same time, the government did not have an easy time in finding private entrepreneurs willing to assume responsibility for modern textile mills.

Most serious, perhaps, were the effects of the inflation on the new land tax. The real purchasing power of government revenue fell drastically, while it did not have the power to siphon off the landowners' windfalls. A public budget crisis was narrowly averted by the introduction of new taxes on sake and tobacco, but expenditures for fostering modern industries and other investments had to be cut down. The targets of the government were in trouble, and optimistic expectations concerning the new national banks were disappointed. These banks, as yet in inexperienced hands, had difficulty in differentiating between commercial and industrial capital, and did little to further MEG. At that time the Japanese economy held slight promise in the eyes of shrewd foreign observers—certainly a bad sign.

In October 1881, Matsukata Masayoshi became Finance Minister. With the installation of this remarkable man, a new era began in Japanese finance, and the targets set in 1868 were safely achieved in 1885. Understanding the corrosions caused by the inflation, Matsukata with great sternness and determination carried out a program of financial orthodoxy: the re-introduction of convertible currency, severe public austerity, and deflation. Public operation of expensive factories and mines was discontinued. Taxes on tobacco and sake were raised, and other indirect taxes were introduced. A redemption program for the public debt, based on government surpluses, was carried out in ten years. Under Matsukata the government succeeded in saving, on the average, 28 percent of its current revenues, and about half of these savings were used for capital formation, the other half being allocated to surplus. Deflation affected government revenues favorably because the land tax was fixed. In sharp contrast to the previous years of inflation, the land tax provided the government with a ready-made vehicle for increasing its real tax revenues. Of course, the disposable income of landowners fell, but this seemed to matter less.

Under Matsukata the quantity of money was reduced by some 20 percent and commodity prices fell sharply. In 1884 the general price level dropped to 75 percent of the 1881 level. Interest rates also declined, and the necessary conditions for convertible currency again came into being. Foreign payments, with the exception of a small deficit in 1881, were also in the black for the first time since the Restoration—and this was not to happen again frequently in the future. Based on these achievements the government could now move toward reform of the banking system. The Bank of Japan was founded in 1885 and took the place of the national banks as the bank of issue. Japan now had a modern currency system and a well-operating public budget structure. It took the government nineteen years to achieve these targets, and now MEG could and did begin.

The Matsukata deflation was the most severe experience of this type in modern Japanese economic history. It was a bold attempt to create the conditions under which MEG could begin—it was a life or death risk. The dangerous inflation which preceded it was the financial result of all the disturbances and hindrances to growth which the Restoration inherited. Private enterprise needed a more rational and elastic currency system, and the government had to have adequate sources of revenue, and both of these came into being largely as a result of the deflation.

Initial Modern Economic Growth, 1886-1905

When MEG begins, in the middle of the 1880's, it becomes convenient to divide the Japanese economy into two sectors: the traditional and modern economy. By traditional economy we mean those sectors which largely preserved pre-modern (indigenous) techniques and organization of production. Agriculture was, of course, the most important sector of the traditional economy, although—in terms of either output or employment—other sectors were not insignificant. The modern economy is largely represented by imported techniques and forms of organization: machinery, factories, corporations, etc. "Modern" and "Western" are almost synonymous. In the real world it is often very difficult to draw a clear line between traditional and modern. We will need a third category, called hybrid, in which traditional and modern elements are combined.

There is little difficulty in applying this classification to Japan. Agriculture, for example, is the clearest case of the traditional economy in operation. In terms of organization of production, there was little change between the end of the Tokugawa era and World War II. The small family farm, land fragmentation, major crops, all these traditional features remained nearly intact. After the Restoration there were important improvement in the general level of agricultural techniques which allowed rapid increases in output and productivity. The most important of these were: (1) more intensive use of fertilizers, and (2) improved irrigation methods, and these improvements applied more widely and intensively the traditional stock of knowledge already available in pre-modern Japan.

Examples of the modern economy are so obvious as to require almost no elaboration. The cotton textile industry, based largely on imported raw materials, imported machinery, and wage labor working in factories, is an outstanding case.

Hybrids become especially numerous in the early years of the twentieth century with the application of the electric motor to small-scale industry. There are also possible example in the Meiji period—for instance seed improvements. We have stated that irrigation and fertilizers accounted for most of the increases in agricultural productivity. While this is true, improvements in seed selection were also of consequence. These were largely the result of the so-called "salt-water method," perfected by Yokoi Tokiyoshi in 1882, at that time head of the agricultural experimental station at Fukuoka. Yokoi's method involved the principles of modern scientific experimentation and knowledge relating to the varying density of salt water. It was, however, inspired by and based on cruder conventional methods long in use by farmers in Western Japan, and therefore is a perfect hybrid.

THE MECHANISM OF MEG IN ITS INITIAL PHASE

We propose to analyze the process of growth during the initial phase in terms of the interrelations between the modern and the traditional economy. The argument can be summarized in the following propositions:

1. In the absence of large capital imports, the initial establishment and subsequent development of the modern economy depended on the accelerated growth of the traditional economy —and also to some extent on the accelerated growth of the hybrid economy.

2. The traditional economy was capable of producing such accelerated growth.

3. However, the growth potential of the traditional economy was limited. When its growth rate begins to decline (1905), the initial phase of MEG comes to an end.

4. By the time the initial phase comes to an end, the dependence of the modern on the traditional economy has greatly decreased—although it has not disappeared.

The validity of the four propositions requires verification. Proposition two requires little argument. A considerable amount of research indicates that the agricultural and non-agricultural traditional sectors of the Japanese economy experienced rising growth rates in the last quarter of the nineteenth century. How to date the beginning of the accelerations is a much more difficult question. We are inclined to believe that they generally started after 1868, and became especially prominent after 1885. Some quickening in these rates may have begun before 1868, but this does not really matter. The major parts of the spurt certainly came after the Restoration.[11]

[11] See, for example, Ohkawa, *Growth Rate of the Japanese Economy,* Bruce F. Johnston, "Agricultural Productivity and Economic De-

We come now to proposition one which asserts that the development of the modern economy depended on the accelerated growth of the traditional economy. This relationship can be seen most clearly if we ask ourselves what the requirements of the modern economy were, and then examine how they could and were in fact met.

1. Most important, perhaps, were the savings-investment needs of the modern sector. The public and private sectors

---

velopment in Japan," *Journal of Political Economy* (December 1951), and also our previously cited article "The Role of Agriculture in Modern Japanese Economic Development."

James Nakamura's paper in this volume (ch. IV) expresses doubt about the figures which we have used as a basis for demonstrating the rapid growth of agricultural production. The differences of opinion which exist between us are in large part of a very technical nature and cannot be adequately discussed at this juncture. (A full treatment is provided in our forthcoming book: *A Century of Growth.*) Briefly, however, we must state our position. The agricultural estimates used by us are based exclusively on the official statistics issued by the Japanese government. Nakamura believes that the official estimates were much too low in the early stages of growth, and he attempts by means of various assumptions to reconstruct what, in his opinion, the level of output *must have been.* We are quite prepared to concede that there may have been some underestimation in the early government statistics, but we do not accept either Nakamura's assumptions or the highly inflated output figures which result.

Our major doubts pertain to the great upward revision of the estimate for rice-yield in the 1870's from the official figure of 1.2 *koku* per *tan* to what seems to us an unjustifiable 1.6 *koku* per *tan.* As Nakamura himself realizes, this is really the crux of the matter; his "bold conclusions" rest in large measure on this assumption. We have re-examined our own sources and looked carefully at Nakamura's evidence. We have also studied new sources, especially the *Chiso kaisei hōkokusho* (Report on the Land Tax Revision) submitted by Finance Minister Matsukata Masayoshi to Prime Minister Sanjō Sanetomi in 1882. Chapter 13 of this report entitled *Kaku fu-ken chiso kaisei kiyō* (Memoir on the Land Tax Reform in the Prefectures) is especially valuable. Our reading of the evidence does not support Nakamura's contentions: the official yield figures perhaps contain a slight downward bias (we would suggest a magnitude of 10-12%), but they are far closer to the mark than the alternatives proposed by Nakamura.

Sometimes Nakamura seems to imply that the growth rates we

needed access to a growing pool of savings which could be turned into social overheads and factories. In the case of the government, during these years, the savings came from agriculture, and the land tax was the mechanism by which they were transferred out of agriculture. This transfer of savings from the traditional sector to the modern sector must have also operated on a private basis, although this is much more difficult to document.

2. The modern sector also needed a labor force, and here again the traditional economy was the only real source of supply. A shift from traditional to modern occupations, from agriculture to industry, depended on increased output and productivity in the primary sector. The output of food and other items had to rise in keeping with a growing population, while labor had to be supplied for industry. If agricultural output had not risen in the face of increased needs (i.e., a growing population and rising incomes) the chances for successful MEG would have been greatly diminished.

3. At this time also the development of modern industry was very dependent on Japan's ability to purchase producers' durables and raw materials abroad. Once the Tokugawa hoards

---

suggest for Japanese agriculture during the Meiji period are so high as to be paradoxical in terms of international experience. But is this implication justified? According to Raymond Goldsmith's calculations, for example, the growth rate of agricultural output in Tsarist Russia between 1860 and 1913 was 1¾-2% per year. (*Economic Development and Cultural Change*, IX, 3 [April 1961], 442.) For the years 1952-61, the countries of the ECAFE region recorded the following average annual growth rates—all cereals (rice, wheat, maize, millet, sorghum, barley) : 2.7%; rice: 2.5%; wheat: 3.3%. Are the Japanese rates so implausible?

Two further points should be added. We have doubts also about some other assertions contained in Nakamura's paper : the revision of the paddy-field area, the extent of double cropping, etc. These points are, however, much less important. Finally, it must also be understood that our exposition of the mechanism of Japanese economic growth does not hinge on a specific or even very high rate of growth of agricultural production. A downward revision, the reasons for which we feel have not been demonstrated, requires no substantial revision of our reasoning.

of precious metals had been depleted, exports were the only rational means of getting foreign exchange for vital imports. And in this period exports were largely composed of traditional output: tea and silk.

4. We have shown elsewhere[12] that even Japanese capital formation can be examined in the light of the modern-traditional dichotomy. Especially during the initial phase of MEG, the government and to some extent the private sector engaged in a great deal of investment of the traditional type, often facilitating investments for modern industry. Examples are road and bridge building, commercial and to a more limited extent residential construction, riparian works, and natural disaster reconstruction. Thus, the traditional economy once again supplied the needs of its modern infant brother.

5. If there had been no increase in the output of the traditional economy, there could hardly have existed any *domestic* market for the output of modern industry. Throughout the initial phase of MEG, over 65 percent of the gainfully occupied population was engaged in agriculture. The sheer weight of this group made them the only sizable domestic market, and cotton textiles, simple domestic utensils, and other such products of the early modern sector must have been sold primarily to these groups. (The export/output ratio of many modern manufactured items was very low at this time.)

We have attempted to establish that during the initial phase of MEG economic progress was primarily supported by the accelerated growth of the traditional sector. However, the expansion potential of the traditional sector was limited, and its rate of growth began to decline around 1905—this being the end of the initial phase. This decline, stated in terms of the growth rate, can be attributed to three principal factors: (1) colonial or empire competition, (2) competition from the modern economy, and (3) endogenous reasons for retardation within the traditional economy.

It is convenient to begin with the endogenous reasons for decline in the traditional economy as typified by agriculture.

[12] Rosovsky, *Capital Formation*, 16ff.

This is a relatively well-researched story. Japan was already in 1868 a densely populated country with a shortage of arable land. As its agriculture grew, using largely traditional methods, it rapidly bumped against this ceiling; and by being forced to use increasingly marginal land faced the steeply rising costs of land reclamation. These conditions were aggravated by the severity of land fragmentation, and the over-all smallness of holdings. In short, given the traditional forms of cultivation, Japanese agriculture had by 1905 reached diminishing returns in terms of the rate of growth.

This leads to an obvious question: why was it not possible to abandon the traditional organization which was now limiting agricultural growth? There were both technical and institutional reasons why this was not possible within the context of early twentieth-century Japan.

Agricultural technology can be conveniently split into two parts—one part relating to improvements of conventional inputs (seeds, fertilizers, nursing, etc.), and the other to improvements of land and capital (irrigation, drainage, machinery, etc.). Between these two parts there exists a complementary relationship: for optimal results, improvements must go hand in hand. Given the character of Japanese agriculture, improvement of inputs was a relatively minor problem. Land and capital improvements, however, became a major problem especially at the beginning of this century. The kinds of investments which were now needed had a "lumpy" character, and due to land fragmentation and the generally small size of holdings were too costly for most landlords.

Institutional limitations were equally severe. Absentee (or, to use the Japanese term, "parasitic") landlordism was on the rise, and the brunt of agricultural difficulties was, to an increasing extent, born by an economically and politically weak peasant class. Consolidation of holdings, one possible method of rationalization, would probably have been resisted by both landlords and tenants, but for quite different reasons. Here one must always keep in mind the factor proportions in Japanese agriculture. Japanese economic growth was very rapid, but it was not rapid enough to modernize the traditional economy. By that we mean that growth was not rapid enough to change the persistently unfavorable man-land ratio. Despite the large exodus of labor to the cities and to modern employment—the pace of this exodus being largely conditioned by the growth rate of the modern economy—the absolute number of workers in agriculture remained nearly the same from 1868 to 1930. Under these circumstances, for the landlords the relative price of capital remained too high (or the relative price of labor was too low) to encourage expensive capital-using modernization. On the other hand, there was always a plentiful supply of people willing, for lack of other opportunities, to assume the burdens of tenancy.

Agricultural competition from the growing empire was another troublesome development, although it became important only after World War I. As Japan experienced increasing difficulties in feeding its growing population, and as rice prices rose alarmingly, the government looked more and more to its colonies for sustenance. Korea and Taiwan became cheap sources of supply, which further increased the difficulties of domestic producers.

Competition from the modern economy as a factor retarding the growth of the traditional economy is an obvious concomitant of MEG in the case of non-agriculture; but its consequences may be quite complicated. In Japan, as modern industry developed, it naturally wiped out numerous traditional crafts. Many examples could be cited. Modern cotton spinning eliminated the native cotton growers because they could not produce raw materials of adequate quality at a competitive price. The modern textile industry in general reduced the levels of home spinning and weaving. In addition, a government system of monopolies and licenses did away with some traditional small-scale production, as was the case with tobacco and sake.

In the non-agricultural sectors of the traditional economy, however, the development of modern industry had both substitution and complementary effects. To some extent, modern small-scale industry—that is to say, modern in some of its techniques and sometimes in its organization—was the heir of traditional non-agricultural industries. As we leave the initial phase of MEG, and especially after World War I, some traditional non-agricultural industries succeeded in integrating themselves into the modern economy. Although their relations with large modern enterprises were nearly always relatively disadvantageous to themselves, they survived and multiplied in their new form. In effect they usually became true hybrids: rather modern in technique (as in their use of electric motors) and rather traditional in their organization (as in the widespread use of non-wage family labor). In this process, the ties between agriculture and traditional (now in good part hybrid) non-agricultural industry became much looser, and in the following phases they must be treated separately.

A slight digression may be helpful at this point. It is an acknowledged fact that in the post-World War II period the rate of growth of Japanese agriculture spurted once again. Does this contradict the assertions made up to now? We do not believe so, for defeat brought many changes and facilitated institutional reform. Land reform became possible, the empire was dissolved, and the government was more active in its support of agriculture. But there was one other very important change, namely, certain advances in technology within the non-agricultural sectors could advantageously be used by agriculture—for example, insecticides, pesticides, vinyl, etc. And this brings to the fore the issue of sectoral reciprocity, a major point. In saying that the traditional economy, during the initial phase, supported the growth of the modern economy, we do not intend to imply that this was exclusively a one-way relationship, although we do say that net support *during the initial phase* flowed from the traditional to the modern economy. After all, what forces can account for the undoubtedly rapid growth of the modern economy from the middle of the 1880's until the Russo-Japanese War? The following appear the weightiest: military expenditures, expanding foreign trade, a slowly developing domestic market, and the competitive strength of modern industry as it innovated and replaced traditional outputs. None of these provided direct support for the traditional economy, and during the initial phase what might be termed modern support was confined to a few technological innovations.

The end of the initial phase of MEG has been defined as the point at which the growth rate of the traditional economy begins to decline, i.e., 1905. This is the end of a phase because from then on the modern economy could no longer count on the same degree of support from the traditional sectors. While the economic relations between the two sectors persisted, the modern economy had to look more to its inner strength or its export capabilities if rapid growth was to be maintained. All this was possible, because, in the twenty years since MEG began, industrialization itself had made considerable progress. Let us briefly review these changes.

1. We had stressed the savings-investment relationship and the role of the agricultural surplus and land tax. By the end of the initial phase, the composition of central government revenues had undergone great changes. Relatively speaking, the role of the land tax had declined, as it was being replaced by excise taxes on consumption, income and business taxes, and customs duties.

2. From the beginnings of MEG until the 1930's the dominant share of the non-agricultural labor force came from agriculture. However, it must also be noted that throughout practically this entire period the rate of growth of the non-agricultural labor force of agricultural origin declines, while that of non-agricultural origin rises. Thus, the natural increases within the modern sectors were beginning to make themselves felt. This is especially noticeable beginning in about 1910. A qualitative factor may be added. The modern economy must have placed an increasing premium on education, and therefore young people of urban origin may have been more valuable to them.

3. The relative weight of traditional exports and modern durable imports had also been altered. By 1905, tea and raw silk exports were being replaced to a considerable extent by the rapid rise of cotton fabrics, cotton yarn, and silk fabrics—all outputs of modern organization and technology. At the

same time, the net import of producers' durables had fallen to about 25 percent of domestic production—from a level of about 200 percent in the 1880's.

4. Another change was in the composition of modern and traditional investments. In 1890 about two-thirds of the investments were traditional in technique. By 1905 the proportion had fallen to one-third. In effect we can say that the modern economy had reached the stage where its facilitating needs could no longer be satisfied by traditional methods.

5. We have also outlined the importance of the domestic market for the development of modern industry, and noted that this largely represented customers in the traditional economy. As the modern economy expanded its output, with the relatively low levels of per capita income of the bulk of its customers, it is clear that the need for other markets increased. Therefore toward the end of the initial phase it is reasonable to find attempts to step up exports in order to tap foreign sources of demand. Statistical evidence for this is available in the rising export/output ratios for many of the products of modern industry. All of these factors yield the same picture—by the end of the initial phase, a modern sector gradually becoming more independent and capable of growing on its own.

One last point of considerable analytical interest remains. The interrelations between the traditional and the modern economy imply that during the initial phase there arises a vital question of timing. We may call this the "crucial interval." Is the traditional spurt long enough to permit the modern sector to establish itself on a sufficiently firm footing? If the spurt is too short and if the degree of the modern sector's dependence remains large, the initial phase could have ended in abortive growth. In Japan there was not much leeway: rapidly diminishing returns appeared all too soon. Would the modern sector have survived if the downturn had come in the 1890's rather than in about 1905? It is far easier to ask the question than to supply the answer.

Differential Structure: Creation, 1906-1930

Beginning about 1906, and continuing for about a quarter of a century, a new feature entered into Japanese economic development. In essence, this feature was the accelerated growth of the modern economy. In turn, this was based on a number of changes occurring at about the same time: an acceleration of the rate of increase of per worker productivity in the modern economy, and, related to this, a rising proportion of investment and an increase in industrial concentration. This process is called the creation of the differential structure because, in this phase, the rate of growth (and allied measures) of the traditional sector no longer accelerates, and therefore a gap grows between the two sectors. One point, however, must be made absolutely clear: the gap results both from the slower growth of the traditional sector and more rapid growth of the modern sector. In fact, the latter was more important than the former. This can be seen if we assume for a moment that "non-agriculture" and "modern," and "agriculture" and "traditional," are the same. In the modern sector, annual rates of increase in output per worker run between 1.1 and 3.2 percent for the initial phase. During this phase, between 1906 and 1930, they fluctuate somewhat but rise to 6 percent. Had agricultural manpower productivity continued to grow at rates of 2-3 percent per year—which it did not—it would have still fallen behind.

Let us, briefly, review some of the major forces in Japanese economic history between 1906 and 1930. We have already commented on the vigorous growth of the modern sector at that time, and now some qualifications must be added. A variety of factors favorable to the development of modern industry appeared shortly after the end of the initial phase. The Russo-Japanese War (1904-1905) greatly stimulated the development of all modern industry directly and indirectly connected with the war effort. This expansion was supported by increased imports, inflation, and rather sizable foreign loans. Government military expenditures during these years were on the increase, and the recently completed nationalization of railroad trunk lines led to further transportation expenditures. We know that the I/GNP proportion begins to rise at about this time, and this must be the reflection of two separate forces. On the one hand, we see here the real beginnings of heavy industry, but it was still tiny and almost exclusively confined to the production of arms. On the other hand, we can also observe the continuing development and modernization of textile production, and especially the substitution of traditional for modern methods (e.g., in raw silk production and weaving). At this time modern industry was also beginning to find an export market in the new empire, while the home market—due to rising per capita incomes— was gradually being strengthened.

And yet all was not well with the Japanese economy—especially with regard to exports and the balance of payments. This can be seen most clearly in the trend of ratios of imports and exports to GNP. Throughout the initial phase, the import ratio shows a sharp increase. During the present phase, it continues to increase though at a somewhat slower pace, reaching a level somewhat higher than 20 percent about 1925. After that, the ratio declines until about 1931 and once again rises sharply. The export ratio kept pace with the import ratio during the initial phase of MEG—both expanded at more or less equal rates. But, beginning in the first decade of the twentieth century, the export ratio—with the conspicuous exception of World War I—began to stagnate at an average level of about 15 percent.

In these terms, the specific experience of Japan in World War I becomes especially interesting. Her major economic weakness had been the chronic imbalance of her foreign payments, and now, all of a sudden, this problem was wiped out. Exports expanded even more rapidly than the growing import requirements, and while the bonanza lasted only from about 1914 to 1919, the effects were of lasting duration. During the period of World War I Japanese modern business circles experienced an unprecedented prosperity. Sales of all items were easy, especially to areas where European competition had been temporarily eliminated. Domestic investment boomed, but there were also less beneficial consequences such as a high rate of inflation.

Japan experienced inflation in part as a result of the export boom and in part due to the lack of an adequate government financial policy. The results included a badly distorted wage structure, with many classes of people experiencing a decline in real income. Food prices rose enormously, and the Rice Revolt of 1918 was an ominous warning to the government. Even the entrepreneurial classes faced new and baffling problems as a result of the boom. Perhaps for the first time in Japanese economic history the unlimited supply of labor was interrupted by the unprecedented expansion of the modern sector. There were labor shortages and the real wages of certain groups of workers rose considerably. "Unlimited supply" usually relates to a long-run concept. The experience of World War I is a good illustration of the much lower supply elasticities prevailing in the short run.

We come now to the aftermath of World War I—the difficult and confusing decade of the 1920's—during which the differential structure became solidified. The termination of the war must have come as an unpleasant shock to many Japanese entrepreneurs. Exports fell sharply, terms of trade improved briefly and then declined, and the rapid inflation turned into a prolonged period of falling prices—after the Matsukata Deflation, the second longest such period in post-Restoration economic history. To this gloomy situation the modern sector responded by adopting a rationalization policy. Essentially this meant attempts to increase productivity and to save labor costs through the introduction of more modern techniques. In an indirect sense, the lessons of World War I had much to do with effecting rationalization. Modern industry had realized the inconveniences of skilled labor shortages. Now, facing a highly competitive international market, the leaders of modern industry also realized that they would have to be more efficient in order to survive. All this meant maintaining a higher level of investment, and the adoption of improved technology. It also led to the oligopolization of Japanese in-

79

dustry and to increased power for the *zaibatsu* (financial cliques or big business).

What did rationalization do to the structure of the Japanese economy? First, it further speeded the increases in product per worker in the modern sector. From 1922 to 1933, product per worker for this group rose by 60 percent—from ¥ 453 to ¥ 726 in 1914 prices. At the same time, the real wages of industrial workers rose slowly, even though the unlimited supply of labor had been reestablished. This was not due to the generosity of entrepreneurs. They depended, now, on more modern skills and a higher degree of commitment. Furthermore, productivity increased much faster than wages. And finally, the labor needs for modern industry declined relatively, and labor's relative share once again declined sharply.

While rationalization was proceeding in modern industry, no similar events took place in the traditional economy. Here, productivity and real wages were no longer rising, and the gap between the two sectors widened enormously. This gap—which we call the differential structure—was brought about by long-run forces already identifiable in the early twentieth century. It was, however, considerably intensified by the rationalization of the 1920's. In oversimplified terms, the following statements are true:

1. Before the establishment of the differential structure:
    a. wages in the traditional and modern sectors were more or less the same;
    b. the productivity gap between the modern and traditional sectors was more or less unchanging; and
    c. the share of the traditional economy in output and labor force was dominant.
2. After the establishment of the differential structure:
    a. there existed a growing wage differential;
    b. there existed a rapidly growing productivity gap; and
    c. the share of modern industry, especially in terms of output, becomes much larger.

The widening gap between the traditional and the modern sectors perpetuated a deep cleavage in Japanese economic life. Manifestations of this change can be readily identified.

1. Two living standards developed—the higher modern and the lower traditional way of life. This had important political consequences. Especially the dissatisfied rural groups, due to their number, exercised considerable political power. They did much to further power ambitions of the military cliques, and in that sense at least Japanese aggression in the 1930's can be related to the internal economic structure of the country.

2. The differential structure perpetuated the unlimited supply of labor because the labor requirements of modern industry were not growing very rapidly.

3. The continuance of the unlimited supply of labor made available to enterprise a continuing source of relatively cheap labor.

4. Given the differential structure, it was difficult to strengthen the domestic market on a continuing basis. In terms of gainfully occupied workers, the largest segment of the economy was condemned to lower productivity and low incomes.

Differential Structure: Economic and Political Consequences, 1931-1952

The demarcation between successive phases of Japanese growth is, as we have seen, reflected in the fluctuations of the annual growth rate of GNP. At the end of the initial phase the growth rate hit a trough, and then shot up with renewed vigor as modern industry expanded. At the end of World War I the growth rate declined, and throughout the 1920's and rationalization the rate stayed at roughly 3 percent—for Japan a somewhat depressed level. A renewed spurt—and a new phase—begins in 1931, and we wish to interpret the next twenty or so years as consequences of the differential structure.[13]

[13] See graph 8 in our previously cited article "Economic Fluctuations in Prewar Japan."

An economic interpretation of the 1930's cannot be one-sided. The Japanese economy grew rapidly partly in response to ordinary economic stimuli. This was especially true of exports. In a world caught in the grips of the great depression, a leading manufacturer of cheap goods (with a recently rationalized industry) had distinct advantages. But this would be a superficial interpretation of the 1930's, because it ignores what might be labeled the "political solution." At the end of the last section we pointed out the grave problems confronting the Japanese economy in the 1920's and indicated our belief that they affected subsequent political action. These actions, more than anything else, explain the brief growth and prosperity of the 1930's.

The political solution which Japan chose ended in disaster. It allowed a few years of relative prosperity, but today few would claim that it was worth the price. In this primarily economic analysis, political judgments may be out of place. We will merely indicate how growth was resumed and how this can be linked with the economic structure of the country.

Once Japan had decided to follow a policy of military expansion, it was a relatively simple matter to step up the growth of the economy, even though the standard of living of the mass of the people did not necessarily maintain the pace. Military expenditures became gigantic in order to fight in Manchuria, Inner Mongolia, China, and in preparation for World War II. The armament industry and associated heavy industries were the leading sectors of this growth. (It did not matter at the time that this was a very artificial expansion for heavy industry, largely based on subsidies creating high-cost producers.) This was accompanied by an expansion drive to the colonies. Colonies were made to take exports, native populations were exploited as food producers, and colonial markets were frequently monopolized for the mother country's benefit. Throughout, the government maintained an expansionary monetary policy with the usual consequences.

In the long run, there is nothing especially interesting in these events, even though they do illustrate vividly the economic background of Japanese imperialism and its relation to the differential structure. The policies of the 1930's logically ended in World War II, a conflict which Japan could not possibly win. Japan might have attempted alternative economic solutions—none would have been easy—but this did not become a realistic possibility until after World War II. The war itself, and the rehabilitation period which followed, defy normal economic analysis. It is generally conceded that the long chain of events which began with the militarism of the early thirties ended between 1952-1954. By that time, Japan had recovered her independence, and most of the abnormal influences of war and occupation had disappeared. Once again the Japanese economy began to spurt, and we must turn to the final historical phase: the years following World War II.[14]

Postwar Growth, 1953—

The Japanese *wirtschaftswunder* has attracted an enormous amount of attention in the postwar world. Since 1954 the economy has expanded at an average rate of somewhat more than 9 percent. No other country has matched this record, and the Japanese have basked in the warmth of international admiration. One cannot argue that this astounding growth is simply the result of repairing the damage of World War II. After all, the war ended in 1945, and our analysis begins only in 1953 when, hopefully, these influences have disappeared. At the same time, from 1953 to the present is not a complete phase of growth. The historical record is shorter than a decade—we have the beginning of a phase as evidenced by the growth spurt, but the end must remain a matter of conjecture. Nevertheless, the current events must be examined critically because they can contribute immensely to an understanding of Japan's historical pattern of growth. One should not, of course, compare the short-term growth of the postwar economy with prewar trends—even though this has been done all too frequently—but even a comparison of different short-term periods yields valuable insights.

[14] We would not wish to imply, of course, that the war and ensuing rehabilitation left the Japanese economy unchanged.

Although the Japanese economy has grown more rapidly during the postwar years than at any other time, there were similar and earlier periods of almost equally rapid growth. For example, the following average annual growth rates apply: 1905-1912, 6.7 percent; 1912-1919, 7.0 percent; 1931-1938, 7.5 percent; 1953-1960, 9.3 percent. The recent average is the highest not so much because peak values have risen (e.g., compare 1918-1919 at 18.8 percent with 1958-1959 at 17.9 percent), but because the postwar troughs have been relatively higher. During prewar spurts negative values are not uncommon, while an annual growth rate of 3.3 percent is the bottom of postwar values.

Behind these aggregate measures exist certain rather fundamental changes observable over time. Postwar growth is distinguished by two factors: a rapid increase in the rate of growth of the gainfully employed population, and an equally rapid increase in the rate of growth of productivity per worker *due to* shifts in the industrial structure. These events are related. The natural rate of increase of the Japanese population quickened in the 1920's, maintained comparatively high levels during the 1930's and World War II, and rose to unprecedented heights in the immediate postwar period. (Since 1949 the pace of natural increase has been declining sharply.) This demographic boom has altered the age structure of the population, so that in the postwar period the proportion of the working age population grew rapidly and reached an all-time high. These forces were intensified by the large number of returnees from the empire in the immediate postwar period.

Where did these increased numbers become gainfully occupied? They were not going into agriculture. The rate of growth of the agricultural labor force has never been as sharply negative as at present. Thus, the new increases, and some of the already gainfully employed workers, were shifting out of agriculture and into manufacturing and services. This sort of transfer means movement from lower to higher productivity occupations, and in large measure this combination of increased numbers and transfer explains the higher rate of over-all growth during the recent decade. The growth rate of "productivity proper," by contrast, has changed much less significantly although what is perhaps most interesting is that it has not *declined* in spite of the large inflow of workers.

In trying to understand what factors in the economy made these happenings possible, one's attention immediately turns to the level of investment, and especially the strength of autonomous investment. It is, of course, true that Japan may have had more than her share of economic good luck in the postwar years—favorable terms of trade, the Korean War, no national defense burden—but this cannot explain enough. Investment was a much more sustaining force. In comparing pre- and post-war capital formation, one is immediately aware of some fundamental differences. First of all, the proportion of gross investment to gross domestic expenditure now stands at an unprecedented level. The average proportion for 1953-1960 was 33.2 percent, and in 1960 it reached an almost unbelievable 38.2 percent. In general, the trend of the capital formation proportion has been rising in Japan, but during the earlier phases of rapid growth it never exceeded 23 percent.

What can account for the postwar level? Essentially it is due to a steep rise in the rate of private investment in plant and equipment, especially since 1956. The role of government investment—always an important magnitude—has also been altered, but here the change has been mainly compositional. Before the war, government accounted for 50 percent of all investment if military investment is included, and for 40 percent if it is excluded. By contrast, in 1960, government investment amounted to only 27 percent of the total. This was not the result of an absolute decrease of public investment—in fact, the ratio of government investment to GNP has been rising virtually since the 1880's—but rather the effect of the more rapid growth of private investment. Of course, it must also be stressed that public investment is today much more "productive," because defense expenditures have fallen to very low levels.

While recognizing the advantages of increased productive investment on the part of the government, it is still clear that what really needs to be explained is the unprecedented vigor of the private sector. The figures indicate great private investment spurts, especially following the rather mild recessions, reaching annual rates of increase in the neighborhood of 55-60 percent during 1956-1957. It must be recognized at the outset that the postwar years were especially suitable for rapid technological progress. Japanese industry, due to the war, had been isolated for more than a decade, and great opportunities existed to reduce rapidly a technological gap. Sometimes this has been called the "catching-up" effect, and some may feel that it is still the best explanation of the current investment wave. This is, however, a much too narrow view. Recently, for example, Japanese entrepreneurs have been concerned about possible trade liberalization and relations with the Common Market. This has quickened the introduction of new techniques and is unrelated to wartime isolation.

Catching-up makes much more sense if we understand the concept in broad historical terms. Then it means the transformation of a semideveloped economy into a mature one, and this is what has been happening in Japan. Underlying this transformation is a shift in the industrial structure from light to heavy industry. Productive investment by the private sector has tended to concentrate increasingly on basic heavy industries, and the dominant proportion of the technical innovations came in these sectors. For example, in 1960 the level of plant and equipment investment was 3.25 times higher than in 1955 for all production, but it was 10.5 times higher for the non-ferrous metals industry, 9 times higher for the iron and steel and metals manufacturing industry, and approximately 7 times higher for the machinery, electrical machinery, and transportation equipment industry.

Quite clearly, the entrepreneur did not lack incentives to promote these heavy investments. In the short run, ordinary private profit considerations can adequately explain the desire to introduce new and better techniques. Private profits were high because domestic and foreign demand was strong, productivity was rising, and wages were lagging behind productivity. The entrepreneur was merely maximizing profits.

In the longer run, the government did much to bolster expectations of continued rapid growth. It compiled several long-range growth plans as guideposts for private business, and all of these anticipated a rate of expansion maintained at very high levels. Our best guess is that Japan will not be able to sustain the postwar average pace of some 9 percent per year for a long time. Some of the things which have stimulated the economy in recent years may lose their force. This is certainly true of the demographic push. It is also hard to visualize investment kept at present levels. The capital-output ratio has been rising, and this could change entrepreneurial incentives; and once the heavy-industry complex is well established, future technological change may proceed at a more deliberate pace. Catching-up—in the short-term sense—will have been accomplished.

We should remember, however, that catching-up does have a long-term meaning, and because of this there are good reasons for believing that Japan will continue to grow, perhaps at a more rapid pace than the 4 percent prewar long-run average. In many ways, Japan is still a semi-developed country. Per capita income levels are still low, the proportion of workers in agriculture is still high, and a dual economy is still very much in evidence. We think that Japan has now entered a second industrial revolution. The first established a modern enclave and a dual economy. The task of the more recent industrial revolution is to abolish the dual economy and to bring about advanced standards of income, consumption, and industrial structure. Our analysis of the postwar years has identified some signs of the process: shifts in the industrial structure, technological progress, and the importance of productivity gains due to transfer. We believe that this is only the beginning; Japan's path to economic maturity still contains many years of rapid growth.

Needless to say, one cannot forget that ever useful disclaimer: "other things being equal." Japan's economic destiny depends very much on the activities of the outside world which we have completely ignored in this analysis. Adverse international economic conditions could easily make a shambles out of our optimistic predictions.

The Longer Phases

Shorter or intermediate-range phases average about twenty years in length, and derive their unity and identifiability from the fact that they represent successive spurts of gross output and a subsequent adjustment mechanism to this phenomenon. At the beginning of each phase—in 1868 (more by induction than by measurement), 1886, 1906, 1931, and 1953—the rate of growth begins to quicken, eventually reaches a kind of peak, and then levels off, until the next phase begins. Within these demarcations we have tried to set forth the major forces accounting for growth. It is also possible to adopt a somewhat wider perspective by combining several phases into one. This sacrifices precision, but it does achieve a clearer historical perspective.

Let us examine first the properties of the so-called first, second, and third phases of MEG. The first phase, 1868-1905, represents the years when the traditional economy is paramount, and when its development is vital to the establishment of the modern economy. A fundamental change takes place with the second phase, 1906-1953, when the modern economy grows on its own base, and securely establishes an up-to-date light (and semi-heavy) industry complex. Finally, the third phase of which we have seen only the bare beginnings, will complete the process of industrialization through the propagation of heavy industries, automation, development of modern services, etc.

Historical phasing is always a hazardous and debatable process, and a degree of overlapping cannot be avoided. Taking an even broader perspective, it may make sense to speak of two industrial revolutions in Japan. The first, lasting from 1868 to 1930, created a semi-developed country possessing a considerable industrial complex, but still characterized by dualism and low per capita incomes. The second industrial revolution, which began abortively in the 1930's and more promisingly after World War II, will transform Japan into a truly mature economy. It does not really matter which one of these schemes is adopted—if any or all of them permit a more systematic presentation of Japanese economic growth, they will have accomplished their purpose.

TABLE 1

Population and Gross National Product for Selected Intervals

	1.1	1.2	2.1	2.2	3.1(2.1/1.1)	3.2
	Total Population	Rate of Increase per annum	GNP	Rate of Increase per annum	GNP per Head	Rate of Increase per annum
	(thousand)	(%)	(million yen [1934-36 prices])	(%)	(yen)	(%)
1879	36,603		2,318		63.3	
1885	38,484	0.8	2,487	1.2	64.6	0.3
1886	38,663		2,979		77.1	
1898	43,275	0.9	4,971	4.1	114.9	3.1
1899	43,736		4,626		105.8	
1905	46,934	1.2	4,616	0	98.4	−1.2
1906	47,322		5,244		110.8	
1919	55,363	1.2	11,340	6.1	204.8	4.8
1920	55,963		8,996		162.5	
1930	64,450	1.4	12,760	3.5	198.0	2.0
1931	64,870		13,887		214.1	
1938	70,530	1.2	21,968	6.8	311.5	5.5
1939	70,850		22,093		311.8	
1944	73,800	0.8	20,113	−1.9	271.4	−2.7
1952	85,750	2.2	20,360	11.0	237.4	8.6
1953	86,983		21,907		251.9	
1960	93,383	1.0	40,466	9.2	433.3	8.1

Source: From 1879 to 1930, based on "List of Continuous Series" (hereafter CS) prepared by the Japanese Economic Development Project, University of California (Berkeley). From 1931 to 1960, based on Japan, Economic Planning Agency, *Kokumin shotoku hakusho 1960* [White Paper on National Income for 1960] (hereafter KH). (Tokyo, 1962.)

Note: Growth rates in columns 1.2, 2.2, and 3.2 are average compound rates for each time interval.

TABLE 2

Ratios of Important Components for Selected Intervals

	4	5	6	7	8	9	10
	% of Gross National Product				Share of Non-Agri-cultural Labor Force to the Total (%)	% of Net National Product	
	Gross Domestic Capital Formation	Personal Consump-tion	Exports	Imports		Agricul-tural Output	Outpu of Factor Manı
1879	n.a.	n.a.	3.1	6.3	17.1	64.4	3.2
1885	n.a.	n.a.	3.9	5.6	20.8	55.7	4.1
1886	11.1[a]	79.0	4.1	5.2	21.5	53.0	5.2
1898	13.5	81.1	6.2	16.8	28.7	52.2	5.9
1899	11.2	80.1	14.0	14.0	21.4	43.0	8.1
1905	13.9	63.9	10.0	32.7	33.4	39.0	9.1
1906	13.8	70.7	10.6	22.0	34.2	41.0	8.9
1919	17.3	74.6	13.2	16.7	46.0	36.5	14.3
1920	22.9	66.9	14.7	16.7	45.5	33.7	14.9
1930	18.8	69.0	17.5	24.4	50.3	18.6	17.3
1931	11.3	78.0	20.8	26.8	49.0	17.4	18.1
1938	21.7	51.8	22.7	21.2	54.0	20.3	26.1
1939	27.1	49.1	23.8	21.1	54.5	24.1	30.4
1944	29.5	34.8	11.5	12.2	57.3	17.8	24.4
1952	22.5	63.4	11.6	10.0	54.7	23.9	25.5
1953	26.3	63.3	11.7	12.3	55.1	22.0	29.5
1960	40.1	53.4	12.8	15.6	65.3	15.1	33.5

Source: Same as Table 1 except for column 10 which is based on Ohkawa K zushi et al., *Growth Rate of the Japanese Economy Since 1878* (Tokyo, 1957) a relevant years of *Kōjō tōkeihyō* [Census of Manufactures].

Note: [a] Due to lack of data, 1887 was substituted for 1886.
[b] Due to lack of data, 1942 was substituted for 1944.
[c] Due to lack of data, 1958 was substituted for 1960.

TABLE 3

SELECTED PHASE INDICATORS I

Phases	1.1 Total Population (thousand)	1.2 Rate of Increase per annum (%)	2.1 GNP (million yen [1934-36 prices])	2.2 Rate of Increase per annum (%)	3.1 GNP per Head (yen)	3.2 Rate of Increase per annum (%)
1879[a]	36,603		2,318		63.3	
1885	38,404	0.8	2,487	1.2	64.6	0.3
1886	38,663		2,979		77.1	
1905	46,934	1.1	4,616	2.4	98.4	1.3
1906	47,322		5,244		110.8	
1930	64,450	1.3	12,760	3.8	198.0	2.5
1931	64,870		13,887		214.1	
1952	85,750	1.3	20,360	1.8	237.4	0.5
1931	64,870		13,887		214.1	
1944	73,800	1.0	20,113	2.9	271.4	1.8
1953	86,983		21,907		251.9	
1960	93,383	1.0	40,466	9.2	433.3	8.1

SOURCE: See Table 1.

NOTE: [a] Data not available before 1879.

TABLE 4

SELECTED PHASE INDICATORS II

		4	5	6	7	8	9	10
								% of Net National Produc
			% of Gross National Product			% of Non-Agricultural Labor Force in the Total	% of Net National Produc	
		Gross Domestic Capital Formation	Personal Consumption	Exports	Imports		Agricultural Output	Outp of Facto Man
Phases								
I	1879	n.a.	n.a.	3.1	6.3	17.1	64.4	3.2
	1885	n.a.	n.a.	3.9	5.6	20.8	55.7	4.1
II	1886	11.1	79.0	4.1	5.2	21.5	53.0	5.2
	1905	13.9	63.9	10.0	32.7	33.4	39.0	9.1
III	1906	13.8	70.7	10.6	22.0	34.2	41.0	8.9
	1930	18.8	69.0	17.5	24.4	50.3	18.6	17.3
IV	1931	11.3	78.0	20.8	26.8	49.0	17.4	18.1
	1952	22.5	63.4	11.6	10.0	54.7	23.9	25.8
IV'	1931	11.3	78.0	20.8	26.8	49.0	17.4	18.1
	1944	29.5	34.8	11.5	12.2	57.3	17.8	13.2
V	1953	26.3	63.3	11.7	12.3	55.1	22.0	29.8
	1960	40.1	53.4	12.8	15.6	65.3	15.1	33.8

SOURCE: See Table 1.

CHAPTER THREE

Japan and Europe:
Contrasts in Industrialization

DAVID S. LANDES

Challenge and Response

FOR THE STUDENT of European economic history, the story of Japanese industrialization has a special interest. Not only is Japan the only example of a non-Western society to effect an industrial revolution, she accomplished the feat with unprecedented rapidity, and even today her economy continues to advance faster probably than any other in the world.[1] This achievement, moreover, is the more remarkable in that Japan had a far longer path to travel than her predecessors—and this without natural resources for economic prowess. Japan is not a land of wide fields and intrinsically fertile soil; nor is it "a land whose stones are iron and out of whose hills thou mayest dig brass." In particular, Japan has nothing like the great coal deposits that provided the fuel for British, American, and German economic expansion.

What is more, Japan accomplished these gains largely on her own; certainly she relied far less on outside help than did the follower countries of Continental Europe. The government did borrow on occasion from Western businessmen and capitalists—small amounts in the difficult years following the Restoration, a succession of much larger sums from 1899 on. It was not long, moreover, before private companies—railways

[1] Everything is relative, of course. Japan's economic growth has been rapid compared to that of Britain, France, or even Germany. Certainly her spurts have been marked by extraordinarily high rates of increase. Yet when all is said and done, she has taken a century to reach her present level of productivity and income, and, as Sydney Crawcour likes to emphasize, there are few if any backward countries today that would be willing to take that long to reach the same position.

and then industrial corporations—followed suit and began selling their own bonds and debentures in Western markets. The practice, still exceptional before the war, gained considerably in popularity in the twenties, only to be abandoned in the stringency of the Great Depression. To this formal import of capital should be added the support afforded Japanese foreign trade by Western merchant houses and banks by means of revolving short-term credits. These were particularly important in the early Meiji period, before the privileged Yokohama Specie Bank came to dominate the field. Also, one can find here and there examples of direct Western holdings in Japanese trade and industry. These were few and far between in the nineteenth century: Allen and Donnithorne mention tea-curing factories, a rice-straw rug enterprise, a toothbrush plant;[2] and there was the Takashima coal mine, the most important in Japan,[3] which was owned and operated by an English company until its sale to the government in 1874. In the years before and after the First World War, however, the number and importance of these foreign enterprises increased significantly. Joint Japanese-Western ventures were established, most of them in the engineering and electrical trades, while General Electric, Ford, General Motors, and other Western giants set up fully owned subsidiaries, often with an eye to getting behind newly raised tariff walls.

Yet foreign capital represented a small fraction of Japanese investment. The early Meiji loans were redeemed quickly; and total government indebtedness abroad, never more than about 30 million yen, fell to a negligible amount in the nineties. It then rose to 195 millions in 1903 and leaped to almost 2,000 millions in 1914—the equivalent of perhaps two or three years of national savings; to which should be added the comparatively small sum of 70 millions in direct foreign holdings. These debits were offset in part, however, by Japanese claims

[2] G. C. Allen and Audrey G. Donnithorne, *Western Enterprise in Far Eastern Economic Development* (London, 1954), p. 226.

[3] See John McMaster, "The Takashima Mine: British Capital and Japanese Industrialization," *Business History Review*, XXXVII (1963), 217-39.

abroad: liquid assets of 246 million yen and long-term investments estimated at 536 millions. Moreover, thanks to the fat earnings of the years from 1914 to 1918, this was the high point (or low point, according to the point of view) for the period before the Second World War. In 1934 foreigners held perhaps 2,200-2,250 million gold yen in long-term claims on Japan: 1,408 million in bonds of the central government, 583 million in municipals and in the securities of private enterprises, 50 millions of miscellaneous domestic issues, 150-200 million in direct holdings—the whole equal to less than one year's savings. Lockwood notes, however, that at least a third of Japanese securities floated abroad had been repatriated by that date, so that gross indebtedness was probably about 1,500 million yen ($750 million). The total was more than offset by Japanese investments abroad, largely in China and Manchuria, which Lockwood estimates at about 3,000 million yen.[4]

A comparison with the experience of the countries of Continental Europe requires some careful distinctions. All of the European countries drew heavily on foreign capital during the early decades of their industrial development. France placed the bulk of her post-Napoleonic liberation loans abroad, and, until the crisis of 1845-1847 frightened foreign investors into dumping their holdings, from one-third to one-half of her railway shares were held in Britain.[5] Belgium, as Cameron shows, built its industrial boom of the 1830's on French support of her new joint-stock investment banks.[6] And Western Germany owed some of its most progressive enterprises of the 1840's and 1850's—in nonferrous metals and textiles particularly—to French, Belgian, and Swiss initiative and money.[7]

[4] William W. Lockwood, *The Economic Development of Japan: Growth and Structural Change 1868-1938* (Princeton, 1954), pp. 253-61. The ratios of foreign borrowing to national savings make use of the estimates in Henry Rosovsky, *Capital Formation in Japan 1868-1940* (Glencoe, Ill., 1961), p. 9.

[5] L. H. Jenks, *The Migration of British Capital to 1875* (N.Y., 1927), pp. 148-49; Rondo E. Cameron, *France and the Economic Development of Europe 1800-1914* (Princeton, 1961), p. 77 n.24.

[6] *Ibid.*, ch. xi.

[7] Cameron, "Some French Contributions to the Industrial Develop-

It is impossible, unfortunately, to aggregate these investments and compare them with rates of saving or total capital. One can, however, say something about the balance of capital movements. All of these countries early arrived at a point where exports of capital exceeded imports. The French performance is the most striking here: from the 1820's on, the balance of payments was almost always favorable, until cumulated holdings abroad amounted to over 50 billion gold francs in 1913 (more than a year's net national product); only Britain, with 3.8 billion pounds, had larger foreign investments. Even rapidly growing Germany, whose perennially higher interest rates reflected her appetite for capital, bought up most outside holdings in the fifties and sixties and went on to export large amounts in subsequent decades; by 1913 her investments abroad amounted to some 23.5 billion marks (half a year's income). In quantitative terms, the Japanese experience seems closest to the German pattern: a shift to net creditor status after about forty years of industrial development.

Qualitatively, however, the picture is different. One can find nothing in Japanese history comparable to the kind of strategic investments in major industries cited above—at least not until the development of heavy engineering, automobiles, and electrical engineering in the years before and after the First World War. The initial Japanese advances—in textiles, metallurgy, even railways—were accomplished with domestic savings almost exclusively.

Moreover, the proper comparison for our purposes is not with countries such as Britain, France, or Germany, but rather with Russia—Europe's late industrializer *par excellence*. From its first hesitant steps on the path to modernity, the Russian economy leaned heavily on outside support: in 1890, about a third of the country's joint-stock capital was in

---

ment of Germany, 1840-1870," *Journal of Economic History*, XVI (1956), 281-321; Franz Kistler, *Die wirtschaftlichen und sozialen Verhältnisse in Baden 1849-1870* [Forschungen zur oberrheinischen Landesgeschichte, Band I] (Freiburg i. Breisgau, 1954), p. 165.

foreign hands, plus extensive direct holdings and short-term credits. At this point there began a period of exceptionally rapid growth, thanks in large part to an unprecedented influx of west European enterprise and money; by 1900, half the joint-stock capital was held abroad, most of it in France, Belgium, and Germany. And this says nothing of the huge public debt, much of it for railway construction, much of it for armaments, pomp and circumstance, and interest on old loans; half of this was owing to foreigners in 1914. French holdings alone amounted to more than 10 billion francs of public or officially guaranteed bonds—more than the entire annual income of Japan in this period.[8]

By the same token, Japan relied far less than European countries on the skills, knowledge, and enterprise of foreigners. Technicians were brought in when required to build railways, construct and break in new plants, operate ships, above all to teach Japanese how to replace their teachers. We have no over-all count of these imported experts, but we do know that in the Meiji period a good many of them worked for the government and that these were more numerous in the early years than later: 127 in 1872, 213 in 1874, 103 in 1880, 29 in 1883, 56 in 1887. (The numbers would be very slightly larger if one added the skilled workers similarly engaged.)[9] In similar fashion although the aggregate number of foreign technicians employed by private enterprise may well have increased over time, reaching a peak in the 1920's, the pattern in individual branches seems to have been an early rise followed by a drastic decline as the Japanese learned their lessons. When the *Nippon yusen kaisha* (Japan Steamship

[8] Based on Rosovsky's figure of 3,885 million yen for the average annual gross national product of the period 1907-16. *Capital Formation,* p. 9. For Russian borrowing, see Olga Crisp, "French Investment in Russian Joint-Stock Companies, 1894-1914," *Business History,* II (1960), 75-90, especially 75, 77 n.2, 90 n.6.

[9] Karl Rathgen, *Japans Volkswirtschaft und Staatshaushalt* (Leipzig, 1891), p. 93; Allen and Donnithorne, *Western Enterprise,* pp. 270-71. Lockwood, *Economic Development,* p. 328, quotes a higher estimate of Griffis: "by 1876 . . . some 400 foreigners had been engaged in government service." Is this a cumulative total?

Company) was formed in 1884, it employed 174 foreigners, whose number increased to 224 during the Sino-Japanese War. By 1920, however, there was not one foreign officer in the Japanese merchant marine.[10]

Incomplete as these figures are, they are far better than anything we have for Europe, where the great majority of migrant technicians hired out as private persons to private enterprises. The British parliamentary inquiry of 1825 into the emigration of skilled artisans—then illegal—heard an estimate of some two thousand Britons active in Continental industry. The number errs, if anything, on the low side, for it does not include the large number of emigrants who had left years before and had been assimilated into their country of settlement. And to this flow from the heartland of the Industrial Revolution must be added a growing stream of French, Belgian, and eventually Swiss and German technicians moving to more backward countries to the east and south. There developed in effect a number of secondary and tertiary centers of technological diffusion, and by the second third of the century skills were moving about Europe as freely as capital.

Moreover, the difference between the European and Japanese patterns was greater than mere numbers would indicate. Few Westerners remained long in Japan, and fewer still founded firms of their own to act as bellwethers to indigenous enterprise. There were no Cockerills, Douglases, Jacksons, Detilleux, Mulvanys, or Hugheses.[11] Rather, outsiders were brought in for specific purposes—Rathgen speaks of "a few

[10] *Ibid.*, p. 329.

[11] The best discussion of the contribution of British technicians and entrepreneurs to European development is W. O. Henderson, *Britain and Industrial Europe, 1750-1870* (Liverpool, 1954), which contains rich bibliographic footnotes. On the French migrants, Cameron, *France and the Economic Development of Europe.* For Belgium, Jean R. Maréchal, "La contribution des Belges et des Français à l'essor de la grande industrie allemande," *Revue universelle des mines,* 8e sér., XIII (1937), 517-31. On the role of John Hughes in developing the south Russian iron and steel industry, see Marshall Goldman, "The Relocation and Growth of the Pre-Revolutionary Russian Ferrous Metal Industry," *Explorations in Entrepreneurial History,* IX (1956-57), 19-36.

experts, 'rented' (as the characteristic and vivid saying has it) today here, tomorrow there"—kept only as long as necessary, and sent away.[12] For one thing, they cost five to ten times as much as roughly equivalent Japanese talent; for another, they neither wanted to nor were allowed to settle and melt into the society. This was in sharp contrast to Europe, where most countries encouraged the immigration of skilled artisans and potential entrepreneurs by all manner of inducements— gifts of land, money, and housing, exemption from taxes and military obligations, monopoly rights and similar economic privileges. Independent European enterprise became a sig- nificant force in Japan only after 1900, and then often in partnership with Japanese ventures. Its role, as we have seen, was concentrated in the new industries of the so-called "second industrial revolution": electrical engineering, internal combustion motors, automobiles, rubber. The older branches that were at the heart of the breakthrough to modern tech- nology—textiles, metallurgy, railway transport—remained as always in indigenous hands. Above all, one finds nothing in Japan like the situation of the Russian iron industry, in which only one of seventeen works that constituted the modern smelting sector in 1898 was entirely Russian.[13]

This largely independent achievement is the more surpris- ing because one would have expected just the reverse. The usual experience has been that, the poorer an economy and the more backward its technology, the greater its dependence on outside aid. The only significant exception seems to have been Soviet Russia, whose repudiation of pre-revolutionary debts more or less cut it off from the international money and capital markets; though even Russia relied heavily on foreign engineers and technicians during the first revolutionary gen- eration. Moreover, insofar as the Soviet Union did do without capital imports, she was able to do so only because she had inherited a substantial industrial plant from the previous regime—extensive railways, modern smelting mills, coal and iron mines, numerous textile factories—much of it paid for,

[12] *Japans Volkswirtschaft*, p. 726.
[13] Crisp, "French Investment," p. 80.

built, or managed by foreigners. It is therefore less of an exception to the rule than appears at first glance.

All follower countries have done their best, however, to limit their dependence on outside capital and skill. In the first place, they have feared that political dependence would follow economic dependence—as it often has. Secondly, foreign aid is often expensive; technicians and engineers in particular will live abroad, in a strange and often less comfortable environment, only for generous remuneration. Finally, this very gap between the emoluments of domestic and imported labor produces friction that is usually aggravated by differences of manner and temperament. The more ambitious and chauvinistic the client country, moreover, the more acutely these differences are perceived and felt. The very hopes and drives that impel a nation to bring in teachers from abroad and listen to them, make it quick to take umbrage and resentful of pupillary status.

GOVERNMENT ENTERPRISE IN INDUSTRY

The ability of industrializing economies to achieve independence without sacrificing growth unduly has always depended on their success in mobilizing their initially meager domestic resources, material and human. Professor Gerschenkron's well-known essay on "Economic Backwardness in Historical Perspective," which deals primarily with the material aspects of this effort, notes that European countries used a combination of a financial innovation, the investment bank and what we would call today the development bank— and government promotion to generate capital for growth. He argues, moreover, from the examples of Germany and Russia that the more backward the economy, the more the reliance on the state rather than on private enterprise.

Japan seems to fit this model well. Henry Rosovsky and others have shown that the government was responsible for an important share of gross domestic fixed capital formation— generally about 30 percent, though rising to about 40 in a few years—for the period 1887-1936.[14] And while we do not have

[14] This excludes military expenditures. The percentages in Rosovsky,

similar data for Europe, it seems unlikely that government share of total investment was so high as in Japan, though it was probably not much lower.[15] On the other hand, a com-

---

Capital Formation, p. 24, Table 7, col. 2, are based on national product less agriculture. When the latter is included, the percentages drop to the level indicated above.

[15] Comparisons are hazardous, but I shall attempt some calculations of extreme estimates for the French economy around 1860 and argue from them *a fortiori*. Marczewski's figure for annual gross physical product in the period 1855-1864 is 14,366 million francs. If we assume that output of services represented as large a proportion of total product as it does in the contemporary United States (it was probably much lower), that is, about 30%, we arrive at a hypothetical gross national product of about 19,000 million francs. (Compare François Perroux' estimate of 19,400 million francs for the net national product in 1859. "Prise de vues sur la croissance de l'économie française, 1780-1950," in S. Kuznets, ed., *Income and Wealth, series V* [London, 1955], p. 61.) Marczewski's figure for annual expenditures of the central government during the same years is 2,148 million francs. Now, in Japan, government investment seems to have accounted for about one-third of total government outlays (compare col. 7 in Table 1 of Rosovsky, *Capital Formation*, p. 2, with Table 3 of Harry Oshima's essay in this volume, "Meiji Fiscal Policy and Economic Progress" [Ch. VIII]). If one assumes that the proportion was substantially lower in France, say 25% (though it may well have been just as high in these years of railway construction), one arrives at an investment by the central government alone of about 537 million francs. To this should be added investment by local governments and by quasi-governmental agencies like the Crédit Foncier, which financed the great projects of urban redevelopment of the Second Empire. Unfortunately, it would seem impossible to calculate and aggregate these sums; at least those historians who have occupied themselves with the subject—Louis Girard and David Pinkney, for example—have studiously avoided any collation or tabulation of statistical data. But Girard, *La politique des travaux publics du Second Empire* (Paris, n.d. [1951]) p. 349, speaks of between 400 and 650 million francs a year in loans by local authorities and quasi-governmental agencies (excluding the state-guaranteed railway bonds) during the period 1861-1865. Adding the lower figure to the 500-plus millions presumably invested by the central government, one gets a total for these years of some 900 million. If then we assume that 10% of national product was invested (1,900 million francs), we have a public contribution of over 47%. If we assume the highly unlikely rate of saving of 15% (2,850 million), we still have government accounting for almost a third

parison of state investment in isolation is misleading; the model is incomplete. In promoting economic growth, government spending is just one of several devices for mobilizing and allocating resources. For backward countries especially, it is linked closely, as we have seen, to imports of capital from abroad, the one complementing the other. When one examines the Japanese experience in this light, one is less impressed by the contribution of the state; one would expect it to have been higher to compensate for the lack of funds from outside. And one is struck instead by the high proportion of investment accounted for by private enterprise.

Once again, to be sure, one must distinguish between quantitative and qualitative effects. Often a relatively small investment by the state yielded a large harvest of technological progress and increased output. One thinks, for example, of the construction of modern cotton mills which showed the way to private enterprise, and of the purchase of modern British spinning machinery which was then resold to private industry at low prices and on easy terms. "It seem clear," Smith remarks, "that without government help of both kinds, private capital would have been no more successful in developing machine cotton spinning in the decade after 1880 than it had been in the decade before; in short, in this field as in all others except silk reeling, the government was responsible for overcoming the initial difficulties of industrialization."[16]

---

of total investment. All of this is intended simply to convey orders of magnitude and proportion. A great deal of work will have to be done before we have figures for western Europe comparable to those we now have for Japan. The Marczewski figures are from his article, "Some Aspects of the Economic Growth of France, 1660-1958," in *Economic Development and Cultural Change*, IX, no. 3 (April 1961), 372.

[16] Thomas C. Smith, *Political Change and Industrial Development in Japan: Government Enterprise, 1868-1880* (Stanford, 1955), p. 63. Cf. John E. Orchard, *Japan's Economic Position: The Progress of Industrialization* (N.Y., 1930), p. 90: "There are few modern industries in Japan today that do not owe their existence to government initiative." And again: "The part played by the government cannot be overemphasized. Japanese industry of the present day owes its state of development primarily to the efforts of a highly paternalistic central government."

The value of easy credit in a country still poor and lacking in a resourceful, responsive capital market is undeniable. The role of official entrepreneurship, as expressed in these early "model" plants, is less obvious. These plants no doubt did much to overcome the initial ignorance of machine technology and factory organization, and in so doing to train Japanese cadres for private enterprise. They were also usually fitted out with the latest equipment. Partly for this very reason, how-ever, they were usually inefficient: relative factor costs hardly warranted the choice of such capital-intensive methods. Most of them seem to have lost money regularly, and when an im-pecunious government sold them off in the 1880's, it received far less than the amount of its investment. Most of these properties subsequently earned substantial profits, so much indeed that some historians have been inclined to see the whole operation as a dilapidation of the public treasury for the benefit of a few insiders. This is not the place to examine such allegations. The important fact for our purposes is the contrast between losses before and profits after, a contrast that throws doubt on the usual assumption of the incapacity of private enterprise to develop successful modern industries without the lesson and example of prior government initiative. To be sure, it may well be that these private profits were simply a conse-quence of the favorable terms of acquisition. We simply do not know. In the meantime, the burden of proof would seem to lie on those who have taken for granted the superiority of government enterprise. Certainly one may well ask whether development would not have been cheaper and more rapid had the state confined its role to that of honest broker and banker, introducing its citizens to the opportunities of the new tech-nology and assisting their ventures with money and in-formation.

In any event, it is worth noting that Japanese experience in this regard closely paralleled that of the countries of Conti-nental Europe. In France, Prussia, Austria, and the smaller German states, the paternalistic regimes of the eighteenth and early nineteenth centuries invested large sums in selected pilot plants. Many of these were entirely government-owned and were managed by crown officials. Others were operated by private businessmen who received outright subsidies or low-cost loans or took in the state as a partner. As in the case of Japan, it is usually impossible to state categorically whether or not these enterprises made money; the officials charged with their surveillance tended to be reticent about their accounts. All the evidence, however, points to mediocre results. Take, for example, the most ambitious program of industrial promotion, that of the Prussian monarchy. Most of its creations of the eighteenth century collapsed when the death of Frederick II deprived them of continuing support. The later ventures of the Seehandlung may have done somewhat better. Yet it is significant that the Director, Christian von Rother, maintained throughout his tenure (1820-1848) that profit and loss should not be the criteria of his success. Rother wanted to set up model establishments that would set an example of technique and efficiency to private enterprise; to reverse the decline of obsolete industries like the rural linen manufacture; and to promote the industrial development of what we today would call "depressed areas" east of the Elbe. Yet even if the Seehandlung is judged against the measuring stick of Rother's aims, its results were mixed. His factories did no better and often worse than comparable private works; his attempts to reverse the course of industrial evolution and to alter patterns of location were largely a misallocation of resources; and his prejudices against vital innovations such as the railway and the joint-stock company were hardly calculated to hasten Prussian economic development.[17]

To be sure, government promotion of industry, whether or not commercially profitable, yielded some beneficial by-products. Even those works that failed could often serve again, and many came to yield a return under more efficient management. A few eventually provided the basis for industrial giants; Le Creusot is the best example.[18] Most

[17] See W. O. Henderson, *The State and the Industrial Revolution in Prussia 1740-1860* (Liverpool, 1958), ch. vii, and the literature cited there.

[18] Though half a century of liquidations and reorganizations inter-

important, these pilot plants trained numerous skilled workers and technicians, some of whom became entrepreneurs in their own right. The state-initiated and state-supported works at Pardubice in Bohemia (later moved to Brno) was a repeated failure in the eighteenth century and drove several syndicates into bankruptcy; but it supplied the men who went out on their own and eventually made Brno the greatest center of wool manufacture in the Austrian empire.[19]

This parallel between the Japanese and the European experience suggests not only that the contribution of government enterprise to Japanese economic development has been overrated but that it is best understood in a different context. Japanese scholars are wont to distinguish, I believe, between the industrial ventures of various *han* (feudal domains) in the late Tokugawa period and those of the central government after *bakumatsu* (collapse of the Tokugawa regime): the former were clearly abortive, perhaps misguided, and in any event of minor significance; the latter were serious and an indispensable prodrome to subsequent industrial advance. The distinction in my opinion rests on extraneous historical circumstances: a change in political auspices. The change made a difference, to be sure, in the scope and content of the promotional effort; centralized direction meant greater resources, some coordination, above all better information. Yet both phases together seem to me to constitute essentially a single prefatory stage, one characteristic of almost all industrializing follower countries before this century, particularly those with strong central governments and an established mercantilist tradition. For all of these, there was a period between the time

vened between its support and abandonment by the French State during the 1780's and its definitive regeneration under the brothers Schneider. Denise Ozanam, "La naissance du Creusot," *Revue d'histoire de la siderurgie*, IV (1963), 103-18; J. Chevalier, *Le Creusot, berceau de la grande industrie française* (Paris, 1925).

[19] H. Freudenberger, "The Woolen Goods Industry of the Habsburg Monarchy in the Eighteenth Century," *Journal of Economic History*, XX (1960), 398-99; also his thesis, "A Case-Study in the Government's Role in Economic Development in the Eighteenth Century: The Brno Fine-Cloth Factory" (Ph.D. dissertation, Columbia University, 1957).

they perceived the necessity and opportunity of an industrial revolution and the time when human and material resources and the institutional structure made such a revolution feasible. This was the season of impatience, when ambition outran capabilities. In the meantime, private entrepreneurs were cultivating their own gardens, with and without assistance from the state.[20] As their resources and knowledge increased, they took over the process of technological advance and gave it a continuity and momentum it had never had and was never to lose. It would be a great mistake simply to assume that *post hoc, ergo propter hoc.*

MOBILIZATION OF HUMAN CAPITAL

The Gerschenkron model of the historical conditions of economic backwardness concerns itself primarily with the mobilization of material resources; but it can and should be extended to the development of human resources as well. In the course of the nineteenth century, the governments of

[20] Smith, *Political Change and Industrial Development,* pp. 52-53, points out that these gardens were small: "private capital was least active in heavier branches of industry. . . . There were a few private shipyards and hundreds of private mines before 1880, but with perhaps one or two exceptions in each industry, all the larger modern enterprises were government-owned. Only in manufacturing did private capital show any considerable initiative. And even in this field private capital chose enterprises calling for no great outlay of capital and in which the productive process was not highly mechanized." Yet this was exactly the pattern one would expect in an economy of scarce capital and abundant labor, and *mutatis mutandis* corresponds closely to the situation of European enterprise in the period preceding the breakthrough to industrialization. Indeed, it might well be argued that those European firms that deviated from this pattern and constituted themselves on a large, capital-intensive scale (Carron, Le Creusot, Van Robais at Abbeville, Cockerill at Seraing) did poorly, not only because their costs were higher but also because their high ratio of fixed to variable capital limited the proportional support they could get from what was then the principal source of industrial credit, the market for short-term bills of exchange. Cf. Sidney Pollard, "Fixed Capital in the Industrial Revolution in Britain," *Journal of Economic History,* xxiv (1964), 307-14. On the question of relative factor costs and optimum investment pattern, see below, pp. 115-19.

Continental Europe devoted considerable money and the energies of some of their most capable civil servants to the creation of complete, integrated systems of public education, ranging from grammar schools to universities and scientific research institutes. Much of this program reflected the conviction that only literate people could be moral, effective citizens of a modern society; much of it, particularly the establishment of scientific, technological, and vocational institutions, had the express purpose of freeing the economy from dependence on imported skills and providing a firm cognitive basis for autonomous growth. The extent of these efforts varied considerably from place to place; but all of these follower countries did far more along these lines than Britain; and the industrial gains of several of these economies—e.g., Germany, Switzerland, eventually Denmark—seem to have been closely tied to their successful development of what is now sometimes called "human capital."

The Japanese government also laid great stress on education as a means of forming the citizenry of a modern society. One thinks of the Imperial Rescript of 1872: "The acquirement of knowledge is essential to a successful life. . . . It is intended, henceforth, that education shall be so widespread that there shall be no house in any village, no person in any house without learning." And the 1963 white paper of the Ministry of Education, *Nihon no seichō to kyōiku* (Growth and Education in Japan), remarks "that one common factor in the development of the rapidly growing societies of the twentieth century—Japan, Canada, Western Germany, Israel, Russia, and America—has been the great attention paid to education, and particularly a conscious awareness of the importance of technological education."[21]

Yet intention is a long way from realization. The Japan of the 1870's was poor, and in those early days the total annual budget of the Ministry of Education was less than a million yen. The burden was therefore thrown on the local districts,

21 For an English language summary of this report see R. P. Dore, "Education in Japan's Growth," *Pacific Affairs*, XXXVII, 1 (Spring, 1964), 66-79.

each of which was required to establish at least one primary school. In spite of considerable prodding, it took decades to approximate this minimal standard. In the meantime, the monthly tuition fee was a serious deterrent to attendance, especially in rural areas; and not until its abolition in 1898 did universal elementary education become a realistic goal.[22]

This long delay in generalizing primary instruction was characteristic of many European nations as well. France did not see free public schools until 1881, at which date 17 percent of her army conscripts and 25 percent of her brides could not read or write.[23] In Great Britain, attendance in primary school was not made compulsory until 1880; by then it was more urgent to civilize the wild offspring of an industrial society than to impart the ability to read and write. Germany, however, was an exception. There the duty of parents to send their children to school had been proclaimed by Luther in 1524, and the more progressive states had taken steps to satisfy this obligation long before industrialization began. In Prussia, the General Landschulreglement of Frederick the Great (1763) had made primary schooling obligatory, though not free, and while it took decades to generalize the habit of compliance, attendance was just about universal by the second third of the nineteenth century. Even so, there were backward states— generally those whose economies were overwhelmingly agricultural—and abolition of fees did not become general until 1888. In all these countries, as in Japan, the rural areas were slow in sending their children to school, not only because of the charges and inconvenience but even more because the children could be used for farm chores. Conversely, the main reason why attendance in the cities and towns picked up

[22] The significance of the 1890's as the threshold to a new era of systematic development of the educational system is apparent from the statistics of government expenditure (central and local):

| 1880 | 6.9 million yen | 1900 | 42.0 million yen |
| 1890 | 10.5 million yen | 1910 | 90.9 million yen |

In view of the inflation of the eighties, the apparent gain in that decade was nil. Figures from Oshima, Table 2, below, p. 370.

[23] Jacques Chastenet, *Histoire de la Troisième République*, Vol. II: *La république des républicains 1879-1893* (Paris, 1954), 74.

earlier is that social legislation increasingly curtailed the ability of parents to turn their children into breadwinners.

What is different about Japan, however, is a certain neglect of scientific and technical education; and this is the more surprising in view of the lateness of the Japanese industrial revolution. To be sure, one can cite a number of important advances in this area: the early establishment of the *Kōgakkō*, later the Imperial College of Engineering; of the College of Agriculture; of several higher technical schools and some tens of specialized secondary and "quasi-secondary" schools in the 1870's and 1880's; and of scientific research institutes. Yet all of these together trained a small minority of Japanese students. As late as 1930, only 4 percent of the boys in secondary schools were studying "engineering"; and the vocational and apprentice training schools, on which Dore lays heavy emphasis, enrolled only 7 percent of the boys of secondary-school age in 1900. Moreover in the ordinary middle schools, the time and resources devoted to science were less than one would expect.[24] By contrast, many of the European countries made a special effort in this sphere: Switzerland, Sweden, above all Prussia, where about 30-35 percent of the high school students attended *Realschulen* in the 1850's and 1860's.[25]

One might argue, perhaps, that Japanese students were the better for not concentrating early, that well-trained generalists make better engineers than premature specialists. Yet university training had long focused on the humanities and was directed primarily to preparing bureaucrats. This, after all, was the quickest path to security and position; for as in

[24] The white paper on education mentioned above offers (pp. 226-27) a table of the content of the curriculum in boys' middle schools at selected dates from 1886 to 1943. The proportion of the total program devoted to natural history, chemistry, and physics (in terms of hours) varied as follows over this period:

1886	8.5%	1919	12.0%
1901	9.5	1931	12–13.0
1911	10.6	1943	13.5

I am indebted to Mr. Dore for help with this material.

[25] L. Weise, *Das höhere Schulwesen in Preussen* (4 vols.; Berlin, 1864-1902), I, 454; II, 554; III, 368.

today's new nations, "there were so few college graduates that those who did finish were virtually assured of a decent place in the government."[26] Science received some attention, but nothing like the devotion it received in the *polytechniques* and *technische Hochschulen* of Europe. Higher technical instruction made headway only after 1900, and then mainly in agriculture and commerce. Not until the 1930's did college-level engineering grow substantially, increasing its share from 9 to 16 percent of the degrees awarded.

All of this raises the question how, in view of her limited employment of foreign experts, Japan developed the skills and techniques required to effect an industrial revolution. Some of the answer, no doubt, lies in the manual address and imitative quickness of the labor force—qualities already developed by the indigenous industrial crafts; some lies in the knowledge and experience brought back by Japanese students assigned to study and work abroad. The most important consideration, however, was undoubtedly the composition of Japan's economic activity in these early decades of growth. For one thing, as Ohkawa and Rosovsky emphasize (Ch. II), much of the increase of manufacturing output derived simply from the pursuit of traditional trades more efficiently and on a larger scale. For another, the modern sector consisted largely of textile manufacture, crude metallurgy, railway construction, and shipbuilding—the mainstays of the classical industrial revolution—which even in Europe continued to rest heavily on on-the-job training and intelligent empiricism. It is no accident that the multiplication after 1900 of licensing agreements and partnerships with foreign firms and the creation of foreign-owned enterprises on Japanese soil are linked to the more complex, science-oriented branches of technology: heavy engineering (including internal combustion motors),

---

[26] Shibusawa Keizō, *Japanese Life and Culture in the Meiji Era* (Tokyo, 1958), p. 299. "In 1885 Tsuboichi Shōyō described typical student-houseboys swaggering down a Kanda street as though they owned it and reminding people that despite their ragged clothes and worn-out hats they would some day be great men. Students liked to point out that the national councillors of the day had all been students once." *Ibid.*, 300-01.

electrical engineering, and organic chemicals (including rubber).

By then, however, the decisive breakthrough to industrialization had been made; and within another generation the Japanese were able to establish their independence in these areas as well. All of which raises the most important question of all: how, with this limited recourse to the usual remedies for backwardness, did this latecomer accomplish these gains so quickly?

THE RAPIDITY OF JAPANESE GROWTH

The answer, it seems to me, lies paradoxically in the severity of the challenge that confronted Japan in the middle of the last century. The steady aggrandizement of Western commercial and political power in the Far East threatened nothing less than the dissolution of the Japanese polity and the reduction of the society to colonial status. All efforts, therefore, had to be applied to enhancing the country's national power, so that Japan could treat with the "barbarians" on equal terms; and this required the adoption of modern military technology and the establishment of a centralized government that could effectively promote and focus the strength of the nation.

These were the immediate objectives. They constituted the irreducible minimum of the reform program in the last years of Tokugawa and received support from reactionaries and progressives alike. The small group that led the overthrow of the shogunate apparently looked no farther at first. It was soon obvious, however, that political and military changes could not be effected in a vacuum and that, if Japan were to match strength with the great Western powers, she would have to accomplish a metamorphosis. Modern armed forces could be equipped and sustained only by a modern economy, and this in turn required an educated, mobile, motivated population. By the same token, a professional warrior class would no longer suffice for the defense of the nation's interests; only a nation in arms could meet the demands of modern war, and this implied a society of citizens rather than of servile subjects. All the pieces hung together, and the men of the

Restoration soon found that they were inexorably engaged on a path whose destination few if any had foreseen. Some of them disapproved and gave up their posts. In the long run, they were replaced by men who accepted the still fuzzy but ever-clearer vision of a new Japan. *Sonnō-jōi* (Revere the Emperor—Expel the barbarians) and *kaikoku* (Opening the country) merged in a national consensus: under the aegis of the Emperor, Japan would take from the foreigner what she needed to maintain her independence and rise to new heights of power.

The integration of economic development in a general program of national enhancement had important consequences for the course and rate of growth. It stimulated and sanctioned productive efforts by all classes, for it conferred a patriotic nimbus on the everyday virtues of diligence, thrift, perseverance, and the like, while making a virtue of acquisitiveness. The evidence concerning the respectability of trade in Tokugawa times is ambiguous: the measures designed to limit the activities and curtail the influence and pretensions of merchants are imbued with scorn and moral disapproval; yet many samurai engaged in business, and numerous businessmen succeeded in attaining samurai status. In any event, insofar as a stigma was attached to moneymaking in the market place, it was subsequently erased by the identification of business success with national aggrandizement. (See the essays of Horie and Hirschmeier below, Chs. IV-V.)

At the same time, the sanction of patriotism apparently facilitated rapid change by dampening the kinds of conflict that usually accompany industrialization. In general, it promoted a sense of duty and a docile acceptance of the burdens of life and responsibilities of citizenship. In particular, it helped dissuade labor from making an issue of the distribution of the social product and thereby fostered a high rate of profit and saving. It may also have done something to reconcile the rural population to their heavy share of the fiscal burdens of reform. In all this, patriotism was seconded by the traditional morality. As Dore has put it:[27]

[27] Ronald Dore, "Some Comparisons of Latin American and Asian

"The Confucian ethic of personal relations was reformulated as the uniquely *Japanese* family system. It served to preserve an image of society as properly hierarchical and based on personal loyalties, and thus to strengthen authoritarian tendencies in general, enhance the docility of the labor force, and hold in check the erosion of the government's traditionally sanctioned authority."

Finally, the hostility between state officials and private entrepreneurs that afflicted the economies of Continental Europe seems to have been largely absent in Japan—at least until expansion in Manchuria and China in the 1930's led to a sharp cleavage between the military and the more responsible elements of civilian society within and without the government. We shall return to this point later.

Severity of challenge is never enough in itself, however, to account for response. For one thing, stimulus clearly does not increase indefinitely with severity of adversity; there is such a thing as too much pressure. For another, response varies from one society to another: the same pressure that crushes one will elicit a vigorous reaction from another. China, after all, was also confronted by the threat of Western domination in the nineteenth century and failed the test. The secret of Japanese success, therefore, must also lie in the internal endowment of the nation—which, in view of the relative penury of raw materials, means individual and social resources.

Here, it seems to me, the position of scholars like Thomas C. Smith and E. Sydney Crawcour (above, Ch. I) is unexceptionable. Tokugawa growth may not have been "modern economic growth" by the criteria of Simon Kuznets, as adopted by Ohkawa and Rosovsky (above, Ch. II). It was certainly not an industrial revolution. But it was a self-sustaining advance that rested on attitudes and values favorable to material development, and as such it provided a basis for a creative and effective response to new opportunities. It was very similar, in this respect, to the gradual development of

Studies, with Special Reference to Research on Japan," S.S.R.C. *Items*, XVII, no. 2 (June 1963), 18.

the economies of Western Europe in the centuries preceding the great inventions of the eighteenth century. There, too, one has the impression of a fundamental contrast between the growth and change of the Industrial Revolution and the immobility of the earlier agrarian society. Yet a closer scrutiny reveals that the first breakthrough to industrialization—in Britain—derived directly from this preliminary development; that the countries of Continental Europe had already proceeded a long way toward a breakthrough when the British achievement thrust upon them the necessity of abridging the process; and that the subsequent success of these responsive revolutions owed much to the autonomous movement that preceded them. The significance of this demonstrated capacity to generate growth and change from within is not to be underestimated. As much as anything, it is this that sets Meiji Japan apart from the underdeveloped countries of the present day.[28]

In the Japanese case, a number of symptoms of progress seem to me deserving of special notice. The first, heavily stressed by Crawcour (Ch. I), is the commercialization and industrialization of the countryside, at least in the more advanced areas. The resemblance to "pre-industrial" England is striking. There the spread of manufacture out of towns into the land had begun very early, so that by the end of the sixteenth century at least half of the output of woolen cloth came from rural cottages. From a by-occupation in times of slack, spinning, weaving, and other industrial activities had become the main support of tens of thousands, whose specialization made them increasingly dependent on markets, peddlers, and shops for their needs. The result was not only an ever-growing output of cheap manufactures that could undersell the better but dearer products of urban guildsmen, both at home and abroad, but an ever-growing national market for more or less standardized products. Supply and demand stim-

[28] Compare the argument of Simon Kuznets, "Underdeveloped Countries and the Pre-Industrial Phase in the Advanced Countries: An Attempt at Comparison," in A. N. Agarwala and S. P. Singh, eds., *The Economics of Underdevelopment* (Bombay, 1958), pp. 140-41.

ulated each other and made possible, in conjunction with growing markets overseas, a spiral of growth that eventually exceeded the productive capacity of dispersed hand manufacture and gave rise to the decisive technological changes that we denominate the Industrial Revolution.

The Japanese economy, closed as it was to outside trade and handicapped by political decentralization, did not proceed this far. But the commercialization and industrialization of rural areas were both a sign and source of expansion, which called forth a technological response on the appropriate scale. This took the form of devices to save labor: the use of the spinning wheel in cotton manufacture, the occasional application of water power in such branches as oil pressing, above all an increasing division of labor and occupational specialization.[29] Most of this seems small by comparison with European innovations at a similar stage or even earlier—fulling mills, blast furnaces, industrial use of coal. Yet it looms large against the technological stagnation of most non-Western societies, which were content to spin with the distaff and made no use of inanimate power.

The significance of these advances, then, lies not in the gains they yielded in productivity, but in the evidence they offer of a rational, economizing mind at work. This was probably the greatest achievement and legacy of the late Tokugawa period: the rise and spread of attitudes conducive to adaptation and growth. The basic ingredients were there to begin with—diligence, thrift, a sense of responsibility; what these decades added was a leaven that made possible a new kind of economic cake.

QUALITY AND COST OF JAPANESE LABOR

The basic virtues should not be underestimated. Once Japan found herself on the path of industrialization, her most valuable resource was her supply of cheap, intelligent, hard-working labor. This, more than anything else, it seems to me—

[29] See, for example, Thomas C. Smith, *The Agrarian Origins of Modern Japan* (Stanford, 1959), pp. 19, 167 n.

more than fiscal measures, more than a high rate of private saving—accounts for Japan's ability to multiply her initially meager wealth so rapidly.[30]

A comparison of the Japanese and European adaptations of technology to relative factor costs is instructive. In Europe, the follower countries made the most of their cheap manpower by building more rudimentary but less expensive equipment, buying second-hand machines whenever possible, and concentrating on the more labor-intensive branches or stages of manufacture. Not until the last third of the century did the Continental economies conform to the usual theoretical model and avail themselves of the opportunity to adopt the latest techniques; and even then they maintained a larger working force per unit of production (spindle, loom, blast furnace) than Britain or the United States.[31] In addition, they tended to be prodigal in their use of labor to manipulate or move materials and goods; for these were activities that were external to those processes of transformation that had been the foci of technical advance (spinning, weaving, smelting, rolling), and methods and equipment were thus not dictated by the requirements of an integrated procedure. Finally, the Continental mills, like the early British factories, worked their equipment as long and hard as possible, into the night even on the Sabbath eve. Sunday morning was set aside for cleaning and oiling the machinery. In time of expansion, the manufacturer added to his capital only as a last resort; it was easier to lengthen the working day; in time of crisis, he did the reverse. Only the introduction of social legislation to protect the health of women and children imposed an upper limit to the demands of the employer or the effort of the worker. Even

---

[30] Some have suggested that Japanese children owe their manual dexterity to their training in calligraphy. I myself am inclined to attribute it to eating with chopsticks. Cf. Jack Baranson, "Adapting Technologies for Developing Countries," *Technology and Culture*, IV (1963-64), 26.

[31] There is an excellent discussion of comparative productivity in G. von Schulze-Gaevernitz, *The Cotton Trade in England and on the Continent* (London and Manchester, 1895), p. 85 *et seq.*

then, the hands were expected to work overtime in periods of lively demand.[32]

Japanese industry operated along similar lines. The best discussion is provided by Gustav Ranis, who emphasizes the "survival of old-fashioned production functions": cottage-based weaving in silk and cotton, dispersion of preparatory and finishing processes in domestic shops, "the retention of traditional, relatively primitive machinery in many areas." In some branches, of course, modern equipment was so far superior to the old as to make factory production profitable and home manufacture unviable; cotton spinning is the best example. In such fields, the Japanese did adopt modern machines and methods, but adapted them to the pattern of relative factor costs by running the equipment for longer periods and at higher speeds, throwing in additional manpower as required to maintain the machines and repair the more frequent breaks in the yarn. Moreover, as in Europe, resources were channeled toward the more labor-intensive branches of manufacture; the processing of raw silk, which financed almost a third of Japanese imports in the period before 1900, was perhaps the most advantageous instance of such specialization. And Ranis notes in this regard the significance of the domestic consumption pattern:[33]

[32] Wolfgang Köllmann, *Sozialgeschichte der Stadt Barmen im 19. Jahrhundert* (Tübingen, 1960), p. 133, writes: "Above all the workers fought against the extra hours that were required in periods of good sales and which made the generally conceded reduction once again illusory." And yet in those occupations where wages were paid by the piece, the adult male workers often opposed any shortening of hours as vehemently as did the employers. See, for example, André Lasserre, *La situation des ouvriers de l'industrie textile dans la région lilloise sous la Monarchie de Juillet* (Lausanne, 1952), p. 132, on the attitude of the spinners of Fourmies after 1848.

[33] G. Ranis, "Factor Proportions In Japanese Economic Development," *American Economic Review*, XLVII (1957), 599-601. See also Lockwood, *Economic Development*, p. 30, who notes that in 1912 Japanese cotton mills used four times as many workers as American mills of the same size using the same equipment. See also the British consul's description of the silk reeling industry in 1878. Smith, *Political Change and Industrial Development*, p. 57.

"It is quite impossible to completely 'hold the line' against mounting pressures of domestic demand during the developmental process. . . . Limited increases in consumption at near-subsistence levels of income do not, of course, necessarily represent a total loss to the nation's productive capacity. Such increases may well enhance people's ability and willingness to work. But, should the new demands be directed towards labor-intensive goods, the capital costs are undoubtedly smaller. Compared with the capital-intensive channels such demands might have taken, the elasticity of substitution stands to benefit—if only in a relative sense."

Here he was anticipating the more extended analysis by Henry Rosovsky of the resistance of traditional tastes in Japan to "the erosions of the consumer demonstration effect."[34]

To be sure, one can have too much of a good thing, and there is considerable evidence that capital saving was pushed too far on occasion in both the West and Japan. In both France and Germany textile manufacturers often adopted techniques less remunerative than the best available, either because they were reluctant to scrap old equipment that was still working or because they were unable or unwilling to venture larger outlays on new machinery. In areas such as Normandy and Saxony, chronic technological backwardness was made possible only by natural and artificial protection from the competition of more efficient producers. It was the shift away from prohibition to freer trade in the 1860's that broke the resistance to the self-acting mule and power loom in French cotton and wool, and to coke-blast smelting in iron-making; and, by the same token, it was the construction of a national rail network, which brought Rhenish and Westphalian manufactures to Berlin and eastern Germany, that forced the rationalization of Silesian metallurgy and the Silesian and Saxon textile industries.

There is evidence of a similar miscombination of factors in Japan, at similar expense. Orchard argues, for example, that Japanese enterprises used too much labor, without regard

[34] *Capital Formation in Japan,* pp. 86-87.

to productivity or costs; that the consequent inefficiency was in effect contagious and "snowballed"; and that cheap labor was thus "a most important weakness of the Japanese industrial system."[35] Looking from the vantage point of the European experience, however, I am inclined to disagree. I have no doubt that Japanese entrepreneurs often overdid the substitution of labor for capital; American producers often sinned in the opposite direction; indeed, few businessmen anywhere calculate this sort of thing accurately. Probably the Japanese also lost certain byproducts of skill and efficiency (as opposed to productivity) in the process. Yet the absence of prohibitive tariffs prevented to some degree misallocation of resources; and on balance the Japanese undoubtedly gained, achieving a far higher rate of growth than they would have, had they adopted the "best," that is, the most capital-intensive practice.[36]

The Process of Reform

THE CASE OF GERMANY

Although the developing Japanese economy of the Tokugawa period finds its closest parallel in the England of the eighteenth century, it is German history that offers the best comparison with Japan's subsequent experience of political challenge and economic response. The facts of the German case are fairly well known. Here was a nation whose territory was fragmented into a veritable mosaic of sovereignties, to the detriment of her political capacity and economic performance. Even more serious, perhaps, than this geographical division were the profound social fissures that set apart the great horizontal *Stände*—nobility, bourgeoisie, peasantry— and were reinforced by a whole complex of legal and administrative impediments to the movement of persons and capital: in most of Germany, no one was permitted, at least in prin-

[35] Orchard, *Japan's Economic Position*, p. 362.

[36] For similar combinations of inputs in similar conditions, see V. V. Bhatt, "Capital Intensity of Industries: A Comparative Study of Certain Countries," *Bull. Oxford University Institute of Statistics,* XVIII (May 1956), 179-94.

ciple, to acquire property or engage in an occupation reserved to members of another class; and intermarriage between nobles and bourgeois was discouraged, particularly in a country such as Prussia.[37] The great mass of the population lived on and from the land, for commerce and industry had suffered severely in the Thirty Years' War and had not fully recovered a hundred years later.

The condition of this peasantry varied considerably from place to place, so much so that any summary must do violence to the reality. Yet this is the kind of violence that character-izes any history that pretends to be more than a congeries of discrete facts; one can only warn the reader and direct him to more extended treatments for nuances and details.[38]

What were the principal features of German agrarian struc-ture in the eighteenth century? In particular, what were the features most relevant to the effort of economic development that is our primary concern? Here I shall try to distinguish between three aspects of the problem: (1) the organization of cultivation (the field systems), (2) the terms of land ten-ure, and (3) the personal status and condition of the peas-

[37] Thus the edict of 1765 against "the all-too unequal or shameful marriages of those of the nobility" of Silesia and Glatz, signed by Frederick II, Schlabrendorff, *et al.* On one occasion, Schlabrendorff was confronted with the case of a Fräulein von Schalscha, who was consorting unworthily, with her mother's connivance, with an economic official. He had the lover conscripted into the army and urged the family to "deposit" the daughter in the Ursuline nunnery in Breslau. Prussia, Preussische Akademie der Wissenschaften, *Acta borussica, Denkmäler der preussischen Staatsverwaltung im 18. Jahrhundert, Behördenorganisation und allgemeine Staatsverwaltung*, XIII (Berlin, 1932), 730. In the pages that follow, I shall focus my attention on Prussia, next to Austria the most important German state of the early nineteenth century and the subsequent leader in German unification and economic development.

[38] Among the most convenient introductions to the question are the old but essentially reliable encyclopedia articles written around the turn of the century: C. J. Fuchs, "Bauernbefreiung," in L. Elster, ed., *Wörterbuch der Volkswirtschaft* (Jena, 1898), I, 297-311; W. Wittich, "Gutsherrschaft," in *Handwörterbuch der Staatswissenschaften* (3rd ed.; 1909), pp. 209-16. These also provide excellent short bibliographies of the older literature.

antry. The distinction is artificial, for historically these three aspects were inextricably related, especially the last two. Yet it has some analytical merit, and in fact, when peasant emancipation did come, the statesmen and lawyers of the day engaged in precisely the same effort of decomposition in an attempt to separate those dues paid by the peasant for his use of land belonging to another and those deriving from personal subordination.

In the most general terms, German field systems fall into two groups—dispersed and compact. In much of the country, particularly the lands west of the Elbe, the former predominated. The holdings of the peasant and even the demesne of the lord were fragmented and scattered among the open fields surrounding the village and manor house. This dispersion increased enormously the labor required for cultivation; while the absence of real separations between the holdings made it extremely difficult for anyone to plant a different crop from his neighbor, the more so as the members of the village community (*Gemeinde*) had a common right to pasture their livestock on the stubble after harvest. By the same token, the community had rights of usufruct over lands not under field crops—pasture land, meadow, woodland, waste—and these posed an obstacle to the expansion of cultivation.

East of the Elbe, the compact holding was the rule. Noble estates (*Rittergüter*) tended to be large, and the demesne was farmed as a commercial enterprise; the bulk of the lord's income came from the sale of cash crops, primarily cereals, both within Germany and abroad. Even peasant homesteads often stood apart and were not subject to the communal servitudes of the open-field system. On the other hand, much of the land—proportionately more than in the West—was kept out of cultivation by communal rights of usufruct.

Under the circumstances, property in land, especially crop land, was rarely complete and indefeasible in the modern sense of freedom of disposition and alienation. In areas of dispersed holdings, even the lord's demesne was frequently subject to common rights and field restraints (*Flurzwang*); and throughout Germany noble estates could be tied up by familial restrictions on indebtedness and transmission. All the more was the content of peasant tenure limited. Property was usufruct rather than ownership, subject not only to communal servitudes but also to an overriding dominion of the lord. The usufruct might be hereditary; and the peasant family might farm the same soil for generations. But it paid for the privilege with rents in money or kind and with labor services, and any change in title or occupancy, via sale, loan, gift, or inheritance, required the consent of the lord.[39]

The burden of this "eminent domain" was unequal in different regions. It was far lighter west of the Elbe, partly because the proportion of Slavs in the population was negligible, even more because the *Herr* was primarily a landlord (*Grundherr*) and hence was more interested in income from rents, fees, and dues than from direct exploitation of the soil. As a result, the labor obligations of the peasant were moderate and had been commuted in part (in some areas altogether) into money payments, while the consent of the lord to changes in the status of the property was in fact automatically accorded in return for stipulated indemnities in money or kind. Moreover, where the obligation to furnish labor remained, it was fixed by custom and even formal agreement, and was often due, not from the peasant to his landlord, but from the village community to the local political authorities—like the corvée in France or parish road duty in England.

In the East, by contrast, the economy of the estate depended on the compulsory labor of the serfs and the size of the area devoted to cash crops. The efforts of the *Gutsherr* were directed therefore toward increasing the services furnished by his peasants and augmenting the size of his personal demesne, either by purchase or by simple eviction (*Bauernlegen*) ; for the obligations of the peasant were essentially undefined and were limited in the last analysis only by physical endurance or the possibility of flight, while tenure was in fact and law precarious, and the only stop to lordly

[39] Actually, there were free peasants to be found throughout Germany, with full title to their land. But with the exception of a few peripheral areas and enclaves, they were few and far between.

appetites was the desire of the state to protect its reservoir of army conscripts. This policy of *Bauernschutz* (peasant protection), be it said, was of only modest effect. It was applied more after the fact than before; and it aimed, not so much at preserving the tenure of a given family, as at keeping *Bauernland* in peasant hands—any peasant hands.

The weight of these burdens in the lands east of the Elbe reflected the character of the bonds between peasant and lord. Throughout Germany in the eighteenth century, the vast majority of peasants were technically unfree—in a state of either hereditary personal dependency (*Leibeigenschaft*) or hereditary estate subjection (*Gutsuntertänigkeit, Erbuntertänigkeit*).[40] It is not easy to distinguish between these two concepts, not only because their real content was often the same but because contemporaries themselves had difficulty differentiating between them and had an unfortunate tendency to use them indiscriminately. In principle the status of the *Leibeigene* was lower, indeed scarcely distinguishable from chattel slavery. He could be sold apart from the land, even apart from his wife and children, for he could not enter into legitimate matrimonial or family ties; he could not own or transmit title to property, for anything he possessed, to the very clothes on his back, was his master's; and he had no right to appeal or complain to any higher authority. In short, he was just a thing, without personal rights or civil status.

By contrast, the *Untertänige* was a person. He could enter into family ties, own and transmit property, go to law even against his lord. His specific stigmata were two: He was bound to the estate (*Gutshörigkeit* or *Gutspflichtigkeit*), could not leave it without permission, and had to accept attachment to such parcel or parcels as the lord assigned him; he had, therefore, no hereditary claim to a given plot of land. Further he and his children were required to furnish services to the lord—both in his house (*Gesindedienst*) and in his fields (*Frondienste*). In return, the lord was obligated to assure him the means of subsistence, and this commitment was ap-

---

[40] Theodor von der Goltz, *Geschichte der deutschen Landwirtschaft* (2 vols.; Stuttgart and Berlin, 1902), I, 433.

parently real enough to deter the peasantry in certain places and times from taking advantage of state programs of emancipation.[41]

Legal definitions, of course, are one thing, and historical reality another. It is one of the cherished doctrines of medieval historiography that serfdom originated in the dim past as a voluntary arrangement between strong man and weak, to their reciprocal advantage. The lord gave protection, work, and bread; the peasant gave labor and its fruits. Whatever the pristine contract may have been, however, the relationship had long been shaped by its intrinsic logic and historical circumstances. On the one hand, the nature of personal attachment was such that it could be maintained and the supply of services assured only if the lord controlled the crucial decisions and junctures of peasant life—choice of occupation, movement, marriage, death and inheritance. On the other hand, the need for such services and, indirectly, of these personal controls was a function, as we have seen, of the economics of cultivation; while the ability to impose and enforce these burdens and restraints was conditioned by the lord's political power. Thus in the lands of *Grundherrschaft* the lord needed little peasant labor or, because of the dispersion of his holdings, could use only part of the labor that was potentially available; and when, in places like Hanover and Bavaria, he tried to increase his claims on his peasants, he found his way blocked by the state, which drew the bulk of its tax revenues from the peasantry and could not stand by and see these resources swallowed by the nobility. By the eighteenth century, therefore, personal services had either disappeared in the West, or were much reduced and their content stipulated. Similarly the occasional obligations of serfdom had been commuted into so many sources of income; the consent of the lord may still have been required for

[41] For the legal and real content of the two statutes, see the excellent discussion by Robert Stein, *Die Umwandlung der Agrarverfassung Ostpreussens durch die Reform des neunzehnten Jahrhunderts*, Vol. I: *Die ländliche Verfassung Ostpreussens am Ende des achtzehnten Jahrhunderts* (Jena, 1918), 252-54, 257-58.

changes in personal status or for the transmission or alienation of wealth; in fact it was accorded as a matter of course
in return for indemnities whose names vary with the purpose
and region (*Hauptrecht, Weinkauf, Sterbefall, Todfall,
Freikauf*).

In the area of *Gutswirtschaft*, however, the Junker was
both estate lord and judge-administrator (*Gerichtsherr*).
This cumulation of the roles of economic master and local
sovereign—as the saying has it, the Prussian state of the
Old Regime ended at the boundaries of the *Rittergut*[42]—gave
him almost unlimited power over the residents of the area.
This in turn enabled him over a period of several hundred
years, from the fifteenth to the eighteenth centuries, to
increase the burdens of his peasants, to appropriate their
land, and to assimilate every free man within reach to
the status of a *Leibeigene*. In Prussia, the process was
slowed and then reversed only in the eighteenth century,
when the state became strong enough to protect peasant holdings against noble encroachment in the interest of military
recruitment. On the other hand, the very same considerations
militated against abandonment or modification of personal
subordination, for the survival of the aristocracy as a seedbed
of army officers seemed to depend on a continued supply of
compulsory peasant labor.[43] Moreover, even the Prussian
state had difficulty in imposing its will on the Junker. In 1709,
1714, and again in 1739, Frederick William I forbade his
Gutsherren to evict their peasants without good reason and
without immediately reestablishing another peasant family on
the land. The very iteration of the decree is evidence of its
inefficacy. Again, in 1724 the Prussian government asserted
that there was no *Leibeigenschaft* in the kingdom, only *Erbuntertänigkeit*, because the peasants were not without rights.

---

[42] Cited by Friedrich Keil, *Die Landgemeinde in den östlichen Pro-
vinzen Preussens* [Schriften des Vereins für Socialpolitik, Vol. XLIII]
(Leipzig, 1890), 41. Keil gives no source, just calls this a *"gehörten
Behauptung."*
[43] On the efforts to reconcile these conflicting concerns, see Otto
Büsch, *Militärsystem und Sozialleben im alten Preussen 1713-1807*
(Berlin, 1962).

The claim was somewhat premature. Though it was not common in eighteenth-century Prussia, as it was in Schleswig-Holstein, Mecklenburg, and Neuvorpommern, to sell peasants without the land they farmed and the cottages they lived in, such cases did occur, especially in areas populated by Slavs; and it was not at all uncommon to sell an estate while retaining some of its serfs, in effect uprooting these from the soil that was the presumed basis of their subordination. In any event, one half-century later (November 8, 1773) the king ordered that all personal serfdom and slavery be abolished in West and East Prussia.[44] Even this was not decisive, and the complaints and violations that come down to us from subsequent years (and we must assume they constitute only a fraction, a small fraction, of the actual abuses) make clear that the so-called "rights" of the *Untertänige* depended in the last analysis on the pleasure of the lord.

The consequences of these social and economic relationships for the health and growth of the nation were extremely deleterious. In the first place, agricultural productivity was low and stagnant, partly because the communal servitudes of the field system posed an obstacle to innovation in technique, even more because compulsory labor was intrinsically inefficient. A free day laborer would do two to three times the work of a serf—sometimes more;[45] and the effort to increase output by augmenting the required services soon passed the point of diminishing returns.

[44] Georg F. Knapp, in his classical study *Die Bauern-Befreiung und der Ursprung der Landarbeiter in der älteren Theilen Preussens* (Leipzig, 1887), p. 28, states that the term *Leibeigenschaft*, as used in Prussian decrees of the eighteenth century abolishing the status, refers not to true personal bondage, but to what he calls *"uneigentliche Leibeigenschaft,"* that is, *Gutsuntertänigkeit* with precarious tenure; and he argues that cases of true *Leibeigenschaft* were "most exceptional." Perhaps so; though enough instances are known to throw doubt on so optimistic a judgment. In any event, the decree of 1773 referred to *Leibeigenschaft und Sklaverei*.

[45] A fact realized even by those most attached to the old system of domination and exploitation. Friedrich Lütge, "Ueber die Auswirkungen der Bauernbefreiung in Deutschland," *Jahrbücher f. Nationalökonomie und Statistik*, CLVII (1943), 368.

Secondly, the system placed serious impediments in the way of geographical mobility. The great mass of peasants were not permitted to move about as they pleased, and even free men, endowed with *Freizügigkeit*, could not settle at will because of the reluctance of numerous village communities to accept potentially burdensome outsiders.

Finally, the injustice and oppressiveness of the peasant condition cut off the great mass of the population from the rest of the body social. In Prussia the peasant lived out a life of poverty and travail in sullen resignation, broken only occasionally by fits of resistance that were quickly suppressed by the troops. As for the latter, they were the brothers and cousins of the serfs at the other end of their bayonets, and their conscription into the army, far from affording them a happier existence, exposed them to the same kind of abuse and humiliation that would have been their lot on the land. Their officers were Junkers, whose sense of superiority and personal dominance was reinforced and twisted by the unlimited authority of military discipline. Harshness, cruelty, even sadism had free rein, to the point where Gneisenau's first prescription for military reform was *"die Freiheit der Rücken,"* freedom of the soldier's back from the rod and his elevation from beast to human being.[46]

Let it not be thought, however, that this degradation of three-fourths or more of the population was the only price of the privileges and comforts of the upper classes. These were

[46] This was a newspaper article, published in the *Volksfreund* of July 9, 1808. The text is reprinted in G. H. Pertz, *Das Leben des Feldmarschalls Grafen Neithardt von Gneisenau* (2 vols.; Berlin, 1864), I, 385-87; also in Hans Bursch, ed., *Die Reformen in Preussen unter Stein und Hardenberg, in Zeugnissen der Zeit* (Breslau, n.d.), pp. 8-10, which gives the date of publication as July 6.

As a result of these abuses, the rate of suicide was four times as high among soldiers as among civilians, and desertion was commonplace. In garrison towns, a special cannon would be fired whenever a soldier was found missing, and the peasants of the surrounding area would set up watch at bridges and crossroads. Whoever brought in the fugitive, dead or alive, received a reward. H. Brunschwig, *La crise de l'état prussien à la fin du XVIIIe siècle* (Paris, 1947), p. 98. This, no doubt, was the peasant's revenge.

also paid for with the brutalization of much of the landowning aristocracy, the resentment and disaffection of the enlightened elements of the bourgeoisie, a widespread ignorance of or indifference to civic responsibilities, an economy operating at only a fraction of its potential performance. In the long run, moreover, the last shortcoming became ever more costly and dangerous. Over the course of the century, population grew at an unprecedentedly rapid and increasing rate—part of an international explosion that struck almost every country from Ireland to Russia. With greater numbers came a rising demand for jobs and food. To be sure, much of East Elbia was still uninhabited, and rulers such as Frederick II made strenuous efforts to encourage immigration and colonization. Yet there were large and growing pockets of overpopulation, especially in the West and the South, and throughout the Germanies, the lack of profitable employment and abusive treatment drove peasants and artisans to flight, mendicancy, and crime.[47] Some of the surplus population was drained off by emigration; in these decades Hungary was the new frontier, and then the virgin steppes of South Russia.[48] Another outlet was military service abroad. Yet these drains were at best palliatives. Salvation in the long run lay only in industrialization—an economic breakthrough to a technology of higher productivity and with it a path of self-sustained growth.

In the meantime, the incentive to increase agricultural output was greater than ever, and experienced observers began to look at the structure of rural society and the system of land cultivation with a critical eye. Their discontent with the prevailing system was fostered by both the example and the ideas of the countries to the West. In the domain of the practical, England, with her "improving landlords," rational farmers, enclosed estates, technological innovation, and high productivity offered a model for imitation. In the ethical sphere, the values of the Enlightenment, developed within by men like

[47] See the discussion *ibid.*, Part II, ch. i. Also Lütge, "Ueber die Auswirkungen," p. 365.

[48] There is a superb brief description of these movements in Karl Helleiner, ed., *Readings in European Economic History* (Toronto, 1946), pp. 25-27.

Lessing, Mendelssohn, and Kant and imported from without, worked their leavening action on both rulers and ruled, pointing up the contrast between the justice and happiness that reason could secure for man and the misery that custom and arbitrary power had brought him.

In consequence of these material and idealistic considerations, which grew increasingly powerful toward the end of the eighteenth century, even some of the landlords were persuaded of their advantage in improving the condition of their tenants. Some of them went so far as to commute labor services into rents. How many did this is impossible to say; nor do we know their social status, though it seems likely that many, if not most, of these enlightened proprietors were bourgeois, who were buying up noble domains in increasing number and brought to their new status the rationality that had marked their rise to wealth.[49] Among the most progressive were the farmers of the state domains, the *Pächter* and *Generalpächter*, who had the capital, the connections, and the business attitudes required to make the most of the new techniques. They formed almost a caste—a small group of intermarried dynasties.[50] But improving landlords were to be found in all classes—among the more enlightened Junkers, of course, and even among the peasants, whose reputation for ignorance and backwardness has probably been overdrawn.[51]

In the meantime, the growing interest in agricultural methods was both cause and effect of a swelling demand for land, which by the turn of the century had assumed the proportions of a boom. A whole range of new purchasers was enter-

[49] Cf. Wolfgang Treue, "Die preussische Agrarreform zwischen Romantik und Rationalismus," *Rheinische Vierteljahresblätter*, XX (1955), 338-39.
[50] Cf. Walter Mertineit, *Die Fridericianische Verwaltung in Ostpreussen* (Heidelberg, 1958), especially pp. 112 *et seq.*
[51] This is a favorite theme of the most recent Marxist research, which is inclined to see the allegedly traditional characterization as an expression, "deliberate or unconscious of the attitude of the ruling bourgeois class toward the capitalistically exploited peasants." H. H. Müller, "Eine bäuerliche Preisschrift," *Jahrbuch für Wirtschaftsgeschichte*, 1963, Teil IV, 244.

ing the market: the same *Generalpächter*, energetically applying the fortunes they had acquired as tenants to the acquisition
of *Rittergüter*; merchants buying financial security and higher
status for their children; civil servants enriched by office;
lawyers and stewards of landed magnates following a path to
wealth and rank as old as hierarchy itself; finally, army officers
returning to civilian life with the earnings of military enterprise—not so much booty as the profits of rationally managed
troop finances.[52]

On one level, one can explain this boom, in which estates
were bought, improved, and resold in a cycle analogous to the
settle-clear-sell-move-on sequence of the American frontier,
as a psychological phenomenon—a product of speculative pas-
sion. It was that in part. But in the last analysis it rested on
rising demand for food and industrial crops and therefore
higher returns from husbandry. Increases in output not only
paid well; they were indispensable to justify the soaring price
of land. All of this tended on balance to intensify the exploitation of the peasantry. It took a real effort of the imagination
to see that the higher productivity of free labor more than
balanced the concomitant uncertainty of supply and price; the
more so as emancipation entailed a loss of psychic income. It
is an unfortunate characteristic of human nature that personal
dominion over one's fellow can be and usually is a source of
considerable gratification. The German Junker enjoyed his
seignorial role. In any event, all landlords, with few exceptions, stuck at relaxation of the peasant's personal bonds; so
that while a number of German states, the most important of
which was Prussia, made repeated efforts to emancipate the
peasantry, the only areas of significant change at the turn of
the century were the king's own domains, where he was
master of his own serfs.[53] If anything, conditions elsewhere
deteriorated as landlords moved to tighten control and squeeze
more work out of their labor force.

[52] Büsch, *Militärsystem*, p. 144 *et seq.*
[53] See especially Knapp, *Die Bauern-Befreiung*, pp. 81-126; Gode-
froy Cavaignac, *La formation de la Prusse contemporaine* (2 vols.;
Paris, 1897), I, 157-65.

There were, to be sure, some bright spots. In the more progressive West—the Rhineland especially, but also Westphalia and Nassau—a number of industrial centers began to flourish from the middle of the eighteenth century, building on the same system of rural manufacture that had made England's fortune.[54] Yet these islands of prosperity, far from sustaining the social order, were a force for subversion, for they undermined the dependence of peasant on land and lord, broke the guild-controlled urban monopoly of production, and raised up a new industrial and mercantile aristocracy. Their success also underlined the comparative failure of the hothouse promotions of the cameralist state.

One reason for this failure of development-from-above was the inefficient convolution of the decision-making and administrative apparatus. Political institutions, even more than industrial plants, have a way of outlasting the functions they were built for; in the absence of pecuniary criteria of profit and loss, scrapping is almost inconceivable. Instead, legislators and administrators tend to engage in an unending series of improvisations, patching here, adding there, touching up everywhere. So it was with Prussia as, beginning in the seventeenth century, the rulers of a small principality superimposed on the feudal institutions of a *Ständestaat* (a state governed by representatives of the major status groups) those of an authoritarian monarchy; as their officials in turn worked to change the resulting autocracy into a bureaucracy; as local and provincial functions and rights were arrogated by the central government; as territories of very different law and social constitution were annexed to the Brandenburger heartland; as new departments and agencies were created to perform the newly conceived duties of the mercantilist state.

---

[54] The best discussions are Max Barkhausen, "Staatliche Wirtschaftslenkung und freies Unternehmertum im westdeutschen und in nord- und südniederländischen Raum bei der Entstehung der neuzeitlichen Industrie im 18. Jahrhundert," *Vierteljahrschrift für Sozial- und Wirtschaftsgeschichte*, XLV (1958), 168-241; and also by Barkhausen, "Der Aufstieg der rheinischen Industrie im 18. Jahrhundert und die Entstehung eines industriellen Grossbürgertums," *Rheinische Vierteljahrsblätter*, XIX (1954), 135-77.

"How can one convey the A.B.C. of these abuses?" asked the Minister von Struensee.[55]

"They arise from ten antique budgets, twenty files, fifty constitutions, a hundred privileges, and uncounted personal considerations, all of which together I alone cannot alter or clear away; for I am not Prime Minister, and my own department is too entangled in the general red tape. And no one is going to be able to do anything about it until a powerful blow from outside forces a change, or the disorder in the inner detritus [sic: *Geschiebe*] becomes so bad that no one understands anyone else and therefore all feel the necessity to resort to new and simple principles. These are the things that will bring us to the season of the one and only Reformer, whom we must wait for and whose way, when he does come, we must bear patiently; whether, because of people's stiff-necked opposition or lack of clear thinking, he does his work of reform roughly, or he does it gently."

By the end of the eighteenth century, German society was in the throes of crisis. Internal frictions were as baneful as ever, while outside ideological pressures had turned into military aggression. Against the strength of a unified revolutionary nation-in-arms, the Germans could oppose only divided forces, sullen conscripts, a population at best apathetic, at worst ready to welcome the invaders as liberators. Prussia, the leader with Austria of German resistance, tried to temporize while rushing long-deferred reforms into execution. Even then, on the brink of catastrophe, these efforts miscarried, for those most aware of the ineptness of the regime and the illness of the body social were not frightened enough. The same Struensee was able to tell himself that "the pastry would hold up a little longer"; and a keen administrator like Vincke, later one of the most effective reformers, could visit Britain and France in the early years of the new century and return home with the conviction that nowhere were people "better

[55] Quoted by Ernst Meier, *Die Reform der Verwaltungsorganisation unter Stein und Hardenberg* (Leipzig, 1881), pp. 132-33.

off, happier, and truly free than in his Prussian fatherland."[56]

So catastrophe came. On October 14, 1806, the French Grand Army routed the main Prussian forces at Jena and Auerstädt and then moved on to capture Berlin. Their rapid advance was facilitated by the alacrity of Prussian commanders to surrender and by the hospitality of the inhabitants, who went so far as to turn their own wounded out to make room for their French guests.[57] The Prussian King fled to East Prussia where he could maintain a semblance of sovereignty. But he was compelled to yield up to Napoleon all of his territories west of the Elbe, and the whole of the state laboriously put together by the Great Elector and his gifted successors was threatened with dissolution.

It was at this point that the King consented in desperation to send away the timeserving, procrastinating advisers he found so congenial and grant the Freiherr vom Stein almost dictatorial powers to transform the government and carry out a program of national regeneration. Stein's term lasted little more than a year (October 1807-November 1808). In that short time, however, he instituted a number of major reforms and thereby opened the way to principles whose subsequent implementation gave a powerful impetus to the development of the Prussian society and economy. The best known of these measures was embodied in the edict of October 9, 1807, which abolished serfdom and did away with all class barriers to movement of capital or choice of occupation. This was followed by a new *Städteordnung* that gave municipalities large powers of self-government. Finally, ministerial government was substituted for the private cabinet rule preferred by Prussia's authoritarian kings. Admittedly, Stein's realizations fell far short of his intentions, and his intentions fell far short of what the situation and the best values of the day called for. Stein was at bottom a conservative who wanted to save the monarchy and the traditional hierarchical society from them-

[56] The words are Meier's, *ibid.*, p. 133.

[57] On the easy surrender of Prussian forces and the subsequent trials by courts martial, William O. Shanahan, *Prussian Military Reforms, 1786-1813* (New York, 1945), pp. 93-96, 104-9.

selves. But he opened the floodgates, and the work was completed over the next generation by men such as Hardenberg and Scharnhorst at the ministerial level, Vincke, Humboldt, Kunth, Maassen, and Boyen at lower administrative levels.[58]

This is not the place to describe in detail the substance of Prussian or German reform: the conversion of a *ständische Gesellschaft* (estate or status society) into a society of free citizens bound by common loyalty to the nation;[59] the abolition of restraints on investment and enterprise; the development of the most advanced system of public education in Europe; the achievement of political, economic, and legal unification. What is of concern, however, is the circumstances in which reform was undertaken and effected, in particular, those aspects that bear comparison with the Japanese experience

[58] A number of German historians have pointed out that the institutional order of Prussia was not ossified before 1806 and that the Stein-Hardenberg reforms were simply the consummation of a long, slow change. Thus Otto Hintze, *Geist und Epochen der preussischen Geschichte* (ed. Fritz Hartung; Leipzig, c. 1943), p. 541. This is true; but insofar as these scholars seek to infer from this fact that reform would have come in the natural course of events, with or without Jena, they are misleading. No doubt change would have come, eventually. But it can make an enormous difference to the development of a nation whether changes of this kind come sooner or later, and both the frustration of emergency reforms in the opening years of the century and the success of reactionary forces in delaying and distorting the implementation of the liberal program after its inception give reason to believe that 1806 was a turning point. Some of the most important Prussian advances were not matched by other German states, though they were more advanced socially to begin with, until after 1848.

[59] This statement should not be misinterpreted to mean the abolition of status lines. All societies are hierarchical in some degree, and to this day German society is sharply divided on the basis of origin, occupation, rank, wealth, and similar criteria. Our concern here is with the fundamental transition from servile to free status, however humble, and from legally sanctioned and enforced social immobility to mobility. It was these changes that were decisive for the development of a sense of participation in the larger society and identification with the national effort—and these are the heart of the matter. The rest is a question of social justice, and no one has ever argued that social justice is a necessary condition of economic growth.

and thus throw light on movements of this kind in general and on the relation between political change and economic development.

PRIME MOVERS OF CHANGE

In both Japan and Germany, unification came about through the efforts and under the leadership of only a part of the nation. In Japan, the key role was played by Satsuma and Chōshū; in Germany by Prussia, in particular the eastern heartland of the kingdom. In both countries, these were paradoxically among the most hierarchical and conservative of states; and their leaders stood to lose the most in the long run from a fundamental political and social revolution. That they behaved as they did is testimony to their limited immediate objectives and, for some, to a misestimate of the ultimate consequences of reform. In Japan, numerous officials resigned when they found the Restoration going beyond what they had anticipated; and some went home to mount rebellions against the Restoration betrayed. In Germany, the differences between reaction and reform-from-above never led to armed conflict; unlike the *han*, the Prussian provinces were long dead as autonomous entities and foci of loyalty. Instead, the two parties fought each other within the government. The sabotage of Stein's reform by the landed aristocracy began as soon as it became apparent that emancipation would not be the occasion for unlimited expropriation of the peasantry; while Stein himself recoiled from Hardenberg's edict of September 1811, which fixed the terms of redemption of peasant land and services, as being subversive of the inner structure of the peasant family.[60] For decades after, moreover, the work of modernization was retarded and thwarted by the covert renitency of vested interests and by overt pressure on a monarchy that took its tone and advisers from the Junkerdom of East Elbia.[61]

[60] G. H. Pertz, *Das Leben des Ministers vom Stein* (7 vols.; Berlin, 1850-55), II. 571.

[61] Blood was shed in Germany, but not over the transformation of the society and economy, for in the long run this left the political

Yet one should not lay everything at the door of unanticipated consequences. In both countries, loyalties to the polity overrode at critical points the prejudices and personal interests of beneficiaries of the old order. In Japan, what we may call the technique of the contagious sacrifice precipitated acceptance of several particularly painful reforms: the most spectacular instance is the surrender by the daimyo of Satsuma, Chōshū, Tosa, and Hizen of their fiefs as a prelude to the transformation of the *han* into prefectures. Nothing like this can be found in the German record to my knowledge; but it is significant that the reformers there were drawn in large measure from the same landed aristocracy that produced their most vehement opponents.

In neither country did reform proceed from the economically advanced regions. In Japan, it was the sea-level plains of central Honshū—the Osaka-Kyoto basin, the Nagoya area, the great Kantō plain around Edo—that had adopted new techniques of cultivation, commercialized much of their crops, developed sophisticated mercantile and banking methods, strewn the countryside with industry. And in Germany it was in the Rhineland, Westphalia, and Hesse that manufacturing and trade were flourishing in the eighteenth century and building up the kind of pressures that had led in Britain to an industrial revolution. Chōshū and Satsuma in Japan, Brandenburg-Prussia in Germany were the Spartas, not the Athens of their respective countries.

---

power of the landed aristocracy intact (more of this later); moreover, in time of social crisis—as in 1848—progressive and reactionary forces within the Establishment united against the threat of reform-from-below. Rather it was national unification that was the broiling point. Where in Japan, unity was implicit in the restoration of the Emperor, in Germany, Prussia imposed national unity on the recalcitrant states about her by economic pressure and eventually by military force. That war did break out, however, was due to the presence of a rival power for German hegemony. Had Austria not existed to focus the resistance to Prussia, the lesser states would have knuckled under without a struggle. It is interesting to speculate what course Japanese history would have followed had Satsuma and Chōshū not joined forces to accomplish the overthrow of the shogunate.

This pattern is not surprising. Reform, however much it may have worked to the advantage of the economically progressive areas, was a political response to a political problem. The initiative lay with the toughest, most powerful units, not with "small fry," however prosperous. Indeed, one might argue that, given the nature and knowledge of government in these pre-industrial societies, strong authority and an innovating, progressive economy were incompatible. In Satsuma, the "Prussia of Japan," free enterprise was sacrificed to a cameralist policy of official monopolies and government factories; while the repudiation of the *han* debts wiped out a good part of the assets of the merchant class.[62] In Chōshū, where the government alternated between the establishment of official monopolies and the granting of monopoly privileges to the guilds, the merchants were looked upon as a necessary evil: their "rightful scope" lay in "serving the *han* without procuring great profits for themselves."[63] As for Germany, it was precisely the fragmentation of the Rhineland into weak political units that enabled industry to develop there along new, free lines and to grow faster than in the mercantilist economies to the East.[64]

Revolutions are never made by the masses. They are made by revolutionaries who see and use the opportunities of public weakness and popular discontent to seize power and effect change. In both Germany and Japan, modernization was the work of a small number of statesmen, advised and seconded by a somewhat larger group of dedicated, hard-working civil servants. In both cases, it was the bureaucracy that actually worked out and then carried out the program of reform—a bureaucracy that had long since won its autonomy from the dictates and whims of the overlord and developed an *esprit de corps* and an impersonal loyalty to the polity. At all levels of

[62] Albert M. Craig, *Chōshū in the Meiji Restoration* (Cambridge, Mass., 1961), p. 72.

[63] *Ibid.*, p. 74f.

[64] The best discussions are Max Barkhausen, "Staatliche Wirtschaftslenkung" (see n. 54 above); and Herbert Kisch, "The Textile Industries in Silesia and the Rhineland: A. Comparative Study in Industrialization," *Journal of Economic History*, XIX (1959), 541-64.

Japanese government under Tokugawa, the nominal ruler was essentially a figurehead: the Emperor, of course; but the shogun also and the great majority of daimyo. All of them had long been accustomed to leave the business of administering such affairs as came within their domain to their officials; and if they occasionally were able to take advantage of power struggles among their vassals to intervene in politics, they were more often the creatures of vassals who influenced the succession to their own advantage. By contrast, Brandenburg-Prussia was ruled by a series of intelligent and active autocrats from the Great Elector to Frederick II,[65] all of whom tended to treat their civil servants as just that—servants. Their successors, however, were far less capable and decisive—such is the biological penalty of inherited rank. So that well before the end of the eighteenth century, "the Prussian bureaucracy, as a body, gained a considerable amount of executive discretion and irresponsible political influence in detachment from, and veiled opposition to, personalized monarchical autocracy."[66]

Ironically, this development was due in part to an administrative policy whose specific aim was to render the bureaucracy more amenable to royal control. In an effort to break down local loyalties, the Prussian crown early established the policy of appointing as provincial officials only people from other areas.[67] The device was effective in the short run, but the ultimate consequences far exceeded intentions. The trans-recruitment of personnel (if I may coin a term) inevitably fostered a sense of national identity, and this in turn conduced to the same substitution of impersonal for personal loyalties. Even more, the rise of Prussian power made the new state a magnet to outside talent. Stein was an independent knight of the Holy Roman Empire, whose tiny castle domain in the

[65] With the exception of Frederick III (King Frederick I), 1668-1713.

[66] Hans Rosenberg, *Bureaucracy, Aristocracy, and Autocracy: The Prussian Experience*, 1660-1815 (Cambridge, Mass., 1958), p. 192.

[67] See, for example, Art. I, Par. 11, of the Instructions of the General-directorium of December 20, 1722. Conrad Bornhak, *Geschichte des preussischen Verwaltungsrechts* (3 vols.; Berlin, 1885), II, 42.

Rhineland was absorbed by the Duke of Nassau in 1803; at that time, he had already served more than twenty years in the Prussian administration. Hardenberg was a Hanoverian; Scharnhorst and Gneisenau, Saxons. Even groups left their home territories to offer their services to the Prussian crown: thus Bischoffswerder and his cohort of Saxons, including the Count von Brühl, son of one of Frederick the Great's fiercest enemies. Behind this flow one can perceive a sense of German identity transcending particularistic allegiances. As a result long before the Prussians themselves were aware of their role, other Germans began to see them as the standard bearers of national unity and regeneration.[68]

DIVERSITY AND CONSENSUS

We have noted that in both Germany (early 1800's) and Japan (1850's and 1860's) the achievement of consensus on the necessity of change was the result of an enduring commitment and an immediate challenge: of a common loyalty to a national ideal transcending private and local interests; and of the necessity to fight off foreign domination and protect the polity from dissolution. Yet when all is said and done, this was a very meager common denominator, and at that, not common to all. Throughout Germany and even in Prussia, there were those who were content, or pleased, to collaborate with the French. And the advocates of resistance were split along lines very similar to the opposition between *kaikoku* and *sonnō-jōi*: there were those who called for reform after the British and French models; and those, like Marwitz, who argued that these Western innovations were the negation of the best and noblest in Prussian society, and that what was needed was a return to antique virtues and selfless loyalty to the King. The reform party itself had its own varieties: visionaries and theorists who enunciated comprehensive pro-

[68] In Japan, a national bureaucracy was not achieved until Meiji. John W. Hall suggests that the change from *han* loyalties to national loyalty was made possible by the earlier separation of the samurai from the land: "Land ownership can be a cause of stagnant provincialism."

grams (like Sakamoto Ryōma); statesmen like Stein who acted on principles that transcended the immediate crisis; politicians like Hardenberg, who also cherished larger aims but subordinated principle to feasibility; practitioners like Gneisenau, whose sole aim was the expulsion of the French and who lost interest in reform once that was accomplished.

That so limited a consensus was in fact transmuted into a purposeful, integrated program of reform owed a great deal to ideological preparation. In Japan, both *sonnō* and *kaikoku* had long antecedents, and although the early advocates of reform, whether in the form of a return to tradition or of an advance to a new and stronger order, had little immediate influence on events, they provided the inspiration and doctrinal nourishment for later policy. It is possible, to be sure, to overemphasize the effect of ideas on action. An early historian of modern Japan wrote of the Mito school: "They did not attempt to give practical effect to their discoveries; their era was essentially academical. But this galaxy of scholars projected into the future a light which burned with growing force in each succeeding generation and ultimately burst into a flame which consumed feudalism and the shogunate."[69] Later scholars have toned down this hyperbole, pointing out that other intellectual traditions were at least as important, and suggesting that, in any event, events and political interest would have created the ideas required.[70] Perhaps. And yet it is hard to believe that the pieces of a largely improvised reform movement—improvised, that is, from the standpoint of the individual political decision and its timing—would have fitted together so well had there been no previous speculation, no blueprints to work by.

In Germany, it is even more hazardous to draw a neat line from ideas to action. For one thing, there is the diversity of inspiration: the English combination of aristocracy, limited

[69] Cited in Frank Brinkley, "Japan," in the *Encyclopaedia Britannica*, 11th ed. He does not give the source of this quotation.

[70] Thus Craig, *Chōshū*, p. 154f.: "It may well be that sonnō thought in Chōshū emerged directly from the orthodox climate of opinion in the han in response to the changing political situation."

monarchy, and increasing laissez faire; the younger, more radical French doctrines of the Enlightenment; the new German thought of people such as Lessing and Kant; the old cameralist tradition renewed by men such as Suarez for loftier ends. For another, there is the diversity of motivation. Even less than in Japan did ferment coagulate into orthodoxy. Once again it would seem the situation selected the ideas it needed and created those that were not already available. Even so, it is significant that in both countries, the reformers sanctioned their programs with an appeal to a morality transcending time and place. The classic statement for Germany is that of Hardenberg's memorandum of October 1807:[71] "Thus a revolution in the good sense, leading directly to the great goal of the ennoblement of mankind, through the wisdom of the regime and not through forceful impulse from within or without—that is our aim, our guiding principle."

More important probably were the human contacts that made possible the exchange of ideas, the selection of those most suited to the circumstances and purposes of the revolutionaries, and their dissemination to distant centers of power; this permitted in short the coalescence of a movement. In this regard, historians have often stressed the separation of the samurai from the land; the land gave him his income, but he did not own it or the people on it, and his horizon was therefore not bound by local residence or interests. Rather, he lived in the castle towns, and his administrative duties or obligations to his lord often took him from his home to Edo, where he met officials from every part of Japan, or Nagasaki, which more than ever after the incursion of Perry was a channel for Western ideas.[72] The importance of these personal encounters is perhaps nowhere so spectacularly illustrated than by the career of Sakamoto Ryōma, who came as a loyalist fanatic to kill the Westernizer Katsu Rintarō and stayed to become his disciple; and who later profited from

[71] Leopold von Ranke, ed., *Denkwurdigkeiten des Staatskanzlers Fürsten von Hardenberg vom Jahre 1806 bis zum Jahre 1813* (4 vols.; Leipzig, 1877), p. 8*.

[72] Marion J. Levy emphasizes the implications of compulsory residence in Edo.

residence in Nagasaki to develop his conception of political reform and his image of a new Japan.[73]

By comparison, the German aristocrat would seem to offer a picture of ingrained parochialism. The Prussian Junker especially drew his material comfort, social status, and self-esteem from his estate and his seignorial relation to its inhabitants. Possessed of some of the attributes of sovereignty— he dispensed low justice within the bounds of his domain— he long preferred to look on his monarch as *primus inter pares* and on the kingdom as a personal assemblage of autonomous provinces. And while the personal authority of the House of Brandenburg had succeeded by the end of the seventeenth century in reducing the provincial estates to ceremonious impotence and in fostering the concept and reality of a centralized autocracy, the horizon of the ordinary Junker remained constricted by his personal ties to the soil.

Yet it would be a mistake to overemphasize the cultural and ideological parochialism of the Prussian nobility. Even the heaths and wastes of East Elbia were not too barren for the seeds of the Enlightenment, which gave forth in Germany a peculiarly Teutonic harvest—the cult of *Bildung*. *Bildung* was both more and less than the French mélange of ideas and ideals seasoned by eloquence and wit. It was sober, pragmatic, academic—the formal and systematic development of human powers. The French ripened their *civilisation* in the salon; the Germans cultivated *Kultur* at home and in the lecture hall. The German took his education seriously and in heavy doses. By the second half of the eighteenth century, the pattern of the student *Wanderjahre*—of training at several universities—was firmly established. Alexander von Humboldt, born and reared in Berlin, attended classes at the universities of Frankfurt a. Oder and Göttingen, the Handelsakademie in Hamburg, the Bergakademie at Freiberg. Ludwig von Vincke, born in Minden, a close friend of Stein and chief administrator of Westphalia from 1815 to 1844, studied at Marburg, Erlangen, and Göttingen. Wealthy families hired

[73] Marius Jansen, *Sakamoto Ryōma* (Princeton, 1961), pp. 162-65, 275, 294.

some of Germany's best teachers and thinkers to tutor their children at home and guide them on educational trips abroad: thus Schleiermacher for the counts of Dohna, Berger for the young Count Theodor von Schön, the later collaborator of Stein and Hardenberg.[74] To be sure, these were exceptions; the average Junker family was indifferent to these frills. Yet when we study the origins of a revolutionary movement, it is precisely the exceptions that we are interested in. Thus a scholarly "brain truster" such as Christian Jakob Kraus, Professor of Practical Philosophy (and later of Cameralistics) at Königsberg at the age of 27, had a remarkable clientele of influential officials and statesmen: Stein's later associate, Friedrich von Schrötter; Hans Jakob von Auerswald, curator of the University and then (1808) Oberpräsident of East and West Prussia and Lithuania; Landschafts-direktor Theodor von Hippel, friend until 1812 of Hardenberg's associate Scharnweber and the man who was to draft the *Landsturm* [citizens' militia] edict of 1813; the above-mentioned Theodor von Schön; and sundry others.

"THE DISCONTENTED"

In one way ideas did directly influence events—by suggesting new standards of social selection and thereby exacerbating class conflict within the traditional order.

More energetic than the German nobility in this pursuit of *Bildung* were the commoners who saw in these new values a path of social ascent. Here was a new "yardstick for 'gauging the degree of social esteem which formerly rank and external glitter alone determined.' . . . Now strange new voices could be heard, uttering self-assertive provocations and revealing an attitude of arrogance rather than deference toward the titled aristocracy."[75] On the other hand, the cultivated nobleman felt toward the *gebildete* commoner a kinship that transcended barriers of birth and rank. There formed "a proud and self-reliant aristocratic fraternity . . . 'a sort of freemasonry, of which all the members continue to recognize one

[74] Brunschwig, *La crise de l'état prussien*, p. 96.
[75] Rosenberg, *Bureaucracy, Aristocracy and Autocracy*, pp. 183-84.

another through certain invisible signs, whatever may be the opinions which make them strangers to one another or even adversaries.' "[76] Nowhere, perhaps, did this change of standards have more impact than in the state administration. Here were the men, of high and low origin, who did most to raise the bureaucracy from a tool of the monarch to an autonomous corporate body guided by a higher loyalty to the ethical state. And it was largely they who instituted and effected the social and political reforms of the nineteenth century.

Compare in this regard Smith's description of "The Discontented" in Japan.[77]

"They were not limited to a single class but existed in every broad social stratum; they were not, on the whole, the oppressed and exploited but in large part able and rising men destined to form a new ruling class who felt unjustly cut off from positions of power and respect; and although emphatically they believed that hierarchy reflected natural inequalities among men . . . they were for freedom of movement within the hierarchy and against birth and other hereditary restraints upon such freedom.

"This attitude is unambiguously expressed in warrior writings on government. Everywhere eligibility for office was largely determined by family rank, and everywhere this practice was bitterly attacked by writers who urged that the appointment and promotion of officials be based on merit alone."

In both Germany and Japan, the confrontation with an outside system encouraged introspection that fostered in its turn dissatisfaction with the status quo. The Japanese were

[76] *Ibid.*, p. 186. The quotation within the quotation comes from *The Recollections of Alexis de Tocqueville* (New York, 1896), pp. 305-06 (also in the J. P. Mayer edition; New York: Meridien Books [paperback], 1959, p. 242). The argument, however, is entirely Professor Rosenberg's, for Tocqueville's point was just the reverse, that is, that he felt "a hundred times more at ease in dealing with aristocrats who differed with me entirely in their interests and opinions than with bourgeois whose ideas and instincts were analogous to mine."

[77] *Journal of Asian Studies*, XXI (1962), 218.

faced by an immediate menace. The Germans of the eighteenth century were under less pressure, but the comparison with richer, freer societies was disturbing and thought-provoking. In both cases, once thoughts came, they fed on themselves and developed a force of their own. This discontent might, of course, have led to unbridgeable cleavages and class conflict, as indeed it was to do in Germany in 1848 and 1918. Under the wider menace to the polity, however, horizontal lines became vertical, drawn between institutional systems rather than class groups. Smith suggests that for Japan, it was partly this very "leaven of class discontent which made possible, within these [vertical] guidelines, new political combinations capable of revolutionary acts."[78] The same was, if anything, even more true in Germany, where over the course of the nineteenth century the bourgeoisie—and eventually even the working class—sublimated their ambitions and assuaged their frustrations in the drive to national unity and aggrandizement.

PRIMACY OF THE POLITICAL

It is important to keep this primacy of the political in mind while steering the bark of historical interpretation. On the one hand is the rock of overexpectation; on the other, the whirlpool of underestimation.

Take the former. Students of German history have noted that the achievements of the reform movement fell far short of the avowed goals of some of its sponsors. Thus one can cite the well-known lines from Stein's "Nassauer Denkschrift" of 1807: "If the nation is to be ennobled, the oppressed part of it must be given freedom, independence, property, and they must be accorded the protection of the laws"; yet note by way of contrast that the emancipation of the serfs and the tenurial changes in agriculture left the peasants heavily burdened and forced many in the long run to give up their holdings to the wealthier landowners.[79] This gap between aims

[78] *Ibid.*, 219.

[79] The passage in question is given in E. Botzenhart, then W. Hubatsch, eds., *Freiherr vom Stein: Briefe und Amtliche Schriften*, II (ed. P. G. Thielen; Stuttgart, 1959), 397. It is cited in part by

and results has led some scholars to speak of failure. Yet such a judgment deforms the underlying character of the reform program by imputing the loftier objectives of a few to the movement as a whole; even for these few, it exaggerates the importance of their "higher" as against their "lower" aims; and it rests on a misunderstanding of the fundamental character of political action. Politics as the cliché has it, is the art of the possible; and there is many a slip on the red tape that litters the path from intention to result. The phenomenon alluded to is a familiar one. Americans, for example, have seen a number of new administrations ride victoriously into Washington, zealous to purge the abominations of the old order and establish a new temple of virtue: New Deal, Fair Deal, the Eisenhower Crusade, the New Frontier. In each case, idealism yielded to pragmatism, principle to compromise, the indispensable to the feasible, the just and right to the lesser or least of evils. So with Prussia. In a sense, all reform movements are failures.

The danger of underestimation is somewhat more subtle. Here one remains aware of the essentially limited objectives of a program requiring the collaboration of many people— again the question of the common denominator—but then argues from this that the consequences must necessarily have been limited. Thus German historians have laid heavy stress of late on the narrow aims of the movement that created the Zollverein. In opposition to the once popular notion that the customs union was established as a device for forcing the political amalgamation of Germany, these historians have

---

W. M. Simon. *The Failure of the Prussian Reform Movement, 1807-1819* (Cornell, 1955), p. 4, who does not explain that the sentence refers not to the German people, but to the Polish nation. One could conceivably argue, however, *a fortiori* that if Stein wanted this much for the annexed Poles, he wanted at least as much for the German peasantry. Still, his official papers make few appeals to higher principles. Cf., *ibid.*, pp. 77-78, the tone of his reply to a petition of the merchants of Königsberg, August 27, 1805: ". . . the Prussian commercial class may rest assured that I shall do everything for their benefit and facility that is compatible with correct financial principles and the other considerations of state."

pointed out that the Prussian government had nothing more in mind than the promotion of the commercial prosperity and political authority of Prussia. From this it is an easy step to the contention that the Zollverein made only a modest contribution to national unification. At the same time some students have come to, or close to, this position from the other side of the question, that is, from the side of consequences. They have been troubled by what seems to be a deterministic view of history, one that postulates an ineluctable sequence from economic union to political unification; and indeed some of them confine themselves to the negative formula that the establishment of the Zollverein did not necessarily entail the creation of a congruent political entity.[80] The content of such an assertion is modest: "necessarily" is a very big word, and it does not take much to argue that history rarely if ever works that way. Yet there are those who do believe in materialistic determinism, and this antimechanistic stance is in large part a reaction against a simplistic, allegedly Marxist interpretation of German history.[81] This is its justification.

Unfortunately the antideterminists often join those who

[80] Thus Wolfgang Zorn, "Wirtschafts- und sozialgeschichtliche Zusammenhänge der deutschen Reichsgründungszeit (1850-1879), *Historische Zeitschrift,* CXCVII (1963), 322: "Surely the view that the Zollverein, with its economic consequences, was on the way, even before 1866, to forcing political unification is untenable." Cf. Friedrich Zunkel, *Der rheinisch-westfälische Unternehmer 1834-1879* (Köln and Opladen, 1962), p. 149 and n. 67. This position has been reinforced by the divergent fortunes of today's movements toward the political unification of Europe on the one hand and her economic unification on the other.

[81] See for example Zorn, "Wirtschafts- und sozialgeschichtliche Zusammenhänge," pp. 318-20. Yet if the examples cited there are indicative, the assertion of an ineluctable sequence from economic to political unity is less an article of Marxist doctrine than the affirmation (or at best, implication) of economists and historians such as Keynes, Benaerts, and Hallgarten. One of the East German historians cited offers a more indirect link between the Zollverein and political unification: the customs union promoted economic growth; economic growth fostered the rise of a proletariat; and Bismarck had to unify and centralize political authority in order to forestall revolution from below.

147

insist on conformity of aims and results, indeed they make use of their argument and throw the good away with the bad by going to the other extreme and denying to commercial union a substantial influence on political events. Such reasoning overlooks what we may call "the uncertainty principle" of historical change. Not only need there not be a neat correspondence between intentions and consequences, but there probably cannot be, for each act produces its own complex of results and reactions, which then act upon one another in an endless sequence of such complexity that foresight and planning are possible only within wide limits. Thus with the Zollverein: whatever the objectives of the bureaucrats, the movement of commercial unification acquired a momentum and logic of its own. Before the Prussians were aware of it, they were armed with a powerful economic and political lever; each advance called forth and made possible another; and consequences inevitably far surpassed anticipations. The lever, moreover, had a curious ratchet effect; not only could Prussia move participants and those she wanted to bring into the union to follow her initiative, but the very fact of membership created a vested interest that far outweighed the discomforts of subordination. Each participant quickly learned that once in, he could not afford to withdraw; and that, while one could advance with Prussia, one could not retreat without her. So that while historians may cultivate their doubts, contemporaries were quick enough to perceive what was going on— either because they saw in customs union a giant step toward the old dream of national unity, or because they understood and feared that customs union with Prussia would mean a German nation dominated by Prussia. They were right.[82]

The above analysis would seem to have some relevance to the interpretation of the Japanese experience. There too historians have exerted themselves to find the connections be-

[82] Some readers may be tempted to infer from the above a belief on my part in some kind of historical inevitability or material determinism. Far from it. To argue in this way is not to say that historical movements follow an inexorable course, any more than an analysis of the moments of physical bodies implies that they are intrinsically irresistible.

tween the large forces—the challenge of Western technology
and power, the material and spiritual resources of Japanese
society, and so on—and the atomistic behavior of individual
actors.[83] There too, one cannot help but be struck by the
contrast between the neat simplifications of broad analysis
and the complex dance of hesitations, tergiversations, advances, and retreats on the political scene. The reconciliation,
imply Sakata and Hall, is to be found in the study of motivations. But I submit that even motivations are not enough:
too much of history is unanticipated consequences. More
significant, it would seem, are the persistent, underlying determinants that tend to focus disparate and even contradictory
efforts, minimize and counteract deviancy, and give a long-run
direction to what seems at times a rudderless vessel. As in
Germany, there was a momentum and logic to Japanese reform. Sakata and Hall write:[84]

"Thus it can be seen that the Restoration was motivated
primarily by the desire to eliminate the despotic Tokugawa
rule. Other than the establishment of a new hegemony, the
Restoration leadership had no clear-cut aims. Social and
economic reorganization was not part of their objective. . . .
Between restoration and reform there was both a change of
motive and a change of leadership. Of these two it was change
of leadership which was of crucial significance."

Can it be that the reason for the greater importance of the
change in personnel lies not in its intrinsic significance, but
in the relative stability of motivation? The primacy of the
political remained; the goal continued to be national aggrandizement; but to achieve it, new men were needed who
realized that social and economic reform was an integral part
of the process.[85]

So in Germany: for all the larger concerns of the ideologues

[83] See, for example, the article by Yoshio Sakata and John W. Hall,
"The Motivation of Political Leadership in the Meiji Restoration,"
Journal of Asian Studies, XVI (1956), 31-50, especially 35.
[84] *Ibid.*, p. 50.
[85] Cf. Craig's analysis, *Chōshū*, p. 373.

and the spiritual rationalization of the reform program by a statesman such as Hardenberg, the prime determinants of decision and action were always political. Economic and social change were not ends in themselves, but means to create a stronger nation that would be capable at first of resistance to the French invader, later, of assuming a role of leadership in Germany and Europe. The early debate concerning the implications of emancipation for agrarian tenure illustrates the point well. On the one side were those like Schön who argued that trade in land should be free of all restraints and that it was a matter of indifference whether or not the peasantry acquired proprietary rights over the plots they had tilled as serfs; the important thing was to maximize output by putting the land in the hands of those who could exploit it most efficiently, in units of such size and form as would make possible this efficient exploitation. On the other side were men like Stägemann and Niebuhr, who argued in the old mercantilist tradition that a strong peasantry is the backbone of a strong nation.[86] No one seems to have raised the issue of social justice—of the right of the peasants to land they had worked under exploitative conditions for generations. Such considerations have been introduced into this context only by later historical research.

EXECUTION OF THE REFORM PROGRAM

This similarity arising out of a common pattern of challenge and response must be modified in one important respect. Where in Japan, reform seems to have been the result of a joint effort of business and government, in Europe the antagonism between a tutelary bureaucracy and a bourgeoisie coming of age and impatient of authority inhibited collaboration and even directly hampered economic development. The same states that lavished subsidies and favors on private businessmen and worked toward freedom of trade and enterprise instituted a mass of regulations and red tape to circumscribe private initiative. The most serious of these obstacles to

[86] Pertz, *Das Leben des Ministers Freiherrn vom Stein*, II, 14.

growth were the numerous restrictions on company formation —banks were a special object of suspicion—and on the conduct of those resource-intensive branches of industry whose activity affected the value of landed property: mining, metallurgy, the chemical manufacture.[87] Vexatious as these interferences were, moreover, they were less serious than the manner of their enforcement, which sometimes took on the character of a crusade against the incursions of a rampant capitalism, sometimes took the more subtle form of passive resistance and procrastination. It must be remembered that in Continental Europe much that we (or the British of that period) would consider private was subject to official scrutiny; and that while approval in some areas came to be given almost as a matter of course, delays cost money, and the bureaucrat could pose a barrier to enterprise simply by losing papers in the administrative labyrinth or on his desk.

Part of the difficulty lay in the diverse social origin of bureaucrats and businessmen. The higher officials were usually noblemen—often small noblemen, the proudest kind—or vintage bourgeois who saw in state careers something more distinguished and dignified than the pursuit of wealth in the market place. To men like these, businessmen seemed crude, pushing, impertinent; while from the other side of the desk, bureaucrats seemed officious, patronizing, systematically hostile. This conflict of background and temperament rested, moreover, on a real clash of material and political interests: on the one hand, there was the aristocracy, whose status and power derived largely from its possession of land and its influence and control over the great mass of the population resident on the land; on the other, the rising bourgeoisie, whose claims to status and power rested on what contemporaries called mobile wealth and its influence over that growing portion of the population employed thereby. Needless to say, social conditions consistently lagged behind this momentous shift in the balance of resources and power. From the

[87] Some of these measures, however, were dictated by considerations of public safety—controls over chemical manufacture, for example—or social welfare.

eighteenth century on, the business classes of Continental Europe, beginning with the most advanced country, France, were increasingly sensitive to the disparity between their fortunes (how better measure their contribution to society?) and the consideration accorded them. Nothing probably was so important as this *ressentiment* in pushing them toward liberal ideas in politics; and this in turn simply defined the conflict and increased the antagonism of conservative administrators.

The process of reciprocal exasperation was most obvious in Prussia, where the economically and socially advanced Rhineland found itself annexed in 1815 to a Junker-dominated polity still struggling to effect the transition from *ständische Gesellschaft* to citizen state.

"The French imperial regime had, to be sure, made heavy demands on the purses of its subjects, but the French administration had not only understood the importance of showing itself ever-solicitous of the economic welfare of its taxpayers, but it had introduced a kind of commerce that at once commanded and conferred respect and thus wrapped up with a certain ribbon the decoration-loving Rhinelanders, with their susceptibility to appearances. Decorations that the Emperor conferred did not trouble the bourgeois conscience, since, questions of genuine self-government aside, they were nevertheless real official decorations, whereas it was soon apparent under the Prussian regime that the bourgeois was still nothing but a bourgeois and that another caste surpassed this group in power, position, influence, and esteem. Even the most respected bourgeois stood in the second rank; if he was decorated, it was so to speak a social preparation which first qualified him to consort with the members of that first class. One perceived in addition the preference which the government was inclined to accord the old Prussian provinces over the new ones; one looked with misgiving and displeasure on the pampering of the old nobility, which in the Rhineland even more than in Westphalia had retreated from its former pre-eminence. . . ."[88]

[88] Mathieu Schwann, *Ludolf Camphausen als Wirtschaftspolitiker.*

In the end, the burghers of Cologne and Aachen and their Westphalian allies made important gains, especially in the sphere of economic policy. But the fight lasted for decades and reflected the difficulty of arriving at a consensus on the economic and political implications of national development and aggrandizement; or put another way, the difficulty of reconciling divergent interests in the context of common aspirations.

Japan was more fortunate on all counts. Leaders of both enterprise and government were recruited to a significant degree from among the former samurai; and, indeed, there was some shifting back and forth between the two spheres in the early years of the Restoration. Moreover, for all the disdain of mercantile activity once nursed by the aristocracy, this prejudice did not rest on a vested material interest in another form of productive activity and economic organization. It was therefore intrinsically weaker, and indeed the landless samurai had often shown himself ready to meet poverty with commercial enterprise. So that not only was the personal prejudice weaker—as against Europe, where it was converted into a matter of high principle—but the barriers to ideological consensus were far lower. In Japan, industrial growth was unmistakably the answer to the menace of foreign domination. In Europe, there was strong dissent on this point right into the twentieth century.

The Course of Economic Development

LINKAGES BETWEEN REFORM AND GROWTH

It is one thing to compare the movements for reform in Germany and Japan and to note the numerous similarities of motivation and timing; it is quite another to link these institutional changes to the actual course of economic development in the two countries. The task is less difficult for Japan, not because the causal relationship between the political and

---

I [Veröffentlichungen des Archivs für rheinisch-westfälische Wirtschaftsgeschichte, Vol. III] (Essen, 1915), 25-26.

social on the one hand and the economic on the other has been analyzed and demonstrated, but because it has been accepted by historians as axiomatic. Since this assumption accords with my own interpretation, I am only too happy to take it over for the purposes of this discussion. But the German experience poses real difficulties. Here there is no historical consensus. If some historians have been wont to associate the reforms of the early nineteenth century with the rapid economic growth that ensued (I use the word "associate" advisedly), others have emphasized the lag between legislation and economic response. If, for example, Stein's decrees of 1807 were so important as often alleged, why does rapid economic growth not begin for another generation?

Part of the difficulty is chronological. Professors Ohkawa and Rosovsky feel that one can mark with some accuracy the starting point of "modern economic growth" in Japan: 1886, the end of the Matsukata deflation.[89] It is harder to be so categorical in the case of Germany. The traditional birth date of the modern economy has been the opening of the Zollverein in 1834; but Rostow places Germany's "take-off" in 1850, and W. O. Henderson has written of the genesis of the German industrial revolution in the eighteenth century.[90] Even the Kuznets criteria (above, pp. 47ff.) do not settle the question. The first of these—the application of "modern scientific thought and technology" to production and transportation—is not very specific; in any event, the introduction of the more important new techniques into German industry dates from the eighteenth century. The Newcomen steam engine came in the 1760's, the Watt engine and coke-blast smelting around the turn of the century, the first spinning machines at the same time. Diffusion, to be sure, was often slow—though, given the zero point of departure, the rate of adoption was high. The point is, it is not easy to mark off chronological

---

[89] Above, Ch. II. I am told, however, that some Japanese scholars do not look upon the year 1886 as a significant divide and see this aspect of the Ohkawa-Rosovsky periodization as possibly misleading.

[90] Wm. O. Henderson, "The Genesis of the Industrial Revolution in France and Germany in the 18th Century," *Kyklos*, IX (1956), 190-207.

boundaries for a continuing and broadening flow of innovation, particularly for those countries that industrialized earlier and moved into the stream while the complex of new techniques that constituted the Industrial Revolution (with capital "I" and capital "R") was still being developed. Demarcation may be easier for a country like Japan, which took over the completed package.

Kuznets' other criteria are not much more helpful. This is not through any intrinsic fault in conception; it is simply that we do not have data good enough to enable us to apply them. With regard to the question of income per head, we know that population was rising rapidly in Germany from the second half of the eighteenth century on. But we have no measures of real product per head, and, though it is reasonable to assume that it was going up from at least the 1830's, the data do not permit us to say whether an earlier point of take-off would not be more accurate.[91] The same is true of the rate of transformation of the industrial structure. The shift of labor from agriculture into industry is difficult to follow because of the confusion of the two categories of occupations in the pre-factory period: where is one to place the rural weaver who spends a good part of his time cultivating his plot and tending his livestock? Moreover, one consequence of technological change was the elimination of numbers of these country weavers and craftsmen from the industrial work force. Some of these went on to work in the city; but some remained on the land to swell the ranks of agricultural labor and confuse the statistical trend. The best measure of change in the industrial structure would presumably be the population of the factory work force and its share

[91] In this regard, the agricultural crisis of the 1820's poses an interesting problem. The decade was marked by considerable hardship, which seems to have spread from the agricultural sector to the rest of the economy. Yet this was a crisis of overproduction rather than crop failures, and it may well be that real product per capital rose. On the other hand, Germany had been a heavy exporter of grain, and the closure of the British market combined with lower world prices meant far lower earnings abroad. The story of this cycle and its consequences for general economic growth deserves study.

in total employment, though these data too are rendered inaccurate by inconsistencies in the definition of factory and by continuing inaccuracies in the assignment of labor by category. For what they are worth, however, the Prussian statistics show an increase of factory-employed from 164,000 in 1802 to 1,574,000 in 1843, at which point they accounted for about 43.5 percent of the industrial work force. We do not have figures for total employment, but for purposes of comparison, population rose in these years by 61 percent—from 9.6 to 15.5 million.[92]

As for the final criterion, the presence of international contacts, the trade of the German area with the rest of Europe is unbroken from the Middle Ages on.

On the whole then, the aggregate figures do not permit us to speak with precision of a lag between reform and response. Moreover, even if we were to rely on such partial quantitative evidence as is available—trade statistics, for example—to postulate a quickening of growth from the mid-1830's on, we would in effect be talking about a lag no greater than that between the Meiji Restoration and the Ohkawa-Rosovsky breakthrough to modern economic growth. The Japanese experience in effect provides negative corroboration for the alleged link between institutional change and industrial development in Germany; that is, it seems to show that even a massive transformation of the political and social order, firmly instituted and conscientiously applied, needs time to work its effects. By contrast, the German reforms were strongly opposed from the start and repeatedly undermined by reactionary influences. Could they be expected to yield comparable results in less time?

Yet negative corroboration is cold comfort. It would be helpful to have direct evidence of the impact of these political and social changes on economic performance, not only for Germany but for Japan. (My limited reading in English has not turned up any systematic analysis of the Japanese relationships.) The trouble is that this sort of phenomenon is not

[92] Karl Abraham, *Der Strukturwandel im Handwerk in der ersten Hälfte des 19. Jahrhunderts* (Köln, 1955), pp. 26, 71, 19 n.23, 55.

easy to specify or isolate, much less to measure. How does one determine the effect of a new sense of dignity and freedom of enterprise on entrepreneurial vigor? How does one separate these influences from the purely economic factors—the availability of new techniques, the opening of new commercial outlets—or from the adventitious political events—the cessation of the Napoleonic wars, for example? There is, of course, a large body of evidence that no status society has ever effected on industrial revolution, presumably because of the limitations imposed on the mobility of human and material resources and because of the prevalence of social values and attitudes unfavorable to business enterprise. All of this accords very well with sociological theory. Yet this just brings us back to the realm of negative, or at best indirect, corroboration.

The reforms whose contributions to German growth are most patent are the establishment of a unified national market, the widening of educational opportunity, and the abolition of serfdom. We need not tarry over the first, whose implications for division of labor and the scale of production are obvious. The long line of wagons that waited patiently in the icy night of December 31, 1833 for the customs barriers to lift are the best testimony to its significance. Nor need we say more about the second than we have already.[93] The third, however, deserves some attention.

AGRARIAN REFORM AND ECONOMIC PROGRESS

An industrial revolution requires a mobile population, able and ready to leave the countryside for the mills, factories, docks, and warehouses of the cities. Such a work force was

[93] See above, pp. 107-10. The significance of formal technical and commercial training in the preparation of entrepreneurs in the Rhineland and Westphalia is well brought out by the table in Horst Beau, *Das Leistungwissen des frühindustriellen Unternehmertums in Rheinland und Westfalen* [Schriften zur rheinisch-westfälischen Wirtschaftsgeschichte, Neue Folge, Band III] (Köln, 1959), p. 68. The schools made their greatest contribution to the science-intensive industries such as chemicals, mechanical and electrical engineering, and optics. The economic pay-off came in the second half of the century.

already available in western Germany in the eighteenth century as a result of the long dissolution of the personal ties between lord and peasant. In eastern Germany, however, hereditary serfdom posed a serious barrier to labor recruitment. The incompatibility of this constraint with modern industrial development was felt most keenly in Silesia, where in the eighteenth century the rapidly growing coal and iron industries were compelled to go far afield for labor, and in those overpopulated areas that were best suited to the kind of rural putting-out so highly developed in the Rhineland. To be sure, these limitations were overcome for some enterprises—in the Silesian mines and mills, for example—by the award of special immunities to their workers. Moreover, there were a number of landlords who made use of their power over their serfs to assign them to industrial tasks. Yet the program of exemptions ran into frequent opposition from Junkers who saw in these derogations a threat to the security of their own agricultural labor supply; the monarchy, in its solicitude for the welfare of the nobility, vacillated between the promotion of freedom and the preservation of bondage; while the servile labor in private industrial establishments performed far less efficiently than free labor would have.[94]

[94] On problems of labor supply in Silesian mining and metallurgy, see Hermann Fechner, "Geschichte des schlesischen Berg- und Hütten- wesens . . . 1741 bis 1806," *Zeits. f. das Berg-, Hütten- und Salinen- wesen,* XLVIII (1900), 392-401; Konrad Wutke, *Aus der Vergangen- heit des schlesischen Berg- und Hüttenlebens* (Breslau, 1913), p. 81; Heinz Kelbert, *Das Bildungswesen auf den fiskalischen Berg- und Hüttenwerken in Preussen am Ausgang des XVIII. Jahrhunderts* (Berlin, 1955), pp. 17-18, 58-59; Otto Hue, *Die Bergarbeiter: His- torische Darstellung der Bergarbeiter-Verhältnisse von der ältesten bis in die neueste Zeit* (Stuttgart, 1910), pp. 337-40; above all, H. W. Büchsel, *Rechts- und Sozialgeschichte des oberschlesischen Berg- und Hüttenwesens 1740-1806* [Veröffentlichungen der Historische Kom- mission für Schlesien, III. Reihe: Forschungen zur schlesischen Wirt- schaftsgeschichte, Vol. I] (Breslau and Kattowitz, 1941), pp. 106-08, 136-39. On the general question of detached serf labor (similar to the Russian *obrok* labor), emancipation, and mobility in Silesia, see Jo- hannes Ziekursch, *Hundert Jahre schlesischer Agrargeschichte* [Verein für Geschichte Schlesiens, Darstellungen und Quellen zur schlesischen Geschichte, Vol. XX] (Breslau, 1915), p. 96 *et seq.*

This situation changed significantly with the establishment of personal freedom. Not only could workers move freely to industrial centers but enterprise could move out into the countryside and take advantage of cheap labor to meet the competition of more advanced producers abroad. An extensive relocation took place. After 1815 the textile industries of Berlin, which had grown behind the shelter of the Continental Blockade, gradually abandoned the city, with its high cost of living, valuable sites, and expensive labor. At first they went to the suburbs, but over the decades they moved farther out, to Silesia, Saxony, and Thuringia. In their place rose a complex of skill-intensive trades like machine building and metal working, which used labor released by the departing enterprises and brought in new recruits from the land. The population of Berlin, almost stagnant in the first two decades of the century, rose from 186,000 to 329,000 from 1820 to 1840.[95]

More important, however, than even this heightened mobility of labor, were the effects of emancipation and land reform on agricultural productivity. After all, it is not impossible to reconcile the personal bonds of serfdom with effective industrial performance, if the serf is freed of his tie to the soil, the work is not compulsory, and the serf is permitted to keep a good part of the fruits of his labor. Many of the early Russian factories operated on this basis, and some were actually owned and managed by serf-entrepreneurs who eventually became rich enough to purchase their freedom —needless to say, at prices appropriate to their wealth. Such arrangements are not the equivalent of a free labor market; in particular, they seriously limit the worker in his choice of employment and weaken accordingly opportunities for and pressures toward rational behavior. But they overcome what is undoubtedly the greatest drawback of servile labor: the lack of personal incentive.[96] In Germany, moreover, there

[95] Alfred Zimm, *Die Entwicklung des Industriestandortes Berlin* (Berlin, 1959), pp. 26, 28, 34.

[96] On serf labor and the serf entrepreneur in Russian industry, see Henry Rosovsky, "The Serf Entrepreneur in Russia," *Explorations in*

was a population of landless peasants (*Instleute*), unattached day-laborers who were free to leave the small plots provided them by the employing landlord and seek their fortune elsewhere. They were still few at the start of the nineteenth century; but their numbers were growing—from 18,000 to 48,000 families in East Prussia from 1750 to 1802 (as against a 40 percent increase for the rest of the peasant population)—and they could conceivably have furnished in time the recruits of an industrial proletariat.[97]

No such remedy was available to agriculture, however. Its manpower requirements were vastly greater, and performance here was a function not only of the motivation of its workers but of the distribution of the land and the constraints on its use. In farming only a radical transformation of the system would suffice to open the way to technological advance and rational production.

Four changes made possible this transformation:

1. Emancipation of the serfs, with consequences for mobility and motivation already described.

2. Redemption of land and seignorial dues by the peasantry. The burden of redemption was generally heavy, often so heavy that the peasant ceded part of his land in payment. But he was master of what he kept and could devote all his energies to its cultivation and improvement.

3. The dissolution of the communal economy of the estate or village. Group lands—meadow, woods, waste—were divided up among the individual proprietors, big and small, noble and commoner, who were thereby enabled to clear them and put them to the plow. At the same time, the constraints of the traditional three-field system were removed, releasing fallow for use and freeing the land for new rotations, crops, and techniques of cultivation.

Entrepreneurial History, VI (1953-54), 207-33; and Reinhard Bendix, *Work and Authority in Industry* (New York: Harper Torchbook, 1963), ch. iii.

[97] Gunther Ipsen, "Die preussische Bauernbefreiung als Landes-ausbau," *Zeitschrift für Agrargeschichte und Agrarsoziologie*, II (1954), 32 n.3.

4. The liberation of the market in land from traditional caste restraints. This fostered the already powerful tendency of wealthy bourgeois to invest in country estates. They brought with them the rationality and inventiveness that had made their fortune in business.[98]

It was one thing to institute these reforms; another, to carry them out. Those cottars and small peasants whose means did not enable them to take advantage of the new laws and establish title to a piece of land generally found it necessary to take employment on the estate of a large holder; there, owing to the personal sway of the proprietor over his people, their dependency was not very different in fact from that of the serf. By the same token, the division of the common lands and the elimination of traditional restraints on cultivation were the work, not of years, but of decades. It was not only that the village economy was solidly rooted in centuries of custom, or that the dissolution of communal ties inevitably gave rise to conflicts of interest. The problem was that the exploitation of the economic opportunities created by these reforms— the cultivation of noble domains once worked by the serfs, of the one-third of the old arable that had formerly lain fallow, of the wastes, meadows, and wood now put to the plow—required a vastly increased labor force that only time and reproduction could create.[99] Conveniently, the demographic response

[98] A small but perhaps necessary caveat: the above is not intended to imply that the purpose of the first two of these reforms—the emancipation of the peasantry and redemption of dues—was to promote rational cultivation and increase agricultural output. These were among their consequences, but their aim was to create a self-respecting, independent peasantry, able and willing to defend the state. Friedrich Lütge, "Ueber die Auswirkungen der Bauernbefreiung in Deutschland," *Jahrbücher für Nationalökonomie und Statistik*, CLVII (1943), 398 n.2, writes: "The emancipation of the peasants had in the last analysis spiritual motives; it created the conditions for the new agriculture, but did not call it into existence." I would not go so far. Spiritual motives there were; for that matter, economic motives also. But these were subordinate to the overriding concern for the regeneration of the nation-state.

[99] For a comparable increase in the demand for farm labor in Britain as a result of enclosures, see J. D. Chambers, "Enclosure and

was implicit in these same reforms: the new demand for labor promoted earlier marriage; and the increased supply of food pushed back the Malthusian limits. The groups showing the most rapid increase were the *Eigenkätner* (small cottagers who generally eked out the income from their own plots by hiring out their labor) and the *Instleute* and *Tagelöhner* (landless day laborers)—respectively 21 and 16 per thousand per year from 1805 to 1867; by comparison, the number of *Hofbauern* (peasant proprietors) rose over the same period by only 3 per thousand.[100]

Over time, the consequences of the reforms were apparent in the increase of agricultural productivity and output. From 1815 to 1864, the area under cultivation in East-Elbian Prussia more than doubled, from 5.5 to 12 million hectares. In Posen, the share of arable rose from 11.9 to 60.6 percent of the land area; in Pomerania, from 15.5 to 52.3 percent. The effect of this extension of cultivation in conjunction with the adoption of new rotations and techniques is apparent in the crop yields:[101]

PRUSSIA (1815 BOUNDARIES): OUTPUT OF FIELD CROPS
(IN 10,000 TONS)

	1816	*1864*
Cereals	508.8	1,097.8
Potatoes	93.0	1,135.2
Beets, turnips, and other roots	——	1,090.0
Animal fodder	——	356.1

Labour Supply in the Industrial Revolution," *Economic History Review*, 2d ser., V (1952-53), 319-43.

[100] Ipsen, "Die preussische Bauernbefreiung," *Zeits. f. Agrargeschichte und Agrarsoziologie*, II (1954), 51. These are not rates of population increase, and it is impossible to deduce from them the fertility of different occupational groups. Yet there is good reason to believe that natural increase accounted for a large part of the growth in the population of the class of landless laborers and that such increase marked a significant departure from an earlier pattern of stability. Cf. Werner Conze, "Vom 'Pöbel' zum 'Proletariat': Sozialgeschichtliche Voraussetzungen für den Sozialismus in Deutschland," *Vierteljahrschrift für Sozial- und Wirtschaftsgeschichte*, XLI (1954), 339-40.

[101] H. W. Finck von Finckenstein, *Die Entwicklung der Landwirt-*

This was a substantial achievement. Not only did the harvest of plant food substantially outstrip the rise in population, but the development of new fodder crops made it possible to nourish livestock around the year, thereby increasing the supply of meat and, more important, of natural fertilizer. And this in turn enhanced the fertility of the soil, which made possible still larger yields of fodder, which sustained a greater number of livestock, which dropped more dung, and so on. The age-old vicious circle of inadequate fertilizer—poor crops —annual slaughter—inadequate fertilizer was finally broken, and a spiral of increasing returns instituted that has continued to the present day.[102]

Yet impressive as these gains were, they fall short of the spectacular achievements attributed to the Japanese peasant: a doubling of output in the thirty-five years from 1878/82 to 1913/17; an increase in land productivity almost as great; and a rise of almost two-and-a-half times in output per man.[103] This, at least, is what the statistics of the Japanese Ministry of Agriculture say. If the figures proposed by James Nakamura in Chapter VI below prove accurate, the above comparison will require drastic revision. Whatever the outcome of this debate, however, it would seem an accepted fact that, thanks to fiscal arrangements that siphoned off a substantial fraction of the income of the Japanese peasant, the government obtained the wherewithal to finance its program of social reform and economic development; that, in fact, it was this oldest and greatest sector of production that paid by its growth and savings for the Japanese industrial revolution.[104]

---

schaft in Preussen und Deutschland 1800-1930 (Würzburg, 1960), p. 326.

[102] On the character and historical significance of this immemorial vicious cycle, see the speculative, stimulating article of V. G. Simkhovitch, "Hay and History," *Political Science Quarterly*, XXVIII (1913), 385-403.

[103] These are the figures given in K. Ohkawa and H. Rosovsky, "The Role of Agriculture in Modern Japanese Economic Development," *Economic Development and Cultural Change*, IX, No. 1, Part 2 (October 1960) [Special number: *City and Village in Japan*], 45-46.

[104] Given the reservations expressed above about the role of the

The German experience would seem to have been the reverse. The land tax provided a far smaller proportion of government revenue (less than 8 percent in Prussia in the 1860's), and insofar as public investment furthered economic growth, it was largely the consumer who paid for it through tariff duties and excise taxes. As a result, the flows of private resources to and from the land weighed more heavily in the allocation of capital than fiscal transfers; and, in Prussia at least, the balance of payments was long unfavorable to agriculture.

On the face of it, this is perhaps surprising. Students of economic development have led us to assume that an agricultural revolution and the surplus it yields are not only promotive of industrialization, but a prerequisite thereof. Yet second thoughts do much to justify the paradox. For one thing, the changes in land tenure and improvements in technique that made possible the increase in German agricultural output required substantial outlays of capital. Land clearing and drainage were so expensive as to be beyond the means of most smallholders, while the costs of consolidation and enclosure apparently drove numerous cultivators into debt and even bankruptcy.[105] For another, if private capital was to

state in Japanese development and the rapid diminution of the share of land taxes in total government revenue from the mid-eighties on, the role attributed to these transfer payments would seem to have been exaggerated. Moreover, one should not forget the five-sixths of farm income that remained after taxes; the hypothesis of agricultural financing for industrial development will not be complete until direct evidence is forthcoming of the transfer to the modern sector of a good part of the savings derived from this income. On the share of land taxes in total government revenue, see the essay by Harry Oshima, below, pp. 353ff.; on the share of taxes in net agricultural income, see G. Ranis, "The Financing of Japanese Economic Development," *Economic History Review*, 2d ser., XI (1958-59), 448.

[105] von Finckenstein, *Die Entwicklung der Landwirtschaft*, p. 134, speaks of costs "arising from the activity of the General Commissions" (enclosure commissions) of "not under 30 marks and seldom more than 100 marks per hectare." And one estimate puts the capitalized value of the additional cost of working the land on the new basis (exclusive of enclosure costs and capital improvements) at 12 marks per hectare, or

flow from agriculture to the modern industrial sector, it had to come largely from the big holdings; given the inchoateness of the capital market and the limited knowledge and aspirations of the peasantry, who either lent on land or hoarded against the day when they could acquire more land, little could be expected from that quarter. Yet many if not most of the big estates were in the hands of noblemen, a class little given to frugality. That they were often wastrels and poor managers is evidenced by the sales of *Rittergüter* (noble estates) to bourgeois: in the haughty society of Junkerdom, such transfers were almost invariably forced, for few aristocrats would voluntarily abandon the land that was the material foundation of their social status. Even when solvent, moreover, Prussian noblemen were usually short of money, and from the mid-eighteenth century on, the provincial estates joined with the monarchy in setting up *Landschaften* (mutual mortgage banks), whose purpose was to secure the credit of the individual Junker by the assets of the group and thus make it possible for him to borrow a substantial fraction of the value of his land at low interest.

These *Landschaften* were at first the only institutional lenders to private individuals in Prussia; and well after the creation of other credit institutions—as late as the railway boom of the 1840's and 1850's—their mortgage bonds (*Pfandbriefe*) constituted the great bulk of private securities on the market. The amount of these bonds in circulation is not a measure of the indebtedness of the Prussian agricultural sector toward other sectors of the economy. Many of these *Pfandbriefe* were bought by landowners; while the money so raised, though intended in principle for improvement of cultivation, also went toward the acquisition of the lands of insolvent proprietors. Some of it was even invested in industry. On the other hand, these bonds constituted only a part, perhaps only a small part, of the debt of the landed sector; most of the *Landschaften* excluded bourgeois realty from their

---

1,200 million marks. G. W. von Viebahn, *Statistik des zollvereinten und nördlichen Deutschlands* (3 vols.; Berlin, 1858-68), p. 1002.

coverage, and the peasant always had to secure funds through private arrangements. On balance, though, their circulation offers the best indication we have of the trend of the payments deficit of agriculture over time.

The amount of *Pfandbriefe* outstanding increased from 151 million marks in 1810 to 202 million in 1822, to 240 million in 1839. At that point the figures decline slightly—in spite of the enclosure costs imposed by the General-Kommissionen and the severe crop failures of the mid-forties. Not until 1849 do they again turn upward, and not until 1852 do they pass the previous high.[106] The explanation for this behavior may lie in part in the increased ability of agriculture to generate savings. More important, in my opinion, was the competition of new forms of investment, in particular railway stocks and bonds. Before this, the modern industrial sector seems to have nourished itself primarily from its own savings, supplemented by those of the commercial and professional bourgeoisie. Not until ' the development of capital-hungry branches like the railroad, deep coal mining, and large-scale metallurgy in the forties and fifties was it necessary to resort to joint-stock companies and draw heavily on the non-business sector. Even then, most of the capital was obtained by the diversion of established currents of investment: those people, largely urban, who had been placing their savings in government bonds, mortgage bonds, and direct mortgage loans, now shifted over to the higher, if riskier, returns of industry and transportation.

The German pattern of capital flows to and from agriculture was not significantly different from that of other western European countries. In Britain also, the increase in the area of cultivation and in yield per acre that marked the so-called "agricultural revolution" of the eighteenth and early nineteenth centuries constituted gains substantially smaller and slower than those attributed to the Japanese peasant. Unfortunately the statistics available are in no way comparable to the Japanese, but such as they are, they have led one

[106] von Finckenstein, *Die Entwicklung der Landwirtschaft*, p. 387 (Table 67).

authority to speculate that "output per head in agriculture increased by about 25 per cent in the eighteenth century, and that the whole of this advance was achieved before 1750." The same source suggests that the real output of the farm sector rose about 43 percent over the entire century, 24 percent during the critical decades from 1760 to 1800.[107] Moreover, as in Germany, the improvement of the land required a heavy investment in fencing, drainage, buildings and equipment, roads and the like. Again, the statistics do not permit us to be categorical. But it would seem that from 1760 to 1815 Britain enclosed millions of acres at an initial cost of redistribution of upwards of £1 per acre and at an eventual cost of anywhere from £5 to £25 per acre, depending on the original condition of the soil and the nature of its use.[108]

It is likely, therefore, that in the years of Britain's industrial revolution, agriculture was taking as much capital as it was giving; indeed, in the period from 1790 to 1814, when food prices rose to record levels, the net flow of resources was probably toward the land. In subsequent years, when both enclosure and the breaking of marginal soil slowed and proprietors and tenants began to reap the fruits of earlier efforts, capital may well have moved out of agriculture into transport and industry; as in Germany, the railway proved a powerful lodestone. Even then, however, a good part of the savings accumulated by landowners was derived from the sharp increase in the value of non-agricultural land, urban sites particularly, which increase was itself a consequence of improvement of transportation and industrial growth. As for the earnings of cultivation, these depended on protection against foreign grain and were only in part a net addition to the savings generated by the economy. In part they were bought at the price of a certain misallocation of resources and a propor-

[107] Phyllis Deane and W. A. Cole, *British Economic Growth 1868-1959* (Cambridge, 1962), pp. 75, 78.

[108] On the cost of enclosure, cf. Great Britain, Board of Agriculture, General Report on Enclosures (London, 1808), p. 97. On costs of subsequent improvement, Albert Pell, "The Making of the Land in England: A Retrospect," *Journal of the Royal Agricultural Society of England*, 2d ser., XXIII (1887), 355-74.

tionate diminution of the national product. Even with protection, the return on investment in land seems to have been distinctly lower than that in other areas; to the point where one scholar has concluded that "the biggest improvers among great landowners were subsidising agriculture, contributing directly to its over-capitalisation, and encouraging further overcapitalisation by the tenants who farmed the improved farms."[109]

The same was true for France. Wheat crops rose somewhat more than half from 1815/24 to 1841/50—51.7 million to 79.6 million hectoliters per annum—while output per acre increased by some 37 percent. At the same time, the harvest of potatoes jumped from 28.8 million hectoliters to 71.3, a gain of 150 percent.[110] This was substantially slower than the Prussian advance, to say nothing of the Japanese, but then population was growing less rapidly in France (29.4 million in 1815 to 35.6 million in 1850), and the outlays on improvement were undoubtedly smaller. For one thing, French agriculture was far less commercialized than the Prussian; for another, there was nothing comparable to the massive, transformation of tenure and distribution of property effected and imposed by the Prussian reforms. In any event, the flow of resources from agriculture to other sectors was thready and, as in Germany, of relatively minor significance for industrial development. Similarly, only a small share of government revenues (some 15 percent in the 1860's) came from taxes on the land, and the role of the state in promoting industry was if anything even smaller than in Germany, for better or for worse; while the same tendency to overcapitalize the soil prevailed as in Britain. The larger landowners placed some of their savings in government bonds and, from the forties on, in railways; yet they constituted a small minority of stockholders and bondholders, who were drawn as elsewhere primarily

---

[109] F. M. L. Thompson, "English Great Estates in the Nineteenth Century, 1790-1914," in *Première conférence internationale d'histoire économique, Stockholm 1960, Contributions, communications* (Paris, The Hague: Mouton, 1960), p. 394.

[110] France, *Annuaire statistique*, XXV (1905), Résumé rétrospectif, pp. 10*, 32*-33*.

from the urban bourgeoisie. The peasant who was able to save held on to his money until it would buy him more land; not until the fifties did the proliferation of guaranteed railway bonds draw him into the capital market. Nor was there until a generation later a truly national money market comparable to that developed in Britain as early as the late eighteenth century, to take the bills of the capital-hungry industrial districts and sell them to the capital-rich countryside.

In general, then, the land did not perform in western Europe the function of generator of savings for industrial development to the same extent as in Japan. On the contrary, not only did it compete for funds with the modern sector on purely rational grounds, but it drew more than its share of capital resources. For land in Europe was more than a factor of production; it was a social good. To the peasant, it was the goal of all his efforts, and he was willing to pay a price for the soil that reflected rates of return the less because he counted the cost of his own labor as nothing. To the bourgeois, land meant status and political influence as well as income. And to the aristocrat, land was the foundation of dynastic continuity and prestige—the only solid and right form of wealth. There is an eloquent letter of advice on this point from the Belgian nobleman Liedekerke-Beaufort to the *parvenu* banker Langrand-Dumonceau that expresses these values as well as anything I know:[111]

"You have four sons and a whole future to open to them. Build it on landed property. It is the land which forms the basis of families. This is true as much of the small rural patrimony of the peasant as of the great landed endowments of the most aristocratic persons. And so, my dear Sir, buy when you can for your children, not pieces of land, but real properties having enough compactness and extent to deserve the name of estate. There you will have solid settings for the generation that will follow you and will sink deep roots into the

[111] Letter of September 28, 1865, quoted in G. Jacquemyns, *Langrand-Dumonceau, promoteur d'une puissance financière catholique*, Vol. III: *Vers l'apogée*: 2. *Organisation et opérations* (Brussels, 1963), 45.

soil. You will have thus built on rock and not on sand. Landed property alone gives distinctive character [*donne du relief*] to families, classifies them in the eyes of all, and confers upon them a solid and permanent influence. That is what instinct, the traditions handed down by my parents, experience, and study have taught me. . . ."

In Japan the system of land ownership and tenure seems to have conduced to other values. The Tokugawa had made it a point to separate the samurai from the soil, thereby depriving them of autonomous control over revenues and manpower. The motives and direct consequences of this policy are well known. After a long period of civil conflict, Japan had come to appreciate the disadvantages of an independent and inevitably insubordinate aristocracy; and under the Shogunate there were to be no Junkers or great barons to exercise local sovereignty and challenge the authority of the central government. But for our purposes, it is the indirect and unintended consequences that are of interest: land ownership never became the symbol of social eminence and prestige, the hallmark of quality, and hence did not have the attraction for new wealth that it had in the West. So that when Japan entered on the path of industrialization, the successful businessman, whatever his social origin, did not feel it necessary to put the seal on his economic ascent by placing a good part or all of his fortune into estates. To be sure, the farmers themselves were not exempt from the characteristically immoderate peasant appetite for soil; and in Japan, as in the West, the wealthier residents of the village often coveted land for the political influence it brought with it. But at least the non-rational flow of entrepreneurial funds out of the modern sector was less than it would otherwise have been; and insofar as there are social differences in the efficiency of capital, this was undoubtedly a major gain.[112]

---

[112] To be sure, the sale and purchase of land is essentially a transfer operation, and much of the capital that left the European modern sector in this manner eventually returned to it. Yet much was lost to investment, for in countries where the prestige of land ownership was high, many proprietors sold only under compulsion, that is, only when

All of this is not intended to depreciate the significance of agricultural improvement for general economic development, but rather to qualify the usual assumptions and put the story in a truer light. It should not be forgotten that thanks to those changes in tenure and technique that we sometimes designate the "Agricultural Revolution," the countries of western Europe were able to fend off Ricardo's stationary state: that end of growth and accumulation wherein the pressure of population on the supply of food has so raised the cost of subsistence and hence wages, that manufacturers can no longer make profit and the wealth of the nation flows as rent to the owners of the land. In short, the land gave men and nourishment to the burgeoning industrial society. Need one ask for more?

FURTHER SIMILARITIES AND CONTRASTS

One could cite other substantial differences between the patterns of German and Japanese economic growth. One of the most obvious is the contrast between their respective natural endowments: Germany, rich in coal and ores, inherited a tradition of skillful metallurgy and metal-working and raised these branches to international preeminence in the course of her industrial revolution. Japan perforce made considerable progress in these areas; her goal of economic independence and parity required it, and one of the strongest motives for her penetration of the Asian continent was the acquisition of the raw materials she lacked at home. Yet the strength of her modern sector lay in light industry, while the heavy branches never showed the same competitive strength on the world market. Significantly, Japan's recent successes in exporting metal products have been concentrated in those branches where labor constitutes the most important input and material costs are relatively low: light machinery, electrical and optical equipment, small vehicles.

---

misinvestment, mismanagement, or excessive consumption had so indebted them that they had no choice. Land purchases, in other words, often served in the last analysis to finance previous disinvestment.

On the general subject of Japanese attitudes to land ownership, I am especially indebted to Henry Rosovsky and Irwin Scheiner.

Another difference between the two countries lay in their technological roles. Germany, thanks to the precocious development of scientific and technical education, was a major innovator even before she was an industrial nation. She was in the forefront of steel technology in the 1840's and pioneered in electrical engineering, chemicals, optics, agronomy—to name only a few areas—from the middle of the century on. Japan, though she could boast of important innovations in the period before the Second World War—the Toyota loom is the one most frequently cited—was much more the imitator.[113] Insofar as she did invent new methods and devices, they were more adaptive than revolutionary; that is, they rendered borrowed techniques more suitable to the circumstances of Japanese production. Much of her skill went to copying the wares of more advanced countries. As a result, she was often accused of lacking originality, and hard-pressed competitors fulminated against the immorality of economic plagiarism. (Compare British outrage against cheap German imitations in the 1890's.) This pattern of technological development reflected in large part the inadequacies of the educational system. Equally important, however, was the structure of factor costs: an economy endowed with cheap, skilled manpower is less likely to seek for improvements in methods or equipment, while the labor-intensive techniques it does employ will throw off less opportunities for or stimuli to innovation.[114]

Yet in the last analysis, the similarities between the courses of development in the two countries are even more striking and more significant than the differences. One of the most obvious is the cleavage in both between the modern and traditional sectors, a cleavage wide enough to warrant the use of term "dualism." Professor Rosovsky and others have analyzed this aspect of the Japanese economy in such detail as to render further comment here superfluous and importunate.

[113] Orchard, *Japan's Economic Position,* p. 252, writes: "The Toyoda loom is patterned after and does not differ materially from an American type of automatic loom."

[114] Cf. H. J. Habakkuk, *American and British Technology in the Nineteenth Century* (Cambridge, 1962), p. 45 *et seq.*

The German example is perhaps less well known: on the one hand, a few branches of industry using the latest techniques, heavily capitalized and organized in large units of production; on the other, a great number of traditional crafts, clinging to hand methods and working in small shops or dispersed cottages; here, one of the most efficient systems of rail transport and inland waterways in the world, and there, peasant carts hauling wood along the muddy roads of the north European plain; in some areas large model estates using the latest discoveries of agronomic science, elsewhere subsistence farms that had not changed in centuries. This was Germany on the eve of the First World War: 95 percent of the enterprises in industry and mining employed ten people or less; and the average number in such enterprises was two. Yet almost half of the work force in this sector was to be found in units employing fifty or more, and in the more modern branches the percentage was far higher: 89 percent in spinning, 96 percent in the manufacture of heavy electrical equipment, 98 percent in the dye trade.[115]

In order to appreciate the significance of this contrast, one must distinguish between two kinds of dualism: the dualism of backwardness and the dualism of rapid growth. The former is typically characteristic of colonial economies, with their small, air-conditioned island of modern villas, shops, office buildings, hotels, country clubs, and comparatively high income per head lost in a sea of heat and rain, thatched huts, primitive tools, and malnutrition. But one can find analogous contrasts in independent but retarded nations: in Spain, where the peasant even today brings his donkey to the Gran Via of Madrid to offer his earthen jugs for sale; in Sicily, where the bourgeoisie of Palermo lives encapsulated within a strange world of endemic poverty and lawlessness; in the Rumania of the interwar period, where luxury hotels lined the main boulevard of Bucharest and chickens scratched for food a block away.

The dualism of rapid growth is very different. Essentially it

[115] Germany, *Statistik des deutschen Reichs*, N.F., Vol. CCXIV, Table II.

is nothing more than the gap implicit in uneven development; and since economic development is never even, all industrializing countries have known some degree of dualism. Productivity gains are inevitably greater in some branches than others, and capital flows are correspondingly selective. Institutional arrangements play a role: some parts of the economy are freer than others to change and grow, because less subject to political or collusive restraints; while competition is never perfect, and pressures to rational allocation of resources are weakened accordingly. And there is always the human factor: peasants, for example, are far more traditional in their outlook and slower to change than businessmen. It would therefore be a mistake to look upon dualism as something that sets Japan apart from European countries.

On the other hand, the size of the gap between modern and traditional in Japan is not to be ignored. Rather, it is important as a particularly good example of a larger phenomenon, which one may almost state as a law: dualism is inversely proportional to the length of preparation for industrialization and directly proportional to the rate of growth in the course of industrialization. The German experience was essentially similar. Nor is it a coincidence that in both countries, industrialization was so closely tied to political aims. In each case, the decision to develop the economy as a means of national aggrandizement implied extensive state intervention, for better or for worse; and intervention in turn meant a certain distortion of capital flows and a preferential development of some branches rather than others. Moreover, these tendencies toward unevenness were accentuated by a natural channeling of talent and effort toward those activities most closely related to the national cause. It was not only that this is where the money was, here lay also prestige and honor.

The same considerations go far to explain the structure of big business in the two countries. I am not thinking here only of the size of the largest German and Japanese firms or even of their vertical and horizontal integration. Similar giants could be found in other countries, including some, like Holland, where the role of the state has always been extremely small and the question of national aggrandizement has never arisen. Rather, I am thinking of the organization of enterprise at the higher levels—the precocious development of collusive restraints on competition, the establishment of powerful professional organizations to mediate between private interests and government, the close coincidence of official and private attitudes on the national character of private enterprise, the preference for big, as against small, business because of its superiority as an instrument of power, the socially accepted importance of order in the market place. Alfred Marshall looked upon this development as "congenial to the temper of [the German] people": "the steadfastness, patience, and amenity to discipline of the Germans inclined them to seek the sheltered haven of a cartel, in spite of the partial loss of freedom, and the troublesome negotiations involved in it."[116] Yet these temperamental characteristics, which resemble mightily the Japanese stereotype, are inseparable from the long collaboration between state and economy that began with the decision to grow and be strong.[117] The one made possible the other, and was in turn reinforced by it.

THE PENALTIES OF AMBITION

The ultimate consequences of politicized economic development in Germany and Japan were enormous. Growth was more uneven than in other industrializing countries and more uneven than it need have been. Economic power was formalized and concentrated to a greater degree than in any other free enterprise system. Private interests were protected and coddled; yet in the last analysis political and military considerations had precedence. The economy was an instrument in the service of the nation, rather than the reverse. It must be said that German businessmen on the whole accepted this sub-

[116] *Industry and Trade* (London, 1919), p. 546.

[117] In both countries this decision preceded the period of social and political reforms. To observe this close collaboration, incidentally, is not the same as saying that the state contributed to the growth of these economies. That is something that has to be examined and tested separately: involvement, intervention, and efforts at promotion are not the same as effective promotion.

ordination; even more, they derived enormous satisfaction from their part and wore their titles of Geheimer Kommerzienrat and their third- and fourth-degree ribbons (higher degrees were reserved for Junker statesmen and generals) with swelling chests.[118] The official history of the Krupp steel works offers a splendid woodcut of Alfred Krupp, booted, riding crop in hand, a new kind of Junker surveying his chimneyed estate. I know of nothing that symbolizes so well the Prussian sanctification of industrial entrepreneurship by assimilating it to the role of the feudal aristocracy.[119] The social and economic significance of these pretensions is in no way vitiated by the unwillingness of the Prussian nobility to accept them at face value. The important thing is that the bourgeoisie took them seriously.

It is human to be vain, and the self-important postures affected by the business magnate may be excused as one more example of a universal weakness. What was more serious was the abdication by the German business community of the liberal role to which they pretended in the days of reform, that is, until around the middle of the century, and their abandonment of the ship of state to the Junker establishment that steered it to military victory. In the other nations of western Europe, the Industrial Revolution was accompanied by political revolution; indeed, the current historical fashion is to speak of the Two Revolutions.[120] Just as the economy was transformed, so were the society and the structure of government. Absolute monarchy gave way to parliamentarism; the balance of power shifted from the nobility to the bourgeoisie, and the reins of government were taken over either by a coalition of the middle classes or by an amalgam of the old aristocratic elite and assimilated *parvenus*.

Up to the First World War, Germany, of all industrial na-

[118] Cf. Friedrich Zunkel, *Der rheinisch-westfälische Unternehmer 1834-1879: Ein Beitrag zur Geschichte des deutschen Bürgertums im 19. Jahrhundert* (Köln and Opladen, 1962), ch. iv, esp. 105-06.

[119] *Krupp 1812-1912. Zum 100-Jährigen Bestehen der Firma Krupp und der Gussstahlfabrik zu Essen-Ruhr* (n.p., n.d.), opp. 108.

[120] Or what Eric J. Hobsbawm, *The Age of Revolution: Europe from 1749 to 1848* (London, 1962), calls "the dual revolution."

tions, had advanced least along this course. Obviously political and social time did not stand still where economic change was so rapid. In spite of strong prejudices and a considerable measure of financial independence, the landed aristocracy showed itself more and more receptive to the blandishments of business wealth: old names began to decorate the boards of corporations; the scions of military families took the daughters of merchants and industrialists to wife. A few bourgeois received noble rank for their services, and even more bought landed estates and assimilated to the Junker class.[121] Like converts everywhere, they were often more papist than the Pope. At the other end of the social scale, the rise of an industrial proletariat provided the base for the largest labor party in Europe.

Yet when all is said and done, the landed nobility retained its status and power throughout. There was far less dilution of the aristocracy than in Britain; the working classes were "defanged" by paternalistic legislation; and the bourgeoisie traded, in effect, its political birthright for the pottage of economic advantage and vicarious prowess. The moment of truth came in the early 1860's, when the Liberals clashed, first with the Regent (from 1861 King William I) and then with Bismarck (appointed Minister-President in 1862), over a proposed increase in the size of the army and in the length of military service. No issue was better calculated to draw the battle lines between Junker and bourgeois. The King and his ministers contended that military affairs were a prerogative of the Crown and that no legislative consent was required; while the Liberals, who took the reasonable position that a matter so closely linked to the lives and fortunes of the citizenry fell within the purview of their elected representatives, countered by refusing to vote the monies needed to pay for the new army. This was the classic *modus operandi* for affirming and establishing parliamentary power; but in this case

[121] By 1856 only 57% of the *Rittergüter* in Prussia were in the hands of noble families. Hans Rosenberg, "Die Demokratisierung der Rittergutsbesitzerklasse," in W. Berges, ed., *Zur Geschichte und Problematik der Demokratie; Festgabe für Hans Herzfeld* (Berlin, 1958), pp. 459-86.

it foundered on the obduracy and resourcefulness of the Minister-President, who collected taxes without consent, spent
the proceeds without a budget, found ways to raise additional
funds without taxes, decreed measures for the control of the
press, and generally comported himself as anachronistic
autocrat.

One cannot but acknowledge the ingenuity and resolve of
Bismarck. Yet it is no diminution of his achievement to recognize that, supported though he was by the King, he probably could not have defeated a bourgeoisie that had made its
own social and political revolution and could lay claim to
power, not only as a natural right, but as a spoil of war. Reform had come from above in Prussia, and the one serious
effort of the bourgeoisie to impose its values, in 1848, had
ended in humiliation. Moreover, the very content of the agrarian reforms had strengthened substantially the power of the
East-Elbian landlords: they had lost some—though by no
means all—of their personal authority over the resident peasantry; but this had been more than compensated by their new
entrepreneurial freedom and the concomitant increase in their
income and wealth. Finally, and perhaps most important, the
mass of the German bourgeoisie was simply not ready to follow its leaders and would-be leaders to war over such issues
as parliamentary supremacy.

The reasons for this indifference are at first consideration
inconsistent, but only at first. On one level—within the sphere
of domestic politics—the bourgeoisie tended to see its rights
and influence as means to the achievement of a legal and administrative environment favorable to enterprise. As an article
of 1864 put it, "economic conditions are the goal of political
rights."[122] In the context of that article, this dictum was used
to justify political activism by the bourgeoisie; but it was also
the expression of a hierarchy of values whose implications
could be, and were in Germany, just the reverse. For if po-

[122] Julius Faucher, "Oesterreich und die Handelsfreiheit," *Viertel-
jahrsschrift für Volkswirtschaft,* II (1864), Bd. IV, 176. The statement is made as part of an argument that the Austrian government
would not be having political difficulties with the Hungarians if it had
only adopted a trade policy suited to Hungary's needs.

litical rights were not a matter of principle, but an instrument, then one could in good conscience use or discard them as convenient or practical. So long as political neutralism paid and business was good, why rock the boat? Better to leave matters of state to those to the matter born. Prussian merchants and manufacturers had in the long run little patience for those who wanted to stand on issues at the expense of public harmony and industrial development. "Whoever seeks to bind trade to party interests," wrote the Hagen Chamber of Commerce in 1865, "commits a crime against the material welfare of his Fatherland!"[123] To be sure, this political renunciation was sometimes given a higher justification. At least some of the bourgeois spokesmen of the day liked to assure their listeners or readers—and perhaps themselves—that economic freedom would inevitably be followed by political freedom. But, after all, first things first. In the meantime the obvious solicitude of Bismarck's government for industrial enterprise and its success in negotiating advantageous commercial arrangements with other states were ideally calculated to appeal to this rationalized self-interest.[124]

On another level—and in the last analysis decisive—were the patriotic sentiments of the bourgeoisie. In this sphere of national, as against party, interests, the long "instrumentalization" of the Prussian economy, going back to the cameralism of the eighteenth century and accentuated by reform-from-above, had consecrated the subordination of economic concerns to *raison d'état*. In this sphere, in other words, economic strength and growth were means to a higher end, and the industrial and commercial classes found compensation for their political tutelage in the psychic rewards of unconditional loyalty and national aggrandizement. To be sure, enthusiasm for the power politics of the Minister-President varied considerably from one part of the kingdom to another. The western provinces, particularly the Rhineland, retained their suspicion of Prussian (that is, East Elbian) militarism and their

[123] Cited by Zunkel, *Der rheinisch–westfälische Untermehmer*, p. 207.

[124] Cf. Walter Bussmann, "Zur Geschichte des deutschen Liberalismus im 19. Jahrhundert," *Historische Zeitschrift*, CLXXXVI (1958), 543.

resentment of Junker arrogance. The scions of business families in cities such as Elberfeld and Crefeld remained indifferent to the prestige of government careers and shunned army duty as though it were a form of penal servitude. Here lay the center of agitation for the right of redemption of military service: Prussia, they argued indignantly, was the only European state that made no distinction between the man "who through years of diligence, through the greatest sacrifice of time and money, had won for himself a place of influence and of extraordinary usefulness to the common weal, and the man who expended nothing for its development and contributes almost nothing to society. . . ."[125] And here was the heart of the opposition to the three-year tour of duty: how could factories run if their best workers were always being pulled out for unnecessary (and expensive) training and exercise?

Yet all this was largely an expression of special interests, such as are to be found in any context of national loyalty. On a higher level—or lower, depending on the point of view— these captains of the counting house were true Germans, accepted the primacy of the *Militärstaat*, and thrilled with the most unregenerate Junker at Bismarck's triumphs of war. In 1864, when the series of conquests had barely begun, so outspoken an opponent of Bismarck as Mevissen assured the King that "the conviction is as strong on the Rhine as anywhere in the Fatherland that the armed strength [*Wehrhaftigkeit*] of the people is the gage of its development, the hope of its future." In reply to which Wilhelm expressed his pleasure at hearing from Mevissen also "that the armed strength of the people is the basis of all material and national [*staatlichen*] greatness."[126] Once Bismarck had proved his point, of course—*la raison du plus fort est toujours la meilleure*—serious opposition disappeared. After all, *Blut und Eisen* worked. The ends of unification, power, and glory were attained and only a mealy-mouthed recreant would quibble

[125] Zunkel, *Der rheinisch-westfälische Unternehmer*, p. 209 f., citing *Der Zollverein* of June 20, 1866 (No. 25).

[126] Joseph Hansen, *Gustav von Mevissen: Ein rheinisches Lebensbild 1815-1899* (2 vols.; Berlin, 1906), I, 742-43.

about the means. In a surge of gratitude, one bourgeois weekly actually rejoiced in the people's subjection to a higher will: these successes were achieved, "not by the people acting as free, conscious citizens, but by the people in arms serving as a masterly tool in the hand of an intelligent, energetic, strong-willed, fearless man, who knew how to manipulate this tool in masterly fashion, for the fame of his King and the greatness of his Fatherland."[127] Germany's revolutions continued to come from above.

One final point. The above discussion is concerned primarily with the apolitical businessman. A full analysis of the readiness of the German middle classes to acquiesce in the Junker grip on political power would require consideration of the attitudes of other fractions of the bourgeoisie—the professionals and academic intellectuals in particular. The reader may consult on this subject the important essay of Fritz Stern, "The Political Consequences of the Unpolitical German."[128] In Stern's analysis, these non-business groups found their mess of pottage—that is, their compensation for political impotence—in *Bildung* and *Kultur* rather than in wealth; and he quotes Hermann Baumgarten, liberal historian and uncle of Max Weber, on the division of labor in German society: "The *Bürger* is meant to work, not to rule, and a statesman's primary task is to rule" (p. 115). And for intellectuals as for businessmen, nothing succeeded like success. The same Baumgarten, referring to the constitutional conflict of the 1860's, avowed: "We have had the unprecedented experience that our victory [that is, the victory of the Liberals] would have been a disaster while our defeat has been an immense blessing" (p. 116).

I am not familiar enough with Japanese history to attempt a parallel statement of the relations between class, economic interest, and government. One has the impression, however, of an analogous division of labor and power between business

---

[127] Zunkel, *Der rheinisch-westfälische Unternehmer*, p. 224, citing *Der Zollverein* of August 22, 1866 (No. 34).

[128] In *History* [a semiannual serial published by Meridian Books, New York], No. 3 (1960), 104-34.

and the military, with each profiting from the prosperity of the other—that is, until the invasion of China increased the stakes of national aggrandizement enormously. The moment of truth for Japan apparently came in the thirties, and there too the bourgeoisie yielded to the apparent success of force. In both countries, the bill for this alliance of intoxicating economic expansion and irresponsible power eventually came due, and the price proved far greater than anyone had dreamed.

Needless to say, these aberrant courses of development had roots that went back before the period of industrialization; indeed, any attempt to offer a full analysis and explanation would require writing something close to a general history of the two countries in the modern period. Such a history lies beyond my means and competence; and this is not the place for it. It seems reasonable to argue, however, that one of the most important sources of this combination of *modus vivendi* and alliance between the political-military and economic were the conditions in which economic growth was decided upon and initiated. It was the State that conceived modernization as a goal and industrialization as a means, that gave birth to the new economy in haste and pushed it unrelentingly as an ambitious mother her child prodigy. And though the child grew and developed its own resources, it never overcame the deformity imposed by this forced nurture.[129]

[129] Mention must be made of T. Watanabe, "Economic Aspects of Dualism in the Industrial Development of Japan," *Economic Development and Cultural Change*, XIII (1964-65), 293-312, which appeared when this chapter was in page proof. This article treats of technological change from 1905 on, specifically, of the balance between labor-saving and capital-saving innovation. Watanabe argues that "despite the existence of an abundance of labor, Japanese industries had continued their efforts to introduce capital-using techniques" (p. 297), and then seeks to explain this "paradoxical pattern" of growth. Yet the pattern is not paradoxical. Given the basic technology of the Industrial Revolution, the optimal techniques available to Japan in these decades of transition were labor-saving—as they had been for western Europe. The point is implicit in Watanabe's own introductory remarks (p. 294, line 12); and he in fact adduces evidence of the Japanese concern to save capital (p. 300).

CHAPTER IV

Modern Entrepreneurship in Meiji Japan

YASUZŌ HORIE

ONE OF THE MOST IMPORTANT aspects of industrialization in its early stages is the role of the entrepreneur. Capital resources, however abundant, cannot be mobilized and productively put to work without initiative and organization. A supply of entrepreneurs (whether public or private) who are able and willing vigorously to perform the key functions of innovation, risk-taking, and management is the decisive element in economic progress.

This essay concerns the rise of modern business enterprise in Japan during the initial stage of industrialization following the Meiji Restoration of 1868. The careers and characteristics of various pioneering individuals will be examined in the light of social and cultural conditions at the time and the influence of the government.

Entrepreneurship means broadly the ability to recognize and exploit economic opportunity. In Japan, as in Western countries in varying degrees, this has been a function of both private and public initiatives joined in complex patterns of interaction. We shall be concerned here primarily with pioneers of modern Japanese business enterprise in the private sector, but always with recognition that the goals and activities of the Meiji state exercised such a pervasive influence as to make unreal any sharp distinction between the two.

Early Industrial Leadership

COTTON SPINNING

Industries of a modern type were initiated by the Tokugawa Shogunate and several of the more important *han* (feudal domain) governments in the closing days of the Tokugawa era (1603-1867). Some, such as shipbuilding and the casting of cannon, were undertaken for reasons of national defense. Others, such as the cotton spinning mills of Satsuma *han*, originated in the needs of feudal domains for additional revenue to meet budgetary needs.

The spinning mills of Satsuma, one at Kagoshima and the other at Sakai, were the work of Ishikawa Masatatsu (1825-1895), acting under the aegis of the *han* regime. A second pioneer entrepreneur of machine spinning was Kashima Mampei (1822-1891) a Tokyo merchant.[1] His plant, built in 1872, was rather small in scale but proved successful in operation, one reason being his use of marketing arrangements available through his wholesale store in Tokyo. Under the patronage of the government, other factories soon followed, and by 1882 ten more were in operation, besides two model plants of 2,000 spindles each set up by the state itself.

The early industrial entrepreneurs who initiated these modern-type ventures possessed qualities we have come to associate typically with business pioneers: a sense of market opportunity, a creative response to change, and a readiness to experiment with new methods.[2] They came typically from families of status and substance: landlords, brewers, merchants. Itō Denshichi (1852-1924), for example, was the son of a sake brewer of Yokkaichi, Mie prefecture, whose father and grandfather had served the Oshi *han* as financiers.[3] Itō first trained himself in the operation of spinning machinery at the Sakai Cotton Spinning Mill, the Satsuma venture that later became a government model factory. Gaining his experience there he returned to his native village to build his own plant, which he equipped with machinery obtained from the government and paid for in annual installments. Another pioneer was Okada Ryōichirō (1839-1915), founder of the Futamata Cotton Spinning Mill in Shizuoka prefecture.[4] He

[1] Kinugawa T., *Hompō menshi bōseki shi* [A History of Japanese Cotton Spinning] (Osaka, 1937), II, 271ff.

[2] Horie Y., "Business Pioneers in Modern Japan," *Kyoto University Economic Review* (hereafter KUER), XXX, 2 (March 1961), 1-16.

[3] Kinugawa T., *Itō Denshichi-ō* [A Biography of Itō Denshichi] (Osaka; 1936), pp. 10ff.

[4] Denda I., *Kindai nihon keizai shisō shi no kenkyū* [Studies in the Economic Thought of Modern Japan] (Tokyo, 1962), pp. 301-04.

was the son of a wealthy landlord who had served as village headman and led a movement to improve village life. Okada aspired to be a local leader, too, and launched many schemes for agricultural improvement such as training former samurai in sericulture. Next he turned to the new cotton industry, and founded the first spinning mill in Shizuoka.

These cotton mills constructed from 1878 to 1882 were built primarily to encourage the production of raw cotton, as well as to increase the supply of cotton yarn for weavers in their districts. Little consideration beyond this was given to market conditions or to the economical location of plants. Not surprisingly therefore, they were rarely successful as business ventures. Nevertheless their promoters shared certain characteristics in common that held promise for the future. Although of differing origins, they were men of means. Second, they were interested not merely in profit but in developing their local districts. And third, they belonged to the educated class.[5] Persons of similar purpose and capacity were to appear increasingly as development gathered headway, not only in the cotton industry but also in other fields of enterprise.

Shibusawa Eiichi was the man responsible for the first large-scale cotton-spinning mill, a plant of 10,500 spindles built in 1882. Shibusawa's remarkable story is told by Johannes Hirschmeier in the essay that follows (Ch. V). His firm, known as the Osaka Cotton Spinning Company, had as its major shareholders former feudal lords and wealthy merchants of Tokyo and Osaka. It proved to be a commercial success, owing in large measure to the talents of its chief technician, Yamabe Takeo (1851-1920).[6] Born into a samurai family of Tsuwano *han*, Yamabe learned English under an English missionary in Yokohama. Later he went to England to study at the University of London with the intention of becoming a businessman. While abroad, he was asked by Shibusawa to become chief technician for a new cotton-spinning company. Accepting the offer, he gave up his studies at the

[5] *Ibid.*, p. 295.

[6] H. Ichikawa, *Kozan no hen'ei* (A Biography of Yamabe Takeo) (Tokyo, 1923).

University and spent several months at a mill in Lancashire. Here he worked with machines and studied managerial techniques under the friendly guidance of the mill owner. The Osaka plant, founded upon his return to Japan, proved to be financially profitable and served as a pilot model for other large mills.

Mill construction increased during the financial boom of the late 1880's, especially in the Osaka area. The founders and shareholders of these new ventures were also mainly ex-samurai and leading merchants who traded in raw cotton or cotton cloth. At first the merchants of Osaka had been slow to embark on new business ventures. Seeing the profitable records of such concerns as the Osaka Cotton Spinning Company, however, they were now drawn increasingly into industrial enterprise, where their financial and commercial experience proved valuable.[7]

SILK-REELING

Just as the Satsuma *han* developed cotton-spinning mills to increase its budget revenue, so the Maebashi *han* turned to silk-reeling as a source of income. The first silk filature of a Western type was built in 1870 by the Maebashi *han* under the direction of a Swiss expert. Hayami Kensō (1839-1913), who was responsible for its construction, was a man similar to Ishikawa of Satsuma in entrepreneurial spirit and capacity.[8] When the *han* was abolished in 1871 and its silk filature was taken over by the newly created prefecture, Hayami accepted an advisory role in the Nihommatsu Silk-reeling Company organized with the backing of wealthy residents in Fukushima prefecture. Later he was appointed president of the Tomioka Silk Mill, a government model factory, and simultaneously headed Dōshinsha, a silk export firm.

The Maebashi silk venture was soon followed by the Tsukiji mill of the Ono Company in Tokyo. This was a project of Furukawa Ichibei (1832-1903), chief clerk of the Ono

[7] Denda, pp. 311-13.
[8] Dai nihon sanshi kai (ed.), *Nihon sanshigyō shi* [A History of Sericultural and Silk-reeling Industries in Japan] (Tokyo, 1935), II, 41ff.

Company, a big silk merchant of Kyoto whose wealth was said to rival that of the Mitsuis.[9] If the Maebashi mill was built to obtain revenue for the *han*, the purpose of the Ono-built mill was private profit. Both operators, however, exploited market opportunities. Since Japanese export silk was selling in the Lyons market at about half the price of the Italian variety because of its inferior quality, each entrepreneur strove to develop a finer quality of silk for export. Unfortunately the Tsukuji mill was doomed because of a shortage of local cocoon supply. Its equipment had to be transferred to Nagano prefecture, where the cocoon industry was now flourishing. Furukawa himself turned to mining, where he later became one of Japan's copper magnates.

The Maebashi and Tsukiji mills, along with others owned and operated by the government—the Tomioka (1872) and Kōbusho (1873)—served as models for others. Managers and skilled workers from these plants scattered over Japan and helped in the wider development of the industry. Many fortune-seekers cast their eyes on silk-reeling. The opening of the country to foreign trade had created a growing overseas market, and silk-reeling, unlike cotton-spinning, required no heavy outlays of capital. Minor changes in technique and equipment brought substantial improvements in quality. As foreign markets grew, silk filatures of all types and sizes appeared like mushrooms after rain throughout the country.

ELECTRICAL APPARATUS

An even more innovative type of industrial enterprise developed in the field of electrical apparatus during these early years. The best examples are the two firms whose subsequent merger gave birth to the well known Tokyo Shibaura Electric Works of today.

The first, the Tanaka works (later renamed Shibaura Seisakusho after being taken over by the Mitsui Bank), was

[9] Itsuka kai (ed.), *Furukawa Ichibei-ō* [A Biography of Furukawa Ichibei] (Tokyo, 1926).

established in 1875 by Tanaka Hisashige (1799-1881).[10] Tanaka came from an artisan family in Kurume *han*. Displaying early a talent for invention, he spent some years in Saga *han*, one of the most advanced of the feudal domains in Western-type industries, serving as an adviser in cannon-casting, building of model steamships, constructing steam boilers, etc. Following the Restoration, he came to Tokyo at the age of 74. There he opened a small shop to manufacture appliances for the telegraph office and soon secured official patronage. Three years later the government purchased the shop, with all its equipment and skilled workers. However, Tanaka with his adopted son, also named Hisashige, continued to manufacture equipment especially for naval use. On his death the firm was continued by his son, and enlarged with reinvested profits so rapidly that by 1882 it came to occupy an impressive brick building in Shibaura, Tokyo.

The other forerunner of Tokyo Shibaura was a firm established in 1890 to manufacture incandescent lamps under the name of Hakunetsusha. It was founded by Fujioka Ichisuke (1821-1918), in partnership with a group of his friends.[11] The son of a middle-grade samurai of Iwakuni, Fujioka was sent by his *han* to study in Tokyo after the Restoration. He first learned English in the Foreign Language School and then entered what is now Tokyo University. Here he studied electrical science under an English instructor. In 1878 he developed an arc lamp, the first electric light in Japan, and thereupon decided to devote himself to its manufacture. Upon graduation from Tokyo University in 1881, he served for a time as a professor, but when the Tokyo Electric Light Company was incorporated in 1885 he accepted an appointment as chief engineer, his main task being to develop the manufacture of electric lamps previously imported from abroad.

For this purpose Tokyo Electric established an experi-

[10] *Shibaura seisakusho 60 nen shi* [Sixty Years' History of the Shibaura Electric Works] (Tokyo, 1962), pp. 14-16.

[11] H. Segawa, (ed.), *Kōgaku hakase Fujioka Ichisuke den* [A Biography of Fujioka Ichisuke, Dr. of Technological Engineering] (Tokyo, 1933).

mental institute that soon became an independent organization headed by Fujioka. Within two years he was able to produce a marketable lamp. Commercial manufacture took longer
to develop, and was not decided upon until 1895. Hakunetsusha was thereupon reorganized as a joint-stock company—
the Incandescent Lamp Manufacturing Company—with Miyoshi Shōichi (1853-1906) as president. Four years later the
firm was renamed the Tokyo Electric Company, and Fujioka
himself assumed the presidency.

The success of this company owed much to the financial
assistance that Fujioka received from Miyoshi Shōichi, whose
own career is of interest.[12] Miyoshi was the son of a low-
grade samurai, likewise from Iwakuni. Graduated from the
Telegraph Training School of the Ministry of Communications in 1880, he soon opened a small shop in Tokyo in which
he manufactured bells, telephone and telegraph apparatus, and
other such appliances. Here he also constructed a 15 kilowatt-
hour generator designed by Fujioka for electric lighting.

Miyoshi was not only an excellent technician but also an
astute business man. He persuaded local leaders to form
electric light companies and in some instances constructed
generating plants for them. While his purpose was to enlarge
the market for his own products, especially generators, his
efforts contributed much to the general spread of electric
power in Japan. Prior to the Sino-Japanese war the Miyoshi
Electric Works was perhaps the biggest and best known company of its type in the country. Unfortunately it was caught
in the depression following the war and plunged into bankruptcy. Miyoshi had always been diligent in training his employees however, and men from his shop became leaders in
the electrical field.

SHIPBUILDING AND SHIPPING

Shipbuilding constituted a fourth industry, one to which
the government attached special importance because of its

[12] *Nihon denki kōgyō shi* [A History of the Electric Industry in
Japan] (Tokyo, 1956), pp. 4-6, 603.

relation to national defense and profitable overseas trade. The great pioneer in the field was Kawasaki Shōzō (1837-1912), founder of the Kawasaki Shipbuilding Yard.[13]

Kawasaki was the son of a former samurai who had given up his rank to become a merchant. While engaged in trade with foreigners in Osaka the young man was impressed by the superior loading capacity and speed of Western ships. He decided to devote himself to shipbuilding, and in 1878 he opened a small yard in Tokyo, investing all the capital that he had acquired through trade. After considerable effort he succeeded in launching his first vessel. However, with the establishment of another yard in Kobe he ran into serious financial difficulties, and also suffered a prolonged illness. Nevertheless, his dream of a shipbuilding empire persisted. Finally in 1887 he purchased from the government the Hyōgo Shipbuilding Yard, originally founded in 1869 by three Kaga samurai. Thus was laid the foundation of the well-known Kawasaki Heavy Industry Company of today.

If the government was interested in shipbuilding, it was no less concerned to foster modern shipping. Shipping of the traditional type was slowly developing, and the Meiji government had been content to leave it in private hands. But Japanese private capital was hardly adequate yet for modern-type enterprise, so that for some years foreign companies virtually monopolized the traffic in Japanese waters, even coastal transport. The government gave its full support to two Japanese firms organized by merchant groups, the Kaisō kaisha and Yūbin jōkisen kaisha, but both failed at the task, and it was only the Mitsubishi Company that finally turned the tide in favor of the government's mercantilist policies.

Mitsubishi was founded by Iwasaki Yatarō (1834-1885), born of a country samurai (*gōshi*) family.[14] A student of Confucianism in his boyhood, his unyielding character was a byword among his neighbors. Entering the employ of his *han* in 1866, he was soon placed in charge of its shipping affairs,

---

[13] *Kawasaki jūkōgyō 60 nen shi* [Sixty Years' History of the Kawasaki Heavy Industry Company, Ltd.] (Kobe, 1959), pp. 15-24.

[14] Y. Irimajiri, *Iwasaki Yatarō* (Tokyo, 1960).

which had fallen into disorder. When the *han* was abolished in 1871 Iwasaki bought up its ships with the capital he had accumulated and established the shipping firm of Mitsubishi Shōkai in partnership with a younger brother.

The Mitsubishi firm, like its predecessors, received full protection from the government and enjoyed the advantage of monopoly for several years after the Saigō rebellion of 1877. Its success, however, was due in good measure to Yatarō's entrepreneurial abilities. His management of the firm was as vigorous as it was shrewd. An autocrat and an empire builder, he recruited to his loyal service many able graduates of Keiō University. His company was distinguished for modern management techniques that differed sharply from those of more traditional firms like Mitsui. His epic struggle with Shibusawa is recounted by Fr. Hirschmeier in the essay that follows.

FOREIGN TRADE

When Japan was opened to overseas commerce merchants from many districts appeared in Yokohama eager to do business with foreigners. Few were foreign traders in any real sense, however; they merely sold indigenous products— chiefly raw silk—to foreign firms in the open ports, and in turn bought foreign goods for resale either to the government or public. Overseas trading itself was a foreign monopoly. This state of affairs was hardly satisfactory, and no time was lost in seeking to wrest control from foreign firms and beginning the direct sale of Japanese goods abroad through Japanese merchants.

Two men figure prominently in this pioneer movement. One was Morimura Ichizaemon (1839-1919), a Tokyo merchant;[15] the other was Ōkura Kihachirō (1837-1928), also a commoner.[16] Morimura was the son of a bag dealer who did

[15] Y. Mishima, "Chūkyō tōjikigyō no kindaika to Morimura Ichizaemon" [Modernization of the Ceramic Industry in Nagoya and Morimura Ichizaemon], *Nihon keiei gakkai 35 kai daikai nempō* [Annual Report of the 35th General Meeting of the Business Economics Society of Japan], 1962, pp. 177-90.

[16] Kakuyu kai (ed.), *Ōkura Tsuruhiko-ō* [A Biography of Ōkura Kihachirō] (Tokyo, 1924).

business mostly with the *daimyo*. He moved to Yokohama as soon as the city was opened, and began trade with foreigners. When civil conflict broke out in the course of the Restoration, he made large profits supplying the government forces with military equipment, but he soon gave up this lucrative business when he was requested—as a privileged merchant—to pay bribes to an official.

Morimura had once been told by Fukuzawa Yukichi, the leader of the Meiji Enlightenment, that Japan urgently needed to develop direct exports to foreign countries and to import specie in return, thus correcting her trade imbalance. Deciding to enter the export trade, he first opened a curio shop for foreigners in Yokohama. Then in 1873 he established an export firm, the Morimura company, in partnership with his younger brother who became manager of its New York office. Morimura exported such products as curios, ceramics, copperware, fans, and lanterns, but ceramics eventually became the main item of business. To finance this export he founded at Nagoya in 1904 the Nihon Tōki Company, maker of Noritake china. Later this industrial enterprise was to make him famous, but he always regarded himself primarily as a trader.

Ōkura Kihachirō, the second pioneer in foreign trade, was the son of a village chief who, though a commoner, was permitted to have a surname and wear a sword. His grandfather, too, had been both scholar and prosperous merchant. After a boyhood education that included Confucian studies and comic *tanka* (31-syllable poems) Ōkura went to Edo at the age of eighteen. He first worked in a dried fish shop, and three years later opened a store of his own for dried goods. The civil disorders of 1865 turned him to dealing in military supplies, reselling imported rifles first to the *daimyo* and *bakufu* (Tokugawa government), and later to the anti-*bakufu* forces as well. The profits were handsome and after the Restoration he determined to move directly into foreign trade.

Following two years of travel in Europe and the United States, Ōkura organized the Ōkura Company in 1873 to enter upon direct trade with England and other Western countries. His firm soon opened a branch office in Korea (1875), and later in India (1884). Ōkura retained trading ties with the government, but also sought, like Iwasaki, to build an independent business empire. He invested his earnings in a wide array of enterprises including mining, civil engineering, shoe manufacture, linen weaving, hotels, and theaters. Only the banking business he scorned, as unsuited to a businessman!

BANKING

Yet banking in fact was the sector of modern business enterprise into which traditional merchant firms moved initially with a minimum of difficulty. During the Tokugawa period, exchange merchants had grown wealthy making loans, handling deposits, and engaging in other financial transactions. After the Restoration, accordingly, the government took no immediate steps to modernize banking except to encourage such firms to form joint-stock companies. The first companies of this type, *kawase kaisha* (exchange banks), were financed partly with government funds and partly with capital put up by the directors.

Soon it became apparent that such institutions could not meet the needs of a modern industrial economy. As a consequence a system of national banks was established in 1872 on the American model, the first four financed by wealthy merchant houses like Mitsui, Ono, and Ichijima-Tokujirō. These banks proved relatively unprofitable, however, for they were required to back their note issues with specie and with government bonds earning only 6 percent. In 1876, therefore, the law was revised to permit banks to issue inconvertible notes to the extent of 80 percent of capital funds deposited in bonds with the government. Meanwhile such bonds were being issued in large amounts to ex-daimyō and ex-samurai in commutation of their feudal pensions. The capitalization of new banks with these pension bonds (*kinroku*) now became very profitable, and the total number soon mounted to 152.

Japan's national banking system thus owes its founding in good part to these ex-aristocrats and their commuted feudal pensions. As the movement grew, however, merchants and landowners of commoner origin joined in through participation both in national banks and in other "private banks" like Mitsui Bank. Hirschmeier tells this story in greater detail below (Ch. V) in recounting the role of Shibusawa.

Social Background

These examples should serve to underscore the fact that the social origins of the new industrial pioneers were diverse. Some were merchants; others came from families traditionally engaged in agriculture; and finally there were the samurai. Statistically it can be shown that the first generation of businessmen after the Restoration came chiefly from commoner families. Included in such data, however, are establishments of a traditional kind, whereas our concern here is with firms that ventured into modern business enterprise. Generally speaking Japan's Industrial Revolution was not pioneered by Tokugawa mercantile families, a point that can be strikingly illustrated by reference to Osaka.

Osaka had been the center of both commercial and financial activities during the Tokugawa period. It was the common belief of the day that Osaka merchants held 70 percent of the nation's monetary wealth. Yet for all its previous renown Osaka furnished few modern business leaders in the early Meiji years. Government officials of the time complained that Osaka merchants were tradition-minded and unresponsive to change. The reason seems to have been that Osaka merchants were accustomed to serving as middlemen and content with the profits derived thereby. Prior to the Restoration many *han* had taken to encouraging local production and marketing the products in Osaka through official monopolies.[17] The merchants of Osaka thereby were able to engage in large-scale transactions without having to invest their own capital or engage in manufacture.[18] No tradition of industrial entrepreneurship had developed among them, and it was not until

[17] Horie Yasuzō, "Han Monopoly Policy in the Tokugawa Period," *KUER*, XVII, 1 (Jan. 1942), 31-52.

[18] Horie Yasuzō, "Business Pioneers of Modern Japan," *KUER*, XXX, 2 (March 1961), 1-16.

the investment boom of the late eighties that they embarked actively upon industrial development.

In Tokyo the situation was different. Even before the coming of Perry, Edo had been a great metropolis thronged with samurai from all parts of the country. When ports were opened to foreign trade the adjacent port of Yokohama became the center of overseas contact, and merchants from Tokyo readily participated in this trade. Among them were many with the enterprise and flexibility necessary to seize upon the new opportunities, in company with new business leaders from other social backgrounds and districts of the country.

On the other hand, the role of samurai families in founding Japan's modern business class can hardly be exaggerated. The reasons are significant. The samurai were the educated elite of Tokugawa society. In the beginning they had been renowned as warriors; but the long peace maintained by the Tokugawa Shogunate had dampened their martial spirit. They had come to take pride in themselves as a cultured class rather than as military figures. Nevertheless they were generally poor; most of them becoming dispirited by poverty sank into obscurity. Others—a minority—turned to Western learning to sustain their ambition and began to engage in political activity. These ambitious samurai, especially those of lower rank, were the men who accomplished the Meiji Restoration. Thereafter, conscious of their elite status and responsibilities, they appeared in every field of new activity including business entrepreneurship.

The spirit of initiative among samurai was heightened by another circumstance. Wealth and rank did not necessarily coexist in Tokugawa Japan. The feudal aristocracy lived on fixed stipends of rice determined by rank. With the rise of a money economy, samurai stipends, especially those of lower ranks, tended to lag behind the rise in income of well-to-do merchants and farmers, but their social status remained superior. It is interesting to note the contrast with China, where rank and wealth continued to coexist more closely in the scholar-official class. Their predicament spurred many samurai to advocate sweeping social changes, not only in their own interest but also for the sake of their country.

Cultural Influence of Confucianism

One common characteristic of Japan's business pioneers, whether of samurai or commoner origin, was their Confucian education. In Tokugawa times Confucianism was more than a learned specialty of scholars and rulers; it was a way of life and thought widely disseminated through every stratum of society. Moreover, Confucianism in Japan differed from that of its mother country, China, in three specific characteristics, as defined by S. Azuma:[19] (a) it was easier to understand and practice; (b) it was blended with Shintoism in certain respects, for instance the virtues of loyalty to the emperor and filial piety were linked together at the center of the national ethic; and (c) it modified *bushidō*, the feudal code of honor and duty, to embrace both the ethic of the warrior and the ethic of the ruler.

Confucianism in its Japanese adaptations thus helped to produce leadership from commoner as well as samurai ranks. Its rationalism bred habits of mind that facilitated the introduction of Western technology. Intellectual discipline coupled with a flexible pragmatism made the Japanese quick to take up Western learning when its practical utility for national defense and other purposes became clear. Yet it also cultivated an instinctive nationalism, even in the process of adopting Western ways. While I would hesitate to say that Confucianism helped to breed the entrepreneurial spirit as actively as did the Protestant ethic in Europe, it certainly provided an intellectual and moral climate that favored the emergence of this new leadership.

In the early Meiji years, although business leaders progressively altered their ways of thinking, they retained the basic ideology built around Confucian ethical and philosophical values. This is revealed in their motivations for entering

[19] S. Azuma, *Kinsei nihon keizai rinri shisō shi* [A History of Economic-Ethical Thought in the Tokugawa Period] (Tokyo, 1944), pp. 113-40.

and pursuing their new careers. A genuine concern for the national interest was characteristic, along with personal advantage. Often they employed as slogans in their business affairs such patriotic injunctions carried over from Tokugawa days as "do your bit for your country." It is easy to suspect that such phrases were used to cover up selfish purposes. But not necessarily. And whatever the motive of the speaker, the maxim was wholeheartedly accepted by the people.

In short, a national consciousness, the sense of national crisis that developed in the closing days of Tokugawa, was carried over into the Meiji era. The slogan *sonno-jōi* (Revere the Emperor; Expel the Barbarians) was altered after the Restoration to *bummei-kaika* (civilization and enlightenment). One way to be "enlightened" was to enter a Western type of business and help to make Japan a rich and strong nation able to hold her own in competition. Gustav Ranis thus characterizes Japanese entrepreneurs in this early stage of industrialization as "community-centered," in contrast to Schumpeter's "auto-centered" entrepreneurs.[20] An outstanding example in Shibusawa Eiichi, the subject of Fr. Hirschmeier's essay that follows.

The Supporting Role of the Government

Several political circumstances further contributed to the rise of a vigorous business entrepreneurship in the early Meiji years.[21]

POLITICAL STABILITY

The Meiji Restoration was directed to making Japan strong and wealthy enough to compete with more advanced Western nations so to safeguard her independence. To achieve this, her economy had to be modernized and industrialized by importing and adopting Western knowledge and techniques. But this

[20] G. Ranis, "The Community Centered Entrepreneur in Japanese Development," *Explorations in Entrepreneurial History*, VIII, 2 (Dec. 1955), 80-98.
[21] W. W. Lockwood, *The Economic Development of Japan, Growth and Structural Change 1868-1938*. (Princeton, 1954), pp. 587ff.

could take place only within a unified nation under a sound central administration. Building on the tradition of centralized feudalism established by the Tokugawa regime, this was the first and greatest achievement of the Restoration. It provided the framework of political stability necessary to encourage long-term investment in fixed capital.

ECONOMIC LIBERALIZATION

A second circumstance favorable to the rise of modern entrepreneurship was the freeing of economic activities from all sorts of feudal restrictions. Greater economic freedom had long been advocated by certain scholars and *bakufu* officials in the late Tokugawa era, and the regime itself had moved in this direction. For example, in 1853 it lifted its ban on the construction of large vessels, and even provided merchants and farmers with subsidies in undertaking large-scale shipping. Following the Restoration, the Meiji authorities moved even more rapidly and decisively to liberalize state policies. The initial steps included: (a) abolition of guilds in 1868; (b) permission to all social classes to engage in any occupation in 1871-1872; (c) permission to farmers to select crops freely for cultivation and to sell their land without restriction in 1872; and (d) prohibition of commercial activities by local governments in 1869.

The withdrawal of local governmental authorities from commercial pursuits deserves added comment. During the Tokugawa era most of the *han*, in the hope of meeting their financial difficulties, had come to intervene extensively in the production and sale of local products. Some even went so far as to monopolize the right of sale. After the ports were opened to foreign trade, many *han* also established their own trading firms through which they dealt directly with foreign firms for the purpose of obtaining arms and other foreign goods. Foreign merchants in fact, preferred to deal directly with feudal lords rather than private merchants because in those days the former's transactions were likely to be larger. Nevertheless, the new Meiji regime moved promptly in 1869 to prohibit such dealings, proclaiming that "government officials should never be in competition with merchants in the pursuit of profits." Such activity was to be henceforth in the private sector.

Why the Meiji authorities should so readily adopt such a liberal principle in the nation's commercial life is not easy to say, but contemporary scholars offer several answers. One, emphasized by Sydney Crawcour in Chapter I, is found in the extensive development of a money economy that had already taken place, in the country as well as in the city. Another is the growing awareness within the traditional economy of the potentialities of liberalizing measures. For example, Sakurada Michi of the Sendai *han* says in his petition to his lord in 1834 that a country will necessarily become rich when commercial transactions are entrusted to merchants. Ōshima Takatō of the Nambu *han*, in a similar petition of 1863, urges liberalization of merchant activity in order to make the nation wealthy, and he links this with the contention that national development should shift from an agricultural to an industrial emphasis.[22] Kanda Kōhei, a specialist in Dutch learning at the Bakufu Institute for the Study of Foreign Books, wrote in *Nō shō ben* [An Essay on Agriculture and Commerce, 1860] that "Oriental countries are persistently poor because they depend on agriculture, while Occidental countries are at all times wealthy because they rely on commerce." He went so far as to say that the Western principle of self-interest was more conducive to benevolent administration than the Oriental one of rule by virtue.[23]

Meiji policies of liberalization thus followed the tendencies already present in Japan, and were reinforced by the observation that the wealth and strength of the West was built on economic liberalism. Neither economic freedom nor capitalism per se, however, was itself the object of policy to be transplanted from the West. Capitalistic organization, as a theory, even "capitalism" as a word, was hardly known yet to the Japanese. The thing they saw and desired was the national

[22] Horie, "Business Pioneers," 1-16.
[23] Horie Yasuzō, "Confucian Concept of State in Tokugawa Japan," *KUER*, XXXII, 2 (Oct. 1962), 26-38.

strength and industrial riches that Western nations had achieved on liberal principles. Liberalism, then, was a pragmatic choice to build Japan's political and economic independence. The same motivation runs through all aspects of cultural borrowing from the West. The great contemporary scholar Fukuzawa Yukichi wrote in his *Outline of What is Meant by Civilization* (1875) that the final objective of the country was national independence, and "civilization and enlightenment" (*bummei-kaika*) was the means to achieve it.[24]

SOCIAL MOBILITY

The third circumstance favorable to the emergence of vigorous business enterprise was increasing social mobility. Liberalization of state policy in favor of private initiative required greater mobility to make it effective. A degree of social mobility was already in evidence in the Tokugawa era, for example in the selection of able men for important public responsibility, and the practice of adopting into a family sons born to a different social status. Shibusawa Eiichi, whose career is recounted in Chapter V, was born into a farmer-merchant family and later became a samurai by chance. Such a case was not rare, especially in late Tokugawa years, nor was the reverse i.e. from samurai to commoner.

Now under the Meiji regime the old feudal social strata were abolished as a hindrance to free social movement. No other single measure was more important in preparing for the new order. With this change went a shift in values from the agricultural emphasis of feudalism to the industrialism of modern Japan, and from an emphasis on social status to economic wealth and power. Traditionally looked down upon in the old society, businessmen now acquired a new respectability that considerably increased incentives for modern business enterprise.

[24] Y. Fukuzawa, *Bunmeiron no gairyaku* [An Outline of What is Meant by Civilization] (Tokyo, 1931), p. 232.

Industrial Promotion

JOINT-STOCK COMPANIES

Liberalization of opportunity for private enterprise, however, could not of itself result in bold investment without provision of more positive aids. Long accustomed to control and
patronage by the State, businessmen facing the new competition from abroad looked naturally to the government for
measures of protection and active support. Liberalism and
protection seem contradictory to each other only apart from
historical context. For the protection now sought was the
opposite of that provided by *bakufu* and *han,* whose aims had
been merely to bolster the finances of feudal lords. Meiji
policy, on the contrary, skillfully utilized the tradition of
state patronage to draw a rising economic class into new
fields of business enterprise, in order to build a new Japan.

One way of doing this was to encourage the company form
of business organization.[25] Knowledge of the joint-stock principle had already been brought back from the United States
by the *bakufu* mission dispatched to ratify the Treaty of
Amity and Commerce. Other travelers to Europe, such as
Shibusawa and Fukuzawa, returned with similar information.
By order of the Shogunate a company was organized by
Osaka merchants to collect funds for modernizing the port of
Kobe. After the Restoration other measures followed, such
as government publication of two pamphlets on company
organization. Through extending subsidies and other privileges, it sought to persuade wealthy people to establish such
firms as *kawase kaisha* (exchange banks), *tsushō kaisha*
(trading companies), *kaisō kaisha* (a marine trading firm),
and *riku'un moto kaisha* (a land transport agency), etc. While
such firms remained rudimentary in company organization,
the national banks authorized in 1872 were companies of
limited liability closely patterned on American and European
banks. Meanwhile modern-style companies were formed here

[25] W. Kanno, *Nihon kaisha-kigyō hasseishi no kenkyū* [A Study of
the Rise of the Company Form of Business in Japan] (Tokyo, 1931),
pp. 32ff.

and there on private initiative, most notably the Maruya Trading Company (predecessor of the present Maruzen Book Store) established in 1869 under the guidance of Fukuzawa Yukichi.

Traditionally business had been conducted on the family principle. The important consideration for the old-style merchant was to maintain the family line and family business. For that purpose he was likely to maintain a close relationship with branch families, on the one hand, and to entrust the management of the firm to a chief clerk recruited from his employees, on the other.[26] This created some familiarity with the principle of partnership. But the development of incorporated business based on limited liability of stockholders was something quite different and could hardly have proceeded rapidly without encouragement and assistance from the government.

FINANCIAL ASSISTANCE

The Meiji State also gave extensive financial subsidies to business enterprise in new fields. An early example was the supply of capital funds to well-to-do people as an incentive to the formation of exchange banks in 1869. To promote export trading firms the government assisted such companies as Ōkura through export funds advanced directly or through the Yokohama Specie Bank. Well known, too, are the huge subsidies, in addition to numerous vessels, given the Mitsubishi Company. To encourage cotton spinning in 1879 the government sold ten units of spinning equipment on easy payment terms, calling for repayment over ten years without interest. And when the Japan Railway Company was established in 1881, it was exempted from the railway land tax and guaranteed annual dividends of 8 percent regardless of profit. Other examples of similar support are too numerous to mention.

There were also the *seishō* (privileged merchants, or businessmen with political affiliations). They appeared first among firms financing the government, especially Mitsui and Ono.

[26] The relationship between employer and employees was as paternalistic as the relationship between master and retainers.

Others were dealers in imported arms, like Ōkura Kihachirō mentioned earlier. In a sense all companies receiving special assistance might be called *seishō*, as they relied on government patronage. The privileged relations between government and *seishō* have been much criticized by historians, yet one must recall that the State had no alternative but to rely on these men of entrepreneurial ability to develop modern forms of business enterprise. They were the chosen instruments of the day.

GOVERNMENT FACTORIES

Model factories established by the government were still another measure of industrial promotion. Already in the closing days of Tokugawa the *bakufu* and several influential *han* had set up shipbuilding yards and arsenals of Western type to strengthen national defense. The Meiji authorities not only took over such establishments but went on to invest large sums in various kinds of government factories. The first was the Tomioka Silk Reeling Mill of 1872, mentioned earlier. By the end of the following year such schemes were put in charge of a Ministry of Civil Affairs, and Ōkubo Toshimichi, just back from a tour of Europe and America, was asked to become the first minister. His career may be compared to that of Colbert in France; it was after he assumed his influential position that most of the government plants were set up—cement, plate glass, fireproof brick, woolen cloth, cotton yarn, etc.

The purposes of these factories varied from one field to another. Generally speaking, however, they were to demonstrate Western factory design and techniques of production, and to furnish some of the new products that previously had to be imported from abroad. Later a third purpose was added, i.e., revenue. (At this time the object was to lighten existing fiscal burdens rather than to add new revenue.) Of the three purposes the first was the most important. It was served incidentally even when the chief object was to supply government needs, for example as in the mint opened in 1871.

In 1880 it was decided to sell off most of these government

plants to private entrepreneurs, except for those affiliated with the Army and Navy ministries. This was the year when the inflation of paper money reached its peak, and one reason for the withdrawal of the government was to get funds to redeem inconvertible notes. Another was to open outlets for private investment, especially by bondholders, i.e., ex-daimyō and samurai. These aims of the government were not actually fulfilled, however, until the investment boom of the late eighties.

GOVERNMENT OFFICIALS AS ENTREPRENEURS

Through such measures of public encouragement to business enterprise the entrepreneurial spirit and talent of public officials was applied to construct a framework for modernizing Japan's economic life. Foreign experts were influential, too, but decisions required the approval and initiative of Japanese officials themselves. Often it is said that Japan's capitalistic development was fostered by "government." But government itself is nothing more than a form of human organization. Although some high officials still advocated spending money not to build railroads but to "expel the barbarians," fortunately they could not prevail over their more enlightened colleagues. Among the latter, called the *shin kanryo* (new bureaucrats), the names of Ōkuma Shigenobu, Itō Hirobumi, Inoue Kaoru, Ōkubo Toshimichi, Matsukata Masayoshi, and Shibusawa Eiichi stand out. Their achievements are too well known to require enumeration here; but one further example may be cited in Maejima Hisoka, founder of Japan's modern postal service.

Maejima[27] (1835-1919) was born of a country samurai (*gōshi*), a scholarly landowner of Echigo (now Niigata). Having learned foreign languages in his youth he was employed successively by the Satsuma *han*, by the *bakufu*, and then by the Meiji government at the same time (1869) as Shibusawa. Though Maejima's rank was low, his office, the

[27] Y. Ichino, *Kōsōkon* (or *Kō no Tsuma'ato*) [A Biography of Maejima Hisoka] (Tokyo, 1926).

Kaisei kyoku (Reform Bureau) was influentially affiliated with both the Ministries of Finance and Public Affairs which was administered by a number of brilliant officials like Ōkuma and Itō. The Finance Ministry was the chief driving force in modernization at the time, and the Reform Bureau served both ministries in an advisory capacity. Maejima's great contribution in this office was his prospectus for the Tokyo-Osaka railway that the government had decided to build. His proposals enabled the new bureaucrats to persuade their conservative colleagues to undertake the project, and his abilities were rewarded the following year when he was appointed vice-director of the Ekitei Ryō (Bureau of Transport and Communications).

While the government had carried on most of the inland transport of goods in the Tokugawa period, the postal service had been a private express-messenger service organized as a guild and confined to the route between Tokyo and the Kyoto-Osaka area. As soon as Maejima took office he observed that the government had been paying heavily for these express messengers. Accordingly he laid out a plan for a modern postal system modeled after the British one. His purpose was first to reduce expenditures and second to provide the public with a cheap and efficient service. The service was inaugurated first between Tokyo and Osaka in 1871, and within three years it had spread across most of Japan. Inland freight transport, on the other hand, was transferred from the government to the private agency Riku'un Moto Kaisha (Overland Transport Company, predecessor of the present Nihon Tsū'un Kaisha, Japan Express Company) in 1872, again mainly on Maejima's advice.[28]

The Japanese government was able to push forward with these modernization schemes because of these energetic officials of vision and administrative talent. Japan thus illustrates again A. H. Cole's remark that "the bearers of entrepreneurial role is in a number of respects one variety of a

[28] *Shashi* [A History of the *Nihon tsū'un kabushiki kaisha*] (Tokyo, 1962), pp. 127-37.

rather large genus of men."[29] While government officials of early Meiji came mostly from the samurai class, their cultural heritage and social environment were much the same as that of business leaders. Not surprisingly a number of them displayed marked entrepreneurial spirit. Thus leader-follower relations developed smoothly between public officials and private businessmen, and the latter could act in harmony with the government. Undoubtedly this was a major reason for Japan's rapid industrialization.

Conclusion

Japan may be said to have reached what is called the "take-off" stage in industrialization about 1888, after two decades of conditioning. Such an achievement would hardly have been possible without a vigorous and pragmatic spirit of enterprise displayed at the top and the strong, disciplined hierarchy of authority extending down to the people. A few words summarizing this leader-follower relationship will serve to conclude this essay.

One clear advantage for Japan lay in the heritage of the commercial society developed during the Tokugawa period.[30] As previously noted the spread of the money economy had infused the whole society with new values and accustomed it to the problems of such an economy. Among leading groups— samurai, merchants, and rich peasants—a rational, pragmatic spirit emerged that enabled them to respond positively to the challenges of the '60's and '70's. Facing this challenge, political leaders in government and business leaders among the people could cooperate in pushing forward, with a minimum of conservative opposition, to the goals of industrialization.

Nationalism, too, was an asset for modernization, resting as it did on ancient territorial loyalties on the one hand, and the spirit of Confucianism on the other. Tokugawa govern-

[29] A. H. Cole, "Entrepreneurship and Entrepreneurial History" Lambie, J. T. and R. V. Clemence (eds.), *Economic Change in America* (Harrisburg, 1954), pp. 18-33.

[30] Y. Horie, "The Feudal States and the Commercial Society in the Tokugawa Period," *KUER*, XXVIII, 2 (Oct. 1948), 1-16.

ment had divided the country into two sectors, one the domain of the shogun and the other the *han* numbering over 250. The latter were small states within themselves ruled by the *daimyō*, ideally as a father rules his children (although the people were often heavily exploited). Moreover, the castle town of each *han* was a local center economically and culturally, as well as politically. From such centers new ways of life had begun to radiate out through the countryside. Thanks to this tradition of unified territorial rule Japan was able to avoid anarchy and disorder when plunged into the crisis of the Meiji Restoration. A developing national consciousness smoothed the transition to the centralized nation state of modern times.

Finally, this national consciousness was further strengthened by the legacy of Confucianism which had been fostered by the *bakufu* to rationalize feudal administration. The essence of Confucianism lay in its political ethic of authority and responsibility, and it was studied in Japan not only by scholars but also by the common people, so that the foundation for a truly national morale was provided, as noted above. More concretely, its contribution to Japan's modernization lay in three aspects:[31] first, it cultivated the intellect, being rational in its interpretation of the universe; second, it valued knowledge for practical use, thus training the people more readily to accept Western science and technology; and third and most important, as interpreted in Japan it served to bolster the nationalism of the Japanese people. It taught that the main aim of government was to build a strong and moral state— strong because it was moral. To achieve this end, the ruler must be prosperous enough to practice beneficent rule, and the nation strong enough to maintain independence.

"Prosperity and Strength" thus was the slogan advanced by influential scholars and the one that guided the economic activities of the *han*. After 1868, as revitalized by the Meiji government, it became the watchword of the country's modernization. "Men of Japanese spirit with Western knowledge" now appeared in increasing numbers at the helm. In short the nationalism of modern Japan emerged from within

[31] Horie, "Confucian Concept," 26-38.

the Japanese themselves; it was not borrowed abroad. With all the revolutionary changes in values and techniques that began with the Restoration, one thing persisted—namely, a nationalism that enabled Japan to escape serious political and social turmoil and possible foreign domination. Having achieved national unity and political stability, Japan could move forward rapidly on the path of modernization.

CHAPTER V

Shibusawa Eiichi: Industrial Pioneer

JOHANNES HIRSCHMEIER, S.V.D.

EARLIER CHAPTERS in this volume set forth the general truth that the Meiji economy was propelled into modern growth by vigorous leadership from government officials and a rising class of modern business entrepreneurs in close cooperation with each other. This essay singles out one outstanding leader in this process, Shibusawa Eiichi (1840-1931). Through his career it seeks to throw light on three questions: (1) how did the Meiji Restoration itself affect the emergence of modern business entrepreneurship; (2) what major problems did the new entrepreneurs face in building modern banks and industries; and (3) what kind of mentality was dominant among the representative and leading entrepreneurs.

Answers to all three questions are suggested in the entrepreneurial portrait of Shibusawa. In his career as government official, banker, and industrialist, and in his life philosophy, we find reflected most of the basic characteristics of the Meiji business elite. He was the acknowledged leader of this rising business community for almost the entire Meiji and Taishō periods and was widely admired and imitated by the younger generation especially.

The term "entrepreneur" is used here in a very broad sense to designate modern-type bankers, foreign traders, and industrialists. Although technology was borrowed by the Japanese from Western countries, most business leaders in the modern sectors of Meiji Japan had to innovate in a secondary sense: they had to adapt that technology to a setting vastly different from that of the West.

The Influence of the Meiji Restoration

Shibusawa Eiichi was born in a village fifty miles north of Edo in 1840, the son of a rich farmer who also carried on a lucrative trade in indigo. Like many rich farmers' sons of late Tokugawa he received a samurai education in fencing, calligraphy, and Confucian philosophy; here he acquired his lifelong love for the *Analects*, which he learned almost all by heart. Although employed in his father's business he had time enough as a young man to become involved in the movement known as *sonnō-jōi* (Revere the Emperor; Expel the Barbarians), and at the age of 24 he participated in a plot to overthrow the Tokugawa government.

Fortunately for Shibusawa the conspirators against the *bakufu* (Tokugawa government) were dissuaded from their premature attempt. To rehabilitate himself Shibusawa used the good offices of a friend to enter the service of the Tokugawa family itself. Attached to the Hitotsubashi branch in Kyoto, he ingratiated himself with Prince Yoshinobu by successfully recruiting five hundred new soldiers for the weak Tokugawa forces in Kyoto. In 1867 he left for France on a good will tour in the entourage of Prince Yoshinobu's younger brother, Minbu. Meanwhile Yoshinobu had accepted the nomination as Shogun, against Shibusawa's advice that he should refuse the post because the cause of the *bakufu* was doomed. Shibusawa now served this Shogun with unswerving loyalty, despite the fact that only a few years before he had attempted to overthrow the hated regime.

Until 1867 Shibusawa's life clearly lacked consistency. He had left his village to overthrow the Shogunate, only to end up as a loyal retainer. After he was made a samurai by Yoshinobu, his career became tied to the Tokugawas; yet he could not abandon his belief that the Tokugawa cause was doomed. He was hardly a weak and inconsistent personality; his later life indicates the exact opposite. Yet here he was, caught like many other young patriots between two forces: loyalty and personal conviction. Early conviction of the evils of the feudal system, as administered by the *bakufu*, had driven him from his farm toward revolutionary action. Many others had done something similar, not only samurai but farmer and merchant sons as well. In the march of events that preceded the Restoration they sensed an acute national crisis summoning them to action. Everybody shouted "Hannibal at the gates!" and the youth of Japan, those who were awake to the situation, came running. But in action, minds were confused. Not only did feudal loyalties prevent a free grouping of men according to convictions but patriots fought on either side convinced that their cause was the cause of Japan.

As in the case of Shibusawa, it was immaterial in the long run where a man first stood, whether on the side of the *bakufu* or of the Restoration, provided only that he became involved. To enter political struggle meant for most patriots cutting loose their ties to traditional occupations, and leaving their homes especially those in the villages. Again and again we find the same thing in the lives of Meiji business leaders. The political tide prior to or after the Restoration undermined their allegiance to tradition and their former economic status and prepared them for something new. Thus it created the condition necessary for them to assume the role of innovating entrepreneur in the new world now taking shape.

Shibusawa accompanied Prince Minbu to France as his financial manager, and it was this journey that became instrumental in turning him from politics to business. As a *jōi*-man he received the shock of his life when he saw the flourishing, industrious business life of Europe. Not only did he realize the futility of any attempt to drive the foreign powers out of Japan by force but, more important, he saw now that Japan could only achieve greatness and equal these advanced countries if she adopted their technology. This meant she must reshape her society by elevating business pursuits to an honored status, and downgrading or abolishing samurai prerogatives. Shibusawa's stay in Europe lasted only one year, but it decided his future career. He vowed henceforth to devote his life to the modernization of the Japanese economy.

Shibusawa's European experience was shared by many Meiji entrepreneurs, though not as universally as his participation in the Restoration movement. Still more was this true of political leaders in the Meiji government; travel to the West almost invariably made these young Japanese ardent advocates of economic modernization and industrialization.

Thus the patriotism energized by the Restoration struggle came to be channeled into concrete and productive activity. This is why the *sonnō-jōi* men could abandon their militarist outlook so quickly and become the planners of Japan's new Industrial Revolution.

When the Restoration had become a *fait accompli* Prince Minbu returned to Japan, and with him came Shibusawa in 1868. Shibusawa accompanied him to Shizuoka, the home territory of the Tokugawa, and began immediately to carry out his resolution to take up economic tasks. Soon he organized a granary for the samurai on a joint-stock basis, insisting that government officials must not interfere in its management.[1] In fact, both the joint-stock form of enterprise and this conviction regarding government non-interference now became two of his abiding business principles. Both had developed into firm convictions during his stay in France.

As one of the few men of samurai status who combined a keen interest in economic matters with first-hand knowledge of the West and practical experience in financial matters, Shibusawa was tailor-made for the Ministry of Finance. Ōkuma Shigenobu, then Finance Minister, came personally to Shizuoka to enlist him, and he accepted on condition that he might resign at any opportune moment to enter the private sector if he chose.[2]

In his new post Shibusawa was extremely successful, and moved up rapidly in rank, despite the fact that the arrival of this young samurai from Musashino apparently was not well received by the Satsuma-Chōshū clique. Not only was he an outsider but he openly criticized the too numerous samurai officials who sat in their offices sipping tea and talking boastfully about the new era, meanwhile doing nothing to usher it in nor even knowing what should be done. Ōkuma put Shi-

---

[1] Shibusawa seien kinen zaidan ryūmonsha [The Shibusawa Seien Memorial Foundation Ryūmonsha], ed., *Shibusawa Eiichi denki shiryō* [Biographical Material on Shibusawa Eiichi] (vols. 1-46; Tokyo, 1958-1963), II, 182-85; hereafter, *Denki shiryō*.

[2] Shibusawa later emphasized repeatedly that he had never planned to become an official and that from the beginning his heart was with private enterprise.

busawa in charge of the Ministry's newly created Bureau of
Reorganization, where he worked on matters such as tax reform, standardization of measures, cadastral surveys of the
whole country, and the disposition of *han* (feudal domain)
debts.[3] Sometimes he would labor through several nights
without sleep in order to complete urgent drafts. Soon he
gained the respect of all and rose within about two years to
occupy the third place in the Ministry.

FOE OF MILITARISM AND BUREAUCRACY

In handling his heavy responsibilities, however, Shibusawa
was handicapped and irritated by two phenomena: militarism
and bureaucracy. Together with Inoue Kaoru, who shared
major decisions in the Ministry of Finance with him, he
viewed these twin problems as grave hindrances if not acute
dangers to efficient economic modernization. Both men kept
urging restraint in military expenditures and sought priority
for those which would stimulate economic growth especially
in the private sector. An open clash occurred in 1871. The
strong man of the regime, Ōkubo Toshimichi, demanded approval of the Ministry of Finance for an armament budget of
over 10 million yen at a time when the total annual revenue
of the government was only about 40 million. Other officials
had given their consent, partly in deference to Ōkubo; but
Shibusawa flatly rejected the request on behalf of Inoue, who
was then absent. The infuriated Ōkubo charged Shibusawa
with slighting the military security of the country; Shibusawa
replied that such outlays were economically irresponsible. His
objection was overruled, and only Inoue's plea prevented him
from resigning then and there. Inoue reasoned that Ōkubo
would soon leave on the large Iwakura Mission to Europe
and that the two of them would then run the Ministry of
Finance according to their own ideas.[4] Ōkubo himself re-

[3] *Denki shiryō*, II, 275-77.
[4] Shibusawa Hideo, *Chichi Shibusawa Eiichi* [My Father, Shibusawa Eiichi] (2 vols.; Tokyo, 1959), II, 30-31. In 1871 many government officials under the leadership of Iwakura Tomomi departed on a
grand study tour of the advanced countries of Europe to learn first-

turned from his extensive sightseeing tour of the West as another staunch advocate of the economy-first principle, but Shibusawa left the Ministry of Finance the next year, 1872.

The young Shibusawa remained much concerned about economic policies and continued to advise and speak out on these matters. Always he opposed the trend toward large armament expenditures and military involvement. At the time of the Formosan Expedition (1874) he told an assembly of the highest state officials in Prince Sanjō's mansion that he could never assent to the proposed expedition because the Treasury had already a deficit of 6 million yen.[5] Prudent counsels of this sort did prevent militarism in its extreme form from gaining control during the Meiji period; the advocates of economy-first could by and large assert themselves. But militarism remained a standing threat, for the former military class was reluctant to place a higher value on the activities and calculation of merchants than armies, or to expect a strong Japan to result from flourishing manufactures and profitable banks rather than daring military exploits.

Equally dangerous for economic growth was bureaucratism, another byproduct of the Restoration. The Tokugawa regime was well known for its bureaucratism, of course; in this respect the *han* differed little from the *bakufu*. The highest offices were occupied by the highest ranking samurai whether they did any work or not. After the Restoration the government was taken over by able and progressive men whose policies introduced the new era of *bummei kaika* (civilization and enlightenment). Meiji officials now became idols in the minds of many Japanese; everything great and exciting in the after-Restoration years tended to be credited to the government. Consequently young and ambitious men of the elite aspired to public office rather than private business. The fact that the government built the first large factories and the rail-

hand about Western civilization; their interest centered notably on modern industry and how they could introduce it into Japan.

[5] Obata Kyugorō, *An Interpretation of the Life of Viscount Shibusawa* (Tokyo, 1937), p. 80.

ways seemed only to confirm the idea that, even in economic life, achievement was to be sought through careers in government.

Shibusawa believed that this over-estimation of public office and contempt for the common people (*kanson minpi*) had to be combatted if a viable economy was to be built. He complained often that students would dream only of political careers and took as their ideal only statesmen such as Gladstone, Bismarck, or some Meiji high official. Indeed, graduates from the technology department of the Imperial University demanded special compensation if they were to work as engineers for city public works instead of being given government appointments.[6] Shibusawa sought to champion the work of businessmen, asserting that it was just as vital for the nation's prosperity as the work of the bureaucracy.

One of the main obstacles to a change in public thinking on these matters was the poor performance, initially, of the merchant class. From the merchant houses that had wielded a dominant influence in Osaka and Edo during the Tokugawa period came little or no initiative; the house of Mitsui was only in part an exception. Thus the private sector in the first decade after the Restoration was almost entirely without enterprise, without leaders, and without organization. Having dealt with many merchants as an official in the Ministry of Finance, Shibusawa saw at first hand that these people would never be able to provide the industrial enterprise needed or to improve the public image of business. This caused him finally to resign his position and become a private entrepreneur.

At the age of 34, when he left public office to enter private life, Shibusawa had thus come full circle. First he had left his father's farm and business to become a revolutionary. Then he changed sides, traveled abroad, and returned with the determination to devote all his energies to the economic progress of Japan, beginning as an official and a very successful one. He now turned once more to the private sector.

[6] Shibusawa Eiichi, *Jitsugyō kōen* [Lectures on Enterprise] (2 vols.; Tokyo, 1913), II, 36-37.

Henceforth he was to remain a businessman, rejecting any return to government even when asked to serve as Minister of Finance.[7] Uprooted by the Restoration and inspired to a new patriotism that never flagged, he chose nevertheless to work for Japan's prosperity where he felt the need was greatest. In reality he could not sever his ties to the government completely, nor was it called for. But he gave wide publicity to his preference for a business career as a way to strengthen the self-confidence of the new business class, and at least one other high Meiji official, Godai Tomoatsu, followed his example by ostentatiously entering private business. He too deplored publicly the superabundance of government officials and the lack of capable and progressive businessmen.

Like Shibusawa most of the modern entrepreneurs of early Meiji were influenced toward their careers by the political events and social changes preceding and following the Restoration. Most of them in common with Shibusawa had voluntarily broken their ties with the past, including their traditional occupations and even their homes. They did not cling desperately to their inherited economic existence until uprooted by the events of the Restoration. Many a merchant family was forcibly displaced of course, and the whole samurai class as well. But for a man to emerge as an entrepreneur in the new order it seems to have been important whether he had moved on his own accord, motivated by patriotism, political ambition, or the quest for economic success in the big cities, or whether he had been overtaken by the course of events in passive acquiescence or outright resistance.

Shibusawa's dramatic resignation from office and his constant stress on independence from government derived from the well-known tendency of the Meiji entrepreneurs to rely on official subsidies and to vie for government commissions and contracts. Favoritism and clique politics were rampant,

[7] Shibusawa Hideo, *op.cit.*, II, 116. In 1901 Inoue was offered the premiership; he made his acceptance dependent on whether Shibusawa would serve as his Minister of Finance. But it seems that Shibusawa's refusal to do so was not the only or even major reason for Inoue's not becoming prime minister.

with the *zaibatsu* (economic cliques) as the chief beneficiaries. It must be remembered that leading businessmen and officials had been shaped by the same political and social forces of change and thus were akin in their mentality. Though their interests and activities were predominantly private, business entrepreneurs often served in a sense as agents of the State.

SHIBUSAWA AND THE RISE OF MODERN BANKING

Japan had come out of the Tokugawa period with a higher standard of living and higher potential savings than most underdeveloped countries of Asia today. Consumption based on feudal dues was first drastically reduced and within ten years almost disappeared, while new government revenues were channeled through government expenditures into military equipment, social overhead capital, and (via subsidies) private industry. For economic development, however, Japan also needed a modern banking system to collect untapped savings on a larger scale and make them available to investors. The Tokugawa exchange houses (*ryōgaeya*) that had served as banks for the merchant community, notably in the large cities, had mostly collapsed prior to or immediately after the Restoration. Those that remained were neither prepared nor willing to adapt to the new needs of foreign trade and industry.

As Professor Horie has already described (Ch. IV), the Meiji government tried in 1869 to mobilize merchant capital and initiative for the financing of foreign trade by encouraging the establishment of exchange companies to act as banks for foreign trade companies. But these first banks of Meiji Japan collapsed after less than one year, for the merchant-bankers had acted only under government orders, and their passive resistance combined with their ignorance of modern banking condemned this first scheme to an early death. Four national banks were then established in 1872 after the model of American banks, again only under strong government pressure. Osaka merchants had intended and promised the government to establish a large bank, but failed to do so. Even the first and most important of the four banks actually established was founded only after the Houses of Mitsui and Ono were told by Inoue and Shibusawa that unless they joined to establish a bank they would lose all the government commissions and favors heaped on them after the Restoration.[8]

At that time Shibusawa had already tendered his resignation from the Ministry of Finance. When he attended the first general meeting of the newly established First National Bank he was elected its general superintendent. He soon gained almost absolute control over policies because the two presidents supplied by the rival houses of Mitsui and Ono could never agree; Shibusawa was therefore free to act as he chose. His memoirs are very critical of the clerks of Mitsui and Ono because of their ignorance of banking matters, as well as their unwillingness to learn. In 1874 the House of Ono went bankrupt, and its bad loan of a million yen almost brought ruin in turn to the Dai-Ichi Ginkō (First Bank). Shibusawa finally managed to retrieve all but 19,300 yen,[9] and in the following year he was made president of the bank, a post of strategic influence in the business community. The Dai-Ichi soon ran into difficulties again, however, when the government withdrew its deposits in 1875. Once more Shibusawa saved it by initiating a series of retrenchment measures. He slashed capital by 1,500,000 yen, closed branch offices, and persuaded the government to withdraw its deposits over a period of two years rather than all at once.[10]

By 1875, as a matter of fact, all four national banks were in distress. Their notes fell rapidly in value, and with them public confidence. Clearly the banking system was in need of reform as well as expansion to serve effectively Japan's expanding industry and trade. Out of this need came the Revised Banking Act of 1876, which now opened the door to samurai initiative. The new statute made it possible for samurai to invest bonds issued to them in commutation of their feudal pensions as share capital in new banks. The government expected thus to solve two problems at once: to estab-

[8] Obata, *op. cit.*, 89-90.
[9] *Ibid.*, 94.
[10] *Denki shiryō*, IV, 139.

lish a modern banking system with the help of the cultured and declassed elite of the nation, and at the same time help them to find a new economic livelihood.

The enthusiastic response of the samurai contrasted strikingly to the reluctance of the merchants. A total of 193 national banks had been chartered by 1893, when further applications were refused. Blocked by this ceiling of 193 charters, eager samurai went on to establish private banks that soon grew even more numerous than the chartered national banks. The former feudal class, nobility and samurai together, thus supplied 76.0 percent of the capital at all national banks, as against 14.9 percent from merchants.[11] The capital of the nobility, 44.1 percent of the total, was chiefly concentrated in the Fifteenth National Bank; it had over 17 million yen, as against 25 million in all others put together.[12] In the system as a whole, however, they were not the chief dynamic element. Nor were the merchants even though typically individual merchants had larger amounts of capital invested than individual samurai. The initiative for establishment, planning, and management of national banks came mainly from samurai.

This outcome resulted from a number of factors: merchants were restrained by tradition from the adoption of joint-stock banking; samurai were held back neither by tradition nor by alternative livelihoods. Nor were they handicapped by house rules and rigid customs like the merchants, who found it difficult to learn and to carry out banking regulations phrased in official and partly literary language. Inexperienced samurai could do better here than in other types of business by simply following instructions. Last but not least the samurai saw in the establishment of banks a unique opportunity to enter the business world without losing "face." The establishment of national banks was proclaimed a service to the country and a sign of modern civilization. Thus it was not only becoming to

[11] Ministry of Finance, ed. *Ginkō kyoku dai niji hōkoku* [Second Report of the Banking Office] (Tokyo, 1879/80), p. 129.

[12] Meiji zaiseishi hensan kai [Meiji Financial History Compilation Committee], *Meiji zaisei shi* [Meiji Financial History] (Tokyo, 1905), XIII, 10-11.

enter banking but even patriotic. Some even argued that every samurai had the duty to join in establishing a bank. Of all fields of modern enterprise, then, banking was the one in which the contribution of samurai was probably most decisive.

The new bankers had to learn, however, and for this there was no better place than the Dai-Ichi Bank. Shibusawa was soon busy training or advising presidents and managers of newly established national banks. Probably as many as a third of all national banks sent their men at one time or another to him. The most primitive banking techniques had to be explained, from the issue of bank notes and calculations of interest to half-year reports and bookkeeping. In 1876 Shibusawa wrote a booklet on banking with down-to-earth explanations and examples that any novice in the field could understand.[13] In a good number of instances he was even consulted prior to the establishment of a bank, or would himself take the initiative. He was particularly interested in having new banks established in areas which he considered backward and in need of development capital, like Sendai.[14] He also guided and protected the new banks with paternal solicitude: he would extend loans when small banks came under pressure, and pleaded with the government officials for patience when a government inspector discovered irregularities.[15]

[13] *Denki shiryō*, IV, 295-312.

[14] *Ibid.*, V, 294-97.

[15] The Sixteenth National Bank was in for a heavy penalty because an inspection had shown that this bank did not keep the required reserve ratio. Shibusawa pleaded pardon for the bank, maintaining that the bankers were still inexperienced. (*Ibid.*, p. 313.) A newspaper article of 1880 throws interesting light on the haphazard treatment of both reserve ratios and government inspections. It says that when an inspection was announced to local banks they would hastily borrow money from each other to replenish their reserves in the vaults. If that should not suffice, or be impossible, the managers would show the officials first one vault and then urge them to have lunch; in the meantime the money would be carried over to the next vault that was to be inspected. (Nakayama Yasumasa, ed., *Shinbun shūsei Meiji hennen shi* [Chronological History of Meiji Compiled from Newspapers] (Tokyo, 1936), IV, 298. Anyone familiar with the way inspections are sometimes carried out in Japan today will not find this incredible.

NATIONAL BANKING POLICIES

The establishment of numerous modern banks was of course only the first step toward a well-functioning monetary system. It became necessary immediately to work toward a general banking policy, to develop efficient techniques suited to the particular needs of nascent industries, and to establish mutual cooperation on the basis of some *esprit de corps*. The responsibility for such over-all guidance and national policy rests usually with a central bank, but the Bank of Japan was not to be established until 1882. Before that, such functions were handled naturally by Shibusawa as president of the Dai Ichi. Already in 1876, the year of the Revised Banking Act, Shibusawa founded the Takuzen Kai (Choose-the-Good Association), the first bankers' association in Japan. Bankers of the Tokyo-Yokohama area assembled monthly in the Dai Ichi Bank to discuss informally their common problems. The chief purposes of this Takuzen Kai were education in banking practices, strengthening of banking morale, mutual cooperation and friendship. In 1880 it was replaced by a more formal Bankers' Association, initially with thirty-two members. Shibusawa served both associations as president.

The first order of business for the new association was education of the general public as well as bankers themselves. People at large and notably many merchants had no clear idea what banks were supposed to do for them; distrustful merchants kept on dealing in cash. Even more than the public the bankers themselves needed instructions and training. Shibusawa had many useful articles from foreign banking journals translated into Japanese and distributed to his colleagues. The *Takuzen kai* had its own periodical, the *Takuzen zasshi*, and beginning with 1885 the Bankers' Association published the *Ginkō tsūshinroku* (Banking Correspondence).

Wider use of *tegata* (commercial bills) was frequently discussed in the Bankers' Association and the Chamber of Commerce. Shibusawa invited city merchants to attend and had specialists explain to them in great detail the advantages of *tegata*. After much negotiation a law was passed in 1882 for the protection of their bills. Following this success Shibusawa and the Bankers' Association worked toward the establishment of a *tegata* exchange, which finally came about in 1890 after the failure of an earlier attempt in 1886. To stimulate further the use of *tegata*, the Chamber of Commerce—its president also was Shibusawa—proposed to lower the interest rates of *tegata* slightly below the going rates, and, in case of repayment prior to maturity, to refund the interest differential.[16]

Assuming the responsibilities of a central banker, Shibusawa constantly opposed the inflationary fiscal and monetary measures of the government. Particularly he objected to the printing of paper money as a means to finance government spending. It is interesting to note that, one year before Count Matsukata as Finance Minister undertook a policy of deflation in 1881, Shibusawa had proposed to the Bankers' Association a four-point program of retrenchment and monetary stabilization almost identical with the actual measures later carried out by Matsukata. Shibusawa's proposals of 1880 may be summarized thus:[17]

1. Of all bank notes outstanding, 20 percent were to be retired and paid back to the Treasury.
2. The banks should pay up to the Treasury their reserves on note issues and receive instead interest-bearing gold certificates.
3. The Treasury should retire 50 million yen of its paper money within four years.
4. After that the Treasury should build up annually, for five consecutive years, a reserve fund of 5 million yen in specie in preparation for full convertibility.

The Matsukata deflation of 1881-1884 caused many businesses to collapse, notably those inefficient and capital-starved industrial ventures that had been started with more enthusiasm than know-how and had relied on government help and easy profits generated by inflation. Although Shibusawa had

---

[16] *Denki shiryō*, XIX, 366-77.

[17] Tsuchiya Takao, *Shibusawa Eiichi den* [Biography of Shibusawa Eiichi] (Tokyo, 1955), p. 182.

advocated radical deflationary measures, he was greatly concerned with industrial stability and growth as the express purpose of the modern banks, and not just sound finance in and of itself. This functional relationship remained strong in the consciousness of all Japan's modern bankers of the Meiji period; they were not only closely associated with industrial entrepreneurs in large lending operations but they often invested directly as shareholders. The Japanese banking structure had been modeled after the Anglo-American system of commercial banks, but practice followed closely that of German banking leadership in industry. Shibusawa himself became an outstanding industrial promoter and encouraged other bankers to do the same.

While expounding this idea of the responsibility of bankers toward modern industry Shibusawa faced a dilemma: long-term lending to industrial entrepreneurs involved high risks which often militated against the required safety of a bank, and Shibusawa was emphatic about safety. One way to avoid high risks was to spread them; large loans for new investments would be split up among several banks. On the other hand, Shibusawa also spoke frequently of the need to accept "personal security." A banker ought to know the entrepreneur, and if the latter were honest and capable the banker ought to grant him a needed loan even if other safeguards for security were lacking. Several cases are known in which Shibusawa continued lending in spite of seemingly bleak prospects because he trusted the man and believed he would finally succeed.[18] This policy was risky if carried too far, of course, but he always insisted that banks must share some of the risks of industrial ventures during the difficult pioneering era of Japanese industry. "Even if there should

[18] When the Ono Company went bankrupt with a bad loan of one million yen to the Dai Ichi Bank, its head clerk, Furukawa Ichibei, handed all Ono assets over to Shibusawa and added to this all his personal property and saved-up salaries, leaving the company with nothing but the clothes he was wearing. Shibusawa retained the highest regards for Furukawa all his life, because honesty was for Shibusawa a cardinal virtue of entrepreneurship. Obata, *op. cit.*, 95-96.

be no profits at all, a bank must assist industry," he maintained, "because this is its first duty."[19]

For Shibusawa there was no real contradiction between the desire to manage banks with the highest possible margin of safety on the one hand and the willingness at times to assume high risks for the sake of industrial growth. Both were born of the same sense of responsibility toward the public. "Banking is the easiest type of business," he once said, "but all the more it must be carried out with the greatest sense of responsibility toward the general public and toward industry, for which the banks exist."[20] In Shibusawa's mind, and in the mind of many other leading bankers, the interest of the general public was finally nothing else but the speedy growth of modern Japanese industry. This is why we find so many Meiji bankers lending on a long-term basis to industrialists, investing directly in large enterprises, and eventually becoming industrial entrepreneurs themselves, as did Shibusawa himself.

SHIBUSAWA IN MODERN INDUSTRY

Japan's modern industries reached self-sustaining growth at different times. First came cotton spinning and the railways, then considerably later heavy industries such as iron and steel. Almost all encountered the same set of problems as illustrated in the examples cited above by Professor Horie. Technological inexperience was usually the greatest hurdle; along with it often came lack of capital; and last, but not least, insufficient domestic demand. How these hurdles were negotiated varied of course from case to case and from entrepreneur to entrepreneur, but the general patterns were similar. Technical ignorance would be overcome either by hiring foreign engineers—infrequent in private industry—or by training native engineers abroad. Capital funds for large-scale enterprises were raised by close cooperation among entrepreneurs and with banks. Efficient management was often achieved by employing university graduates or other young

[19] *Denki shiryō*, IV, 397.
[20] *Ibid.*, 593.

and energetic men able to absorb new ideas. Insufficient domestic demand plagued some industries for many years, notably paper manufacturing, leather, cement, glass, and at times even cotton spinning. Here solutions came only gradually through improved quality and marketing.

Entrepreneurial leaders of the early and middle Meiji period characteristically spread themselves thin over a wide range of industrial ventures. They changed from one task to another and often left the details to others; they give the impression of having always been in search of something new. Shibusawa was an extreme case in point. In one capacity or another he was connected with over 500 diverse enterprises—mostly industrial firms—as president, director, adviser, or major shareholder. He was both a professional banker and an amateur industrialist, though his chief interest in the latter role was in breaking bottlenecks. As soon as major initial difficulties were solved he apparently lost interest. Details of routine management never engaged him; he was a strategist of modern industrialization, as the following pages will show.

COTTON SPINNING

Shibusawa's entrepreneurial achievement in the field of cotton spinning first deserves our close attention. Although he never managed a spinning mill and probably knew very little about the technology of mechanized spinning, his judgment and policy recommendations gave a decisive turn at several critical junctures to Japan's first successful modern industry. Observing his role in cotton spinning, one sees several crucial problems facing that industry at successive stages of its growth.

He first became concerned with cotton spinning after the Satsuma Rebellion of 1877. As president of the Dai Ichi Bank he worried about Japan's unfavorable balance of payments arising from domestic inflation. Cotton yarn and cloth constituted over one-third of total imports; yet all government efforts to promote mechanical cotton spinning were achieving only meager results. The few existing mills of 2,000-spindle size set up with government subsidies were inefficient, and many of them operated at low profits or actual losses. The reasons were numerous, chief among them being technical inexperience; small-scale, poor location; reliance on water-power—an irregular source of energy—and lack of funds to expand or even to maintain existing capacity. Moreover, in spite of low wages, labor cost was high due to inefficient use of both machinery and labor.

Shibusawa did not know the answer to all these difficulties, but he saw that the industry was in a critical situation. Something drastic must be done lest the early enthusiasm for cotton spinning turn into irreparable pessimism. His first order of business was to secure sufficient capital for a large-scale mill which he planned for Osaka, the center of the cotton trade. A total of 250,000 yen was subscribed by a few top industrialists and nobles. (Existing mills were capitalized at only about 40,000 yen on the average.) The next step was to improve production methods, and here Shibusawa did not trust the technicians of any of the existing mills, some of which did not even have an engineer of their own.[21] As described already by Professor Horie, he requested a student of technology, Yamabe Takeo, who happened to be in London at that time (1878-1879) to take up cotton spinning as a special study and gain some practical experience in Manchester. Shibusawa paid the expenses out of his own pocket. This young technician returned to Japan in 1880 and directed the construction of the Osaka Spinning Mill. Using steam power, it was equipped with latest machinery and operated its 10,500 spindles on day and night shifts. In 1883 it began its operations, and the next year dividends of 18 percent on capital were paid! A second plant was added in 1886 with another 20,800 spindles. In 1888 capital was raised to 1.2 million yen and 1,100 workers were employed in an operation that had now become one of the largest industrial establishments in Japan.[22]

Through his phenomenal success with the Osaka Spinning Mill, Shibusawa came to be considered one of the leaders in

[21] *Ibid.*, XXVI, 125-30.
[22] *Ibid.*, X, 119; the whole account *ibid.*, 5-120.

cotton spinning. His advice was frequently sought by others, as in the case of the Mie Spinning Mill.[23] That plant had been established in 1886, but labored under many difficulties, and finally its president came to Shibusawa for advice. Shibusawa suggested the same approach that had made the Osaka mill so successful: large scale operation, location close to the market, and employment of a top expert. The firm consequently moved to the port city of Yokkaichi, raised additional capital, and employed an engineer whom Shibusawa handpicked from the engineering department of Tokyo University and sent abroad for special training. As a result, this mill also became in a few years one of the most successful textile ventures in Japan.

Other mills quickly learned the lesson of the Osaka Spinning Mill, and with this turn of events Japanese cotton spinning entered its first boom period. Between 1886 and 1894 some 33 new plants were established, of which 10 were located in the vicinity of Osaka.[24] Though a few small-scale operations persisted, the pattern that now became dominant was large-scale and efficient organization utilizing the latest technology. Profit rates rose well above 10 percent as compared with only 4 to 5 percent prior to the establishment of the Osaka Mill.

Important as was this breakthrough at the level of plant operations, other difficulties of the cotton industry remained unsolved. Chief among them were marketing problems, and the cotton spinners, now growing every year in numbers, proceeded with a new self-confidence to tackle them in cooperation. As late as 1890 Japanese cotton spinning still labored under an outmoded tariff system: import duties were imposed on raw cotton and export duties on yarns. The home-grown cotton which these duties protected was not suitable for finer yarns; yet the Japanese mills had to produce the finer counts in order to compete effectively with imported yarn. Shibusawa became one of the leaders in the fight of the Spinners'

[23] *Ibid.*, 121-30.
[24] Kinugawa Taiichi, *Honpō menshi bōseki shi* [A History of Japanese Cotton Spinning] (7 vols.; Osaka, 1937), IV, 237-39.

Association for the abolition of these tariffs, and here his close association with government officials was a great asset. In the course of the struggle he sent delegations to China, Indochina, India, and the United States to study cotton qualities and import possibilities. Some patriots objected to the proposed purchase of foreign cotton on the ground that whatever could be produced in Japan ought not to be imported. Shibusawa replied that it was foolish to grow cotton in Japan if other crops, like indigo (he had been an indigo farmer), could yield more profits on the same land. Moreover, he stressed, everything must be done to promote Japanese industry.[25] After a ten-year struggle the tariffs were finally abolished in 1896, and the Spinners' Association presented a congratulatory document to Shibusawa.

Another trouble source, though a less important one, was Japan's exclusive reliance on the services of the Peninsular & Oriental Shipping Company for importing raw cotton. Not only were its freight rates high but the P&O could jeopardize any attempt of Japanese spinners to compete with English firms in the world market. Shibusawa hated monopolies in principle but he preferred a Japanese monopolist to a foreign one. He arranged with the Nihon Yūsen Kaisha (Japan Steamship Company) to establish a freight service for raw cotton from India for the benefit of Japanese mills. The P&O representative protested and threatened reprisals that frightened most cotton spinners. Only five firms, in which Shibusawa's influence was strongest, signed the exclusive shipping agreement with the NYK in 1893. Other mills followed later, however, and the termination of the P&O shipping monopoly lowered raw cotton prices considerably.[26]

With technical progress, ample capital, and cheaper raw cotton of improved qualities, the way was open for Japanese cotton yarns and fabrics to enter the world market. Shibusawa was not much involved in this next stage of development, but his interest continued in cotton spinning. He continued to urge expansion into foreign markets, notably China

[25] Tsuchiya, *op. cit.*, 201.
[26] *Denki shiryō*, X, 394-442.

and Korea, which he considered natural outlets for Japanese industry. And despite his aversion to monopolistic arrangements he was instrumental in establishing an export cartel to stop cut-throat competition between Japanese mills in these overseas areas, especially Korea.[27]

RAILWAYS

As mentioned previously, a major boom in railway building coincided with rapid expansion of the cotton industry. Yet these two modern sectors differed considerably in their particulars and in the approach chosen for their development. Cotton spinning was independent of government subsidies for all practical purposes, and it was exposed to foreign as well as domestic competition. Yet it achieved high rates of return on invested capital after the breakthrough of the Osaka mill. All was different in the case of railways: they could not dispense with government aid; they faced no competition; and yet they achieved on the average very low returns on invested capital.

Shibusawa's interest in railways dated back to his first journey to Europe. He considered them to be necessary for industrialization and consequently became their champion. When Baron Maejima tried in 1873 to organize the first railway company to build a line between Tokyo and Aomori, Shibusawa joined as treasurer. Although the scheme did not actually materialize until 1882, Shibusawa went on record in 1873 stressing two important reasons for building the Aomori line: it should provide a valuable stimulus to development of that backward northern area, and it should serve as a reminder to Russia that Japan had a stake in its northern frontier and would not tolerate intrusions there.[28]

As in other sectors of modern industry, the government sought to stimulate railway building by first constructing lines of its own to serve as models. Its intention was not to create a network of state railways but rather to encourage a good deal of private building. The first two lines completed

[27] *Ibid.*, 497-525.
[28] *Ibid.*, VIII, 371.

by the government served the crowded Tokyo-Yokohama and Kyoto-Kobe routes. On completion they paid handsome profits of 15 to 20 percent.[29] The government now prodded the nobles interested in the Tokyo-Aomori line to go ahead, offering subsidies as well as a guarantee of a 7 percent minimum return on invested capital. The company was started in 1882 with 20 million yen of capital. The next year, with the first sector in operation, it paid a dividend of 10 percent. This success finally ended the timidity of private investors and started a fever of railway promotion that reached its climax in the mid-1890's.

Like the national banks, railways initially seemed to offer an especially attractive investment opportunity because they provided both prestige and high returns. In the early years we find Shibusawa connected with no less than 34 railway companies, some of which, however, never went beyond the planning stage. In most cases he was a member of the organizing committee or one of the founders. These projects ranged from a railway in Hokkaidō for the coal mining industry to a projected line in Taiwan.

In the rush many railways were badly planned, poorly constructed, and inefficiently managed. The government kept extending subsidies, notably in the form of tax exemptions. By 1892 private railways operated 1,320 miles and government lines 550 miles. But the average returns of private lines over their construction cost (not including operating expenses) amounted to only 5.6 percent.[30] Disappointed shareholders demanded high dividends, at the expense of repairs and capital reserves. Some hastily established companies even ran out of funds in the phase of construction. Shibusawa was sometimes to be found playing the role of mediator between impatient shortsighted shareholders and managers.

Though opposed in principle to government enterprise, he soon saw that private initiative was functioning badly in rail transport. Before long he became one of the advocates of

[29] Ministry of Railways, ed., *Nihon tetsudō shi* [A History of Japanese Railways] (Tokyo, 1935), I, 92-93, 113.
[30] *Ibid.*, 972-73.

nationalization—the policy finally adopted in Japan at the turn of the century. His views on this issue are contained in a memorandum sent to both Houses of Parliament by the Chamber of Commerce, of which he was president. Its argument was as follows: Nationalization is needed because railways are vitally important for the military security of the nation as well as its economic development. In the hands of the government, railways ought to become an instrument for subsidizing industry by granting a discount on industrial freights. Private railway building is absorbing too much capital that is badly needed in other areas of the private industrial sector.

These reasons for nationalization of the private railways are interesting. Low profits are not touched upon at all because nationalization itself could hardly change the rate of return on invested capital. Instead, the reasons are tailor-made for government officials and also reflect much of the mentality of Meiji entrepreneurs. First comes the stress on military security, which was then linked with economic development, Shibusawa's own special concern. He did not advocate hasty nationalization without due planning; he cautioned repeatedly against measures that would upset monetary stability, for example a proposed issue of railway bonds in the amount of 291 million yen. He insisted also that purchases be made with full consideration of the rights of private property and that prices be set according to average profits over the preceding few years. Finally he worried lest government monopoly lower operating efficiency.[31] Despite these concerns, however, and his well-known predilection for private enterprise, Shibusawa stood with those who favored railway nationalization.

THE JOINT-STOCK FORM OF ENTERPRISE

In the private sector Shibusawa must have been deeply impressed by the joint-stock companies in Europe. He had seen large industrial ventures impossible to construct without

[31] *Denki shiryō*, IX, 567, 573; XIX, 664-84.

joining the capital resources of many individuals. The first thing he did on his return to Shizuoka in 1868, as noted earlier, was to establish a granary on a joint-stock basis, and in 1871 he published two booklets on company system. Often thereafter he deplored the lack of interest by merchants in the cooperative establishment of large enterprises. Some large houses, such as the Mitsui, operated on a partnership basis with all branch families pooling their resources, but cooperation outside the family on a joint-stock basis was unknown to Tokugawa merchants. When the company form of enterprise was propagated by the Meiji government, largely through the efforts of Shibusawa, merchants often did nothing more than change their store name from *ya* (store) to *kaisha* (company).

Samurai had less difficulty in accepting this new form of enterprise. They had no fixed business tradition, nor had they any choice but to pool their meager resources in the form of cash or commutation bonds. When the government undertook to provide loans for unemployed samurai to start new enterprises in its relief program of 1878-1888, the condition of such loans was that the enterprise be a joint-stock venture. By and large the samurai were the pioneers of joint-stock enterprise, while merchants continued with their family businesses and partnerships.

Reviewing the development of joint-stock companies in 1899, Shibusawa maintained that the astonishing progress of Japanese industry and banking was due largely to this new form of enterprise. When he had started it in 1873, he said, few people had any idea what was meant. Even as late as 1899, when he was writing, joint-stock companies showed many shortcomings. Too many managers behaved like owners in disregard of the rights of shareholders; they ignored regulations and sought quick profits rather than healthy long-range development.[32] Nevertheless, Shibusawa claimed that the reason for Japan's industrial progress in contrast to China's backwardness lay in her success in corporate activity. It was not that the Japanese were more profit-minded or clever than the Chinese; rather, in his opinion, it was because

[32] Shibusawa Eiichi, *op.cit.*, I, 331-33.

they had learned how to pool their resources and cooperate, while the Chinese remained economic individualists.[33] This interesting view deserves closer examination. Whatever the handicap of the Chinese, unquestionably the fast spread of joint-stock enterprise in Meiji Japan was one important factor of success in modern industry, banking, and commerce.

As the chief advocate of the joint-stock company Shibusawa was repeatedly at odds with lone-wolf entrepreneurs who scorned cooperation and preferred to build their own family empires. Notably, older men among the Meiji entrepreneurs who came from merchant background or had entered business from *han* trading monopolies or politics were prone to go it alone. The most outstanding example was, of course, Iwasaki Yatarō, the founder of Mitsubishi. His first company was a continuation of the former Tosa *han* shipping and trading company, whose authoritarian and monopoly character was thus inbred in Mitsubishi. Although Iwasaki drew other samurai associates into his growing empire of shipping and industry, he ruled alone; it remained essentially an Iwasaki family enterprise. The Mitsubishi house rule written by Yanosuke, Yatarō's younger brother who continued to control Mitsubishi after the latter's death in 1886, put this succinctly:[34] "Although this enterprise calls itself a company and has company structure, in reality it is entirely a family enterprise and differs therefore greatly from a company with joint-stock capital. Consequently everything that pertains to this company, praise and blame and all, are exclusively the responsibility of the president. All profits return to the person of the president and the losses, too, are borne by him alone."

THE CLASH OF POWER AND IDEALS

Shibusawa thus represented one principle and Iwasaki the exact opposite. A clash of the two giants of enterprise was unavoidable, and it came rather early. In 1877 Iwasaki was

[33] *Ibid.*, II, 89-91.
[34] Mitsubishi honsha hensan kyoku [The Compilation Section of Mitsubishi Main Office], ed., *Shashi* [Company History] (Tokyo, 1917), No. 14.

reaping tremendous profits from government contracts; he is said to have received about 27 million yen of subsidy in that year alone on account of his shipping services during the Satsuma Rebellion.[35] He now invited Shibusawa to a geisha party and suggested that they join hands to run the Japanese economy. Shibusawa refused, protesting the necessity of co-operation with many others. Iwasaki shrugged off Shibusawa's opposition with the remark that "if many captains run the ship, it will founder." The two top entrepreneurs parted as enemies.[36]

Not long after this incident occurred one of the most pub-licized and deadliest episodes of cut-throat competition in Japanese economic history. Principles, power, money, and politics were all involved. Shibusawa could not bear the monopoly practices of Mitsubishi and called on Masuda—of Mitsui Bussan (Mitsui Products)—to help him establish a rival shipping company. Mitsui had suffered the most under Mitsubishi's outrageous monopoly pricing and gladly cooper-ated in founding the new Tokyo *Fūhansen* (Sailing Ship) Company in 1880, with capital of 300,000 yen. When it proved to be no match for Mitsubishi, Shibusawa in cooperation with Inoue and Masuda worked out a merger with other smaller companies. In 1882 the *Kyōdō unyu* (United Transport) Company was born. Meanwhile in 1881 the protector of Mit-subishi in the government, Count Ōkuma, had been ousted, and the enemies of Iwasaki got the upper hand. To *Kyōdō unyu's* 3.4 million yen of private capital the government now added 2.6 million of its own, and supplied it with trained crews as well. In the fierce competition that ensued passenger fares between Kobe and Yokohama dropped in two years from 5.50 yen to 0.25 yen.[37]

Iwasaki meanwhile carried on a smear campaign against Shibusawa, hinting that he was working for foreign interests.

[35] Takahashi Kamekichi and Aoyama Jirō, *Nihon zaibatsu ron* [Treatise on the Japanese *Zaibatsu*] (Tokyo, 1938), pp. 52-53.

[36] Shibusawa Hideo, *op. cit.*, II, 59-62.

[37] Tsuchiya Takao, *Nihon no seishō* [Japan's Political Merchants] (Tokyo, 1956), p. 106.

Others called Iwasaki an enemy of the State, so that Iwasaki once threatened in his fury to gather his fleet in Shinagawa Bay and burn it. By 1885 both companies were completely exhausted. Shibusawa proposed that the government begin to regulate competition, to set prices and control operations. Iwasaki, however, had bought up secretly over half of the shares of *Kyōdō unyu*, and when he died in 1886 the two companies were finally amalgamated under his brother Yano-suke. Neither Shibusawa nor Masuda received initially any position of importance in this new Nihon Yūsen Kaisha (Japan Shipping) Company. However, Shibusawa could not rest satisfied with this dramatic defeat. Although one of the chief shareholders of the NYK—a joint-stock company after all—he helped Asano Sōichiro establish a new shipping company in 1887. When this one collapsed, he became the chairman of the founding committee of still another firm in 1896, assuming the position of controller and superintendent while Asano was president.[38]

The fight against Iwasaki was the most dramatic clash between Shibusawa and a leading entrepreneur. However, another occurred in 1888, this time with Mitsui; it was a minor one but very painful for Shibusawa. He had established Japan's first large paper factory in 1875, the Ōji Paper Company. It was his most cherished industrial enterprise because he had to see it through a host of difficulties ranging from difficult production techniques to insufficient market demand. Finally by about 1885 these twin problems had been overcome. Shibusawa had his talented nephew, Ōkawa, study paper production abroad, and under the latter's technical management the factory became highly efficient around 1890. Shibusawa now persuaded Mitsui to invest more capital in Ōji Paper, whereupon Nakamigawa Hikojirō, then chief manager of the Mitsui combine, used the majority of newly acquired shares to oust Ōkawa and with him also Shibusawa. Ōji was then incorporated into the Mitsui empire and staffed with Mitsui men. It was a personal tragedy that the great

[38] Tsuchiya Takao, *Shibusawa Eiichi den*, 224.

Shibusawa should have lost his finest enterprise to a Mitsui newcomer, Nakamigawa, who only a few years back had been teacher of English at Keiō College. Despite this misfortune at the hands of a ruthless rival, Shibusawa in 1891 had his mansion built close to the Ōji plant. Here the smoke from its chimneys was such a nuisance that it sometimes brought complaints from his family. His son recalls that his father would reply: "Why do you complain? The smoke comes from the chimneys of the factory which I built with the greatest of efforts. Therefore, no matter how it may smoke, bear with it patiently."[39]

Though Shibusawa was probably the most talented and farsighted of all Meiji entrepreneurs, he never accumulated wealth on the scale of Iwasaki, Ōkura, Yasuda, or even entrepreneurs of secondary rank. Why was this? Why did he not establish an industrial family empire of his own? Part of the answer lies, of course, in his attachment to the joint-stock principle, but this is certainly not the whole answer. On the contrary, he could have acquired tremendous riches and power through majority holdings in many companies; and even had he refrained from majority ownership and control he might have become tremendously wealthy. Another contrast lay in the fact that the success of the entrepreneurs depended substantially on their combine banks as strong and independent sources of capital. Shibusawa owned no bank. He was only president, not owner of the Dai Ichi. Still another factor was probably his generous support of hopeful new entrepreneurs such as the two mentioned above: Yamabe in cotton spinning and Ōkawa in paper manufacturing. A good number of others, too, gained success through his support.

In the final analysis, however, the answer lies probably in Shibusawa's personality and life goals. He was not a single-minded, profit-maximizing entrepreneur. He was successful as banker and as industrialist, but his ambition never centered on wealth. This may seem like a contradiction for a

[39] Shibusawa Hideo, *op. cit.*, II, 105-13.

man who pioneered in so many fields of enterprise, but his concern went far beyond money or even personal power. In some respects he acted like a statesman, in others like a philosopher, and in still others like an educator. People often get what they singlemindedly strive for, whether it be learning or power of money, when they are also gifted toward these ends. The *zaibatsu* (financial cliques) secured riches and power because they often cared for little else. Shibusawa won something more: his memory lives on in the minds of many Japanese as the great father of modern enterprise. He "ruled" the business community of Japan through the Meiji period as elder statesman, not primarily by money but by persuasion and example.

A New Business Mentality

Reading Shibusawa's speeches and writings one might think that here was a social philosopher or the preacher of a new business ethic, but hardly a banker occupied around the clock with practical business affairs. As a matter of fact, he had little time to prepare his many extemporaneous speeches, and they therefore lacked precise formulation. But his chief ideas were forcefully put and frequently repeated. He was clearly aware of the need to inculcate a new mode of thinking with respect to business activity. In his mind the success of Japan's industrialization depended primarily on the formation of an entrepreneurial elite who would not only master technical know-how but would also share his progressive outlook. Modern businessmen had to become different from the old merchants with respect to both personal attitudes and social status.

Shibusawa realized further that economic development required not merely capital and modern technology, but essentially the acceptance of a new business rationality. Non-economic values clinging to tradition and contemptuous of the merchant class had been characteristic of Tokugawa society. The Meiji Restoration had undermined a good deal of this status quo mentality, but did not itself raise the social status of business pursuits. In fact, as we have seen, there was some tendency to extol political leadership and government bureaucracy in a way that made the foot-dragging merchant appear all the more backward. As already observed, merchants in general showed a passive attitude toward change, because many had suffered grievous economic losses in the years before and after the Restoration. The British Consul commented in 1868 on the passivity of the Osaka merchants: "Few of the wealthier native merchants have turned their attention to foreign trade; indeed, this class of people in Osaka is the last to recognize any benefit in foreign relations."[40]

Shibusawa contributed much to raising the status of the business community by publicizing its social responsibilities and its contribution to the welfare of the nation. To be sure, he was an idealist, and many others followed different approaches, as illustrated in his clash with Iwasaki. Yet he was able to speak for the modern business group as a whole in many matters. He set up a public image that served businessmen both as an ideal to imitate and as a façade that protected them from the public eye. He addressed himself often to the general public, notably in his later years when he came to be admired by the whole nation, and to colleagues in the Bankers' Association and the Chamber of Commerce. Like a philosopher of old he also had his own school of disciples, to whom he tirelessly expounded his business philosophy. They listened avidly and propagated their master's words, preserving them for posterity. Probably he was well aware that only the younger men were capable of absorbing fully his own new modes of business rationality.

A small group of these young men closely identified with Shibusawa soon established an association, which by 1885 had 50 to 60 members. They met once a month and discussed practical and theoretical problems of business under his guidance. Beginning in 1886 they edited their own periodical, the *Ryūmon zasshi* (Ryūmon Journal) dedicated chiefly to the spread of Shibusawa's business ethic. With the rise of his public prestige, all sorts of people connected with his enter

[40] Commercial Reports of Her Majesty's Consuls in Japan, London, 1868, p. 22.

prises became members of this Ryūmonsha (literally: Dragon Gate Society). Consequently, stricter admission requirements were established, confining membership to men who really subscribed to his ethical principles.[41] The *Ryūmonsha* continued its activity under changed conditions after Shibusawa's death and still functions today. Its unaltered purpose is to educate Japan's youth to high business ethics through its periodical *Seien* (Shibusawa's pen name) and through sponsoring research on problems of business morals.

According to the Ryūmonsha of the 1890's a modern businessman in the Meiji period had to fulfill five requisites: education, honesty, virtue, personality, and a synthesis between the Analects of Confucius and the abacus. These five requisites mirror Shibusawa's thinking, and also indicate in their negative form the weaknesses of the traditional business class. The need for education and honesty are apparent enough, but the other three virtues too, he felt, called for radical changes in Tokugawa merchant mentality. Actually in his terminology these five requisites were embodied in *bushidō* (The Way of the Samurai). This meant that he proclaimed *bushidō* now as the "Way of the New Merchant."

GAKUMON (LEARNING)

Shibusawa's strong emphasis on *gakumon* as a requisite for a successful modern business career was echoed by almost all modern entrepreneurs of the Meiji era. The reason is obvious: modern technology and business methods were being imported to Japan through the medium of either travel in the West or study of the new learning in Japan. For the new entrepreneur apprentice-type training would no longer suffice; consequently any aversion to book learning could form a real barrier to modernization. This lack of *gakumon* prevented many merchants from grasping the new era and its modern technology. In establishing national banks, as already noted, the samurai had shown a greater willingness to learn from books and to follow written regulations. Shibusawa

[41] *Denki shiryō*, XXVI, 445.

scored the merchants for their contrary attitudes:[42] "They [the merchants] were only concerned to lower their posture and to show deep respect to me as a higher government official; they had neither *gakumon* nor self-respect, and gave not the slightest thought to things like regulations, new projects or the improvement of capital structure. I was so disgusted with this state of affairs that I decided to renounce my position and to strain all my energies toward the development of trade and industry." In his insistence on high standards of education for the modern businessman Shibusawa would at times go to extremes and deny support to entrepreneurs who were otherwise capable but failed to fulfill this one condition.[43]

To promote *gakumon* for business Shibusawa became active in education. He saved the first commercial high school in Tokyo from being closed down by the city on account of its yearly deficit of 10,000 yen and started a collection drive to provide the needed funds. Subsequently he remained an influential patron of this school, which developed eventually into Hitotsubashi University, today Japan's outstanding university in the field of economics. At the first graduation ceremony in 1889 he spoke before foreign diplomats and ministers of state. He explained that merchants used to neglect education and consequently had become unfit for modern business activity, but the graduates before him should not fall into the opposite error of neglecting business. Learning should serve

[42] Tsuchiya Takao, *Nihon shihonshugi no keiei, shiteki kenkyū* [Studies in the Managerial History of Japanese Capitalism] (Tokyo, 1954), p. 182.

[43] An example shall illustrate this point: A candy dealer and self-styled entrepreneur, Suzuki Tōsaburō had after many trials succeeded in producing refined sugar. He intended to start production and further improvements on a large scale and approached Shibusawa for a loan. One of Shibusawa's first questions was, according to Suzuki, from which school he had graduated. When Shibusawa heard that Suzuki had no higher education he flatly rejected any further consideration of a loan, maintaining that a man without school training could not succeed in modern enterprise. Shibusawa was wrong in this case because Suzuki became eventually one of the leading men in sugar refining. Suzuki Gorō, *Suzuki Tōsaburō den* [Biography of Suzuki Tōsaburō] (Tokyo, 1956), 104-07.

some practical purpose, or merchants would continue to say that "theoretical reasoning may be very lofty but it is of no use for daily life."[44]

Gakumon traditionally had been the class prerogative of the samurai and had tended toward non-practical, theoretical concerns. Confucian philosophers would hardly stoop to inquire about business principles at a time when trade was considered a parasitic occupation designed to exploit the ruling feudal class and the productive peasantry. The traditional bent of Japanese education was oriented more to the training of government officials than businessmen. This bias continued far into the Meiji period; as late as 1900 Shibusawa complained in a speech to principals of commercial high schools that students were taught lofty theories like how to rule a country, but after graduation they did not know the most elementary requirements of business life.[45] He suggested in 1905 at a meeting of the Tokyo Teachers Association that the total time of studies ought to be shortened. Japanese life expectancy, he said, might be 40 to 45 years, but before a graduate of a senior high school could engage in business activity he was 24 or 25 years old; if he graduated from a university, he was 27 or 28 years old. Yet junior high school education was generally not considered a sufficient education for business. As a remedy he suggested less memory work and more stimulation of the students' active thinking and self-education.[46]

It is open to question whether education through senior high school was needed, in fact, for many practical business activities. But almost uniformly the outstanding entrepreneurs insisted on high school education, and several of them built or supported commercial high schools. It is well known that the *zaibatsu,* notably Mitsubishi and Mitsui, preferred to recruit their managerial personnel from Keiō and Waseda Universities and that some of the chief managers and inno-

[44] *Denki shiryō*, XXVI, 579.
[45] *Ibid.*, 829-36.
[46] Shibusawa Eiichi, *Jitsugyō kōen*, II, 39-43.

vators in both these *zaibatsu* firms were either students of Fukuzawa at Keiō or had taught there.

Apart from this primary function as Shibusawa and other entrepreneurs saw it, education served another important purpose. *Gakumon* had always been the status symbol of the samurai class. When rich peasants and merchants bought books and had their sons study Confucian philosophy, they sought to emulate the samurai and share their prestige. When the new entrepreneurial elite kept stressing education to such an extent, this also underlined the dignity and raised the social standing of the new businessman. For samurai who had turned to business it likewise meant a preservation in part of their status dignity; they could escape the stigma of having become a member of the "ignorant" merchant class. Leading entrepreneurs publicized the new business class as educated in the best tradition of the samurai, thus strengthening the motivation of ambitious youth to enter business.

THE ANALECTS OF CONFUCIUS AND BUSHIDŌ

During the Tokugawa era *gakumon* was almost synonymous with Confucian studies. Even when Western studies became important toward the end of the Tokugawa, they were carried on by Confucian scholars more often than not. The strong Confucian emphasis on theory served a purpose similar to that of humanistic studies of Greek and Latin, and scholastic philosophy in the West. It was a formal training of the mind that shaped basic mentalities.[47] Sometimes Confucian studies of the Tokugawa period are now looked upon solely as obstacles to modernization and as the main support of the status quo. But Confucian philosophy also inculcated high respect for *gakumon* and, one step closer to the practical, molded *bushidō*. This code of samurai ethics comprised the best of Japanese tradition and retained its importance far into the modern era. In a sense *bushidō* consciousness inspired the feeling of

---

[47] I agree here very much with the views of Professor Horie Yasuzō, as expressed in his essay, above, and elaborated in greater detail in his: "Confucian Concept of State in Tokugawa Japan," *Kyoto University Economic Review* XXXII, 2 (Oct. 1962), 26-38.

ethical superiority over the "Western barbarians" who had to be "expelled" from the sacred soil of the gods. Viewed in this way, Confucianism served an important role in the making of modern Japan, providing in the *jōi* idea ("expel the barbarians") the dynamite that exploded the old system.

Shibusawa was anxious to project Confucian ethics into the Meiji era by making *bushidō* the model for modern businessmen. He explained that the essence of *bushidō* consisted of justice, integrity, chivalry, magnanimity, and courtesy. This was the *Yamato damashii* (the Japanese spirit) which had to be brought back to life in the modern business elite. Only with integrity, justice, and responsibility toward public interest could Japanese businessmen eventually gain the respect of the Western world and triumph in the competitive race. *Bushidō* which gave victory to samurai in the heroic ages should equally inspire modern merchants working for the welfare of their country.[48]

Such reasoning is nothing but the *jōi* idea turned from the sword to the abacus. Here we come to the common ground of many if not all of the important entrepreneurs of Meiji. Despite many diversities of approach, fields of endeavor, and private motivations they held one great ambition in common: they all wanted to "expel the barbarians" in the sense of competing successfully against them and making Japan an equal partner with the West rather than a trade colony. Other entrepreneurs seldom quoted the Analects of Confucius to buttress their *jōi* and *bushidō* in business. Many stressed newness at the expense of tradition; for example, Fukuzawa and the managers he trained in Keiō looked for inspiration to Western philosophers, notably British thinkers of the liberal persuasion, like Adam Smith and J. S. Mill. But Shibusawa said that he wanted "to build modern enterprises with the abacus and the Analects of Confucius." He was fully convinced that Western capitalism alone would not be

---

[48] Shishaku Shibusawa Eiichi, jutsu [Spoken by Viscount Shibusawa Eiichi], *Rongo to soroban* [The Analects and the Abacus] (Tokyo, 1928), 304.

beneficial for Japan without the ethical basis of Confucianism. He warned that virtue would decline if *gakumon* ever became completely dominated by profit considerations. The evils apparent in Western societies would then certainly spread to Japan.[49] Thus Shibusawa was opposed to both extremes: to making *gakumon* subservient to business, as well as separating it from practical life.

Yet the Analects that he loved to quote contain in themselves a strong tendency to scorn commerce. Here Shibusawa had to come up with some original interpretations. Replying once to the charge that the Analects hold virtue and business to be incompatible, he replied:[50] "Morality and economy primarily were meant to walk hand in hand. But as humanity has been prone to seek gain, often forgetting righteousness, the ancient sage, anxious to remedy this abuse, zealously advocated morality on the one hand, and on the other, warned people of profit unlawfully obtained. Later scholars misunderstood the true idea . . . they forgot that productiveness is a way of practicing virtue. . . . This misunderstanding tended to separate learning from practical living."

From the Confucian concept of the individual's obligation toward the community Shibusawa further argued that the businessman ought to subordinate his private interests, if need be, to the welfare of the nation. Just as the samurai class had benefited from feudal society by receiving feudal stipends, so its best traditions called upon the individual to serve society even at the sacrifice of his life. Similarly, insisted Shibusawa, a modern businessman is essentially a servant of his country, a promoter of economic—notably industrial—progress. Thus he would score monopolistic and self-seeking empire builders like Iwasaki along with old-type merchants. His ideal of a *jitsugyōka*, the word coined around 1890 for the modern-type businessman and best rendered as "entrepreneur," was that he work selflessly and with dedicated honesty to further economic progress. Not only did he talk this way, he acted accordingly. Once when a chemical fertilizer plant which he

[49] *Denki shiryō*, XXVI, 29.
[50] Obata, *op. cit.*, 266-67.

had established was in great difficulty with continuous losses, the shareholders proposed to scrap the plant. Shibusawa replied:[51] "This enterprise should not be looked upon from the angle of profit-making alone. If the majority of shareholders decide to scrap it, I shall for the good of the country take over the affairs of the company alone by buying up all the shares that are left."

In such dedication to the common good even when it cost him a profit, Shibusawa had few if any equals among the Meiji entrepreneurs. Many used similar phrases to camouflage their real intentions. But this in itself is a sign of deference to the *bushidō* ideal. Constant reference to the welfare of the nation when pursuing private purposes with the aid of government subsidies shows the formal adherence of businessmen to the Confucian ethical ideal as their myth of legitimacy. By "building modern enterprise on the abacus and the Analects," Shibusawa thus sought to combine the best of the West with the best of Japanese tradition: economic rationality in the service of the community. Speaking to bankers in 1892, he remarked that the reasons why some of the ills of Western capitalist society had not yet appeared in Japan were reverence for the Emperor and loyalty to old traditions. Confucian mentality was the bulwark; if modern education should eradicate the influence of Confucian tradition and ethic, those ills would appear in Japan too. The bankers, he concluded, had the moral responsibility to prevent such a development from taking place.[52]

Summary and Conclusions

This brief essay has focused upon one Meiji entrepreneur: his career, his approach to modern enterprise, and his business mentality. The great Shibusawa influence the new business community far beyond the range of his own ventures and even beyond his own lifetime. Unique as he was, we gain from his career valuable insights into the forces that shaped the new

[51] *Ibid.*, 126.
[52] *Denki shiryō*, VI, 323.

Meiji entrepreneurs as a class.[53] They may be summarized as follows:

1. The typhoon of socio-political changes that swept over Japan with the Restoration as its center was the single most decisive factor determining the entrepreneurial revolution. Only men decisively uprooted from past traditions and occupations, and driven by a good deal of nationalistic emotion, could fulfill the preconditions for successful entrepreneurship in the new era.

2. Nationalism in Meiji Japan, while an important positive force, constituted also an obstacle to the emergence of entrepreneurs, and thus to industrial development. For it tended to attract potential leaders primarily into the political and military arena. Consequently private business needed an upgrading of status through a new image of the patriotic businessman whose activity was no less of value to the nation than that of political leaders and generals. For this purpose education and the Confucian samurai ideals were stressed by Shibusawa, the outstanding Meiji entrepreneur, as distinctive marks of the new business class. The samurai image of service for the public welfare was thus transferred to the modern entrepreneur. This in turn made it easy for samurai to become "merchants of the new era" while it also attracted talented men from other walks of life into modern business.

3. The stress on samurai ideology does not thereby imply that samurai predominated among the leading entrepreneurs. On the other hand, the experience of the national banks suggests that samurai found it easier and preferable to enter new modern-type enterprises than traditional trades. The dispute among historians over the role of the samurai in the private sector has to be solved by distinguishing clearly between modern and traditional types of business, and again between banking, trade, and industry in the modern sector itself. While samurai dominated modern banking, they were less prominent in industry, and least active in foreign trade.

[53] For a more extended treatment the reader is referred to the author's *The Origins of Entrepreneurship in Meiji Japan*, Harvard East Asian Series No. 17, Cambridge, 1964.

4. Shibusawa's approach to modern industry was pre-eminently that of a general policy maker, strategist, and promoter rather than innovator in the sphere of production itself. Like many other Meiji entrepreneurs he hurried from one venture to another, driven on by the realization that there was so much to be done with so few to do it.

This scarcity of entrepreneurs was one of the critical bottle-necks of the Meiji economy. It was solved chiefly in two ways: entrepreneurs spread themselves over a vast number of ventures, leaving details as well as control to lesser men who eventually would acquire know-how and entrepreneurial stature; and economic power was concentrated in great clusters of operating firms, the *zaibatsu*. They were so regarded by the government and supported accordingly.

In the mid-twentieth century most people might prefer direct government planning and control over private empire-building by men like Iwasaki. If underdeveloped countries want to avoid this alternative, they must explore ways and means to enlarge the supply of dynamic entrepreneurs. To this end Shibusawa's efforts and methods may not have lost their significance even for nations which otherwise are a world away from the Meiji Japan of a century ago.

CHAPTER VI

Growth of Japanese Agriculture, 1875-1920

JAMES I. NAKAMURA

1. Introduction and Summary

MANY SCHOLARS and Japanese government officials have warned against the uncritical use of Japanese government statistics of the Meiji period. The most authoritative of such warnings appears in the second volume of the *Tōkei nenkan* (1886) [Statistical Yearbook][1] as follows: "It is extremely difficult to obtain reliable statistics because people, fearing increased taxes, conceal the truth and because [land and crop] measurement techniques have not been sufficiently improved."[2] Significantly, this caution appears in the introduction of the section on agricultural statistics.

All existing estimates[3] of income and rates of growth in

I am indebted to colleagues at the Estes Park conference for valuable suggestions and criticisms which have led to substantial revision of the conference draft of this paper. Particular mention is due to William W. Lockwood, Harry T. Oshima, Ohkawa Kazushi, and Alan H. Gleason. I am similarly indebted to Hemmi Kenzo and Ouchi Tsutomu of Tokyo University, Fujino Shozaburo and Umemura Mataji of Hitotsubashi University, Simon Kuznets of Harvard University, and Arthur R. Burns, Herschel Webb, William S. Vickery, and Carl S. Shoup of Columbia University. This paper is a condensation of a part of a Ph.D. dissertation completed at Columbia University.

[1] *Tōkei nenkan* is the abbreviated name of Japan's pre-World War II statistical yearbook, *Nihon teikoku tōkei nenkan,* published by the Cabinet Bureau of Statistics. All references to it will be in this shortened form.

[2] *Tōkei nenkan,* II, 41.

[3] Three well-known studies may be mentioned (cited in the order of publication) : Yamada Yūzō, *Nihon kokumin shotoku suikei shiryō* [Japanese national income estimates] (Tokyo, 1951) ; Bruce F. Johnston, "Agricultural Productivity and Economic Development in Japan," *Journal of Political Economy,* LIX, 6 (December 1951) ;

agriculture or in the primary sector are based on government statistics without correction for errors. Although considerable differences exist in the results obtained by different investigators owing to methodological and other variations, they are all characterized by a rapid rate of growth of agricultural production during the period from around 1880 to 1920. This growth can be regarded as a result of increases in two variables; the area planted to crops and the yield per unit area of various crops. Previous investigators have hesitated to correct the official statistics because they would then be forced to rely on "extremely vulnerable and risky statistical and analytical procedures."[4]

In this writer's view, new studies have been made and new data have become available in the past ten years or so that reduce the range of probable errors that may be expected from corrections of government statistics.[5] These studies by government (Ministry of Agriculture and Forestry) and private (both Japanese and Western) researchers deal with arable land measurement and yield estimation for both the Meiji and the Tokugawa periods. In particular, Tokugawa period studies have made imperative a reexamination of production data for the Meiji era. However, there is no denying that precise corrections are impossible because what is being attempted, in effect, is to measure the extent of tax evasion for which the responsible parties could scarcely have been expected to leave records.

The basic proposition examined in this paper is that land tax evasion practices caused a significant understatement of agricultural production during the Meiji period. The opportunity and incentive to landowners and villages to underreport production were provided in various land valuation legislation and statistical reporting practices of the Meiji era. The basic Meiji land tax legislation enacted in 1873 revised the land

---

Ohkawa Kazushi, *The Growth Rate of the Japanese Economy Since 1878* (Tokyo, 1957).

[4] The quoted passage is from a statement by Ohkawa Kazushi.

[5] The new studies and data will be cited in later sections where relevant.

levy system from a harvest tax to a land value tax. The land value was determined by capitalizing at the prevailing interest rate the gross value of production less certain costs.[6] The value of production, in turn, was determined by the area of cultivated land, the yield per unit area, and the price level. To minimize their tax burdens the landowners and villages would have had to understate production, or, more specifically, underreport the area of cultivated land, the yield per *tan*[7] or both.

The original land value assessment was made during the cadastral survey of the 1870's. The opportunity to understate the area of cultivated land and the yield per *tan* was provided by the 1873 land tax act, which made the landowner and the villages responsible for the original survey report for each lot on which the area, total harvest, and the land value were entered. The total harvest was the product of the land area and the estimated yield per *tan* of the lot. The land value was, of course, a function of the harvest. Although the land survey was conducted under the supervision of tax officials, and all entries were subject to review by officials responsible to the national tax office, it is clear that some amount of understatement was expected and *tolerated*. The best evidence of toleration is the law itself which permitted the acceptance of reported land values which, in the judgment of the officials, did not understate the market value by more than 10 percent.[8] How flexible was the judgment of the officials is a debatable point, but some flexibility was the rule as will be evident from a later discussion of specific tax evasion practices.

Two practices understated the arable land area—concealment (discussed in Section 2) and undermeasurement (Section 3). Concealment was eliminated during the land survey of the 1880's, but undermeasurement continues to exist even today. But once a given lot is assigned an area, it does not

[6] The national land tax, the local surtax, and the costs of seeds and fertilizers were deductible from the gross value of production.

[7] One *tan* is equal to 0.245 acres.

[8] *Dajōkan fukoku 272 bessatsu: chihōkan-kokoroesho* (July 28, 1873), Article 6.

change, and the opportunity for further undermeasurement exists only for lots that have been reclaimed or are being remeasured. However, the underreporting of yield (Section 4), the third tax evasion practice, can continue indefinitely for all arable land as long as the incentive remains and an annual estimation of production is made, as did happen.

The incentive to underreport yield continued to exist because the land valuations were not fixed once and for all by the land tax act of 1873. In 1874 an amendment to the 1873 act provided for a quinquennial revaluation of land beginning in 1880 to conform with changing market values.[9] In fact, periodic revaluations were never carried out, and the amendment was scrapped in 1884 because it became clear that such revaluations would be costly, time-consuming, and would provoke political friction. However, land revaluations under special legislation did occur. Whether the yield actually helped determine the new values is a moot point, but, as long as the possibility existed that it might, the landowners and villages did have incentive to underreport yield.

In revising production statistics, ideally the statistics of area planted and yield per unit area—neither of them complete—should be corrected where required for all agricultural crops. This is quite impossible, however. Official data for all crops are not available even today, and in early Meiji production data were collected only for the most important crops. Even when official data are available, the bases on which a revision can be made are either nonexistent or not sufficiently reliable for individual crops, with the exception of paddy rice. For these reasons much of the revision undertaken here is based on assumptions guided by judgment built on historical evidence and understanding of agricultural techniques and practices.

The model for the estimation of production is a simple one. (1) The value of agricultural production (V) is taken to be the sum of the values of paddy rice production (V_1) and of all other agricultural production (V_2). (2) V_1 is equal to the

[9] *Dajōkan fukoku* 53 (May 12, 1874).

product of the output of rice (O_1) and the price of rice (P_1). Analogously, $V_2 = kO_2P_2$, where k is a constant coefficient, O_2 is a production index, and P_2 is a price index. (3) O_1 is equal to the product of the area planted to rice (A_1) and the yield per unit area of rice (H_1). Analogously, $O_2 = A_2H_2$ where A_2 is the area of fields planted to dryland crops and H_2 is a yield index. Therefore the value of agricultural production in time period t is $V_t = (P_1H_1A_1)_t + k(P_2H_2A_2)_t$. The overriding reason for dividing agricultural production into the two categories of paddy rice production and all other production is that it made possible the estimation of area planted and yield per *tan*.

Since the objective was to obtain the value of production in constant yen, the actual procedure involved the determination of three basic sets of figures. They were (1) the construction of two quinquennial indices of area planted; (2) the construction of two quinquennial indices of yield per unit area; and (3) the estimation of base year (1913-1917) values of paddy rice production and of other agricultural production. Given the above sets of figures the value of agricultural production in constant yen and the growth rate of agricultural production can be estimated.

The value that is obtained for a particular year is not the actual value of production in constant yen because the particular level of that value is determined by such factors as weather, improvements in technology, and the amount of fertilizers used—factors for which allowances cannot be made with the techniques of estimation used here. The value that is obtained here will be called the corrected value. It assumes normal weather conditions and a stable improvement or increase in yield-increasing factors other than weather. Deviations of normal value from the actual value (in constant yen), if the latter were known, would largely be a result of weather conditions. The corrected value, therefore, is less useful in obtaining precise changes in levels of agricultural production than it is in determining the rates of growth, because like the latter it reflects trends, not short-term fluctuations. Nevertheless, it is believed that the corrected value (despite a probable small understatement in 1913-1917 period) is a better approximation of the actual constant yen value of agricultural production than existing estimates.[10] The corrected value estimates are given in Section 5. No further attention will be given to them in this section, since our main concern is the determination of the rate of growth of agricultural production.

The growth rate in Japanese agriculture is estimated here to range from 0.8 to 1.2 percent with an average of 1.0 percent over the period 1873-1877 to 1918-1922.[11] The selection of a single value for the growth rate is precluded by the uncertainties that attend the estimation of the changes in arable land area and yield per unit area. The particular points of uncertainty are discussed in later sections. An attempt was made to confine the range within reasonable limits. The conclusions and implications that are drawn from the analysis follow.

1. The corrected estimates of agricultural production differ radically from previous estimates. We select for comparison the estimates made by Bruce F. Johnston, who pioneered in Western studies about the relationship between agriculture and economic development in Japan, and by Ohkawa Kazushi and associates in *The Growth Rate of the Japanese Economy Since 1878* (to be called the Ohkawa estimates henceforth).

The Johnston estimates show a 77 percent increase in agricultural production in a thirty-year period as follows:[12]

[10] Extreme caution must be exercised in the use of the corrected value. In addition to the qualifications noted in the text, another characteristic of the normal value can be indicated. Corrected value estimates for the middle one-half of the period from 1873 to 1922 are likely to be significantly understated because it is assumed that yield per unit area grew at a constant rate despite indications to the contrary (Section 4), and because weather conditions also appeared to depress yields around the turn of the century.

[11] In the first draft of this paper discussed at the Estes Park Conference, the growth rate of agricultural production was estimated to be 0.8%. The new estimates are derived from a modification of yield estimates based on criticisms by conference colleagues. I am particularly indebted to Professors Harry Oshima, Ohkawa Kazushi, and Alan Gleason in respect to this point.

[12] Computed from Johnston, "Agricultural Productivity and Eco-

Period	Index	Period	Index
1881-1890	100	1901-1910	146
1891-1900	127	1911-1920	177

The annual growth rate is 1.9 percent. This is about twice the median growth rate of the corrected values given here.

Even more startling is the contrast with the Ohkawa values which increased 136 percent in a thirty-five-year period as follows:[13]

Period	Value in 1913-1917 prices	Index
1878-1882	766 million yen	100
1883-1887	891 " "	116
1888-1892	1075 " "	140
1893-1897	1123 " "	147
1898-1902	1309 " "	171
1903-1907	1433 " "	187
1908-1912	1616 " "	211
1913-1917	1806 " "	236

This increase is equivalent to an annual growth rate of 2.4 percent which is double the maximum growth rate of the corrected values presented here.

Figure 1 compares the changes in the Johnston, Ohkawa, and corrected values of agricultural production. The Johnston

---

nomic Development in Japan," p. 499. The Johnston production index is a quantity index based on six agricultural food crops. It, therefore, suffers from incompleteness but avoids the pricing problem, a sticky one during the Meiji period.

[13] Computed from Ohkawa, 58, 126-27. The reader should understand that Professors Ohkawa and Henry Rosovsky, whose essay on "A Century of Japanese Economic Growth," appears in this volume, do not accept the corrected values and growth rates presented here for the early decades. They concede (pp. 68-69, fn. 11) that the statistics on which their own estimates are based may understate farm output for the early Meiji years, thus exaggerating subsequent rates of growth in some degree. But they are unable to accept either the revised estimates offered here or the reasoning on which they are built, and they regard the issues as too technical to settle here.

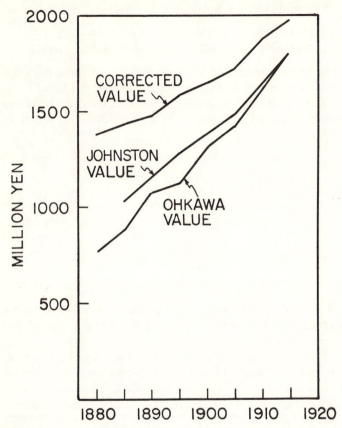

FIGURE 1

Comparison of Ohkawa, Johnston, and Corrected Values of Agricultural Production in Japan (at 1913-1917 Prices).

SOURCES:

1. Corrected value from Table 14, Column (3).
2. Ohkawa value from page 6.
3. Johnston value was converted from the production index by using the 1913-17 Ohkawa value as the Johnston 1915 value. Johnston production index taken from page 6.

production index was converted into value terms by assuming that the 1913-1917 value was identical with that of the Ohkawa estimates. The corrected value assumes median paddy rice yields of 1.6 and 1.95 *koku* (4.96 bushels) per *tan* in 1873-1877 and 1918-1922, respectively. A remarkable difference in the values of production at the beginning of the period is evident in the chart. As corrected here the value in 1878-1882 is actually 76 percent higher than the Ohkawa value of the same period.

2. The significance of the downward revision of the agricultural growth rate for the economy as a whole is that it will downgrade the growth rate of the latter also. Since present income estimates of the secondary and tertiary sectors are probably understated also in the Meiji period (see Oshima's remarks, below, p. 355), it is difficult to say how much downward revision is needed for the economy as a whole. But because early in the Meiji period the agricultural sector accounted for more than 50 percent of total production, a very substantial reduction will be required if our estimates are accepted. The downward revision will be more pronounced in the period prior to 1900 because agricultural production appears to have grown more rapidly after 1900 than before it.[14] In this event Japan's growth rate will be at a higher level in the period after 1900 than before it.[15] These figures indicate that the so-called early spurt of the Japanese economy was

[14] The growth rate of agricultural production from 1873-77 to 1898-1902 according to our estimates is 0.8, and that for 1898-1902 to 1918-22 is 1.2% when the average rate for the two periods is 1.0%. (Computed from Table 15.) However, it is probable that the growth rate of yield per unit area which is assumed to be constant was much lower in the period before 1900, therefore making the growth rate of agricultural production lower before 1900 than indicated by the above figure.

[15] The growth rate of the Japanese economy computed from a previous study is 4.9% in the 20-year period from 1878-82 to 1898-1902, and 3.3% in the 20-year period from 1898-1902 to 1918-22. (Ohkawa, p. 17.) The growth rates of gross agricultural production in the same two periods were 2.7% and 1.9% respectively as computed from data in the same study.

not as remarkable as previously believed. Indeed they create a doubt that such a spurt took place at all.

3. Historically, peasant economies have been observed to respond very slowly to stimuli. Japanese agriculture before World War I was typically that of a peasant economy producing under the condition of a limited land supply. We have just noted that the growth rates of agricultural production derived from previous estimates are remarkably high. In the pre-World War I period, according to one study, the growth rate of Japanese agricultural net product per worker ranked among the highest of any nation,[16] including nations where farming was highly commercialized and took place under virtually unlimited land supply conditions. This seeming paradox, of a peasant agriculture under limited land supply conditions growing at a faster or as fast a rate as commercial agriculture producing under unlimited land supply conditions, is resolved by the finding that Japanese agriculture grew at a slower rate than previously believed.

4. The growth rates of agricultural production of 0.8 to 1.2 percent are more consistent with the Japanese population growth rate than previous estimates. The Japanese population rose from 35.6 million in 1875 to 56.0 million in 1920, an annual growth rate of 1.0 percent, which is equal to the average growth rate of our agricultural production estimates. This does not mean that the Japanese ate no more in 1918-1922 than in 1873-1877. In fact, if the growth rate of agricultural production was 1.0 percent, the per capita food consumption could have risen substantially, owing to imports and better distribution. For example, net rice imports in 1915-1925 were more than 10 percent of domestic production, and very substantial amounts of other food products were imported, including wheat, soy beans, sugar, and animal products. The fact that the estimated growth rates of agricultural production were roughly equivalent to the rate of population growth explains why Japan became a substantial

[16] Ohkawa Kazushi and Henry Rosovsky, "The Role of Agriculture in Modern Japanese Economic Development," *Economic Development and Cultural Change*, IX, 1, Part 2 (October 1960), 44, 65-66.

net food importer by 1915-1925, after having been a net food exporter until around 1895. If agricultural production grew at rates of 1.9 and 2.4 percent per annum, Japan probably would have increased its food exports rather than become a net importer.

5. In a nation where long-term comparative advantage does not lie in food production, food production cannot normally be expected to grow at a very much faster rate than the population. Therefore, the conclusion that agricultural production (over 80 percent devoted to food production) grew at about the same rate as the population is not surprising. What is noteworthy is that the agricultural growth rate from the 1870's to the 1920's is about ten times the rate of about 0.1 percent that prevailed during the Tokugawa period (Tables 10 and 11). This is evidence that Japan's farmers adapted themselves with remarkable rapidity to new techniques, new crops, and new market conditions after having emerged so recently from feudal social and economic relations. The fact that this adaptation occurred with very little government financial aid[17] and under a condition of limited land supply makes it all the more notable.

6. The "unlimited supply" of labor made available to the non-agricultural sector was not the result of an extraordinarily rapid growth of agricultural production as previous investigators have held. The principal reason was probably a better allocation of labor. During the Tokugawa period more labor was tied to agriculture in almost all *han* (feudal domains) by institutional and other restraints than would have been the case in their absence. The result was more than adequate supply of food in normal crop years and the insurance of a tolerable supply even in poor years, short of a serious crop failure. The *han* maintained this policy to reduce the incidence of famines and social disorders and as a defense measure. Usually crop failures affected a section of the nation, but due to poor transportation facilities reliance on supply in other sections of the nation was extremely costly.

When the restraints on labor mobility were lifted after the

[17] See Harry Oshima's analysis below, Ch. VIII.

Meiji Restoration, a reallocation of labor occurred. But such movements are expensive, as they require changes in the capital structure of the economy. Therefore an overnight shift of labor is not possible, and a more efficient allocation could only be achieved over a period of time. Nevertheless it is apparent that the movement occurred with sufficient speed so that the agricultural sector was not obliged to absorb additional labor, and an "unlimited supply" of labor was made available to the other sectors.

7. No doubt the rapidity of Japan's industrialization required an early, huge, and continuing accumulation of capital, particularly in view of the very rapid increase of labor force in the non-agricultural sectors. Because the agricultural sector produced a very high proportion of income in the early stage of Japan's development, a large part of savings necessarily had to come from this sector. A very attractive proposition that has won wide acceptance is that a high rate of increase of agricultural production accounted for a substantial part of Meiji savings.[18] It follows from the radical downgrading of the growth rate in this paper that increasing agricultural productivity was less important as a source of savings than claimed above. However, despite the qualification, it was an important source.

8. If agriculture in early Meiji had more than enough resources to supply the nation's need for agricultural products, investment in agriculture could not have been sufficiently attractive to induce most agricultural savings to remain in it. The outflow of savings from agriculture in this early period therefore was as much a result of overallocation of resources to agriculture in the late Tokugawa period as was the outflow of labor.

9. The discussion in this paper suggests a theory of savings for which empirical verification has been attempted elsewhere.[19] The Meiji reform caused a revolutionary transfer of income from the Tokugawa ruling class to the landowners, a

---

[18] Johnston, "Agricultural Productivity and Economic Development in Japan," pp. 511-12.

[19] James I. Nakamura, "The Place of Agricultural Production in the

transfer made possible because the agricultural sector was producing a substantial surplus above subsistence. This was a transfer from a class with a high marginal propensity to consume to one with a lower propensity; that is from the ruling class to the landowners and to the new investment-minded government. As a consequence, in the first decade or so of the Meiji period the nation's average propensity to save jumped to a new level which, by itself, could have been adequate to generate sustained growth. The argument that savings increased contradicts the previous belief that Japan's economic development occurred with relatively little capital. Evidence indicates that the landowners not only saved but were directly involved in a great deal of the investment that occurred in early Meiji years. Therefore it is further argued that private investment played a substantially greater role in Japan's economic development than existing quantitative estimates indicate.[20]

10. Although Japan was clearly a traditional agriculture-based economy, she did not behave accordingly in one respect. When the production capacity of her agriculture and economy rose during the Tokugawa period, her population did not increase, but remained constant owing to voluntary population control. It is probable that per capita income would not have increased substantially were it not for the limitation of population, because a classic Malthusian response could otherwise have been expected. Since the level of per capita income was unquestionably an important factor in Japan's modern growth, voluntary population control of the Tokugawa period was an important precondition of that growth.

2. Concealment of Arable Land

We now begin an examination of the various practices that led to the understatement of agricultural production, and we

Economic Development of Japan" (unpublished Ph.D. dissertation, Department of Economics, Columbia University, 1964), Chapter 8.

[20] This supports one of the main themes in William W. Lockwood's *The Economic Development of Japan* (Princeton, 1954) that the investment of small and medium enterprisers played a major role in Japan's growth.

will construct also indices of area planted and yield per unit area that are intended to correct the understatement. This section treats concealment, Section 3 will deal with undermeasurement, and Section 4 with underreporting of yield per *tan*. In the final section we will estimate the base-year values of paddy rice production and of all other agricultural production, and also obtain our estimates of agricultural production from 1873-1877 to 1918-1922 and the growth rate over the period.

In this section more specifically, we will construct indices of the area planted to paddy rice and of the area planted to dryland crops that correct the understatement introduced by concealment.[21] In the process we will attempt to demonstrate that the arable land area was understated owing to concealment before the land survey of the 1880's, and that as a consequence the areas planted to crops were also understated.

Concealment of arable land will be defined as the practice of hiding such land from official notice by not registering it. Concealment was attractive to landowners because it reduced the tax burden. This practice is important for the purposes of this paper because production from concealed land was frequently omitted from government statistics.

In 1872, before the Meiji cadastral survey began, the area of arable land as reported by the various domains was 3,234,-000 *chō*.[22] This area cannot be compared with any subsequent area data because it was based on feudal domain measures, which were not always uniform. The post-survey area—which is a part of a continuous series and will be referred to hence-

---

[21] Some criticisms have been voiced about my area-planted indices. The indices necessarily had to be on the basis of assumptions which appear reasonably realistic to me but are subject to attack on perhaps equally reasonable basis. However, I am fairly confident that the indices will not change significantly, given any other set of reasonable assumptions. Moreover, my assumptions about the area planted to crops create biases that tend to increase the growth rate of agriculture production.

[22] Ministry of Finance, *Meiji zenki zaisei keizai shiryō shūsei* [Collection of Early Meiji Financial and Economic Materials] (21 vols.; Tokyo, 1932-36), VII, 346. Henceforth to be cited as MZZKSS. One *chō* is equal to 2.45 acres.

forth as the Taxed Arable Land Area[23]—was 4,493,000 *chō*,[24] an increase of 1,259,000 *chō*. This increase can be attributed to reductions in concealment and undermeasurement. Nevertheless, it was evident that in some areas the landowners had followed the practice of Tokugawa peasants and underreported their arable land holdings. A land survey[25] was undertaken in the years 1885 to 1889 for the primary purpose of eliminating concealment of arable land. The government apparently was less concerned with undermeasurement and made little or no effort to correct it during this survey. Between 1885 and 1889 the Taxed Arable Land Area changed from 4,527,000 *chō* to 5,027,000,[26] an increase of 500,000. Almost all of the change occurred between 1886 and 1888; the Taxed Paddy Field Area rising by 123,000 *chō*, and Taxed Upland Field Area by 379,000. These are relative increases of 4.7 and 20.1 percent, respectively.

There does not appear to be even a remote possibility that real increases in arable land area could have accounted for a substantial part of this change. Professor Nasu Shiroshi notes two estimates of additions to arable land area by reclamation from 1880 to 1885. One showed an annual increase of 9,000 *chō*, the other, said to be the more reliable of the two, showed an annual increase of 2,500 *chō*.[27] Even if the larger estimate is accepted, no more than about 20,000 *chō* of land could have been expected to be added by reclamation in any two-year period.

An analysis of prefectural data shows that the increases tended to be concentrated in certain prefectures and in a

[23] This was a series maintained by the Ministry of Finance for tax purposes. It is the sum of the Taxed Paddy Field and Taxed Upland Field Areas (Minyū yūsochi ta oyobi hata).

[24] Computed from MZZKSS, VII, 81.

[25] *Ibid.*, 400-06.

[26] The arable land area figures used in this paragraph from 1880 on are from MAF, Agr. and For. Eco. Bur., Stat. Sec., *Nōrinshō ruinen tōkeihyō 1868-1953* [Annual Statistics of the Ministry of Agriculture and Forestry] (Tokyo, 1955), p. 10. This reference will be cited as NRT henceforth.

[27] Nasu Shiroshi, *Aspects of Japanese Agriculture* (New York, 1941), pp. 72-73.

single year. In Yamaguchi the reported paddy field area increased 35 percent in a single year from 1886 to 1887. In Kyoto a 16 percent increase occurred between 1885 and 1886. The increases in Kagoshima, Kumamoto, and Okayama of 10, 11, and 8 percent, respectively, occurred between 1887 and 1888.[28] Five-year increases from 1885 to 1890 for each of the above are 35, 18, 12, 12, and 11 percent, respectively, as shown in Table 1. The five-year increase from 1885 to 1890 in the Taxed Paddy Field Area of the ten prefectures with the highest percentage increases is 74,000 *chō*, which is 66 percent of the 112,000 *chō* increase for the nation. These prefectures averaged a 12.2 percent increase in the five-year period in contrast to a 1.8 percent increase for the rest of the nation. A similar pattern of increases being concentrated in certain prefectures and in a single year exists for Taxed Upland Fields, except that the percentage increases are greater.

It is clear that these reported increases of both types of land occurred in the year, or years, when land survey results were reported to the national government. Real increases of arable land of the pattern described above are most improbable. Furthermore, a rapid increase in agricultural labor force or in agricultural investment was not discernible in any prefecture in the year when its taxed area increase occurred. There is hardly any question that almost all of the reported increase in the period under discussion results from the uncovering of concealed arable land. It will be so assumed henceforth.

Nominal changes in arable land area need not necessarily cause changes in production statistics, or, more specifically, in the reported area planted to crops. Because we know that the reported increase in the Taxed Arable Land Area is almost entirely fictitious, it can be assumed that the actual area planted to crops remained almost unchanged. But if arable land was concealed before the land survey as a device to

[28] The percentage changes are computed from MAF, Agr. and For. Eco. Bur., Stat. Sec., *Nōsakumotsu ruinen tōkeihyō: ine, 1881-1956* [Agricultural Crop Statistics: Rice, 1881-1956] (Tokyo, 1957). To be cited as NRTHI henceforth.

minimize taxes, it is virtually certain that the area of crops planted on concealed land was not reported so that the concealment could be successful. When the concealment was eliminated in the 1880's, the need to prevent the discovery of concealment evaporated. Therefore, when the Taxed Arable Land Area increased as a result of the elimination of concealment, the reported area planted to crops can be expected to have also increased. We now turn to statistical evidence to determine whether the two areas did increase as expected.

TABLE 1

COMPARISON OF PERCENTAGE CHANGES IN TAXED PADDY FIELD AREA AND REPORTED AREA PLANTED TO PADDY RICE IN SELECTED PREFECTURES, 1885-1890

efecture	Taxed Paddy Field Area 1885 (1000 chō)	Area 1890 (1000 chō)	% Change	Paddy Rice Area 1885 (1000 chō)	Area 1890 (1000 chō)	% Change
	(1)	(2)	(3)	(4)	(5)	(6)
maguchi	58.6	79.0	34.8	51.7	78.1	50.9
oto	40.3	47.6	18.1	38.6	45.7	18.3
goshima	48.7	54.6	12.1	47.8	51.4	7.6
mamoto	58.1	65.0	11.9	60.3	65.8	9.1
ayama	75.0	83.0	10.7	74.3	83.5	12.3
kuoka	96.9	106.5	9.9	96.1	107.5	11.9
yazaki	35.6	38.8	9.0	35.1	38.8	10.6
a	46.2	49.7	7.6	45.1	48.6	7.6
gano	65.5	70.0	6.9	61.9	67.6	9.2
ragi	81.2	86.0	5.9	78.9	83.6	6.0
Prefectures ion less	606.1	680.2	12.2	589.8	670.6	13.7
Hokkaidō ion less	2641	2752	4.2	2572	2711	5.4
o Prefectures nd Hokkaidō	2035	2072	1.8	1982	2040	2.9

 source: Columns (1), (2), (3), and (4) computed from MAF, Agr. and For. . Bur., Stat. Sec., *Nōsakumotsu ruinen tōkeihyō: ine, 1881-1956* [Agricultural p Statistics: Rice, 1881-1956] (Tokyo, 1957).

CORRECTION OF AREA PLANTED TO PADDY RICE

An examination of the reported area planted to paddy rice reveals a pattern of increase from 1885 to 1890 similar to that for Taxed Paddy Field Area, with a slight lag as a rule. Excluding Hokkaidō because its area planted to crops grew much more rapidly than the rest of the nation, the area indices for the two classes of land from 1885 to 1890, with 1885 as the base year, are shown in Table 2. The greater increase in the reported area planted to paddy rice can be attributed to the narrowing of the gap between the areas of the two classes of land by 27,000 *chō* in the five-year period.

TABLE 2

COMPARISON OF CHANGES IN TAXED PADDY FIELD AND REPORTED AREA PLANTED TO PADDY RICE, 1885-1890

Year	Taxed Paddy Field Area (1000 chō)	Index	Paddy Rice Area (1000 chō)	Index
1885	2640	100.0	2572	100.0
1886	2652	100.5	2586	100.5
1887	2697	102.2	2606	101.3
1888	2776	105.2	2657	103.3
1889	2751	104.2	2693	104.7
1890	2752	104.2	2711	105.4

SOURCE: Statistical Appendix: Tables 1A, 2A.

Even more revealing is a study of prefectural statistics. We take the ten prefectures with the highest percentage changes in Taxed Paddy Field Area and compute for each the percentage changes in the reported area planted to paddy rice in the five-year period from 1885 to 1890. The results are shown in Column (6) of Table 1. The percentage changes in the two classes of land area for each of the ten are closely related. If the ten prefectures are taken as a group to cancel out much of the random fluctuations that smaller universes are subject to, we find that the Taxed Paddy Field Area increased by 12.2 percent and the reported area planted to paddy rice by 13.7 percent. For the rest of the prefectures, excluding Hokkaidō, the increases were 1.8 and 2.9 percent. For the nation as a whole, the changes were, respectively, 4.2 and 5.4 percent. It is concluded that the changes in the two areas are closely related, that the changes in the reported area planted to paddy rice were almost entirely fictitious, and that the actual area planted to paddy rice changed very little in the five-year period from 1885 to 1890.

The estimation of the actual area planted to paddy rice requires that the reported area planted to paddy rice be corrected for the years before the completion of the land survey of the 1880's. Although the survey was completed in 1888, and the Taxed Arable Land Area fully reflects the elimination of concealment in its 1888 area, the reported area planted to paddy rice apparently does not adjust fully until 1890. Therefore, the area planted to paddy rice will be revised for years 1878 through 1889. The revised areas are obtained by extrapolating the reported area planted to paddy rice, including Hokkaidō, by use of a straight line least-squares trend line based on 1890-1910 data. It is believed that the 21-year period is sufficiently long to establish a trend and short enough so that the trend would not be seriously effected by changes in supply and demand conditions.[29] The corrected five-year averages of areas planted to paddy rice during nine periods for the nation, for Hokkaidō, and for the nation less Hokkaidō, are shown in Table 3. A national area index with 1873-1877 as the base year is also shown in the table.

In addition to the principal crop, rice, a second crop is grown on many paddy fields. Between 1903 (when surveying of multiple cropping commenced) and 1922, the proportion of paddy fields grown to second crops fluctuated between 29 and 31 percent with no clear trend.[30] If landowners deemed

[29] From around 1910 the government land improvement policy began seriously to affect the paddy field area.

[30] Computed from Kayō Nobufumi (ed.), *Nihon nōgyō kiso tōkei* [Basic Statistics of Japanese Agriculture] (Tokyo, 1958), p. 72. The proportion does not include green manure crops which, if included, would bring the proportion to 35-40%. (*Ibid.*)

TABLE 3

Corrected Paddy Rice Area and Index, Five-Year Averages, 1878-1922

Period	National Area less Hokkaidō (1000 chō)	Index 1873-77 = 100	Hokkaidō Area (1000 chō)	National Area (1000 chō)	Index 1873-77 = 100
	(1)	(2)	(3)	(4)	(5)
1873-1877	2603	100.0	0	2603	100.0
1878-1882	2632	101.1	0	2632	101.1
1883-1887	2662	102.3	1	2663	102.3
1888-1892	2699	103.7	2	2701	103.8
1893-1897	2712	104.2	4	2716	104.3
1898-1902	2745	105.5	11	2756	105.9
1903-1907	2779	106.8	19	2798	107.5
1908-1912	2820	108.3	36	2856	109.7
1913-1917	2867	110.1	54	2921	112.2
1918-1922	2890	111.1	83	2973	114.2

Source: Column (1): The annual data for the 5-year averages were obtained from two sources. The 1873-1889 areas were computed from the following estimating equation: $Yc = 2750 + 5.878X$ with 1900 as the origin and X unit equalling one year. The equation is a least-squares trend line based on 1890-1910 data. The 1890-1922 areas are from Statistical Appendix: Table 3.

Column (3): The annual data on which the 5-year averages are based are from Statistical Appendix: Table 3.

it desirable to adjust the reported area planted to paddy rice to the Taxed Paddy Field Area, they probably tended to adjust the area planted to the second crops for the same reason. It will be assumed that 30 percent of the area of paddy fields was grown to second crops prior to 1903.

CORRECTION OF AREA PLANTED TO DRYLAND CROPS

The construction of a corrected index of area planted to all other crops (that is, excepting rice) obviously poses a greater problem than that for the reported area planted to paddy rice. The area planted to all other crops includes all upland field areas including Hokkaidō and that part of paddy fields on which two crops are grown.[31] It has already been assumed that double cropping occurred on 30 percent of the corrected paddy field area.

With respect to upland fields we must determine whether the increase in registered upland field area affected the reported production of dryland crops. The problems in doing so are different and more difficult to resolve than those associated with paddy fields. Almost all paddy fields were and are put into rice, and because of the established boundaries of paddy fields the problem of determining the acreage planted to each crop was probably not a difficult one for village statistical reporters. But on upland fields, serious estimation problems arise due to six circumstances that differentiate the planting pattern of these fields from that on paddy fields. On upland fields (1) many more varieties of crops were grown; (2) crops were more readily changed from year to year; (3) a field might be planted to more than one crop at the same time; (4) multiple cropping was more extensive and intensive; (5) new crops were being introduced; all upland field crops were not surveyed and the number of crops surveyed tended to be fewer in the earlier years; and (6) some land that was used in shifting agriculture was classified as upland fields. Because the cycle of use as cultivated land could vary from a few years to many years for these fields and because they were typically located in remote mountain districts, tabulation of crops grown on these fields probably occurred erratically, if at all.

Given the conditions under which crops were raised on upland fields, accurate reporting would require the measurement of the area planted to each crop. Such an undertaking would require the services of many men and would also arouse the suspicion of the farmers. The villages lacked the resources for the former and certainly did not wish to evoke the latter; moreover, they were not fully aware of the importance of accurate statistical reporting. For these reasons the estimations of the area planted to various crops on upland fields

[31] We can ignore double cropping of paddy rice in Kōchi Prefecture, which was an insignificant part of the total double cropped area.

were probably no more than informed guesses at best. The Ministry of Agriculture and Forestry studies that were made between 1948 and 1952[32] reveal a high probability of error in reporting the area planted to crops. The ratio of reported area to that actually planted for the three principal grains other than rice (wheat, barley, and naked barley) was 78 percent; for soy beans, 72; for rapeseed, 56; and for peanuts, 53. As was to be expected, the rate was highest for rice, at 93 percent, because almost all paddy fields were grown to rice and the area of individual paddy fields was known except for the average undermeasurement of about 7 percent.

There are 15 dryland crops for which data are available for 1884, 1892, 1902, and 1912. As generally unreliable as the area planted data may be, the increases shown by these crops between 1884 and 1892 for the nation, less Hokkaidō, appear to validate the contention that the reported planted area of upland fields tended to adjust to the Taxed Upland Field Area. The 15 crops can be divided into winter and summer crops.[33] The percentage changes between the eight-year period from 1884 to 1892 and in two following ten-year periods for the two classes of crops can be tabulated as shown in Table 4. The 15-percent increase for summer crops, the 16-percent increase for winter crops, and the total increase of 15 percent are sufficiently differentiated from subsequent percentage changes to warrant the conclusion that they were largely influenced by the increase in Taxed Upland Field Area. A distinction is made between winter and summer crops because a large part of the winter crops was grown on paddy fields. The years 1884 and 1892 were selected because they are the closest years to 1885 and 1890 for which data are available for the greatest number of crops.

[32] Hatanaka Kōichi, "Waga kuni ni okeru sakuzuke to kōchi ni kansuru tōkei chōsa no genjō" [Present State of Statistical Reporting with Respect to Crop Area and Arable Land Area in Japan], *Nōgyō tōkei kenkyū*, III, 3 (February 1956), 2n.

[33] The fifteen dryland crops consist of four winter crops—wheat, barley, naked barley, and rapeseed—and 11 summer crops—upland rice, sweet potatoes, white potatoes, foxtail millet, barnyard millet, proso millet, buckwheat, soybeans, indigo, cotton, and mulberry.

TABLE 4

PERCENTAGE CHANGES IN REPORTED AREA PLANTED TO
FIFTEEN DRYLAND CROPS

	1884	1892	1902	1912
Summer crops (1000 *chō*)	1413	1619	1743	1835
% change from previous period	—	15	8	5
Winter crops (1000 *chō*)	1650	1911	1961	1910
% change from previous period	—	16	3	−3
Total dryland crops (1000 *chō*)	3063	3530	3704	3745
% change from previous period	—	15	5	1

SOURCE: Computed from MAF, Agr. and For. Eco. Bur., Stat. Sec.,
Annual Statistics of the Ministry of Agr. and For., 1868-1953.

Because the data on area planted to dryland crops are
incomplete, and because rapid shifts in reported areas planted
to specific crops occurred, statistics of reported area planted
cannot be used to construct an index of the actual area planted
to dryland crops. The only other reasonable basis for estimating the planted area is by assuming that it is functionally
related to the Taxed Upland Field Area. This area, excluding
Hokkaidō, is almost a constant between 1889 and 1917,
showing only a slow upward drift of 52,000 *chō* in the twenty-
seven-year period.[34] The area before 1889 was obtained by a
least-squares straight line trend. Statistical Appendix: Table
1B, reveals a sharp decrease in Taxed Upland Field Area in
1891 and 1892. This is due to the failure to include data from
Aichi and Gifu prefectures in both years and from Mie in
1891, following a severe earthquake in the three prefectures.
Because in these two years reports on area planted were made
by these prefectures and the reports are comparable to those
of other years, a straight line interpolation of the national
data using 1890 and 1893 areas as bases was made for these
years.

Five-year averages and the index (1873-1877 = 100) of
the corrected arable land area on which dryland crops were

[34] Statistical Appendix: Table 1B.

grown are shown in Table 5. This area is the sum of the corrected upland field area, Hokkaidō upland field area, and 30 percent of the corrected paddy field area. The total change in area from 1873-1877 to 1918-1922 was 930,000 *chō*. Most of this change can be attributed to the increase in the area of Hokkaidō upland fields. A significant qualitative difference exists between Hokkaidō and other upland fields: Hokkaidō upland fields grow one crop per year, whereas most upland fields in the rest of the nation grow two or more crops. This

TABLE 5

Corrected Area of Dryland Crop Fields and Index, 1873-1922
(1000 chō)

Period	Corrected National Upland Field Area less Hokkaidō	Hokkaidō Upland Field Area	Double Cropped Paddy Field Area	Corrected National Area (1)+(2)+(3)	Index 1873-77=1 %
	(1)	(2)	(3)	(4)	(5)
1873-1877	2244	—	806	3050	100.0
1878-1882	2254	—	806	3060	100.3
1883-1887	2264	25	807	3096	101.5
1888-1892	2276	45	810	3130	102.6
1893-1897	2281	96	815	3192	104.7
1898-1902	2283	225	827	3335	109.3
1903-1907	2317	324	839	3480	114.1
1908-1912	2322	497	857	3676	120.5
1913-1917	2311	626	876	3813	125.0
1918-1922	2340	748	892	3980	130.5

Source: Column (1). The annual areas on which the five-year averages are based are obtained as follows: 1) the 1873-88 annual areas are computed from the following least-squares trend equation: $Yc = 2299 + 1.95X$ with 1903 as the year of origin and X units equal to one year; 2) annual areas for 1889-1922 are from Statistical Appendix: Table 1B, except for 1891 and 1892, which are straightline interpolations of the national data between 1890 and 1893 to correct for the omission of data from three prefectures.

Column (2). Statistical Appendix: Table 3.

Column (3). This is 30 percent of Table 2, Column (4).

same qualitative difference exists between double-cropped paddy fields and upland fields excluding Hokkaidō: double-cropped paddy fields also grow one dryland crop per year. This means that a *chō* of Hokkaidō upland field (or a double-cropped paddy field) produces less dryland crops on the average than a *chō* of upland field in the rest of the country. Because the areas of Hokkaidō upland fields and double-cropped paddy fields were growing more rapidly than the area of upland fields in the rest of the nation, an index of the change in the total area of the three groups of dryland crop fields would overstate the increase of the total area planted to dryland crops—unless of course, the proportion of upland fields planted to more than one crop increased sufficiently to offset the upward bias caused by the greater increase in single-cropped dryland crop fields. Some offsetting factors did exist. The area put in more than one crop tended to move northward over time, and, in zones where multiple cropping took place, land utilization was further intensified as urbanization progressed, transportation improved, and fertilizer use increased. At least partially offsetting the above tendency toward more intensive land use was the tendency for upland field reclamation, excluding Hokkaidō, to occur in the northern part of Japan where single cropping predominated.

On balance it seems reasonable to conclude that the index of the corrected area of dryland crop fields probably overstates the increase in the area planted to dryland crops. However, the Meiji period land utilization rate (defined as the ratio of area planted to crops to the area of cultivated land) for upland fields is not known and the land utilization indices for later periods tend to raise more questions than they answer because the concept is not a precise one in the economic sense. Therefore no attempt will be made to allow for the land utilization factor. We will assume that the index of corrected area of dryland crop fields on Table 5 is also the *index of the corrected area planted to dryland crops*, which will be used to obtain the dryland crop production.[35]

[35] If it is assumed that the land utilization rate was 60% on upland fields excluding Hokkaidō and that it stayed constant, the 1913-17

3. *Undermeasurement of Arable Land*

The main objective of this section is to obtain indices for paddy fields and upland fields which will offset the bias in production data introduced by undermeasurement. Undermeasured land is defined as registered land, the registered area of which is less than the true area. Undermeasurement, like concealment, was a practice intended to reduce the land tax burden, and for this reason it tends to reduce estimates of agricultural production.

Undermeasurement was an institutionalized practice in the Tokugawa period known and sanctioned by the authorities as a safeguard for the peasantry against over-zealous tax officials. The rate of undermeasurement was apparently not firmly fixed. However, "the usual practice on land measured for the first time was to permit a 10 percent undermeasurement of the length and a 20 percent undermeasurement of the width of a piece of land."[36] A linear undermeasurement of 10 and 20 percent causes an area undermeasurement of 28 percent. Other relatively minor allowances caused further undermeasurement. What the precise undermeasurement was in the Meiji period before the cadastral survey of the 1870's cannot be known. According to a December 1873 Ministry of Finance document[37] the undermeasurement was 20 to 30 percent.

Although one of the purposes of the Meiji cadastral survey was the accurate measurement of land, the government apparently disregarded it. In view of the Tokugawa period practices, the only way accurate measurement might have been attained would have been land measurement by tax officials dispatched from the national office and given strict

---

index would be 18% rather than 25%. This adjustment would reduce the annual rate of growth of agricultural production by about one-tenth of 1%. The land utilization rate including Hokkaidō in 1955 was 48%. (MAF, Agr. and For. Eco. Bur., Stat. Sec., *Statistical Yearbook of Ministry of Agriculture and Forestry*, Vol. 32 [1955], 166. Henceforth to be cited as *MAF Yearbook*.)

[36] Andō Hiroshi, *Tokugawa bakufu kenji yōryaku* [Outline of the Provincial Administration of the Tokugawa Shogunate] (Tokyo, 1915), p. 178.

[37] MZZKSS, VII, 336.

instructions to measure accurately. What happened in fact was that landowners and the villages were held responsible for land measurement, which was subject to spot checks by tax officials. Owing to the unsettled political conditions in the provinces, the Meiji leaders believed that the policy on under-measurement, which had been flexible during the Tokugawa period, should continue to remain so, with considerable discretion given to field officials who were dispatched from the national office.

It is a matter of record that the registered arable land area increased from 3,234,000 to 4,493,000 *chō* as a result of the cadastral survey of the 1870's.[38] A major part of concealment and undermeasurement was probably eliminated during the survey. Nevertheless, it is a certainty that a very substantial amount of undermeasurement remained, as will be shown below.

In his reminiscences about the Meiji land tax reform, Mr. Ario Keijū, a tax official during the cadastral survey, stated that, during the cadastral survey of the 1870's, undermeasurement of up to 10 percent was permitted at first. Later the tolerance was reduced to 3.3 percent.[39] He stated also that during the land survey of the 1880's those fields were investigated where undermeasurement occurred such that "one *tan* was recorded as 0.8 *tan*, or 0.8 *tan* was recorded as 0.7 *tan*."[40] Without systematic remeasurement of all land it is unlikely that errors of 15 or 20 percent could always be detected. Therefore, it is probable that only flagrant undermeasurements were investigated by tax officials.

A Ministry of Finance report on land measurement of the land survey of the 1880's also attests to the survival of undermeasurement. The document states that owing to the crude techniques used in measurement during the cadastral survey of the 1870's, errors of measurement can be expected in every parcel of land upon remeasurement.[41] However, it adds that

[38] *Supra*, pp. 262-63.

[39] Ario Keijū, Hompō chiso no enkaku [A History of Japan's Land Tax] (Privately printed by the Hypothec Bank of Japan, 1914), p. 76.

[40] *Ibid.*, pp. 142-43.

[41] MZZKSS, VII, 402.

the purpose of the land survey of the 1880's was not to correct these "small" errors.

The only reliable estimates of undermeasurement available are those made by sampling by the Crop Statistics Section (CSS) of the Ministry of Agriculture and Forestry.[42] The survey undertaken in 1956 shows undermeasurement separately for paddy fields and upland fields. The ratio of the true area to the registered area will be called the "undermeasurement index" (UI). The utility of the UI is that the product of the registered area and the UI is the true area. The national paddy field UI was found to be 1.069, and the national upland field UI, 1.049.[43] The CSS estimates were made by sampling 1,440 districts. Interestingly, 324 of these districts had arable land UI of 1.10 or greater, and of these, 14 had UI of 1.30 or greater. These figures appear to indicate a considerable variation in the tolerance of undermeasurement during the land surveys of the Meiji period.

Although the UI of the 1950's may be known, this does not tell us what it actually was after the land survey of the 1880's. Moreover, there appears to be no way of determining the exact UI of the Meiji period. Therefore, it will be assumed that the UI's existing in 1956 were the lower limit of a probable range of values. There appears to be reasonable basis for this assumption. Whenever an arable field was converted to other land classes, the undermeasurement associated with that field was deleted from the undermeasurement of arable land. The total deletions from arable land area in the 15-year period from 1926 through 1940 were 544,000 *chō*.[44] Thus a very substantial amount of undermeasurement was almost certainly eliminated between 1889 and 1956. Accurate remeasurement of arable land would also tend to reduce the UI, and such remeasurement did occur under the provisions of the Arable Land Adjustment Laws of 1899 and 1909. The total land

---

[42] Hatanaka Kōichi, *Kōchi tōkei no kakuritsu* [Establishment of Reliable Cultivated Land Statistics] *Nōrin tōkei chōsa*, VII, 10 (October 1957), 14. See also Statistical Appendix: Table 4).

[43] Statistical Appendix: Table 4.

[44] *MAF Yearbook*, III-XVII.

area involved in adjustment was 1,238,000 *chō*.[45] Although not all undermeasurement was eliminated in the adjustment districts,[46] a very substantial amount of undermeasurement was eliminated as evidenced by the fact that the area of the adjustment districts increased by 65,000 *chō*.[47] Increases in undermeasurement could have occurred when there were additions to arable land area. Gross additions to arable land area in the 15-year period from 1926 to 1940 was 702,000 *chō*.[48] It is not possible to determine how much of the added area was undermeasured nor what was the proportion of undermeasurement. But the net effect of the three changes discussed probably was a decline in the UI from 1889 to 1956. However, it will be conservatively assumed that the CSS values of 1.069 and 1.049 for paddy field and upland field UI's held true during the Meiji period and through 1922.

One further assumption will be made about these indices. The values given above exclude Hokkaidō. Because the exact undermeasurement in Hokkaidō is not known, it will be assumed here that the undermeasurement in that prefecture was identical to that in the rest of the nation.

4. Underreporting of Yield

Whether the bold conclusions drawn in Section 1 stand or fall depends largely on whether the objectives of this section are realized. We will attempt to justify here the hypothesis that yield was underreported and to obtain indices of yield per *tan* for paddy rice and dryland crops. The underreporting of yield is defined as the act of reporting agricultural crops as less than they were in reality. It is irrelevant whether this was done intentionally or unintentionally. It is believed, however, that most Japanese underreporting was done by design, and, even when apparently unintentional, the inclination toward

[45] *Ibid.*, XVII, 5.
[46] Tōbata Seiichi, and Morinaga Toshitarō (eds.), Nihon nōgyō hattatsu shi [History of Japan's Agricultural Development] (10 vols. plus 2 suppl. vols.; Tokyo, 1953-59), VI, 166. Henceforth to be cited as NNHS.
[47] *MAF Yearbook*, XVII, 6.
[48] *Ibid.*, III-XVII.

underreporting probably played a role in determining the direction of the error.

There was greater opportunity for underreporting yield than land area. The latter was subject to an irrefutable check: remeasurement. But the estimated yield was a less certain quantity. Since accurate records were not kept as a rule, if a farmer or a village insisted that a certain yield was the average, the tax officials had little basis to refute it. As for annual village production reports after the cadastral survey, they were submitted by village statistical reporters who were either village officials or leading farmers who regarded appointment to the post as an honor. If reflection of village policy in statistical reports was desired, it could be expected in either case.

The incentive to underreport yield continued to exist until 1898. The reporting of yield after the cadastral survey was, of course, a village function. The incentive arises from the likelihood that land might be revalued with yield as one of the determinants of value. This prospect was present from 1874 when an amendment to the Land Tax Revision Act of 1873 provided a quinquennial revaluation of land beginning in 1880. Revaluation did not occur under the provisions of the 1874 amendment as the planned 1880 revaluation was postponed to 1885; and quinquennial revaluations were abandoned in 1884 by the enactment of the Land Tax Law of 1884, which stipulated that existing land values would not be changed except when land class changes occurred.

Land revaluations did occur after 1884 under special legislation. In all, there were four such arable land revaluations.[49] The final one came in 1898-1899 following the passage of a revaluation bill which in one form or another had been introduced annually in the Diet since its establishment in 1890. Paddy field value was largely determined by three variables: the interest rate, the price of rice, and the yield per *tan*. Of

[49] *Meiji zaisei shi hensankai* [Meiji Financial History Compilation Committee], *Meiji zaisei shi* [Meiji Financial History] (15 vols.; Tokyo, 1904-05), V, 403-10, 623-60, 660-83, 683-726. Henceforth to be cited as MZS.

these three the landowners had some control over yield and very little, if any, over the other two. Because the arable land revaluations were not completed until 1898-1899, the landowners' incentive to underreport yield persisted until around the turn of the century. Therefore, if underreporting did take place, it can reasonably be expected to have lasted to at least around this time.

TABLE 6

PADDY RICE YIELDS PER TAN BASED ON GOVERNMENT STATISTICS, FIVE-YEAR AVERAGES

Period	Yield per *tan*	% Change from Previous Period	Period	Yield per *tan*	% Change from Previous Period
	(1)	(2)		(1)	(2)
1878-82	1.166	—	1903-07	1.626	7.2
1883-87	1.297	11.2	1908-12	1.734	6.6
1888-92	1.428	10.1	1913-17	1.843	6.3
1893-97	1.371	−4.0	1918-22	1.927	4.6
1898-1902	1.516	10.6			

SOURCE: Computed from MAF, Agric. and For. Eco. Bur., Stat. Sec., *Annual Statistics of the Ministry of Agriculture and Forestry, 1868-1953*, p. 24, except the yield per *tan* for 1878 which was computed from data in *Tōkei nenkan*.

UNDERREPORTING OF PADDY RICE YIELD

Most of the discussion will center on paddy rice yield, for which data are more plentiful and reliable than for other crops. The paddy rice yields based on government statistics appear on Table 6 as five-year averages for periods from 1878-1882 to 1918-1922. It will be argued that all of these averages, with the possible exception of the final figure, were understatements of the actual yield. Because of its importance it may be desirable to obtain an average based on a longer time period for the final figure. Over an 11-year period from

1915 to 1925 the average was 1.894 *koku*[50] per *tan*, which was slightly less than the 1918-1922 average of 1.927. The two can be rounded off to 1.9 *koku*.

The clearest statement on the underreporting of yield as a factor in the unreliability of Japanese agricultural statistics was made by Professor Yokoi Jikei in an address to the Imperial Agricultural Association in 1914.[51] He said:[52]

"Although there are statistics in Japan, they cannot be relied upon. The reason is that the reporting standards were established when harvests were first surveyed.[53] At that time the village office fearing that taxes would be excessive if the true harvest were reported, reduced the figure by several tenths.[54] . . . In succeeding years, harvest reports were based on and tended to vary around the original reported harvests. . . . However, in recent years, particularly since the Russo-Japanese War (1904-1905) conditions appear to have changed, and now the farmers want harvests to show an increase. One reason for this is that increased harvests show the agricultural improvement program to advantage. Another is that they simply want to show good reports. In this fashion, the reported harvests have gradually increased."

The implication of the final statement, substantiated by later comments, is that the reported production was increasing at a faster rate than the actual production. The reliability of Professor Yokoi's statement—which, if not true, is slanderous—cannot be seriously questioned because it was carried in the official organ of the Imperial Agricultural Association. An English observer of rural Japan, J. W. Robertson Scott,

[50] One *koku* equals 4.96 bushels.
[51] Yokoi Jikei, "Nōkai ni tsuite" [In Regard to the Agricultural Association] *Teikoku nōkai hō*, IV, 4 (April 1914), 1-10.
[52] *Ibid.*, 5.
[53] It is clear that the survey refers to the cadastral survey of the 1870's.
[54] The implication of this statement is that since other villages can be expected to underreport their harvests, failure to underreport would invite excessive taxes. "Several tenths" is our translation of *"nanwari."*

notes that in 1915-1916 rice production was underreported. He states,[55] ". . . the statistics show a production 15 per cent less than the actual harvest. Formerly the underestimation was 20 per cent. The practice has its origin in the old taxation system." Because precise yields are not necessary if records are to be falsified, the percentages quoted are probably very crude. It is reasonable to infer from the statement, however, that underreporting of yield per *tan* of paddy rice persisted well into the twentieth century.

The above accounts indicate that the farmers in most cases successfully thwarted government attempts to obtain accurate harvest reports during the cadastral survey. In reality, the government seems to have permitted a downward adjustment of reported yield. This resulted from a global revenue target established by the government for the nation as a whole. The total revenue was apportioned to the prefectures, which in turn apportioned their shares to the cities and villages.[56] The global target appears to have been a fixed money revenue.[57] For paddy fields the government anticipated an average per *tan*[58] value of around 40.80 yen and a per *tan* revenue of 1.22 yen. This was based on an expected average paddy rice yield of 1.6 *koku* of rice per *tan*, an average rice price of 3 yen per *koku*, and an interest rate of 6 percent.[59] The interest rate did average around 6 percent[60] because the government estab-

[55] J. W. Robertson Scott, *The Foundations of Japan* (London, 1922), p. 87.

[56] Ono Takeo, *Meiji zenki tochi seido shi ron* [Treatise on the Early Meiji Land System] (Tokyo, 1948), p. 95. To obtain brief descriptions of how different prefectures determined the average yield of a village, see *ibid.*, pp. 86-95.

[57] Ario, p. 52. The anticipated revenue shown in one document is 33.5 million yen against a pre-revision revenue of 37.4 million. (MZZKSS, VII, 346). The pre-revision revenue was primarily a tax in kind, in which case, the money value is a conversion at the prevailing price of rice. By "pre-revision revenue" is meant Meiji government revenue before the tax revision.

[58] We work with per *tan* values rather than totals because totals are dependent on land area which was not a firm figure.

[59] Ario, p. 53.

[60] The rates for the various prefectures and districts within prefec-

lished this figure as the norm. The average price of rice, however, was nearly 40 percent greater at 4.185 yen[61] instead of 3 yen. With this change, if the yield averaged 1.6 *koku*, the land value would have risen to about 57 yen per *tan*; or if the land value was maintained at 40.80 yen, the yield would have dropped to 1.14 *koku* per *tan*.[62] What occurred in fact was that the paddy field value ended higher and the yield lower than expected. In 1881 the value averaged 46.37 yen per *tan*,[63] which was 14 percent more than the original per *tan* value target of 40.80 yen. It follows that the yield per *tan* had to be about 19 percent less than the expected yield, or about 1.3 *koku* per *tan* assuming interest rate constant, which is about what the land valuation yield averaged.[64] It may be no accident that the per *tan* value of paddy fields after the four revaluations was 40.01 yen, which is close to the original land value target of 40.80 yen per *tan* for paddy fields.

There is no reason to doubt that the farmers and the government adjusted the yield to the revenue target of the government.[65] This target apparently rose in response to a price inflation, but the rise was considerably less proportionally than the increase in the price of rice. The fact that the average yield was revised downward during the inter-prefectural land value adjustment of 1898-1899[66] is further evidence

---

tures varied closely around 6% with many prefectures reporting a flat 6% rate. (MZZKSS, VII, Appendices 7, 8, p. 442ff.)

[61] MZS, V, 373.

[62] The relationship between the three variables can be expressed by the following equation: $V = kQP$, where V = land value; Q = yield; P = price; and k = constant coefficient when the interest rate is given. (*Ibid.*, pp. 345-46.)

[63] Computed from *Tōkei nenkan*, II, 13.

[64] One estimate of production per *tan* from paddy fields during the cadastral survey of the 1870's is 1.32 *koku*. (Horie Hideichi, "The Agricultural Structure of Japan in Meiji Restoration," *Kyoto University Economic Review*, XXXI, 2 [October 1961] 15.)

[65] This point is strongly argued in Niwa Kunio, *Meiji ishin no tochi henkaku* [Land Reform of the Meiji Restoration] (Tokyo, 1962), pp. 427-29.

[66] MZS, V, 663-64.

that the government regarded the land valuation yield as a purely nominal figure.

For convenience government policy on land valuation has been discussed in terms of paddy field valuation. However, the same general statements as were made about paddy fields can be made about upland fields with one qualification: upland field valuation was regarded as relatively less important than paddy field valuation, and even less precision was demanded in determining the yield. For example, despite the widespread practice of multiple cropping, upland field yield was taken to be that of one principal crop.[67]

Another approach to the question of whether the land valuation yield was an understatement is to obtain actual yield reports that are independent of government data. This applies during the Tokugawa period as well as the Meiji era because underreporting appears to have been practiced successfully in that time also. The following three sets of data are relevant: (1) yield in early Meiji; (2) yield in late Tokugawa; and (3) yield in earlier periods if yield tended to increase over time, or if the trend in yield was known.

A number of studies that have attempted to obtain actual yield per *tan* are available. In the early Meiji period the best of these may have been the cost-of-production surveys conducted during the Matsukata deflation of the 1880's, which severely depressed the agricultural sector. For example, average paddy rice yields of 1.619, 2.546, and 2.5 *koku* per *tan* were reported, respectively, in villages in Niigata (1884-1889) and Tokyo (1890) prefectures and in Kofu valley of Yamanashi prefecture.[68] Over the same years the official yields in the above prefectures were 1.256, 1.633, and 1.364 *koku* per *tan*, respectively.[69] A study of rent burdens in 48 communities in various parts of Japan showed an average yield on medium grade paddy fields of 1.871 *koku* per *tan*

[67] MZZKSS, VII, 340.

[68] Ono Takeo, *Nōson shi* [History of Rural Japan] (Tokyo, 1941), pp. 116, 119, 121.

[69] NRTHI, relevant pages.

toward the end of the Tokugawa period.[70] Above are a small sampling of the kind of data that may be found. They are, of course, scattered data and cannot be regarded as conclusive. They are, nonetheless, suggestive.

Earlier records of paddy rice yields also exist. Curiously, the reported yield in each of three widely separated periods in Japan—Kamakura period (1192-1333), Bunroku period (1592-1596), and Jōkyō period (1684-1688)—was the same; 1.3 *koku* per *tan* for medium grade paddy fields,[71] which can be assumed to be the average for all fields. This unanimity seems to indicate that land productivity had remained constant for around 400 years. However, we find that the yield was not constant because the dimensions of the *tan* had decreased over time—Kamakura *tan* was 20 percent greater and the Bunroku *tan*, 10.25 percent greater than the Jōkyō *tan*, which is equal to the modern *tan*. The capacity of the *koku* has remained almost constant after a change in the Kamakura period.[72]

The meaning of the nominal constancy of yield per *chō* is that Japan, like any traditional society almost entirely dependent on agriculture for its basic needs, has maintained policies which have caused the average family unit to have sufficient land to pay taxes and feed itself. The area so determined can be taken to be one *chō*, consisting roughly of equal shares of paddy and upland fields, and it was believed necessary that paddy fields average 1.3 *koku* of rice per *tan* for the family

[70] Yamada Moritarō, *Nihon shihon shugi bunseki* [An Analysis of Japanese Capitalism] (7th ed.; Tokyo, 1955), p. 187.

[71] Ministry of Finance, *Dai nihon sozei shi* [Annals of Taxation in Japan] (3 vols. and supplement; Tokyo, 1926), II, 248, 267, 283. To be cited as DNSS henceforth.

[72] Actually the dimensions of the *tan* and the capacity of the *koku* often differed in different prefectures. The Kamakura period *koku* appears to have varied from 49.32% to 98.63% of the modern *koku*. (Hōgetsu Keigo, *Chūsei ryōsei shi no kenkyū* [A Study of the Feudal Weight System] (Tokyo, 1961), p. 103.) It is certain that the Kamakura *koku* used in establishing the 1.3 *koku* yield per *tan* as the average for medium grade fields was very close in capacity to the modern *koku*.

to carry out its obligations.[73] As land productivity rose, the dimensions of the *chō* were changed in the years noted.

Using modern *tan* and *koku* units we find that yields have been increasing as shown below:[74]

PERIOD	Yield per *tan* of medium grade field
Kamakura (1192-1333)	1.0 *koku*
Bunroku (1592-1596)	1.2 *koku*
Jōkyō (1684-1688)	1.3 *koku*

There are no national per *tan* yield records to show what the increase was after the 1680's. However, according to most scholars in this field, a gradual but very substantial increase occurred in paddy field output per *tan* in the 200 years following the Jōkyō period. Professor Thomas C. Smith has summed this view as follows:

". . . Japanese agriculture . . . underwent notable technological (though not mechanical) changes long before the modern period. Between 1600 and 1850 a complex of such changes greatly increased the productivity of land. . . .

"Few changes were the result of invention; most resulted from the spread of known techniques from the localities in which they had been developed to areas where they were previously unknown or unused."[75]

[73] The Malthusian process appears to have been operating to decrease the real size of family holdings as the productivity of land increased.

[74] Katō Tadataka, *Suiden shukoku seisanryoku no tenkai* [The Development of Productivity in Paddy Field Grain Production] (*Nihon nōgyō bunseki shiryō*: 3 [Materials for the Analysis of Japanese Agriculture: 3]) (Tokyo, 1960), p. 177.

[75] Smith, Thomas C., *Agrarian Origins of Modern Japan* (Stanford, 1959), p. 87. The outstanding authority on Tokugawa agricultural developments, Professor Furushima Toshio, has done some of the most important studies on technical change and agricultural productivity. See, for example, his *Kinsei nihon nōgyō no tenkai* [Agricultural Development in the Tokugawa Period] (Tokyo, 1963), which collects a number of studies under one cover.

He states that the increasing publication of technical treatises had led to the exchange and diffusion of agricultural innovations.[76] For example, commercial fertilizers, which were probably the most important of all innovations in raising yields had become supplements to natural fertilizers almost everywhere by the nineteenth century. There had also occurred an enormous increase in rice plant varieties and a widespread awareness of existing varieties.

Other evidences of growing agricultural productivity include the following: increased production of industrial crops; accelerated development of rural industries;[77] growth of urban centers and castle towns;[78] the development of an extensive network of trade; and an amazingly high level of literacy.[79] Because Japan's population and arable land area remained roughly constant from around the beginning of the eighteenth century to the middle of the nineteenth century, the above trends imply that rural workers were being released from the production of food and that per capita income was rising in Japan.

If yield per *tan* continued to rise as argued and if the Bunroku and Jōkyō yields are accurate, the official yield of 1878-1882 of 1.166 *koku* per *tan* must be an understatement, since this was somewhat less than the Bunroku yield of almost 300 years before. There is no reason to believe that the earlier yields were not reasonable approximations of actual yields. One evidence of the reliability of the Bunroku yield is that it was published in 1595,[80] well toward the end of the land survey which began in 1583 and ended in 1598.[81] This indicates that most of the surveying had been completed before the

[76] Smith, 87 ff.

[77] Crawcour, E. S., "Changes in Japanese Commerce in the Tokugawa Period," *Journal of Asian Studies*, XXII, 4 (August 1963), 397.

[78] Hall, John W., "The Castle Town and Japan's Modern Urbanization," *Far Eastern Quarterly*, XV, 1 (November 1955), 47.

[79] Dore, R. P., "The Legacy of Tokugawa Education" (Paper presented at the Conference on Modernization of Japan, January 1962).

[80] DNSS, 235.

[81] Sansom, George, *A History of Japan, 1334-1615* (Stanford, 1961), p. 316.

yield was determined. Another reason for confidence in the reliability of the Bunroku yield is that it was used as a basis for grading land for tax purposes. Owing to strong peasant resentment of the survey, the government would not have dared to be less than fair in yield estimation.[82] The same observation applies equally to the Kamakura and Jōkyō yields.

Scattered yields are available for the period after the Jōkyō era. A document written in the Meiwa period (1764-1772) records paddy rice yields in villages of average productivity in Chikuzen province (part of present Fukuoka prefecture). For superior grade fields, the average yield is recorded as 1.818 *koku* per *tan*; for medium grade, 1.515; for inferior grade, 1.212; and for very inferior grade, 0.909.[83] Averaging the four gives a yield of 1.363 *koku*. Whether this is the true average depends on the relative areas of the various grade fields which are not given. It is possible that the yield of the medium grade field—because medium suggests average—is a better approximation of the average for the province. Given a probable rise in yield in the next 100 years, whether the actual Meiwa yields were 1.363 *koku*, 1.515, or any intermediate figure, the actual Chikuzen average in 1878-1882 would have been considerably greater than the national average of 1.166 or the Fukuoka prefecture average of 1.287 in 1881-1885.[84] Furthermore, because the Meiwa data are taken from official records, it is probable that they understate yield.[85]

[82] *Ibid.*, 317-18.

[83] Ono Takeo (ed.), *Kinsei chigata keizai shiryō* [Provincial Economic Materials of the Tokugawa Period] (10 vols.; Tokyo, 1932), I, 174.

[84] Computed from NRTHI. Earlier prefectural data are not available.

[85] Understatement of area and yield in the leased holdings of one landlord in Kawachi province (part of present Osaka prefecture) is revealed by a comparison of official village records and data in the family journal. The time is around 1850. The officially recorded leased area was 37.464 *tan*. The area from which rent was collected, as revealed in the journal, was 52.731 *tan*, which can be taken as the probable true area. The undermeasurement index is 1.41. The *kokudaka* —the officially recorded yield for tax purposes—was 60.862 *koku*, making the official yield per *tan* 1.625 *koku*. Although the total pro-

Studies of family records (which are more likely to be accurate than official records) by Professor Furushima Toshio show yields much in excess of 1.166 *koku*. The journal of the Imanishi family of Kawachi province (present Osaka prefecture) shows paddy rice yields averaging 2.31 *koku* in the 15-year period from 1798 to 1812.[86] The average officially reported yield per *tan* in Osaka prefecture in 1881-1885 was 1.496 *koku*.[87] This family also rented 31.721 *tan* of paddy fields, all of which produced one crop per year. The annual production is not given but the rent was 39.715 *koku*,[88] which on a per *tan* basis is 1.25 *koku*. The yield per *tan* probably was about the same as for fields farmed by the family, that is, about 2.31 *koku*. Professor Furushima also estimates (with extreme reservation because of limited data) that the rent on one-crop paddy fields in the northeastern part of Honshū was 0.8 to 0.9 *koku* in the Tokugawa period.[89] If this is correct, the average actual yield in that area could hardly have been less than 1.5 *koku* per *tan*.

Since government statistics are being questioned, it is necessary to examine them to see whether the reported yield changes are consistent with our hypothesis. The reported annual yield and a five-year moving average are shown in Figure 2. In the early 1880's, the average yield was less than 1.2 *koku* per *tan*; in fact, the annual yield tends to decline from 1879 to 1884. A sharp rise occurs in the late 1880's, and then the average yield remains roughly constant until about the turn of the century, from which time the reported yield climbs

---

duction of the leased area is not given, the rent expressed as *koku* of rice is given. This was 86.141 *koku*, 42% higher than the official yield. Dividing this by the probable true area gives a per *tan* rent of 1.634 *koku*, which is more than the official yield per *tan*. The true yield per *tan* must obviously be considerably greater than the rent; a possible minimum may be 2.5 *koku*. (Basic data taken from Furushima, p. 535, Table 35.)

[86] *Ibid.*, p. 345, Table 2.
[87] Computed from NRTHI, p. 58.
[88] Furushima, p. 352, Table 7.
[89] *Ibid.*, p. 522.

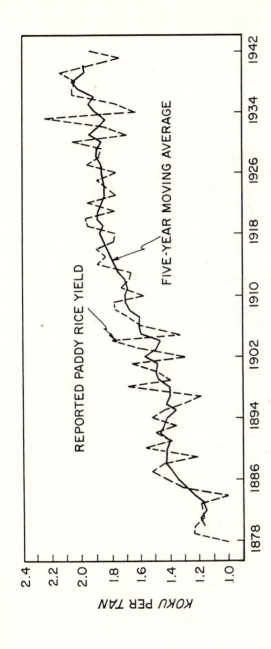

FIGURE 2

Reported Paddy Rice Yield in Japan, 1879-1942.

SOURCE: Ministry of Agriculture and Forestry, Agriculture and Forestry Economics Bureau, Statistics Section, *Nōrinshō ruinen tōkeihyō, 1868-1953* [Historical statistics of the Ministry of Agriculture and Forestry, 1868-1953] (Tokyo, 1955), p. 24.

fairly steeply until another plateau is reached about twenty years later.

Without other evidence the observed plateaus and rises in yield can perhaps be regarded as typical of the kind of changes that occur in agricultural production. It has been observed, however, that the incentive to underreport weakened around the turn of the century when the 20-year rise in yield commenced. It is also known that Professor Yokoi stated that the villages tended to inflate the increases from around the time of the Russo-Japanese War (1904-1905) in order that statistical support might be available to show the effectiveness of the agricultural aid program.

One probable reason for the sharp rise in the reported paddy rice production per *tan* of about 20 percent that occurred in the late 1880's is the establishment of new statistical regulations, procedures, forms, and detailed instructions by the Ministry of Agriculture and Commerce from 1883 to 1886,[90] following the creation of the Ministry in 1881. In 1884, statistical forms were standardized, much more detailed instructions were issued on the collection of statistics, and directions were given for more comprehensive surveys of the most important crops. For example, information sought on rice included the area planted, production, planting and harvesting dates, and area of damaged crops. In 1886, instructions were issued for pre-harvest reports on growing conditions (including the effects of the weather and pests), expected harvest, and expected deviation from the normal harvest of rice, wheat, barley, naked barley, tea, cotton, and rapeseed. A second reason for the sharp rise probably was the greater importance placed on reliable statistics at this time, as is evident from the care put into its collection. This attitude toward statistics was at least partially related to the depression of the 1880's when the suffering of farmers and other segments of the population drew much attention. A

[90] The basic authority was given in the *Nōshōmushō tasshi 32* (December 28, 1883) whose descriptive designation is *Nōshōmushō tsūshin kisoku* [Statistical Regulations of the Ministry of Agriculture and Commerce].

final reason that may be mentioned is the abandonment in 1884 of the policy of revaluing land every five years, which may have caused a temporary weakening of the incentive to underreport.

In 1889 the instructions for pre-harvest reports were abolished. During this year also the first inter-prefectural revaluation occurred and about this time the farm sector had emerged from the depression. Probably due to these reasons the need for reliable statistics appears to have faded around that time, and for the next decade the rice yield remained constant. Starting around 1895 Japan became a food-importing nation, and once again she became conscious of the need for reliable statistical reports. The second and final inter-prefectural arable land revaluation occurred in 1898-1899. It was also about this time that the yield per *tan* started the 20-year rise.

Doubt is cast upon the argument being developed here by two articles which attribute the rapid growth of agricultural production in the Meiji era to three technical factors: the more intensive use of fertilizers, particularly commercial fertilizers; the improvement of seed; and the diffusion of farming techniques through experienced farmers.[91] Of these, the intensive use of fertilizers is regarded as by far the most important cause of increased per *tan* yield of rice. It will be argued here that the above three factors were not as effective as previously believed.

Gains from fertilizers are both observable and calculable to the cultivator. A direct relationship may usually be noted between the quantity of fertilizers used and the yield per unit area. If the relationship held true in Japan—and it did as a rule—fertilizers could hardly have been a significant factor in the reported production increases before 1905. Table 7 shows

[91] Bruce F. Johnston, "Agricultural Development and Economic Transformation: A Comparative Study of the Japanese Experience," *Food Research Institute Studies*, III, 3 (November 1962), pp. 223-76; and R. P. Dore, "Agricultural Improvement in Japan, 1870-1900," *Economic Development and Cultural Change*, IX, 1 (October 1960), 69-91.

TABLE 7

TREND OF FERTILIZER CONSUMPTION, FIVE-YEAR AVERAGES

Period	Value in 1934-36 Prices (million yen)	Index 1883-87=100	% Change from Previous Period
	(1)	(2)	(3)
1883-1887	212.0	100.0	—
1888-1892	218.8	103.2	3.2
1893-1897	231.9	109.4	6.0
1898-1902	248.2	117.1	7.0
1903-1907	270.5	127.6	9.0
1908-1912	322.6	152.2	19.3
1913-1917	362.2	170.8	12.3
1918-1922	410.4	193.6	13.3
1923-1927	451.9	213.2	10.1
1928-1932	516.0	243.4	14.2

SOURCE: Hayami Yūjirō, "Hiryō tōkaryō no suikei" [Fertilizer Consumption Estimates], *Nōgyō sōgō kenkyū*, XVII, 1 (January 1963), 253.

average five-year changes in fertilizer consumption. Commercial fertilizers constituted less than 15 percent of total fertilizers used in the nineteenth century, and self-supplied fertilizers, therefore, constituted more than 85 percent. The fact that the latter made up the bulk of all fertilizers requires caution in the use of Table 7 because rather risky assumptions necessarily had to be made in estimating their value.

Column (3) of Table 7 reveals that the percentage increase in the use of fertilizers climbed steadily from 3 percent to 9 percent from period to period through 1903-1907. Then a very sharp increase to 19 percent occurs, after which increases drop to 12 and 13 percent. What is clear is that increases in fertilizer use were greater after 1903-1907 than before it. In contrast to this, Column (2) of Table 6 shows percentage increases in paddy rice yield to be substantially higher prior to 1903-1907. Greater increases could have been expected after this period on the basis of the trend in fertilizer consumption, yet Table 6 shows an almost unbroken decline in the percentage increase of paddy rice yield from 1878-1882 to 1918-1922.

Benefits from seed improvement are much more difficult to determine than gains from fertilizers. Seed improvement can lead to several changes, the two most important of which are increase in yield per unit area and improvement of quality. The latter is indeterminate, and even the former is difficult to gauge. Although a new seed may be shown to yield a given percentage more rice per *tan* than another under experimental conditions, its performance in the field can be quite different. Even if it lives up to expectations, it may in time succumb to a new disease or a mutant form of an old one.

Although seed improvement is difficult to measure, it is now a commonplace that application of scientific principles and methods has tended to accelerate the development of desired varieties. During the Tokugawa period, when the search for more and better seeds went on widely,[92] the principles of genetics were unknown, and the appearance of a new variety was the result of a fortuitous variation of a plant that an observant cultivator set aside for seed. The application of Mendelian principles to plant breeding in the government experimental stations started around 1910, about a decade after its introduction into Japan.[93]

Intensive experimental work on seed improvement did not start until the Taishō period (1912-1926). By that time prefectural experimental stations had also matured and much of the selective breeding, which was the most important accomplishment of the times, was undertaken by them.[94] From around 1925 the stress shifted to cross breeding, which led

[92] Smith, pp. 94-95. Because a given seed tends to become less productive in a locality over time, it is desirable to have a continual stream of new improved seeds being developed.

[93] NNHS, II, 438.

[94] *Ibid.*, IX, 85-103.

to the development of many superior varieties of rice, most of these being notable for their heavy yield.[95]

It is hardly necessary to discuss the role of experienced farmers in raising land productivity. Their role in raising yield per *tan* had to be almost entirely through bringing to the attention of other farmers the benefits of fertilizers and new, improved seeds, which have already been discussed. One observation may be made, however. The use of experienced farmers to educate other farmers was a continuation of a Tokugawa practice of diffusing techniques used by farmers who obtained superior results.[96] These results were obtained usually by exceptional circumstances of soil, location, sheer diligence by the farmer, or some combination of the three. Applied under different circumstances and with less care and effort the results could have been detrimental. One of the critics of indiscriminate use of experienced farmers was Finance Minister Matsukata (later Prime Minister), who deplored the absence of theory in their instructions.[97]

Another technical reason to believe that agricultural production tended to increase slowly is that Japan was primarily an innovator in respect to improvement in the agricultural sector. This contrasts strongly with the modern manufacturing sector, where Japan was an avid imitator, adopting modern industrial techniques imported from abroad which made possible a high rate of growth in that sector. Japan did not find most Western agricultural techniques suitable to her needs because they were adapted to dryland or large-scale farming. She needed techniques suited to her type of small-scale farming where particular interest has always been placed on increasing the productivity of paddy fields. Lacking models to follow, Japan could have been expected to go through a relatively slow and labored growth which is the usual lot of innovators in production.

[95] *Ibid.*, pp. 109-11.

[96] Ono Takeo, *Nōson shi*, p. 201.

[97] Kojima Toshihiro, "Meijiki nōgyō tōkei no mondai ishiki" [Problems in Meiji Period Agricultural Statistics] Nōgyō sōgō kenkyū, XII, 4 (October 1958), 93.

Some conclusions can be drawn about the impact of technical factors on agricultural production. The analysis of trends in paddy rice yield and fertilizer consumption not only does not negate the hypothesis that yield was understated but strongly supports our argument that there was a progressive decline in the degree of underreporting over time. The examination of progress in experimental stations also indicates that increases in yield could have been expected toward the end of the period under study, particularly in the Taishō period and later. Both the fertilizer consumption and seed improvement factors point to a more rapid increase in yield in the latter half of the period from 1878-1882 to 1918-1922. The fertilizer consumption trends, in particular, indicate a rapid increase beginning around 1908-1912.

In the discussion of underreporting up to this point such matters as incentive and opportunity, statements by scholars, government policy, empirical investigations of yield, and a study of technical factors that affect yield have been covered. Two conclusions can reasonably be drawn on the basis of the evidence thus presented. The first is that a substantial understatement of yield per unit area exists in government statistics of the Meiji period. The second is the gradual decline of underreporting over a period of time. Since the major objective of this paper is to revise the estimates of agricultural production and growth rate, these conclusions are not sufficient. An index of the change in yield must be constructed. To accomplish this for paddy rice yield we propose to estimate the absolute yields for the periods around 1880 and 1920.

ESTIMATION OF PADDY RICE YIELDS

The average government yield in 1918-1922 was around 1.9 *koku* per *tan*. Can this be accepted as a reasonable approximation of the actual yield? There are at least five grounds for believing so. (1) Statements by Professor Yokoi and Mr. J. W. Robertson Scott indicate that the degree of underreporting had been declining. (2) Incentive to underreport had probably disappeared, and was probably replaced by an incentive to show inflated yields, as Professor Yokoi indicated. (3) Examination of Figure 2 shows that reported yield climbed sharply until around 1920 and then leveled off, suggesting that the period of inflated increases of yield had come to an end around that time. (4) A study of per capita calorie consumption also suggests that the underreporting of yield might have ended around 1920. According to Table 8, which is based on government statistics, Japanese consumed (per capita daily) 1,351 calories from grain, potato, pulse, meat, eggs, and dairy product sources in 1878-1882. This

TABLE 8

Calories Available for Consumption per Day per Capita
From Selected Foods, 1878-1937

Period	Grains, Pulses, Potatoes	Meat, Milk, Eggs	Total
1878-1882	1349	1.7	1351
1883-1887	1520	2.5	1523
1888-1892	1830	2.8	1833
1893-1897	1876	6.6	1883
1898-1902	1941	7.4	1948
1903-1907	2006	7.6	2014
1908-1912	2119	8.9	2128
1913-1917	2084	10.3	2094
1918-1922	2189	12.1	2201
1923-1927	2031	14.9	2046
1928-1932	1866	38.8	1905
1933-1937	1815	47.2	1862

Source: Nakayama Seiki, "Shokuryō shōhi suijun no chōki henka ni tsuite" [Long term trend of food consumption in Japan, 1878-1955], *Nōgyō sōgō kenkyū*, XII, 4 (October 1958), p. 25.

Note: 1. Calories available for consumption are computed by deducting food used as fodder, loss in processing, and seed requirements and allowing for changes in stock and for exports and imports.

2. By grains is meant rice, wheat, barley, naked barley, corn, foxtail millet, barnyard millet, proso millet, and buckwheat. Pulses include only soy beans and *azuki*.

consumption had climbed to 2,114 calories[98] in 1915-1925, and then fell to around 1,900 in the next decade. The calorie supply in 1915-1925 might have been around 2,300 if omitted sources (fish, vegetables, fruit, and other unenumerated sources) are added. Consumption of 1,351 calories from the sources mentioned above is an obvious understatement of the actual consumption, but 2,300 calories may be roughly what underdeveloped countries consume today and what Japan may have consumed then. A noted authority on food consumption believes, for example, that India's probable calorie consumption was around 2,200 calories in 1953-1955.[99] In view of above considerations it is not unlikely that yield was accurately reported around 1920. (5) Accurate reporting was also made easier when, in 1914, statistical forms and procedures for estimating the harvest of rice, wheat, barley, and naked barley were revised.[100] The survey procedure was made much more detailed in the effort to obtain accuracy. Among other things, the village was divided into a number of survey districts, which made possible a better appraisal of village yield. Moreover, the village yield was to be estimated by three or more appraisers who were scientific experts or men of experience, or, alternatively, by taking sample harvests from fields determined to be the village average. This survey procedure became effective in 1915. Because it takes a few years to adjust to changes of this kind, underreporting may not have been immediately eliminated, even if the villages were inclined to make accurate crop reports, as appears to have been the case.

However, a nagging question remains about underreporting of yield around 1920. Mr. Robertson Scott's statement,

[98] Adjustment is not made for undermeasurement. If the undermeasurement adjustment is made the supply would have been somewhat more than 100 calories higher.

[99] Helen Farnsworth, "The Role of Wheat in Improving Nutritional Status and Labor Productivity in Lesser Developed Countries," *International Wheat Surplus Utilization Conference Proceedings* (Brookings, South Dakota, 1958), p. 57.

[100] *Nōshōmushō kunrei 13 bessatsu: nōshōmu tōkei yōshiki* (November 21, 1914), notes to Forms 1 and 2.

made on information obtained around 1915, that rice production was understated by 15 percent seems to suggest that production around 1920 may also have been substantially understated. Actually paddy field undermeasurement probably accounts for about 7 percent of the understatement, seemingly leaving 7 percent attributable to the underreporting of yield per *tan*. It is possible that the 8 percent figure actually applies to an earlier period, because a lag may be expected between practice and knowledge of its quantitative impact when the practice itself is changing. If this is so, since the practice was that of reducing the degree of underreporting, the underreporting of yield could have been eliminated by around 1920. Aside from this lag factor it must also be borne in mind that Mr. Robertson Scott's figure must necessarily have been a very crude estimate, because it is not likely that accurate yield estimates were made when it was intended to falsify the reported figures anyway. If underreporting continued to remain in yield statistics of the period around 1920, it is likely that it had become an unimportant factor.

In addition to the two possibilities that the 1.9 yield may be correct or be an understatement, there is a third possibility—that the yield was overstated. Since a desire to inflate yield reports apparently existed up to around 1920, mention of the third possibility is not merely an attempt to touch all bases. Neither Yokoi's statement nor the movement of government yields around 1920 are inconsistent with this possibility. However, we will conservatively assume that yield was not overstated around 1920.

The average paddy rice yield of 1.166 for the period around 1880 has been discarded. There is no set of national data on which new estimates can be based (since government yield statistics are not acceptable). There remain only less certain and less direct methods of estimation.

The probable range of values within which the new estimate would lie can be obtained. The minimum cannot be less than 1.3 *koku*, which is the estimated average yield in the Jōkyō period (1684-1688), given our conclusion that yield increased during the Tokugawa period. The maximum value cannot be more than 1.9 *koku*, which is the yield around 1920. There is one figure within this range for which a better case can be made than for any other figure. It is 1.6 *koku*, which, fortuitously, is the average of 1.3 and 1.9. According to Ario, the previously mentioned tax official who participated in the cadastral survey of the 1870's, the government expected an average paddy rice yield of 1.6 *koku* per *tan* to emerge from the survey.[101] The fact that the government used the 1.6 *koku* yield in its instructions[102] for computing the paddy field value during the survey appears to confirm the official's statement. Where did the government obtain this figure, for it had not even started the survey when the instructions were published? There is no record of how this was done, but it may have been obtained by consulting Tokugawa tax officials in various parts of the country. These officials were highly skilled specialists who were trained from childhood for their function of appraising harvests and the productivity of fields.[103] If the Meiji government did obtain the yield figure in this way, it was probably a good approximation of the actual yield. If Tokugawa practices were followed in appraising land, the appraisal could well have been an underestimation because allowances were made for costs of transportation, frequency of natural disasters, poor irrigation facilities and climate conditions, scarcity of natural fertilizers, slope of land, and the like—some of which probably tended to push the yield down below the average for a given field.

None of the factors examined thus far appears to be inconsistent with the 1.6 *koku* hypothesis—with the exception of Tokugawa and early Meiji yield data. The latter suggest that the yield was greater than 1.6 *koku* during the cadastral survey. However, the yield data consist of scattered samples of limited areas, and it is possible that the yields are all taken from superior fields with the exception of the Chikuzen province yield which is said to be the average for the province.

[101] Ario, p. 53.
[102] *Dajōkan fukoku 272 bessatsu: chihōkan kokoroesho* (July 1873), Article 12.
[103] MZS, V, 294.

Nevertheless, the possibility that the actual yield during the 1870's was higher than 1.6 *koku* does remain, particularly because the 1.6 *koku* yield expected by the government may have been a conservative figure.

One check for plausibility of the 1.6 hypothesis is to estimate the yield per *tan* required to meet the food needs of the Japanese population in 1878-1882. This approach is particularly applicable to Japan since almost all of her calorie requirements come from plant sources.[104] Estimates of calories available for consumption made by Dr. Nakayama Seiki[105] using government statistics will be employed in our analysis. Table 8 shows calories supplied per day per capita from grains, pulses, potatoes, meat, dairy products, and eggs from 1878-1882 to 1923-1927. The supply in 1878-1882 was 1,351 calories from all sources. In 1918-1922 it had increased to 2,201 calories. If we conservatively take a 15-year period from 1913-1917 to 1923-1927 as a base, the supply was 2,114 calories, an increase of 56 percent from the 1878-1882 supply. In Dr. Nakayama's computations some sources of calorie supply (principally sugar, fish, vegetables, fruits) were omitted but they probably accounted for less than 10 percent of the total.[106] The omitted part, however, became proportionally more important over time; therefore, if it were possible to include all sources of calorie supply, the percentage change in supply would probably have been greater than 56 percent.

---

[104] Bruce F. Johnston, *Japanese Food Management in World War II* (Stanford, 1953), p. 70.

[105] Nakayama Seiki, "Shokuryō shōhi suijun no chōki henka ni tsuite" [Long-run Trend of Food Consumption in Japan, 1878-1955], *Nōgyō sōgō kenkyū*, XII, 4 (October 1958), 13-37.

[106] In 1930-34 three of these sources—fish, fruits, vegetables— accounted for about 7% in a food balance sheet prepared for the U.S. State Department. (U.S. Dept. of State, Office of International Research, *Japan's Food, Beverage, and Tobacco Position, 1928-36* [OIR Report No. 4126, 1948], p. 88, Table 42.) Since these sources furnished a greater proportion of calorie intake as the national income rose, it is probable that they accounted for less than 7% in earlier years. Sugar accounted for about 2% or 3% of the total calorie supply in early Meiji according to S. Nakayama's judgment, expressed in an interview in Tokyo in 1964.

Let us assume that the actual calorie supply per day per capita in 1878-1882 was 2,114. We will disregard the under-measurement factor because it is assumed to affect both periods equally. The 1878-1882 calorie supply must be adjusted for concealment since it does not affect the 1915-1925 supply. This adjustment requires an upward revision of the 1,351 calories by about 10 percent, which makes the calorie supply 1,486. The remaining difference of 628 calories is assumed to have been a result of the understatement of yield per *tan*. The adjusted total of 1,486 calories must be raised by 42 percent to obtain 2,114 calories. If the recorded yield of 1.166 *koku* per *tan* is increased by 42 percent, the result is 1.656 *koku*. This is somewhat more than the yield that the government expected during the cadastral survey, according to Mr. Ario. If the assumption of constant calorie consumption and the area adjustment are correct or have offsetting biases, this analysis tends to confirm the hypothesis that the yield per *tan* was around 1.6 *koku* in early Meiji period.

The area adjustment is likely to be tolerably accurate. The assumption of a constant calorie consumption is probably tenable also. To be sure there are circumstances that seem to indicate that calorie consumption increased during the Meiji period. An increase in physical size, other things being equal, increases calorie requirements for the obvious reason that carrying more weight requires a greater energy use. Japanese have grown in stature over the years although the change up to around 1920 was relatively small. Another factor usually associated with increased food consumption is a rise in per capita income. It is a fact, however, that the average real income did rise somewhat, and food consumption may have risen as a result. But this increase need not necessarily be an increase in calorie consumption except in countries where the initial staple food supply did not adequately feed the population. In such countries most of the increase in food expenditures would probably go toward the purchase of calorie-rich foods. In others increases in income have been accompanied by a change in the composition of foods consumed. The shift is typically from the grains and potatoes to the meats, dairy products, vegetables and fruits. A shift away from carbohydrates is suggested by Table 8 which shows that the consumption of meat, eggs, and dairy products increased at an extremely rapid rate.

The principal reason for the belief that early Meiji food supply per capita was equal to or higher than in later years is that the Tokugawa period policy of producing more staple foods than required in normal crop years almost certainly carried over into the Meiji period. This food policy, necessitated by the inadequacy of storage techniques and facilities, was maintained as a safeguard against famine and social disorder and as a means to maintain *han* self-sufficiency in food for defense purposes. Moreover, the fact that transportation was prohibitively expensive except along the main transportation routes made such a policy highly advisable for economic reasons. Except in *han* near large population centers where agriculture had become highly commercialized, the peasants for the most part could have been expected to support this food policy insofar as they were almost completely self-sufficient, and famine was the principal threat to their well-being. To enforce it, where acquiescence was not forthcoming, drastic measures were taken. These included "attempts to stop immigration to Edo and even to return recent immigrants to their villages; to prohibit the migration of labor from one lord's jurisdiction to another; to prevent labor in the village from following occupations other than farming; to stimulate the birth rate, to fix wages, and much else."[107]

Following the Meiji Restoration, self-sufficiency in food for security reasons ceased to be a *han* problem. However the threat of hunger and social disorder still confronted the government and the people since storage, transportation, and communications facilities were yet poorly developed. Moreover the rice surplus probably tended to persist for the additional reason that the farmers needed more cash income than in the past in order to make money payments for taxes (previously mostly paid in kind), fertilizers, and other goods and

[107] Smith, pp. 111-112.

services becoming increasingly available. For most farmers rice remained the most important and certain source of money income.

As time passed, however, certain food saving effects operated which made it possible to feed an increasing number of people with a given supply of food until these effects were fully realized. Soon after the Meiji Restoration all commercial barriers between *han* were abolished. Although this did not immediately cause an abundant flow of food within the *han*, since trade requires the build-up of service industries, it paved the way for an improved flow in the future. The commencement of foreign trade in the 1850's eased the threat of severe famine and reduced somewhat the need to maintain a policy which would produce a food surplus in normal crop years. But, the food saving effects could only be fully realized with the improvement of national transportation facilities and storage facilities and the institution of a more efficient national (as opposed to *han*) administration of emergency food measures. In respect to storage facilities Lockwood states that decay and infestation of grain in storage can easily run up losses of 5 to 10 percent.[108] This implies that food savings up to 5 to 10 percent are possible by improvement. The improvement of transportation also lowered the prohibitively high costs of transporting food over most of the country. All these measures required time to become effective, however.

It is also probable that a higher food supply per capita was needed in the earlier years because a higher average consumption per capita over the years tends to be required when the food supply is less stable from year to year.[109]

For the reasons given above, although Japan did not have a long-run comparative advantage in food production, she

[108] *Op. cit.*, 192, 247.

[109] Professor E. J. Hobsbaum states that it is quite possible for a citizen of an industrial society to be worse fed on the average than his predecessor, so long as he is more regularly fed. (Hobsbaum, E. J., "The British Standard of Living, 1790-1850," *Economic History Review*, Second Series, X, 1 [April 1957], 46.)

continued to be a rice exporter until the 1890's, when a rough balance in rice supply and consumption was reached.

It has been argued above that there are grounds for accepting a 1.6 *koku* per *tan* yield during the cadastral survey of the 1870's, and a 1.9 *koku* per *tan* yield around 1920. However, because of the uncertainties attached to yield estimation even under the best of circumstances, a range of yields will be selected for each period instead of a single figure.[110] For the 1918-1922 period the range will be 1.9 to 2.0 *koku* on the ground that underreporting might have existed at the time but that if it did it probably was by a small percentage. The range selected for the 1873-1877 period is 1.5 to 1.7 *koku*. Given estimated yields of 1.3 *koku* in the 1680's and 1.9-2.0 in 1918-1922, and considering agricultural developments from the 1680's to the 1920's, the yield could scarcely have been greater than 1.7 or less than 1.5 *koku* in the 1870's. If the yield ranged from 1.5 to 1.7 *koku* in 1873-1877 and from 1.9 to 2.0 in 1918-1922, it increased by 11.8 percent at the least, and by 33.3 percent at the most in the 45-year period. If the median yields of 1.6 and 1.95 *koku* are taken, the increase is 21.9 percent. On Table 9, quinquennial yields are estimated on the assumption that yield increased at a constant rate.[111]

ESTIMATION OF DRYLAND CROP YIELDS

The argument that the increase in paddy rice yield was partially fictitious applies with equal strength to dryland crops. A case can be made that the gain in yield per *tan* of dryland crops was slower than that of rice with the possible exception of cocoons, wheat, and barley. In general, much greater attention was given to the care and fertilization of

[110] Originally I was disposed to take a single most reasonable figure for each period. I am much indebted to Professor Harry T. Oshima for persuading me of the wisdom of selecting a range of values. Professor Ouchi Tsutomu of Tokyo University offered criticism along similar lines.

[111] It is probable that yield per *tan* increased at a faster rate in the latter half of the period under study. The constant rate assumption is made because no firm basis exists for adopting any other rate.

TABLE 9

INDICES OF CORRECTED PADDY RICE YIELDS PER TAN UNDER VARYING
ASSUMPTIONS OF YIELD IN 1873-1877 AND 1918-1922

Assumed Paddy Rice Yields (*koku*):	1.7 in 1873-77 1.9 in 1918-22		1.6 in 1873-77 1.95 in 1918-22		1.5 in 1873-77 2.0 in 1918-22	
	Yield	Index 1873-77 = 100	Yield	Index 1873-77 = 100	Yield	Index 1873-77 = 100
	(1)	(2)	(3)	(4)	(5)	(6)
1873-1877	1.700	100.0	1.600	100.0	1.500	100.0
1878-1882	1.721	101.2	1.636	102.2	1.549	103.3
1883-1887	1.743	102.5	1.672	104.5	1.599	106.6
1888-1892	1.764	103.8	1.709	106.8	1.651	110.1
1893-1897	1.786	105.1	1.747	109.2	1.705	113.7
1898-1902	1.808	106.4	1.786	111.6	1.760	117.3
1903-1907	1.831	107.7	1.826	114.1	1.817	121.1
1908-1912	1.854	109.0	1.867	116.7	1.876	125.1
1913-1917	1.877	110.4	1.908	119.3	1.937	129.2
1918-1922	1.900	111.8	1.950	121.9	2.000	133.3

NOTE: Constant growth rate is assumed in all cases.

paddy fields than to that of upland fields, with the major exception of mulberries. In respect to seed improvement, dryland crops have received much less attention than rice,[112] with the exception of cocoons, which technically are not a dryland crop. A more important reason to suspect that dryland crop yields were more frequently understated than paddy rice yield in the early Meiji period is that tax officials paid relatively little attention to the valuation of upland fields, thus probably providing landowners with greater opportunity for understatement. This is evident from the cursory attention that the problem of upland field valuation received in communications and instructions relating to the cadastral survey

[112] NNHS, III, 678.

recorded in Volume 7 of *Meiji zenki zaisei keizai shiryō shūsei* (Collection of Early Meiji Financial and Economic Materials). If understatement of dryland crop yields is proportionally greater than paddy rice yields, a more rapid rate of increase of the former might be expected in government statistics.

However, there are offsetting factors. The importation of foreign seed, for example barley and wheat, which were widely grown in economically developed countries, might have increased yields in Japan. But this practice was not an unqualified success. Despite superior yield, the Kinai region experimental station reported in 1908 that imported barley and wheat seed were almost worthless for use in Japan because they matured late.[113] Two other reasons have been given for their failure to be adopted: susceptibility to wind and rain damage and incompatibility with the practice of growing crops between rows owing to their height.[114] Limited planting of foreign varieties did occur in Hokkaidō and the Kantō region,[115] where weather conditions and farming practices were more suitable.

There is no question that very serious attention was paid to the improvement of sericulture by the government and by private individuals. Early in the Meiji period disease control, improvement of quality, mulberry culture, and other aspects of sericulture became a major concern of the national government, and particularly the prefectural government of Nagano.[116] The fact that improvement could occur at more stages in cocoon than in rice production suggests that cocoon yield per *tan* of mulberries rose more rapidly than rice yield per *tan*. Government statistics also show cocoon yield to have been greater than that of rice, which points to the same conclusion.

Government statistics indicate that dryland crop yield per *tan* generally rose more rapidly than paddy rice yield. Sta-

[113] *Ibid.*, p. 40.
[114] *Ibid.*, p. 197.
[115] *Ibid.*, p. 24.
[116] *Ibid.*, V, 547-48, 562-75.

tistics are available for a number of important dryland crops prior to 1885, when the change in statistical reporting policy occurred. Although the yield series for many of these crops are broken between 1885 and 1894, sufficient information is available to make a few observations. The increase in the yield per *tan* of seven out of ten dryland crops over the period from 1879-1884 to 1915-1925 is greater than that of rice.[117] A weighted average of ten crops reveals an 86.3 percent rise[118] in the period, against an increase of 64 percent for rice.

Is the higher value for dryland crops a result of a greater understatement in 1879-1884? Did the understatement of yield decline as rapidly as for paddy rice? These are questions that cannot be answered on the basis of available information about dryland crops, and for this reason a direct estimate of dryland crop yield cannot be made. The only alternative is to base it on the estimated paddy rice yield. In establishing a relationship between the two there are perhaps three considerations that may serve as guides. First, the dryland crop yield, as computed above, increased 86 percent compared to 64 percent in the case of paddy rice. Second, yield improvement of dryland crops, except for cocoons, received less attention than that for paddy rice. Third, foreign seed imports may have increased the yield of wheat, barley, and possibly other crops. If the second factor is relatively more important, an assumption that the change in dryland crop yield was the same as that for paddy rice becomes attractive. If the first and third factors are given greater weight, then the assumption might be made that the actual percentage increase in dryland crop yield exceeded the percentage increase in the corrected paddy rice yield by the ratio of the 1915-25 dryland crop yield index of 186.3 to the paddy rice yield index of 164.0. This works out to be 13.6 per cent. The second assumption will be regarded as the more probably correct of the two.[119]

---

[117] Statistical Appendix, Table 6. The ten crops are wheat, barley, naked barley, sweet potatoes, white potatoes, soy beans, foxtail millet, barnyard millet, buckwheat, and cocoons.

[118] *Ibid.*

[119] Originally I made the assumption that the percentage increase of

Under the first assumption, the yield increases for dryland crops would be 11.8, 21.9, and 33.3 percent, depending on the assumptions made about paddy rice yields in 1873-1877 and 1918-1922. Under the second assumption the dryland crop yield increases would be 27.0, 38.5, and 51.4 percent when the paddy rice yield increases are 11.8, 21.9, and 33.3 percent, respectively. Table 10 shows the indices of dryland crop yields under the second assumption. Under the first assumption the yield indices would be the same as that for paddy rice.

TABLE 10

Indices of Corrected Dryland Crop Yields per Tan Under
Varying Assumptions of Paddy Rice Yield in 1873-77 and 1918-22
(1873-77 = 100)

Assumed Paddy Rice Yields (*koku*)	1.7 in 1873-77 1.9 in 1918-22	1.6 in 1873-77 1.95 in 1918-22	1.5 in 1873-77 2.0 in 1918-22
	(1)	(2)	(3)
1873-1877	100.0	100.0	100.0
1878-1882	102.7	103.7	104.7
1883-1887	105.5	107.5	109.7
1888-1892	108.3	111.5	114.9
1893-1897	111.2	115.6	120.3
1898-1902	114.2	119.9	125.9
1903-1907	117.3	124.3	131.8
1908-1912	120.5	128.8	138.1
1913-1917	123.7	133.7	144.6
1918-1922	127.0	138.5	151.4

Note: Constant growth is assumed in all cases.

An examination of rice yields since the Kamakura period suggests that our yield assumptions may not be off the mark—

dryland crop yield was the same as that of paddy rice yield. I am indebted to Alan H. Gleason for the suggestion that dryland yield be reexamined.

it is assumed that paddy rice yields per *tan* are representative of changes in yields of all agricultural crops—since peace and order became more firmly established and communications improved as time passed, a gradual increase in the growth rate could have been expected. Indeed this seems to have occurred according to the data on Table 11.[120] The annual growth rates of 0.44 percent for the period from 1873-1877 to 1918-1922 and that of 0.66 percent for the period from 1918-1922 to 1955-1961 appear compatible with the earlier discussion of yield-increasing factors. If the average yield per *tan* in 1918-1922 is assumed to be 1.90 *koku*, the growth rates are 0.38 and 0.75 percent in the two respective periods. With a yield of 2.00 *koku* the rates are 0.50 and 0.59 percent.

TABLE 11

GROWTH RATE OF RICE YIELD PER TAN, SELECTED PERIODS

Period	Yield (*koku*)	Annual Growth Rate of Yield from Previous Period %
Kamakura (1191-1333)	1.00	—
Bunroku (1592-1596)	1.20	0.06
Jōkyō (1684-1688)	1.30	0.09
1873-1877	1.60	0.11
1915-1925	1.95	0.44
1955-1961	2.50	0.66

SOURCES: Kamakura, Bunroku, and Jōkyō data from supra, p. 30. The 1915-25 data is computed from *NRT*, p. 24. The 1955-61 yield is computed from data in *Nihon tokei nenkan*, 1960, p. 86, and Jiji tsū-shinsha, *Jiji Almanac 1963* (Tokyo, 1962), p. 873.

5. *Index of Corrected Value Agricultural Production*

To obtain adjusted indices of agricultural production with the methods employed here, it will be necessary to obtain the corrected values of paddy rice production and of dryland crop

[120] The 1955-61 yield was selected to represent the postwar period because yields in these years were obtained by a well-planned random sampling method, and as such are regarded as reliable.

production, the latter being assumed to represent all other agricultural production. The adjusted quantity indices of the two categories of agricultural production can now be computed, since they are the products of the adjusted area and yield indices. To obtain the estimated values of the two, there remains only the computation of their base-year values.

Although it is desirable as a general rule to select a later period because statistical refinements occurred with time in Japan, in order to avoid war and post-war price and production distortions 1913-1917 will be taken as the base period rather than 1918-1922. By 1913-1917 previous estimates of the value of agricultural production can be assumed to have become reasonably accurate if adjustments are made for undermeasurement of land. Some understatement owing to unreported crops and underreporting of yield probably existed, but these are believed to be within tolerable limits in view of the relatively wide margin of error that must be allowed for the estimates being made. Moreover, because the purpose of this paper is primarily to determine the growth rate of agricultural production, it is less important to obtain the correct absolute values of paddy rice production and all other agricultural production than it is to obtain the correct relative values of the two in the base period.

The average annual value before correction of all rice production including paddy and upland rice, computed from Ohkawa's *The Growth Rate of the Japanese Economy Since 1878* (GRJE), is 911.3 million yen in the 1913-1917 period.[121] The pre-correction value of paddy rice production of 892.7 million yen is obtained by deducting the value of upland rice, which is estimated to be 18.6 million yen.[122] Since the uncorrected average annual value before correction of all agricul-

[121] Ohkawa, p. 86.

[122] The 18.6 million yen is the product of the average harvest of 1,251 thousand *koku* and the assumed price of upland rice of 14.87 yen per *koku*. This price is 91% of the price of all rice, which is a percentage that held true for the five-year period of 1923-1927. (Computed from MAF, Minister's Secretariat, Stat. Sec., *Nōrinshō ruinen tōkeihyō, 1873-1929* [Annual Statistics of the Ministry of Agriculture and Forestry, 1873-1929], pp. 8-9.)

tural production in 1913-1917 is 1,806.4 million yen according to GRJE estimates[123] and the unadjusted value of paddy rice is estimated at 892.7 million yen, the pre-correction value of all other agricultural production is 913.7 million yen. Livestock production is included with the latter in order to include all agricultural production.[124]

Two adjustments are made to change the Ohkawa base year values to corrected base year values. They are an adjustment for undermeasurement of area planted to crops, and another for underreporting of yield. The adjustment for undermeasurement of area planted to paddy rice and dryland crops is made by inflating with their respective 1956 undermeasurement indices of 1.069 and 1.049, which are assumed to have remained constant. The yield adjustments are less simple. The reported average paddy rice yield in 1913-1917 is 1.843 *koku* per *tan*.[125] The assumed yields in the 1913-1917 period are 1.877, 1.908, and 1.937 *koku*, depending on the specific assumptions made about yields in 1873-1877 and 1918-1922. The yield inflators for each of these assumed yields are 1.018, 1.035, and 1.051, respectively. It is assumed that other agricultural production was underreported by the same proportions and is properly inflated by the same set of yield inflators. The corrected base year values in million yen under various yield assumptions are given below:

Assumed yields	*1.7-1.9*	*1.6-1.95*	*1.5-2.0*
Paddy rice prod.	971.5	987.7	1003.0
Other agric. prod.	975.8	992.0	1007.4
Total agric. prod.	1947.3	1979.7	2010.4

Having obtained the corrected indices of the volumes of paddy rice and other agricultural production and the corrected base year values, we may now compute the corrected

[123] Ohkawa, p. 87.

[124] Since computing it separately, or even excluding it, can only minutely affect the growth rate of agricultural production, it was believed unnecessary to treat livestock separately.

[125] Computed from Statistical Appendix Table 5.

value series. The new values of paddy rice production under various yield assumptions are given on Table 12; those of agricultural production less paddy rice on Table 13; and those of total agricultural production on Table 14. The percentage

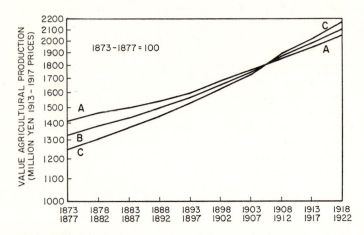

FIGURE 3

Total Agricultural Production in Japan, 1873-1922, Corrected Estimates Under Varying Assumptions

SOURCE: Table 14.

Note: Underlying the three estimates are the following assumptions regarding paddy rice yields in 1873-1877 and 1918-1922, as given in Table 14:
(a) 1.7 and 1.9 *koku* per *tan*
(b) 1.6 and 1.95 *koku* per *tan*
(c) 1.5 and 2.0 *koku* per *tan*

increases in the latter under the three yield assumptions are 44.7, 57.7, and 72.5.

The annual growth rates of the corrected values of agricultural production in Tables 12-14 range from 0.8 to 1.2 percent. The median rate is 1.0 percent, which is also the arithmetic average of the two extreme rates.

TABLE 12

CORRECTED VALUE OF PADDY RICE PRODUCTION IN 1913-17
PRICES UNDER VARYING PADDY RICE YIELD ASSUMPTIONS,
FIVE-YEAR AVERAGES

sumed addy Rice elds[a] (*oku*)	1.7 and 1.9		1.6 and 1.95		1.5 and 2.0	
	Produc-tion Index	Value[b]	Produc-tion Index	Value[b]	Produc-tion Index	Value[b]
	1873-77 = 100	million yen	1873-77 = 100	million yen	1873-77 = 100	million yen
	(1)	(2)	(3)	(4)	(5)	(6)
3-1877	100.0	784	100.0	738	100.0	692
3-1882	102.3	802	103.3	762	104.4	722
3-1887	104.9	822	106.9	789	109.1	755
3-1892	107.7	844	110.9	818	114.3	791
3-1897	109.6	859	113.9	840	118.6	820
3-1902	112.7	883	118.2	872	124.2	859
3-1907	115.8	908	122.7	905	130.2	901
3-1912	119.6	937	128.0	944	137.2	949
2-1917	123.9	971	133.9	988	145.0	1003
4-1922	127.7	1001	139.2	1027	152.2	1053

)URCES : Column (1) : Product of Table 3, Column (5), and Table 9, Column (2).
ᴉmn (3) : Product of Table 3, Column (5), and Table 9, Column (4). Column
: Product of Table 3, Column (5), and Table 9, Column (6).

ɔTES : [a] Assumed paddy rice yields are respectively for 1873-77 and 1918-22.
ᴉumns (2), (4), and (6) were computed by converting base year value with
production indices. The base year values used were 971.5, 987.7, and 1,003.0
on yen.

TABLE 13

CORRECTED VALUE OF AGRICULTURAL PRODUCTION LESS PADDY RICE IN 1913-17
PRICES UNDER VARYING PADDY RICE YIELD ASSUMPTIONS,
FIVE-YEAR AVERAGES

Assumed Paddy Rice Yields[a] (*koku*)	1.7 and 1.9		1.6 and 1.95		1.5 and 2.0	
	Prod. Index	Value[b]	Prod. Index	Value[b]	Prod. Index	Value
	1873-77 = 100	million yen	1873-77 = 100	million yen	1873-77 = 100	millio yen
	(1)	(2)	(3)	(4)	(5)	(6)
1873-1877	100.0	631	100.0	594	100.0	557
1878-1882	103.0	650	104.0	617	105.0	585
1883-1887	107.1	676	109.1	648	111.3	620
1888-1892	111.1	701	114.4	679	117.9	657
1893-1897	116.4	735	121.0	718	126.0	702
1898-1902	124.8	788	131.1	778	137.6	767
1903-1907	133.8	845	141.8	842	150.4	838
1908-1912	145.2	916	155.2	921	166.4	927
1913-1917	154.6	976	167.1	992	180.8	1007
1918-1922	165.7	1046	180.7	1073	197.6	110

SOURCES: Column (1): Product of Table 5, Column (5), and Table 10, Column (1). Column (3): Product of Table 5, Column (5), and Table 10, Column (2). Column (5): Product of Table 5, Column (5), and Table 10, Column (

NOTES: [a] Assumed paddy rice yields are respectively for 1873-77 and 1918-
[b] Columns (2), (4), and (6) were computed by converting base year values w the production indices. The base year values used were 975.8, 992.0, and 1,0 million yen.

TABLE 14

CORRECTED VALUE AND INDEX OF TOTAL AGRICULTURAL PRODUCTION
IN 1913-17 PRICES UNDER VARYING PADDY RICE YIELD ASSUMPTIONS,
FIVE-YEAR AVERAGES

Assumed Paddy Rice Yields[a] (*koku*)	1.7 and 1.9		1.6 and 1.95		1.5 and 2.0	
	Value	Production Index	Value	Production Index	Value	Production Index
	million yen	1873-77 = 100	million yen	1873-77 = 100	million yen	1873-77 = 100
	(1)	(2)	(3)	(4)	(5)	(6)
1873-1877	1415	100.0	1332	100.0	1249	100.0
1878-1882	1452	102.6	1379	103.5	1307	104.6
1883-1887	1498	105.9	1437	107.9	1375	110.1
1888-1892	1545	109.2	1497	112.4	1448	115.9
1893-1897	1594	112.6	1558	117.0	1522	121.9
1898-1902	1671	118.1	1650	123.9	1626	130.2
1903-1907	1753	123.9	1747	131.2	1739	139.2
1908-1912	1853	131.0	1865	140.0	1876	150.2
1913-1917	1947	137.6	1980	148.6	2010	160.9
1918-1922	2047	144.7	2100	157.7	2154	172.5

SOURCES: Column (1): Sum of Table 12, Column (2), and Table 13, Column (2). Column (3): Sum of Table 12, Column (4), and Table 13, Column (4). Column (5): Sum of Table 12, Column (6), and Table 13, Column (6).

NOTE: [a] Assumed paddy rice yields are respectively for 1873-77 and 1918-22.

315

STATISTICAL APPENDIX

TABLE 1A

TAXED PADDY FIELD AREA, 1880-1922

(1000 *chō*)

Year	Nation	Hokkaidō	Nation less Hokkaidō	Year	Nation	Hokkaidō	Nation less Hokkaidō
	(1)	(2)	(3)		(1)	(2)	(3)
1880	2623	—	2623	1905	2823	4	2819
1881	2631	—	2631	1906	2835	5	2830
1882	2631	1	2630	1907	2836	5	2831
1883	2644	1	2643	1908	2844	5	2839
1884	2642	1	2641	1909	2852	5	2847
1885	2641	1	2640	1910	2842	5	2837
1886	2653	1	2652	1911	2849	5	2844
1887	2698	1	2697	1912	2851	5	2846
1888	2777	1	2776	1913	2961	5	2856
1889	2752	1	2751	1914	2855	5	2849
1890	2752	—	2752	1915	2872	6	2866
1891	2532	0	2532	1916	2892	7	2885
1892	2602	—	2602	1917	2889	7	2882
1893	2734	0	2734	1918	2909	8	2901
1894	2744	0	2744	1919	2914	9	2905
1895	2748	0	2748	1920	2922	10	2912
1896	2732	0	2731	1921	2927	12	2915
1897	2739	0	2738	1922	2935	13	2922
1898	2735	0	2735				
1899	2745	2	2743				
1900	2764	3	2761				
1901	2780	4	2776				
1902	2800	4	2796				
1903	2806	4	2802				
1904	2818	4	2814				

SOURCE: Computed from *Tōkei nenkan*. Okinawa data are not included.

NOTES: Data for Aichi, Gifu and Mie prefectures are missing in 1891 and tho for Aichi and Gifu are missing in 1892 owing to a severe earthquake which c curred in 1891.

Up to and including 1899, the date of record is December 31. From 1901 it January 1. To maintain an unbroken series, January 1 data are taken to be those the previous calendar year.

Areas of less than 500 *chō* are designated by 0; — indicates that the data w not entered in the *Tōkei nenkan*.

TABLE 1B

TAXED UPLAND FIELD AREA, 1880-1922

(1000 *chō*)

Year	Nation	Hokkaidō	Nation less Hokkaidō	Year	Nation	Hokkaidō	Nation less Hokkaidō
	(1)	(2)	(3)		(1)	(2)	(3)
1880	1847	—	1847	1905	2344	27	2317
1881	1855	—	1855	1906	2358	30	2328
1882	1876	8	1868	1907	2358	30	2328
1883	1883	9	1874	1908	2356	28	2328
1884	1882	10	1872	1909	2358	28	2330
1885	1886	12	1874	1910	2349	28	2321
1886	1894	13	1881	1911	2347	30	2317
1887	1987	14	1973	1912	2345	30	2315
1888	2274	14	2260	1913	2343	30	2313
1889	2291	14	2277	1914	2324	31	2293
1890	2278	0	2278	1915	2337	35	2302
1891	2150	1	2149	1916	2367	41	2326
1892	2174	—	2174	1917	2361	41	2320
1893	2279	1	2278	1918	2402	68	2334
1894	2285	1	2284	1919	2447	110	2337
1895	2289	1	2288	1920	2496	155	2341
1896	2277	1	2276	1921	2550	206	2344
1897	2282	1	2281	1922	2597	253	2344
1898	2257	1	2256				
1899	2286	16	2270				
1900	2299	16	2283				
1901	2307	16	2291				
1902	2334	19	2315				
1903	2324	21	2303				
1904	2334	25	2309				

SOURCE AND NOTES: Same as for Table 1A.

TABLE 1C

TAXED ARABLE LAND AREA, 1880-1922

(1000 *chō*)

Year	Nation	Hokkaidō	Nation less Hokkaidō	Year	Nation	Hokkaidō	Nation less Hokkaidō
	(1)	(2)	(3)		(1)	(2)	(3)
1880	4470	—	4470	1905	5167	31	5136
1881	4486	—	4486	1906	5193	35	5158
1882	4507	10	4497	1907	5194	35	5159
1883	4527	10	4517	1908	5200	33	5167
1884	4524	12	4512	1909	5210	33	5177
1885	4527	13	4514	1910	5191	33	5158
1886	4547	14	4533	1911	5196	35	5161
1887	4685	15	4670	1912	5196	35	5161
1888	5051	15	5036	1913	5204	35	5169
1889	5043	15	5028	1914	5179	36	5143
1890	5030	0	5030	1915	5209	41	5168
1891	4682	2	4680	1916	5259	48	5211
1892	4776	—	4776	1917	5250	48	5202
1893	5013	2	5011	1918	5311	76	5235
1894	5029	2	5027	1919	5361	119	5242
1895	5037	2	5035	1920	5418	165	5253
1896	5009	2	5007	1921	5477	218	5259
1897	5021	2	5019	1922	5532	266	5266
1898	4991	2	4989				
1899	5031	17	5014				
1900	5063	19	5044				
1901	5088	21	5067				
1902	5134	23	5111				
1903	5130	25	5105				
1904	5152	29	5123				

SOURCE: Columns (1) and (2). Computed from Tables 1A and 1B.

TABLE 2

AREA PLANTED TO PADDY RICE, 1878-1922

(1000 *chō*)

Year	Nation	Hokkaidō	Nation less Hokkaidō	Year	Nation	Hokkaidō	Nation less Hokkaidō
	(1)	(2)	(3)		(1)	(2)	(3)
1878	2490	—	2490	1903	2772	16	2756
1879	2536	—	2536	1904	2790	18	2772
1880	2558	—	2558	1905	2800	19	2781
1881	2544	—	2544	1906	2810	20	2790
1882	2559	—	2559	1907	2820	22	2798
1883	2583	0	2583	1908	2831	27	2804
1884	2573	1	2572	1909	2843	31	2812
1885	2573	1	2572	1910	2850	35	2815
1886	2588	2	2586	1911	2868	40	2828
1887	2608	2	2606	1912	2885	46	2839
1888	2659	2	2657	1913	2903	50	2853
1889	2695	2	2693	1914	2902	44	2858
1890	2713	2	2711	1915	2924	55	2869
1891	2717	2	2715	1916	2935	59	2876
1892	2708	2	2706	1917	2945	64	2881
1893	2724	3	2721	1918	2953	67	2886
1894	2681	3	2678	1919	2961	74	2887
1895	2725	4	2721	1920	2978	82	2896
1896	2730	5	2725	1921	2986	91	2895
1897	2720	6	2714	1922	2990	102	2888
1898	2745	7	2738				
1899	2763	9	2754				
1900	2749	9	2740				
1901	2762	12	2750				
1902	2758	16	2742				

SOURCE: Computed from MAF, For. and Agr. Econ. Bur., Stat. Sec., *Annual Statistics of the Ministry of Agriculture and Forestry, 1868-1953*, p. 10. Okinawa data are not included.

319

TABLE 3

ARABLE LAND AREA IN HOKKAIDŌ, 1878-1922

(1000 *chō*)

Year	Arable Land	Paddy Field	Upland Field	Year	Arable Land	Paddy Field	Upland Field
	(1)	(2)	(3)		(1)	(2)	(3)
1878				1903	286	15	271
1879				1904	329	17	312
1880				1905	344	21	323
1881	12	1	11	1906	346	21	325
1882	15	1	14	1907	410	22	388
1883	23	1	22	1908	436	28	408
1884	27	1	26	1909	510	38	472
1885	26	2	24	1910	538	38	500
1886	25	2	23	1911	580	44	536
1887	31	2	29	1912	618	49	569
1888	35	2	33	1913	632	56	576
1889	41	2	39	1914	654	58	596
1890	45	2	43	1915	683	60	623
1891	52	2	50	1916	717	63	654
1892	56	3	53	1917	747	67	680
1893	66	3	63	1918	795	71	724
1894	79	3	76	1919	816	74	742
1895	97	4	93	1920	839	84	755
1896	115	5	110	1921	855	93	762
1897	143	6	137	1922	853	94	759
1898	170	7	163				
1899	216	9	207				
1900	241	10	231				
1901	266	13	253				
1902	289	19	270				

SOURCE: Columns (1) and (2). Kayō Nobufumi (ed.), *Nihon nōgyō kiso tōke* [Basic Statistics of Japanese Agriculture] (Tokyo, 1958), p. 607. Column (3) i the difference between Columns (1) and (2).

TABLE 4

Undermeasurement Index of Paddy Fields and Upland Fields
by Prefectures, 1956

Prefecture	Paddy Field UI	Upland Field UI	Prefecture	Paddy Field UI	Upland Field UI
Aomori	1.143	1.086	Osaka	1.012	0.987
Iwate	1.139	1.068	Hyōgo	1.112	1.078
Miyagi	1.117	1.199	Nara	1.024	0.998
Akita	1.024	1.046	Wakayama	1.040	1.038
Yamagata	1.072	1.056	Tottori	1.067	1.084
Fukushima	1.073	1.054	Shimane	1.038	1.047
Ibaragi	1.067	1.008	Okayama	1.044	1.043
Tochigi	1.019	0.999	Hiroshima	1.096	1.084
Gumma	1.045	1.021	Yamaguchi	1.013	1.007
Saitama	1.037	1.027	Tokushima	1.046	1.041
Chiba	1.047	1.031	Kagawa	1.093	1.064
Tokyo	1.054	1.054	Ehime	1.035	1.041
Kanagawa	1.009	1.010	Kōchi	1.112	1.118
Niigata	1.139	1.090	Fukuoka	1.042	1.009
Toyama	1.047	1.024	Saga	1.088	1.094
Ishikawa	1.055	1.045	Nagasaki	1.103	1.048
Fukui	1.065	1.000	Kumamoto	1.089	1.094
Yamanashi	1.037	1.024	Ōita	1.075	1.056
Nagano	1.087	1.061	Miyazaki	1.093	1.051
Gifu	1.058	1.026	Kagoshima	1.079	1.056
Shizuoka	1.078	1.070			
Aichi	0.998	0.995	Nation		
Mie	1.085	1.045	(minus		
Shiga	1.071	1.019	Hokkaidō)	1.069	1.049
Kyoto	1.090	1.030			

Source: Taken from a mimeographed worksheet provided by Hatanaka Kōichi of ᴛʜᴇ Crop Statistics Section of the Ministry of Agriculture and Forestry.

TABLE 5

Yield Per Tan of Selected Crops, 1879-1925

Year	Paddy Rice	Wheat	Bar-ley	Naked Bar-ley	Sweet Pota-toes	White Pota-toes	Fox-tail Millet	Barn-yard Millet	Soy Beans	Buck-wheat
	(*koku*)	(*koku*)	(*koku*)	(*koku*)	(*kan*)	(*kan*)	(*koku*)	(*koku*)	(*koku*)	(*koku*
1879	1.249	0.521	0.814	0.687	167	91	0.824	0.996	0.516	0.47
1880	1.223	0.630	0.969	0.885	163	99	0.770	0.954	0.551	0.44
1881	1.169	0.566	0.874	0.696	175	83	0.682	0.885	0.509	0.43
1882	1.173	0.650	0.965	0.897	184	142	0.702	0.962	0.543	0.43
1883	1.177	0.639	0.964	0.754	173	140	0.717	0.934	0.505	0.45
1884	1.047	0.679	0.998	0.858	209	119	0.643	1.095	0.530	0.42
1885	1.312	0.606	0.896	0.775	—	—	—	—	—	—
1886	1.426	0.797	1.174	0.974	—	—	—	—	—	—
1887	1.524	0.779	1.135	0.987	253	172	1.058	1.265	0.698	0.70
1888	1.444	0.767	1.124	0.874	—	—	—	—	—	—
1889	1.216	0.739	1.134	0.836	—	—	—	—	—	—
1890	1.576	0.536	0.834	0.478	—	—	—	—	—	—
1891	1.392	0.831	1.249	1.007	—	—	—	—	—	—
1892	1.513	0.707	1.042	0.932	234	184	1.260	1.250	0.701	0.71
1893	1.354	0.753	1.099	0.939	—	—	—	—	—	—
1894	1.547	0.898	1.315	1.105	208	215	0.912	1.187	0.675	0.69
1895	1.450	0.888	1.306	1.044	209	190	0.943	1.196	0.734	0.67
1896	1.310	0.803	1.206	0.882	284	175	1.027	1.214	0.680	0.63
1897	1.196	0.832	1.255	0.946	256	202	0.957	1.081	0.712	0.56
1898	1.701	0.898	1.351	1.081	268	92	1.069	1.165	0.645	0.66
1899	1.414	0.890	1.295	0.968	247	172	0.929	1.124	0.749	0.56
1900	1.482	0.908	1.345	1.087	279	188	1.012	1.192	0.778	0.76
1901	1.669	0.898	1.386	1.072	265	190	1.122	1.316	0.859	0.71
1902	1.315	0.817	1.262	0.936	257	128	0.885	0.805	0.673	0.57

TABLE 5 *continued*

Yield Per Tan of Selected Crops, 1879-1925

Year	Paddy Rice	Wheat	Barley	Naked Barley	Sweet Potatoes	White Potatoes	Foxtail Millet	Barnyard Millet	Soy Beans	Buckwheat
	(*koku*)	(*koku*)	(*koku*)	(*koku*)	(*kan*)	(*kan*)	(*koku*)	(*koku*)	(*koku*)	(*koku*)
1903	1.649	0.399	1.134	0.627	265	162	1.048	1.302	0.784	0.702
904	1.817	0.841	1.370	0.994	236	173	0.927	1.440	0.830	0.701
905	1.339	0.794	1.275	0.950	263	231	0.892	1.109	0.711	0.681
906	1.616	0.894	1.410	0.993	278	242	1.127	1.223	0.763	0.747
907	1.707	1.003	1.539	1.085	315	251	1.160	1.344	0.777	0.743
908	1.798	0.981	1.466	1.100	317	253	1.133	1.325	0.785	0.746
909	1.808	0.994	1.472	1.124	308	257	1.146	1.389	0.785	0.810
910	1.600	0.968	1.498	0.994	284	262	1.104	1.329	0.710	0.838
911	1.762	1.004	1.568	1.125	342	265	1.072	1.391	0.755	0.805
912	1.703	1.004	1.637	1.162	334	264	1.030	1.262	0.738	0.680
913	1.689	1.081	1.705	1.274	337	250	1.196	0.921	0.630	0.687
914	1.920	0.938	1.549	0.991	322	280	1.037	1.630	0.789	0.847
915	1.862	1.045	1.721	1.160	343	278	1.227	1.567	0.809	0.814
916	1.934	1.107	1.674	1.156	353	271	1.332	1.531	0.804	0.787
917	1.810	1.194	1.708	1.277	322	283	1.199	1.514	0.830	0.655
918	1.807	1.134	1.579	1.220	350	245	1.211	1.512	0.799	0.625
919	1.996	1.160	1.841	1.179	372	313	1.343	1.757	0.915	0.829
920	2.056	1.103	1.531	1.225	371	238	1.312	1.709	0.897	0.876
921	1.794	1.083	1.707	1.059	347	275	1.304	1.698	0.875	0.868
922	1.980	1.142	1.735	1.160	345	242	1.316	1.682	0.821	0.873
923	1.800	1.064	1.590	1.041	345	235	1.270	1.705	0.807	0.864
924	1.869	1.123	1.759	1.055	331	248	1.252	1.120	0.793	0.765
925	1.926	1.306	1.933	1.415	348	267	1.319	1.630	0.909	0.901

SOURCE: MAF, Agric. and For. Econ. Bur., Stat. Sec., *Annual Statistics of the Ministry of Agriculture and Forestry, 1868-1953*.

NOTE: In years marked by —, national data were not compiled for the crops indicated.

TABLE 6

ESTIMATION OF INDEX OF DRYLAND CROP YIELD
IN 1915-25, 1879-84 = 100

Crop	Average Area Planted 1918-22 (1000 *chō*)	(1) as % of Total	Ratio of 1915-25 Yield to 1879-84 Yield	Weighted Yield Increase (2) x (3)
	(1)	(2)	(3)	(4)
Wheat	535	15.5	1.85	28.5
Barley	528	15.4	1.83	28.2
Naked Barley	648	18.8	1.48	27.8
Sweet potatoes	311	9.0	1.94	17.5
White potatoes	123	3.6	2.35	8.5
Soy beans	450	13.1	1.60	21.0
Foxtail millet	142	4.1	1.77	7.3
Barnyard millet	48	1.4	1.63	2.3
Buckwheat	134	3.9	1.79	7.0
Cocoon	523	15.2	2.50	38.0
Total	3442	100.0		186.3

SOURCES: Column (1). Computed from MAF, Agric. and For. Eco. Bur., Stat. Sec., *Annual Statistics of the Ministry of Agriculture and Forestry, 1868-1953*.

Column (3). Computed from Statistical Appendix: Table 5, except for the cocoon yield ratio. The only problem associated with estimating the cocoon yield ratio was in obtaining the area planted in 1879-84. It was assumed that this was 230 thousand *chō*. The average cocoon production at this time was 11.8 million *kan*. (1 *kan* = 8.27 lbs.) The average yield per *chō* of mulberries is 50 *kan*. The average yield in 1915-25 was 125 *kan* (area = 512 thousand *chō* and yield = 65.9 million *koku* computed from same source as Column (1)). The ratio of 125 to 50 is 2.50.

The assumption of 230 thousand *chō* planted to mulberries is probably an overstatement. Any lower estimate will, of course, raise the per *tan* cocoon yield in 1879-84 and reduce the increase in yield, therefore lower the dryland crop weighted yield increase.

CHAPTER VII

Innovation in Japanese Agriculture, 1880-1935

SHŪJIRŌ SAWADA

THE LITERATURE on Japanese agriculture since 1868 has tended to contrast the slow processes of change in agrarian Japan with rapid technical progress and social change in other sectors of national life. Much has been said too about agriculture's role in fostering industrialization through making available in the countryside "unlimited" supplies of labor for industrial employment. Also stressed is the financing of industry through investment funds siphoned out of agriculture in the form of land taxes and rental and interest incomes.

On the other hand, it is a truism that in Japan, no less than elsewhere, "take-off" from traditional levels in national economic development required a certain process and level of modernization in agriculture and other extractive industries themselves. Ohkawa and Rosovsky in their "Century of Economic Growth" (above, Ch. II) argue that Japanese agriculture in fact achieved a growth rate in keeping with that of other industries almost until the end of World War I.[1] Even if James Nakamura's downward revision (above, Ch. VI) be accepted in whole or part, agricultural progress was substantial. Only in this way was the Japanese economy provided with sufficient supplies of food and raw materials, as well as labor and capital, to effect the critical transition to industrial society.

This essay concentrates on technological developments in Japanese agriculture from 1880 to the eve of World War II— the first half century of industrialization. The discussion

[1] See also Ohkawa Kazushi and Henry Rosovsky, "The Role of Agriculture in Modern Japanese Economic Development," *Economic Development and Cultural Change*, IX, 1, Part II (1960), 43-67.

focuses on (1) the economic implications of technological change in agriculture, (2) entrepreneurial incentives and leadership, and (3) the limitations imposed by the social background of traditional village society.[2]

Production Coefficients in Agriculture

LAND AND LABOR

Technological innovations in Japanese agriculture throughout the prewar era were both land-saving and labor-saving in nature. Taking land, first of all, one finds that the arable area is estimated in index terms to have increased from 100 in 1878-1882 to 135 in 1933-1937. Meanwhile general agricultural production concurrently rises from 100 to 246, according to the index computed from official data.[3] On these

[2] Special gratitude is due Professor K. Ohkawa, Hitotsubashi University, Professors K. L. Robinson, J. W. Mellor, and R. Barker, Cornell University, Professor A. M. Tang, University of California, and members of the Estes Park Conference, especially Professors William W. Lockwood and Johannes Hirschmeier, for helpful comments and criticism. I am also indebted to Professor L. B. Darrah and Dr. J. H. Marshall for assistance in preparing this paper at Cornell, and Mr. I. Iwama, Kyūshū University, for aid in the collection of data.

[3] Several writers give different time-series of the gross output in Japanese agriculture as follows: (Here we employ the second estimate below, by the Ministry of Agriculture.)

Indices of Gross Output in Japanese Agriculture

	1878-82	1933-37
(1) Ohkawa Kazushi, et al.	100	311
	1878-82	1933-37
(2) Ministry of Agriculture and Forestry	100	246
	1880-84	1935-39
(3) Yamada Saburō	100	212

SOURCES:

(1) Ohkawa Kazushi, et al., *The Growth Rate of the Japanese Economy since 1878* (Tokyo, 1957), table 16, p. 32. Table 16 shows real national income produced in primary industry, deflated by sectoral deflators. The author derives gross output through dividing net income

326

findings the land coefficient index, measuring changes in the ratio of land area to its output, declined from 100 to 55 over this half-century or so. To turn it around, physical output per acre nearly doubled in physical terms. If we accept Nakamura's argument that official statistics underestimate yields in the early years (above, pp. 277ff.) the coefficient for land drops less substantially, though its movement is still downward.

Labor productivity in agriculture, similarly defined, likewise rises steadily through the period, though not at a uniform rate. The number of people gainfully employed in agriculture, at least part-time, probably changed comparatively little from 1880 to 1935, though the data are unsatisfactory.[4] If so, the labor coefficient fell more or less in proportion as output grew, i.e., as much as 60 percent if official output statistics are used.

Concealed here may be a considerable change in man hours per year devoted to agricultural work by people enumerated in the agricultural labor force but actually only at work part-time. Their work was seasonal, and most of them were family workers who combined agricultural employment with subsidiary work in proportions that may have altered appreciably over a half-century. No data exist on real labor inputs over this period. From 1922 to 1937, however, according to the Farm Household Survey, farm-family labor hours devoted to agricultural operations dropped about 20 percent. Mean-

---

by net income ratios as shown in tables 10 and 12, pp. 64, 70.

(2) Kayō Nobufumi, ed., *Nihon nōgyō kiso tōkei* [Basic Statistics of Japanese Agriculture] (Tokyo, 1958), pp. 68, 220.

(3) Yamada Saburō, "Nōgyō ni okeru tōnyu sanshutsu no chōki hendō" [Long-term Changes in Agricultural Inputs and Outputs], in Ohkawa Kazushi, ed., *Nihon nōgyō no seichō bunseki* [Economic Growth and Agriculture in Japan] (Tokyo, 1963) p. 88.

[4] S. Hijikata's labor force estimates put 16.1 million people in agriculture, forestry, and fishing in 1878-82, and 16.4 million in 1886. K. Hemmi's more recent estimate sets the figure for 1886 at 14.9 million—probably closer to the truth. Census data yield a figure of 14.7 million for 1933-37, little below Hemmi's estimate for the eighties. Ohkawa, *Growth Rate*, pp. 142-49.

while the number of family workers enumerated as principally employed in farming remained constant. Very likely over the entire period 1880-1935 the labor coefficient expressed in labor hours decreased more than that reflected in the numbers of people gainfully employed in agriculture. Probably it fell even more than the land coefficient, though Japan's population nearly doubled in the meantime. To cite one other clue, labor hours devoted to rice culture per *tan* (.245 acres) fell from 32 days a year toward the end of the Tokugawa regime[5] to 23 days in 1922 and 20 days in 1937.[6] For the prewar era as a whole, however, neither the statistics of farm output nor those of labor inputs before 1920 are reliable enough to permit any firm conclusions.

CAPITAL

What change occurred in the coefficient for fixed capital? (The term as used here excludes land.) Such calculations are difficult, too, particularly in physical terms and over a long period, since new kinds of capital goods are introduced and old ones disappear. On small-scale farms like those in Japan, also, capital goods often take the form of hand tools and semi-mechanical equipment having only a very subjective evaluation. Finally, buildings and other capital goods are sometimes used for both farm and family purposes, making it difficult to measure accurately their net contribution to farming. A few observations can be made, nevertheless, on the trend of the capital coefficient in real terms.

Cattle and horses are the only capital inputs for which quantitative data are available throughout the period 1885-1935. Excluding land and buildings, they were the most important component of fixed capital anyway, particularly in the early years. Sheep, goats, and hogs have appeared in the statistics since about 1899; poultry since 1906; and cows since 1922. Thereafter enumerations of newly-recorded kinds of livestock and poultry indicate that their numbers must

[5] Nōgyō gijutsu kyōkai, ed., *Meiji ikō ni okeru nōgyō gijutsu no hattatsu* [The Development of Agricultural Technology in Japan since the Meiji Period] (Tokyo, 1952), p. 124.

[6] Kayō, p. 404.

have been almost negligible at the beginning of the Meiji era. To simplify matters here, different kinds of livestock and poultry are aggregated by using the standard unit of livestock of the Ministry of Agriculture and Forestry. Assuming a negligible quantity other than cattle and horses at the outset, the index of livestock units rises from 100 in 1878-1882 to 236 in 1933-1937. (Even if some poultry and livestock other than cattle and horses did exist at the beginning of the Meiji era, this error in the index is more than offset by marked improvements in quality which are also not reflected in the statistics.) Since the official production index rises from 100 to 246 during the same period, the capital coefficient in terms of livestock and poultry alone remains virtually constant on this calculation. The same conclusion holds true regarding the more limited period from 1911-1915 to 1933-1937, when the enumeration of livestock and poultry is more complete. Here the capital-coefficient index in these terms rises from 100 to 112, while the general production index rises from 100 to 116. Again, then, the coefficient of fixed capital remains more or less constant in terms of this major component, if we accept the official statistics of production.

Next we turn to mechanical equipment. Some kinds of plows and rotary weeders have been used in Japanese agriculture since the middle of the Meiji era, and stamping rotary threshers since World War I. Since about 1920 there are some statistics of farm machinery; for example, electric motors and oil engines increased from 2,468 in 1920 to 192,301 in 1937, and mechanically powered equipment along with them. Taking farm equipment and livestock together, we may conclude that the capital coefficient in this sector increased through the period.[7]

[7] Recently, an estimation of fixed capital in agriculture during the period under review has been completed by Umemura Mataji and Yamada Saburō in "Nōgyō kotei shihon no suikei" (An Estimation of Fixed Capital in Agriculture since 1875), *Nōgyō sōgō kenkyū* (Quarterly Journal of Agricultural Economy), XVI, 4, National Research Institute of Agriculture (Tokyo, 1962). According to their estimate, the real input of fixed capital excluding buildings rose from 100 in

As for working capital, a tremendous increase develops in the use of chemical fertilizer. If the consumption of fertilizer in 1878-1882 is taken as 100, the index in 1933-1937 stands at about 11,500.[8] Meanwhile the quantity of manure decreased in relative terms, being superseded by much larger applications of chemical fertilizer. Other agricultural chemicals came into increasing use also, though no data are available for the entire period. It seems likely that the coefficient for working capital of all types increased considerably during the period.[9]

From these fragmentary data we may infer that the over-all coefficient for farm capital (excluding land) rose substantially in Japan from 1880 to 1935. It should be emphasized that these computations all rest on official statistics of agricultural output as emphasized in the indices cited above. To the extent that James Nakamura's upward revision of production data for the earlier years is accepted (above, Ch. VI), the growth rate in agriculture from 1880 to 1920 is accordingly reduced, and the capital-output ratio rises still more.

1878-82 to 220 in 1933-37, in index terms. The official production index rose up from 100 to 246 during the period as in the text. Considering the error which is inevitable in any such estimation, the fixed capital coefficient might well be said to have remained almost constant during the period.

[8] Shishido Hisao, "Nōgyō seisansei no hatten to donka" (Development and Retardation of Agricultural Productivity) in Tōbata Seiichi, and Ohkawa Kazushi, eds., *Nihon no keizai to nōgyō* (Japanese Economy and Agriculture), (Tokyo, 1956) I, 91.

[9] An estimation of working capital in agriculture during the period under review was recently completed by Yūjirō Hayami, in "Waga kuni nōgyō ni okeru keijōzai tōkaryō no suikei" (Measurement of Current Input in Japanese Agriculture: 1878-1940 and 1957-1961), *Nōgyō sōgō kenkyū* (Quarterly Journal of Agricultural Economy), Vol. 17, No. 4, National Research Institute of Agriculture (Tokyo, 1963). He concludes that the real input of working capital increased from 100 in 1878-82 to 312 in 1933-37, in index terms, while the official production index rose from 100 to 246. On this calculation, accordingly, the working capital coefficient increased from 100 to 127 during the period.

Technological Developments and Their Economic Implications

LAND-SAVING ASPECTS

Before World War II Japanese agriculture had attained the highest production per acre in the world. Net product in agriculture per hectare of agricultural land was valued at $146 just before the war, according to Ohkawa's estimate. This put Japan at the top of 51 countries, with a figure seven times that of the United States.[10] How had such economies in land been effected, and what were their economic implications?

Agricultural land in Japan is almost all arable land and is used mostly to raise crops for final use, particularly human food. The total agricultural area was accurately measured for the first time only in 1950, when cultivated land was found to comprise 82 percent.[11] This high ratio is attributable partly to the demarcation measure of 1876, which excluded extensive community grasslands and placed them in the category of national forest land. However, the percentage of agricultural land cultivated seems to have increased still further since then, owing to reclamation and deforestation.

This shift to tillage doubtless raised land productivity, since output per acre is generally low on grassland, and at this time was rising on cultivated land. On the other hand, there was an economic offset in terms of the replacement of grassland by labor to get manure. The farmers' routine was to procure grass or young leaves from distant areas almost every morning from early summer to fall, using hand-sickles and bamboo baskets. Such areas were often forest or grassland belonging to village communities, riverbanks, etc. The grass or leaves gathered were used as roughage (fodder), or plowed into arable land directly as grass manure called *kari-shiki* or *kasshiki* (cut and spread). But available grassland was so scarce that it was often over-used; most of it deteriorated in quality, owing to this abuse and mismanagement. More and more labor was thus required to get a given quan-

[10] Ohkawa Kazushi, *International Comparison of Productivity in Agriculture* (Tokyo, 1949).
[11] Kayō, p. 73.

tity of grass. Increasingly, then, Japanese farm manure became the product of labor rather than of land. This contrasts
with Western practice, in which soil fertility is maintained by
retaining much land in pasture and meadow, and using it to
raise livestock. In Japan land has been used mostly for final
crop cultivation, and it is farm labor that has been relied upon
increasingly to provide the necessary roughage.

More recently farmers have come to use more and more
fish-meal fertilizer, and this seems to have replaced grass
manure to some extent. In fact, *karishiki* had already almost
disappeared toward the end of the Meiji era. In this sense
land may be said to have been replaced by working capital.
However, fertilizer was more than a mere substitute for land
and labor, since it could also be used in increasing amounts to
raise yields. This has been one of the most efficient means of
saving land, especially as fertilizer prices declined relative to
those of farm products in the latter half of the period under
review. In addition, the tendency to decreasing returns in
fertilizer use was offset to some extent by technological developments such as improvement of varieties of crops and
deep-plowing. However, a tremendous increase occurred in
the use of chemical fertilizer, particularly after World War I;
as noted earlier if the consumption of fertilizer in 1878-1882
is taken as 100, the 1933-1937 index stood at 11,500.[12] Despite
these improvements the use of fertilizer seems to have approached a limit; moreover, the tremendous increase of chemical fertilizer created a problem of maintaining soil fertility.
To these problems we shall return shortly.

A second form of land-saving was its more intensive utilization, that is, to produce two or more crops per year. Double-
cropping of paddy fields, usually with rice in summer and
wheat or barley in winter, was developed gradually along
with the improvement of land, crop varieties, and methods of
cultivation. Nurseries for early rice planting have greatly
extended double-cropping, because farmers can germinate
rice seedlings for a couple of months while the winter crop is
still in the field. This double-grain system is rare in other

[12] Shishido estimate cited earlier.

countries but became a normal pattern of paddy utilization in Japan. Again difficulties arose, however. First, a great demand for labor appeared at the moment of changing from one crop to the other. The bottleneck was in the fall, when the paddy field had to be shifted to an upland condition for the wheat or barley, with as little delay as possible. Even in the warm southwest districts of Japan the sowing of winter crops was often delayed in order to harvest the rice, particularly as the growing period of rice was extended to get better yields. One of the hardest tasks in prewar Japanese farming was to dig up the moist soil of the paddy field, pile it up in furrows, and harrow it. In many districts the first two laborious jobs were often done with a simple hoe.

These tasks became somewhat easier when an efficient plow was introduced along in the middle of the Meiji period, though harrowing remained a drudgery throughout the period. (Now these problems are rapidly being solved by the tremendous increase in power-driven tillers since World War II.) Such implements as stamping rotary threshers, too, tend to reduce the seasonal peak of labor demand. In many districts the development of electrical pumping has lessened still further the peak demand for labor; its efficiency has permitted farmers to delay the transplanting of rice seedlings by a couple of weeks and reduce losses from the rice-borer that spawns early in June. Before World War II the latter often caused serious damage to the rice crop.

Another problem which came along with intensive land utilization was how to maintain soil fertility. Fertility can be sustained rather easily on paddy fields if used only for rice culture, since the paddy is irrigated and produces much straw to be used as manure. However, the introduction of the second crop created difficulties. While rice culture benefits from irrigation, the second crop grows mainly with manuring. Farmers tried to use as much manure as possible for the second crop, but came nevertheless to rely increasingly upon chemical fertilizer to raise yields. Over-exploitation of the soil in this fashion threatened its long-run fertility. One solution was increased production of livestock and poultry, both to raise farm income and maintain soil fertility. From their own land, however, farmers could not produce their own feed, a necessary intermediate product, without turning large amounts of precious arable to low-yield livestock farming. In prewar years over one million tons of feed began to be imported annually from China and other countries, furnishing almost 80 percent of the feed used by cows and chickens. Again intensive utilization of land in crop farming required compensating allocation of factors to other uses—in this case, exports.

The third form of land saving was improvement in its quality. The well-to-do farmers led in early improvement, and later such gains became widespread following the Land Adjustment Law of 1899 and a subsidy measure enacted several years later. By 1937 the total area of improved land under the law was 652,431 *chō*,[13] some 20 percent of the entire paddy area. The improvements of the early years, including those accomplished before enactment of the law, were mainly adjustment through regional planning which facilitated use of an improved plow; improvements in irrigation and drainage came later.

One of the purposes of land improvement was *nawanobi* (to lengthen a measuring rope). This did not mean the actual enlargement of land area; rather, it was better official measurement and recording of the actual acreage. Usually the gain was around 6 percent in the acreage formerly recorded.[14] The main purpose, however, was to raise and stabilize yields per acre. Yields could be increased by combining land improvements with other innovations such as deep plowing with the improved plow, better varieties of seed, and more fertilizer. It is difficult to say in what degree yields were increased by improved land use. Some records show a 10-20 percent increase in rice yield per acre; others report a gain of 100 percent or more, besides changes making it possible to cultivate a second crop. By thus raising output per acre such improvements economized land, and it is not surprising that expendi-

[13] 1 *chō* = 2.45 acres.
[14] Kayō, p. 70.

tures for this purpose rose rapidly. Real improvement costs approximately doubled during the first 30 years after the Land Adjustment Law was enacted in 1899.[15] Toward the end of the period under review they seem to have approached their limit, and only improvements far larger in scale of organization could continue economically to raise productivity still further.

LABOR-SAVING ASPECTS

Land saving is the major concern of technological developments in Japanese agriculture, needless to say. What motivation can there be for labor-saving improvements in a country said to be so overpopulated as Japan?

Briefly, in farming as in other industries technology tends to vary with different endowments and relative prices of the factors of production. If labor becomes increasingly scarce, farmers feel its shortage keenly until a new kind of technology is developed economizing on its use. Such shortages have occurred in two ways: one was the attraction of labor into other industries, raising the wage rate of hired labor; the other was a rise in the imputed marginal value of family labor, as farm incomes gradually increased. Typically both effects have occurred simultaneously; the time when much labor was being attracted into other industries was often the time when farm prices were favorable. Thus labor shortages have occurred even in Japanese agriculture where it is said to be so plentiful, and have stimulated economies in the use of labor.

As regards labor-saving improvements, several historical developments are significant. First, while we commonly associate labor saving chiefly with machinery, in prewar Japanese agriculture more working capital and better tools and semi-mechanical implements also saved much labor. Fertilizer was responsible not only for increasing yields per acre, as mentioned above, but also for saving labor by replacing in part the use of grass manure, especially manure from ma-

[15] Tōbata Seiichi, *Nihon nōgyō no tenkai katei* [The Development Process in Japanese Agriculture] (Tokyo, 1938), p. 260.

335

terials obtained away from the farm. Consequently some grass-land fell into disuse. According to a survey by the Ministry of Agriculture and Forestry in 1950, a time when villages were still overpopulated as before the war, mountainous villages were leaving unused some 35 percent of their grassland, because of the shortage of labor. For semi-mountainous and semi-flat villages the figure was 33 percent.[16] *Karishiki* had almost disappeared in Japan as long ago as the early part of this century. Increasing use of insecticides was still another way in which labor was economized, for farmers previously had had to employ very laborious methods to prevent insect damage.

Power-driven machinery came into use on Japanese farms only toward the end of the prewar era. The earlier manually operated implements such as the improved plow, hand rotary weeder, and stamping rotary thresher saved much toil, but always required some skilled labor and generally additional hand work. Some of the improved plows had no base[17] and needed very skilled operation. Those most widely adopted had a short base, and, although more stable, they required considerable skill as well. Weeding by the hand-rotary weeder required in addition about two hand weedings with *ganzume* (hand-forks). Again, the rotary thresher could not move over a field like a combine; harvesting had to be done by hand with a sickle. Labor-saving accomplished by such tools or simple machinery thus needed skilled labor and much hand work, and this undoubtedly helps to explain continuance of small-scale farming throughout the period.[18] Even so, some

[16] Kayō, p. 91.

[17] The part touching the ground.

[18] The social system and technical methods of production interact upon each other in their development, of course. In prewar Japanese agriculture the former strongly influenced the latter; this is the main contention of this paper. This passage, however, refers to the counter-action. Such influences of technology upon the social framework and organization of agriculture were always present. In prewar Japan their influence upon traditional village society seems relatively weak because of the continuing abundance of labor and the slow accumulation of capital mainly in the form of working capital.

of the hardest jobs, such as digging the paddy field with hoes, weeding with *ganzume* under the blazing sun, etc., were greatly eased by such labor-saving improvements.

As previously noted, labor saving was always accompanied by economies in land that increased yields per acre of land or facilitating multi-cropping.[19] A growing need to economize labor prompted the introduction of implements which at the same time had a land-saving effect. The absorption of labor into other growing industries thus seems to have resulted not only in raising labor productivity in agriculture but also in providing the national economy with higher yields and outputs of farm products.

In grain crops, labor in use per acre could be reduced comparatively easily through mechanization, and the labor thus economized used for other enterprises with a higher return per capita.[20] The latter included sericulture, tobacco culture, horticulture, and the keeping of livestock and poultry. Through such shifts the productivity of labor was increased, particularly when grain prices fell. Sometimes these newer products likewise tended to overproduction, as the government encouraged their spread through many districts. Nevertheless this process of raising productivity through diversification has been one of the principal avenues of labor saving and remains a strong tendency in the Japanese countryside.

CAPITAL-USING ASPECTS

At a time when the surplus of agricultural income over the living necessities of farmers and their families was still very small, and institutions still undeveloped for finance and marketing, the formation of capital directly on the farm was the principal way of adding to production facilities. That meant the mobilization of labor to produce capital goods on an indi-

[19] Umeki Toshimi, *Effects of Power-tiller Use on Farm Income in the Saga Plain Area, Saga Prefecture, Japan.* English Bul. No. 3, Dept. of Ag. Econ., Kyūshū Univ. (Fukuoka, 1961).

[20] Otsuki Masao, *Labor Productivity and Employment in Japanese Agriculture,* English Bulletin No. 4, National Research Inst. of Agriculture (Tokyo, 1961).

vidual or a community scale, as was characteristic of pre-modern Japanese agriculture. Ever since 1868 this type of capital formation has brought major advances. Many irrigation reservoirs such as those covering about 20 percent of the whole irrigated area today were formed with labor investments in the early days. Soil fertility, too, was often improved by the continuous effort for many years of farmers who applied great quantities of manure to land after digging or plowing it deeply. Other land improvements as well, including river utilization, were effected in large measure with local farm labor. Much labor was likewise required to enlarge stocks of cattle and horses, as well as handmade implements and buildings.

Fertilizers, tools, and implements were introduced characteristically in complementary relationships with each other and with land improvements. For example, increasing use of fertilizer required improved varieties of plants, including varieties that were not vulnerable to diseases caused by heavy use of fertilizer. Disease-resistant varieties were generally of the multi-panicle type having short stems and many strong roots; they could therefore absorb large amounts of nutrients and produce high yields. Thus improved varieties and greater fertilizer inputs worked together, along with other innovations such as land improvements and improved plows. The last-mentioned were indispensable for deep plowing, which allowed the roots to grow into the soil widely and deeply. A long-based plow could plow only about two inches deep, whereas the short-based plow could reach a depth of three or four inches.

Deep plowing also created a new demand for draft animals. Before the improved plow became popular, cattle and horses had been used mainly for transporting crops, fodder, and miscellaneous goods, or for stamping manure into paddy fields. As they came into use for plowing, they became one of the essential means of production. In fact they became all-purpose assets, providing draft power and manure, and bringing forth young. Moreover, they could be raised in farmyards, and even their salvage price was a source of income. Such all-purpose capital goods fit well into the capital-scarce economy of Japanese farmers. However, the versatile use of these animals often reduced their efficiency for any single purpose, and since World War II they are gradually being supplanted by milk cows and power-driven tillers.

In many ways, then, Japanese agriculture intensified the use of capital goods. Beginning with an emphasis on more working capital, it went on gradually to build stocks of fixed capital as well. A major problem then developed in the rapid increase of costs due to fixed capital charges in small-scale farming. For instance, a power-driven threshing machine, most efficient for harvesting crops of 15 hectares, was used on one- or two-hectare farms. This illustrates the contradiction between the modernization of agriculture and traditional small-scale farming—a problem to which we shall return at the end of the next section.

Incentives and Leadership

Fundamental to this long record of innovation in Japanese agriculture was the supply of leadership and incentives, either from within or without the agrarian order. In exploring them we shall distinguish, first, the Meiji era, and, second, the years between World War I and World War II.

THE MEIJI PERIOD, 1868-1911

Substantial and cumulative modernization required, first of all, destruction of the feudal system. Among the major reforms that followed the Meiji Restoration were the abolition of restrictions on the permanent sale of land, on cultivation of various kinds of crops, and, above all, on the free trade and communication between districts. These new freedoms were fundamental to technological development, as noted in earlier essays in this volume. Improved varieties of rice were now widely marketed, for example, whereas in feudal times fear of the shortage of good seeds had led to the strict prohibition of export of improved seed from one *han* (feudal domain) to another, and sometimes even between villages in the same district. With the Restoration such barriers were removed, and improved varieties and better culture methods were now rapidly developed by veteran farmers in various districts. The *Nōdan kai*, farmers' associations first organized in 1874, contributed substantially to such communications, especially after it began in 1881 to hold national meetings in Tokyo sponsored by the central government.

The spreading use of fertilizer illustrates this dissemination of improved techniques. Some fertilizer in the form of fish meal had come into use even in feudal times. Made chiefly from herring in Hokkaidō, it was confined in the main to commercial crops like cotton, rush, indigo plant, and tobacco that were cultivated in the western districts in Japan. Its use now increased greatly as communication became free and active between districts and was extended to rice cultivation clear across Japan. Later, soybean cake began to be imported from China, ushering in the so-called golden age of soybean fertilizer.

Rōnō (veteran farmers) traveled throughout the country after 1868, teaching improved methods of culture that were based initially on their own experiences rather than scientific experimentation. Some of what they taught was excellent. At first they seem to have been invited mostly by local governments, but in 1885 the central government established the Farm Visiting Teacher System, and many prominent veteran farmers traveled in numerous districts. The *Kannōsha*, a private school of farming established by Enri Hayashi in Fukuoka prefecture in 1883, also sent staff members throughout the country. Some 464 members were so engaged between 1885 and 1893, and this group is credited with introducing the improved plow throughout the country.

Those who first adapted the improved methods of cultivation and took the leadership in spreading them throughout their neighborhoods were the *gōnō* (wealthy farmers). The above-mentioned *rōnō* belonged mostly to this prosperous class. Though not many in number, the *gōnō* each operated a considerable acreage of land—several hectares—with hired workers who served ordinarily in a servant-master relationship to the operator and his family. Some of the *gōnō* accumulated

340

much land, particularly during the period of deflation which began in 1881 and drove many peasants into tenancy and toward the end of the Meiji era they changed increasingly into non-operating landlords. The social status of the *gōnō* is significant: they came mostly from the families of village headmen and other leading families in their districts. Characteristically they were leaders in village affairs, for reasons both of ability and means. Some of them sought to invite *rōnō* from a distance, and some went to great lengths to accomplish land improvements even before measures for subsidy were enacted. As agricultural entrepreneurs they were, so to speak, "dynamic landlords."[21] Later some of them became members of prefectural assemblies; many took leading positions of country or prefectural farmers associations; and others became officials of local governments. As a class they were influential both as formulators and mediators of government policy in the countryside.

It is well known that social overhead capital and other subsidizing encouragements to manufacturing industry were provided by the government with revenues raised mainly from the land tax.[22] Few similar measures to subsidize agriculture were undertaken before World War I. Mention might be made of programs for the settlement of ex-samurai, though their purpose was essentially political. National land was given or sold at a low price to tremendous numbers of displaced aristocrats now deprived of their feudal stipends. Furthermore the large sum of 6 million yen—the national budget was only 50 million yen at that time—was used around 1878 for low-interest loans to help them enter farming. However, the purpose of this program was to employ and pacify the former samurai class rather than to promote the agricultural economy per se, and in spite of such subsidies few ex-samurai became successful farmers.

Last to be mentioned are direct incentives to the adoption of the improved plow and other implements around the middle of the Meiji period. The wage rate in agriculture rose con-

[21] Tōbata, p. 79.
[22] See Oshima's discussion, below, pp. 357ff.

siderably in those years, owing to a growing shortage of labor as other industrial employments developed. Higher wages created a difficult problem for large farms like those of the *gōnō*, which depended upon numbers of hired workers. The difficulty was twofold: first, the labor shortage itself, and second the breakdown of the master-servant relationship which ruled the traditional farm.

The district where plows were first improved and widely used was the northern part of Kyūshū, where the shortage of labor was acute owing to the rise of the mining industry. The private farm school known as the *Kannōsha* was located there, and staff members were invited to many districts to teach the so-called "Southwest" method of farming with the aid of the improved plow. These districts, too, tended to be ones experiencing a growing shortage of labor. Thus M. Umemura classifies all prefectures at this time according to the change in the number of farm families, labeling them R, S, or G, that is, "recessive," "standstill," or "growing" in population. He also divides the whole period under review into two sub-periods, before and after 1910. He identifies the labor situation of the two periods for each prefecture by such symbols as RR (recessive in both periods), SR (standstill in the first, recessive in the second), GG, etc.[23] From other records we can check which prefectures invited staff members of the *Kannōsha*.[24] If we assume that prefectures labeled RR, SR, and GR are the labor-short prefectures, and GG, SG, and RS are the less-labor-short prefectures, the relationship is as follows: 9 of the 19 labor-short prefectures invited *Kannōsha* members ten times and more, as compared with only 4 of the 26 less-labor-short prefectures. The former is 47 percent; the latter, 15 percent of the total.[25]

[23] Umemura Mataji, *Chingin. koyō, nōgyō* [Wages, Employment, and Agriculture] (Tokyo, 1961), 123.

[24] Nōgyō hattatsu shi chōsakai, ed., *Nihon nōgyō hattatsu shi* [The History of the Development of Japanese Agriculture]. (Tokyo, 1953), I, 395.

[25] The labor-short prefectures were also the more prosperous, and were in centrally located areas where new production methods most easily spread. Fr. Johannes Herschmeier has observed that the im-

Two further points are of interest regarding farm entrepreneurship in this early era of modernization. First, *gōnō* families are said to have retired almost entirely into the status of non-operating landlords toward the end of the Meiji era. The main reasons were apparently as follows: the new methods of farming which they introduced were of a sort that required close management and skilled operation, and this kind of farming was better adapted to small-scale farms. It became more profitable, therefore, for *gōnō* to rent their land in small parcels to tenant farmers, obtaining a high rent from the intensive farming methods they had themselves helped to improve. Meanwhile the land taxes they paid were reduced relative to their rent incomes. For rent was set generally as a fixed amount of rice per unit of land, and the price of rice drifted upwards in the late Meiji years. Meanwhile the land tax rose only moderately or not at all, leaving the landlord with a wider margin of retained income. In some districts, however, this tendency was held in check by low productivity stemming from poorer land or inferior marketing conditions. These districts were mostly in northern Honshū, some parts of Kyūshū, and mountainous areas in other regions. Here some wealthy farmers remained as landlord farmers, exercising local leadership and entrepreneurial initiative as in the past.

A second development of significance was the active initiative assumed by the government in developing agriculture toward the end of the Meiji period. National agricultural experiment stations were established in 1893. The Land Adjustment Law of 1899 (revised in 1909), the Agricultural Association Law of 1899, the Industrial Cooperative Law of 1900, and other agricultural laws were established one by one. Some subsidies to agricultural improvement were also undertaken.

---

proved plow was pioneered in such prefectures not merely because of rising labor costs but because also in these more progressive, accessible districts new knowledge was diffused more readily than in more remote regions. Before long, however, some 30 prefectures invited staff members of the *Kannōsha*, or 64% of the total number. By that time the *Kannōsha* was widely known throughout the country.

In 1901 legislative measures and provincial administrative orders were also introduced to prescribe the best methods for cultivating rice. In some prefectures policemen seem to have checked on how well the prescribed procedure was being followed. Agricultural associations developed around 1900 from the *Nōdan kai* into a large organization backed by a special law and equipped to play an important role in extension work in close contact with the central and local authorities. Their village branch offices were often in buildings located near village government offices. Strong governmental leadership of this sort in the modernization of technology continued until World War I, when mounting wartime inflation shifted attention increasingly to problems of marketing and price control.

THE INTERWAR YEARS, 1918-37

The years after 1920 were difficult years for Japanese agriculture. Cheap rice began to be imported from Korea and Formosa, where rice cultivation had been encouraged by the Japanese government following the food shortage of World War I and the rice riots that resulted in 1918. Labor absorption into other industries ceased for a time with the postwar depression. The number of those gainfully employed in agriculture actually increased by 2.2 percent between 1923-1927 and 1933-1937, in contrast to its 1.5 percent decline in the preceding decade.[26] Meanwhile agriculture itself fell into a prolonged economic depression from which it slowly emerged only in the thirties. As shown in Figure 1, the gradual decline in the farm labor force appears to have been interrupted after 1925, and instead a tendency appeared for people to pile up on the farm during the next decade of the Great Depression and its aftermath.

The only development favorable to agriculture at this time was the expansion of the ammonium sulphate industry so that the relative price of fertilizer fell considerably. The price ratio of chemical fertilizer to agricultural products declined

[26] Hemmi Kenzō, *Nōgyō yūgyō jinkō no suikei* [An Estimate of Gainfully Employed Population in Agriculture], in Tobata and Ohkawa, p. 415.

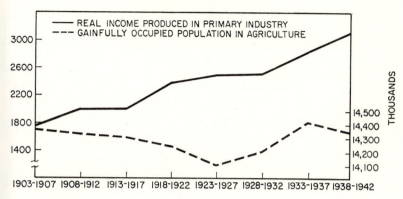

FIGURE 1

Primary Production and Agricultural Employment in Japan, 1903-1942

SOURCE: Tōbata Seiichi and Ohkawa Kazushi, eds., *Nippon no keizai to nōgyō* [Japanese Economy and Agriculture] (Tokyo, 1956) I, 23, 415.

by about one-third, and its consumption increased rapidly. In fact, the amount of fertilizer (including non-chemical fertilizer) used per acre of arable land greatly increased during these years. This more intensive use of fertilizer and labor to raise acreage yields was the main technological change to occur in the interim period. Older varieties of rice such as *shinriki* were discarded in favor of *asahi* and others that responded better to additional fertilizer. Deep-plowing also spread as a means to get high yields. Encouraged by the government, farmers also diversified their farming with second crops, livestock, and processing of farm products. Such technological innovations offset or postponed the tendency of diminishing returns in Japanese agriculture.

The increasing reliance on heavy applications of fertilizer, and its relation to the availability of cheaper supplies, is illustrated in Figure 2. Here is depicted the change in the regression coefficient for the relation of the amount of ferti-

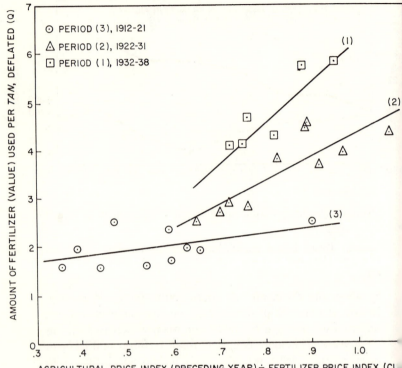

Figure 2

Fertilizer, Technology, and Agricultural Prices in Japan, 1912-1938.

Source: Calculated from the data provided in Tōbata Seiichi and Ohkawa Kazushi, eds.. *Nippon no keizai to nōgyō* [Japanese Economy and Agriculture] (Tokyo, 1956), I, 191, 410; II, 227.

lizer used per *tan* to the price ratio of agricultural products and fertilizer as follows:

Where Q is the amount of fertilizer used per *tan* (deflated value of fertilizer bought by farmers per *tan*), and P is an index of the ratio between the price index of agricultural products in preceding year to that of fertilizer in current year for periods,

(1) 1912-21, $Q = 1.251 + 1.270\ P$ $r = 0.529$
(2) 1922-31, $Q = -0.534 + 4.890\ P$ $r = 0.854$
(3) 1932-38, $Q = -1.805 + 8.115\ P$ $r = 0.898$

Significantly the coefficient of P rises over the periods, which means that the amount of fertilizer used per *tan* increases from one period to the next for the same increment in the price ratio of agricultural products to fertilizer. This clearly reflects technological changes making the slope of the marginal productivity curve of fertilizer less steep in successive periods.[27]

The relative share of labor in agricultural net income also increased from 40 to 50 percent during the interwar years.[28] This may have been the result partly of thousands of tenancy disputes which occurred during the years of farm depression. From only 85 throughout the country in 1917 the number of such disputes rose to 6,824 in 1935, though the number of persons involved in each dispute became smaller. One factor at work here was the gradual change in the traditional relationship between landlords and tenant farmers. The landlords tended more and more to become mere absentee rent-collectors, and at the same time traditional high rents gradually declined. These shifts were only beginning to take place, however, and labor's relative share of income still did not rise above 50 percent. It was the growing demand for rural labor

[27] Consistent with the data also would be the conclusion that the elasticity of the supply function had increased over a period of time. This was pointed out by Anthony M. Tang, University of California. However, assuming that the demand function has shifted slowly over time, and the supply function comparatively rapidly, the author's conclusion appears warranted as regards the shift in the slope of the derived demand function of fertilizer (the marginal productivity curve). Under this assumption the price-quantity data express mainly the demand function. Such was the actual situation at the time, as technological development occurred only slowly in agriculture, while the fertilizer industry underwent rapid expansion.

[28] Umemura, p. 85.

in non-agricultural employment that was working mainly to undermine the traditional framework of the village, but these forces were still weak in relation to the pressure of a growing population on the farm.

Technological developments tended also to increase the relative share of labor in agricultural income. Land improvements spread more extensively throughout the country, and steady improvements in seeds and crop practices adapted to local conditions tended to level up the yields of marginal land. Many such technological developments tended to improve the marginal productivity curve of labor and to raise its relative share of agricultural income.

Yet it is significant that the technological development which had extended back to early Meiji seems now to have been approaching its limit in the thirties. Agriculture could not continue to extend these limits without breaking down its traditional structure, particularly the small family farm with its reliance upon supplies of working capital, simple tools, intensive hand labor, and various institutional and economic relationships that provided its social framework. (See Ohkawa and Rosovsky, above, pp. 77ff.)

Thus, in spite of determined efforts the rice yield per *tan* increased only slightly from 1918 to 1937 as shown in Table 1.[29]

TABLE 1

AVERAGE RICE YIELD PER TAN (PADDY FIELD)
IN JAPAN, 1918-37

	koku
1918—22	1.929
1923—27	1.878
1928—32	1.911
1933—37	2.008

SOURCE: Statistics of the Ministry of Agriculture and Forestry.

[29] Rice culture was encouraged in this period by the high price of rice relative to other farm products. Kanazawa Natsuki, *Inasaku no tenkai kōzō* [The Structural Development of Rice Culture] (Tokyo, 1958), p. 6.

The relation between rice yields and fertilizer used per *tan* from 1922 to 1937 is shown in Figure 3. Increasing input of fertilizer did not increase yields per *tan* much over 2.5 *koku* (1 *koku* = 4.96 bushels) per *tan*, and in most years it was used in this maximum amount.

Significant, too, is the fact that increased capital investment appears no longer to have had any marked effect in raising output within the existing framework of technology and economic and social relations. Some increase in fixed capital did take place during this period, as mentioned earlier. Often it is said that Japanese agriculture was being starved for lack of capital—a great barrier to increases in output. According to T. Noda's cross-comparisons of farms analyzed in the Farm Household Survey, however, the evidence points the other way.[30] A slight increase in capital is associated with decreased efficiency and increased costs of production; the capital coefficient rises considerably with an increase in farm capital. Surprisingly, the capital coefficient in Japanese agriculture at this time seems larger even than in the agriculture of the United States. Small-scale farming as now practiced in Japan could no longer absorb efficiently increasing capital investment.

Conclusion

From this survey of prewar Japanese agriculture we see a steady growth in output achieved by a long, slow process of technical innovation. These innovations, both land-saving and labor-saving, were achieved within an economic and social framework that preserved the basic traditional features of the small family farm. Increasing investment of capital supported technical progress, first through better working capital and tools and semi-mechanical equipment, and then with mechanization, which set in toward the end of the period.

As the traditional structure of the Japanese village and small-scale farming remained basically intact, however, further advances in land yields and labor productivity became

[30] Noda Tsutomu. *Nōgyō no shihon keisū* [Capital Coefficient of Agriculture], Tōbata and Ohkawa, p. 228.

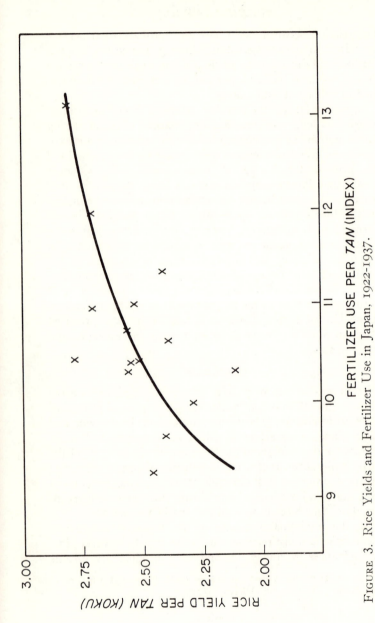

FIGURE 3. Rice Yields and Fertilizer Use in Japan, 1922-1937.

SOURCE: Imperial Agricultural Assn., *Kome seisanhi chōsa, jisaku* [Rice Production Cost Survey, Owner Farmers], 1922-37.

... in the total expense of fertilizer including manure, estimated by ingredient prices

increasingly difficult to achieve in the later decades, 1918-1937. Not until the land reform and other structural changes of the era after World War II did it become possible to break through this ceiling to new levels of production and technical efficiency. (See below, p. 450).

CHAPTER VIII

Meiji Fiscal Policy and Agricultural Progress[1]

HARRY T. OSHIMA

THE GENERALLY ACCEPTED JUDGMENT in the current literature is that fiscal policy in the Meiji era (1868-1911) was a noteworthy success on the whole from the point of view of developing the Japanese economy.[2] The general tenor of this thinking may be summarized as follows: despite the low productivity levels of the economy, Meiji fiscal policy was able to raise large amounts of funds internally to finance the enormous expenditures required for the development and modernization of the economy. It did this mainly by taxing heavily the agricultural sector, without interfering with the healthy growth of the sector. The upshot was that the Meiji economy grew at a rate of about 4 percent per year.

The arguments presented in this essay contradict this line of thinking. No one can maintain that Meiji fiscal policy was a total failure, of course, for a degree of success was achieved in several respects—e.g., the modernization of transportation

[1] I wish to acknowledge the assistance of Mr. T. Sakiyama and Mr. K. Niiro in the compilation of data. In revision of the original paper, my greatest debt is to Professor William Lockwood, whose comments were most helpful in the preparation of the final version. I also benefited very much from comments by Hugh Patrick, Henry Rosovsky, and Ohkawa Kazushi. Mr. Sakiyama, a junior fellow at the East-West Center, is presently engaged in the revision of the Taishō-Shōwa estimates of functional expenditures. Though the Taishō-Shōwa data used here are preliminary and approximate, they are thought to be adequate for present purposes.

[2] See, e.g., Thomas C. Smith, *Political Change and Industrial Development in Japan: Government Enterprise, 1868-1880* (Stanford, 1955); also Hugh Patrick, "Lessons for Underdeveloped Countries from the Japanese Economic Development," *Indian Economic Journal,* IX, 2 (October 1961), 156-59. See also articles by Ranis, Ohkawa, Rosovsky, et al., cited by Patrick.

and communications, the extension of education and the mechanization of industries like textiles and a few heavy industries. But shortcomings considerably dim the luster of the achievements. In particular, the extraction of large sums of money from the farm population was generally detrimental to the healthy development of agriculture, especially as so much was used relatively unproductively for military purposes. If we are to profit fully from the Meiji experience this aspect needs to be studied.

Achievements and shortcomings are matters of degree, of course. Some may argue that it was more or less inevitable that large expenditures should be appropriated for military purposes, given the configuration of events and pressures that characterized the Meiji period. With this view I disagree. In any case, the purpose of this study is not to evaluate the historical impact of fiscal policies in this era but to learn from the Meiji experience whatever lessons may be useful in shaping the policies of underdeveloped countries today.

Those who may be inclined to dismiss outright the view presented in this paper should ponder some important recent findings. It has been generally held that the growth of Meiji agriculture was rapid and that, paralleled by the even more rapid expansion of the non-agricultural sectors, this resulted in a growth rate of about 4 percent for the economy as a whole. This optimistic judgment is now being challenged. Scholars both in Japan and the United States have been critically reexamining the official statistics of agricultural output and increasingly doubt their reliability. Many are puzzled by the extremely low calorie levels implied by the official statistics of agricultural output for the early Meiji period. They suggest something like 1,400-1,600 calories per day per person for the 1870's and 1880's, compared to more than 2,000 for India today. We now have a detailed study by James Nakamura, part of which is presented above in Chapter VI. Nakamura finds that the official statistics significantly understate agricultural output in the early part of Meiji. He estimates (p. 254) that agricultural output rose by only about

1.0 percent per year from 1875 to 1920, as compared to Ohkawa's figure for primary production of 2.9 percent.[3]

Though challenged by Ohkawa and Rosovsky (above, pp.
68-69)—the whole matter is still very uncertain—Nakamura's findings go beyond the agricultural sector in their implications. They tend to cast doubt, in my opinion, on the
growth rate of the whole economy for the entire Meiji era.
As Professor Ohkawa notes in *The Growth Rate of the Japanese Economy Since 1878*, "our estimates . . . of net product in
manufacturing . . . should be understood as being far weaker
than that of primary industry," and as for the tertiary sector
". . . the measurement of the tertiary production represents
the greatest statistical difficulties. . . ."[4] If one examines the
secondary sector in Ohkawa's data for the Meiji period, the
estimation of the very important small industry sector is
hardly more than guesswork based on certain assumptions
(see pp. 90-94). The extremely high rates of growth exhibited for the period 1878-1900, around 8 percent per annum,
are consequently largely arbitrary. Even if the assumptions
turn out to be correct, the estimates contain a large element
of upward bias because they fail to "include the output of
peasant households in their supplementary and subsidiary
activities"—output which is of major consequence in early
Meiji Japan.[5]

For the tertiary sector, i.e., the rest of the economy, Ohkawa's estimates are largely dependent in turn on the estimation of the primary and secondary sectors. For he has taken
the "average of the weighted average of per capita income
and wages in the goods-producing sector (primary and sec-

[3] See Ohkawa Kazushi et al., *The Growth Rate of the Japanese
Economy Since 1878* (Tokyo, 1957), p. 21. In my "Survey of Various
Long-Term Estimates of Japanese National Income," *Keizai kenkyū*,
IV, 3 (July 1953), 249, it is argued that Meiji official agricultural
figures appear to be too low.

[4] Ohkawa, pp. 94, 100.

[5] See my paper cited in n. 3, p. 249. As growth takes place, household
production declines and there is a shift of production to factories,
whose output becomes recorded in the industrial statistics.

ondary industries").[6] In short, the growth rate of about 5 percent per annum shown for the tertiary sector cannot be taken to be reliable either.

The upshot of the foregoing is that we do not know whether the growth of the Meiji economy was rapid or slow. Yet much discussion takes rapid growth for granted because of existing national income estimates. In the light of Nakamura's criticism of the official agricultural data and because of the shakiness of the Ohkawa estimates for the secondary and tertiary sectors, this view is unwarranted. One may not assume that Meiji growth was rapid and then proceed to explain it. As matters stand now, it could have been as low as 1 or 2 percent. Under these circumstances, a reexamination of the period from a different point of view may be worthwhile.[7]

[6] Ohkawa, p. 101. In a paper entitled "Notes on an Alternative Method of Estimating the National Income and Expenditure of Japan, 1881," *Keizai kenkyū*, VIII, 3 (July 1957), 243-51. I attempted a detailed estimate for a single year, using a method different from that used by Ohkawa and others. My estimate for 1881 was about 25% higher than Ohkawa's. The higher total was mainly due to the secondary and tertiary sectors. Though not satisfied with Ohkawa's primary gross output figure, I had no adequate basis for revising it.

[7] In reviewing Ohkawa's book in the *American Economic Review*, XLVII, 4 (September 1958), 685-87, I pointed out that if Ohkawa's growth rates were accepted, a puzzling question would be posed: what happened to all the increases in product and productivity implied by the high growth rates, inasmuch as Japan's per capital incomes in the late 1930's or mid-1950's were so low compared to those of European and other countries. One guess was that much of the growth was dissipated in military activities and war expenditures. Partly, in an attempt to study this possibility, I undertook the study of Meiji Japan's budget statistics. I speculated also that Japan's per capita income at the end of the Tokugawa period may have been extremely low. But if we assume that Meiji growth rates were low, it may be that Tokugawa per capita incomes may not have been so low.

Such a rate is not very impressive, compared to the 4% in the Philippines, Thailand, Malaya, Taiwan, India, etc., in the decade of the 1950's. The interpretation of the Meiji period has influenced the construction of other theories of underdevelopment (e.g., the Ranis-Fei model, the Hagen theory, etc.), so that we need to know much more about the period than we do at present. The views presented in

In the pages to follow, we discuss first government revenues and their sources and the impact of Meiji tax policies on agriculture. We then analyze the expenditures of the Meiji government as a whole. In both cases, not only the central government budgets are considered but those of all local governments are consolidated with the central government budgets. Because previous studies were based on expenditures of only the central government, they have tended to give a somewhat distorted picture of Meiji fiscal policy.

On the other hand, certain limitations on this study need to be stressed at the outset. Fiscal activities exclude regulatory and other non-financial activities of the government. "Government," as the term used here, excludes public enterprises such as railroads, postal services, etc., and public financial institutions. Because of this, our conclusions are restricted to a narrower range of activities than is usually associated with the term "government" However, in view of the important role of government banks in financing industries during the Meiji period, it is not possible to ignore them. We consider their role toward the end of the analysis.

The Meiji Land Tax

PRODUCTIVITY AND INCIDENCE OF MEIJI LAND TAX

Table 1 and Figure 1 show the importance of the land taxes (levied on rice fields, dry fields, residential land, salt fields, mineral springs, forests, and pastures) in the consolidated revenue of all governmental bodies in the Meiji period. The percentage share contributed by land taxes declines sharply, as against relative stability in the shares of indirect taxes and the rise in the shares of other direct taxes and non-tax revenues. Despite the sharp fall in the share of land taxes in the total public revenue, the absolute amount of revenue from the land taxes remained high throughout the nineteenth century; it then rose in the first two decades of the twentieth.

---

this paper should be taken to be more intuitive than scientific and are intended to provoke further work on the period.

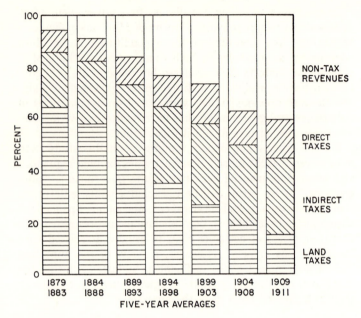

FIGURE 1

The Share of Land and Other Taxes in the Consolidated Government Revenues of Japan, 1879-1911

Source: Table I.

These taxes comprised about one-tenth of income originating in agriculture, 1879-1911. Since the agriculturists paid many levies other than land taxes, the burden on the agricultural sector was enormous indeed.

This is by no means the complete picture. The Meiji period began in 1868. It is possible to obtain a rough notion of the importance of the land tax during 1873 to 1878. In this period, the share of land taxes in central government revenues averaged 80 percent. Since in 1879 land taxes comprised 55 percent of total local revenues, the 80 percent amounts roughly to 72 percent for all governments for the period 1873 to 1878, if 1879 proportions are assumed. This compares with

64 percent for the period 1879-1883. If one assumes that 72 percent also holds for 1868-1872, one may conclude that, in the entire Meiji period, the share of land taxes comprised two-fifths of the revenue of all governments. (Table 1.)

TABLE 1

CONSOLIDATED GOVERNMENT REVENUES IN JAPAN, 1879-1911

(million yen)

Five-Year Averages[a]	Land Taxes	Other Direct Taxes[b]	Com-modity Taxes[c]	Enter-prise Taxes	Other Indirect Taxes	Non-Tax Reve-nues	Total Reve-nues
1879-1883	60.7	8.0	17.1	2.7	0.7	5.1	94.6
1884-1888	57.4	9.6	20.7	3.8	0.1	8.3	100.1
1889-1893	53.4	12.1	27.5	4.3	0.4	18.7	116.5
1894-1898	59.2	20.2	38.2	9.0	2.3	40.8	169.9
1899-1903	84.9	50.1	76.5	18.4	6.1	86.2	322.1
1904-1908	114.7	86.2	140.9	36.9	8.5	231.0	618.4
1909-1911	126.2	127.8	185.1	49.5	6.9	338.0	841.9
Average for:							
1879-1911	79.5	44.8	72.2	17.8	3.5	104.0	323.4

SOURCES: See Appendix.

[a] Except 1909-1911, a three-year average.

[b] Includes personal income tax, residence tax, corporate income tax, inheritance tax, and house tax.

[c] Includes taxes on sake, tobacco, soy sauce, drugs, scales, sugar, textile, bever-ges, and transportation and custom duties.

Even this proportion may be an understatement. In the period before 1879 most of the revenue of local governments came from a levy called *minpi*. According to Fujita Takeo (*Nihon chihō zaisei seido no seiritsu* [The Formation of Provincial Fiscal Systems of Japan] Tokyo, 1941), most of this comprised taxes on land.

Of course, not all land taxes were agricultural land taxes. Data on the distinction between taxes on crop land and other (including residential) land are not available. An approxi-mation may be obtained from central government budget data which make the distinction from 1880. In the ten-year period,

1880-1889, 90 percent of the land tax was derived from farm land, 6 percent from rural residential land, 2 percent from urban residential land, and the rest from a miscellany of land. This pattern probably holds roughly for local governments, which used surtaxes on national taxes.

INCIDENCE OF THE LAND TAX

Before the effect of the land tax on agriculture itself is discussed, something must be said regarding its incidence. The land tax was levied on the owner of the land. Unlike the farm real estate tax in the United States (which is treated as an indirect tax in the United States Department of Commerce national income accounts), the tax was actually based on the average normal net yield of the land, though nominally assessed on land values. This was because most agricultural land had no actual sales value in Japan at this time owing to the absence of real estate markets. Such a tax is probably difficult to shift in the short run.

In the long run, complete or partial forward shifting may be possible if a peasant can withdraw from production so that the supply curve of farm products can shift to the left. But for Japanese agriculture in the Meiji period, the type of entry and withdrawal assumed for the highly dynamic economy of the United States is probably not realistic. In the basically subsistence economy of Meiji Japan, tradition, ignorance, poverty, social pressures, inadequate transportation, and the absence of alternative employment considerably limited the mobility of the peasant. Moreover, most of the peasant's crop was intended for home consumption, not for sale; the aim of production was primarily for use (subsistence) and secondarily for profit maximization. It was not possible for him to abandon rice production just because its price was low or because his profits had diminished because of high taxes. Even though the farmer was incurring losses, he had no choice but to continue working his land. It is safe to conclude that forward shifting of the land tax (from farmer to the consumer) probably was not possible under conditions of the Meiji economy.

In this period about one-third of the total farm area was tilled by tenant farmers. Was the tax levied on landowners shifted backwards to tenants in the form of higher rents? In the absence of adequate data the question is difficult to answer with any degree of certainty. It is likely that increases in productivity were largely claimed by the landlords since the absolute share of the tenant per *chō* (.275 acres) of rice-land seems to remain constant. Since the land tax rate in the Meiji period was no higher than in the Tokugawa period, the problem of tax rate increases being shifted to the tenant does not arise as far as Meiji Japan is concerned. Whether in principle land taxes are shiftable backward or not, it is clear from the foregoing discussion that the heavy land taxes were borne by the farming sector.

THE LAND TAX AND FARM BENEFITS

The success of the land tax in providing finances for the growth of the nonagricultural sector is obvious. But the Japanese experience should not be evaluated solely by the revenue-effect of the land tax. If this experience is to be a valuable guide to policies for underdeveloped countries, the impact of land taxes directly on agriculture must be considered. This is, of course, a broad subject, and we can indicate no more than the rough direction which such an analysis may take.

The issue of certificates of ownership, clearly establishing ownership rights and opening the way to the sale and purchase of land, undoubtedly contributed to the security of tenure which was prerequisite for investment in long-term improvements by the cultivator. Also, the tax was based on land values which were fixed for a stated period of time (five years) and uniform throughout the nation, without the arbitrariness and uncertainty that seemed to characterize land tenure in the Tokugawa period.

Other aspects of Meiji policy were less favorable to agricultural productivity, e.g., the high level of taxation, its regressive character, and the requirement of cash payment. The rates were high relative to the productivity levels of the period. If productivity is measured by calorie intake (to facilitate international comparisons), the per capita intake per day in Japan was reported to be no more than 1,400 to 1,600 units a day.[8] Even if an upward adjustment of 30 percent is made to the agricultural production data, the intake is no more than 1,800, which is about the level in India today. If the total revenue from land taxes is computed as a percentage of income originating in agriculture and forestry, as noted above it averages about 10 percent or more. Although income from agriculture is by no means the total of peasant income (since subsidiary economic activities loom large in the Japanese countryside), still this was a substantial burden for the farm households in the middle-income and lower brackets of the Meiji period. For American farmers, a 10 percent tax payment is not a difficult matter. But with low productivity, taxable income over and above living expenses may be very small, if any. For a large number of the peasants those rates left very little for farm improvements and investments.

The structure of rates was regressive with respect to net income—net after payment of actual and imputed wages. Since a flat rate was levied on each yen of assessed value, the tax was proportional to the total value of land owned. This proportionality was probably equivalent to regressivity with respect to net income if the unequal distribution of land ownership is taken into account, assuming that the bigger landowners tended to possess better land. It was highly regressive with respect to monetized net income since the poorer peasants who were forced to sell at harvest time received a lower price for their product than others.

Above all, the provision that taxes be paid entirely in cash strained the resources of the rural economy. Despite the rapid extension of the money economy during the Tokugawa period, the Meiji economy was basically a subsistence economy in

[8] S. Nakayama, "Shokuryō shōhi suijin no choki henka ni tsuite," [On Long Term Changes in Food Consumption Levels, 1878-1955], *Nōgyō sōgyō kenkyū*, XII, 4 (October 9, 1958), 13-37. Nakayama's estimates of Japanese food consumption per capita, 1878-1937, are given by Nakamura (above, Table 8, p. 296), in connection with his discussion of food output in the Meiji period.

which economic activities were conducted without the use of money. (For example, tenants still paid their rents in kind.) The sudden imposition of cash payments brought severe hardship, especially to the small land peasant. Since taxes were due in the harvest months, the rice markets were flooded with crops to be sold for tax payments and prices fell disastrously, but richer peasants and landlords were able to withhold their crops until prices improved.

It has been argued that cash payment of taxes promoted usefully the monetization and commercialization of the rural economy. But aside of the tax system itself and the sale of a larger share of the crop, it is not clear that the cash requirement for tax payments did much to promote monetization and commercialization. As discussed below, the Meiji patterns of revenue and expenditure point to a fairly substantial drain of cash from the rural to the urban areas, leaving the countryside short of liquidity. Cash flowed out of the rural areas in the form of land taxes, and most of the proceeds from these taxes went to the urban areas in the form of administrative and military expenditures, leaving less cash on balance than before. If this generalization is valid, tax payments, in cash, coupled with Meiji expenditure patterns, could have retarded the movement toward monetization and commercialization by draining cash from the countryside.

Table 1 shows that around the middle of the Meiji period, i.e., in the later 1890's, the sum of indirect taxes and non-tax revenues begin to exceed land taxes in importance.[9] This does not mean a decline in the absolute burden of taxation on agriculturists, for the proceeds of land taxes continued to rise, doubling from the late 1890's to 1910. The rise in the indirect taxes (on sake, tobacco, soy sauce, drugs, sugar, textiles) and non-tax revenues (surpluses from enterprises such as railroads, tobacco, post and telegraph, etc.) reflects in part the expenditure needs of urbanization, militarization, and industrialization. Although it is true that these taxes bore heavily on the urban population, it is not true that the rural

[9] See also William W. Lockwood, *The Economic Development of Japan* (Princeton, 1954), 522-23.

population was able to avoid them. Per capita the urbanite paid a very much greater amount, but since the rural population was larger than the urban population, the total paid by the rural population may have been as great, if not greater. This is the conclusion of a detailed study of Meiji taxes by U. Kobayashi (with the assistance of T. Kushida) in a volume on the impact of war and militarization on the economy, sponsored by the Carnegie Endowment for International Peace (Oxford University Press, 1923), Chapters 2, 3, and 5 of Part II. Kobayashi views most of the indirect taxes after 1894 as a consequence of the two Meiji wars and argues that they weighed most heavily on workers and peasants. Though the analysis is rather simple and crude, Kobayashi's detailed description of the excise taxes renders his conclusion plausible.

Certain features of the land tax were favorable to growth, e.g., the relatively fixed character of the tax base, the lump sum method of payments. Nevertheless, these were of relatively minor consequence when compared with the size of the tax payments. Data on the impact of the land tax on saving and investment are not available. Except for the larger landowners, however, a tax that took as large a sum of cash as 10 percent of the income of the average peasant, which was hardly more than bare subsistence (as indicated by the calorie figures), can only mean that for the vast majority of the farming population saving and investment were almost out of the question. Though savings and investment data are lacking, the frequency of disputes, uprisings and riots, the rise in unpaid taxes and land confiscated in lieu of tax payments, the increase in debts and mortgage foreclosures, and the rapid rise in the amount of tenanted land (from around 30 percent of the total cultivated land to 45 percent by the end of the Meiji period) were clear signs of the difficulties experienced by the majority of agriculturists in the period.[10] The fact that

[10] See volumes sponsored by the Carnegie Endowment for International Peace cited below. Rice prices rose up to 1881 but fell sharply after 1881. Prices began to rise around the last years of the Meiji period, just before World War I.

the percentage share of the consolidated tax receipts contributed by the land tax fell sharply from about 60 percent in
1880 to 15 percent in 1910 did not necessarily lessen the tax
burden. In fact, it might have increased the burden since a
substantial portion of the indirect taxes fell on the peasants as
purchasers of the taxed products.

If the difficulties caused by the land tax had been confined
to the economic sphere, our discussion could end at this point.
But a comprehensive policy such as the land tax has ramifica-
tions far beyond the rice paddies of rural Japan. The land tax
law comprised the very backbone of the Meiji government's
agrarian policy, and that policy in turn was a basic part of
the government's entire socio-political-economic policy. The
woes of the peasantry were also a crucial element of social
unrest, contributing much to the instability of Meiji governments. While many factors went into the decision of the
Meiji oligarchy to embark on the road to military adventures
abroad, it is difficult to dismiss the part played by peasant
distress. And once on this road, turning back was almost
impossible.[11]

R. P. Dore has discussed the links between agrarian
distress and the rise of totalitarianism at home and military
expansion abroad. While his summary of the arguments is
intended to apply mainly to the twenties and the thirties, it
is not inappropriate for the Meiji era. Dore evaluates seven
processes by which agrarian difficulties are linked to militarism; of these he regards two as particularly noteworthy.
First, overseas military expansion diverts attention from dire
poverty at home to emigration abroad, where more land and
economic opportunities are available, and it channels disaffection at home into search for national glory overseas.
(Indonesia's Sukarno recently told his hungry people to stop
complaining about the price of rice and to eat corn instead;
this was the only way victory over Malaysia would be
possible.) Second, low rural incomes and low urban wages
restrict the domestic market for manufactured goods, com-

[11] Shibusawa Keizō, *Japanese Society in the Meiji Era* (Tokyo,
1958), pp. 90-94.

pelling industrialists to look for more profitable markets abroad. If both arguments are valid, poverty must be assigned an important role in the rise of militaristic expansion, though by no means the sole factor involved. By contributing to increasing tenancy and to low wages in the urban areas (via low labor incomes in the rural areas), the Meiji land tax both directly and indirectly must be regarded as a major contributing factor in the entire process which finally led to the disasters of the last war. It is, of course, not possible to assign any precise weight to the tax in the configuration of causal factors. But the frequency with which the land tax crops up as a controversial political topic in the annals of Meiji Japan suggests that it was not a minor element.[12]

Military and Civil Expenditures

The quantitative effects of tax policy on growth cannot be assessed without a consideration of the uses made of tax receipts. If most of the enormous contributions by the farm sector to the nation's treasury had flowed back to the farm, the tax burden on the agricultural sector might have been offset by benefits. Unfortunately, data for the precise measurement of sector benefits are not available. But some insight into this problem can be gained from the functional classification of expenditures. Such a classification groups expenditures by their objectives. While there are certain problems in the classification, it comes closest to meeting the needs of development analysis. (See Appendix for details.)

In one sense Meiji fiscal policy was a success. Consolidated government expenditures as a percent of GNP (see Appendix) rose steadily from 10 percent in 1879-1883 to 15 percent in 1884-1895, 20 percent in 1896-1904 and 25 percent in 1905-1912. Compared with similar data from countries such as India or the Philippines, these over-all percentages attest to the efficiency of the Japanese system in raising revenue.

The pattern of expenditures of Meiji governmental bodies

[12] R. P. Dore, *Land Reform in Japan* (Oxford, 1959), Ch. 5, "Tenancy and Aggression."

is shown in the tables and diagrams below. In Table 2 a detailed picture is given for four selected years. Table 3 gives comparisons with similar patterns for an earlier Meiji period, 1873-1877, and for 1920, 1925, 1955, and 1960. Figure 3 depicts broad groups in which the preponderance of state services is noteworthy. From Table 2 this category can be seen to comprise mainly military, fiscal, and executive expenses. The largest of these is clearly military expenditures (see Fig. 2). If the extraordinary outlays of the Russo-Japanese War are included, military expenditures rise to about one quarter of the total spending of all Meiji governments, 1879-1912. Compared with the other broad categories, social and economic (Fig. 3), the direct productivity effect of expenditures on state services upon the growth of national income was relatively small. In later years expenditures on social and economic services rise significantly faster (Fig. 3).

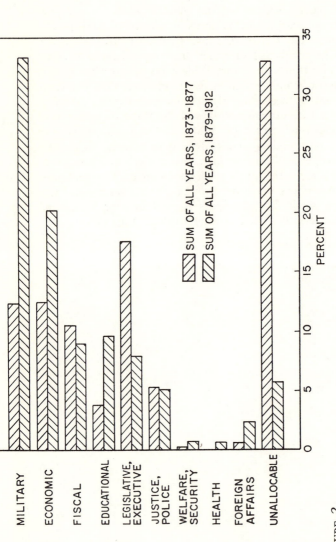

FIGURE 2

Functional Classification of Major Government Expenditures (Consolidated) in Japan, 1873–1877 and 1879–1912.

NOTES AND SOURCES: For sources, 1879–1812, and for central government data, 1875-77, see Appendix. (Fiscal years, not calendar years.) Local government data are based on Ministry of Finance, *Nihon fu-ken*

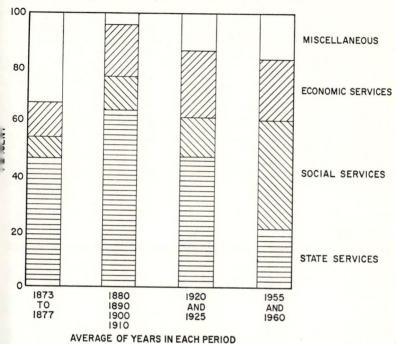

FIGURE 3

Functional Classification of Central and Local Government Expenditures in Japan: Broad Categories at Intervals, 1873-1960.

SOURCE: Tables 2 and 3.

TABLE 2

FUNCTIONAL CLASSIFICATION OF CENTRAL AND LOCAL GOVERNMENT
EXPENDITURES IN JAPAN, 1880, 1890, 1900, 1910

	1880		1890		1900		1910	
	Million Yen	%	Million Yen	%	Million Yen	%	Million Yen	%
TOTAL	92.0	100.0	126.7	100.0	425.4	100.0	834.1	100.0
State Services								
Legislature, Executive	19.0	20.7	19.6	15.8	29.4	6.9	49.4	5.9
Fiscal	25.0	27.2	24.8	19.6	50.8	11.9	62.5	7.5
Foreign Affairs	1.0	1.1	0.7	0.8	11.1	2.6	24.1	2.9
Military	12.0	13.0	26.0	20.5	131.7	31.0	349.4	41.9
Justice, Police	8.0	8.7	13.0	10.3	19.9	4.7	29.7	3.6
TOTAL	65.0	70.6	84.4	66.6	242.9	57.2	515.1	61.8
Social Services								
Education	6.9	7.5	10.5	8.3	42.0	9.9	90.9	10.9
Research, Scientific	—	—	—	—	1.8	0.4	1.5	0.2
Health	1.0	1.1	0.7	0.6	6.0	1.4	3.0	0.4
Welfare, Security	1.3	1.4	0.9	0.7	0.7	0.2	3.9	0.5
Religion, Culture	0.5	0.5	0.3	0.2	0.7	0.2	0.7	0.1
Other	0.9	1.0	0.9	0.7	0.8	0.2	13.5	1.6
TOTAL	10.7	11.6	13.3	10.6	60.3	14.0	113.6	13.6
Economic								
Transportation	7.1	7.7	15.0	11.8	57.5	13.5	57.6	6.(
Communication	1.5	1.6	4.5	3.6	20.4	4.8	34.6	4.?
Primary Industries	4.0	4.3	5.6	4.4	15.7	3.7	29.0	3.
Secondary Industries	1.4	1.5	0.5	0.4	7.6	1.8	8.3	1.
Tertiary Industries	0.1	0.1	0.1	0.1	1.1	0.2	1.9	0.
Other Industries	0.1	0.1	0.1	0.1	1.5	0.4	3.8	0
TOTAL	14.2	15.4	26.0	20.5	103.8	24.4	135.4	16
Unallocable	2.3	2.5	1.6	1.3	11.4	2.7	44.8	5
Excluded expenditures	0.1	1.0	0.4	0.3	7.1	1.7	25.3	?
TOTAL	2.4	2.6	2.0	1.6	18.5	4.3	70.1	8

SOURCES: See Appendix.

TABLE 3

Functional Classification of Central and Local
Government Expenditures in Japan, 1873-1877, 1920, 1925, 1955,
1960

	Average 1873-1877	1920	1925	1955	1960
Total	100.0	100.0	100.0	100.0	100.0
Legislature, Executive	17.7	3.7	3.5	5.7	4.8
Fiscal	10.6	21.8	24.5	8.1	3.2
Foreign Affairs	0.7	0.5	0.5	0.1	0.2
Military	12.5	23.4	10.2	3.4	2.3
Justice Police	5.4	2.5	3.0	2.5	2.0
Total (State Services)	47.0	52.0	41.7	19.8	12.4
Education	3.9	9.6	11.0	11.2	10.1
Research, Scientific	—	—	—	0.5	0.2
Health	—	2.1	1.7	4.2	3.7
Welfare, Security	0.3	0.5	0.8	7.3	7.7
Religion, Culture	0.9	0.1	—	—	—
Other	2.3	—	4.1	1.9	0.9
Total (Social Services)	7.5	12.2	17.7	25.1	22.6
Transportation	7.3	7.4	8.8	4.5	8.7
Communications	0.4	4.5	7.6	1.0	1.1
Primary Industries	1.9	2.6	2.9	26.3	31.0
Secondary Industries	1.8	2.3	2.4	0.3	1.0
Tertiary Industries	0	5.6	3.8	0.1	—
Other	1.2	0.5	0	1.2	2.1
Total (Economic)	12.6	22.5	25.6	33.4	44.0
Unallocable	30.7	5.8	5.6	12.5	7.8
Excluded Expenditures	2.2	7.4	9.4	9.2	13.1
Total	32.9	13.2	15.0	21.7	21.0

Notes: 1. For 1873-1877 data, see Appendix.

2. 1920 and 1925 figures were based on data from the Ministry of Finance *Shōwa zaisei shi* [History of Fiscal Policy in Shōwa] Vol. 14 (Tokyo, 1914) Statistics Bureau, *Teikoku tōkei nenkan* [Statistical Yearbook] Vol. 47 (Tokyo, 1929), and Tōyō keizai shimpō sha, *Meiji zaisei sōran* [Meiji Abstract of Public Finance] (Tokyo, 1915).

3. 1935, 1955, and 1960 figures are based on Ministry of Finance, *Zaisei tōkei* [Financial Statistics] 1958 and 1959 Vols. (Tokyo, 1957, 1958), and *Teikoku tōkei nenkan*, Vol. 55 (Tokyo, 1936).

4. Calendar years for 1873-1877; fiscal years for others, April-March.

5. K. Niiro and T. Sakiyama assisted me in the estimates for 1920, 1925, 1955, 1960.

PRODUCTIVITY OF MILITARY EXPENDITURE

Military expenditure, by far the largest item in the Meiji budget, is the least significant category in its direct contribution to economic productivity. It may make some contribution, of course: military and military-related industries no doubt played a useful role as model plants where Japanese gained training and know-how in the operation of modern technology and organization. But government investment in most other peace-time industries could have had similar advantages. Military expenditures also created demand for a variety of products through inter-industry linkages, e.g., demand for woolen blankets, uniforms for soldiers, etc. But again so would government investment in most other peace-time industries. These advantages are not peculiar to military enterprises.

Another justification advanced for military expenditures is their effect on aggregate demand. If this be an advantage, then again it must be pointed out that all expenditures, military or civil, tend to be demand-generating. Under conditions of underdevelopment, where substantial unemployment generally does not exist, however, is the shortage of effective demand a problem? There was nothing in the character of the underdeveloped Meiji economy which resembled a Keynesian world continually moving toward an under-consumption equilibrium with sizable unemployment, due to over-saving. The consensus among economists today is that the basic problem confronting underdeveloped countries is not so much a shortage of aggregate demand but rather a shortage in the aggregate supply of goods.[13] If this be so, the demand-generating effect of any expenditures is a disadvantage rather than an advantage. And so it was for most of the Meiji period, as these massive military expenditures formed the major impetus to the inflationary tendencies of the era.

[13] See, e.g., W. A. Lewis, *The Theory of Economic Growth* (Illinois, 1955), Ch. 5. B. Higgins, *Economic Development* (New York, 1959), Ch. 21. Robert E. Baldwin, and Gerald M. Meier, *Economic Development* (New York, 1957), pp. 303-10.

In fact, a case can be made that war expenditures in the Meiji era were the very cause of the relapses in business activity which followed both the Sino- and the Russo-Japanese Wars. In the most detailed study of Meiji military expenditures, Ono Giichi concludes with the statement:[14] "Often we have met with such cases in the foregoing consideration of the relation between our economy and the expenditures for military affairs, as where there appeared activities in the market, after the Satsuma Rebellion, the Sino-Japanese War and the Russo-Japanese War, the rise of a speculative fever and spirit, a boom in the stock market, the production of luxuries, the heavy increase of imports, the prodigality of capital and its following dearth, the failure of enterprises, excessive precaution among enterprising people, the decrease of general consumption, and at length extreme inactivity in the economic world. Is it not then, sufficient to state that on the whole war and armament expenditures would be found rather productive of unfavorable effects on these points if careful investigation were made broadly in the field of study?"

In terms of modern economic analysis, what happened during each war and its aftermath might be interpreted as follows: Through the large deficit financing of the wars the government injected a large amount of excessive purchasing power into the economy at large. This caused economic expansion extending even into the immediate postwar years, despite the fact that indirect taxes were weighing heavily on the large majority of lower income receivers and causing income distribution to be increasingly unequal. Once deficit financing ceased after the wars, the relative fall in the aggregate money incomes of workers and peasants created a deficiency of aggregate demand which brought on a recession. If this is a valid analysis of the underlying causes of the expansion and contraction connected with wars, then the

[14] Ono Giichi, *War and Armament Expenditures of Japan* (Oxford, 1922), pp. 256-57. This volume appears to have been written by Ōuchi Hyōyē. See also: Ogawa Gotarō with Y. Takata, and H. Ōyama, *Expenditures of the Russo-Japanese War* (Oxford, 1923), 251-252.

shortage of effective demand in the recession is itself caused by war expenditures and is not the Keynesian type of unemployment equilibrium.

In essence, the *direct* productivity effect of military expenditures is small relative to other expenditures because the *end products* of military expenditures, i.e., munitions, arms, fortifications, naval vessels, training to fight, and fighting itself, do not serve in the main a useful purpose from an economic point of view. Expenditures to build and operate a fertilizer factory, a railroad, a textile factory, a school, or a hospital are substantially more productive as they serve an economically useful purpose.[15] Compared to these end products, byproducts like those mentioned above are of minor consequence and are neither peculiar nor unique to military outlays.

It may be contended that victorious war may win a bountiful indemnity, as was the case in the Sino-Japanese War. And it is probably true that the indemnity from the Sino-Japanese War was used effectively for Japan's development needs in the postwar period. But indemnities represent losses for a defeated nation; from the consolidated point of view of the two warring nations they do not represent a net gain. Such economic benefits the world can well do without. Certainly it would be wrong to point to such reparations as a possible justification for military adventures by underdeveloped countries. This is one lesson from Meiji experience that scholars do well to ignore.

So far the discussion has been confined to direct effects of military expenditure. There are important *indirect* consequences on growth and development, too. It is clear that

[15] It was, I believe, Quesnay and the Physiocrats who first brought out clearly the distinction between productive and unproductive expenditures and incorporated this distinction into their model, the *Tableau Economique*. Besides military expenditures, they included luxury expenditures. In another of the seven-volume works sponsored by the Carnegie Endowment for International Peace, entitled *The Conscription System in Japan* (Oxford, 1921), Ogawa Gotarō discusses the unproductive nature of soldiers and armaments. This volume appears to have been written by Takata Yasuma.

Japan could not have survived as an independent nation in the international environment of the Meiji period without some degree of military strength. And without autonomy and independence it is plausible to suppose that her development would have been greatly retarded. What is not clear is how large a military expenditure was necessary to maintain this independence. These conjectural issues are difficult to resolve. Nevertheless, it does not seem plausible to argue that the enormous expenditures for the preparation and conduct of both the Sino- and the Russo-Japanese Wars were necessary for national defense. Nor was it necessary for a relatively poor Japan to maintain a military establishment which strove to rival or to "catch up" with the richer, powerful Western nations. If the military expenditures for the two wars are excluded, something like one-half of the total military spending of the entire Meiji period remains. This might well have sufficed to keep Japan an independent nation, and the savings from such a reduction in military expenditure could have been used to reduce the burden of land taxes by one-half.[16]

Outlays for these two wars, moreover, produced victories which "brought about a complete change in the way of thinking of the Japanese," in the words of one writer.[17] Constructive nationalism was transformed into a militant, chauvinistic ultra-nationalism. The Japanese people began to think of themselves as invincible and began to dream of the glories of empire, a dream which was not to be shattered until World War II.

[16] The estimate of one-half was arrived at by Mr. T. Sakiyama as follows: during the three decades, 1884-1912, total military expenditures reached 4.7 billion yen, of which expenditures from the special military accounts for the two wars comprised about 2.1 billion yen, or 45%. An alternative method using different assumptions—that the proportion of military expenditures to the central government budget for the peacetime years 1884-1893 (about 28%) was adequate for defense, and that anything beyond this percentage in the war-affected years, 1894-1912, was excessive—yield also a figure of around 45%.

[17] Takayama Chogyū in *Meiji shisō no hensen* [The Changing Pattern of Meiji Thought], quoted in Shibusawa, p. 92. Also see Ono Giichi (and Asada Keiichi), *Expenditures of the Sino-Japanese War* (Oxford, 1922), concluding chapter, esp. pp. 321-24.

In concluding this brief discussion of the impact of military expenditures on the Meiji economy, one must note that many aspects, such as their impact on prices, taxes, money and credit, public debt, foreign trade, and wages, have not been mentioned. This may be justified by the fact that seven volumes on these topics were published in 1922 under the sponsorship of the Carnegie Endowment for International Peace. While the economic and statistical analyses in these volumes are rather simple and crude by present-day standards, these studies are notable for their detailed facts and figures relating to Meiji military expenditures. They attempt judiciously to weigh the advantages and disadvantages of military outlays for the Meiji economy. All of the seven volumes (with the possible exception of *Military Industries of Japan* by U. Kobayashi) conclude that the net effect was not favorable.[18]

ADMINISTRATIVE VS. EDUCATIONAL OUTLAYS

Another outstanding feature of Meiji public finance was the heavy spending for fiscal purposes (Table 2, Fig. 2). Together with expenditures on foreign affairs, justice, police, legislative and executive functions, military and fiscal expenditures make up the total of state services, as distinct from social, economic, and miscellaneous services. Because of the size of military and fiscal expenditures, nearly 55 percent of the total consolidated national and local expenditures for the entire Meiji period was spent on state services. This is a phenomenon unparalleled in the financial annals of modern nations, especially for a period as long as half a century.[19]

[18] On the harmful effects of loans contracted for wars and armaments, see Kobayashi Ushisaburō, *War and Armament Expenditures of Japan* (Oxford, 1922), Ch. VI.

[19] See, for example, studies of the National Bureau of Economic Research, Solomon Fabricant, *Trend of Government Activity in the U.S. Since 1900* (New York, 1952), and Alan Peacock and Jack Wiseman, *The Growth of Public Expenditure in the United Kingdom* (Princeton, 1961).

The total of about 20% shown in the diagram for fiscal expenditures may be too high for the later Meiji period. Some of the interest

Such large fiscal and other non-military state expenditures cannot necessarily be justified as essential for an efficient and modernized administrative system. First of all, there need not be a close association between the size of such expenditures and administrative adequacy. Indeed, if much of the expenditure is for corrupt purposes, as in certain underdeveloped countries, there may even be a negative association between expenditure and efficiency. It is true that a modern system of taxation, courts, diplomacy, police, etc., requires expenditures for buildings, for adequate salaries, for travel, for equipment, etc., as part of the indispensable infrastructure of a modern state. But all this could have been accomplished in Japan more cheaply, if we judge by the budgets of some underdeveloped countries today.[20] While certain basic minimum expenditures for state services are necessary for efficient, adequate administration, the amounts spent by Meiji governments appear to have been far in excess of this minimum.

Of about three billion yen of expenditures for fiscal, legislative, executive, foreign affairs, justice, and police (Table 2, "state services") during the entire Meiji period, just about one-third was spent for fiscal purposes. And of this amount, roughly three-fourths went to pay interest and amortization on the public bonds issued to the nobility for the commutation of pensions and the like. It may be argued that the payment of such sums was necessary to maintain political stability, i.e., to keep the nobility from joining in a revolt against the Meiji government during the transition. For an economist to evaluate this argument is difficult. The maintenance of po-

---

payments included in fiscal expenditures from 1904 may be for loans contracted for the Russo-Japanese War. Perhaps something like 10% may be more appropriate. The over-all percent for state expenditures of 55% will not change, however.

[20] I plan to present the data for these countries in another study now under preparation. Of course, for countries such as Taiwan and South Korea, which receive large amounts of assistance from the U.S., military expenditures (and therefore state expenditures) are as large as Japan's in the Meiji era. For these countries, however, to the extent of the military assistance from the U.S., there should be a deduction from military expenditures.

litical stability in respect to the nobility was at the expense of the peasantry in the form of the land tax, so that political stability on one front was purchased at the expense of insta- bility on another, i.e., the peasantry. The cost of this type of unrest is in part reflected in the large expenses for justice and police functions, which comprised two-thirds of a billion yen for the entire Meiji period. It is worth noting in Figure 2 that expenditures on legislative and executive affairs, and also on fiscal affairs are about equal to educational expendi- tures in the social service category, roughly one billion yen each. None of the countries in Asia for which consolidated functional expenditures are available (Malaya, Burma, Cey- lon, Taiwan, India, South Korea, Philippines, Thailand, and Pakistan) shows such a pattern of functional expenditure. Indeed, countries such as the Philippines, where educational expenditures are high, show such expenditures alone to be nearly as large as the total outlay for state services.

This result is not surprising. The compulsory, universal education of the period for which the Meiji leaders are lauded was largely financed by the peasants and townspeople over and above the taxes they paid. For the tuition charged was ex- tremely high, resulting in widespread resistance to compulsory education. The tuition could be as high as 50 sen per month per child, "at a time when the average annual income per employed worker was no more than about 21 yen."[21]

Inasmuch as the Meiji government could not adequately finance universal, compulsory education, was it necessary to introduce it so rapidly? One may believe firmly in the im- portance of education in economic growth—of this there can be no doubt—and yet question the wisdom of Meiji policy. General education is an expensive institution for an economy as poor as Meiji Japan. It is also a great luxury for an econ- omy which throughout the whole of the period (and even into the Taishō era) was overwhelmingly traditional in technique and organization. Under these circumstances, was there a

[21] See Shibusawa, pp. 11, 294-300. Also, Ministry of Education *Nihon no seichō to kyōiku* [Japan's Growth and Education] (Tokyo, 1962), p. 33.

need to force peasants to pay for so much of the education of their children? A large majority of them were hardly in a position to make use of the learning in their own lifetime, not even to read the newspapers (which they could not afford). As a result the acquired knowledge commonly tended to atrophy.

On this and other matters one can only speculate; yet it might have been more prudent in the Meiji period to initiate a system of *selective* compulsory education almost entirely paid for by the state. Perhaps in the beginning, one child in each family, then later two, could have been given free education, with universality introduced in the late twenties. This would have enabled the peasants to shift the funds used for educating their children to meet farming needs, while the number educated would have been adequate for the needs of modernization.

A word should be added about the lending activities of the government-controlled banks. Fujino Shōsaburo, Assistant Professor of Economics of Hitotsubashi University, Tokyo, has compiled statistics classifying the loans of the three government banks, *Nihon kangyō ginkō, Nōkō ginkō*, and the *Hokkaidō takushoku ginkō*, according to industrial sectors.[22] During the Meiji era, these banks in the aggregate loaned 764 million yen to agriculture, 378 million yen to industry, 26 million yen to commerce—a total of 1,314 million yen (including miscellaneous loans). These are impressive sums. But for the purpose of a study focused on public finance, they need not be taken into consideration since only a small portion, something like 10 million yen, was contributed by the government itself. These loan funds appear to have come largely from bonds issued by banks, and savings and other deposits by individuals.[23]

[22] See S. Fujino (and H. Ōshima), Mimeographed Statistical Material (*Shiryō*) *C6*, Institute of Economic Research, Hitotsubashi University (Tokyo, 1963).

[23] Dr. Asakura of the Bank of Japan research staff and a leading authority on Meiji banking has pointed out to me that very little of the agricultural loans of the *Nōkō ginkō* (which make up the bulk of

Implications of Meiji Experience

Our conclusions run somewhat counter to the usual pre-
scriptions offered to underdeveloped countries on the basis of
the Meiji experience. It appears that the Meiji economy actually did not grow as rapidly as has been thought, certainly
not at the rate of 4 percent. Perhaps the rate was closer to
2 percent. A persistent drag is found in heavy expenditures
made for state-administrative purposes, especially military.
The Meiji government could have cut military expenditures,
perhaps by one-half, by staying out of the Sino-Japanese and
Russo-Japanese Wars, and yet possessed a defense adequate
for national independence. Further cuts in other state expenditures would also have been possible, e.g., by extending
the maturity dates of pension bonds beyond World War I.
Such reductions would have permitted a considerable decrease in land taxes and an increase in the expenditures for
economic purposes, especially for agriculture. Despite the
enormous contributions made by the agricultural sector to the
revenues of the government, it received back in expenditures
a pitifully small amount, something like 4 percent of the total
public expenditure. This is consistent with the findings of
James Nakamura in Chapter VI that Meiji agriculture did
not grow as rapidly as has been believed. Greater encouragement of agriculture, together with greater assistance to industry (via increased taxes on urban real estate, and excise
taxes on luxuries and semi-luxuries from the early decades
of the Meiji period) would have produced a growth rate for

---

the bank loans to agriculture) was in fact invested in agricultural
activities. Landlords borrowed on the security of their land holdings
but used the funds to invest in banking, commerce, and industry.

In this paper, I have not discussed expenditures on economic activities (public works, transport, etc.). The implicit assumption is that
such expenditures are highly productive. Meiji economic expenditures
when related to total government expenditures and national income
are about 20% and 5%, respectively. These are significantly lower
than those of South and Southeast Asian countries in the early 1960's,
which are around 30% and 7%, respectively. I hope to analyze elsewhere the nature of Meiji economic expenditures.

the Meiji era appreciably larger than that which actually materialized. More important, it would have reduced the rural unrest and tension which contributed in a real way to the militarism of the Taishō and prewar Shōwa eras.

Meiji experience, of course, does not argue against the use of the land tax by underdeveloped countries. It is a tax which is easy to administer and difficult to evade. It is a good source of revenue because the wealth of underdeveloped countries is predominantly in agricultural land, though Japanese experience points to moderation in its use. The current practice in underdeveloped countries errs in the other direction; the land tax is rarely used extensively enough to yield adequate sums.[24] Other lessons that can be derived from Japan are (1) the need for a degree of progression in the rates, if an unfavorable income redistribution effect is to be avoided; and (2) the desirability that a portion of the taxes to be paid in kind, if not offset by a system of government loans, to avoid the denuding the rural areas of liquidity.

Above all, the most important lesson of Meiji public finance is that rapid economic growth and rapid militarization of the economy are fundamentally incompatible. Underdeveloped countries, whether capitalistic, socialistic or communistic, must choose one or the other.

APPENDIX

Sources, Methods and Concepts

The definitions of functional categories (see below) are generally those of the United Nations Fiscal Division, *A Manual for Economic and Functional Classification of Government Transactions*, N.Y., 1958, but with several important exceptions. These are discussed in detail in Appendix 2 of my paper, "National Accounts for the Analysis of Asian Growth," presented to the Asian Conference, University of Hongkong, August 1960, and to be published by the International As-

[24] H. P. Wald, ed., *Agricultural Taxation and Economic Development* (Cambridge, Mass., 1954), pp. 300-01.

sociation for Research in Income and Wealth, Yale University. There are a number of difficulties pertaining to the functional classification, especially in dealing with expenditures with multi-functions, but most expenditures are classifiable into one or the other categories. When a predominant function cannot be singled out (as in the case of secret expenditures), such expenditures are classified as unallocable. In certain cases (as in the case of debt repayments), expenditures are excluded from the functional classification.

The figures for the Meiji period are taken from (or based on) two statistical papers of mine entitled "Preliminary Summary Table: Functional Classification of Meiji Central Government Expenditures, Meiji 1 to 45," p. 46, October 1961, and "Preliminary Summary Table: Functional Classification of Choson Table For All Prefectures, Meiji 13, 23, 33 and 43," p. 49, March 1962, both mimeographed by the Hitotsubashi Institute of Economic Research. In compiling these statistics, I had the assistance of Haehara Takashi, Kaya Tomoji, Haramu Fujiko, Kazuno Keiko and Nomuro Katsue. The compilation would not have been possible without the invaluable assistance from and discussions with the entire staff of the Institute on matters of concept and source material. I am grateful also to the Ministry of Finance for making available to me the complete set of the *Kessan sho* (settled accounts) on which are based the compilation of the central government accounts. The local government accounts for Meiji 13, 23, 33, 43 were based on the voluminous *Ken tōkeisho*, collection of the Hitotsubashi Library supplemented by the *Sorifu Tōkei kyoku* collection.

Expenditures of local governments for other years were obtained by interpolations, using appropriate time series compiled from *Chihō zaisei Gaiyō*, *Meiji zaisei hyōran* and the *Teikoku tōkei nenkan* and taking Meiji 13, 23, 33, 43 as benchmarks. Mr. K. Niiro assisted me in this work.

The figures in these tables purport to be consolidated quantities, i.e., inter-governmental flows are counted once only, the original receipts on the revenue side and the final expenditure on the payment side of the accounts. The consolidated totals include all governmental units, central government, prefectural, municipal, town and village governments. Both general and special funds are included but public enterprises are excluded. Excluded also are the Russo-Japanese War special fund expenditures. Full details of the statistics and methods, sources and concepts will be given in a forthcoming volume on the revenue and expenditures of Japanese governments, 1868-1960.

Where the text compares taxes, etc., with gross national income or product, the latter has been calculated as follows: Professor Ohkawa's estimates of national product at market prices (*Growth Rate of the Japanese Economy*, Tokyo, 1957) are used to extend GNP for 1930 (as estimated by the Economic Planning Agency) back to 1872. These figures are averaged for each year with James Nakamura's higher figures (due to higher agricultural production estimates) found in his essay above, Chapter VI. The resulting estimates give values of GNP which are mid-points of the Ohkawa and Nakamura estimates. All this is unsatisfactory, but at the present state of our knowledge of Meiji incomes, it cannot be helped.

FUNCTIONAL CLASSIFICATION : DETAILED DEFINITIONS

I. General Administration: Activities relating mainly to the needs of the States.

1. *Legislative and Executive*

a. Legislative: expenditures relating to the function of lawmaking. Besides legislative bodies, agencies attached to legislatures such as audit boards, commissions, and electoral bodies are included. For example: cost of research for revising election laws, cost of supervision of general elections, expenses of House of Councilors, House of Representatives, and Board of Audit, cost of inspecting legislative and government buildings.

b. Executive: expenditures in connection with the functions of heads of State and governments at various levels, such as Emperor, Prime Minister, governor, mayor, village head, and commissions and bodies attached to them. For example:

cost of visits by Imperial Household members, expenses of Cabinet Library, cost of state funerals, cost of issuing and printing Imperial rescripts.

2. *Fiscal*: expenditures relating to "the collection of taxes, raising of public money, management of public debt and control over the disbursement of public funds (other than by bodies acting on behalf of legislative)." For example: cost of issuing and printing national bonds, expenses for disposing tax delinquent cases, expenses for general administration, contribution to the Inter. Assn. for Tariff Rate Compilation, cost of control of treasury notes and finance, cost of research on tariff rate determination, cost of collecting China Incident reparation, cost of revising value of residential land, payment of stipend to former daimyos.

3. *Foreign Affairs*: expenditures for protecting and promoting the interests of a nation abroad, including expenses of all agencies stationed abroad, contribution to international organizations, and grants, subsidies, loans to foreign governments, but excluding military expenditures. Territories such as foreign areas and their special accounts are excluded. For example: expenses for general administration, cost of revising international treaties, attending international conferences and reception of official guests.

4. *Military Affairs*: expenditures for maintaining the army, navy, air force, and civilian defense units and for activities relating to war.

a. Army: for example; cost of army divisions, regiments, schools, hospitals, military police, prisons, horse administration bureau (*Basei kyoku*). Disabled Soldiers' Home (*Haihei in*), armed forces sent to Korea, China, Manchuria, Karafuto; cost of postwar adjustment, rehabilitation, rewards for Korea and China incidents, map printing, maneuvers, research, intelligence agencies, protection against contagious diseases, construction of forts, arsenals, suppression of Taiwan bandits, expropriation of estates for military use.

b. Navy: for example, cost of naval division, bases, academy, hospitals, warships, harbors, expeditionary forces abroad, reception of foreign squadrons, maneuvers, pilot boats, rescue of foreign naval ships, printing of military maps, grants and rewards for Russo-Japanese War, transfer to Naval Arsenal Fund Account and Naval Mining Fund Account and research on aeronautics.

5. *Justice and Police*: expenditures relating to the maintenance of internal and civilian law and order. This group is divided into law courts, police, prisons and all other (including general administration and detention and correction but excluding expenditures on the maintenance of law and order abroad and in the army and navy).

a. Law courts: for example, expenses of administrative courts, expenses of civil and criminal courts.

b. Police: for example, expenses of the Metropolitan Police Board, prefectural and local police bureaus, police schools, lost and found service, expenditures on detectives and secret service.

c. Prisons: for example, cost of transfer of prisoners by prefectural agencies, expenses of prisons.

d. All other: for example, expenses of general administration, cost of examinations for lawyers, cost of research on and grant for reformatories, cost of criminal correction of administrative maladjustment in prefectural governments.

II. Social Services: activities relating mainly to the needs of households.

6. *Education*: expenditures for teaching and learning the existing body of knowledge and for transmitting culture, including expenditures on institutions of higher learning, technical training institutes, schools, kindergartens, adult education, schools for the deaf, dumb, and blind, libraries and museums. The educational element is secondary in reformatories and child care centers which are classified elsewhere. Specialized schools, institutes and libraries which are so integrated with various government agencies that they are not opened to the general public are regarded as in-service training agencies and are included elsewhere. Where in institutions of higher learning, the search for new knowledge and culture

predominates over the function of teaching and transmission, they should be regarded as research organs.

7. *Research and Scientific Services*: expenditures promoting the search for (including the import of) new knowledge and culture, excluding research which are linked to the provision or promotion of any particular type of service. The latter are included elsewhere as auxiliary to other functions.

For Japan, these are divided into:

a. Physical Science research: for example, expenses of Research Committee against Earthquakes, International Latitude Observatory, Central Meteorology, Geology Committee.

b. Research in the social sciences and humanities: for example, expenses for attending International Demographic Conference, cost of compiling demographic statistics, expenses of the Bureau for compiling Historical Material on the Meiji Restoration, Japan Academic Assn. and Committee for Document Catalogue Compilation, expenses for attending International Academic Assn. and International Science Conference, cost of research on the Japanese Language, cost of compiling war history, contribution to International Statistical Conference.

c. All other.

8. *Health*: expenditure on facilities or services for preventing and curing human illness. Health services for members of the armed forces and administrative services are classified elsewhere. Veterinary services are shown under agriculture. For Japan these are divided into:

a. Hospitals: for example, maintenance of hospitals for contagious diseases in Hokkaidō, expenses of school hospitals.

b. All other: for example, costs of national examination of physicians and pharmacists, expenses of Institute for Contagious Disease Research, attending International Medical Conference, International Tuberculosis Conference, International Opium Conference, International Leprosy Conference and International Life-Saving Conference, expenses for protection against contagious diseases and research on trachoma, cost of quarantine by prefectural authorities.

9. *Social Welfare and social security*: expenditures concerned with the alleviation of physical, social and economic distress of individuals, other than those shown under health and community services. Labor unions are not regarded as welfare institutions but mainly economic institutions (17). Pensions and annuities of government employees are shown elsewhere. Includes payments to individuals for damages due to floods, fire, typhoons, etc.

For Japan, these are divided into:

a. Social Welfare: for example, expenses of local governments for the care of insane persons, grants to emigrants, cost of survey on emigration.

b. Natural damages: for example, loans for rehabilitation due to fire, expenses of rehabilitation and grants for flood, fire and earthquake damages, subsidies to prefectures for interest payments on reconstruction bonds.

c. Social Security.

10. *Religion, Recreation, and Culture*:

a. Religion: expenditures relating to shrines, temples, and other institutions of worship.

b. Recreation: expenditures relating to sports, amusements and entertainments.

c. Culture: expenditures relating to artistic activities.

11. *Other social services*:

a. Sanitation: expenditures relating to sewerage and drainage systems (urban), collection and disposal of garbage and refuse, street cleaning, smoke regulation, public baths, comfort stations, disinfection, inspection of food and drugs, and the like. For example, expenses of sanitation laboratory and local sanitation projects, cost of inspection of slaughter houses.

b. Water Supply: expenditures relating to the collection, purification and distribution of water. Irrigation and drainage systems in rural areas are predominantly economic in function and are shown under agriculture.

c. Fire protection: expenditures relating to the prevention of fires, excepting forest fires. Excludes rehabilitation (9b).

d. Housing: expenditures relating to dwellings including slum clearance but excluding housing of military personnel.

III. Economic Services: activities relating mainly to the needs of enterprises.

12. *Transportation*: expenditures relating to the function of carrying passengers and freight including facilities closely related to this function such as warehouses, lighthouses, traffic controls, harbours, terminals, etc.

13. *Communication*: expenditures relating to the function of transmitting information such as through post, telegraph, radio, telephone, and newspaper. Radio broadcasting and TV are regarded to be mainly media of entertainment and are classified elsewhere.

14. *Promotion of primary industries*: expenditures to promote the development of agriculture, fishery, forestry, and mining.

15. *Promotion of secondary industries*: expenditures promoting the development of manufacturing, construction, and gas and electric industries.

16. *Promotion of tertiary industries*: expenditures for promoting the development of industries in trade, finance and services.

IV. Miscellaneous:

17. *Unallocable expenditures*: due to difficulties of determining a single, predominant function (mainly because of the multifunctional nature with no single function predominating), these expenditures are not allocable. For example, distribution of medals, pension and annuity payments made to former government officials, army and navy officers, soldiers, police officers, teachers and others, grants to projects on local improvement, secret expenses for Hokkaidō and other prefectural agencies, miscellaneous expenses of the latter, grants and tax redemptions to foreigners, and grants to towns and villages, grants and awards for miscellaneous incidents, capital expenditures (and losses, if any) of Printing Bureau.

18. Payments excluded from functional classification: include: Intra-central government transfer: payments which are made from one agency to another within the central government and are thought to be duplication, debt repayment, purchase of negotiable financial claims, etc.

CHAPTER IX

Economic Growth and Consumption in Japan[1]

ALAN H. GLEASON

THE HIGH RATE of economic growth of Japan since the Meiji Restoration has stimulated much comment and analysis. Considerably less attention, however, has been paid to the extent to which this growth has resulted in rising levels of consumption. Statistical indicators of consumption levels have been rather sparse and indirect and the discussions have perforce been largely speculative of inferential in character. So far, opinions of Japan's progress in improving levels of consumption up to World War II have been generally pessimistic. Various writers have given the impression that consumption has risen slowly compared with both the growth in Japan's gross national product and the historical improvement in living levels in other industrialized countries. It is held that growing inequality has caused certain groups in Japan to lag seriously behind the population as a whole. Among the factors frequently cited as retarding a rise in prewar consumption levels among the

[1] I am grateful to Professors Emi Koichi, Hisatake Masao, William W. Lockwood, Ohkawa Kazushi, Hugh T. Patrick, and Henry Rosovsky, and to Dr. Ōkita Saburo and Mr. M. Nagasawa of the Economic Planning Agency for very helpful comments and suggestions during the preparation of this paper. In addition, much benefit was gained from the discussion of a preliminary draft by members of the Conference on the State and Economic Enterprise of Modern Japan held in Estes Park, Colorado, June 1963. I am especially indebted to Professor Ohkawa and his associates at the Institute of Economic Research of Hitotsubashi University for making available to me much of the statistical data on which my analysis is based. I also wish to thank Mr. Ishiwata Shigeru, and Misses Kido Yoshiko, Kuge Takako, and Oda Yori for their valuable assistance in the collection and preparation of materials. Responsibility for the use of all material is, of course, completely my own.

largest economic groups are exploitation of the peasant through heavy taxation and high rents; exploitation of the industrial worker through the excessively low wages made possible in part through the poverty of the peasant; a high rate of personal saving; inflationary policies which reduced the purchasing power of money incomes; and the rapid growth of population which absorbed much of the increase in consumer goods production.[2]

[2] These views are illustrated by the following quotations:

"Industrialization and scientific progress slowly raised the standard of living of the average Japanese well above that of his Asiatic neighbors, but this improvement was scarcely commensurate with the rate of industrial and commercial development. This was probably in part because the ruling group was interested in developing a powerful nation rather than a prosperous people, but a much more basic reason was the economic drag of an impoverished peasantry and the countercurrent created by a rapidly expanding population. Japan as a nation was growing rapidly in wealth, but as a result of increasing economic opportunities and improved health conditions and medical care, the population of Japan shot up from 30,000,000 in the middle of the nineteenth century to over 70,000,000 by 1940. Because of this phenomenal growth, the per capita gain in wealth remained relatively small." Edwin O. Reischauer, *Japan Past and Present* (Tokyo, 1953), pp. 132-33. And, in another book, Reischauer said that, "While Japan as a whole became a modernized and industrialized nation, her peasant masses were left behind, living not far above the miserable economic levels of feudal days. Moreover, by threatening to glut the labor market, they kept urban labor down to these same pitiful levels. The result has been something new and as yet unique in the world—an industrialized nation supported by the toil of people living not far above the subsistence level." *The United States and Japan* (Revised edition, New York, 1957), p. 62.

"Despite industrialization, Japan could barely bring her huge and growing population above the level of subsistence, even before the destruction wrought by the war." Solomon B. Levine, *Industrial Relations in Postwar Japan* (Urbana, 1958), p. 9.

Takahashi Masao refers to Japan's economic development during the Meiji period as making "the small people poorer and the rich ever richer." "Kyūshū's Role in the Japanese Economy" (Paper presented at the Kyūshū International Cultural Conference, November 1962), p. 4.

"On the face of it, the meager livelihood of the masses of people in Japan at the end of the prewar era, even the dire poverty of millions of tenant farmers and unskilled workers, seems to challenge the evidence

392

Lacking so far has been adequate statistical evidence either supporting or refuting the various contentions. Recently, however, the work of Ohkawa Kazushi, Henry Rosovsky, and their associates at Hitotsubashi University has provided statistical information, along with Economic Planning Agency data, to permit a preliminary analysis of historical changes in consumption in Japan since the middle of the Meiji period.[3]

. . . as to the expansion of national output. How could a growth of such apparent magnitude have left most of the population so close to the minimum of subsistence, as Westerners would regard it?" William W. Lockwood, *The Economic Development of Japan, Growth and Structural Change, 1868-1938* (Princeton, 1954), pp. 139-40. In this passage, the qualifying phrase, "as Westerners would regard it," suggests that the impression of extreme poverty may reflect some cultural bias on the part of Western observers. For example, the traditional Japanese house for all classes of society is unpainted and constructed of wood, but, in the United States, such characteristics in combination are apt to be associated with the shacks of the poorest members of society. It is interesting to note that while Lockwood began his discussion of Japan's living conditions on a somber note, he concluded his analysis of the factual evidence by saying that "There can be no doubt that the great expansion of Japan's productive powers [by the 1930's] had raised the general level of economic well-being appreciably above that of Commodore Perry's day despite a doubling of the population." *Ibid.*, p. 150.

The above quotations are all taken from studies written in the postwar period and represent primarily Western views. Judged by a limited sample, there was a tendency for Westerners writing in the prewar period to present a brighter picture. Phrases like "substantial improvement" appear more frequently. Those Japanese writers who are oriented toward Marxist thinking understandably tend to take a critical view of the condition of the masses at any stage of Japanese history.

[3] Ohkawa Kazushi et al., *The Growth Rate of the Japanese Economy Since 1878* (Tokyo, 1957); Henry Rosovsky, *Capital Formation in Japan* (New York, 1961); Ohkawa Kazushi and Akasaka Keiko, *Kobetsu suikei no sōgōka* [Integration of Estimated Components] (Working Paper D 11, December 18, 1961); and Ohkawa Kazushi, and Akasaka Keiko, *Kobetsu suikei no sōgōka* (Working Paper D 21, September 28, 1962). The latter two references are successive revisions and extensions of parts of the first two works. They are the sources of the data for our indices of consumption and gross national product up to 1930.

We have used these data to construct an index of real personal consumption per capita extending from 1887 to 1962. The results appear in Figure 1 and Appendix Table 1, together with an index of real gross national product per capita for purposes of comparison.

Our measure of consumption has its conceptual defects. It omits the consumer services provided by the government and therefore differs from the flow-of-goods concept used by Simon Kuznets.[4] Except for housing service, as measured by rent, it does not include the flow of services from consumer durable goods. Still, it should provide a fairly satisfactory index of long-term trends in quantitative consumption levels. In addition, the recent calculations of yen-dollar purchasing power equivalents[5] have enabled us to obtain initial estimates of the *absolute* differences between the real consumption per capita in Japan and in the United States from the middle of the Meiji period to the present time. These estimates are shown in Figure 2 and Appendix Table 2. Since the statistical data on which our various series are based are in the process of revision, conclusions drawn from them must necessarily be regarded as tentative.[6]

[4] See *Capital in the American Economy* (Princeton, 1961), pp. 467-69.

[5] Watanabe Tsunehiko and Komiya Ryutarō, "Findings from Price Comparisons Principally Japan vs. the United States," *Weltwirtschaftliches Archiv*, Band 81, Heft 1 (1958), and Kumano Hideaki, *Beidoru to Nihonyen no kōbai ryoku heika* [American Dollar and Japanese Yen Purchasing Power Equivalents], *Tsūshō sangyō kenkyū* [International Trade and Industry Research], IX, 1 (January 25, 1961). A revised English version of the latter article was published in *The Journal of Economic Behavior*, I, 2 (October 1961). The English version will be used in subsequent citations.

[6] A drastic revision of the Japanese data prior to World War I is proposed by James I. Nakamura in Ch. VI, above. His estimates for agricultural production are much higher than the Ohkawa estimates for 1878-1882. The difference diminishes over time so that the revision results in a growth rate falling within a range markedly below the rate estimated by Ohkawa for the period prior to 1920. The use of Nakamura's revised estimates would, of course, result in a reduced rate of growth for both GNP and consumption during the period involved. In my opinion, Nakamura is right in claiming that previous

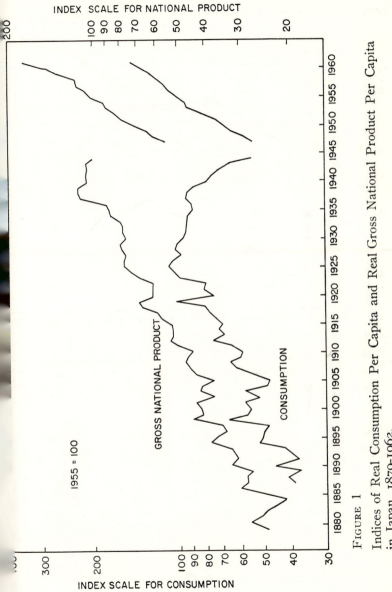

FIGURE 1

Indices of Real Consumption Per Capita and Real Gross National Product Per Capita in Japan, 1879-1962.

SOURCE: Appendix Table I.

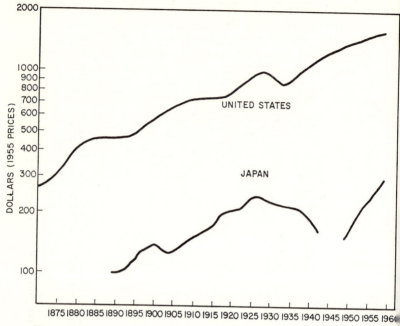

FIGURE 2

Real Consumption Per Capita in Japan and the United States, 1871-1960 (1955 Dollars, Five-year Moving Averages)
SOURCE: Appendix Table 2.

Our main objective here will be to show what has happened to consumption during the process of growth. A thorough analysis of why it happened is beyond the scope of this paper, but various hypotheses will be suggested. It is hoped that these will serve as a framework for a more definitive study later. In limiting the scope of the study, we have also omitted detailed

---

estimates of agricultural production for the early period are too low (and the estimated growth rate too high) as a result of being based on government data which are biased because of underreporting of land area and crop yields. But I suspect that even the upper limit of Nakamura's growth rate (above, p. 254) range may be too low.

consideration of changes in consumption patterns and of the effects of changes in consumption on growth. Specifically, we shall seek preliminary answers to the following questions: 1) Has Japan's process of industrialization been accompanied, as some have held, by a tendency for consumption to lag behind the rate of economic growth? 2) Has inequality in the distribution of consumption goods shown a long-run increasing trend? 3) To what extent have farmers and urban workers benefited from rising productivity? 4) Have government policies encouraged or retarded the rise in consumption levels? 5) How does Japan's growth in consumption compare with that of other industrially advanced countries? Here the analysis will be confined to a comparison with the United States. In dealing with these questions, our index of consumption will be our main statistical tool, but we shall also use other quantitative and qualitative information provided mainly by older studies.

Figure 1 reveals three distinct statistical phases in the long-run growth of consumption since 1887: 1) a phase of generally rising trend from 1887 to 1925; 2) a phase from 1925 to 1945, during which the upward trend was markedly checked and which included at least two pronounced declines; 3) a phase of rapid increase since 1945. These phases are not intended to represent stages which follow certain laws of development. They are purely descriptive in character and are designed only to divide our analysis into convenient parts.

We shall discuss each phase in turn, but most of our attention will be devoted to the first phase, where the need for a new analysis seems to be greatest. Only brief sketches will be given of the second and third phases. Our emphasis will be on long-term tendencies rather than on short-run variations, some of which may represent erratic changes reflecting statistical inadequacies rather than actual causal factors.

Phase I (1887-1925)

In view of rather pessimistic opinions concerning Japan's growth in consumption during her early development, the

statistical results may seem surprising. In terms of quinquennial averages for 1887-1891 and 1923-1927, real consumption
per capita increased by 154 percent during Phase I, a period
of a little less than forty years.[7] Furthermore, it kept pace
with the growth in GNP. In real per capita terms, GNP increased by 155 percent from 1887-1891 to 1923-1927, an
insignificantly greater growth than that of real consumption
per capita. At first sight, this may seem unreasonable, since
real gross domestic investment, a major component of GNP,
grew more rapidly than real consumption during the same
period. Recent estimates show that for real investment (including government investment other than military investment), the quinquennial average for 1923-1927 was 4.9 times
the average for 1887-1891.[8] The corresponding figure for real
consumption was 3.8. However, net foreign investment, which
showed a slight surplus during the period 1887-1891, developed a large deficit during the period 1923-1927. Government expenditures (excluding government investment other
than military investment) increased only slightly as a proportion of GNP.[9] Statistically speaking, therefore, gross
domestic investment, during the period under consideration,
expanded largely at the expense of net foreign investment.
The ratio of real personal consumption to real GNP declined

[7] During that period, three short-term swings may be noted: 1) a
moderate growth until the end of the nineteenth century; 2) a brief
declining tendency during the first few years of the twentieth century;
3) a period of relatively rapid advance beginning about 1905. The
declining tendency around the turn of the century is associated with a
decline in the general growth rate of the Japanese economy at this time
(see Ohkawa et al., pp. 21-24).

[8] Computed from investment data in Ohkawa and Akasaka, *op. cit.*
(Working Paper D 21, Addition of Nov. 15, 1962), pp. 1-3, using as a
deflator the investment goods price index in *ibid.* (Working Paper
D 21, Sept. 28, 1962), pp. 18-19. The ratio of real gross domestic investment (excluding military investment) to real GNP was 12.9%
in 1887-91, and 16.4% in 1923-27. In current prices, the corresponding
ratios were 15.0% and 18.3%.

[9] *Ibid.* (Working Paper D 21), pp. 18-19, and (Addition of Nov.
15, 1962), pp. 1-2.

only slightly from 78.1 percent in 1887-1891 to 77.7 percent in 1923-1927.[10]

During Phase I, then, Japan achieved not only rapid per capita economic growth but, in real terms, an almost matching rise in per capita consumption. It seems fair to say that if one regards Japan's per capita rate of growth as remarkable, one must regard the rise in per capita consumption as equally remarkable during the period under discussion.

Japan's achievement can be better appreciated if a comparison of consumption levels is made with other countries, though the scope of this paper permits only a limited comparison of this sort. We have selected the United States for this purpose, both because of the availability of adequate data and because of the frequency with which American development is used as an international yardstick. The results shown in Figure 2 and Appendix Table 2 may appear startling to some. During Phase I, at least, the rate of growth in real consumption per capita in Japan not only kept pace with the rate in the United States; it exceeded it. For Japan, the quinquennial average of 1925 was 2.54 times the quinquennial average of 1889. For the United States, the corresponding figure was 2.06.[11]

[10] In current prices, the corresponding ratios were 76.4% and 75.5%. The consumer goods price index rose a little more rapidly during the period than the investment goods price index. It should also be noted that since real gross domestic investment was a much smaller proportion of real GNP than was real personal consumption, a substantial percentage increase in the investment proportion, even if entirely at the expense of consumption, would result in a relatively small percentage decrease in the consumption proportion.

Within the period, considerable fluctuations in the various components of GNP took place with the consumption proportion in current prices ranging from about 70% to 77% in terms of quinquennial averages.

[11] If the figures for Japanese agricultural output proposed by Nakamura were used (above, p. 315), the difference between Japan and the United States would be much less. A rough recalculation of real personal consumption per capita in Japan in Phase I using Nakamura's lowest agricultural-output growth estimates for 1888-92 to 1913-17 gives a percentage increase during Phase I almost identical with that of the United States.

It is true that we are comparing different stages of development here. By 1890, the United States had already undergone several decades of industrialization and had attained a per capita level of income which was probably second only to that of Great Britain, the most developed country of the time.[12] Japan, starting rapid industrialization from a very low level only one or two decades before 1890, might be expected to experience relatively high percentage rates of growth after 1890. W. W. Rostow expresses the opinion that the "take-off" period for the United States extended from about 1843 to 1860, while he very tentatively suggests 1878-1900 for Japan.[13] Kuznets' series for the United States begins in 1869 so that we cannot compare Japan and the United States during similar early stages of industrialization. The closest we can come to this is to compare the change in the quinquennial average for Japan from 1889 to 1925, our Phase I period, with the change for the United States from 1871 to 1907. In this case, the increase for the United States is 164 percent as against 154 percent for Japan for the 36-year period beginning in 1889. The slightly higher rate for the United States is largely due to the unusually rapid change during the 1870's, a rather remarkable phenomenon considering that the period included a severe depression. In general, even after making allowances for the roughness of the statistical estimates and lack of comparability in the stages of growth, Japan's progress in raising levels of real consumption per capita during Phase I can scarcely be termed "slow" relative to that of the United States.

Other evidence of Japan's improvement in general consumption levels during Phase I comes from non-monetary indicators and the subjective observations of contemporary writers.

John Orchard, who studied Japan in the 1920's, used changes in food consumption as an indicator of changes in the level of living. His results are reproduced in Table 1.[14] Or-

---

[12] See Colin Clark, *The Conditions of Economic Progress* (Third Edition, London, 1957).

[13] *The Stages of Economic Growth* (Cambridge, 1960), p. 38.

[14] According to Lockwood, the official statistics on which Orchard's

TABLE 1

Estimated Average Annual per Capita Consumption
of Selected Food Products

Commodity	Years	Quantity (lbs.)	Index
Rice	1887-1891	296.0	100
	1921-1925	349.0	118
Wheat	1892–1896	31.0	100
	1923-1927	48.0	155
Barley and Rye	1892-1896	106.0	100
	1923-1927	77.0	73
Meat	1889-1893	0.9	100
	1922-1926	4.0	444
Fish	1900	29.0	100
	1924-1926	82.0	283
Sugar	1896-1898	10.4	100
	1922-1926	13.0	125

Source: John E. Orchard, *Japan's Economic Position* (New York,
1930), p. 18. Corrections have been made for some arithmetic errors
found in the original table.

chard concluded that "rapidly as the population has grown,
the increase of the food supply has more than kept pace with
it. During the modern period, there has been no recurrence of
famine, and the standard of living has advanced materially."[15]
Other figures show rice consumption per head increasing by
42 percent from 1880-1884 to 1925-1929.[16] The apparent shift

figures are based probably overstate the gain in consumption because
of more complete reporting at the end of the period than at the
beginning (*op.cit.*, p. 146, supplemented by comments in a letter to the
author dated July 24, 1963).

[15] *Japan's Economic Position* (New York, 1930), p. 17.

[16] Computed from figures cited in G. C. Allen, *A Short Economic
History of Modern Japan* (Second Revised Edition, London, 1962),
p. 201. The peak was reached in 1925-29. Since that time, consumption
per head has shown a long-term declining trend.

The gain may be exaggerated, however, since the data are based on
government production figures which Nakamura argues are seriously

from barley and rye to rice is regarded by several writers as indicative of a rising level of living since rice was considered at the time to be the superior grain.[17] Even back at the turn of the century, a Western missionary noted that ". . . the standard of living is rising. American wheat flour is being imported by shiploads. Beef, potatoes, cabbages, turnips are favourites with those who can afford them."[18]

The per capita intake of food was about 2,300 calories per day in 1926 and remained at that level during the following decade.[19] Its failure to increase might be interpreted as an indication of Japan's inability to do more than keep pace with a rapidly growing population. Certainly compared with the per capita consumption of about 3,500 calories per day in the United States in 1930, the Japanese intake appears grossly inadequate.[20] What is sometimes forgotten is that caloric needs vary greatly from one country to another and even over time within a given country. A postwar FAO study

---

understated for the early 1880's (above, Ch. VI). The same may be said for the substantial caloric gains shown by Nakayama Seiki in the consumption of grains, potatoes, pulses, meat, milk, and eggs from 1878 until the 1920's (*Long-term Changes in Food Consumption in Japan*, CTES No. 26, The International House of Japan, Inc., Tokyo [1962], translated from "Shokuryō Shōhi Suijun no Chōki Henka ni Tsuite"), *Nōgyō Sōgō Kenkyū*, XII, 4 (October 1958). Nakamura, in discussing Nakayama's figures (above pp. 300-301), takes the position that calorie consumption per capita in the early Meiji period may have been about the same as in 1913-1927.

[17] See, for example, Allen, p. 115; Orchard, p. 18; and Lockwood, p. 146. In the current postwar period, rice consumption per capita is declining, but this time the shift is interpreted as an indication of a rising standard as wheat, meat, and dairy products are being substituted for rice.

[18] John H. De Forest, *Sunrise in the Sunrise Kingdom* (New York, 1904), pp. 44-45.

[19] Lockwood, p. 147.

[20] Since 1930, the caloric consumption in the United States has shown a long-run decline and recently was about 3,150 calories per person per day. Bureau of the Census, *Statistical Abstract of the United States: 1959* (Washington, 1959), p. 84. At best, changes in caloric consumption are a shaky indicator of changes in levels of living.

reported that when climate, body weight, age, and sex composition of the population are taken into consideration, the
estimated daily requirement per person in Japan is only
2,330 calories.[21] If we accept this estimate as applying to
earlier decades, then we may conclude that by 1926 Japan
had reached an adequate level of food intake in terms of
calories and that this, rather than population pressure, accounts for the stability of the intake during the following
decade.[22]

GROWTH AND INEQUALITY

Up to this point we have been concerned mainly with
changes in average levels of consumption. A most difficult
question remains to be answered. How were the nation's
consumer goods shared during Phase I? Did the rise in the
general level merely mean a rapidly growing inequality in
distribution, with the rich experiencing a phenomenal improvement in living level and the less fortunate masses little
or no change?

No one doubts that income was very unequally distributed
during the whole period. The Lorenz diagram (Fig. 3) shows
a substantial amount of inequality in 1930, especially when
compared with a recent year. At the same time, consumption
expenditures were presumably more equally distributed than
incomes, since in Japan, as elsewhere, the upper income groups
save a higher percentage of their income than the lower
income groups.[23]

[21] UNFAO, *Second World Food Survey* (Rome, 1952), cited in
Horace Belshaw, *Population Growth and Levels of Consumption*
(New York, 1956), p. 19.

[22] Some attempt has been made to assess the level of consumption
through analysis of household budgets. For the period with which we
are presently concerned, the family income and expenditure survey of
1926-27 is a source of fruitful information. An excellent analysis of
this survey is provided in Lockwood, pp. 420-33.

[23] The family budget study of 1926-27 showed that those in the top
income group of wage-earner families with an average monthly
income of 231 yen saved about 24% of their income. These families
were probably close to the top 10% for the nation as a whole in
income level. (Estimated from data cited in Lockwood, pp. 272, 426.)

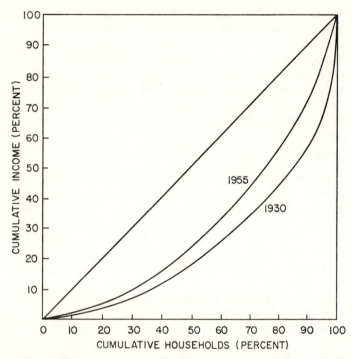

FIGURE 3

Income Distribution in Japan, 1930 and 1955 (Lorenz Curve).

SOURCE: For 1930, U.S. Department of State, *National Income of Japan* (Washington, 1945), p. 233, cited in William W. Lockwood, *The Economic Development of Japan* (Princeton, 1954), p. 272. For 1955, Economic Planning Board, *Economic Survey of Japan: 1955-1956* (Tokyo, September 1956), p. 204. The income figures are before taxes.

The mere existence of inequality per se, however, does not mean that the poor fail to experience the same percentage increase in consumption as the rich.[24] The questions that must

[24] What is meant here is that if families are ranked according to consumption expenditures and the lower 50% makes, say, 30% of the expenditures and the upper 50% makes 70% of the expenditures, doubling the amount of expenditures of each group will still leave the

be answered are: 1) Did relative inequality of incomes increase substantially during Phase I? 2) Did the proportion of income devoted to savings and direct taxes change for different income groups in ways to increase or decrease inequality in consumption? Reliable data are unfortunately very scanty on both of these points. Lockwood comments that "whether income and wealth were more or less unevenly distributed in 1880 than in 1930 we do not know. . . . One can only guess what the curve of income distribution during the early Meiji period was. The events attending the Restoration undoubtedly had a certain levelling influence in that they destroyed the great feudal incomes of the ruling class. On the other hand, the nobility were pensioned off, not wholly expropriated, and their clan debts to the merchants were shouldered by the government. These obligations, as subsequently commuted by the State, together with mercantile wealth carried over from the old days, provided the start for a new aristocracy of wealth to be erected on the foundations of the new capitalistic order. The new regime was therefore characterized in all probability by a fairly high degree of inequality from its early days, so far as the upper tail of the income distribution curve was concerned."[25]

Even though we may grant that inequality of personal incomes increased somewhat through the Meiji period, we cannot assume inequality of consumption increased at the same rate. Changes in the income tax system, especially during the second half of Phase I, may have affected the rate of change in the inequality of disposable incomes and hence consumption expenditures, assuming no offsetting shifts in rates of saving. A national personal income tax with progressive rates was introduced as early as 1887, but special treatment of property income, widespread evasion, and a very low maximum rate

---

percentage shares of each group unchanged. The absolute amount of increase, of course, would be less for the poor than for the rich if there were equal percentage increases in consumption under conditions of inequality.

[25] Lockwood, pp. 141, 271.

made it of slight importance until after World War I.[26] In 1922, it provided 26 percent of the total tax receipts of the national government as compared with about 10 percent in 1914.[27] In 1926-1927, at the end of Phase I, revisions increased the burden on upper income groups.[28] To the extent that it became more progressive through revisions, the income tax during Phase I may have retarded the rate of increase in consumption expenditures of the wealthy relative to the poor, through its impact on disposable incomes.[29]

It is difficult to determine whether the average propensity to save changed for different income groups as national income levels rose and thereby affected inequality in consumption. One cannot assume that because for short periods of time a higher income means a higher percentage of saving, the same thing will be true for longer periods during which consumption standards may rise. Although many writers stress the Japanese philosophy of frugal living at all income levels, there is strong evidence that standards of consumption, in the sense of what people wished to have, rose steadily among all classes.[30] Certain traditional patterns of consumption remained, but, within these patterns, changes of both a quantitative and qualitative nature took place. Fish consumption increased, but so did meat consumption. Kimonos were still worn, but better quality and more variety were sought. Houses might still be traditional in style, but larger and constructed with better materials. Increasing quantities of foreign consumer goods were evidently added to traditional items. New forms of recreation were sought. Harold G. Moulton, who observed Japan in 1930, wrote that "life in Japan today in many ways bears a striking resemblance to that of occidental countries. The system of universal education has not

[26] *Ibid.*, pp. 521-22.

[27] Harold G. Moulton, *Japan: An Economic and Financial Appraisal* (Washington, 1931), p. 576.

[28] *Ibid.*, pp. 217-18, and Lockwood, p. 524.

[29] The probability of an increase in the consumptive gap between landlords and tenants in rural areas is discussed below.

[30] Lockwood deals in some detail with this point (*op.cit.*, pp. 430-32). In Keynesian terms, the consumption schedule shifts upward.

only virtually eliminated outright illiteracy but, what is more significant, it has spurred the ambitions of millions to attain a higher plane of living. In the range of recreational and cultural activities open for the enjoyment of many, Japan now compares not unfavorably with leading countries of the West."[31] Preservation of much that was traditional in the way of life may have contributed to a continuously high level of personal saving, but this did not necessarily mean a rising average propensity to save for the population as a whole as income levels rose over the long term; nor did it necessarily mean changes in the relative inequality of consumption among various income groups.

On the whole, the preceding type of analysis permits no firm conclusions on the extent to which less privileged groups shared in the general improvement in consumption levels. More direct evidence is needed. This is provided for urban workers by real wage statistics. Following an examination of these statistics, we shall discuss the results of an experimental indicator of the consumption level of farm cultivators.

Long-term estimates of real wage changes in manufacturing industries are given in Figure 4 and Appendix Table 3. They show a strong upward trend during Phase I after 1905. From 1905 to 1925, in terms of quinquennial averages centered on those years, real wages rose 84 percent.[32] This compares with an increase of 90 percent in national real personal consumption per capita during the same period. It may also be contrasted with an increase of only 37 percent in the real hourly earnings in manufacturing in the United States during the same period.[33]

Prior to 1905, our series shows no perceptible improvement

[31] Moulton, p. 346.

[32] A more recent index computed by Umemura Mataji shows an increase of 136% during the same period. *Chingin, kōgyō, nōgyō* [Wages, Employment, Farming] (Tokyo, 1961), p. 65.

[33] Calculated from data in Bureau of the Census, *Historical Statistics of the United States: Colonial Times to 1957* (Washington, 1960), pp. 91-92, 126-27.

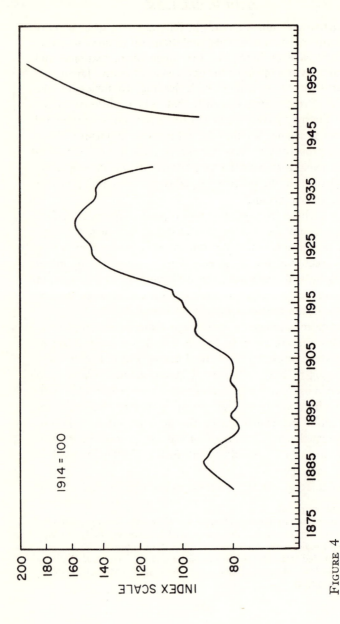

FIGURE 4

Index of Real Wages in Manufacturing in Japan, 1881-1959
(Five-year Moving Average).

SOURCE: Appendix Table 3.

in real wages.[34] This lag in real wages behind real personal consumption per capita before 1905 may be due partly to the very high percentage of female workers used in manufacturing. In 1900, women constituted 61 percent of workers in factories employing ten persons or more.[35] As is well known, a large proportion of these women were young girls from rural areas, working in textile mills for a limited period before returning to the farm. Wage increases for members of this group were probably limited by their susceptibility to exploitation, their frequent turnover, and a possible downward pressure on their wages due to the initial struggle of the textile industries to establish themselves in the highly competitive world market. By 1910, the silk and cotton textile industries, Japan's main sources of exports, were well established and increased in prosperity during most of the following two decades. World War I brought an expansion of heavy goods industries and a sharp increase in higher-paid male workers in manufacturing. Between 1914 and 1919, the proportion of male workers increased from 40 percent to 46 percent.[36] Part of the increase in real wages after 1900, therefore, may be attributed to a change in the labor force structure as the percentage of male workers in manufacturing increased. Another contributing factor may have been the adoption of the "permanent employment" system and the automatic annual wage increase system during the World War I period, especially in the new heavy industries where a stable, well-trained male work force was needed.[37]

Granting the limitations of real wage indices as indicators of changes in real consumption levels, the evidence suggests that at least during the second half of Phase I, as a permanent wage-earning class developed, Japanese urban workers not

[34] Umemura's index mentioned above shows a slight improvement of about 10% from 1883-87 to 1903-07.

[35] From Department of Commerce and Industry data cited in Allen, p. 197.

[36] *Ibid.*, p. 197.

[37] See Economic Research Institute, Economic Planning Agency, *Employment Structure and Business Fluctuations* (Bulletin No. 2, Tokyo, July 1959), p. 19.

only experienced an upward trend in their level of living, but did not fall substantially behind the population as a whole.[38]

Our next task is to examine changes in rural consumption levels. Roughly 80 percent of the gainfully occupied population were engaged in agriculture and forestry during the 1870's, and the proportion did not drop below 50 percent until after 1930.[39] Many recent studies have stressed the vital role of agriculture in Japanese economic development at least until World War I.[40] The principal thesis is that a rapid growth in agricultural productivity with relatively little capital investment provided a surplus which could be used for capital formation in other sectors.[41] This surplus, it is said, was tapped largely through a very heavy tax on land and invested by the government. It is sometimes held that, in this process, the improvement in consumption levels of farmers was greatly retarded. For example, Johnston and Mellor state that "Japan is probably the clearest example of a country where agriculture contributed significantly to the financing of development. . . . The impressive increase in farm output and productivity in Japan between 1881-90 and 1911-20 required only small capital outlays and but moderate increases in other inputs. Consumption levels of the farm population increased much less than the rise in productivity in agriculture, so that

[38] We have not dealt with the large group of self-employed and family workers in the non-agricultural sector. According to Ministry of Labor statistics, this group constituted about 36% of the non-agricultural labor force as recently as 1955. To the extent that long-term occupational mobility exists, the net real earnings of this group have probably followed the trend of real wages.

[39] Ohkawa et al., Table 2, p. 145.

[40] See especially Ohkawa Kazushi and Henry Rosovsky, "The Role of Agriculture in Modern Japanese Economic Development," *Economic Development and Cultural Change*, IX, 1, Part II (October 1960); Gustav Ranis, "The Financing of Japanese Economic Development," *Economic History Review*, XI, 3 (April 1959); and Bruce F. Johnston and John W. Mellor, "The Role of Agriculture in Economic Development," *American Economic Review*, LI, 4 (September 1961).

[41] Nakamura claims that this view rests upon statistics which greatly overstate the rate of growth of agricultural production during the Meiji period.

a substantial fraction of the increment in product in agriculture could be used to finance capital formation in the capitalist sector of the economy."[42]

Taxation of agriculture was said to be the "principal device used to siphon off a part of this increase in productivity." The large proportion of total direct tax revenues contributed by agriculture as compared with non-agriculture was mentioned. Many others have commented on the sizable proportion agriculture contributed to national and local government tax revenues during the Meiji period, but this fact in itself is not sufficient to tell us what the burden was in terms of farm income and whether or not that burden was increasing or decreasing over the years. This information has been provided by Ohkawa and Rosovsky and is reproduced in Table 2 with some modification.[43] As Ohkawa and Rosovsky point out, the weight of the burden shows a long-term declining tendency.[44] This was due in large part to the fact that the famous Meiji land tax was essentially a lump sum tax whose amount changed little over most of the years for a piece of property of a given classification.[45] The drop was especially rapid up to 1893-1897, after which the burden remained fairly stable until 1913-1917, when the downward tendency was resumed. There is no question about the greater tax burden on agriculture as compared with non-agriculture; but since the burden declined over time it is difficult to understand how it can be argued that heavy direct taxes per se caused consumption levels of the agricultural population as a whole to lag behind agricultural productivity.

To arrive at some estimate of changes in agricultural consumption levels, net income produced should be adjusted not only for direct taxes but for personal savings and business savings (investment). Data are lacking on personal savings,

[42] Johnston and Mellor, pp. 577-78.

[43] Ranis also computed a similar set of figures (*op. cit.,* p. 448).

[44] Ohkawa and Rosovsky, p. 62.

[45] Some land revaluations occurred. See Nakamura's discussion, above, pp. 278-79, 282. The most significant rate changes were during the period 1899 to 1905 when three increases took place.

TABLE 2

RATIOS OF DIRECT TAXES ON AGRICULTURE
AND OF GROSS AGRICULTURAL INVESTMENT
TO NET INCOME PRODUCED IN AGRICULTURE[a]

Year (Annual Average)	Direct Tax Ratio[b] (%)	Gross Agricultural Investment Ratio[c] (%)
1883-1887	20.2	10.1
1888-1892	14.1	9.3
1893-1897	11.3	9.2
1898-1902	11.2	8.8
1903-1907	10.4	8.1
1908-1912	11.6	8.1
1913-1917	11.0	8.0
1918-1922	8.3	7.9
1923-1927	9.4	8.6
1928-1932	8.9	9.1
1933-1937	7.1	7.6

NOTES AND SOURCES:

[a] The data for net income produced are from Ohkawa Kazushi et al., *The Growth Rate of The Japanese Economy Since 1878* (Tokyo, 1957), pp. 72-73. They include forestry.

[b] The direct tax estimates were originally provided by Tsunematsu Seiji and cited by Ohkawa Kazushi and Henry Rosovsky, "The Role of Agriculture in Modern Japanese Economic Development," *Economic Development and Cultural Change*, IX, 1, Part II (October 1960), p. 62. Their ratios differ slightly from those in this table since they used as the ratio base the income of agriculture excluding forestry.

[c] The estimates of gross agricultural investment are from a revision of figures in Ohkawa Kazushi and Akasaka Keiko, *Kobetsu suikei no sōgōka* [Integration of Estimated Components] (Working Paper D 11, December 18, 1961), pp. 21-22. They include construction of farm housing, farm land improvement, and farm equipment.

but recent estimates for agricultural investment are now available. It is generally accepted that the remarkable increase in agricultural productivity in the prewar period in Japan was accomplished with relatively little investment expenditure. This is evident from Table 2. What is more important for estimating changes in income used for consumption pur-

poses is the declining ratio of investment to net income produced from the 1880's until World War I. It rose only slightly
during the early 1920's.

Although no data are available which would permit an adjustment for personal savings, the information on investment
and direct taxes enables us to construct an index of real disposable income per member of the agricultural labor force
roughly comparable to the real wage index for urban workers
which is also unadjusted for personal savings.[46] In preparing
this index, we have deducted direct taxes and gross agricultural investment from net income produced in agriculture
(including forestry), deflated with a rural consumers' price
index, and divided the results by estimates of the number of
gainfully occupied persons in agriculture (including forestry).
The results are shown in Table 3 together with indices of
real income produced and the agricultural terms of trade.

Some of the limitations of the procedure should be pointed
out. First, income produced is not necessarily identical with
income received during a given period. Secondly, no adjustment has been made for the rents received by non-cultivating
landlords which reduced the income available for consumption by the cultivating population. Such landlords, of course,
paid the land tax and sometimes contributed to agricultural
investment. The rents they received, less their contributions
to agricultural investment and direct taxes, should be deducted from our estimates of disposable income of cultivators;
but no adequate data exist for doing this. R. P. Dore provides some indication of the importance of the non-cultivating
landlords through his estimates of the percentage of tenanted
land they controlled immediately after World War II. He
suggests, as a rough approximation, that ". . . in mid-1947
about 18 per cent of the total tenanted land was owned by
absentee landlords, [and] another 24 percent by non-farmers
living in the same village or town as their landholding or in
a neighbouring village or small town. . . ."[47] Since tenanted

[46] It is assumed that during Phase I direct taxes paid by urban wage
earners were generally relatively small in amount.
[47] R. P. Dore, *Land Reform in Japan* (London, 1959), p. 23.

TABLE 3

Indices of Estimated Real Disposable Income and
Real Income Produced per Gainfully Occupied Person in
Agriculture, and Agricultural Terms of Trade
1883 to 1937

(1913-1917 = 100)

Year (Annual Average)	Real Disposable Income per Gainfully Occupied Person in Agriculture[a]	Real Income Produced per Gainfully Occupied Person in Agriculture[b]	Agricultural Terms of Trade[c]
1883-1887	42.2	48.4	101.2
1888-1892	56.3	55.1	106.9
1893-1897	66.8	59.9	114.4
1898-1902	77.0	71.4	109.2
1903-1907	81.3	76.0	106.7
1908-1912	90.6	90.6	100.7
1913-1917	100.0	100.0	100.0
1918-1922	121.7	117.6	100.1
1923-1927	120.0	113.3	105.1
1928-1932	103.4	125.1	82.1
1933-1937	131.6	138.4	90.4

Notes and Sources:

[a] Disposable money income was estimated by subtracting direct taxes on agriculture and gross agricultural investment from net income produced in agriculture (including forestry). The sources are given in Table 2. The deflator for 1883-1936 is the rural consumer price index given in Ohkawa and Akasaka, *Kobetsu Suikei no Sōgōka*, [Integration of Estimated Components] Working Paper D 11, December 18, 1961, pp. 16-17, with the rural consumer price index of the Economic Planning Agency used for 1937. The figures for gainfully occupied persons in agriculture (including forestry) are from Ohkawa Kazushi et al., *The Growth Rate of the Japanese Economy Since 1878* (Tokyo, 1957), p. 245.

[b] Data for real income produced in agriculture (including forestry) were obtained from Ohkawa et al., *Growth Rate*, p. 72 and divided by the same figures for gainfully occupied persons used in n.a. above.

[c] Computed by obtaining the ratio of the price index of agricultural commodities (Ohkawa et al., *Growth Rate*, p. 130) to the rural consumer price index used in n.a. above.

land constituted about 46 percent of the total cultivated land, this would mean about 19 percent of total cultivated land was owned by non-cultivators.[48] Doubtless their rent income after taxes and investment was a substantial amount. It would not affect our index of disposable income, however, if it remained a constant proportion of our estimates of disposable income. Thirdly, supplementary income of farmers from non-agricultural occupations is not included. Presumably this income expanded as the economy developed, though not necessarily at the same rate as our index. Fourthly, interest on farm debt is not taken into account. According to one estimate, interest charges paid by these engaged in agriculture to persons outside of agriculture constituted about 9 percent of net agricultural income in 1930.[49] Undoubtedly the total amount of interest increased secularly during Phase I, but whether the rate of increase was greater than that of disposable income we do not know.

With these limitations, as well as those inherent in the data themselves, the index must be regarded as no more than a very tentative and experimental indicator of changes in the real disposable income of cultivators.

The results show a striking increase until the middle of the 1920's. In comparison with real wages of urban workers, real disposable income per agricultural worker rose more rapidly up to 1905 and then less rapidly as urban wages surged upward. For Phase I as a whole, real disposable income per worker in agriculture kept pace with real personal consumption per capita for the nation as a whole up to 1918-1922. Our data, of course, tell us nothing about the relative levels

[48] The cultivators formed a highly mixed group. Some were pure tenants who owned no land; others owned some land and rented some land; and still others owned some land, part of which they worked themselves and part of which they rented to others (see Dore, Ch. II). A portion of the total rent, therefore, was transfer income among cultivators.

[49] Computed from data in U.S. Department of State, *National Income of Japan* (Washington, 1945), pp. 161, 171, cited in Lockwood, pp. 57, 100. Since this was a year of severe agricultural depression, the percentage may have been unusually high relative to most of the years of Phase I.

of living of urban and rural workers. It seems evident, however, that both groups shared in the rise in general consumption levels but experienced their most rapid gains at different
times. On the whole, the statistical evidence supports Shiro
Kawada's assertion in the 1930's that "it is hardly possible
to deny that the agrarian standard of life has been raised to
a much higher level than obtained formerly, for agricultural
communities have had their share in the general increase in
wealth experienced in the capitalistic age. As a matter of fact
there is a considerable gap between the modern standard of
rural life and that of the feudalistic period, or even between
the present standard and that of the period preceding the Sino-
Japanese War and the Russo-Japanese War."[50]

Our data also permit us to make a preliminary test of the
hypothesis that consumption levels lagged behind productivity in agriculture during Phase I. Table 3 provides a comparison between our index of real disposable income per
worker and an index of real income produced per worker in
agriculture. If we may regard our index of real disposable
income as a rough indicator of changes in consumption levels,
then it is clear that for Phase I as a whole (1888-1892 to
1923-1927) there is no support for the theory that productivity outran consumption. Real disposable income actually
increased slightly more than productivity. The relationship
between the two indices is a function of the direct tax and
agricultural investment ratios shown in Table 2, and the
terms of trade index shown in Table 3. On the basis of the
decline in the direct tax and investment ratios during Phase I,
one would expect real disposable income to outstrip productivity to a much greater extent. Offsetting the effect of these
two ratios, however, was a decline in the agricultural terms
of trade for the period as a whole, especially in the middle
years. The terms-of-trade index was computed by dividing
the agricultural commodities price index (used in deflating
the income produced) by the rural consumers' price index

[50] "The Income and Living Standards of the Agrarian Population
in Japan," *Journal of the Osaka University of Commerce*, 4 (December 1936), p. 13, quoted in Lockwood, p. 150.

(used in deflating disposable income). A decline in the ratio meant the prices of what the farmer consumed were rising faster (or falling more slowly) than the prices of what he produced. In such a case, this meant, in real terms, an increasing amount of production required to finance a given amount of consumption. If one makes a shorter-term comparison using a different starting point such as 1893-1897, real disposable income lagged markedly behind production until 1908-1912, but this was due to the sharp drop in the terms of trade during the period and not to the effect of the tax system.

The possible impact of the land tax on changes in the distribution of disposable income and consumption in the rural areas requires some comment. Since the amount of the land tax for a given piece of agricultural property changed little after 1878, it declined as a percentage of income as incomes rose. It was paid by the landowners and not by the tenants. The tenants, on the other hand, were subject to heavy rents. These rents were usually paid in kind and did not vary much with crop yields. Rising rice prices during most of the Meiji-Taishō period meant a tendency for the money value of the rents to increase. The combination of the land tax system, the rent system, and rising rice prices therefore may have increased the disposable income and consumption gap existing between landlords and tenants. Dore explains this point in some detail. In commenting on the introduction of the land tax in 1873, he points out that "Rents for tenanted land . . . showed no reduction with the change in the taxation system. They continued to be paid in kind and continued to represent about half of an average crop. The reduction in the land tax did not affect such tenants, and the rise in the price of rice brought them little or no advantage (since the amount of rice they marketed was small), while greatly benefiting the landlords who received the same amount of rice in rents and had to devote a proportionately smaller portion of the proceeds of its sale to the payment of taxes. The gap between the economic status of the landlord and the tenant consequently grew."[51]

[51] *Op. cit.*, p. 17.

On the basis of this and other observations, Dore reaches the pessimistic conclusion that "There were, therefore, many factors at work to make the rich richer and the poor poorer in Japanese villages."[52] But a little further on, he notes the great increase in agricultural productivity from about 1880 to 1940 and feels "it represented a net gain for the tenant as well as for the owner-cultivator, since, apart from a limited amount of sharecropping in the north, rents were generally in the form of a fixed amount of rice, and custom imposed certain limits on the extent to which the landlord could raise that amount."[53] He finally concludes that, "Allowing for the increase in the cultivated area and for the increased profits of the landlords it seems certain that this meant some rise in the levels of living of the cultivators too, . . ."[54] The increase in tenancy during the Meiji period may have slowed this rise for a growing proportion of cultivators since the rents on the average imposed a greater burden than the land tax.[55] Judged from the widely varying estimates available, most of the shift took place before 1890, when the amount of tenanted land reached approximately 40 percent of the total. It tended to stabilize at about 45 percent after 1900. Estimates of the proportion of cultivators who were pure tenants, with no land of their own, run around 30 percent in 1910-1915 as against about 20 percent before 1880.[56] During the years of Phase I,

[52] *Ibid.*

[53] *Ibid.*, p. 19. Rosovsky points out that while the rents were nominally fixed in absolute amounts, "the final rent paid tended to fluctuate according to yield changes" (*op. cit.*, p. 84).

[54] *Op. cit.*, p. 20. The systems of fixed tax and fixed rent provided a strong incentive to increased productivity for both tenants and owners in periods of rising prices, but an equally strong depressing effect in periods of falling prices. Dore states, "Under the old feudal system reductions in the rice tax had been made in years of bad harvest. The new land tax was invariable and a crop failure meant that a peasant might be forced into debt to meet his tax obligations." (*Ibid.*, p. 16.) Fortunately for Japan's early development, there was only one prolonged agricultural depression prior to 1925. That was the depression of the 1880's.

[55] Lockwood, p. 98.

[56] Based on figures cited in Allen, p. 64; Dore, pp. 17, 19; and Rosovsky, p. 82.

therefore, it seems unlikely that the shift toward tenancy was sufficiently great to have had much impact on the distribution of income and consumption.

Summing up our discussion of consumption distribution in agriculture, the combination of a declining land tax burden for landowners and a fairly constant rent burden for tenants during the generally inflationary years of Phase I suggest a growing inequality in the distribution of disposable income in the rural areas. To the extent that changes in the average propensity to save and in the relative interest burden did not offset this trend, the consumption levels of the pure tenant group probably rose more slowly than the consumption levels of the owner group.

Phase II (1925-1945)

The upward surge in national consumption levels during Phase I was sharply checked after 1925 through a series of highly inter-connected economic and political events. A glance at Figure 1 shows, (1) an absolute decline in real per capita consumption setting in before the World Depression got underway; (2) only a slight recovery during the 1930's, while aggregate production boomed; and (3) the disastrous drop precipitated by involvement in total war. As a result, by the end of World War II, Japan's real per capita consumption had dropped below the level attained as far back as the turn of the century. In comparison with the United States, the gap in consumption levels between the two countries, after narrowing for several decades, began to widen (see Fig. 2). United States consumption was hit harder by the depression, but resumed its upward trend after 1933. This rising trend continued even during World War II, an achievement partly attributable to the fact that the United States began the war effort at a time when large amounts of human and capital resources were unemployed.

The decline which followed immediately after 1925 appears to be related to the beginning of a severe agricultural depression. While real wages of urban workers continued to rise, farmers experienced two serious blows which occurred simultaneously. First, the price of rice began a steep decline in 1926, reaching a trough in 1931 from which it did not emerge until 1935.[57] The decrease from 1925 to 1931 was 56 percent.[58] Among the contributing factors were the growing imports of rice from Korea and Formosa encouraged by the government, four large crops in succession beginning in 1927, and a weakening of urban demand as the industrial depression got underway after 1929.[59] Secondly, raw silk prices also began to fall after 1925.[60] From their postwar high in 1925, they dropped 32 percent by 1929. The collapse of American demand during the depression administered the *coup de grâce* and in 1931 silk prices were only one-third of their 1925 peak.[61] They remained low throughout the 1930's.[62] Cocoon prices were similarly affected.[63] Rice and cocoons were the two major sources of income for farmer, providing together 66 percent of the total value of agricultural output in 1926.[64] A simultaneous collapse in prices for both of these products was consequently an economic disaster for cultivators. The value of the net product of agriculture fell 58 percent between 1925 and 1931. The 1925 level was not regained until 1939.[65] The farmer's cost of living, on the other hand, declined only 28 percent from 1925 to 1931 and then began to rise.[66] The effect on real disposable income per worker in 1928-1932 is seen in Table 3.

Meanwhile, real wages increased until 1930 (Fig. 4 and Appendix Table 3).[67] The continued rise during the depres-

[57] Dore, p. 21.

[58] Computed from data in Lockwood, p. 56.

[59] Allen, pp. 114-15.

[60] Allen associates the initial fall with a rise in the exchange value of the yen (*ibid.*, p. 117).

[61] Computed from data in Lockwood, p. 56.

[62] Allen, p. 139.

[63] Lockwood, p. 57.

[64] From data given by E. F. Penrose in *The Industrialization of Japan and Manchukuo* (E. B. Schumpeter, ed., New York, 1941), p. 131, cited by Allen, p. 202.

[65] Ohkawa et al., p. 73.

[66] Ohkawa and Akasaka, *op. cit.* (Working Paper D 11), p. 17.

[67] The Bank of Japan Index shows the peak in 1931. See Allen, p. 221.

sion was the result of the urban cost of living falling even more rapidly than money wages. This is partly attributable to the rapid decline in the price of rice. The gain of the urban workers therefore was, in part, at the expense of the farmer. It appears from our analysis that the declining trend in national real consumption per capita from 1925 to 1930, in the face of rising real wages, was due largely to the drop in consumption levels of rural workers.

After 1931, Japan recovered from the industrial depression as military expenditures increased and the volume of foreign trade expanded with the depreciation of the yen. Real wages, which had shown some rise during the depression, now showed a substantial fall during industrial prosperity. Allen, in his analysis of this phenomenon, points out that the change in the average real wage conceals a marked change in wage structure. Workers in the rapidly growing heavy industries became better off, while the real wages of workers in the light industries declined about 30 percent between 1929 and 1936.[68] According to Allen, "The members of agricultural families were driven by the depression to offer themselves in increasing numbers for industrial employment in the towns. The girls who had previously found jobs in the silk-reeling mills in rural areas now competed for jobs in other textile factories, especially the cotton mills. Yet, as technical improvements had reduced the number of workers required for a given output in the cotton industry, the demand for workers in that trade did not rise to an extent corresponding to the increase in output. Thus the persistent agricultural depression impelled a large-scale transference of workers from agriculture to industry and from rural to urban trades, and it exercised a powerful influence in keeping down industrial wages."[69] The cessation of the fall in rice prices after 1931 and their later rise also contributed to the fall in real wages.

During the 1930's, agriculture began to revive. The government made some attempt to support rice and silk prices, to relieve the burden of the farm debts which had accumulated

[68] *Ibid.*, p. 139.
[69] *Ibid.*, pp. 139-40.

rapidly during the depression, and to encourage the growth of agricultural cooperatives.[70] Monetary demand for farm products by urban workers improved as money earnings stopped declining after 1933 and then gradually rose. Expanding industrial demand for labor facilitated the flow of rural workers into non-agricultural occupations. It helped to absorb the natural increase in the agricultural labor force and, in addition, to reduce the total number of workers in agriculture (and forestry) by about 3 percent between 1932 and 1940.[71] Moreover, the percentage of investment to net income produced declined (Table 2). The effect of these various factors on rural real disposable income per worker, after adjusting for direct taxes and investment expenditures, is seen in Table 3.

The combination of the declining trend in real wages and the improvement in real disposable income per worker in agriculture is consistent with the tendency of real personal consumption per capita for the nation as a whole to remain fairly stable from 1931 to 1938.[72] From the aggregative standpoint, the failure of national consumption to keep pace with the growth of GNP has been attributed to the increasing proportion of the national output devoted to government military

[70] For details, see Dore, pp. 98-106.

[71] Calculated from data in Ohkawa et al., p. 246.

[72] Consumption may have risen more during this period than is shown by our estimates, which are based on EPA data. A preliminary series by Ohkawa and Akasaka shows an increase of over 30% from 1931 to 1937 in real consumption per capita (see Note 2, Appendix Table 1 for details). Lockwood estimated that the consumption of goods and services per capita rose about 10% from 1930 to 1936 (*op. cit.*, p. 74). Our figures show a 6% decline for the same period. Expenditures for consumption by military personnel are excluded from our figures, although military personnel residing within Japan are included in the population figures used in obtaining per capita estimates. I do not believe, however, that adjusting for this discrepancy would affect our index appreciably prior to 1937 unless the consumption per capita by the armed forces in Japan was very much greater than that of the civilian population, and the number of members was a large and changing percentage of total population. Actually the members of the armed forces in Japan were less than 1% of the total population from 1930 to 1937, according to data cited in Lockwood, p. 465.

expenditures and to private investment. Gross domestic capital formation, including military expenditures, rose from 18.4 percent of GNP in 1922-1931 to 25.0 percent of GNP in 1931-1940.[73] Another factor sometimes mentioned is the deterioration in terms of trade in the 1930's following the depreciation of the yen. This meant exporting a greater quantity of goods in order to import a given quantity of goods, and hence, *cet. par.*, a rise in real GNP more rapid than real domestic personal consumption and capital formation.[74]

While the growing gap between GNP and personal consumption during the 1930's may be attributed partly to government policies such as increased military expenditures and an export drive through depreciation of the yen, this does not necessarily mean that such policies made consumption less than it would have been otherwise. The increase in government expenditures and in the physical volume of exports, coming as it did during a time of depression and unemployed or underemployed resources, may well have provided a stimulus which contributed to some recovery in consumption after several years of decline. It was not until after the war in China was vigorously renewed in 1937 that the war drain on resources, which were by then more fully employed, led to a marked drop in the absolute level of consumption per capita.

Although the growth in her consumption level was checked sharply after 1925, Japan ranked fairly high among major nations of the world in 1934-1938, according to a non-monetary comparison by M. K. Bennett. While Japan stood below such countries as the United States, France, and Argentina, she ranked above Italy, Spain, and the U.S.S.R.[75]

The extent to which Japan's increasing involvement in war after 1937 was at the expense of the living level of her population is clear from Figure 1. The final disaster of defeat, as is well known, reduced large numbers of people to

[73] Rosovsky, pp. 9, 15.

[74] See Allen, p. 140 and Lockwood, pp. 74, 140.

[75] "International Disparities in Consumption Levels," *American Economic Review*, XLI, 4 (September 1951), pp. 632-49. See Lockwood's discussion, *op. cit.*, pp. 147-48.

virtual starvation. This painful episode needs no further comment except to point out that Japan's level of living in the postwar period needed to recover not only from the losses of World War II but also from a deterioration in per capita consumption beginning as far back as 1925, a deterioration from which there was apparently no substantial recovery prior to the war.

Phase III (Postwar Period)[76]

Japan's spectacular growth in the postwar period has been matched by an almost equally spectacular rise in consumption per capita (Fig. 1 and Appendix Table 1). By 1955 the highest level of the 1930's was reached; by 1957 the 1925 peak had been exceeded. How much higher the 1957 figure would have been in the absence of Japan's military adventures beginning in 1931 is, of course, a matter of conjecture. A rough projection of a linear trend[77] based on the period prior to 1931 would give a figure about 55 percent higher than the actual value for 1957. There is no reason to believe, however, that the trend would have remained linear. Since the end of the war, consumption has continued to grow at a prodigious pace. By 1962, it stood in quantitative per capita terms at 291 percent of its 1947 level and about 142 percent of the prewar peak in 1925.[78]

Real wages, which had to recover from a level well below that of the 1880's, rose 430 percent from 1947 to 1963 (Fig. 4 and Appendix Table 3). From 1950 to 1962, however, the percentage increase was only 83 percent compared with 127 percent for national real consumption per capita. One might be tempted to conclude from this lag in real wages that since 1950 the consumption level of workers has lagged behind that of the nation as a whole. The data in Table 4, however, are more reassuring and are probably a more accurate indicator

---

[76] Lockwood's essay below on "Japan's 'New Capitalism'" chapter X in this volume, also includes considerable data on changes in consumption during the postwar period.

[77] Exponential on an arithmetic scale.

[78] 150% of the prewar peak for quinquennial averages in 1924-28.

TABLE 4

INDICES OF REAL HOUSEHOLD CONSUMPTION
EXPENDITURES, URBAN AND RURAL, 1952-1963
(1934-1936 = 100)

Year	Urban	Rural	Ratio of Rural to Urban (%)
1952	80.2	116.6	145.4
1953	94.0	123.2	131.1
1954	100.0	127.5	127.5
1955	106.5	129.7	121.8
1956	112.0	133.6	119.3
1957	116.9	134.9	115.4
1958	124.4	138.3	111.2
1959	131.1	143.7	109.6
1960	137.4	153.9	112.0
1961	146.4	165.9	113.0
1962	154.9	176.5	113.9
1963	162.5	187.0	115.1

SOURCES: Statistics Section, Research Bureau, Economic Planning Agency, cited in Office of the Prime Minister, *Japan Statistical Yearbook: 1955/56* and *1963*, pp. 384 and 399, respectively, and in the *Oriental Economist*, Vol. XXXII, No. 647 (September 1964), p. 636. Beginning in 1955, the data are adjusted for changes in the number of household members.

of changes in the quantitative consumption of middle and lower income urban groups. They show an increase of nearly 93 percent in the real consumption of urban households from 1952 to 1962 compared with 85 percent for national real consumption per capita during the same period.[79] On the other hand, Table 4 shows only a 51 percent increase during the period for rural households. This suggests a growing inequality between urban and rural families. In this connection,

[79] Real wages showed an increase of only about 52% during the same period. Part of the difference between the real wage increase and the real consumption increase of households is attributable to a rise in the labor force participation rate of family members during the period.

Table 4 provides some interesting additional information. Compared with 1934-1936, rural households apparently improved their position relative to urban households. The Ministry of Finance expressed the opinion that, in 1956, the household consumption levels in rural and urban areas were virtually the same.[80] If this is true, then, according to Table 4, rural levels exceeded urban levels for a time prior to 1956. This seems reasonable since the devastation of the war was concentrated mainly in the urban industrial areas. In addition, rural material welfare was greatly advanced after the war by the land reform, rapid growth in agricultural productivity, elimination of farm debts through inflation, and government price supports for certain staple food products. After 1956, the ratios of rural consumption to urban consumption in Table 4 show a gap developing in favor of the urban areas. But, after 1959, the trend was reversed, and, by 1963, the gap (assuming equality in 1956) was insignificant. This relatively rapid progress in the rural areas is of unusual interest. It may be associated with the recent remarkable shift in the labor force from rural to urban areas and the technological change that has accompanied this shift.

Our evidence supports the hypotheses that (1) the war and events of its immediate aftermath not only eliminated prewar inequality between rural and urban consumption levels but temporarily gave rural areas a relative advantage; (2) the rural advantage was wiped out sometime during the years following the war; (3) a consumption gap in favor of urban areas may have developed since 1956. This gap, however, could be eliminated if the recent rates of unusually rapid progress in the rural areas are maintained.

The improvement in the relative position of the farmers and the destruction of sources of property income during and immediately after the war helped to reduce inequality of income distribution. Probably, though not necessarily to the same degree, it also lowered the inequality in the distribution of consumers' goods compared with the prewar period (Fig.

[80] *General Survey of the Japanese Economy* (Tokyo, September 1957), p. 46.

3). In 1955, the degree of inequality in Japan was about the same as that in the United States.[81]

There are many other evidences of the material benefits which Japan's postwar development has conferred upon the population. The boom in purchases of household equipment has been called Japan's "Consumption Revolution." (See below, pp. 451-55.) Its most visible symbol is the forest of TV antennas one encounters even in rural districts. Electric slippers, blankets, rice-cookers, toasters, washing machines, *ko-tatsu* heating units, and refrigerators are readily available. *Insutanto* (instant) food preparations, often catering to the traditional dietary habits, ease the burden of the Japanese housewife.[82] Housing in urban areas is still overcrowded, however, in spite of government efforts to alleviate the shortage through vast low-rent apartment projects.[83] The infant mortality rate, considered by some as a good non-monetary indicator of national well-being, has dropped greatly since the end of the war and stood at 26.5 per thousand in 1962 as compared with rates of 25.3, 22.4, and 40.8, for the United States, United Kingdom, and Italy, respectively.[84]

These great gains leave one wondering how well off Japan is at present relative to other advanced countries. Customary comparisons using foreign exchange rates as factors for conversion to common monetary units show Japan at a great disadvantage even today compared to countries like the United

[81] For Department of Commerce data on income distribution in the United States, see Bureau of the Census, *Statistical Abstract of the United States: 1959* (Washington, 1959), p. 316.

[82] Japan's postwar boom in consumption moved Rostow to proclaim Japan's entrance during the 1950's into the "age of high mass-consumption" (*op. cit.*, pp. 11, 87-88).

[83] This problem is discussed in my "Postwar Housing in Japan and the United States: A Case Study in International Comparisons," published in Japanese in *The Journal of Social Science* (International Christian University), 2 (March 1961), and in English in Richard K. Beardsley, ed., *Studies on Economic Life in Japan*, Occasional Papers No. 8, University of Michigan Center for Japanese Studies, Ann Arbor, 1964. The English version will be used in subsequent citations.

[84] Statistical Office of the United Nations, *Statistical Yearbook: 1963* (New York, 1964), pp. 52-53.

States. Foreign exchange rates, however, are often inadequate indicators of the relative purchasing power of currencies.[85] Consequently, direct estimations of purchasing power equivalents are being used to an increasing extent. Most of these estimations employ the binary comparison method through which the product of each country is valued in terms of both its own prices and the prices of the other country or other countries with which a comparison is to be made.[86]

An attempt to estimate the purchasing power equivalent of the yen in terms of the dollar for consumer goods was recently made by Kumano Hideaki.[87] His study included both sides of the binary comparison, though it lacked a few items, including housing, education and medical services. Combining his results for 1955 with my own estimate of the housing service purchasing power equivalent[88] yields an average of ¥231.9 = $1. If we use this rate instead of the foreign exchange rate to convert Japanese personal consumption expenditures per capita into equivalent dollars, we obtain a result of $243 for 1955. This compares with $1,557 for the United States, or a ratio of 6.4 to 1 in favor of the United States in 1955. This is still a substantial quantitative disadvantage for Japan, though the ratio is much less than the 10 to 1 ratio obtained by using the foreign exchange rate of ¥360 = $1.[89]

[85] Milton Gilbert and Irving B. Kravis have an excellent discussion of this point in *An International Comparison of National Products and The Purchasing Power of Currencies* (Paris, 1954), pp. 14-17.

[86] See Gilbert and Kravis, *op. cit.*, for a detailed explanation of the technique and its application.

[87] See n. 5 above.

[88] The derivation of the housing service purchasing power equivalent is given in my "Postwar Housing in Japan and the United States," *op. cit.*, pp. 12-18. It is based on estimates of the space rental value of an average Japanese house in the United States and Japan.

[89] It is my belief that the national income accounts understate the house-rent component of personal consumption expenditures, but not enough to make a great difference in the above results. Adjusting for the estimated understatement in 1955 would give a figure of $256 for personal consumption per capita. My calculations for rent are given in "Postwar Housing in Japan and the United States," *op. cit.*, pp. 6, 25.

It is possible to use our results in comparing the absolute levels of consumption per capita of Japan and the United States from the middle of the Meiji period. This has been done in Appendix Table 2 and Figure 2 by a method which amounts to multiplying an index of real consumption per capita for each country, based on 1955, by the 1955 values of $243 and $1,557 for Japan and the United States, respectively.[90] Appendix Table 2 and Figure 2 consequently serve a dual purpose. They permit comparisons both of changes over time and of absolute levels at any given time.

Comparing quinquennial averages for 1887-1891, the beginning of Phase I, the ratio of the levels of consumption of the two countries was 4.7 to 1 in favor of the United States.[91] Japan's disadvantage, therefore, was less at that time than in 1955. This conclusion is not surprising when it is recalled that Japan's prewar peak in consumption per capita was reached in the middle of the 1920's after which a long-term decline took place. Even after rapid postwar recovery, the figure for 1955 was still below the level achieved by 1925. During Phase I, Japan actually narrowed the consumption gap existing between her and the United States. In terms of quinquennial averages centered at 1925, the ratio between the United States and Japan was 3.8 to 1. Japan's level in 1923-1927, however, was still a bit below real consumption per capita in the United States in 1869-1873.

Since 1955, continued rapid recovery in Japan has further

Lockwood estimates (below, p. 455) that by 1963 real national *income* per capita in Japan was 25% of income in the United States, 40% or so of that prevailing generally in Western Europe, and about the level of Italian income in 1957.

[90] This method makes the heroic assumption that the 1955 weights used in calculating the purchasing power equivalents, as well as the price structures of the two countries, were unchanged throughout the period. The method is, of course, subject to all the usual limitations of the basic data and deflators.

[91] If Nakamura's highest and lowest estimates of agricultural production in 1888-92 were used (see above, n. 6), the ratio would be roughly 3.9 to 1 and 4.1 to 1, respectively. Nakamura's estimates represent trend rather than actual production.

narrowed the gap existing between her and the United States. By 1962, the United States-to-Japan ratio had dropped to 4.6 to 1, thus restoring Japan to roughly the relative position she held in the middle of the Meiji period. This gives the rather discouraging impression that Japan has been in an Alice-Through-The-Looking-Glass situation, running as fast as she could to stay in one place vis à vis the United States. It should be kept in mind, however, that Japan, in a sense, is still recovering from the long-term decline from 1925 to 1945. Her recovery is continuing at a rapid rate relative to most other advanced countries and the consumption gap is narrowing.

With respect to the size of the gap, our statistics probably exaggerate the actual differences in material welfare existing between Japan and the United States. First, Japan is still far more agricultural than the United States. In spite of the steady movement of people from rural to urban centers and occupations in Japan, 33 percent of the labor force was still employed in the primary sector as recently as 1961.[92] In the United States the corresponding figure for 1961 was 8 percent.[93] Estimates of rural consumption have tended to be understated relative to urban consumption largely because of the difficulty of taking into proper account the products and services produced and consumed directly on the farm. The effect of this understatement on national consumption estimates is probably stronger in the case of Japan than in the United States and makes Japanese consumption appear to be lower than it actually is relative to United States consumption. Furthermore, the greater degree of urbanization in the

[92] Office of the Prime Minister, *Japan Statistical Yearbook: 1961* (Tokyo, 1962), p. 46.

[93] From Bureau of Labor Statistics data in Bureau of the Census, *Statistical Abstract of the United States: 1962* (Washington, 1962), p. 215. The Japanese figure is somewhat overstated relative to that of the United States because of the inclusion in Japanese labor force statistics of a large group of family workers, laboring less than 15 hours per week, who are excluded in United States data. In Japan, the proportion of these workers is greater in agriculture than in the rest of the economy. (See my "Chronic Underemployment: A Comparison between Japan and the United States," *The Annals of the Hitotsubashi Academy*, X, 1 [August 1959], 70.)

United States means that a greater proportion of national consumption expenditures must be devoted to meeting certain costs of urban living which do not occur to the same extent on the farm and which do not add to material welfare.[94] Secondly, our measure of quantitative consumption does not take into account the differences in consumption patterns and basic needs existing among countries. We have already mentioned that Japan's calorie requirements per head are less than in the United States. The climate south of Hokkaidō is more moderate than it is in northern Europe and northern parts of the United States. This permits relatively cheaper housing and reduces fuel and clothing requirements in Japan. On the whole, it is likely that Japan can achieve as high a level of material welfare as the United States with a lower level of quantitative consumption per capita.[95]

Concluding Observations

In this brief study are sketched the major changes in Japan's quantitative level of consumption from the middle of the Meiji period to the present time, with main emphasis on the period prior to 1925. No definitive interpretation of these changes has been attempted, although various hypotheses have been suggested. The principal findings include the following:

[94] Lockwood discusses these effects of urbanization in evaluating the rise in income and consumption levels in Japan (*op. cit.*, p. 141). It seems likely that the process of urbanization has proceeded more rapidly in the United States than in Japan since the Meiji Restoration. If so, then our statistics of changes in quantitative consumption would tend to understate Japan's rate of growth in material welfare relative to the United States.

[95] I made an experimental attempt to measure statistically the yen cost of an urban worker family budget which would be considered "socially adequate" in Japan. This was compared with the dollar cost of an urban worker family budget in the United States estimated by the Bureau of Labor Statistics. The resulting purchasing power equivalent was only ¥63 = $1 for 1952. With this rate, the consumption per capita ratio in 1952 would be only a little over 2 to 1 in favor of the United States. The procedure and results are explained in "The Social Adequacy Method of International Level of Living Comparisons as Applied to Japan and the United States," *The Journal of Economic Behavior*, I, 1 (April 1961), 3-20.

1. During Phase I, from the middle of the Meiji period to the end of the Taishō period, Japan experienced a rise in the general level of real consumption per capita which matched the growth in her real gross national product per capita. Although government emphasis during this period was on rapid industrialization through strategic expansion of investment, this expansion was achieved without sacrifice of consumption, if one means by "sacrifice" a long-run decline in the proportion of the national product devoted to consumption. What made this possible was not a conscious national policy. The increasing proportion of domestic investment was statistically offset by a declining trend in net foreign investment, moving from positive figures at the beginning of the period to a heavy deficit at the end. In the 1930's, Japan was forced to make a strong effort to reduce this deficit. She did this through expansion of exports relative to imports by means of depreciation of the yen and other measures at a time when a depression existed in some of her major export markets.

2. Not only did farm productivity increase rapidly during Phase I but the nature of the tax system and the declining proportion of agricultural investment may have resulted in an equally great increase in quantitative consumption per person in agriculture, in spite of a declining tendency in the agricultural terms of trade. Pure tenants probably lagged behind land-owning cultivators with respect to the improvement in the level of living.

3. While there is no clear evidence of marked improvement in the real wages of workers in manufacturing prior to 1905, in the following years until the end of Phase I, real wages seem to have risen almost as rapidly as real consumption per person for the nation as a whole. Part of this increase was probably the result of a shift in the labor force structure in manufacturing as the proportion of male workers increased rapidly during World War I.

4. The question of whether or not rapid population growth retarded the rise in per capita levels of consumption is not answered in this analysis. But during Phase I, at least, rapid population growth did not prevent Japan from experiencing a per capita improvement in real consumption which com-

pares favorably with that of the United States during the same period.

5. About 1925, the period of rapid growth in real consumption per capita came to an end, and Japan entered Phase II, a period in which consumption levels either declined or showed only slight improvement. During most of this period, which extended to 1945, the gap between GNP and consumption greatly widened. The fall in consumption levels after 1925 was checked during the 1930's but the downward course was resumed after 1937. Rural consumption apparently began to fall after 1925, with recovery beginning in the early 1930's. Real wages on the other hand, showed a reverse trend, rising until 1931 and then falling until 1937, when a brief recovery occurred. A variety of causal factors were at work during Phase II. They fall into four broad groups: a) an agricultural depression which began in 1925; b) the World Depression following 1929; c) the military build-up from 1931 to 1937; and d) the renewal of hostilities in China in 1937 followed by involvement in total war.

6. During Phase II, the net effect on consumption levels of government policies up to 1938 is difficult to determine. The encouragement of imports of rice from Korea and Formosa during the 1920's helped to depress prices received by farmers and probably hurt cultivators more than it helped urban dwellers who benefited from more and cheaper rice. The militaristic build-up during the 1930's contributed to the growing gap between GNP and consumption. Whether consumption levels in absolute terms would have improved more in the absence of the stimulation to the economy of such expenditures at that time is difficult to say. The same comment applies to depreciation of the yen and the effects of resulting deterioration in terms of trade. The government made some direct, but apparently not very effectual, attempts to aid farmers during the 1930's. After 1938, consumption levels could no longer be sustained in the face of expanding military effort and the destructive effects of war. A precipitous decline to a level as yet unmeasured took place.

7. Consumption has so far increased very rapidly throughout the postwar period. Japan, however, has had the task of

recovering not only from the effects of World War II but also from the impact on consumption of the agricultural depression beginning about 1925 and the World Depression in the 1930's. The government in the postwar period has made a strong effort to assist farm cultivators in improving their level of living. Largely as a result of this policy, farm households, so far, have experienced a greater rise in their consumption level than urban households relative to 1934-1936. A gap in favor of urban households may have developed by 1959, but it has been narrowed since then by rapid progress in the rural areas.

8. Japan's absolute level of quantitative consumption per person, measured in dollars for 1962, was only about 22 percent of the corresponding level in the United States for the same year, using a conversion factor which shows the yen to have considerably more purchasing power than the foreign exchange rate indicates. At the present rates of change in the two countries, Japan will probably not achieve equality with the United States in purely quantitative per capita terms until after the year 2000. But if differences in cultural patterns and physiological needs are taken into consideration, an equal level of material well-being may be attained considerably sooner.

APPENDIX

TABLE 1

INDICES OF REAL CONSUMPTION PER CAPITA
AND REAL GROSS NATIONAL PRODUCT PER CAPITA
1879-1962
(1955 = 100)

Year	Real Consumption Per Capita	Real Gross National Product Per Capita	
1879	—	24.2	
1880	—	27.3	
1881	—	25.0	(24.4)
1882	—	23.7	(23.7)
1883	—	22.1	(23.2)
1884	—	20.6	(24.1)
1885	—	24.7	(25.0)

Year	Real Consumption Per Capita		Real Gross National Product Per Capita	
1886	—		29.4	(26.2)
1887	38.9		28.0	(27.4)
1888	41.1		28.1	(28.9)
1889	37.7	(40.3)	26.8	(29.1)
1890	46.2	(40.6)	32.2	(29.8)
1891	37.7	(40.8)	30.4	(30.6)
1892	40.5	(43.6)	31.5	(32.8)
1893	41.9	(44.4)	32.1	(33.6)
1894	51.8	(46.8)	37.8	(34.2)
1895	50.1	(48.3)	36.2	(34.8)
1896	49.9	(53.2)	33.6	(37.2)
1897	47.6	(54.2)	34.4	(37.7)
1898	66.6	(55.2)	43.9	(38.6)
1899	56.7	(56.9)	40.4	(40.5)
1900	55.3	(57.7)	40.9	(41.0)
1901	58.3	(55.9)	42.8	(40.6)
1902	51.4	(54.2)	37.2	(40.7)
1903	58.0	(52.6)	41.6	(40.0)
1904	47.9	(51.7)	41.3	(39.9)
1905	47.7	(53.8)	37.1	(41.4)
1906	53.6	(55.2)	42.3	(42.4)
1907	62.0	(57.5)	44.8	(43.3)
1908	64.7	(59.8)	46.6	(44.7)
1909	59.7	(61.9)	45.8	(46.1)
1910	59.1	(64.5)	43.8	(47.7)
1911	63.8	(65.1)	49.4	(48.7)
1912	75.0	(67.0)	52.8	(49.8)
1913	67.8	(69.4)	51.6	(51.4)
1914	70.9	(71.4)	51.6	(52.9)
1915	69.4	(71.8)	51.8	(54.1)
1916	74.0	(76.4)	56.9	(57.0)
1917	76.9	(82.8)	58.4	(62.3)
1918	90.6	(83.8)	66.3	(64.3)
1919	103.0	(85.1)	78.2	(65.1)
1920	74.6	(85.6)	61.5	(65.7)
1921	80.2	(87.1)	61.1	(65.8)
1922	79.4	(87.1)	61.3	(64.8)
1923	98.1	(94.0)	67.0	(68.0)
1924	103.2	(98.8)	73.0	(71.2)
1925	108.9	(102.3)	77.7	(74.3)

Year	Real Consumption Per Capita		Real Gross National Product Per Capita	
1926	104.3	(102.9)	77.2	(76.6)
1927	96.9	(102.3)	76.6	(77.9)
1928	101.3	(99.5)	78.7	(77.5)
1929	99.9	(97.3)	79.1	(77.4)
1930	95.2	(96.4)	75.7	(77.4)
1931	93.1	(94.6)	76.9	(77.5)
1932	92.5	(93.0)	76.8	(78.9)
1933	92.4	(91.6)	78.8	(81.1)
1934	92.0	(90.8)	86.1	(83.5)
1935	88.1	(90.9)	87.0	(89.9)
1936	89.2	(90.9)	88.6	(96.4)
1937	92.8	(90.1)	109.1	(101.7)
1938	92.5	(88.0)	111.8	(105.0)
1939	87.9	(85.2)	111.9	(108.4)
1940	77.9	(80.7)	103.7	(107.4)
1941	75.0	(75.3)	105.3	(105.9)
1942	70.0	(68.5)	104.1	(103.5)
1943	65.5		104.6	
1944	53.9		99.5	
1945	—		—	
1946	—		—	
1947	53.1		54.5	
1948	58.4		61.0	
1949	63.6	(63.1)	63.6	(64.8)
1950	68.2	(69.2)	68.8	(70.5)
1951	72.3	(75.9)	75.9	(76.2)
1952	83.4	(82.0)	82.9	(81.7)
1953	91.9	(88.4)	89.5	(87.9)
1954	94.3	(95.2)	91.1	(93.9)
1955	100.0	(100.9)	100.0	(100.4)
1956	106.6	(105.9)	106.2	(105.3)
1957	111.5	(111.8)	115.2	(113.8)
1958	116.8	(118.5)	114.1	(124.0)
1959	123.9	(126.0)	133.7	(137.3)
1960	133.8	(134.6)	150.7	(150.9)
1961	143.8		173.1	
1962	154.7		183.2	

NOTES AND SOURCES:

(1) Figures in parentheses are five-year moving averages at the center year of the average.

(2) Real personal consumption per capita: For 1887 to 1930, the

index was computed from personal consumption expenditures in current prices in Ohkawa Kazushi and Akasaka Keiko, *Kobetsu suikei no sōgōka* [Integration of Estimated Components] (Working Paper D 21, September 28, 1962), pp. 1-3. The series was derived by the residual method. Estimates of government expenditures and gross investment were subtracted from estimates of gross domestic expenditures. Ohkawa's and Akasaka's preliminary calculations include two series. In one, Rosovsky's estimate of gross unadjusted domestic investment including military investment was used, with military investment excluded from the government figures. In the other series, military investment was included in government expenditures rather than in gross investment. The results for consumption differ, however, since inventory investment is estimated by applying a ratio to the non-agricultural, non-inventory investment whose magnitude differs according to the inclusion or exclusion of military investment. Where military expenditures are included in investment, therefore, inventory investment is larger, total investment is larger, and consumption, as a residual, is smaller. I decided to use the series which is based on the assumption that military expenditures are excluded from investment mainly because this corresponds to the EPA concept, and it was necessary to link the EPA series and the Ohkawa series. The deflator is a weighted average of a rural consumer price index (excluding rent) and an urban consumer price index (including rent) given in Ohkawa and Akasaka, *Kobetsu suikei no sōgōka* (Working Paper D 11, December 18, 1961), pp. 16-17. For 1930 to 1962, the index is based on personal consumption expenditures estimated by the Economic Planning Agency and given in its *Shōwa 36 nendo kokumin shotoku hakusho* [White Paper on National Income, 1961] (Tokyo, 1963), p. 57, and in the Bank of Japan, *Economic Statistics of Japan: 1963* (Tokyo, 1964) p. 325. The deflator is a weighted average of the urban consumer price index and rural consumer price index from *ibid.*, p. 100, for 1930 to 1950; and from Economic Planning Agency, *Keizai yōran* [Economic Handbook] (Tokyo, 1964), p. 48 for 1951 to 1962. In combining the rural and urban indices, I used the Ohkawa post-1930 weights of .33 for the rural index and .67 for the urban index, instead of the EPA weights of .4 and .6. The EPA weights appear to me to exaggerate the probable relative spending power of the rural area, except perhaps for a brief period after World War II. Fiscal year data for 1946 to 1950 were converted to calendar year figures for 1947 to 1950 by linear interpolation.

Population data used in obtaining per capita results are from the following sources: For data prior to 1920 and for 1946 to 1962, Office of the Prime Minister, *Japan Statistical Yearbook: 1963* (Tokyo, 1964), 10-11; for 1920 to 1945 Ministry of Welfare, *Vital Statistics: 1960*, I (Tokyo, 1961), p. 241. Okinawa is included up to 1945 and excluded after 1945 to provide consistency with the personal consump-

437

tion expenditure estimates. Figures for July 1 were obtained through linear interpolation.

The problem of deciding at what point or period of time to link the EPA series with the Ohkawa series was especially difficult. During the period 1930-1938 in which the two series overlap, the Ohkawa series for real consumption per capita shows a very strong rising trend from 1931 to 1937 (over a 30 percent increase). The EPA series shows an almost level trend from 1931 to 1937, moving slightly downward until 1935 and then rising slightly. Both series dip somewhat in 1938. I decided finally to use the EPA series beginning in 1930 and to extrapolate backwards using the Ohkawa series. The result appears to give a picture which is fairly consistent with the evidence of declining real wages during the period of 1930's, combined with apparent improvement in real incomes in the agricultural sector during the same period. It may, however, somewhat understate the recovery in the 1930's.

(3) Real gross national product per capita: For 1879 to 1930, the index is computed from the gross national product series in current prices in Ohkawa and Akasaka, *op.cit.* (Working Paper D 21), pp. 18-20, deflated by a weighted average of a consumer goods price index and producer goods price index taken from the same source. For 1930 to 1962, the index is computed from real gross national product estimates of the Economic Planning Agency in *White Paper on National Income, 1961*, p. 94, and in the Bank of Japan, *Economic Statistics of Japan: 1963* (Tokyo, 1964) p. 326. Fiscal year data for 1946 to 1950 were converted to calendar year figures by linear interpolation. Population data used in obtaining per capita results are the same as in the case of personal consumption.

TABLE 2

REAL CONSUMPTION PER CAPITA IN JAPAN
AND THE UNITED STATES IN 1955 DOLLARS, 1871-1960
(FIVE-YEAR MOVING AVERAGES)

Year on Which Moving Average Is Centered	Japan (1955 dollars)	United States (1955 dollars)
1871	—	266
1872	—	275
1873	—	286
1874	—	301
1875	—	312
1876	—	325
1877	—	344

Year on Which Moving Average Is Centered	Japan (1955 dollars)	United States (1955 dollars)
1878	—	373
1879	—	397
1880	—	421
1881	—	438
1882	—	451
1883	—	453
1884	—	459
1885	—	459
1886	—	461
1887	—	461
1888	—	459
1889	98	462
1890	99	466
1891	99	470
1892	106	469
1893	108	479
1894	114	483
1895	117	491
1896	129	501
1897	132	525
1898	134	539
1899	138	566
1900	140	587
1901	136	613
1902	132	627
1903	128	647
1904	126	664
1905	131	685
1906	134	688
1907	140	703
1908	145	714
1909	150	719
1910	156	723
1911	158	743
1912	163	744
1913	168	743
1914	173	747
1915	174	749

Year on Which Moving Average Is Centered	Japan (1955 dollars)		United States (1955 dollars)	
1916	185		747	
1917	201		759	
1918	203		776	
1919	207		789	
1920	208		808	
1921	211		840	
1922	211		874	
1923	228		898	
1924	240		927	
1925	248		955	
1926	250		975	
1927	248		992	
1928	242		1005	
1929	236		995	
1930	234		965	
1931	230		928	
1932	226		890	
1933	222		876	
1934	220		887	
1935	221		923	
1936	221		957	
1937	219		994	
1938	214		1031	
1939	207		1064	
1940	196		1084	
1941	183		1115	
1942	166		1146	
1943	—		1185	
1944	—		1230	
1945	—		1278	
1946	—		1321	
1947	—	(129)	1353	(1362)
1948	—	(142)	1382	(1363)
1949	153	(154)	1392	(1373)
1950	168	(165)	1407	(1432)
1951	184	(175)	1431	(1424)
-1952	199	(202)	1452	(1438)
1953	215	(223)	1478	(1484)

Year on Which Moving Average Is Centered	Japan (1955 dollars)		United States (1955 dollars)	
1954	231	(229)	1508	(1475)
1955	245	(243)	1539	(1557)
1956	257	(259)	1557	(1579)
1957	271	(271)	1590	(1591)
1958	288	(284)	1610	(1576)
1959	306	(301)	1626	(1639)
1960	327	(325)	1650	(1657)
1961		(349)		(1659)
1962		(375)		(1712)

NOTES AND SOURCES:

(1) Figures in parentheses are for the year.

(2) For Japan, per capita personal consumption expenditures in current prices for 1955 were converted to dollars using the rate of ¥231.9 = $1. This rate was calculated by 1) obtaining the geometric average of Hideaki Kumano's estimated purchasing power equivalents for consumer goods in Japan and the United States for 1955 (¥200 = $1 with Japanese quantity weights and a maximum probable value of ¥275 = $1 with United States quantity weights), given in "American Dollar and Japanese Yen Purchasing Power Equivalents," *The Journal of Economic Behavior*, I, 2 (October 1961), pp. 113-26; 2) adjusting the geometric average (¥234.5 = $1) for its omission of the housing service component by introducing into the average my own estimate of the purchasing power equivalent for housing service for 1955 (¥179.4 = $1), given in "Postwar Housing in Japan and the United States," *Studies on Economic Life in Japan* (Richard K. Beardsley, Editor), Occasional Papers No. 8, University of Michigan Center for Japanese Studies (Ann Arbor, 1964), p. 18. I used a weight (4.7 percent) based on the ratio of house rent to total personal consumption expenditures (Economic Planning Agency estimates). The personal consumption expenditures per capita in dollars of 1955 purchasing power were then extrapolated for prior years and for later years using the index of real consumption per capita given in Appendix Table 1.

(3) For the United States, I computed an index of real consumption per capita for 1871 to 1929 using Variant III of Simon Kuznets given in his *Capital in the American Economy* (Princeton, 1961), pp. 635-36, in five-year moving averages. (Annual figures for real consumption from 1920 to 1955 are found in *ibid.*, p. 487.) I then calculated a series for personal consumption per capita in 1955 prices for 1929 to 1962 using Department of Commerce estimates of personal

consumption expenditures in 1954 prices and in current prices, given, for 1929 to 1955, in Bureau of the Census, *Historical Statistics of the United States: Colonial Times to 1957* (Washington, 1960), pp. 143, 178; and, for 1956 to 1962, in Bureau of the Census, *Statistical Abstract of the United States: 1962* (Washington, 1962), pp. 314-15, and in *Survey of Current Business*, Vol. 44, No. 11 (November 1964), p. 30. In calculating per capita figures for 1929 to 1962, I used Kuznets' population estimates for July 1, given in five-year moving averages, for 1929 to 1953 (*op.cit.*, pp. 625-26). Armed forces overseas are excluded. Kuznets' estimates are census figures adjusted for underenumeration of the age group 0 to 4 years. For the 1954 to 1960 five-year moving averages of population, I extrapolated Kuznets' series using five-year moving averages of Bureau of the Census population figures for July 1. I followed similar procedures in obtaining annual population estimates used in converting the annual consumption figures for 1947 to 1962 to per capita terms. Population and personal consumption figures for 1960 to 1962 include Hawaii and Alaska.

Finally, I extrapolated the Department of Commerce series in 1955 prices backwards from 1929 using the index previously computed from Kuznets' estimates. Kuznets' concept of flow of goods to consumers differs from the Department of Commerce concept of personal consumption in that it excludes the estimated value of services provided without payment by financial intermediaries, and adds an estimate of the value of government services rendered directly to consumers. The net result of the subtraction and addition makes only a slight change in Department of Commerce figures. For 1929, it added $1.4 billion (1.8 percent) to the Commerce figure (Kuznets, pp. 467-69; 478).

TABLE 3

INDEX OF REAL WAGES IN MANUFACTURING

1879-1963

(1914 = 100)

Year	Average for Year	Five-year Moving Average	Year	Average for Year	Five-year Moving Average
1879	82	—	1886	90	91
1880	78	—	1887	91	89
1881	73	80	1888	93	88
1882	79	82	1889	87	85
1883	87	84	1890	77	82
1884	92	87	1891	78	79
1885	87	90	1892	78	78

Year	Average for Year	Five-year Moving Average	Year	Average for Year	Five-year Moving Average
1893	77	79	1929	157	157
1894	81	80	1930	161	158
1895	81	80	1931	161	156
1896	82	79	1932	154	153
1897	77	79	1933	147	150
1898	74	79	1934	143	145
1899	81	79	1935	143	143
1900	81	80	1936	140	143
1901	83	81	1937	142	141
1902	83	80	1938	147	134
1903	80	80	1939	132	127
1904	76	80	1940	111	116
1905	80	81	1941	103	—
1906	82	83	1942	87	—
1907	85	87	1943	—	—
1908	93	91	1944	—	—
1909	96	94	1945	—	—
1910	98	95	1946	—	—
1911	95	94	1947	43	—
1912	93	95	1948	69	—
1913	91	97	1949	94	92
1914	100	99	1950	121	112
1915	106	100	1951	131	129
1916	104	102	1952	145	141
1917	100	103	1953	152	149
1918	100	107	1954	153	158
1919	104	114	1955	163	165
1920	128	123	1956	177	171
1921	136	132	1957	178	179
1922	145	141	1958	183	187
1923	147	145	1959	194	194
1924	150	148	1960	202	203
1925	146	148	1961	215	212
1926	151	150	1962	221	—
1927	149	152	1963	228	—
1928	155	155			

NOTES AND SOURCES:

For 1879 to 1942, computed from the money wage index in Ohkawa

443

Kazushi et al., *The Growth Rate of The Japanese Economy* (Tokyo, 1957), p. 244, and the urban consumer price index for 1879 to 1936 in Ohkawa and Akasaka, *Kobetsu suikei no sōgōka* (Working Paper D 11, December 18, 1961), pp. 16-17. For deflating the money wage index for 1937 to 1942, I used the cost of living index in Ohkawa et al., p. 244.

For 1947 to 1963, Ministry of Labor index of real cash earnings (1934-36 base) of regular workers in manufacturing firms of more than 30 workers, cited: for 1947-55, in Office of the Prime Minister, *Japan Statistical Yearbook: 1957* (Tokyo, 1957), p. 343; and, for 1956-63, in Bank of Japan, *Economic Statistics of Japan: 1963* (Tokyo, 1964), p. 313.

PART THREE

Growth, Stability, and Welfare
in Japan Today

CHAPTER X

Japan's "New Capitalism"

WILLIAM W. LOCKWOOD

THE FIRST CENTURY of Japan's modernization ends, as it began, in a remarkable burst of practical energies. The parallels are arresting, even if the world of today bears scant resemblance to the world of a hundred years ago, when the boy Emperor was placed upon the throne to open the Meiji era.

Once again, as in 1868, Japanese leaders look abroad upon an external world that offers both promise and threat. Once again within the nation an industrial revolution gathers headway under the force of private and public initiatives. And once more in politics the Japanese grope their way toward some new constitution of authority that will fit evolving traditions yet prove adequate to the new needs of the sixties.

The social order emerging from this second "Renovation" is no easier to characterize than was that of Meiji Japan. It is a modern industrial society, yet with striking divergences from that of France or America or the Soviet Union. It is private-enterprise capitalism, but its enterprise structures range from myriads of tiny farms and shops to great empires of corporate industry enjoying a quasi-public status. It is parliamentary democracy, more truly than anywhere else in the non-Western world. Yet its political ideals and behavior evolve toward an uncertain, and not necessarily democratic future. And in foreign affairs the nation lingers ambivalently between the roles of neutral and Free World ally, pulled this way and that by calculations of the moment, yet still half-immobilized by memories of the recent catastrophe of war.

Incontestably a Great Power, Japan's conservative leaders shrink from the reality of this power in the affairs of East Asia. At home, meanwhile, they divide their energies between factional struggles within the Liberal-Democratic Party, and

447

collective pursuit of national policies that will assure economic prosperity and the ascendancy of their party. Facing them are the renovationists of the Left, a rising political challenge, though one still weakened by attachment to Marxian doctrines that evoke battles of the past rather than the realities of the present. Between the conservatives and the renovationists stand the masses, hardly enamoured of either, lethargic in public affairs, and mostly voting conservative so long as prosperity showers its blessings. The poverty of political discourse contrasts oddly with the technical dynamism of industrial progress.

To assess the situation more closely one begins naturally with Japan's great postwar achievement in the economic realm. From this analysis emerge three problem areas of political economy during the sixties:

1. in external relations, her opportunities East and West;
2. in industrial enterprise, her blend of State and private initiatives;
3. in politics her capacity to handle the strains upon her parliamentary order.

The viability of Japan's "New Capitalism" depends upon its success in these three spheres.

High-Pitched Growth

RISING CAPACITY TO PRODUCE

Through the Occupation years Japan struggled up from the ruin of defeat and postwar disorder. When the Allies withdrew in 1952 her economy had at last regained its prewar level of output. Since then it has thrust forward with a vigor unequalled in her prewar history. Real national output nearly tripled from 1951 to 1963, growing at over 9 percent a year.[1] (Table 1.) It advanced in three wavelike surges, each

---

[1] Miss Saganami Yoko of the Department of Economics, Keio University, has rendered excellent assistance in assembling the statistical materials utilized in this paper. A preliminary version was published in Japanese as *Nihon no atarashii shihon-shugi,* tr. by Miyoshi Masaya (Tokyo, 1964).

TABLE 1

INDICES OF JAPAN'S ECONOMIC GROWTH, 1934-1963

(1934-36 = 100)

Year	Real National Income Total[a]	Gain over Previous Year (%)	Per Capita	Production in Agriculture, Forestry, Fishing[b]	Manufacturing Industry[c]	Volume of Exports[d]	Real Consumption per Family[e]
1934-36	100.0	—	100.0	100.0	100.0	100.0	100.0
1951	107.1	—	86.8	109.6	100.8	35.8	84.8
1952	117.5	9.8	93.8	118.2	108.7	38.0	98.4
1953	124.1	5.8	98.0	106.7	134.5	41.2	105.7
1954	127.8	2.8	99.4	114.8	147.6	54.8	111.0
1955	142.4	11.4	109.5	135.6	159.7	71.6	115.1
1956	156.2	9.7	118.9	130.6	197.2	86.0	118.4
1957	167.4	7.2	126.3	138.3	233.7	95.2	124.4
1958	175.7	5.0	131.7	141.0	234.7	98.7	129.6
1959	204.2	16.3	151.3	145.3	295.8	117.3	133.4
1960	236.1	15.6	173.3	149.7	377.3	133.5	142.3
1961	263.9	11.8	191.9	152.8	452.4	143.5	151.8
1962	286.3	8.5	206.1	157.7	490.9	170.7	158.0
1963	314.9	10.0	224.6	146.9	540.0	191.5	166.5

[a] Net national income deflated by a price index of consumer goods (75% weight) and producer goods (wholesale prices, 25% weight). Economic Planning Agency, *Shōwa 31-nendo no kokumin shotoku* [National Income, 1956] (Tokyo, 1958), pp. 20-21; Bureau of Statistics, *Japan Statistical Yearbook, 1961* (Tokyo, 1963), 399; Bank of Japan, *Economic Statistics Monthly*. Fiscal years, except 1934-36, which is calendar.

[b] *Japan Statistical Yearbook, 1962*, p. 205; *Economic Statistics Monthly*. Shifted from 1950-52 to 1935 base.

[c] *Japan Statistical Yearbook, 1961*, p. 198; *Economic Statistics Monthly*. Shifted from 1955 base.

[d] *Ibid.*, p. 256; *Economic Statistics Monthly*.

[e] *Japan Statistical Yearbook, 1962*, p. 397; *Economic Statistics Monthly*. Fiscal years. Real consumption per capita rose 59.4% from 1934-36 to 1961, according to national income data corrected for prices. Economic Planning Agency. *Shōwa 36-nendo kokumin shotoku hakusho* [White Paper on National Income, 1961] (Tokyo, 1963), p. 99.

of which culminated in a balance of payments crisis that slowed expansion, but only momentarily. Per capita income grew at 8 percent or more a year, a record unmatched elsewhere on either side of the Iron Curtain.

Leading the boom were the manufacturing industries; they quintupled in volume from 1951 to 1963. Services, too, have held their own as a group and still account for nearly half of national output. (Table 2.) Only the traditional occupations

TABLE 2

Distribution of National Income and Labor Force by Industrial Sectors, 1934-1936, 1952, 1962 (%)

	National Income[a]			Labor Force[b]		
	1934-36	1952	1962	1934-36	1952	1962
Agriculture, forestry, fishing	19.8	24.9	14.3	47.4	45.3	29.9
Manufacturing, mining, construction	30.8	31.4	39.1	23.2	23.6	30.4
Commerce, professions, other services	49.4	46.2	46.4	29.4	31.1	39.7
	100.0	100.0	100.0	100.0	100.0	100.0

[a] Economic Planning Agency, *Shōwa 36-nendo kokumin shotoku hakusho* [White Paper on National Income, 1961] (Tokyo, 1963), pp. 78-79; Bank of Japan, *Economic Statistics Monthly*, March 1964, pp. 155-56.

[b] Bureau of Statistics, *Japan Statistical Yearbook, 1961* (Tokyo, 1962), pp. 46-47; Economic Planning Agency, *Japanese Economic Statistics* (November 1963), pp. 76-77.

of agriculture, forestry, and fishing continue to lose ground relatively, as they have for a century or more. The source of over half of the nation's income in the old days, before 1900, they are now reduced to less than 15 percent. Even so, farm output grew by two-fifths during the fifties as agricultural prosperity broke all records. With the spread of mechanization, meanwhile, the farm labor force began to dwindle by over half a million workers (4 percent) a year in response to the boom of the cities—a turn of revolutionary significance.

As Japan moves forward in the sixties, then, she has already raised her productive powers twofold above their prewar level. Viewed against the ruin of war this is an impressive achievement. Per capita output has doubled, with the gain shared between higher consumption and higher investment.[2]

In the world perspective of a quarter-century, it is true, the advance is more modest. The Japanese have reached only the income level they might have anticipated had they remained at peace and forged ahead at their prewar pace. Thanks to the heavy losses of World War II, their gains in per capita income from 1935 to 1962 (rate, 2.3 percent) were no more than in most of Western Europe, and less than in the United States and the Soviet Union. Virtually the whole advance in labor productivity has occurred since 1955; it took that long just to repair the war damage. The dazzle of the past decade, then, should not obscure the sacrifice of the lost years. Nevertheless, Japan has now entered the family of nations that have banished poverty of the abject and degrading variety for the bulk of their people. In this sense her Industrial Revolution has at last come of age.

REVOLUTION IN CONSUMPTION

The Japanese themselves talk of a consumption revolution in the past decade. They mean two things: materially, the rise in incomes and Westernization of taste; and psychologically, the spread of expectations among great masses of people that the amenities of middle-class life may at last come within reach.

The material gain is easier to measure. Real consumption doubled from 1951 to 1963. (Table 1.) By comparison with prewar levels it rose two-thirds.

All classes have shared in this advance, but differentially, of course. One striking shift is the gain in labor incomes rela-

[2] Consumption expenditure (public and private), however, fell from 81.0% of gross national expenditure in 1934-36 to 62.8% in 1959-62. Gross domestic investment rose meanwhile from 19.0% to 37.2%. See below, Table 8, p. 466. Alan H. Gleason discusses these trends in consumption at greater length in Ch. IX, above.

tive to property incomes. Rent, interest, and dividends still account for less than 10 percent of personal income thanks to the wartime destruction of wealth, the postwar inflation, the redistribution of farmlands, and other Occupation reforms. (Table 3.) For a decade or so the rentiér class was virtually

TABLE 3

DISTRIBUTION OF PERSONAL INCOME BY TYPES, 1934-1962[a] (%)

	1934-36	1951-53	1960-62
Employee's labor income	41.5	49.1	58.2
Proprietor's income (unincorporated)	33.4	46.5	30.3
Rent, interest, dividends	23.7	3.9	9.7
Total personal income	100.0	100.0	100.0

[a] Economic Planning Agency, *Shōwa 36-nendo kokumin shotoku hakusho* [White Paper on National Income, 1961] (Tokyo, 1963), pp. 62-63; Bank of Japan, *Economic Statistics Monthly*, March 1964, pp. 155-56. Certain minor categories are not listed.

wiped out. Another change is the new well-being of the countryside, traditionally at a disadvantage in relation to the city. A third consequence has been a tight labor market in which a relative advance of wages in small enterprises has reduced longstanding inequities of Japan's "double-decker" economy. Finally both wage earners and farmers have gained over the white-collar class. Indeed, the latter have shared little in the advance from prewar levels—a factor no doubt in the political disaffection of many intellectuals.[3]

[3] The finding of the 1959 *Kokumin seikatsu hakusho* is summarized as follows by the *Oriental Economist*, January 1960, p. 13; "Comparing the pay for the white collar worker with the manual worker of the same age (a primary school graduate before the war, and a middle school graduate after the war) the former was three to five fold higher than the latter before the war [1934-36]. After the war, however, the former has dropped to the level . . . only about 35.0% higher. . . . The income level of the white collar worker as it is today is less than two-thirds of the prewar mark, justifying the general complaint that the monthly pay of a university professor today is substantially equal to the like pay of an assistant professor some 20 odd years ago."

The urban industrial boom may again re-open the gap between country and city, just as it is again increasing property incomes relative to labor. But for the present at least the old urban-rural differential of 25-30 percent in favor of city families has been substantially reduced in most parts of the country. More persistent are the inequalities among different regions of Japan. They still reach 2:1 or more as between the central, urban districts and remote, rural prefectures, despite the tide of migration to the growth areas. (Table 4.) Within the crowded cities, too, millions of underprivileged families remain under heavy handicap. Great new fortunes have been amassed by business magnates who have risen to the top in the more open competition of the postwar era. But at the bottom remain some 500,000 worker families largely unemployed and eking out their life on meager relief allowances from the government.

TABLE 4

REGIONAL DIFFERENTIALS IN LIVING LEVELS, 1959[a] (%)

	All Japan	Tokyo	Kagoshima
Consumption	100.0	130.9	72.1
Household Wealth (saving, durable goods, housing)	100.0	164.6	58.6
Environment (water, electric power, schools, hospitals, roads, etc.)	100.0	206.3	88.2
"Westernization" (bread, meat, milk, desks, Western cloth, etc.)	100.0	131.6	89.1

[a] Economic Planning Agency, *Kokumin seikatsu hakusho* [White Paper on National Life] (Tokyo, 1961), pp. 144-46.

Within the growing middle class, nevertheless, the "Westernization" of taste proceeds space. Food preferences, long resistant to change, are now shifting toward more meat, dairy products, processing foods, and dining out. Clothing fashions turn toward higher-grade fabrics, mostly synthetics, and more diversified wardrobes. New leisure pursuits absorb rising increments of family income. Spending on movies, baseball, and other such entertainment tripled in the fifties. Weekend trains and holiday spots swarm with holiday crowds. The gay life of the Ginza prospers as never before, nourished by ample expense accounts. More significantly, the average family reads one newspaper a day and ten weekly journals a month, as people increasingly gain the benefits of a high-school education. At the same time the Japanese home is being invaded with mechanical appliances; housemaids are beginning to disappear except in well-to-do families. TV sets, washing machines, refrigerators, electric fans, and rice cookers have become accepted conveniences and status symbols. (The most conspicuous lag is housing itself, still very scarce and very expensive in cities.)

This upsurge of optional family spending, aided by installment credit, prods Japanese businessmen into competition for the consumer yen to a degree unknown before the war. The new accent on marketing appeals boosted advertising outlays fivefold in the decade ending 1962. Firms long preoccupied with export markets, as in textiles, have begun to go after the new opportunities at home as never before.[4]

With the consumption boom are also associated radical innovations in the technology and structure of production. On the one hand, rising productivity since 1955 has furnished much of the increment of goods and services catering to new tastes. On the other, rising consumption joins with vigorous investment activity and export expansion to maintain a high level of aggregate demand. It has channeled a major share of growth toward the domestic consumer market, despite strong competition from investment demands and exports. Especially notable is the soaring output of consumer durables, which grew 29 percent a year from 1956 to 1963. They accounted for nearly one third of the total growth in industrial output for final-demand use in the late fifties, and for about the same share of the increased *domestic* demand for manu-

---

[4] Hitachi and Toshiba, the big producers of electrical appliances, even organize women's clubs and "home life" centers (with music) to plug their wares. By 1963 Japan was fifth in the world in advertising expenditures per capita ($7.22).

factures.[5] In agriculture as well, the growing market for fruit, meat, dairy products, and vegetables is shifting farmers toward larger-scale operations of a more specialized, capitalistic nature. Together with the labor shortage on the farm and related technical improvements—three out of four farm householders now own a power tiller—it has set in motion structural changes here too of far-reaching importance.

No less significant are the social and psychological accompaniments of expanding consumption. Rising incomes, wider communications, and greater economic security bring a new mobility occupationally and socially, a new reach of aspirations, and generally a more confident outlook. Three out of four families now regard themselves as belonging in some sense to the middle class. These are powerful supports to the democratization of Japanese society in its non-material aspects as well.

MIDDLE-RANK INDUSTRIAL POWER

In the limited terms of economic measurement, where has this decade of growth brought Japan in the international scale of wealth and income? Three brief comparisons may be offered.

First, her real income per capita in 1963 stood at about two-thirds of the Italian income level (adjusted for price differences) or about as high as Italy's in 1957. It was 40 percent or so of the level prevailing generally in Western Europe, and 25-30 percent of that in the United States. The actual figure was only $509 at the current yen-dollar exchange rate, compared to $2,515 in the United States. Adjustments for relative buying power, however, bring the Japanese level up to the neighborhood of $700 at U.S. prices.[6]

[5] Ministry of International Trade and Industry, *Nihon sangyō no genjō* [The Present State of Japanese Industry] (Tokyo, 1960) pp. 29ff. Television sets approached the saturation point as output grew from 140,000 units in 1955 to 4,885,000 in 1962. By 1964 they could be found in four out of five urban homes and two out of three farm households, and manufacturers were busy opening a market for the "second home set."

[6] The dollar-exchange value of Japanese income is adjusted to dollar-buying value with price equivalents computed in *Analysis of*

Wage comparisons still put Japanese industrial wages at little over a fifth of the American level (adjusted for purchasing power) and 50-75 percent of those in Western Europe. But another decade of comparable growth will raise wages and real incomes to present European figures. In modern plants of over 500 workers Japanese wages are already close to the general industrial level of France and Italy, even at current exchange rates. Here at any rate her export industries no longer enjoy any great wage advantage.[7] Small- and medium-size firms are another matter; plants of 5-29 workers still pay only half the wage of these big establishments. But even there the margin of advantage in export competition is narrowing as labor scarcities bid up wages. Small producers are under increasing pressure to improve efficiency or go out of business.

Finally it is of interest to appraise Japan's industrial economy with respect to its aggregate scale, as bearing on industrial efficiency and military potential. Today her manufacturing industries produce far more than those of either Italy

---

Price Comparisons in Japan and the United States, Economic Bulletin 13, Economic Research Institute, Economic Planning Agency (Tokyo, September 1963). For 1960 the average retail price equivalent for consumer goods and services lies between 182 yen per dollar (Japan weights) and 235 yen (U.S. weights). Investment goods tend to be more expensive relatively in Japan; the ratio for 1959 was about 370 yen in wholesale prices (Japan weights). Combining these two estimates with weights of 2:1 (below, Table 8) yields an adjusted value for national income of 245-280 yen per dollar. In other words, yen incomes buy 30 to 45% more in Japan than when converted to dollars at the current exchange rate (360) and spent in the United States. This is a crude calculation that omits certain major sectors such as housing and machinery, which tend to be expensive in Japan, and services, which tend to be cheap. It is inherently ambiguous in any case. Nevertheless it gives a more meaningful comparison than mere exchange rates. For further discussion of the changing consumption gap between Japan and the United States see Alan Gleason's comments, above, pp. 396, 399-400, 427-31, 438-42.

[7] *Ibid.*, pp. 238-39. Labor costs declined 14% in Japanese industry from 1953 to 1960, but this took place despite a 64% rise in money wage payments per worker, and a 32% rise in real wages. See below, Tables 5, 6.

or France, or the United Kingdom. She has drawn abreast of West Germany, perhaps even passed her—these comparisons are imprecise. Ahead of her by a wide margin are still the world's giants, the United States and the Soviet Union. Probably her manufacturing production is still no more than a third of American output. Nevertheless, she now ranks third or fourth among industrial powers of the world.[8] By this criterion, too, after a century of development Japan's industrial revolution has come of age.

Springs of Growth

POLITICAL OPPORTUNITY

Nations have phases of growth—like adolescents, someone said. The propelling forces are not easy to understand. Japan's high-pitched growth after World War II is no exception, if

[8] Based on the inter-country production index of Shinohara Myohei for 1956, adjusted here to 1963 as follows:

	Industrial Income Index (dollar values at exchange rates)	Industrial Production Index (at average U.K./Japan weights)	Increase in Industrial Production (%)	Industrial Production Index
	1956	*1956*	*1956-63*	*1963*
United States	100.0	100.0	24	100.0
Japan	5.2	17.6	155	36.2
West Germany	13.2	27.8	48	33.1
United Kingdom	17.8	24.8	20	24.0
France	12.5	14.9	45	17.4
Italy	6.0	12.1	89	18.4

To construct his 1956 inter-country index (Column 2) Professor Shinohara weights quantity outputs of 62 commodities by value added in production and then, in the index selected above, averages U.K. and Japan weights. He shows that dollar values (Column 1) grossly understate West European output relative to American levels, and Japanese output relative to both. *Growth and Cycles in the Japanese Economy* (Tokyo, 1962), p. 30, table 4.

we seek its fundamental causes. But the more proximate forces and processes are apparent enough.

The paramount circumstance must be defined as political, something outside the usual growth models of the economist. First, the Allied Occupation encouraged a unified, liberalized political order congruent with other authority structures in postwar Japanese society and stabilized with little challenge after the Occupation ended. In this order a vigorous business class wields preponderant though not exclusive power and allies itself with a state bureaucracy that also exercises pragmatic initiatives for economic growth. Other classes too, in the main, have found security and expanding opportunity sufficient to keep down revolutionary tension, despite the trauma of recent military defeat. Sporadic riots on one issue or another have failed seriously to disturb the internal security or external ties of the nation. Again therefore, as in Meiji times, the political requisites for rapid economic growth have been recreated with that pragmatic blend of public and private initiatives that is the special aptitude of the Japanese.

Second, the international milieu has been favorable on the whole to Japan's economic resurgence. A constructive aid-granting policy on the part of the victorious Allies after the war helped the initial process of postwar recovery. Thereafter United States policy sought to reintegrate Japan into the international economy of the West under the security umbrella of American power. Japan has remained at peace, largely rid of armament, and free to re-enter an expanding network of world trade and investment without the encumbrances of empire, and despite the underlying insecurities of East Asia (below, pp. 475ff.).

In this setting, then, the Japanese could participate fully in the progress that marked virtually all industrial nations after World War II. For postwar recovery was more rapid almost everywhere in industrial societies this time than after World War I—thanks to the world's new engineering and chemical technologies and the more far-reaching initiatives of government in economic life.[9] In part Japan has only shared in these new efficiencies and opportunities. More than that, however, she proceeded to stage a remarkable catching up process as she moved energetically to repair the technological lags of a generation.

PRODUCTIVITY AND WAGES

From 1935 to 1950 Japan's industries had been largely cut off from the laboratories and drafting boards of the West. The whole economy had become progressively dislocated and demoralized by war and defeat. Now, with peace and trade restored, she proceeded avidly to rebuild it on new technologies imported from the West. From 1950 through 1963 some 2,487 contracts were licensed for the purchase or use of foreign patents and technical assistance by Japanese industrial firms. Seventy percent were with American companies, and about the same proportion were concentrated in machinery, electrical goods, and chemicals. In those new growth sectors, such products as high-octane gasoline, cold rolled steel, plastics, TV tubes, high performance boilers, and scores of others were introduced or improved on a scale that added enormously to the productivity and competitive efficiency of Japanese industry.

Technical borrowing is nothing new in Japan. But this time it has been accelerated by the spirit and skills of a developed industrial society exposed to powerful "demonstration effects" from abroad. Just as pent-up desires for a Western standard of living have furnished a major impetus to growth from the demand side, so the repair of this technological gap in science and engineering has rapidly enlarged the nation's productive capabilities.

Not the least of the benefits is the stimulus to industrial research within Japan itself. Here and there borrowing may have delayed indigenous efforts by providing the simple and quick alternative of purchase abroad. Mainly, however, it

[9] Wolfgang F. Stolper, "West German Development in an Expanding World Economy," *World Politics,* IX, 1 (October 1956), 98-117.

has driven home the need to keep pace with the advancing world frontier of technology, and equipped Japanese industry better to do so. Nothing is more important for a nation that must live by its wits. After 1955 business outlays for research rose rapidly until they now rival those of West Germany and Britain. In major enterprises they are not far from those of American firms of comparable size as a ratio to gross sales (3 percent).[10] There is even a certain historic irony in the news that Sony, manufacturer of transistor radios, is appealing to the Japanese government to protect it against design piracy abroad.

The key process of growth, of course, has been a sustained rise in the productivity of labor, supported by a level of demand sufficient to put resources more fully to work. The work force has grown rapidly in absolute numbers, too; due to high birth rates a generation earlier it advanced at 1.9 percent a year from 1953 to 1963, well above prewar rates. Mainly, however, economic progress has come about through output gains per worker, resulting from fuller employment and better equipment, management, and working conditions. In the economy generally this productivity gain was running at nearly 7½ percent a year during the decade ending 1961. In industry the advance was even faster, doubling output per worker. (Table 5.)

So strong is the economy's technical dynamism, in short, that it has put to work huge reserves of people hitherto poorly employed in agriculture and traditional trades, while absorbing also the big influx of new hands into the labor force at rising levels of efficiency. This has been achieved mainly by productivity gains across the board in agriculture, manufacturing, and the services. But a distinctive feature of the postwar boom, by comparison with earlier ones, has been a somewhat more rapid structural shift from lower-productivity to higher-productivity trades. Such shifts from agriculture to

[10] *Economic Survey of Japan (1962-1963)*, cited, p. 234; *Nihon keizai shimbun*, March 10, and December 15, 1964. Total Japanese expenditures for research and development, public and private, amounted to $1,100 millions in fiscal 1963.

TABLE 5

Manufacturing Wages, Output, and Labor Costs,
by Size of Plant, 1952-1960[a]

(indices, 1952 = 100)

Size of Plants	Total Annual Cash Payment per Worker (1)	Real Output per Worker (2)	Wage Cost per Unit of Output (1 ÷ 2)
30-99 workers	173	162	107
100-499 workers	156	169	93
500-999 workers	155	216	72
1000- workers or more	171	243	70
All Plants	164	190	86

[a] Data from Economic Planning Agency, *Seizōgyō ni okeru chingin bukka rōdō seizansei no sui-i* [Changes in Wages, Prices and Labor Productivity in Manufacturing], vol. ii (Tokyo, 1962), Tables 17, 18, pp. 21-23. Output per worker and labor cost in plants of 30-99 workers were also representative of trends in still smaller plants through 1958, the last year for which data are available.

the manufacturing and service sectors as aggregates have accounted for about one-fifth of the over-all gain in labor productivity.[11]

These processes of technical and structural change reveal themselves at work within each major sector of the economy as well. In agriculture, for example, farm output has risen by two-fifths as Japan moves close to self-sufficiency in food grains and shifts production increasingly to meat, fruits, dairy products, and vegetables. Yet the farm labor force actually dwindled 10 percent in the fifties, so great was the pull of labor off the farm into industries where productivity and income gains were still greater. Among non-agricultural employments the same kind of shift is observable. Banking has doubled in relative net product among the service occupations; department and chain stores take over more and more of urban

[11] Ohkawa Kazushi and Henry Rosovsky, "Recent Japanese Growth in Historical Perspective," *American Economic Review*, LIII, 2 (May 1963), 581.

retailing; machinery grew from 18 percent of manufacturing output in 1955 to 35 percent in 1961. Owing to the boom in investment and consumer durables, the industrial scene is now dominated by the metallurgical, machinery, and chemical trades. Together they produce twice as much as all the "light" industries put together. Accompanying their rise is a shift from smaller- to larger-scale capitalistic processes, characteristically with higher output per worker. Such changes have been in progress since the early thirties, but now they are energized by civilian needs and expectations, not armament.[12]

Three influences from this wave of innovation have been felt in the labor market:

First, wage rates cannot fail to respond to the growing demand for labor, especially for young skilled workers. Real wages rose 86 percent in manufacturing industry from 1952 to 1963. Yet wages have lagged sufficiently behind production to reduce labor costs in manufacturing as a whole; in some chemical and equipment industries the drop has been 25-35 percent or more. (Table 5.) Through 1963 (except briefly in 1961-62) Japan thus managed to avoid the wage cost-push inflation experienced by many Western nations. In export competition this has conferred a significant advantage. (Table 6.) In domestic labor controversies, on the other hand, it invites charges of exploitation. Abroad, too, it furnishes arguments to support the restrictions of Japanese goods. Although productivity was growing less rapidly in other sectors of the economy than in manufacturing, industrial wages hardly kept pace even with the *average* rise in GNP per worker before 1961.

Second, the job market has grown apace, despite the spread

[12] Structural changes of this magnitude required mobility in the work force, geographic and occupational. Some 5.2 million people migrated to new residences in one year alone, 1959-60, half of them to different prefectures. Tokyo alone is now adding 250-300,000 people a year, creating a congestion that is fast becoming a major national problem. See Ōkita Saburo's paper on "Regional Planning in Japan Today," below, Ch. XIII.

TABLE 6

CHANGES IN MANUFACTURING OUTPUT, WAGES, AND LABOR COSTS:
INTERNATIONAL COMPARISONS, 1953-1959[a]

(1953 = 100)

	Japan	United States	United Kingdom	West Germany	Italy
Production	220	114	121	165	159
Employment	155	94	105	131	105
Output per worker	142	122	115	126	152
Wages per worker	138	125	143	141	131
Wage costs per unit of output	93	103	124	111	86
Real wages per worker	126	115	119	127	116

[a] Economic Planning Agency, *Seizōgyō ni okeru chingin bukka rōdō seisansei no sui-i* [Changes in Wages, Prices, and Labor Productivity in Manufacturing], vol. ii (Tokyo, 1962), Table 6, pp. 6-7.

of labor-saving devices. Manufacturing employment rose 4.5 percent a year from 1953 to 1963, absorbing most of the increment in the labor force. Happily it has relieved or postponed fears that work cannot be found for the half-million or more people being added (net) to the working population each year.

Third, labor shortages have begun to reach even into indigenous and small industries, traditionally the "blotting-paper" trades. Here many enterprisers must either adopt labor-saving improvements or raise prices (as has happened generally with service fees). Small industrialists have felt keenly the wage competition of bigger plants, where productivity advances more rapidly. (Table 5.) Income differentials are shrinking for young workers, and as between men and women, too. Thus the gaps in income and technology that have long separated the modern and indigenous sectors of the economy are being narrowed appreciably.

CRESCENDO OF INVESTMENT

Huge sums of capital are required for this enlargement and rationalization of industry. The greater part has gone into the metal, machinery, and chemical trades. Steel firms have added great strip mills, and have reduced their blast-furnace ratios of coke consumption to pig iron output until they are the most efficient in the world—below 0.6. Mammoth tankers and ore carriers have been built in Japanese yards to reduce shipping costs; a petrochemical industry has arisen to supply synthetic fibers and fertilizers; output of passenger cars grew from 14,472 units in 1954 to 448,000 in 1963. Such familiar trades as hotel services, breweries, and food canning are also expanding to meet new demands. Gourmets are vaguely troubled to read that the nation's leading producer of seasoning will now substitute petroleum for wheat and beans as its raw material.

Less spectacularly, new processes have also been acquired by thousands of small- and medium-scale industrialists. With characteristic flexibility small enterprisers have turned from silk to nylon stockings, from wooden clogs to plastic sandals, from toys to auto parts. In the aggregate their capital demands are still enormous. (As late as 1958 plants of less than 300 workers still comprised 99.5 percent of the country's 450,000 manufacturing establishments, employed 70 percent of all persons engaged in manufacturing, and produced 51 percent of total output.) And as private investments mushroom, large and small, governmental agencies struggle to fill expanding requirements for technical schools, roads, port facilities, water supply, and other essentials of social overhead capital.

Gross domestic investment rose under the combined stimulus of these demands to 27.3 percent of national product in the years 1951-1955, and to 31.8 percent in 1956-1960. (Table 7.) Spurred on by trade liberalization, and the buoyant atmosphere of the government's income-doubling plan, it increased still further to approximately 40 percent in 1961-1963. Three quarters of this capital formation was private. Of that only a tenth was residential construction. The rest was mostly plant and equipment, especially industrial equipment.

Such a tempo of investment is remarkable in a peacetime economy operating so largely on voluntary principles. It has reinforced other factors making for a sustained rise in aggre-

TABLE 7

GROSS INVESTMENT AND SAVINGS, 1956-1960 (%)[a]

Gross Domestic		*Gross Total Savings*		100.0
Investment	100.0	Personal savings		37.3
Private	73.7	Government surplus		21.0
Residential construction	7.3	Corporate saving		15.7
Producers' equipment	54.4	Depreciation		30.5
Inventories	13.1	Net foreign balance	(–)	0.4
Government	26.3	Error	(–)	4.1
National public		*****		
enterprise	8.7	Gross domestic saving÷		
Other national		gross nation product		32.4
government	7.6	Personal savings÷		
Local government	10.0	disposable income		17.2
*****		Government surplus÷		
Gross domestic investment÷		current receipts		31.9
national product	31.8			
Net domestic investment÷				
national product	27.7			

[a] Data from Economic Planning Agency, *Shōwa 35-nendo kokumin shotoku hakusho* [White Paper on National Income, 1960] (Tokyo, 1962), pp. 86-87, 140ff.

gate demand. The main components are summarized in Table 8 for the years 1950-1962.

Domestic consumption remains preponderant in total demand. Its shift toward new products such as electrical appliances has spurred on the equipment industries in particular. Overseas markets take a smaller share of Japanese goods and services than before the war. (Of course, their strategic role as payment for essential imports goes far beyond their quantitative importance, only 8-12 percent.) It was the crescendo of investment activity after 1955, however, that furnished the largest increment of total demand. This investment spending was itself a response to (1) the growth in consumer and export markets, (2) the deepening of investment in the new technology of the chemical, oil, and metal-working indus-

465

TABLE 8

Total Demand for Goods and Services, Changing Shares,
1950-1962 (%)[a]

	Total Demand	Con-sump-tion	Invest-ment	Ex-ports	Increase in Inven-tories
Total demand, 1950	100.0	65.7	16.1	10.9	7.3
–increase, 1950-55	100.0	65.1	16.7	12.8	5.5
Total demand, 1955	100.0	65.4	16.4	11.6	6.3
–increase, 1955-62	100.0	53.5	40.4	8.3	–1.3
Total demand, 1962	100.0	57.2	27.3	10.9	4.6

[a] Economic Planning Agency, *Shōwa 36-nendo kokumin shotoku hakusho* [White Paper on National Income, 1961] (Tokyo, 1963), pp. 90-91; *Shōwa 37-nendo kokumin shotoku hōkoku* (Tokyo, 1963), pp. 64-65. Total demand is equal to gross national expenditure plus foreign purchases of goods and services and other receipts on current account. Fiscal years.

tries,[13] and (3) the "chain effect" of investment inducing still more investment. Equipment outlays induced in this last-mentioned manner amounted to 42 percent of total equipment investment in 1960.[14]

The frantic pace of industrial capital formation during 1958-1964 suggests a good deal of hasty calculation and waste. Fears multiply that the race of enterprisers to win advantageous new positions in the growth industries is leading to serious over-capacity in various markets. Beyond a temporary dip in 1961-1962, however, business remains buoyant. Whatever the long-term future, Japanese industrialists are operating vigorously to mobilize huge sums of capital and channel them into productive use. During 1951-1955 the marginal capital coefficient of private equipment investment stood at 1.09 in relation to gains in GNP (9.0 percent a year). During the next five years it increased only to 1.90 as the growth

[13] For example, oil refinery investment per barrel rose from 50,000 yen in 1955 to 80,000 yen in 1960.
[14] *Economic Survey of Japan (1960-1961)*, cited, p. 201.

rate accelerated to 9.7 percent.[15] No immediate bottlenecks appeared to block expansion except as a shortage of foreign exchange again imposed a temporary slowdown in 1961-1962.

The State has played a crucial financial role in all this. True, private sources have furnished most of the capital, and owner-ship of the new wealth remains largely in private hands. But the government and its agencies have been accounting for as much as a quarter of all investment spending. (Table 7.) This is a high percentage for an advanced industrial economy based so largely on private enterprise. Mostly this investment has gone into roads, land improvement, schools, railways, and tele-communications and various local undertakings. Public agen-cies furnish half of the business of the whole construction industry and 15-20 percent of machinery orders. Japan, in fact, ranks with underdeveloped rather than developed nations in the share of public expenditure devoted to capital invest-ment. For government and public enterprises together the figure was 48 percent during 1957-1961, because of these large efforts to improve the social and economic environment.[16]

More than this, the government additionally lends large sums to private borrowers year after year for investment in key industries, export financing, and other such purposes. These sums originate partly in tax revenues. But mostly they come from private savings invested in various government banks and public life insurance, postal savings, and annuity funds. Such government lending activities were of crucial importance during the early postwar years. At that time they were focused on reconstruction of the steel, coal, power, and shipbuilding industries. Later they were spread over a wider front where they have supported a variety of welfare schemes and productive activities inadequately financed by the private banking system. Through these governmental channels came 8.2 percent of all long- and short-term investment funds

---

[15] *Ibid.*, p. 206. The marginal capital coefficient rose in response to the growing need for indirect production facilities, e.g., sites, and for a larger scale of operations in the face of sharpening competition at home and abroad.

[16] *Ibid.*, pp. 151-52; *ESJ (1961-1962)*, p. 275; *ESJ (1962-1963)*, p. 128.

(excluding corporate savings) supplied directly to companies in industry, transport, and trade during the decade 1952-1961. (See below, Table 9.)

TABLE 9

Supply of New Capital Funds to Corporate Business, 1959-1961[a]

	Annual Average 1959-61 (billion yen)	Percent
Total supply of new funds	*5,126*	*100.0*
Foreign funds	*205*	*4.0*
Domestic funds	*4,921*	*96.0*
Internal sources	*1,725*	*33.7*
Depreciation	913	17.8
Retained earnings	812	15.9
External sources	*3,196*	*62.3*
Stocks	595	11.6
Corporate debentures	227	4.4
Loans and discounts from financial institutions	2,374	46.4
Private	(2,153)	(42.1)
Governmental	(222)	(4.3)

[a] Fiscal years. Includes new equipment and operating funds (increase or decrease) supplied to companies (excluding financial institutions) in mining, manufacturing, transport, commerce, agriculture, forestry, and fishing. Data on capital from "external sources" are from Bank of Japan, *Economic Statistics of Japan, 1961*, pp. 33-34, and Bureau of Statistics, *Monthly Statistics of Japan*, August 1962, pp. 21-22. Data for domestic internal and foreign funds (including operating funds) are by courtesy of Miyoshi Masaya, of the Federation of Economic Organizations, and Fujino Hirotake, of the Ministry of Finance, Tokyo.

All in all, the State has been controlling at least one third of the nation's investment spending during the boom of the past decade. This is in addition to the influences it exerts through central bank credit, foreign exchange controls, tax incentives to modernization and exports, and pervasive pressures one way or another on the investment decisions of bankers and industrialists. Its responsibilities in the sphere of capital formation approach those of the government of West Germany, which has likewise been directly financing 40 percent or so of that nation's capital investment.[17]

HIGH-LEVEL SAVINGS, PUBLIC AND PRIVATE

To a surprising degree these investment and lending activities of the government have been financed by public savings. Year after year despite tax reductions the government has piled up a surplus in its current accounts. From 1951 to 1960 tax receipts (central and local) tripled, and 25 percent or more was steadily set aside for loans and investments. From this source came 21 percent of the nation's savings for the decade —a share comparable with that provided by Meiji government budgets from 1890 to 1910. And here the government has lately found as much as two thirds of the funds it needed for all its own investment spending. (For 1956-1960 see Table 7.)

To finance its activities, then, the State has competed little with private investors in the capital market for borrowed funds. Here the Japanese record contrasts with that of many countries—India for example—where public investment has had to be financed largely by borrowing, and often borrowing that is inflationary.[18] It helps, of course, that defense expenditure is now so low. Before the war it rarely fell below 2 percent of national income. It soared from 7 percent in 1934-1936 to 68 percent in 1944, during the Pacific conflict. Now it is below 1.5 percent. Its former place in the government's general-account budget—47 percent of expenditure in 1933-1935—is now filled by spending on economic development, social welfare, and education. By comparison,

[17] Karl W. Roskamp, "Competition and Growth—The Lesson of West Germany: Comment," *American Economic Review*, 501, 5 (December 1960), 1016.

[18] Gross investment by government and public enterprises in India was 12.3% of gross national product during 1957-59, while government saving was a mere 1.1%. This was more or less characteristic of other Asian countries excepting Communist China. See the admirable study of the "Financing of Economic Growth" in United Nations, *Economic Survey of Asia and the Far East, 1961* (Bangkok, 1962), pp. 41-64.

defense expenditure was taking 4.7 percent of national income in West Germany in 1959, and 8-10 percent in France, Britain, and the United States.

Still another heritage left by the war and the Occupation was high taxes, supported by painful memories of inflationary borrowing. Tax cuts were made repeatedly after 1951 in response to political pressures. Yet central and local levies continue to capture 20 percent of national income, as the growth of the economy keeps pushing up yields beyond expectations. In 1962, for example, the figure was 22 percent despite a heavy reduction in income and commodity taxes. Very likely the cuts themselves have stimulated growth and raised yields in turn. In any event government revenues have kept pace with national income;[19] otherwise the State could hardly have made such notable contributions to capital formation—a fifth of the nation's savings and a quarter of its investment outlays—without more pervasive and more inflationary interference in economic life.

Notwithstanding the role of government, Japan's new capital resources are predominantly private in origin and ownership. Their sources and institutional channels may be summarized as follows:

First, the inflow of foreign capital has been quantitatively small, however significant in other respects. Table 7, covering the years 1956-1960 is not unrepresentative of the entire decade after 1953 in this regard; the net foreign balance has been slight. Long-term foreign investment in Japan totaled $2,254 millions from 1950 through 1963—hardly 2 percent of the domestic funds poured into industrial construction and equipment. In the later years high interest rates also attracted

---

[19] The tax burden in Japan relative to that in other advanced industrial countries was as follows in 1961 (*Economic Survey of Japan, 1962-1963* p. 355):

Tax receipts ÷ national income		Tax receipts ÷ national income	
France	30.5	Italy	26.7
United Kingdom	32.1	United States	27.6
West Germany	32.6	Japan	22.2

large inflows of bank funds, so that short-term liabilities reached $2,559 millions at the end of 1963.[20] Even so, this was only a small fraction of Japanese capital sums invested in corporate business enterprise over these years. (See Table 9.) Among big enterprises about 10 percent of equipment funds have come from abroad, mostly in loans. The overseas business tie-ups that sometimes accompany such long-term investment have helped Japanese industries to achieve major gains in technology and foreign markets, and are cautiously approved by the authorities on a case-by-case basis. Mainly, however, Japan has financed her own development since the Occupation. In this respect, as in others already noted, her government and the business community have again reverted since the war to the pattern that characterized her whole century of development during the years 1896-1913.[21]

Second, personal savings have provided nearly two-fifths of national savings in recent years. (See Table 7.) If the appropriate share of depreciation charges is allocated to this sector, the total actually reached 48 percent during 1959-1960.[22] This share is swelled by the business savings of myriads of small, unincorporated proprietors in industry, trade, and farming. Less important than they once were, they still furnish upwards of half the nation's personal saving in a prosperous year. The general public, too, continues to display a high propensity to save, running to 15 percent or so of disposable income even among worker families except in the lower wage brackets.[23] A traditional virtue, and still the chief

[20] Japan attracted $1,408 millions of U.S. private short-term funds during 1960, 1961, and the first quarter of 1962, or 45% of the total outflow from the United States. Hal B. Lary, *Problems of the United States as World Trader and Banker* (Princeton, 1963), p. 38.

[21] William W. Lockwood, *The Economic Development of Japan* (Princeton, 1954), pp. 253-62.

[22] *Shōwa 35-nendo kokumin shotoku hakusho*, pp. 80-81.

[23] E.P.A. data put the average propensity to save from disposable income at 15.4% in Japan (1958) by comparison with 6-8% in the U.S., U.K., Germany, and France (1956-58). However, when social security premiums (relatively very low in Japan) are added in, the Western ratios are increased. The German figure in particular reaches

471

family safeguard against sickness, old age, and disaster, saving has lately been accentuated by the rapid rise of income above customary consumption levels.

Thus personal savings (including those of incorporated businessmen) increased from 14.6 percent of disposable income in 1956 to 21.4 percent in 1961-1962, despite the consumption boom. Strong inducements have prevailed, of course, in the form of high interest rates and profits, a pervasive network of financial institutions, and a stable price level. Investment trusts have mushroomed until they hold 10 percent of the country's listed shares. By the end of 1962 one out of every 6.5 families owned some stock, though 94 percent of them were holdings of less than 5,000 shares that aggregated altogether only 28 percent of shares outstanding. The spread of stock investment has led commentators, somewhat ingenuously, to hail the "new peoples' capitalism," even though here as elsewhere wide stock ownership tends if anything to concentrate control.

Finally the flow of funds into corporate business is depicted in Table 9 for some 15,378 billion yen ($42.7 billions) invested during 1959-1961. One-third came from internal company sources in the form of retained earnings and depreciation. The balance was furnished in large measure, as through Japan's modern history, by financial institutions, mostly private banks and trust companies. Security flotations are a growing share, as public security markets come into wider use. Even so, banks continue as intermediaries to furnish most of the long- as well as short-term capital raised from outside sources. And the public for its part retains its preference for

---

13.7% for worker households as against 15.5% in Japan. *Economic Survey of Japan (1959-1960)*, pp. 202-06. Especially high was the income elasticity of savings in rural Japanese households at this time. In 1960, for example, they absorbed 32% of the year's income gain, according to sample data in *Kokumin seikatsu hakusho*, cited p. 39. See also "A Study of Consumption Function Derived from Family Budget Data," Economic Planning Agency, *Economic Bulletin*, 7 (June 1961); and "Recent Growth of Personal Saving in Japan," Bank of Japan, *Monthly Economic Review* (September 1962), pp. 8-10.

banks and other financial institutions as the place to put its savings.

The continued dependence of industries on banks even for long-term capital is recognized as a weakness in financial structure. It makes interest costs often a heavy charge, and loads banks with illiquid investments. But the insatiable demand for new funds leaves little alternative under the circumstances, even though some shift from indirect to direct financing is now taking place. A good deal of control power remains therefore with the big city banks, and still more with the Bank of Japan to which they are normally indebted.

It appears then that the commercial banking system has operated successfully to mobilize huge credits for investment, drawing more or less continuously on the central bank to fill the gap in its own resources. The joint powers of the Bank of Japan and the Ministry of Finance have been employed—not always in harmony or with sufficient foresight—to minimize business fluctuations. A recurrent drain on foreign balances is the signal sooner or later for the central bank to raise discount rates, or to apply "window guidance" and other restraints. Three mild recessions have interrupted the postwar boom, in 1954, 1958, and 1962 (Table 1) but slackened only briefly the forward movement of the economy. Each gave way before long to the buoyant optimism that has marked the era—"the fourth dimension" of growth. (All these matters are discussed in some detail in Hugh T. Patrick's "Cyclical Instability and Fiscal-Monetary Policy," below, Ch. XII.)

If credit controls have not been wholly successful this is hardly surprising in view of the growth-conscious, inflationary bias that has long characterized the Japanese government and business community. Wholesale prices have drifted up only moderately, nevertheless, thanks to gains in productivity, the high level of voluntary savings, the responsiveness of tax yields, and monetary policies that were flexible and occasionally firm. The index moved annually within a range of 5 percent from 1952 through 1963; at the end of 1963 it stood only 3 percent above its 1952 base. Consumer prices were now recording sharp increases but mainly because continued growth was raising wages markedly in traditional industries and service trades and reducing progressively the old dualism of the Japanese economy.

To summarize, then, the stimulus to growth has come both from rising consumption demands at home and market opportunities abroad. Vigorous initiative in both business and governmental circles to make the most of them; a spirit of cooperation blending pragmatically the efforts of public and private sectors; a labor force that grows rapidly in numbers and skills; a willingness to refrain from consuming income (or spending it on arms) and to pour resources into the technologies of the new industrial era; credit restraints that moderate excesses and wastes without flattening out the curve of growth—these are elements in the equation of enterprise that have tripled the Japanese economy over the years 1951-1964. No single determinant or dynamic impulse can well be singled out unless it is something called the "will to develop," —a phrase that says very little and yet sums up as well as any other the whole record of Japan since 1868.

INCOME-DOUBLING IN THE SIXTIES?

Whether the 1960's will repeat the 50's seems problematical as the decade progresses. True, an expansive "growth mood" has now been built into the political posture of the Liberal-Democratic Party, as dramatized by campaign slogans promising to double national income from 1961 to 1970. The Economic Planning Agency in 1960 translated this promise into a "Long-Range Economic Plan" that projects parameters and programs deemed necessary to achieve a 7.2 percent growth rate through the ensuing decade.[24] Given the nature of Japan's enterprise system, however, the plan can hardly be more than a charting of hopes and expectations, accompanied by a budget of public investment programs. Through the latter the various Ministries are to provide facilities and supplementary programs to sustain the dyna-

[24] Economic Planning Agency, *New Long-Range Economic Plan of Japan (1961-1970)—Doubling National Income Plan* (Tokyo, 1961).

mism of private enterprise and disperse its benefits more equitably among the population.

Implementation of the plan thus rests necessarily on the vigor of private sector in large degree. Pessimists note periodically the weakening of various growth impulses—the slackening of demographic increase, the "catching up" process in technology, sharpening competition in export markets, and above all the latent problem of excess capacity in Japanese industry. An investment boom has for several years been generating its own demand as investment induces still more investment, but the resulting enlargement of supply threatens sooner or later to outrun the needs of both domestic and foreign markets and precipitate a slump. If growth seems likely still at a rate in excess of the prewar average (4.5 percent), one wonders how much longer it can continue at a figure twice that high.[25]

Continuing economic progress depends on developments in several broad areas of public policy. One is trading opportunity overseas; a second, the vigor of industrial enterprise at home. These two interact upon each other, of course, and depend in turn on a third. This may be defined as political stability, e.g., a tolerable state of security abroad, and a viable parliamentary consensus at home. The remainder of this chapter offers an assessment of these problems.

Overseas Need and Opportunity

Long overdue is some correction of Japan's proverbial image as a poor, have-not nation searching for chances to trade abroad in the face of heavy obstacles in order to provide a meager living for her swarming population.

Today she is one of the world's affluent societies, still lacking in natural resources but fourth in the scale of industrial

[25] In mid-1964, nevertheless, the Economic Planning Agency forecast continuing growth in the national economy through 1968 at a rate as high as 9.1% (real) per annum. For further discussion of this issue see the remarks of Ohkawa and Rosovsky, above, pp. 85-87, Patrick, below, pp. 612-18, and Bronfenbrenner's essay on "Economic Miracles and Japan's Income-Doubling Plan," below, Ch. XI.

power and preeminent in rate of growth. Crucial to her post-war success has been her rapid re-entry into markets all over the world, hardly ten years after her whole trading structure was reduced to ruin. From 1951 through 1963 her exports grew three times as fast as world exports, advancing 15 percent a year. (Table 1.) They would have grown even more rapidly had it not been for her own restriction of imports. Ironically in view of the forebodings that followed upon her defeat, the stripping away of the Empire has meant more gain than loss in dollars and cents. Solemn predictions, too, that she could never regain her prewar living level without continuing American aid were falsified; she has raised it by two-thirds.

DIMINISHED OVERSEAS DEPENDENCE

Surprisingly, Japanese dependence on overseas raw materials is even sharply reduced, though her industries now turn out five times as much as before the war. (Table 10.) Much that was once essential has been displaced by new industrial synthetics and by the changing structure of demand. Or it is now a smaller proportion of total resources employed, as fabrication is carried to more advanced stages. Import ratios remain high in the case of industrial materials, by comparison with those of European industrial nations, but this is offset by low ratios in machinery, foodstuffs, and other consumer goods. And even raw material imports are growing much more slowly than industrial production since the war. As for total imports of all goods and services, which stood as high as 24.3 percent of GNP in 1934-1936, they were only 12.2 percent in 1960-1962. Quantitative dependence has been reduced over-all by one-half, in other words.

Aggregate import dependency is once again slowly rising, it is true, if allowance is made for a relative decline in import prices which has kept the value ratio down. Trade liberalization may increase this dependency further. But many nations live satisfactorily with dependency ratios much higher than Japan's. Hers may even begin to drop again with the growth of her heavy and chemical industries, and general advance of

TABLE 10

OVERSEAS TRADE BY COMMODITY GROUPS 1934-1962[a]

	Exports			Imports		
	1934-36	1953	1962	1934-36	1953	1962
Total value						
($ mill.)	936	1,275	4,916	980	2,410	5,637
Quantum index						
(1953=100)	243	100	414	121	100	291
Dependency ratio						
(% of GNP)[b]	20.0	6.7	9.2	20.5	12.7	8.8
Commodity						
Distribution:[c]			(percentages)			
All commodities	*100*	*100*	*100*	*100*	*100*	*100*
Foodstuffs	9	9	7	23	26	13
Coal and petroleum	—[d]	—[d]	—[d]	6	12	18
Textiles & materials	50	36	26	32	28	13
Metals & manufactures	7	15	15	11	7	13
Machinery & equipment	6	15	25	4	7	14
Chemicals & pharma- ceuticals	3	6	5	5	4	5
Other	25	19	22	19	16	24

[a] Values and quantity index are from Bureau of Statistics, *Japan Statistical Yearbook, 1961* (Tokyo, 1962), pp. 256-57, and *Monthly Statistics of Japan, passim.*

[b] Based on foreign exchange receipts and payments in commodity trade.

[c] As compiled in Federation of Economic Organizations, *Economic Picture of Japan, 1961* (Tokyo, 1962), pp. 41-42, and Ministry of International Trade and Industry, *Shōwa 38-nen tsūshō hakusho (kakuron)* [White Paper on Trade (Details) 1963] (Tokyo, 1963), pp. 730ff.

[d] Included in Other.

technology. In any event, little reason exists to anticipate any ceiling on economic growth in this regard, except in short-run terms.[26]

[26] This issue is documented at length in the annual *Tsūshō hakusho* [White Paper on Trade] of the Ministry of International Trade and

In short, when the Japanese bargain abroad for markets today they do so as a powerful, prosperous people no needier of markets than many others. They can hardly plead for trading opportunities abroad unless they are prepared to grant reciprocal benefits at home. While the impulse to economic growth has not come mainly from the expanding world market, foreign markets have grown *pari passu* with domestic markets to sustain the tempo of technological progress and to furnish the necessary materials and equipment from overseas.

Nevertheless, overseas trading needs and problems stand in the foreground of public policy issues in Japan, as they have throughout modern history. The reasons are easy to understand. Imports and exports, now running at $5,000-$7,000 millions each, are intimately tied into the functioning of the economy at all points. From abroad comes 90 percent of the nation's iron ore, a third of its coking coal, a quarter of its steel scrap, and virtually all of its oil, bauxite, phosphate, cotton, wool, and rubber. Machinery imports still run twice as high as machinery exports (excluding vessels), although small by the standard of European industrial competitors.[27]

The *New Long-Range Economic Plan* of 1960 calls for foreign trade to grow at 9-10 percent a year from 1961 to 1970 in order to sustain a 7.2 percent growth rate in national income. Oil imports, already one-third of total energy supplies, are scheduled to quadruple until they furnish one-half. Total exports are to triple, and machinery shipments to rise fourfold. All in all, heavy industrial and chemical goods are counted on to furnish as much as 61 percent of the total growth in exports to 1970.[28] These targets hardly seem overly

---

Industry, and in the Economic Planning Agency's annual *Economic Survey of Japan*. Patrick's emphasis on the balance of payments constraint (below, pp. 612ff.), it should be noted, relates primarily to short-term cyclical fluctuations.

[27] Imports of machinery during 1956-60 were only 8% of machinery production—a low figure for an industrial nation and one hardly possible for Japan without tight import controls.

[28] *New Long-Range Economic Plan of Japan (1961-1970)*, pp. 74-77. See also the policy emphasis in the MITI White Paper, *Tsūshō hakusho*, p. 7.

ambitious, given the record. Yet no area of public policy arouses more worried discussion in business and political circles than Japan's prospects in the evolving structure of world relations. A century of modernization has failed to allay chronic anxiety over external dependence and insecurity.

In the realm of international politics this anxiety has yet to generate any very positive initiative from Japanese political leaders since the war. Security through arms and empire proved a mirage that led the nation to catastrophe. The postwar revulsion against a "positive" foreign policy has re-insularized the Japanese psychologically for a generation. This emotional backwash from the war expresses itself both on the Right and on the Left in an attitude of non-involvement—an inclination, albeit apprehensively, to remain in a passive role for the present. For the first time in fifty years, as one critic put it, "Japan walks softly, and lacks a big stick."

Similar public anxieties pervade the international economic outlook as well. But here paradoxically they have spurred an energetic technical innovation and vigorous commercial drives to reestablish Japan's place in the world on terms that serve her expanding needs for markets, materials, technology and capital.

DUAL OUTREACH: EAST AND WEST

One such area of initiative is the cultivation of new trading relations with southern Asia, where the Japanese seek slowly to repair the hostility left by the war. This region still takes 20-25 percent of Japan's exports, mostly finished manufactures sold in Southeast Asia. (Table 11.) It supplies a seventh of her imports, including raw materials like coal, metals, petroleum, lumber, and rubber. Trade hopes in this theater have prompted her to expand programs of foreign investment and economic cooperation.[29] They also sustained

[29] Japanese economic aid overseas (including reparations and private investments) came to $265 millions in 1963, bringing her total stock of long-term assets abroad to $1,853 millions. Included here were $1,012 millions of export credits and $277 millions in subscriptions to international agencies. Long-term business investments totaled $564 mil-

TABLE 11

OVERSEAS TRADE BY REGIONS, 1934-1962 (%)[a]

	Exports to			Imports from		
	1934-36	1953	1962	1934-36	1953	1962
All countries	100	100	100	100	100	100
Industrial countries	24	32	49	34	48	51
United States	16	18	28	24	31	32
Europe[b]	8	13	18	10	8	14
Non-industrial countries	76	68	51	66	52	49
Asia (inc. Near East)	64	51	34	53	33	29
Mainland China	(18)	—	(1)	(10)	(1)	(1)
South & South-east Asia	(18)	(30)	(22)	(16)	(23)	(13)
Latin America	3	9	7	3	8	8
Africa[b]	6	6	6	3	2	4
Oceania	3	1	4	7	9	9

[a] Data are from Economic Planning Agency, *Shōwa 38-nendo keizai hakusho* [Economic White Paper, 1963] (Tokyo, 1963), p. 432.

[b] Liberia is classified here with Europe, since large Japanese exports were mainly ships of European ownership under Liberian registry. Ministry of International Trade and Industry, *Shōwa 38-nen tsūshō hakusho (kakuron)* [White Paper on Trade, Details, 1963] (Tokyo, 1963), pp. 730ff.

her reparations payments to six Southeast Asian neighbors—$477 millions by April 1964—long after one might expect such obligations to be forgotten.

Trading prospects in southern Asia remain modest, nevertheless; its economic growth is slow and its politics uncertain. Balance of payments difficulties also handicap further expansion of Japan's sales to the area, which are already 50 percent in excess of her purchases. It seems likely that this trade can continue to grow modestly in scale, especially if Japanese industrial interests develop new sources of raw materials in

lions, of which about a half were in properties being developed to supply raw materials for Japanese industry, mostly in southern Asia, the Persian Gulf, Brazil, and Alaska.

the region to balance exports. Contrary to expectations, however, southern Asia has not held its own in Japanese trade over the past decade, and may well continue to diminish in relative importance.

As for the Communist bloc, the attitude of Japanese businessmen and politicians varies between cautious hostility and eager negotiation. Trade with the Soviet Union rose sharply after 1961, and Russian agents promised bigger orders still if the Japanese would only extend 10- to 15-year credits on ships and other equipment sales. Mainland China, too, continues to sustain hopes for the future, at least the distant future. Sooner or later it can hardly fail to return to a central role in Japanese external relations by virtue of its size, proximity, and coming industrialization. For the moment, however, economic contacts are held to slight proportions by Peking's political hostility and its economic tribulations, as well as Japan's opportunities elsewhere, and her deference to American wishes as regards the isolation of China. With Japan's world commerce (imports and exports) running at $12,183 millions in 1963 neither her Chinese trade ($137 millions) nor even her Soviet trade ($320 millions) yet bulked very large.

For the present, then, the significance of trade with China is more political than economic. In fact, the Communist bloc as a whole did not account for more than seven percent of Japan's trade in 1964. Though eager for new opportunities wherever they appear, businessmen generally view with suspicion the political hazards of dealing with totalitarian economies. "Honey is sweet, but the bee stings . . ." said an industrialist when Peking abruptly terminated trade with Japan in 1958 on the pretext of an insult to the Chinese flag in Nagasaki. For the present anyway attractive opportunities are being found elsewhere.

It is upon trade with the West that Japan's eyes are much more closely fixed in the early sixties. Developments here offered both challenge and opportunity. What particularly arouses concern is the vision of great new blocs taking shape around the world. Long accustomed to bargaining at some disadvantage with the American giant, integrated and protected, and with the far-flung Commonwealth group, Japanese now see taking shape a six-nation European Economic Community, paralleled by the seven-nation European Free Trade Association. Should the EEC ever absorb the United Kingdom it would rival America and the Soviet Union in size and competitive strength. Meanwhile modest moves toward regional integration can be observed also in Latin America and in Africa, where the United States and Europe are likewise closely involved. Most important, America itself is seeking to forge new links with the EEC, armed with the negotiating powers of the 1962 Trade Expansion Act. And, of course, there are the Soviet and Chinese constellations to reckon with.

By comparison, Japan's leaders see their own economy as geographically isolated and economically vulnerable, offering no match to these giants in economic or political power. Its traditional advantage in cheap labor slowly fades as wages approach European levels. Energy and raw-material costs are comparatively high, particularly where distant sources add freight charges running to 40-70 percent of costs.[30] The sense of exposure is heightened by doubts that Japanese business structures, more open and competitive than in the days of the *zaibatsu* (the prewar financial combines) will prove a match for new aggregations of industrial power taking shape in the West. Many Japanese industrialists voice confidence that they can compete successfully in a growing·Europe, and reap supplementary benefits elsewhere. For them it spells opportunity. Others fear that they may be not only excluded from Europe but put under pressure at home and in third markets as well. American moves to link up with Europe only heighten anxiety.

The nightmare of Japanese planners, in short, is an At-

[30] Japan's cost advantages characteristically increase at later stages of processing. Relative to U.S. prices, for example, Japanese prices in 1960 were 68% in textile yarns but 46% in fabrics, 132% in copper ingots but 71% in sheets, 173% in iron ore but 63% in wire. *Oriental Economist*, 28,600 (October 1960), 562.

lantic bloc minus Japan. No answer is seen in compensatory moves toward an Asian Common Market under Japanese leadership. Something may be done in Asia multilaterally to evolve special payments arrangements, to specialize industries by countries, and to correct freight structures that now discriminate against intra-regional trade.[31] Yet proposals looking in this direction, under the auspices of the U.N. Economic Commission for Asia and the Far East, draw little response from Tokyo. Asia is deeply divided by political rivalries, cultures, and religions. Its economic level remains far below that of the Western World and is rising more slowly. South and East Asia (excluding Japan and the Communist bloc) bought no more than 7.8 percent of world imports of manufactures in 1960, by comparison with 33.8 percent purchased in North America and Western Europe. Nor can Japan's own share of these Asian imports, some 22 percent, be expected to grow rapidly at the expense of her competitors.[32]

Once again it is being demonstrated that the advanced industrial nations are each other's greatest markets as well as competitors. The Japanese *Long-Range Plan* forecast that shipments to advanced countries would rise from 36 percent of total exports in 1956-1958 to 46 percent in 1970. The share of underdeveloped countries, it predicted, would fall from 61 percent to 49 percent. Horizontal division of labor, not vertical, holds the greater promise of the future.[33]

[31] "Scope for Regional Economic co-operation in Asia and the Far East," United Nations, *Economic Bulletin for Asia and the Far East*, 12, 3 (December 1961), 52-75.

[32] *Shōwa 37-nen tsūshō hakusho*, pp. 136-39. Free Asia's difficulties in sustaining even a 5% growth rate in production and exports, and the implications for Japan, are spelled out in "Foreign Trade Aspects of the Economic Development Plans of ECAFE Countries," *Economic Bulletin for Asia and the Far East*, XIV, 1 (June 1963), and "Japan's Trade with Western Europe and Asia," United Nations, *Economic Survey of Asia and the Far East, 1962* (New York, 1963), pp. 119-33.

[33] This thesis is argued at length in the MITI White Paper cited above, *Shōwa 37-nen tsūshō hakusho*. Japanese exports to North America and Western Europe grew twice as fast as exports to non-

JAPAN AND THE ATLANTIC COMMUNITY

Economic opportunity, then, no less than political orientation is drawing Japan to seek closer ties with the West. America, of course, has long shared with China the leading place in her overseas trade. Together they gave the country that outreach, East and West, which immensely benefited Japanese development through the prewar decades.[34] Trade with the United States was revived rapidly after the war. Now Japan has come to furnish a 1.5-billion-dollar market for American goods—a market second only to Canada's, and the fastest growing of all. Alone she buys twice as much as the whole Near East, and half as much as all of Latin America. The American market in turn takes over a quarter of Japan's entire exports, nearly $1.5 billion in value during 1963.

Sharp influxes of low-priced Japanese manufactures into the United States, concentrated in narrow lines of consumer goods, have been a chronic source of political friction. The solution adopted has been the "voluntary" quota, accepted and enforced under protest by export associations in Japan as the price of warding off still more restrictive American tariffs. Trade disputes have been kept within manageable bounds by the concern of both governments to remain on good terms and to cultivate trading ties. In some degree the force of American protectionist arguments against low-wage com-

---

industrial nations during the fifties (p. 131).

	Annual Growth, 1951-60 (%)		
	Total Imports (A)	Imports from Japan (B)	*(B) ÷ (A)*
Industrial countries	5.45	21.17	3.88
Non-industrial countries	3.37	10.39	3.08
E. and S. Asia	2.87	7.74	2.70

Developing countries nevertheless provide an important market for Japanese machinery and metal products. Leaving aside the Communist bloc, in 1962 the developed industrial nations bought 38% of Japan's exports in this sector, while developing nations took 55%, of which two-thirds went to South and East Asia.

[34] *The Economic Development of Japan*, pp. 398ff.

petition is now beginning to shift away from Japanese goods (textiles, for example) and toward the products of still lower-wage competitors like Hong Kong and India. Yet a third of all Japanese exports to the United States are still covered by semi-compulsory control in Japan. Expedient as it is, the system violates all the proclaimed principles of the U.S. Government. It is secretive; it is restrictive quantitatively in a one-way fashion; and it is a monopolistic restraint on competition with government blessing. That Japan's trade with America is nevertheless of such proportions, and continues to grow by leaps and bounds, testifies to powerful forces of comparative advantage for both countries.

Now the emergence of the EEC as a dynamic force in the West opens new vistas. True, Japan's trade in Western Europe has hitherto amounted to little. Of Western Europe's external trade Japan accounts for hardly 3 percent, while its share in her own commerce is about 12 percent. Western Europe imports three times as much as the United States, but it imports from Japan only half as much. Employing import quotas as well as tariffs, its restrictions on Japanese goods had long been heavy. On the other hand, Europe's economy like Japan's is now growing steadily in scale and efficiency. Both are improving their marketing structures and diversifying their demands. The two regions, differently endowed, should be able to capitalize on the gains of product specialization in industries producing equipment, chemicals, and consumer sundries.

Moreover, Japan's current imbalances in regional trade will be reduced if she can sell more in Europe to cut her import deficit with the West, while also importing more from Asia to finance her exports there. Her foreign trade has long been bilaterally unbalanced to an exceptional degree. It therefore plays a major role in the world's system of multilateral clearing, though by the same token this heightens Japanese feelings of commercial insecurity.[35] More commerce with Eu-

[35] *Shōwa 37-nen tsūshō hakusho*, pp. 16ff. Japan's role in multilateralism is brought out in Michael Michaely. "Multilateral Balance in International Trade," *American Economic Review*, 52, 4 (September 1962), 685-702.

rope would also reduce her heavy reliance on trade with the United States, one of the world's slower growing economies in the fifties. The general objective of a trade offensive in Europe therefore enlist arguments of national economic security as well as business advantage.

Japanese industrialists and economic diplomatists have lately been energetically exploring the new Europe. Led by the Prime Minister himself, missions to the continent have followed one another in steady succession. The bigger firms are opening sales offices, and several are erecting branch plants—Sony in Ireland, Honda Motors in Belgium, Yashica in France, Matsushita in Germany, etc. Essential to the development of an export market, however, is the reduction of barriers to trade. Most European nations, with the chief exception of West Germany, long refused most-favored-nation treatment to Japan, invoking Article 35 of the General Agreement on Tariffs and Trade for the purpose. Others like Italy have achieved the same end by different means.

Japanese efforts to reduce these barriers met with some success in 1962-1963, and trade with Europe rose sharply in response. Led by the United Kingdom, one country after another abandoned discriminatory quotas on Japanese goods under the escape clause of Article 35, and Japan ceased to be the one industrial nation singled out for such overt handicaps. In practice, however, restrictions of one sort or another are still widespread, especially on textiles and sundries, and are commonly discriminatory against Japan either in severity or in number.[36] Just how heavily they bear today is hard to say,

[36] The United Kingdom, for example, although granting Japan most-favored-nation treatment, reserved freedom to restrict imports on a sensitive list, and has Japan's consent to self-regulation of Japanese exports of 61 commodities. Britain's policy on imports of "cheap labor" manufactures from Asia, however, is less restrictive than those of Europe generally. Like the United States, she actually buys a sizable share of her imports of textiles, clothing, and footwear from Asia. By contrast, Asia furnishes very little of such imports into France, Germany, Italy, or the Benelux nations. At the end of 1964 France still discriminated against 68 items from Japan, West Germany 20, Italy 116, and Benelux 33.

for other factors of distance and competitive circumstance are limiting factors, too, as well as Japan's own trade controls. Her sales to Europe, in any case, doubled from 1959 to 1962, and to the industrial nations of the West in the aggregate they rose almost 50 percent.

Judged broadly by the goals of the Free World, it is desirable economically to spread the benefits and the dislocations of Japanese trade competition around the globe. Politically, too, it is of capital importance that Japan be granted full equality in her relations with the West. The status symbols are at least as important as the economic substance if she is to be integrated as a partner. It is not enough if she prospers yet feels excluded from the circle of Western powers where she thinks she belongs by right of interest and responsibility. Reassured that the Atlantic Alliance is not a White Man's Club, she may turn to a more creative policy in Asia, where her mood of detachment deprives her allies of positive support and initiatives they greatly need. No less does it contradict the realities of her own destiny.

Sponsored Capitalism: Post-War Model

LIBERALIZATION

Counter-obligations devolve upon the Japanese, too, if they are to develop a new relation with the West. The most difficult one lies in the realm of competition within the Japanese market. For Japan has always been strongly protectionist. Imports are feared when they compete seriously with indigenous products, or when their competitive pressure encourages "excessive" competition among domestic producers.

After World War II the chief instrument of protection came to be foreign exchange control, not the tariff. A license had to be secured to import anything on an extensive list of items. The regulation of trade in such an import-dependent economy confers wide powers in turn on the government to influence domestic prices, investment, and output. Import quotas were justified primarily as necessary to protect foreign exchange reserves. But their effect was also to shore up industries otherwise unable to stand up against foreign competition. Further, quota controls permitted restraints upon domestic competition through the device of rationing raw material imports.

By 1959 Japan's balance of payments was displaying such strength that it became increasingly difficult to justify these special safeguards. Now she came under increasing pressure from the International Monetary Fund to free her imports from controlled allocations of exchange and to join other nations under Article 8 of the IMF Charter in abandoning such controls as a normal practice. Liberalization of long-standing restrictions on international capital and service transactions became likewise a condition of admission into the Organization for Economic Cooperation and Development. Even had this not been the case, wider access to her market by foreign competitors was the price of successful bargaining for markets abroad.

Accordingly, in April 1964 Japan joined the OECD and accepted the IMF obligations of Article 8, a long step toward restoring the yen to free convertibility. By this date exchange restrictions had been removed on products making up in value some 93 percent of Japan's commodity imports in 1959, as compared with only 43 percent in October of the latter year. The restriction that continues, however, is greater than this seems to imply, for in 1959 trade in many manufactures and farm products was closely limited. Still controlled on April 1, 1964, were 174 items produced in industries thought to be vulnerable. Apprehension is expressed as one item after another is freed from exchange control—TV sets, lemons, film, outboard motors, etc.—and intensive political pressures are mobilized on behalf of industries believed to be threatened. Several difficult issues of policy do indeed confront the authorities in this whole matter of liberalizing commercial and financial transactions with the outside world.

First, deprived of exchange control, can the government handle its responsibility for the balance of payments and make sure the country lives within its means? Continuous oversight and prompt action are of special importance in an economy where, as in 1961, the current accounts can go from a surplus of \$522 millions to a deficit of \$338 millions. Other instruments may need to be strengthened for this purpose, or at least used more resolutely than in the past. (See Patrick's discussion below, Ch. XII.)

Second is a collateral issue: how far should opportunities for foreign capital in Japan be liberalized? The entry of alien funds was closely restricted for some years under the post-war Foreign Exchange Control and Foreign Investment Laws. The ostensible reason, plausible for a time, was to protect the balance of payments from undue repayment burdens. Advance assurance that foreign owners of Japanese stocks might repatriate their capital without any waiting period was refused until April 1963; only then was the last restriction lifted. After 1956, nevertheless, the inflow of long-term funds steadily mounted. They reached a peak movement of \$947 millions in 1963, before the proposal for a U.S. tax on foreign security issues sharply curtailed the American supply. Loans and bond purchases have provided over 70 percent of the total, but stock acquisitions have grown too. By the end of 1963 foreign acquisitions of Japanese shares totaled \$623 millions. While these sums remain very small in the total financing of Japanese industry as noted above (pp. 470-71), they pose a problem of some consequence in foreign economic relations.

Significantly, though foreign holdings of Japanese stocks have grown rapidly, the gain has been mainly in purchases for straight investment purposes, not management participation. The latter are no more than half the total, for such foreign entry with the purpose or the possibility of industrial control has been restricted under the Foreign Investment Law. The government decides license applications case by case, requiring strong justification in terms of the technical benefits for Japanese industry. Equity participation in joint ventures has rarely been permitted to exceed 50 percent; more often it has been held to 35 percent or less. Foreign purchases of company shares have likewise been limited to 10-15 percent of the stock outstanding.

A good deal of trepidation prevails in Japan over this whole matter, despite the growth of Japanese industry in scale and maturity. Partly this is concern over the latent instability of long- and short-term capital flows in and out of the country. Beyond that is the wider implication of foreign ownership of Japanese industry. Is it contrary to national interest, for example, that half the oil refinery business is in the hands of companies with a 50 percent foreign equity? Does it matter that 10-20 percent of the stock outstanding in the rubber and nonferrous metal trades is alien-owned, even if the figure for industry in general is under 3 percent?

Leftist politicians and union spokesmen look suspiciously on any intrusion of "monopoly capital" from abroad, particularly from America. Business attitudes are mixed. Foreign capital is generally welcome when it comes as an investment operation, now that repayment anxieties are no longer acute. It is branch plants and joint enterprises bringing managerial participation by foreigners that arouse misgivings. The Socialists are not alone in voicing anxiety over Japanese "autonomy." Business competitors, particularly smaller ones, fear the advantage accruing to a joint venture enjoying the prestige and resources of a big foreign firm. Alien ownership, too, might disturb the traditional norms of competition and labor relations in the domestic market. And the foreigner hardly fits easily into the web of relations between business and government that is so uniquely and elusively Japanese.

Rigorous licensing of foreign direct investment by the authorities suggests that the government will be slow to depart from its traditional controls—controls that run all the way back to Meiji times and before. On the other hand, the pressures to open Japan to freer investment and closer business ties from abroad can hardly be ignored. Capital is scarce and capital costs high. Foreign tie-ups for technical borrowing and assistance are still needed. In fact they were negotiated during 1958-1963 at a rising tempo. In some fields at least Western concerns are growing less disposed to make their know-how available in return for fees and royalties, and more insistent on equity participation. Finally, Japan finds it more difficult to forge ever closer trading ties with the West so long as she insists on insulating her economy from those interlocking investment relations now characteristic of industrial nations like Germany, Italy, and Belgium. In West Germany, for example, one in five corporations has a foreign minority interest, and foreign ownership of industry as a whole reaches 15 percent—far beyond Japan.

The easing of restrictions on foreign entry into Japanese industry seems therefore, to follow from the logic of Japan's situation. The technical needs of her industry, the easing of balance of payments anxieties, and the concessions required of her in return for economic opportunity in the West—all push the authorities in this direction, despite their traditional fears and inclinations.

The third issue posed by liberalization is how and in what degree to assist industries claiming they will be driven to the wall if competitive imports are de-controlled. This includes new industrial products such as passenger cars, heavy electrical goods, machine tools, and cosmetics, as well as older, high-cost ones such as sugar and pulp. It even extends to such consumer goods as toothpaste, soft drinks, Italian hosiery, lipsticks, and leather shoes, where one might suppose that Japanese manufacturers could easily compete. Moreover, it is not just a matter of imports of like products; the threat can come from desirable substitute, as in the switch from domestic coal to imported petroleum, from domestic oranges to imported lemons, or from beer to gin.

De-control proceeded cautiously and selectively amid much public discussion in the early sixties. Characteristically consumer interests figure little in the deliberations. They have little say, unless they are themselves big producer groups like industries consuming imported fuel oil or wood pulp or steel. No one seriously proposes sacrificing any important industry on the grounds of comparative advantage. Many tariff duties have been raised to replace or supplement exchange control; in fact, a sweeping upward revision of tariffs was quietly begun in 1961. For some items like passenger cars, coal, and various farm products liberalization has been postponed at least for a year or two. Meanwhile the dangers (and opportunities) of de-control add fresh impetus to the surge of new investment and technical renovation that developed after 1958. One company after another, one industry after another, has redoubled its efforts to rebuild its plants, to rationalize its operations, and to enlarge its scale or otherwise improve its competitive position. So intense and widespread has been this response to the new "Open Door economy" that one commentator likens it to a second coming of Perry's "black ships" to Japan.

PATTERN OF INDUSTRIAL ORGANIZATION

Trade liberalization has thus brought to a head issues of business and public policy long latent in Japan's "double-decker" industrial structure.

In small industry stiffer import competition threatens to intensify pressures already severe. With wage costs rising, many a small producer faces the alternatives of modernization or going out of business. Government agencies, sensitive to political pressures from these quarters, have prepared new plans to enlarge modestly various programs of government aid. These include larger supplies of cheaper credit, tax relief, stronger cooperative organs, and other measures to modernize equipment. Small- and medium-scale business remains an important source of employment, income, and exports, even though it gives way slowly to larger structures of enterprise. In 1958 97.5 percent of all incorporated firms (nonfinancial) were capitalized at less than 10 billion yen ($27.7 million). Together they accounted for 27 percent of company assets, 42 percent of sales, and 58 percent of all workers. The *Long-Range Plan* for 1961-1970 foresees little reduction in the relative economic status of the small firm. On the political front, indeed, its importance is bound to increase with the sharpening competition of the Liberal-Democratic and Socialist parties for the middle-class vote.

More controversial is the whole issue of industrial competition and public control in large-scale business enterprise. From the debacle of the war a vigorous new structure has

492

emerged once more. It closely resembles the "sponsored capitalism" of prewar years,[37] yet differs significantly on several points.

First, there is little public ownership of industry, even less than before the war. The State still operates the telephone and telegraph industry, the revenue monopolies in tobacco and salt, and two-thirds of the nation's railways. More important it has a dozen financial institutions engaged mostly in financing private enterprise like the Japan Development Bank, the Export-Import Bank, the Small Business Finance Corporation, and the Housing Loan Corporation. Under the Occupation the government was stripped of its big steel monopoly and most of its other wartime operations and controls except in foreign trade and finance. Shipping, shipbuilding, oil refining, and electric power distribution as well as steel once again became wholly private, though their rebuilding was heavily financed with public funds, and on major decisions they still consult closely with the Ministries.[38] Even the railways, the airlines and the radio and television industries have substantial private sectors.

This restricted scope of government ownership suits the dominant Liberal-Democratic Party, with its business allies. They have no confidence in bureaucratic capacities in this sphere. Nor does even the Socialist Party put forward any vigorous demand for nationalization. It attacks Big Business vehemently, but not so much for inefficiency as for plutocratic exploitation at home and war-breeding alliances abroad. It seeks reform less through public ownership than tighter "socialization" of economic controls.[39]

[37] *The Economic Development of Japan*, cited ch. 10; also G. C. Allen, "Japanese Industry: its Development and Organization to 1937," in E. B. Schumpeter, et al., *The Industrialization of Japan and Manchukuo, 1930-1940* (New York, 1940), pt. ii.

[38] The government continues to own most of the stock in the Electric Power Development Co., a company formed jointly with private interests in 1952 to plan and develop new generating plants and transmission lines feeding the nine private regional distributors.

[39] "Platform of the Japan Socialist Party," *Japan Socialist Review*, 4 (December 16, 1961), 23-46.

In its avoidance of State operation of industry, Japan is to be compared with Belgium rather than the United Kingdom. The government's involvement in industrial finance, however, as well as in foreign trade, still gives it wide powers and responsibilities. To be sure, its supply of capital funds to the private corporate sector has fallen from 10.6 percent of corporate investment in 1953 to 4 percent in 1959-1961 (Table 9). And with this relative withdrawal has gone some reduction in regulatory influence conferred by such activities. Nevertheless, the State is heavily engaged in sustaining the pace of industrial growth. It has been involved directly in at least a third of the nation's gross capital formation from year to year (see above, pp. 467-68). The lack of public ownership of industry is far from being a policy of *laissez-faire*.

A second characteristic of industrial organization worth noting is the absence of product monopoly. This also was true of prewar Japan. The prevailing pattern in large-scale business is oligopoly, with patterns of concentration varying widely from one sector to another. Studies of the Fair Trade Commission through 1958 establish that the concentration of production in a few firms, marked as it commonly was, has declined from prewar days. It was lower in 30 out of 45 industries surveyed, and higher in only 13—mostly older trades such as sheet glass, rayon, and property insurance.

Concentration of industrial control also declined moderately from 1952-1955 to 1958, judged by output attributable to five leading companies in 81 industries. On the average the top five accounted for 63 percent of output in their respective fields during 1958. Since then the evidence is inconclusive but points to no marked drift either way. Characteristic is the domination of three to ten firms, trailed often by numerous smaller companies competing successfully in one stage or another of the production process. Thus the 1958 survey of 122 industrial products showed 11 items where three firms produced over 90 percent, another 34 where five firms accounted for over 80 percent, another 33 where 10 firms produced over 80 percent, and a final group of 29 where it took 10 firms to aggregate as much as 50 percent. Noteworthy, too, is the fact that 10 big companies again handle 50 percent of the nation's imports and exports, as before the war.[40]

Whether large or small, enterprisers vie strenuously for the market. Where sellers are few, competition is usually less keen in pricing than in other ways. Vigorous rivalry to build new plants and stake out positions in new fields has generated an investment boom reminiscent of an armament race. Leading groups spread out their commitments from one sector to another in interlacing patterns of investment that appear often to disregard market limitations. Here again the diversified groupings that have emerged are a reminder of prewar Japan, though with important differences.

THE COMBINES AGAIN

Three old *zaibatsu*—Mitsui, Mitsubishi, and Sumitomo—have long since re-formed under their old banners. Gone are the old families at the top, however. Gone, too, are the holding companies (now outlawed) that long furnished the key instruments of control. Where once the Big Four (including Yasuda) accounted for 24.5 percent of all paid-up capital in corporate industry and finance, there are now eight or ten such groups loosely clustered around big banks.

If the old combines are less tightly put together than before, the newer groupings formed around banks such as Dai-Ichi, Sanwa, and Nippon Kōgyō are even more fluid and uncoordinated in structure. In addition, there are now huge independent firms like Toshiba (electrical goods), Yawata (steel), and Toyota (motors). Each has its own ring of subsidiaries but lacks the complex interlocking ties characteristic of the old combines.

Significantly, the newer enterprises largely occupy the new

[40] The above data are from two detailed studies, one by Misonō Hitoshi of the FTC research staff, entitled *Nihon no dokusen* [Monopoly in Japan] (Tokyo, 1960), especially pp. 75-94, and the other an earlier FTC report on industrial concentration, *Nihon sangyō shūchū no jittai* [The Actual Conditions of Industrial Concentration in Japan] (Tokyo, 1957). Concentration data on the 122 industries during 1954-58 will also be found in the FTC's 1960 report, *Shōwa 35-nendo nenji hōkoku* [Annual Report, 1960] (Tokyo, 1962), pp. 143-49.

growth industries. The veteran *zaibatsu* are more important typically in the older, less dynamic trades. They are stronger in coal than oil refining, in copper rather than steel and aluminum, in shipbuilding rather than autos. In fact the eight biggest industrial concerns of Japan, ranked by sales in 1961, included not one firm closely associated with Mitsui, Mitsubishi, or Sumitomo. As for banking, the big city banks hold 60 percent of all bank assets. (The war years eliminated hundreds of small local institutions.) But there are now 13 of these city banks, all in sharp competition. No other industrial nation except the United States has so many. "In prewar days," said Kaneko Toshi, President of the big Fuji Bank, "a few financial leaders were able to decide things, but . . . you can not do that now."

Within the combines, even the old ones, internal controls are less centralized than before the war. Banks have now replaced the holding companies as nuclei. But they neither desire nor are capable of the old unified control of operations. Cross-holdings of stock among firms within the three old combines run only to 11-21 percent, most of it held by financial institutions. (Before dissolution the figure was 25-30 percent of company stocks held by the ruling family and holding company in Mitsubishi and Sumitomo, and 53 percent in the case of Mitsui.)[41] Operating affiliates typically get about 30 percent of their loans from the group bank, judged by 1961 data on eight such groupings old and new.[42] The group banks in turn commit no more than 10-25 percent of their loans to affiliated concerns. They also furnish executive personnel; a 1956 survey of 450 companies counted 311 former officers of the eight big banks in top jobs.[43] Then again there is the nexus of the trading company. Mitsubishi Shoji and

[41] "Stockholding and Consolidation of Enterprises by Old Zaibatsu Companies," Fair Trade Commission, *Fair Trade*, 1, 4 (August 1958), facing p. 8.

[42] "630 sha no kin-yū keiretsu" [Financial Relations of 630 Companies], *Tōkei geppō*, 22, 2 (February 1962), 2-18; also "Business Groupings and Bank Loans," *Oriental Economist*, 30, 617 (March 1962), 139-44.

[43] *Nihon no dokusen*, p. 254.

Mitsui Bussan once more handle 30 percent and 15 percent of their respective group's business. Sumitomo relies on two such companies, and there are still other big traders each with its circle of clients.

A certain community of interest is embodied in these relations, of course. It is expressed in preferential buying, selling, financing, and personnel exchange—just how preferential, it is impossible to say. Especially when a concern gets in trouble such supports can be important. Yet most big companies are now too large to rely on one or two banks or trading companies. Financial institutions, too, prefer to diversify their loans and to adhere to the role of banker rather than combine operator. They compete for deposits, loans and investments wherever they can find them. As for monthly meetings of company presidents, said to be a coordinating device in the old-line groups, they are no substitute for the prewar, vertical discipline of the holding company. Nor are the personal loyalties of younger executives any longer those of the old *zaibatsu* managers; "business first" is their slogan of independence.

Significantly, there is even sharp industrial competition among affiliates within combines, for example among several Mitsui chemical firms. Rivalry among officers makes cooperation difficult. Mergers are reportedly blocked by disputes over which president should head the new concern and how the merged executive staffs should be ranked. How much more difficult then must be mergers between firms from rival combines, or those within newer groupings even less coherent in structure!

Clearly such groupings are much reduced both in internal unity and in external importance from prewar days, large and powerful as they remain. In part the change is traceable to the deconcentration reforms of the Occupation, its purges and capital levies, and the whole dislocation of the war era. Mainly, however, it reflects the growth of Japan's industrial economy in scale and complexity. Along with this goes increased freedom from banking control, especially control by the primary bank. The 200 largest firms may still account for 39 percent of total company assets and 33 percent of total net profits, as the FTC found in 1958,[44] but controlling decisions can no longer be made in the same degree by a few clusters of financiers and executives—no longer, that is, unless State power can be invoked to give them the force of law. Powerful as Big Business may be, and close as are its relations with the Ministries, it is itself divided in its interests and counsels. Only on the broadest issues can it present a united front. In politics, too, it faces a more open and competitive situation in which strong, though often unequal, countervailing forces come into play from other sectors of Japanese society. On this score there are marked changes, even revolutionary changes, from the old order of the twenties and thirties.[45]

CARTELS AND COMPETITION

As for actual patterns of business behavior in the market, relations among rival firms in large-scale industry are characterized on the one hand by keen competition, which is qualified by much consultation, back-stage collusion, price leadership and other such restraints, on the other. Excessive concentrations and other monopolistic practices contrary to the public interest are forbidden under the Occupation-made Anti-Monopoly Law still carried on the statute books and watched over by the Fair Trade Commission with some deterrent effect. However, the revisions of 1949 and 1953 considerably weakened this law. Enforcement is weak, too, and this whole idea of policing competition in the public interest is basically foreign to Japanese tradition.

Monopolistic practice takes the form usually of cartel and cartel-like agreements, formal or informal, rather than single-

[44] *Ibid.*, p. 80.

[45] The foregoing observations on industrial organization are based on interviews conducted in Japan in 1956 and 1962 and on published materials. Among the latter, besides those already cited, might be mentioned at least one other informative series of articles by Fujisawa Ichirō, "Ginkō Shihon no Shihai-ryoku" [The Dominance of Bank Capital], *Ekonomisuto*, 34, 40-44 (October 6-November 3, 1956).

seller dominance. In fact, as noted above, there is stubborn resistance to outright mergers as a way to concentrate control. While some 1,016 mergers were validated by the FTC under the Anti-Monopoly Law in 1960-1962, they were virtually all minor in scope, and the more important ones occurred mostly among firms already closely affiliated.[46] Standing in the way are rivalries among directors and officers, lifetime commitments to the labor force, differing wage scales, and sometimes a belief that two concerns merged will fare less well together than separately in winning government allocations of import quotas, etc. A classic instance is the shipping industry. Depressed and heavily indebted to the government as it is, its ninety-odd firms were able for years to defy strong pressures from the Ministry of Transportation to force through a reorganization, mobilizing powerful political support for the purpose.[47]

In the realm of inter-firm agreements, on the other hand, the recession of 1961-1962, like its predecessors, gave rise to a rash of proposals to restrict new investment and output, fix prices, and the like. By 1959 there were already some 70 major cartel agreements in mining, metallurgy, machinery, chemicals, textiles, etc. Some of these cartels restrict output as much as 50 percent. A number are "advice" cartels, put forward with the blessing of MITI and the reluctant acquiescence of the FTC, though usually without legal sanction against recalcitrants. Others have been approved by the FTC as legal exceptions to the prohibitions of the Anti-Monopoly Law in the interest of rationalization and stabilization. Still others are formed under special laws exempting foreign trade,

[46] "Anti-monopoly Policy," *Oriental Economist*, 30, 618 (April 1962), 194. For earlier years see *Nihon no dokusen*, p. 68.

[47] The shipping industry finally was induced in 1963 to accept a plan by which 97 firms agreed with government support to consolidate themselves into six major groups. In this year occurred also a decision to merge two of the bigger banks, Dai-Ichi and Asahi, as well as to put back together the three Mitsubishi firms into which the great Mitsubishi Heavy Industries had been broken up during the Occupation. Meanwhile the Fair Trade Commission reported a sharp rise in the number of mergers, evidently in response to the pressures of trade liberalization.

small industry, and other particular sectors in some degree from the ban on joint action. Finally there are monopolistic industries like glass and beer, where informal price leadership and other forms of collusion are a matter of course.

No less evident is the difficulty often of keeping such inter-firm agreements in force. Most of them seem to be short-lived, and some never really take effect except on paper. Listings such as one finds in the literature are therefore deceptive.[48] Evasion and sabotage are commonly present, especially from smaller firms that are eager to grow and see an advantage in non-compliance.

Even the steel industry with its giant producers and its close MITI contacts has found this to be so. Three big firms engaging periodically in restriction of output and price agreements saw their share of steel capacity decline from 85.5 percent in 1953 to 76.3 percent in 1957. Meanwhile four small companies in the Kansai area raised their share from 10.2 percent to 18.3 percent. Again in the recession of 1961-1962 efforts by seven large firms and 33 smaller ones to curtail steel output by 20 percent of capacity, with government approval, ran into difficulty because of "selfish dissidents." (By this time the seven leaders were producing only 70 percent of steel ingots.) Price stabilization in steel has not been very successful either, despite monthly meetings to agree on quotations. In 1962, for example, as inventories accumulated, price quotations maintained nominally since 1960 were actually being undercut 20 percent or more. Neither production control nor the buying up of stocks seemed to solve the problem. The industry thereupon sought approval for a scheme to formalize an "anti-recession cartel" to control sales and prices under the Anti-Monopoly Law. With the upturn of 1963 the pressure for formal government-sanctioned restrictions was again relaxed, although consultations on output, prices and

---

[48] See, for example, the listings in the FTC annual reports, *Nenji hōkoku*, and the excellent study already cited here, Misonō's *Nihon no dokusen*, App. 2. Misonō is careful to stress the limited force of many agreements to restrict output. He finds also that administered prices even in concentrated industries remain sensitive to business fluctuations (p. 122ff.).

import of raw materials remain a standard practice among the big firms under the somewhat critical eye of the FTC and MITI.

These difficulties are even greater in industries where entry is easier than in steel or oil, and where personal relations and Ministerial "guidance" are less potent. Cotton spinning may be cited as an example. This is one trade in which a well-established cartel has intermittently restricted output and capacity for some decades. Such restrictive practices were revived in the recession that followed the Korean War. Some success was achieved, because MITI cooperated by allocating foreign exchange for raw cotton imports only to cooperating spinners. But the 10 big spinners steadily lost ground to scores of smaller firms, as the restriction did not apply to companies with less than 10,000 spindles, and black marketing was rife. The big spinners' share of total spindleage dropped from 89 percent in 1950 to 50 percent in 1957. To tighten controls a law was enacted in 1956 to permit the "mothballing" of all facilities deemed surplus by a government-sponsored cartel. In 1959 this practice was extended to chemical and synthetic fibers as well, along with various other restraints. It remained thereafter the chief reliance for production control as raw cotton and wool were freed from import quota allocations. Increasingly, however, it has failed to check expansionist competition in a manner that preserved satisfactorily the international position of the industry. It has artificially maintained natural fibers against the inroads of synthetics, and in various ways handicapped the Japanese textile industry in cutting costs and improving quality. By 1963, with the production cutback rate still standing at 34 percent in cotton yarn, a move was under way to return the industry to a freer competitive basis, to shift the control of synthetic fibers to "voluntary restraint," and to permit textile producers to adapt their plants more freely to the exigencies of international competition.

THE HAND OF GOVERNMENT

Crucial to this whole matter obviously is the attitude and

involvement of government. True, its statutory authority to control business is less extensive than in most industrial nations. Outside the familiar realms of fiscal and monetary management and the protection of labor, its most sweeping powers had hitherto consisted in regulating imports of goods, capital, and foreign technology. In certain industries, as noted earlier, it has also been a big lender of capital funds through public financial institutions. Beyond this, of course, it has various other specific responsibilities. With reference to the problem under discussion here, for example, it has certain statutory obligations to combat monopoly, while on the other hand it feels called upon also to encourage restrictive agreements in the interest of exports, public health, the protection of small business, and the stabilization of the economy.

The regulation of foreign trade and the supply of capital have conferred latent powers on the Ministries to reach widely into all sectors of business for a variety of purposes. Though both powers are now reduced in scale they make possible a good deal of centralized direction where the authorities are so minded. Or, to turn it around, they enable business groups when they can enlist help in the Ministries to invoke political authority in support of their own programs. This is presumably what has been happening when import controls—with lending powers in reserve—have been employed to regulate internal as well as external competition through the restriction of exchange allocations for imported raw materials in industries such as cotton and wool textiles, petroleum, soap, sugar, and leather goods.

Yet unanimity in such matters is hard to achieve among banks, industries, and government, or among the various Ministries and government lending agencies. Elements of rivalry and cross-purpose are everywhere evident when it comes to specific action. Within the government this can be seen, for example, in the long deadlock between the Finance Ministry and Bank of Japan over the question how and by whom monetary policy is to be conducted. The possibilities of disagreement are only widened when joint action is extended to MITI, the FTC, or big city bankers, not to mention the politicians who head rival cliques in the Liberal-Democratic Party. Within business, too, there are countervailing balances at work, inadequate as they often are. Shipbuilders resist the fixing of steel-plate prices, copper fabricators oppose the tariff demands of domestic mining interests, etc.

The metaphor that comes to mind is a typical Japanese web of influences and pressures interweaving through government and business, rather than a streamlined pyramid of authoritarian control. Perhaps it is just as well. Business is somewhat shielded from government dictation by inter-agency and inter-group tensions. Its own disagreements in turn tend to diffuse its counter-influence in politics. The danger, of course, is a tendency to indecision and drift where national interest may call for clearcut solutions. Only the biggest decisions go up to the Cabinet. There they may still encounter interfactional and inter-Ministerial rivalry, as in the annual contest over the budget. Even then opportunities for noncompliance down the line are considerable. A web it may be, but a web with no spider. What makes the system as workable as it is, no doubt, is a strong *esprit de corps* in the higher ranks of the civil service, and a common social background and university training among leaders in both government and industry.

The hand of government is everywhere in evidence, despite its limited statutory powers. The Ministries engage in an extraordinary amount of consultation, advice, persuasion, and threat. The industrial bureaus of MITI proliferate sectoral targets and plans; they confer, they tinker, they exhort. This is the "economics by admonition" to a degree inconceivable in Washington or London. Business makes few major decisions without consulting the appropriate governmental authority; the same is true in reverse. The Ministries list 300 consulting committees for this purpose!

On fundamentals both businessmen and bureaucrats are in sufficient agreement to avoid the kind of stalemate that often befuddles policy in the United States. Their values are mostly in common, and their attitudes instrumental. Yet within this pragmatic consensus goes on a vigorous and often

503

unruly competition for power and advantage. Civil servants can be stubbornly resistant to business pressures, even though many look forward to business sinecures on retirement. Businessmen on their part view bureaucratic interference with suspicion where it opposes their own calculations and does not merely sanction them. "Creative tension" within and between government and business is the term once used to describe the dynamism of Meiji enterprise. Perhaps it is no less applicable now, nearly a century later.

FREE ENTERPRISE AND NATIONAL POLICY

By the tests of innovation and growth the Japanese enterprise system today is performing remarkably well. While it confers its benefits first of all upon the capitalists, it also serves the worker and consumer. Nevertheless, intensive debate has developed over reforms in industrial structure. Initiated by MITI, this debate is joined in from various viewpoints by business groups.

In the background is alarm on several counts. There are ailing industries like coal, first of all, where lagging efficiency is a drag on the economy and a canker in labor-management relations. The new growth industries, on the other hand, display a burgeoning of firms and plants with little regard to what the traffic will bear—or so the critics fear. Intensifying the whole issue is a third development: the international challenge. Japan must now gird herself to meet new circumstances such as the rise of the EEC with its self-strengthening integration; she faces keener competition in markets around the world, not excluding the Japanese market itself. What is feared is not just foreign competition based on lower production costs, but also superior financial resources and connections enabling giant Western concerns to take over markets and exclude Japanese firms not similarly endowed.

Influential spokesmen for MITI press openly for the rationalization and cartellization of industry under the aegis of the government. They decry "excessive" competition, calling for curbs in the interest of efficiency; only thus can the Japanese

504

make their way successfully against their giant competitors abroad. Already the force of the Anti-Monopoly Law has been pervasively weakened. A growing list of industries has been exempted by statute from its application altogether. Now advocated is a widening of such exemptions still further, and then an application of the State's authoritative powers in one way or another to effect the needed reorganization of various industries on a more consolidated pattern. Government "guidance" is the euphemism—that is, guidance by MITI.

Three types of industries are differentiated in making this case. First are "national policy" industries such as petroleum, steel, and power. Too important to be left to private initiative, it is argued, they should be formed into an "intermediate sector." Neither public nor wholly private, this sector should be operated by private capital with close public support and surveillance. Ample precedents for this exist in the strategic industries of prewar and wartime Japan. Now a new Petroleum Industry Law of 1962 is regarded as the postwar prototype, with its broad grant of authority to the State to influence major operating decisions (and restrict foreign influence).

Second are the "sick" industries—coal above all, but also nonferrous metals and others in varying degree. These are high-cost trades suffering a decline in markets or unable to stand unprotected against foreign competition. The problem varies from one case to another. In coal it is basically the shift to petroleum as an energy source, but the industry's plight is worsened by the existence of over 300 firms, many submarginal, outdated in technique and suffering from labor unrest. The remedy sought is curtailment and modernization fostered by subsidy, price fixing, control over oil imports, and other appropriate action.

Third are those industries of rapid growth where competition threatens to multiply plants and firms needlessly and to keep them below optimum size or optimum rate of utilization. The forecast of over-capacity is debatable; for one thing it depends on selling price. Some argue that facilities already exist in numerous industries to satisfy demand for several years to come. Others point more optimistically to growth factors in foreign and domestic markets. However that may be, it is clear that key industries are uneconomically fragmented. The new petrochemical plants, for example, are much smaller than comparable installations in the United States and unit costs are accordingly high. The same is true in branches of textiles.

One striking case of a market divided among small competing firms is the automotive industry. While 1,108,996 trucks were turned out in 1964, production of passenger cars was still only 579,660 units—four weeks' output in the American industry. Production is now growing rapidly, it is true, and may soon reach a million cars. This is enough to support three or four firms fairly economically, if they specialize in only a few models; for example, Italy's Fiat produced 570,000 cars in 1961. In Japan, however, there are as many as nine firms all competing with numerous models at costs that would spell trouble if the tight restrictions on foreign-car imports were to be relaxed. Even Toyota, the industry's leader, is still a midget; it produces no more than a twelfth of the domestic output of General Motors (which accounts for half the U.S. industry). And this is characteristic of many trades. Judged by sales, Japan's four largest chemical concerns are only one-sixth the size of the 11 largest American companies on the average, and one-eighth the size of nine big European firms. Her two leading chemical companies averaged one-eighteenth of DuPont's sales in 1960; her two biggest steel companies averaged little more than one-seventh of the business of U.S. Steel (although now in the world's top 10) ; and her two larger oil refiners sold less than one-thirtieth as much as Standard Oil of New Jersey.[49]

To be sure, plant size is apt to be more significant for production efficiency up to a certain point than the size of the multi-plant firm. Here the disparities between Japanese installations and those in the West are less marked, of course, than the company comparisons cited above. Yet the Japanese themselves are inclined to stress the importance of scale in

[49] *Economic Survey of Japan* (*1961-62*) cited, p. 372, "Japan's Chemical Industry," *Oriental Economist* 31,631. (May 1963), pp. 268-71.

capital resources and management too; particularly they look with misgiving on the progress of business consolidation in Europe.

Behavior patterns in Japanese industry, at least in the boom era 1955-1963, seemed to encourage numerous firms pushing forward in each field to build new plants and stake out as large a share of the market as possible. No single factor accounts readily for this circumstance. The lifetime commitment of a firm to its labor force is sometimes a factor. Another is the tendency of banks to carry their clients in hard times. A third is widespread resort to market-sharing practices. Firms are thus kept in being when otherwise they might be squeezed out or deterred from entering in the first place. Then, too, the way MITI has awarded licenses for equipment imports may sometimes have fragmented industries and diversified enterprises; it is not easy for Ministry officials to stick to the chosen-instrument principle of development in the face of all the business and political pressures. There are also technical linkages among industries that sometimes argue for group diversification; for example, steel companies have begun to enter certain chemical trades in order to utilize their by-products. The combine tradition, finally, seems to have frustrated rather than assisted consolidation within the single industry. Between combines, mergers are almost unheard of, and even within the single group, as already noted, they are apt to be blocked by executive rivalries and differing wage scales.

It remains to be seen how far all this is a reflection of the buoyant mood of the "income-doubling" era, and what would happen if a prolonged depression should set in. Previous recessions have always produced a wave of failures among small businesses while among large firms they have led characteristically to cartel negotiations looking to output restriction and price maintenance in a number of trades. As remarked earlier, however, these restraints prove difficult to enforce without legal sanctions. If a fear of the cold winds of competition inclines Japanese businessmen naturally to restrictive practices, a vigorous spirit of enterprise is apt to disrupt their smooth operation. Yet a good many investments in new capacity during this boom era seem imprudent except on the expectation that markets can be collusively sustained and shared in one way or another, so as to permit survival for most competitors whatever their cost differentials.

PRESSURES FROM GOVERNMENT

MITI's prescription is unambiguous. It is to suspend or abridge the Anti-Monopoly Law and empower its own industry bureaus in cooperation with business groups to concentrate and specialize production, to force mergers where necessary, to rationalize subcontracting among small firms, to standardize parts and models, to expand markets by installment selling and export credits—and in some degree perhaps to supervise profits as well. In textiles, in steel, in oil, in autos, constant pressure is exerted in this direction.

Business opinion is divided. Spokesmen concede the vulnerability of Japan's industrial structure in the face of import liberalization. They, too, relate this to "excessive" competition, creating a tendency to overcapacity and undue fragmentation. They agree further that voluntary agreements are notoriously weak and subject to breakdown, even where the government applies moral suasion, as in the regulated oil industry. But here counsels diverge. Some go a considerable distance in accepting government regulation as the price of stability. Others—and they are in the majority—view all such proposals with suspicion, seeing in them the revival of a statism they fear. Voluntarism is preferable even if it means some disorder. Business committees speak out against bureaucratic control even in key industries such as petroleum, steel, and shipbuilding. It is plain they will put up a stubborn resistance.

Faced with this opposition, MITI spokesmen stress joint cooperation between government and business. Even here they meet opposition from the Fair Trade Commission. It insists on keeping the statutory safeguards of the Anti-Monopoly Law against monopolistic mergers and cartels that unduly restrict competition. Moreover, the FTC can count on a good deal of support from farmers, small business and labor, at least to keep the law on the books. Several times since 1953 Liberal-Democratic leaders have sought to weaken it still further only to be frustrated by public opposition, led by the Socialists in the Diet.[50] MITI now proposes to detour this roadblock by enacting legislation exempting still more individual industries like steel, motors, and chemicals, without frontal attack on the anti-monopoly statute itself. Planning and oversight of the whole reform would be given to a Council on Industrial Structure, formed jointly by government and business. Characteristically the details would not be spelled out in legislation; they would be left to MITI and cooperating business groups, with a broad delegation of power in the best Japanese tradition. Business, however, responds warily to all such proposals that put the government in more than an advisory role in regulating, say, additions to industrial capacity.

It appears then, that steps will be taken only cautiously in the direction of concerted efforts to reorganize the structure of certain industries and to increase the degree of government-sponsored cartellization. If the government chooses to press the issue it will not lack inducements to offer business, ranging from financial aids to the threat of further import liberalization in vulnerable industries. Cartel-type actions to control investment and market decisions, however, usually require legal sanctions to make them effective over any period of time. That will call for statutory powers well beyond those now permitted the bureaucracy if attempted on any scale.

The danger as many see it is that anxieties over "excessive" competition, both domestic and foreign, are leading in this direction. Should this trend continue, it is asked, will it seriously weaken the dynamism of Japanese enterprise that has been the mainspring of postwar economic growth? The industry specialists of MITI, competent as they are in routine affairs, have never given promise of becoming captains of industry with daring and foresight. Already widespread in

[50] See the excellent review by a former FTC Chairman, Ashino Hiroshi, "Experimenting with the Anti-Trust Law in Japan," *Japanese Journal of International Law*, 3 (1959), 31-51.

Japanese industry is the tendency to rig markets and fix prices at levels that cover the high-cost producer. A more rational industrial structure implied resisting such practices, not re-inforcing them. Nor does cartellization seem a promising way of equipping Japanese industry to face international competition if its effect is to shelter the weak against the strong.

The dilemma is a familiar one in modern industrial organization. Monopoly is apt to stagnate, but unrestrained competition among the giants of modern industry and finance also has its inefficiencies and disorders. The problem is how to keep oligopoly efficient—large enough to achieve the full benefits of scale, under continuous pressure to innovate, and adjusting its investment and production schedules in some prudent relation to expanding markets. Back of that is the issue as to who should decide, and how should action be taken.

Once again the Japanese will doubtless seek an answer in some blend of State and private initiative, reconciling the exigencies of foreign competition with the play of internal forces. In principle, greater liberalism in foreign economic policy implies *greater* freedom of enterprise at home, not less. In practice, too, the first effect of import liberalization is to weaken the government's control powers over the industrial economy. Added to that, industry is now less dependent on the State for investment capital than in the earlier postwar years, and correspondingly less amenable to "guidance." Amid all the conflicts of interest and principle, a new industrial order is taking shape not as one coherent blueprint but through a series of groping experiments. Short of a war or serious depression no radical change seems in prospect.

Industrialism and Parliamentary Democracy

A third area of public life on which depends the future of Japan's "New Capitalism" is successful operation of the parliamentary government that furnishes its political framework. Capitalist industrialism and liberal politics are each the counterpart of the other. The stability of one depends on the stability of the other. And the vigor of each requires open, competitive participation by diverse elements within the consensual limits of a free society.

Despite her problems Japan in the early sixties is living under the strongest and most mature parliamentary govern- ment in the non-Western world. Its most ardent supporters among the Japanese are prone to dwell on its shortcomings. Often they are discouraged over its future, and one can see why. But they can take heart if they measure their achieve- ment less against the abstract norm of democratic theory and more against its imperfect realization in the West. Certainly they can recognize how far Japan has come if they look back fifty years into their own history, or, if they compare their politics with the unstable, authoritarian regimes of the con- temporary non-Western world where democracy is voiced as an aspiration but denied in practice.

What makes for or against democratic politics is a question that can engage one at length. Some of the determinants are rooted in political and cultural heritage, as Japan herself well illustrates. Despite the vogue of Marxism among Japanese intellectuals, no nation of the modern world offers more striking testimony to the autonomy of politics from overriding economic determinism. Yet essential, too, for the rise of demo- cratic capabilities is sustained economic progress from pre- industrial levels of poverty.

WIDENING OF POLITICAL COMPETITION

Initially the Meiji political order was highly authoritarian, of course. Very likely this accelerated Japan's industrialization in the nineteenth century since her new leaders were ambitious to modernize. Certainly it spared her some of the difficulties that have plagued other developing nations in the twentieth, when democratic demands have spread more rapidly than the capacity to fulfill them. No less important, however, Meiji leadership was sufficiently unified and flexible to permit a slow, peaceful widening of oligarchy as economic progress brought into play new interests and aspirations. This diversi- fication and broadening of elites, within a strong framework of authority, was the secret of rapid industrial growth and political stability.

Meanwhile the Industrial Revolution slowly transformed Japanese society. As it did so it began to bring into being the requisites of a more responsible system of government. Greater margins of material well-being, higher rates of literacy and social mobility, new structures of economic and social power, growing experience with parliamentary institutions—these changes worked in Japan as they had in the West to diffuse political power and make it more accountable. During the interwar years 1919-1939, indeed, they built up such a challenge to the old authoritarian order, such conflicts between civil leaders and military, between Diet and bureaucracy, between conservatives and radicals, that the drift toward full-scale party government was abruptly terminated. Japan plunged into a decade of military counter-reaction at home and imperialist adventure abroad. Once again it was demonstrated that sustained economic progress is never a sufficient condition of democratizing political power, however necessary a one.[51]

The bitter experience of World War II, followed by the reforms of the Occupation, permitted the nation once more to resume the trend interrupted in 1931. Political reform cleared away legal and administrative obstacles to the emergence of liberalizing forces. Reforms in economic life—land redistribution, encouragement to unions, the dissolution of combines, tax revision, etc.—sought more positively to diffuse power and wealth and to widen economic opportunities. Related changes in education decentralized controls and fostered equality of opportunity.

What has really stabilized the new order and moved it steadily toward its goals is the remarkable economic progress that has ensued. Economic gains have consolidated the "experimental democracy" of the postwar years far beyond what any but the most naïve well-wishers of the Occupation dared to hope in 1945. The range of popular aspirations, and the more open structure of classes, has now become fairly char-

[51] A fuller discussion will be found in the author's essay, "Economic and Political Modernization: Japan," in Robert E. Ward and D. J. Rustow, eds., *Political Modernization in Japan and Turkey* (Princeton, 1964), pp. 117-45.

acteristic of middle-rank industrial nations everywhere, with allowance for cultural differences. Politics in turn comes to reflect higher levels of income and education and the more diversified structure of interest groups through which demands are now articulated in the political arena. There are still gross imbalances among these interests, of course, but far wider sectors of the population than ever before can now participate with some effectiveness in politics and hold their elected rulers somewhat accountable.

BUSINESS AND POLITICS

Today the power elite of this society, on its dominant conservative front, consists mainly of the officers and directors of big banks and industrial concerns, the upper cadres of the civil service, and the top politicians of the Liberal-Democratic Party. Business maintains close liaison with the Ministries. Together they speak with a powerful though not always united voice in the councils of the ruling party. There they join and support groups of professional politicians many of whom have also been recruited from earlier careers in the civil service, or in business, law, and journalism. For example, the 32 new MP's elected to the House of Representatives on the Liberal-Democratic ticket in 1960 included 11 businessmen, 10 ex-bureaucrats, and others drawn from local politics such as ex-mayors and governors.

Most businessmen avoid political life, however; they prefer to remain in the background. For political influence they rely on personal relations, on financial power, and on their possession of entrepreneurial skills required for economic growth and therefore for political success. Personal relations between business and party leaders vary over a wide range. But it is safe to say that Prime Ministers are not likely to make major decisions, certainly not in economic affairs, without consulting business magnates from the Tokyo and Kansai areas. Nor can large industrial concerns do without a Tokyo headquarters equipped with a fat expense account to facilitate their numerous political and governmental contacts.

This managerial elite is only in moderate degree a social

elite. A good family still counts, but the prime requisite to entry on the ladder is education. Younger members share above all the distinction of coming from Japan's front-rank universities. Other factors of talent and opportunity then condition success, and one, of course, is wealth. Yet the ownership of corporate wealth is increasingly institutionalized in banks, trust funds, and government agencies, so that Japan like other advanced industrial societies is becoming a "society beyond property." The "New Capitalism" is the term widely used to describe the postwar economy. Yet capitalism in reality describes better the nature of enterprise in the more traditional sectors of agriculture and small industry than the structure of authority within the managerial elites of corporate big business, with their involvements in politics and public decision-making.

Business is far from becoming socialized in the sense that the profit motive no longer dominates. Nevertheless, one can see working here, albeit more slowly, the logic of technological change familiar in the West. Decisions as to how best to make money are taken with increasing consideration of the public image, of long-run productivity and profit, and of the relation of business needs to national economic concerns. In a degree perhaps this has always been more true of Japanese business leaders than their Western counterparts, owing to their greater community orientation and the closer relations between government and business.

This is not to say that cooperation between industrial interests and the politicians who circulate among the top offices of the party and move in and out of the Cabinet has any smooth, monolithic character. Nor does it mean that the public interest is necessarily uppermost in the calculations of party or business leaders. To be sure, both groups share with the bureaucracy a basic consensus in support of the existing structure of power. If necessary to preserve it, elements of all three groups might go far to abridge parliamentary rule. Within this consensus, however, individuals and groups are free to maneuver in shifting coalitions of interest and ideology. Such rivalries make for a good deal of instability in political leadership at the top of the Liberal-Democratic Party (LDP). Often this brings uncertainty in national policy with respect to taxes, labor relations, trade treaties, and the like. The controversy over import liberalization and industrial structure described earlier is a case in point.

Thus neither business nor government speaks with one voice, singly or jointly. They form what has been called elsewhere a "homogeneous, bargaining leadership." Between business and the LDP are certain standing sources of friction. Guarding its political ascendancy in the Diet, the LDP often has to cater in some degree to interests other than those of industrialists. Farmers, for example, are now well organized and powerfully represented in the party. Government funds continue to be devoted to the public support of rice prices long after most businessmen ceased to find any public justification. More than this, business leaders are apt to find the style of politicians distasteful. They are dismayed by factional intrigue among the six or eight groups that maneuver within the LDP at the top for political advantage, and by decisions taken in Cabinets full of career politicians too often preoccupied with personal interest to the neglect of public responsibility. Political leaders, on their part, see businessmen as apt to be narrow in outlook, identifying public interest with profit advantage.

Then there is friction over political funds. Business concerns find they have to donate not only to the coffers of the LDP but to the campaign needs of individual party leaders and their factions. Some contribute to the Socialist Party as well—in amounts that are surprisingly large. In Japan no more than in most free societies has there been found a satisfactory solution to the financing of political parties, and the problem gets steadily worse as television and intensified political competition pushes up the cost of a Diet seat above the 30-million-yen ($83,000) mark. On the other hand, the financial dependence of the rank-and-file MP upon largesse from his well-heeled faction leader is the principal instrument of factional discipline. It also means party discipline when the leaders agree—and rigid deadlocks when they fail.

Seen in this light, both business and the Liberal-Democratic Party, and the top civil service as well, are networks of elitist elements, bargaining vigorously within a framework of a consensus on Japan's basic institutions. Built into the system are enough checks and balances to afford some range of choice to leaders at intermediate levels who serve as political brokers for wider segments of the electorate. Neither the LDP itself nor the business federations that cooperate with it, nor certainly the bureaucracy, could be described as representative in the sense of being openly, systematically accountable to wide constituencies. Still, they have moved a long way from the tightly disciplined, elitist authority structures of prewar Imperial Japan.

COUNTERVAILING FORCES FROM THE LEFT

Outside their own ranks, in turn, conservative leaders meet powerful constraints in the wider arena of parliamentary politics.

One power center of the old Japan is gone, to be sure. The military with their ultra-rightist allies have been purged from the scene, at least for a generation. This displacement, and with it the transfer of decision-making power in substantial degree from the bureaucracy to the Diet, is the major change from prewar days. It enlarges the influence of business in one dimension at least by removing one of its most formidable rivals (as well as erstwhile collaborator).

To the Left stand the parties representing the industrial working class, organized for political action as never before. Here, too, in the role of opinion-makers are the teachers and students, the editors, writers, and commentators so prolific on the air and in the press. With access to a full panoply of mass communications these intellectuals articulate and influence public attitudes, though otherwise they seem remote from the real levers of power in Japanese society. To an outside observer, what appears lacking for the building of consensus is a closer dialogue between intellectuals, on the one hand, and businessmen and their political allies, on the other, or between all of them and the new professional military. Many teachers and writers seem prisoners of their long-held views of Japanese society and slow to recognize the transformation before their eyes. Equally, the poverty of political discourse and imagination in the LDP reflects its isolation from the nation's intellectuals. Such compartmental-ized elites are characteristic of developing societies, but in developed Japan one looks for more lateral communication and mobility. Nothing seems more needed if public life is to become creative as well as orderly.

The Socialist Party is the chief political action group for the renovationist forces of the nation, supported as it is by Sōhyō (the General Council of Trade Unions). No major challenge is offered by its rival to the left, the Communist Party, though the latter's influence in union leadership is greater than its electoral weakness or its membership (95,000 in 1963) might suggest. Nor did the dissident right wing, the Democratic Socialist Party, carry much Socialist support away when it broke off in 1959. In 1964 the party line-up in the House of Representatives stood at 23 seats for the Demo-cratic Socialists and 144 for the Socialists, as against 294 for the Liberal-Democrats (and 5 for the Communists).

Factions of the Socialist Party continue in varying degrees to cling to dogmas of the class war at home and the threat of American imperialism abroad, fighting vigorous sectarian battles on points at issue. Under these ideological banners, too, they wage an unceasing struggle against the Liberal-Democratic majority in the Diet, using parliamentary obstruc-tion or extra-parliamentary violence as tactical calculations dictate. Personal and factional rivalries among Socialists are hardly less bitter than among conservatives. And they are so mixed with doctrinal antagonism as to make it hard to tell where one leaves off and the other begins. Together with still other rivalries among affiliated trade unions they make the whole Socialist movement an unstable coalition of forces that splits and merges and shifts its appointive leaders with the tides of political advantage. Meanwhile the Communists too opened a yawning cleavage within their party as the breach widened between Peking and Moscow in 1963-1964.

On the Left, nevertheless, as on the Right, are countervailing forces within and among the parties that now exert a powerful influence on the making of political decisions. Taken together, with all their weaknesses, these forces serve to disperse political power in Japan and widen the range of choice open to the electorate. One danger from all this is a certain headlessness, a tendency to veto government by countervailing blocs; much of the time since the war this has given a lustreless, leaderless tone to Japanese politics in curious contrast to the dynamism of its industrial progress. In the Diet, it is true, the balance is still heavily conservative. Neither in seats nor in popular vote are the radical parties left of center able to break through a ceiling of 35-40 percent. In local politics, their disadvantage is even greater. But the Socialists and Communists had developed tactics of mass agitation that work to modify conservative rule and keep the Liberal-Democratic Party at least in a state of apprehension lest it alienate public support. Critics of the Socialists remind them, of course, that for a working parliamentary system it is not enough to neutralize old centers of power, even by electoral process. What is needed is some more widely responsible, yet still coherent, center of decision-making. This has yet to come into being.[52]

THE GREAT MIDDLE

The Great Middle of Japanese politics comprises the mass of farmers, hosts of small shopkeepers and industrialists, and those large sections of the wage and salaried class that decline to identify themselves necessarily with either major party. Mostly they tend to be apathetic in politics except when some specific group interest is directly involved, or the sentiment of nationalism can be evoked (as in the Tokyo riots over the Security Treaty in 1960). Otherwise this public at large is less concerned with general political issues than with urban traffic congestion, the housing shortage, garbage disposal, typhoon relief, etc.

[52] For a closer study of labor and socialist thinking see "Labor and Politics in Postwar Japan," by R. A. Scalapino, Ch. XV, below.

In elections—and especially in the countryside—people still vote mainly at the behest of influential community leaders in a way reminiscent of traditional authority. Neither the Socialist Party nor even the Democratic Socialists have made any large inroads on the vote of peasants and small businessmen. Large sections of the salaried class are equally suspicious of their class slogans and disruptive tactics. It is these groups who give the LDP its consistent two-to-one majority in the Diet and its overwhelming preponderance in local affairs. Their politics are mainly non-ideological, the incremental politics of more or less. They are now organized in complex interest-group structures that represent them in local and national politics and afford useful two-way channels of communication with government.

Untested as yet is the success that the Socialist Party might achieve if it should move decisively away from its narrow orientation as a party of the "working class" and make a broad appeal to the masses in the middle. This price of political success its leaders have mostly been reluctant to pay. Yet the same circumstances that pushed their sister parties in Europe in this direction are now at work in Japan. With 40 percent of the electorate already voting to the Left, pragmatic calculations of power will move the party in the same direction provided this can be rationalized as involving no betrayal of its historic mission. In fact, theories of peaceful "structural reform" within the existing system began to gain ascendancy in the party in the early sixties. A straw in the wind is the "new vision of Socialism" enunciated by the party's Secretary General Eda Saburō, in 1962, as a move to disarm public suspicion of the party's radicalism. The new vision combines America's high living standard, Russia's social security, Britain's parliamentary democracy, and Japan's "peace Constitution." Such eclecticism can be attacked as sloganeering devoid of analytical content, but hardly as revolutionary Marxism!

If the Socialists have potential appeals that they are only now commencing to exploit, the Liberal-Democrats too are not without reserves to draw upon. They possess resources in money and organization far beyond what they had yet needed to stay in office. They control the spending Ministries, too, and can resort to the public pork barrel as need be when votes are at stake—as in rural relief expenditures, support prices for rice, loans to small businessmen, etc.

Liberal-Democratic leaders take an essentially pragmatic view of politics. Rarely do they voice any coherent philosophy of public interest. But they make pronouncements from time to time that look generally to the model of the British Conservative Party in affirming the middle-class welfare state. Of course, they would like to keep on making the policies, and they would like the policies to cost as little as possible. Their norms of welfare are hardly those of the Socialists. Even so, social welfare outlays under their rule were raised to 7 percent of national income in 1961; the land reform has now a built-in permanency; unions remain powerful, with over nine million members; and no determined campaign has been mounted to reverse most other basic reforms of the Occupation. The pressures of political competition in Japan's "one-and-one-half-party system"—to borrow R. A. Scalapino's term—are slowly creating the profile of a welfare state, i.e., private enterprise plus a widening sphere of social responsibility. Prime Ministers from the LDP resemble in many respects their British counterparts in the way they seek and wield power. As yet, however, they face no such formidable opposition as the British Labor Party.

To conclude, Japanese democracy has been consolidated at a level far beyond its prewar attainment. Its success owes much to "high-pitched" economic growth since 1950, and it in turn has made an essential contribution to that growth. Political life, though still strongly oligarchic, is more open and competitive than before, reflecting the spirit of a more affluent, equalitarian society. Yet it still lacks legitimation to the point where its future is assured. Extremists on the Left and Right make use of its freedom with the avowed purpose of suppressing it if they get the chance. And too few even among its well-wishers seem to realize how quickly such forces unopposed can destroy the system which has taken so long to build.

If democracy should fail in Japan it seems that it will come about through two unhappy developments in combination:

First, deepening anxieties over the nation's external security could again undermine civil liberties and free government. It is no accident that the worse riots and assassinations of 1960-1961 were precipitated over issues of foreign policy. Nationalism has always been the foe of Japanese liberalism. It could destroy it again in a crisis over foreign dangers, real or imagined.

Second, internal tensions generated by the ills of modern industrial society as it comes of age are still acute. Capital and labor are only on the threshold of evolving a constitutional order for the handling of disputes. Such issues, too, could break down civil government by parliamentary process if the economy for any reason should cease to grow. When Left-wing bitterness against the Establishment bursts out in violence, Right-wing extremists are not slow to respond with their own brand of terror. Indeed, violence from the Right, if history teaches anything, is a threat that the Socialists would do well not to provoke.

Whether such forces may again subvert parliamentary government no one can say for certain. The drift of party politics in the second decade following World War II is encouraging. Slowly the Liberal Democrats are being pressed to take over the programs of moderate Socialists and make them their own; this is the price of staying in power. Meanwhile the Socialists, too, are being pressed by the logic of events toward the center. Intellectually their old dogmas asserting the impoverishment of the proletariat are no longer relevant, if they ever were. Politically they can hardly remain content with the minority role to which they confine themselves by a narrow class appeal, when a broader platform would put them within reach of power.

In short, the same forces that have operated in the West

are also at work in Japan to build a parliamentary order supported by the rising well-being and consensus of a middle-class society. The process is far from complete and is capable of interruption. But it is already well advanced. The great question mark is not within Japan so much as in the international sphere. Can the world be made secure enough, and Japan sufficiently integrated, to stabilize her new political and industrial order?

Josef Stalin forecast after World War II that Japan and Germany would prove to be the Achilles heel of the non-Communist alliance. Their victorious capitalist rivals would never be able, he said, to fit them back into a cooperative, prosperous relationship. The record since 1952 is a denial of this forecast, and a promise for the future. It gives substance to Prime Minister Ikeda's vision of Japan standing with North America and Western Europe as "three pillars of the Free World."

CHAPTER XI

Economic Miracles and Japan's Income-Doubling Plan

MARTIN BRONFENBRENNER

"The figures prosper; the people suffer."
—GEORGE PAPANDREOU

WHILE OVERSEAS "economic miracles" of "free enterprise" are accepted less credulously in the U.S. of 1964 than three or four years previously, they retain a measure of interest in view of America's laggard performance in economic growth and high employment. The Japanese case is of especial interest because it now purports to combine "free enterprise" with a 10-year "doubling-income plan," and also because the resulting boom has not yet altered appreciably the drift to Socialism associated with the falling average age and rising urbanization of the Japanese population.[1]

This study supports a minority of students of contemporary Japan in believing that a relatively simple and aggregative "dynamic growth model," specifically the one associated with Sir Roy Harrod in Britain and Professor Evsey Domar in the United States, can go a long way toward explaining what has happened in Japan and indicates some likely trends in the near future.[2]

[1] See Herbert Passin, "The Sources of Protest in Japan," *American Political Science Review* (June 1962), pp. 391-93, for a statistical summary.

[2] Professors Anne Krueger (Minnesota), Y. T. Kuark (Denver) and Dr. Robert Z. Aliber (Committee for Economic Development) have been particularly insistent that I broaden my analysis to include models more complex than the Harrod-Domar ones. I have also profited from critiques by, and arguments with, Professors William W. Lockwood (Princeton), Ohkawa Kazushi (Hitotsubashi), Harry T. Oshima (Hawaii), Hugh T. Patrick (Yale), and Mr. Minabe Shigeo (Kobe).

How Unique is the Miracle?

How miraculous, after all, is the Japanese record since 1953, in view of the entire sweep of Japanese economic history since the Perry visit a century earlier? And in what sense, if any, can a doubling-income plan be more than a pious hope or projection in a capitalistic society like the Japanese? This section attempts to answer each of these questions.

As part of their forthcoming *magnum opus* on the last century of Japanese economic history, the international partnership of Professors Ohkawa Kazushi and Henry Rosovsky have compared income growth rates in Japan's four major booms since 1900.[3] (Table 1.)

TABLE 1

<small>GROWTH RATES IN FOUR JAPANESE BOOM PERIODS, 1905-1960</small>

	Russo-Japanese War	World War I	Manchurian Expansion	Post-Korea
Growth Rate of Gross Domestic Product	1905–12	1912–19	1931–38	1953–60
Average	6.7%	7.0%	7.5%	9.3%
Maximum	16.5% (05–06)	18.8% (18–19)	11.0% (31–32)	17.9% (58–59
Minimum	–3.0% (09–10)	–0.9% (12–13)	2.5% (33–34)	3.3% (57–58

SOURCE: Ohkawa and Rosovsky, *op.cit.*, Table 1, p. 579.

The first three periods are associated, successively, with pent-up demand after the Russo-Japanese War; with Japan's quasi-neutrality during World War I; and with yen devaluation and Manchurian adventures in the 1930's. The most recent boom, despite feed-back from the Cold War, is the least dependent of the four on Japanese involvement in international crisis situations; it is the most massive of the four and exemplifies greater evenness and continuity. The minimum figure (for 1957-1958), for example, exceeds the American average for the late 1950's and early 1960's.

[3] Ohkawa Kazushi and Henry Rosovsky, "Recent Japanese Growth in Historical Perspective," *American Economic Review*, LIII, 2 (May 1963), 578-88.

There is some doubt as to the representativeness of the 1953 starting date. Recovery from wartime destruction may still have been incomplete,[4] or the Japanese Government during the Occupation (1945-1952) may have understated Japanese recovery in the interests of greater American aid and lower "termination of war" expenses. Offsetting this, however, is the special readjustment forced upon the Japanese economy by the reduction of American procurement following the Korean War and the transfer of American armed forces from Japanese to other Asian bases.

Four reasons seem to explain why the boom has not yet slowed down the shift to the left in Japan's post-Korean voting patterns. (1) There is doubt as to the boom's permanence, including the realism of the doubling-income plan. (2) There is suspicion that prosperity is still linked, even in Japan, with armaments and war preparations. (3) There is dissatisfaction with the distribution of the gains from the boom, too much going to the holders of stocks and urban lands. (4) As in the underdeveloped countries, expectations have risen along with incomes. (See also p. 546 below.)

[4] "Professor Milton Friedman has recently stated . . . that he knows of a sure formula for promoting rapid growth. Destroy the greater part of a nation's fixed capital in war activity and dislocate the whole economic structure. Eventual recovery from this chaotic state of affairs will be rapid, giving a growth rate of 8-10 per cent annually. West Germany, Japan, and the Soviet Union are striking examples of this type of growth. Perhaps there are structural changes in each case, allowing the countries concerned to grow at rates far above their secular paths for a long time." Lawrence R. Klein, "A Model of Japanese Economic Growth. 1878-1937," *Econometrica* (July 1961), p. 291.

Without commenting on "Friedman's Law" in general, we may point out that Japanese real national income surpassed its highest prewar level in 1952, while real income per gainfully occupied individual did so in 1955. Ohkawa et al., *The Growth Rate of the Japanese Economy Since 1878* (Tokyo: Kinokuniya, 1957), Appendix Table 2, p. 234.

Klein's latest econometric model for Japan abandons trend lines for a dummy variable, which is zero for prewar and unity for postwar years. L. R. Klein and Shinkai Yōichi, "An Econometric Model of Japan, 1930-1959," *International Economic Review* (January 1963), pp. 8-10.

Is It a Plan?

In discussing the nature of the doubling-income plan, the first thing to remember is that it is not the first but possibly the twelfth such plan since the surrender of 1945 by Professor Tsuru's reckoning,[5] and that its immediate predecessor, covering the period 1958-1962 inclusive, had proved overly cautious. A full English text, in which a few inconsistencies remain, has been published under the auspices of the official Japanese *Keizai kikaku chō* (Economic Planning Agency, or simply EPA).[6] It calls for a doubling of the Japanese national income over the 10-year period 1961-1970, or an average growth rate of 7.2 percent compounded annually. One of Premier Ikeda Hayatō's most influential economic advisers, Dr. Shimomura Osamu of the Japan Development Bank, believes that even this rate is too low; an increase to 2.5 percent or even three times the 1961 level is possible by 1970, in his view.[7]

But before passing to the "growth," or, as it is sometimes called, the "Shimomura" controversy, let us return to the main path of this argument: In what sense, if any, can a doubling-income plan be more than a pious hope or projection in a capitalistic society like the Japanese?

Economic plans can be subdivided into five categories, although the boundaries between them are blurred to such an

[5] Tsuro Shigeto, "Formal Planning Divorced from Action—Japan," in Everett E. Hagen, ed., *Planning Economic Development* (Homewood, Ill.; Irwin, 1963), ch. 5, p. 119. Shinohara Miyōhei," Evolution of Economic Plans in the Japanese Economy" (unpublished Ms.), sets the figure at 15.

[6] Economic Planning Agency, Japanese Government, *New Economic Plan of Japan (1961-1970)* (Tokyo: *Japan Times,* 1961).

[7] Two of Shimomura's larger works are *Nihon keizai seichō ron* [An Essay on Japanese Economic Growth] Tokyo, 1962, and *Keizai seichō jitsugen no tame ni* [For the Realization of Economic Growth] (Tokyo, 1959). His essay, "Consumer Price Problems" appeared in English in *Oriental Economist* (November and December 1963). Another translation, "Basic Problems of Economic Growth Policy," was prepared under the auspices of the Indian Statistical Institute (Translation Series No. 37; Calcutta, 1961).

extent that classification is occasionally difficult. (The French speak of our first category as *planification impérative,* and lump the next two together as *planification indicative.*)

1. "A plan is a command." This quotation, purportedly from Stalin, applies to a centralized macro- and micro-economic plan in a society dominated, like the Soviet or the Chinese, by its public sector. Such a plan is reducible to an input-output table, plus a firing squad, plus a monopoly of propaganda.

2. Somewhat less extreme, and also less detailed in its micro-economics, is the concept of a plan as a set of directives or guidelines for public agencies operating direct controls over credit, foreign exchange, rationed materials, and the like. Planning of this type is commonly found in a society which is attempting a major structural change, as from light to heavy industry or from a small to a large public sector. Its attitude toward existing private industry is more often directed to prevent expansion of "undesirable" activities than to promote expansion of "desirable" ones. The Second and Third Plans of India fall into this category.

3. A step closer to economic liberalism, and still less detailed in its micro-economics, is a plan viewed as a guide to the private planning of private business. It encourages the kinds of expansion that firms make more readily if their customers, suppliers, and competitors are expanding too than if undertaken independently. It also insures them against "bottlenecks" of social overhead capital in the public sector. Planning of this type is definitely expansionary in its approach to private industry as a whole, although it includes public projects competitive with one or another branch of enterprise. French planning under the technical aegis of Monnet and the political aegis of DeGaulle appears to be predominantly of this type.

4. Almost entirely aggregative (macro-economic) are the monetary and fiscal plans of the American Council of Economic Advisers, which aim at full employment, price stability, and an adequate growth rate for the economy as a whole.

5. At the opposite extreme from the "command" type of micro-economic centralized planning are the systems of targets and projections of the "what if" type, as practiced by unofficial agencies like the American National Planning Association.

On this scale, Japanese planning as envisaged by Shimomura falls into the fourth category of aggregative planning only, which depends on private enterprise for its detailed implementation. (A special case, in 1963-1964, was interest rates, which Shimomura favored lowering, even at some cost in direct controls, to reduce capital costs in export and import-competing industries.) For this reason, namely Shimomura's antipathy to detailed *dirigisme*, the Japanese term *keikaku* is sometimes translated as "projection" rather than "planning" when his influence is recognized. On the other hand, the Finance Ministry and the Ministry of International Trade and Industry (MITI) are more impressed with French *planification*—our third category, a detailed guide to the private planning of private firms. In the EPA itself, there is some planning of our second type, directives or guidelines for direct controls in restraint of the private sector, since many Japanese economists, in the universities particularly, advocate planning on this level. The combination or "mix" of Shimomura *plus* the Ministries *plus* the EPA is extraordinarily difficult to categorize or pigeon-hole, and many observers have mistakenly blamed Shimomura, because of his personal prominence, for enlarging direct controls which he would have preferred to minimize.

A Little Growth Theory

Using an elementary production function like $Y=f(N,K)$, where Y is income, N employment, and K the capital stock (somehow defined), in a regime where the government budget and international balance permit equality of private saving and investment, a Harrod-type equation for the growth rate G of the national income Y:

$$\bar{G} = \frac{dY}{Y} = \frac{S}{Y}\frac{dY}{I} \quad \text{or simply } G = a\sigma dt \qquad (1)$$

Here S is saving, I investment, a the ratio of savings to income, and σdt the productivity of investment (df/dK or dY/I) per time period.

If we write (1) as

$$\frac{dY}{Y} - a\sigma dt = 0$$

the resulting differential equation has the solution:

$$Y = Y_0 e^{a\sigma t} \qquad (2)$$

where Y_0 is national income at the start of the growth process.

At the same time, we may differentiate the production function to obtain

$$\frac{dY}{Y} = \left(\frac{\delta Y}{\delta N} \frac{N}{Y} \right) \frac{dN}{N} + \left(\frac{\delta Y}{\delta K} \frac{K}{Y} \right) \frac{I}{K}$$

remembering that net investment (I) is by definition the increment to the capital stock (K). Under pure competition, the expressions in parentheses are the relative shares s_N and s_K of labor and capital, respectively. More generally (dN/N) and (I/K) may be written G_N and G_K, the respective growth rates of labor and capital. Using G for the growth rate of income as before, we have:

$$G = s_N G_N + s_K G_K \qquad (3)$$

A similar process yields a relation between σ and the ordinary "marginal productivity" of capital ($\delta Y/\delta K$):

$$\sigma = \frac{dY}{I} = \frac{\delta Y}{\delta K} + \frac{\delta Y}{\delta N} \frac{dN}{I} \qquad (4)$$

so that σ exceeds the marginal efficiency of investment and the rate of interest if, as is normally the case, investment requires additional net employment to put it to productive use.

Domar has shown, using elementary Keynesian analysis, that investment has a "multiplier" effect on income equal to (dI/a). Its effect on output is $I\sigma dt$. Along an equilibrium growth path, the two expressions are equal. Solving the resulting differential equation, (dI/a) − $I\sigma dt = 0$, we obtain an equilibrium growth rate for investment paralleling (2) for income, and suggesting a constant capital-output ratio:

$$I = I_0 e^{a\sigma t} \qquad (5)$$

The Harrod and Domar equilibrium growth paths are however unstable. If income and investment exceed their equilibrium values (2,5), the excess will increase aggregate investment demand more than aggregate supply, driving income
and investment in the next period still further above (2) and
(5), respectively. If income and investment fall below their
equilibrium values, similarly, a cumulative fall is set off in
the absence of counteracting measures.

Most of this is common knowledge among economists; all
of it is both general and abstract. The issues for Japan concentrate, in my view, around the σ term, the productivity of
capital. Can it be maintained or even raised as capital ac-
cumulates year after year? Or will diminishing returns take
hold, possibly in the Marxian form of a falling profit rate?
[If a falls, the growth rate will presumably fall, as per equations (2) and (5)]. Furthermore, if σ is maintained or raised,
will purchasing power be adequate to absorb the increased
output and to avoid cumulative decline, on terms not involving downward pressure on the saving ratio a? In Marxian
terms, can Japanese planning avoid simultaneously the alleged capitalist tendencies to over-production and to a falling
rate of profit, alternatively or in combination?

Three Digressions

Before tackling these basic issues, however, let us digress
for a trio of minor ones. (1) In terms of formulas (2) and
(4), wherein lies the formal explanation of the difference between Japanese and American growth rates since the Korean
War? (2) Should the Japanese spurts outlined in Table 1
be regarded as disequilibrium or equilibrium phenomena, as
departures from long-term growth rates or as *shifts* in these
rates? (3) How is the current Japanese boom related to the
long-run Japanese growth rate? Following as it does upon
some 15 years of wartime and postwar dislocation, when will
it cross the long-term trend extrapolated, and what significance may be attached to the point of intersection?

1. The main difference between the Japanese and American results for recent years lies in the higher capital produc-

tivity (now called more frequently the *lower* "capital co-efficient") in Japan. This condition contrasts with the pre-war situation, when the Japanese capital productivity was lower and the Japanese capital coefficient higher than the American.[8] Estimates for the 1950's by Professor Komiya are reproduced in Table 2.

TABLE 2

COMPONENTS OF GROWTH RATE IN REAL GROSS DOMESTIC PRODUCT, JAPAN AND U.S.A., 1950-1960

		Japan	U.S.A.
Gross Domestic Saving Ratio	a	29.9%	18.3%
Gross Capital Coefficient	$1/\sigma$	3.1	5.4
Gross Capital Productivity	σ	0.32	0.19
Growth Rate	$G=a\sigma$	9.5%	3.3%

SOURCE: Komiya Ryūtarō, *Taxation and Capital Formation in Post-war Japan* (Mimeographed: Tokyo, 1963), Tables 2, 4, pp. 4f., 13.

Turning to the capital productivity estimates (σ) and equation (4), the Japanese-American differential may be due to the following factors: (a) Higher marginal productivity of capital ($\delta Y/\delta K$) in Japan. This is attributable to the higher Japanese ratio of labor to capital, the high American loading on long-range research and development (of which Japan, too, takes advantage), the American practice of rapid depreciation and obsolescence, and the higher degree of excess capacity in America. (b) Concentration on output-increasing investment in Japan, as against cost-reducing investment in America. This results in higher employment factors (dN/I) in Japan. The (dN/I) term may even turn negative when investment results in net labor displacement, as in some auto-mation cases. On the other hand, there is no doubt that the marginal productivity of labor ($\delta Y/\delta N$) has remained higher in America than in Japan.

Table 3, derived from the Japanese *Keizai Hakusho* (Eco-nomic White Paper) for 1962, presents similar information in marginal form.

[8] Comparisons of capital coefficients between Japan (1928-40) and the U.S.A. (1939) are available in Ohkawa et al., *op.cit.*, pp. 223-27.

TABLE 3

Percentage Distribution of Increments of GNP in Japan and U.S. after Korean War (Approximations)

	Percentage of GNP Increment	
Economic Sector	Japan, 1955–61	U.S., 1953–59
Personal Consumption	32	68
Private Domestic Investment	54	22
Fixed Capital Formation	(46)	(10)
Inventory Investment	(8)	(12)
Government Expenditures	7	5
Exports	7	5
Total	100	100

Source: Toshio Ono, "Japan's Economy and Regional Co-operation," *American Economist* (December 1962), p. 7. See also Economic Planning Agency, "Report of National Income Accounting Research Committee," *Economic Bulletin* 12 (December 1962), Table I-9, p. 11.

2. Professor Shinohara Miyōhei, in his *Growth and Cycles in the Japanese Economy*,[9] treats Japan's four great booms as disequilibrium phenomena, an interpretation fitting the unstable or "knife-edge" character of the Harrod-Domar equilibrium path of equations (2) and (5).[10] Two quotations from Shinohara summarize his position, although the italics are ours:[11]

"In the upswing of the long cycle, Japanese firms always expand their investment at an extraordinary tempo, thus bringing about a steep rise in the investment—GNP ratio. This entails a balance of payments difficulty as well as over-capacity in the end, leading to a situation in which wage-cut,

[9] Tokyo, 1962. The Japanese version (which omits Part III) is entitled *Nihon keizai no seichō to junkan*.

[10] Instability arises because movements above the equilibrium path give rise to shortages of goods, which in turn inspire more rapid production (and vice versa). A number of writers, the best known being Robert M. Solow, have shown that this instability may disappear when account is taken of substitution between capital and labor in the productive process. Solow, "A Contribution to the Theory of Economic Growth," *Quarterly Journal of Economics* (Feb. 1956), esp. pp. 65-73.

[11] Shinohara, *op. cit.*, pp. ii, 107f.

price deflation, and even a sharp deterioration in the terms of trade must ensue. Investment boom—over-capacity—price deflation—deterioration of terms of trade—strengthening of export growth potential; such was the sequence making up the long swings. . . . In other words, we see a process of rapid economic growth through explosive investment behavior and downward price adjustment. It seems to be important to recognize the role of such a *disequilibrating mechanism* in causing the exceptionally high rate of growth, for *without this unstable mechanism we could not have attained such a rapid development. . . .*

". . . Japan's high rate of growth was attained only through such a *disequilibrating process* as a sequence of excessive investment, over-capacity, price deflation, and the aggravation of the terms of trade. This is a *high rate of growth by means of an unstable oscillation of investment and prices,* and *not as smooth-going a process as is formulated in modern economic growth theory."*

Other Japanese economists dispute this interpretation of Japan's earlier boom periods, but we shall question only the application of this analysis to the current "economic miracle" —Chapter 5 of the Shinohara book. Our differences with Shinohara are presented diagrammatically on the equilibrium growth paths of Figure 1. If we understand Shinohara correctly, he interprets the points P_i on the upper line (more rapid growth) as merely unstable departures of increasing magnitude from the lower one (long-term growth). An alternative interpretation is that they lie on a new and higher growth path, resulting from a long- or short-run rise of the productivity of capital from σ_1 to σ_2.

3. Japan's long-term growth rate, shown in logarithmic form as line I in Figure 2, proceeded at an average annual rate of approximately 4.3 percent over the 60-year period 1878-1938.[12] At this point, represented by t_1 in the figure, the Japanese GNP first stopped growing and then fell off rapidly until t_2, in consequence of World War II and the

[12] Ohkawa, et al., *op. cit.,* Tables 6-7, pp. 21, 24.

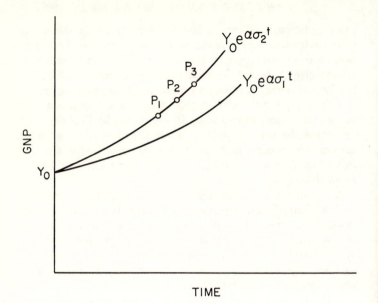

FIGURE 1

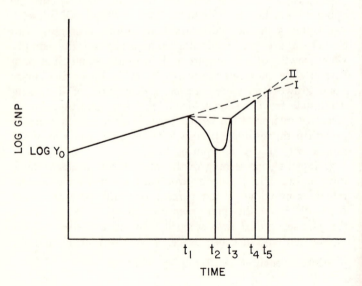

FIGURE 2

strain of immediate postwar reconstruction. (In the diagram t_2 is 1945, but the decline in GNP continues for some months thereafter.) The subsequent "Friedman's Law" recovery, furthered by American aid and the Korean War, brought GNP back to its 1937-1938 level by approximately 1953 (t_3 on the diagram). Subsequent growth has proceeded along line II to t_4 at an average growth rate of 9.3 percent as estimated by Ohkawa and Rosovsky, but still below the extrapolation of line I. When lines I and II are both extrapolated, they are expected to cross at t_5, which has been estimated as "some time in the mid-sixties." (Let us set it at 1965.) What is the significance of the intersection at t_5? Are we to agree with Klein that the long-term trend of line I, adjusted for structural changes to yield a 5.3 percent growth rate between 1958-1962 and 1968-1972, provides "a better framework for future planning than does the official program with the target of doubling real national income in ten years?"[13] Or should we, with Shimomura,[14] discard all such analysis as unduly mechanical and follow line II where it leads, or better, follow the analysis which has resulted in this higher growth rate without concern for the prewar situation?

Doubling Income—Domestic Strategy

We resume our main theme, the strategy of the Japanese doubling-income plan itself, in terms of equation (1), by which the income growth rate is the product of the saving ratio a and the capital productivity σ.

As regards the saving ratio, nothing more is involved than a holding action, despite "demonstration effects" and the extension of consumer credit. That is to say, the plan anticipates a to be maintained at its level, extraordinarily high for a low-

[13] Klein, *op. cit.*, p. 291f. Friedman rationalizes this view (in conversation) by relating the growth rate inversely to the rate of change in a "technological gap" between Japan and the West, with a 3 or 4% rate associated with a constant gap (zero rate of change). Friedman's argument implies that line II of Figure 2 applies only to periods of rapid closing of the technological gap, which must naturally end quite soon.

[14] Shimomura, interview with the writer, May 19, 1962.

income country,[15] or even to continue rising with the aid of a steady shift from progressive to indirect and payroll taxes,[16] while public expenditure is held at an approximately constant percentage of the gross national product. In consequence, the Japanese, especially the corporation and the businessman, has enjoyed a direct-tax rate reduction every year since 1950, which has gone in part to keep up the saving ratio.

Active Japanese development policy is concerned with raising σ, the productivity of investment (or, as more commonly put, in lowering the capital coefficient $1/\sigma$), while minimizing simultaneously the twin threats of excess capacity and a falling rate of profit. A key role is played by an optimistic assumption as to the elasticity of Japanese exports with respect to the total volume of world trade. (See the next section.)

It is well known, and illustrated for Japan by the Tsuru-Ohkawa data cited in note 8, that the productivity of investment in fixed plant and equipment exceeds that of investment in inventories. In terms of equation (4), this inequality holds even when the marginal productivities of the two types of investment are equal, so long as the incremental employment (dN/I) is greater for fixed capital than for inventories. In Japan this may not have been true in the immediate postwar

[15] Shinohara (*op. cit.*, ch. 10) ascribes this high saving ratio to the high proportion of independent entrepreneurs in the Japanese labor force, to the Japanese practice of channeling large amounts of labor income in semi-annual bonuses whose amounts cannot be anticipated with any precision, to the incomplete Japanese social-security system, and to the lack of consumer or even mortgage credit for the ordinary Japanese.

[16] Professor Kogiku and I summarized in 1957 the early stages of this development, which also includes special privileges for interest income, dividend income, depreciation, and capital gains, as a retreat from the "equitable" tax policies of the American Occupation to the "capital-formation" emphasis of Japanese business circles and the Liberal Democratic Party. See M. Bronfenbrenner and K. C. Kogiku, "The Aftermath of the Shoup Tax Reforms," *National Tax Journal* (September and December, 1957). Later summaries are found in the Japanese Ministry of Foreign Affairs pamphlet, *Factors in Japan's Economic Growth* (1962), pp. 16-18, and in Komiya Ryūtarō, *Taxation and Capital Formation in Post-war Japan* (*op. cit., passim*).

period, when the retention and payment of "surplus labor" were commonplace in domestic industry, but was more than half true by 1953 and is certainly true in 1963.

It is this statistical truism which Shimomura proposes to utilize in maintaining the Japanese growth rate. He wishes to see Japan's controls over credit and foreign exchange eased materially as regards the construction and equipping of new industrial facilities. For fixed capital during the cost-cutting and automating decade of the 1950's, Shimomura, playing the role of a Japanese Colin Clark, estimates capital coefficients of 0.9 to 1.2 (σ from 0.83 to 1.11) with a one-year time lag; his estimates are based on American, British, and West German experience, as well as Japanese.[17] There has arisen a so-called "inventory controversy" regarding Shimomura's figures, particularly regarding the extent to which they were biased by inflation of industrial prices.

Liberalizing foreign exchange will curb inventory speculation (which has been concentrated in brief intervals of freedom). This in turn, Shimomura's supporters believe, will change the investment mix and raise the productivity of investment as a whole. In the same way, incidentally, Shimomura believes he can minimize Japan's recurrent foreign-exchange crises.[18] "Bureaucratic" elements in both the Finance Min-

---

[17] Shimomura, "Basic Problems of Economic Growth Policy," pp. 7-10. For criticisms, see Shinohara, *op. cit.*, pp. 122-26. Shimomura also presents a subsidiary argument, which Takahashi Akira (East-West Center, Honolulu) has analyzed in an unpublished paper. In this confirmatory argument, Shimomura obtains his capital coefficient of 1.2 by multiplying an average profit rate (30%) and an average value-added-total profit ratio (4.0). (Both figures are for Japanese manufacturing industry in the 1950's.)

[18] On these crises, the London *Economist* (March 8, 1958) expresses the conventional view:

"As the hectic boom [of 1955-57] progressed, the swollen demands of industry for imported raw materials came up headlong against Japan's inability to pay for them by selling enough exports. As the reserves of foreign exchange fell, the government was forced to slow the economy down.

"This experience was a sample of the dilemma Japan faces. The nation's industry can give the Japanese a steadily improving standard

istry and MITI, however, would prefer to accomplish the same purpose by tightening controls, avoiding free periods, and postponing liberalization. The situation is not clear, but Shimomura is not to blame for the policies of his intellectual opponents.

Returning to equation (5) and Figure 1, the question arises: Will demand continue available, at profitable prices, for the output of Shimomura's stepped-up σ? To paraphrase Domar's statement of the saving-investment dilemma:[19] If today's saving is not invested today, we have not growth but depression today. If today's saving is invested today, there will be excess capacity tomorrow, and depression the day after. Shimomura has been criticized for evading this issue, e.g., by Kurihara:[20]

"The Shimomura model takes the conditions of demand as given and concentrates on the supply side—as if supply created its own demand *à la* Say's Law, or . . . as if the Japanese economy were so completely planned as to equate its demand and supply sides as a matter of course. To be sure, the shortage of capital . . . made the Japanese economy temporarily and understandably behave . . . like an under-developed economy needing . . . productive capacity [more] than effective demand. But that abnormal period is over, and the Japanese economy is once again confronted with the common problem

of life—if Japan can pay for enough raw material from abroad. If it cannot, the same process may occur again and again; first an acceleration of investment and production, to keep pace with the population statistics, and then a painful thud as the balance of payments runs into trouble."

Shimomura regards this as unduly pessimistic. He argues that this year's inventory imports are reflected automatically in next year's exports, so that most payments crises can be taken in stride.

[19] E. D. Domar, "The Problem of Capital Accumulation," in *Essays in the Theory of Economic Growth* (New York: Oxford University Press, 1957), p. 118.

[20] Kenneth K. Kurihara, "Observations on Japan's Ten-Year Growth Plan," *Kyklos* (1962, Fasc. 4), pp. 789f. (Kurihara goes on to derive a less aggregative version of our equation (5) in his (1.5) appended to note 13 on p. 790.)

of all advanced market economies, namely: that of equilibrating effective demand and productive capacity."

The doubling-income plan itself includes a balance of aggregate income and expenditures (reproduced as Table 4);

TABLE 4

INCOME AND EXPENDITURE TARGETS FOR THE JAPANESE ECONOMY, 1970, IN F.Y. 1958 PRICES
(billions of yen)

Gross National			Gross National		
Product		29,727.9	Expenditures		29,726.9
National Income		21,323.2	Consumption		
Primary Industry	2,161.4		Expenditures		17,484.4
Secondary "	8,241.1		Personal	15,116.6	
Tertiary "	8,471.9		Government	2,367.8	
Public Utilities	2,448.8		Investment Expenditures		8,283.2
Adjustment Items		4,676.8	Plant and		
Overseas Payments		3,726.9	Equipment	4,374.8	
			Residential	992.6	
			Inventory Change	856.5	
			Government	2,059.3	
			Overseas Receipts		3,959.5

SOURCE: Economic Planning Agency, Japanese Government, *New Long-Range Economic Plan of Japan (1961-1970)*, pp. 14f. (Inconsistencies in original source.)
NOTE: The corresponding GNP figure for the base year (the average of fiscal years 1956-58) was 11,051.8 million. (The Japanese fiscal year runs from April 1 to March 31.)

it relies heavily on increased exports.[21] The Shimomura solution is not, however, apparent on these documents, which he did not himself prepare; but Kurihara and other critics are perhaps too harsh when they doubt that such a solution exists. It is actually simple—to cut taxes and/or expand credits to whatever extent may be necessary to maintain demand.

In the Ministries, however, the bureaucratic planners have apparently preferred reliance upon the peculiar institutions of the Japanese *Yūdō keizai* (guided economy) to permit the country to live with periodic bouts of excess capacity— meaning, to endure them with minimal discouragement for

[21] Economic Planning Agency, *op. cit.*, Tables 3-4, pp. 14f.

new investment until the excess is liquidated by exports and/or by further growth. Such new investment, however, plays in the short run the role of private pyramid-building, since it is of immediate value for its a-effect (on income and purchasing power) rather than it σ-effect (on output).

What are these "peculiar institutions of the Guided Economy"? They vary from one industry to another, but in general and in resistance to Occupation nudges toward free competition, they consist of alliances between trade associations (cartels) and the appropriate sections of a Ministry, normally MITI. These alliances divide responsibility for maintaining profitable prices and allocating output limitations in case excess capacity plagues the industry. When output quotas or reductions are imposed on individual firms, as often happens during recessions, a traditional basis has been the maintenance of "historical" market shares. More recently, capacity has been taken into greater account, so that in hard times each firm works at approximately the same percentage of its rated capacity.

The larger the weight attached to capacity (as against market shares) in a given industry's "guidance" pattern, the greater is the temptation for *katō-kyōsō* (excessive competition) to expand capacity and insure each firm against decline in its relative position in its industry during the next recession; and conversely, the greater is the danger of losing one's market share, in bad times or good, by what would seem in a freer economy "sound" investment policy. By carrot rather than stick, the Japanese firm is kept under constant expansionary pressure—but by Ministry bureaucrats, not by Shimomura.

Such a system of "constant expansionary pressure," in which Shimomura, like Macbeth "Wouldst not play false, and yet wouldst wrongly win," retains the Domar a-effect, and indeed permits a (the savings ratio) to rise. The same system minimizes any indirect Domar σ-effect on profits through over-capacity, while advancing technology and conservative inventory policy keep σ itself at a high level. The system maintains $a\sigma$, the growth rate. Hence come investment, employment, and, of course, growth—of productive capacity, if not of final output. The piling up of capacity in advance of demand is comparable—however "practical" it may be—to other sorts of made-work, public and private, including leaf-raking, boondoggling, and pyramid-building, except for one important special feature. It almost entirely avoids deleterious effects on the morale of individual workers. Resources may be misallocated in this system of private pyramid-building, but they are not thrown away; also human skills are maintained intact.

Candor impels the admission that, judging by results, the system of private pyramid-building is far from completely developed. In the relative recession of the last half of the 1962-1963 fiscal year, for example, a Bank of Japan report[22] accordingly indicated declines of 3-4 percent in both inventory and plant and equipment investment. Interestingly enough, a *rise* in completely new investment was contemplated over the 1962 level; the decline involved discontinuance or scaling down of projects already under way.

The Ministry of International Trade and Industry includes in its monthly publication *Tsūsan tōkei* two groups of quarterly series from which estimates of the changing rate of capacity utilization in the manufacturing sector of Japan's economy can be estimated.[23] (Table 5.) One group is a set of quotients of index numbers of *output* to index numbers of *capacity*, by industries, with a 1955 base of 100. (1955 was a year of mild recession.) The higher these quotients, the higher the rate of capacity utilization (as compared with 1955) and vice versa.[24] The second group of statistical series consists of

[22] Statistics Department, Bank of Japan, *Ōyō kigyō no tanki keizai kansoku* (Short-Term Economic Survey of Principal Enterprises), No. 23. This report includes forecasts for January-June, 1963), pp. 5f.

[23] A selection of these figures is also available in EPA, *Economic Survey of Japan (1961-62)* (Tokyo: *Japan Times*, 1962), Annex 23, p. 400. Detail on concepts and methods is available in a MITI publication, *Waga kuni seizō kōgyō no seisan nōryoku to shihon kōzō* (Productive Efficiency and Capital Structure in Japanese Manufacturing Industry) (Tokyo; March 1963).

[24] This statement is not strictly correct; insofar as the new facilities are presumably more productive or efficient than the pre-existing ones, the quotients have an upward bias as estimates of capacity utilization, even on the arbitrary 1955 base.

direct estimates of the percentage of capacity utilized. The results do not always gibe perfectly, and we produce as Table 5 both series for the two years 1961-1962; the generally falling rate of capacity utilization seems obvious in most branches of Japanese manufacturing.

TABLE 5

DECLINING CAPACITY UTILIZATION RATES, JAPANESE MANUFACTURING INDUSTRIES, 1961-1962

Industry	(Year and Quarter) 1961				1962			
	I	II	III	IV	I	II	III	IV
All Manufacturing	116.6 (87.1)	114.1 (85.2)	111.7 (83.4)	115.3 (86.1)	116.2 (86.8)	109.9 (82.1)	106.4 (79.5)	110.? (82.7
Iron and Steel	133.0 (85.1)	140.0 (89.6)	134.6 (86.1)	139.1 (89.0)	130.4 (83.4)	116.5 (74.5)	117.2 (75.0)	115.. (73..
Non-Ferrous Metals	110.7 (94.6)	111.9 (95.7)	106.6 (91.1)	114.7 (98.1)	110.1 (94.1)	104.0 (88.9)	98.6 (84.3)	96.? (82.?
Machinery	152.6 (87.6)	153.0 (87.8)	152.3 (87.4)	162.8 (93.4)	157.9 (90.6)	153.8 (88.3)	145.4 (83.5)	149.? (86.?
Ceramics	112.5 (89.0)	91.1 (92.1)	102.0 (80.7)	107.0 (84.6)	123.3 (97.5)	90.2 (71.3)	105.4 (83.4)	104.? (82..
Chemicals	112.0 (70.1)	106.1 (66.4)	102.1 (63.9)	111.1 (69.5)	109.8 (68.7)	109.4 (68.5)	99.3 (62.2)	103. (64.
Petroleum and Coal Products	125.2 (99.2)	120.9 (98.8)	97.3 (77.1)	105.6 (83.6)	112.0 (88.7)	104.8 (83.0)	84.9 (67.2)	115. (91.
Rubber and Rubber Products	131.4 (88.0)	133.2 (89.2)	129.0 (86.4)	134.3 (90.0)	134.3 (90.0)	134.3 (90.0)	132.5 (88.8)	128. (86.
Pulp and Paper Products	108.0 (88.9)	100.6 (82.8)	97.4 (80.2)	101.1 (83.2)	99.3 (81.7)	94.5 (77.8)	94.5 (77.8)	98. (80
Textiles	100.0 (79.8)	102.6 (81.9)	104.1 (83.1)	97.2 (77.6)	100.6 (80.5)	100.3 (80.0)	99.6 (79.5)	100. (79.

SOURCE: *Tsūsan tōkei* (May 1963), Table 16, pp. 47f.

NOTES: Figures in parentheses are direct estimates of percentage of capacity utilized. Other figures are quotients of index numbers of output and capacity (1c = 100).

Export and Inflation Problems

A weakness in the econometrics of the doubling-income plan is its international involvement. On the basis of the brief post-Korea period, Shimomura estimates the elasticity of Japanese export volume relative to the total world GNP between 3.0 and 3.5. With world GNP rising at an average rate of 3 percent per year, this permits a rise of Japanese exports amounting to between 9 and 10.5 percent per year (in real terms).[25] This is a cavalier procedure, in view of the small number of statistical degrees of freedom available, not to mention the special problems created for the 1960's by the proliferation of trading blocs, such as the European Common Market. With respect to the export structure, the official plan envisages a concentration on machinery exports with a 1970 target of 5.7 times the 1956-1958 average as against 3.5 times for exports as a whole, and a correlative concentration on exports to North America and Europe of "more than four times" the same base period.[26] As regards imports, Shimomura estimates the Japanese marginal propensity to import at only .09.[27] Possibly led astray by an unusually favorable balance in 1959, Shimomura accordingly anticipated declining balances through 1964 with equanimity. (He anticipates increasingly favorable ones during the next five years.)

As pure economics, one of the most original and arresting features of Shimomura's thought is a theory of inflation which has led him to regard with unconcern increases in con-

[25] Shimomura, "Basic Problems of Economic Growth Policy," pp. 25f. Compare Klein and Shinkai's estimating equation for Japanese exports (*op. cit.*, p. 9), which is in 1934-36 yen rather than in elasticity terms:

$$F_e = -2.92 + 3.917T_w + 2.457(p_w/p_j) - 3.37D \quad (R^2 = 0.85)$$

(Here F_e is Japanese exports, T_w world trade, p_w and p_j world and Japanese price levels, and D a shift variable, zero for prewar and unity for postwar observations.)

[26] EPA, *New Long-Range Economic Plan of Japan (1961-1970)*, pp. 75-77.

[27] This contrasts sharply with the Klein-Shinkai estimate of .26 (*op. cit.*, p. 13). Shimomura may have equated average with marginal values.

sumer prices. He argues that the consumer price index combines an index of *goods* prices and another index of *service* prices; in Japan, the weights of the two components are 70 and 30, respectively. The goods component, Shimomura says, moves approximately with the wholesale price index and also with the prices of internationally traded goods. The wholesale price index has not risen, and there is no reason why it should fall; Japan's international position does not require it to fall. Because of its international importance, moreover, the *wholesale* price index (whose movements roughly parallel the consumer price index for goods alone) is the appropriate index of inflation. It has not risen; *ergo*, no inflation.

Economic development adds to the productivity and hence the value of labor. It follows that real wages must rise, or what is development for? If deflation is to be avoided (constant wholesale price index), money wages must rise too. If money wages rise, so does the service component of the consumer price index. (Productivity rises less rapidly in services than in the production of goods; furthermore, there is no need to force wholesale prices down.) If the goods component of the consumer goods price index is stable, while the services component follows wages upwards, it follows that the consumer price index must rise as a whole in the course of economic growth, both relative to its base period and relative to the wholesale price index. In addition, runs Shimomura's argument, the higher the level of development, the higher are consumer prices (relative to wholesale). The more rapidly development is proceeding, the more rapidly consumer prices eventually rise, once unemployment is taken up and workers begin moving from low-wage sectors (in Japan, agriculture and small firms) to high-wage sectors of the economy, leaving labor shortages behind them.

Shimomura has accumulated a substantial amount of statistical evidence supporting his theory of rising consumer prices as both a *necessary* and a *non-inflationary* factor in economic growth. He presents this material in the *Oriental Economist* essay cited in note 7. For example, the ratios of consumer to wholesale prices, and of service to goods prices, are higher in the U.S. than in Western Europe, higher in Western Europe than in Japan, and so on, correlating almost perfectly with "relative development." His "stylized facts" of parallel movements between the wholesale price index, the goods component of the consumer price index, and the index of internationally traded goods prices are open to question. For example, the wholesale index has a downward bias, due to its heavy weighting with commodities whose technology has improved; the international index shares (in Japan) the same bias, because Japanese terms of trade have been improving *vis-à-vis* raw-material-producing underdeveloped countries in particular.

It is clear that the Shimomura policies have required a large expansion of money. Using the conventional definition (currency plus bank deposits), the Japanese money supply rose from ¥3,711 billion at the end of 1959 to ¥6,157 billion three years later. An "expanded" definition, which includes time deposits, indicates a rise from ¥10,947 billion to ¥19,517 billion in the same period.[28] The percentage increases are 65.9 (conventional) and 78.3 (expanded), all within three years. To a simple-minded quantity theorist, the wonder is not that prices have risen, but that they have not risen more!

Can It Last?

The implication of these paragraphs has been that the doubling-income plan can succeed in numerical terms, even if at the cost of some private pyramid-building and the creation of some excess capacity. Two points often raised against such solutions are: (1) What happens to the productivity of investment, σ, when a substantial portion of capital is left unused or rendered obsolete? (2) How can the rate of profit be maintained on facilities erected in advance of demand for their output? Will not this rate also fall below the rate Japanese businessmen consider endurable?

[28] U.N.—ECAFE, *Economic Bulletin for Asia and the Far East* (June 1963), p. 98.

1. Proliferation of excess capacity does lower the productivity of new capital. Domar speaks of a fall from σ to some smaller percentage, which he calls s. If capital is simultaneously deepened, however, as in the increasing Japanese stress on modernization and heavy industry (as against inventory accumulation), this fall need not be large. A rising saving ratio might also offset it, since the growth rate of income is $a\sigma$, not σ alone.

In such a high-saving economy, excess capacity might concentrate in final-product industries serving consumers directly, while investment turns to the deepening and modernization of capital—"mills to make more mills forever." The more closely the Japanese economy approaches this particular Nirvana (in defiance of conventional welfare economics), the more stable will be the boom—but the less believable, too, in terms of the consumption standards of the average Japanese.

This involves us in one of the "contradictions" of the Japanese economic miracle. The more closely it is associated with rising living standards, the greater the danger of downturns as the markets for washing machines, automobiles, and television sets are satiated periodically. The more it is stabilized by private pyramid-building, the less meaning it has for the standard of living of the ordinary Japanese. No combination of stability and consumer-directedness yet worked out has thus far checked the rise of Japanese Leftism. Public spending particularly in housing, public utilities, and disaster prevention may be the best answer, despite its low σ.

2. Turning to the rate of profit, this appears to be maintained, despite the rise of excess capacity, by one factor in particular: the failure of Japanese wages to keep pace with rising productivity.

While few Japanese economists accept the Cobb-Douglas function ($Y = bL^k C^j$) as the foundation of their aggregative distribution theories, the function seems to fit the Japanese economy well from the statistical viewpoint.[29] Let us consider an expanded form, which allows not only for the dy-

[29] The evidence is summarized in Shinohara, *op. cit.*, ch. 13.

namic effects of technological change but also for a variable percentage x of capital actually in use. Thus, if C is available capital, we may write, in our notation:

$$Y = A^t N^k (xC)^j \qquad (6)$$

where Y (income) is Douglas' P, and N (employment) is Douglas' L.

From (6) we may take the ratio of the competitive real wage $(\delta Y/\delta N)$ to average labor productivity (Y/N). Denoting this "share ratio" by s, we have:

$$s = \frac{\delta Y/\delta N}{Y/N} = \frac{kA^t N^{k-1} (xC)^j}{A^t N^{k-1} (xC)^j} = k \qquad (7)$$

which is a constant, therefore independent of x, C, and t. In words, the relative share of labor under pure competition, given the Cobb-Douglas production function, should remain constant over time, despite capital accumulation and changes in the rate of capital accumulation. (As has been pointed out repeatedly, however, the use of the A^t term to represent the effects of technological innovation implicitly limits such innovation to "neutral" types in which the relative marginal productivities of capital and labor are left unchanged.)

Regardless of the cogency of (6-7), however, the ratio s has tended steadily to decline for Japanese manufacturing in the course of the post-Korea "economic miracle." This has been pointed out recently in Professor Bela Belassa's study of the American balance of payments, and in most detail by Ohkawa's analysis of the Japanese wage structure.[30] We reproduce as Table 6 Belassa's over-all Japanese data, together with comparisons with the U.S. and Great Britain.

Detailed EPA data on Japanese national income by distributive shares points in the same direction. The combined

[30] Bela Belassa, "Recent Developments in the Competitiveness of American Industry and Prospects for the Future," in U.S. Congress, Joint Economic Committee, *Factors Affecting the U.S. Balance of Payments* (Washington: U.S. Government Printing Office, 1962), Table 3, p. 36; Ohkawa, "The Differential Employment Structure of Japan," *Annals of the Hitotsubashi Academy* (April 1959). See also Arisawa Hiromi, "Low Wages and the Structure of the Japanese Economy" (mimeographed) (Tokyo: Committee for Translation of Japanese Economic Studies, No. 25).

TABLE 6

Indexes of Man-Hour Productivity, Hourly Earnings, and Labor Costs in Manufacturing—United States, Great Britain, and Japan, 1953-1961

(1953 = 100)	1953	1954	1955	1956	1957	1958	1959	1960	196
United States									
Man-Hour Productivity	100	99	106	107	107	109	117	120	12
Hourly Earnings	100	102	107	112	118	121	126	130	13
Labor Costs	100	103	101	105	110	111	107	108	10
Great Britain									
Man-Hour Productivity	100	104	108	108	110	112	116	122	12
Hourly Earnings	100	107	116	124	133	137	142	155	1(
Labor Costs	100	103	108	115	121	122	123	127	1
Japan									
Man-Hour Productivity	100	107	113	119	128	123	150	173	1
Hourly Earnings	100	106	109	120	126	125	136	148	1
Labor Costs	100	100	96	100	98	102	91	85	

Source: Bela Belassa, "Recent Developments in the Competitiveness of American Industry and Prospects for the Future," U.S. Congress, Joint Economic Committee, *Factors Affecting the U.S. Balance of Payments* (Washington, 1962), Table p. 36.

shares of "Compensation of Employees" and "Proprietors' Income—Agriculture, Forestry, and Fisheries" fell from 68.2 percent of national income (1958) to 64.5 percent (1959) and 62.5 percent (1960), while "Corporate Profits" (before taxes) were rising from 9.0 percent (1958) to 14.0 percent (1959) and 16.5 percent (1960).[31]

[31] EPA, "Report of National Income Accounting Research Committee," *Economic Bulletin 12* (December 1962), Table I-7, p. 9.

Professor Baba Masao, in a study entitled "Keizai Seichō, kumiai soshiki ritsu, oyobi shotoku bumpai" [Economic Growth, Unionism, and Income Distribution],[32] has prepared ratios of wage payments to gross value added by manufacture in a number of branches of Japanese manufacturing industry, and computed the trend of these "wage-income ratios" over the decade 1951-1960. He has also compared the average annual rates of change (slope coefficients) in the two halves of the decade, and showed that (in general) wage-income ratios were affected adversely as the growth rate picked up speed. I take the liberty of reproducing his figures as Table 7.

TABLE 7

DECLINING WAGE-INCOME RATIOS IN JAPANESE MANUFACTURING
INDUSTRY, 1951-1960; TIME COEFFICIENTS IN TREND EQUATIONS

Industry	1951-60	1951-55	1956-60
Transportation Equipment	−3.56%	−2.21%	−5.40%
Electrical Machinery	−1.40	−0.65	−2.40
Other Machinery	−1.72	−1.45	−1.85
Iron and Steel	−1.86	−3.13	+0.47
Non-Ferrous Metals	−0.56	−0.26	−0.49
Petroleum and Coal Products	−0.24	+1.16	−2.12
Rubber and Rubber Products	−1.08	−3.27	+0.66
Chemicals	−0.99	−1.35	−1.72
Printing and Publishing	+0.13	−0.60	+1.21
Pulp and Paper	+0.12	+1.20	−0.75
Textiles	+0.15	+0.08	−0.17

SOURCE: Baba Masao, "Keiza seichō, kumiai shoshiki ritsu, oyobi shotoku bumpai," in Komiya Ryūtarō, *Sengo nihon no keizai-seichō* (The Economic Growth of Postwar Japan), ch. 11.

These figures combine to suggest that some form of employer exploitation has kept Japanese earnings in manufacturing from following man-hour productivity. Or in the more technical terms of equations (6-7), exploitation seems to have

[32] This article forms ch. 11 of Kojima Ryūtarō (ed.), *Sengo nihon no keizai-seichō* (Postwar Japanese Economic Growth) (Tokyo: Iwanami, 1964).

lowered the labor share in some manner inconsistent with the ordinary competitive market. (A parallel development occurred in France at approximately the same time, associated with the return of General De Gaulle to power.) It is difficult to avoid the hypothesis that private pyramid-building has been "financed" by the monopsonistic exploitation of Japanese labor. This in turn has been politically possible because Japanese hourly earnings have simultaneously gained on hourly earnings abroad. Rapid increase in labor productivity, associated with technological "catching-up" and the utilization of what was previously surplus labor, is crucial to this analysis. It can hardly be expected to continue indefinitely.

Epilogue, 1964

In Japan during 1964 one found the mainstream of economic discussion shifted away from *Wirtschaftswunder* to the "after-care" of an "over-heated economy." By these phrases the Japanese mean moderation of consumer price rises, aid to small business and agriculture unable to raise productivity in line with wage rates, and redistribution of the gains from growth—away from holders of land and securities to the remainder of the population. Pessimists foreign and domestic, liberal and Marxist, have enjoyed a field day at the expense of Premier Ikeda and Dr. Shimomura; the latter has become almost a voice in the wilderness in his continued enthusiasm for rapid growth. The majority of his critics would gladly trade a couple of percentage points on the growth rate for an equal number on the consumer price index. There was a crescendo of talk about scrapping the whole doubling-income plan for a more conservative model. The Opposition slogan of "Bukka baizō" took on more and more meaning, while the government's "Shotoku baizō"[33] took on less and less.

"There are probably more econometric models (in existence or far along in the process of construction) of Japan than of any other country in the world," including "the largest and most ambitious econometric project ever undertaken . . . a

---

[33] These expressions mean, respectively, "doubling of prices" and "doubling of income."

detailed quarterly model covering the postwar period."[34] The most authoritative model yet published, while admittedly forecasting "too low" for 1959-1961 on the basis of data through 1958, concludes that "unless large amounts of foreign capital can be obtained . . . the experience of the first years [of the 1960's] has not assured that the 7.2 percent rate can be maintained."[35]

Under these circumstances one is tempted to join the Cassandras. However, having erred consistently on the pessimistic side since 1945,[36] I propose instead to indicate certain conditions under which, with luck, the miracle may continue for the remainder of the decade.[37]

It is unfortunately not enough to rely on the Harrod-Domar model to keep the Japanese economy safe for private pyramid-building. This model assumes unlimited supplies of all sorts of labor and ignores the complications of international trade, whereas the Japanese have developed increasingly shortages of particular skills (whence much of the rise in consumer prices) and have not maintained their favorable payments balance of 1959. Let me suggest, however, that postwar Japan *can* avoid these complications (which does not necessarily mean that she *will*).

Labor shortages are avoidable in the fairly short run by diverting Japanese youth from admittedly overcrowded academic education to underdeveloped vocational training. Similar Western programs of subsidized human-capital investment sometimes founder on trade-union restrictionism and on irrelevant standard-raising in skilled trades, but these roadblocks are still avoidable in Japan.

Turning to the endemic Japanese balance of payments

[34] Klein and Shinkai, *op. cit.*, p. 1.

[35] *Ibid.*, p. 21.

[36] M. Bronfenbrenner, *Long-Range Projections of the Japanese Economy* (Santa Barbara, Cal.: TEMPO, General Electric Company, 1958), pp. 14-26, criticized EPA plan targets for 1962 as unduly ambitious. They were largely attained by 1960.

[37] The following paragraphs expand my "Comment" on the Ohkawa-Rosovsky paper (n. 3, above), *American Economic Review* (May 1963), pp. 599-601.

problem, I hesitate to estimate its real severity, above and beyond the effects of European and American discrimination against Japanese exports. If it should amount to more than this—or if net liberalization of restrictions is not forthcoming —Japanese reaction may take the form of intensifying its own illiberal practices, now concentrated in quasi-dumping of exports via the tax system.[38] MITI, suspicious of trade liberalization, favors stringent exchange controls over raw material inventories and imported consumption goods. I have myself argued elsewhere[39] for a quasi-dual currency system via exchange taxes (on imports), or subsidies (on exports), and need not elaborate that argument here.

To insure the continued profitability of private pyramid-building, it is also important to keep man-hour productivity rising faster than hourly wage cost, despite the "ethical" concern with present trends manifested even by the conservative Japan Productivity Center.[40]

Suffice it to conclude that, granted the over-simplifications of the Harrod-Domar model, it not only applies to contemporary Japan but suggests continuation of the present boom through the private pyramid-building of excess capacity. Labor and foreign-exchange shortages, along with trade union resentment of "exploitation" and conventional welfare preferences, e.g. schools and houses as against idle factories, make continuation more difficult in the real world than it is on paper. But the existence of these "contradictions" does not assure their triumph over the forces making for the extension of Japan's economic miracle through the 1960's—after which

[38] "Quasi-dumping" refers to a system whereby full Japanese corporate income taxes do not apply in export industries, and in which export-type goods are subject to heavy excise taxes if sold in the home market.

[39] M. Bronfenbrenner, "Thoughts on the Yen-Dollar Exchange Rate," *Keizai Kenkyū* (April 1959).

[40] See Kaneko Yoshio, "Seisansei, chingin, bukka ni tsuite" [On Productivity, Wages, and Prices], in Nihon seisansei hombu (Japan Productivity Center) *Seisansei to chingin Bukka* (*Productivity and Real Wages*) (Tokyo: Nihon seisansei hombu, 1962), pp. 16-22.

we must await the next projections of Dr. Shimomura or the EPA.[41]

[41] Criticizing this relative optimism, Professor Ohkawa feels that the present essay includes insufficient *differentiation* of the current boom from its predecessors to justify the anticipation of longer life. I can answer explicitly with regard only to the Manchuria-North China boom of the 1930's, where the shoe may be on the other foot. By this I mean that, had the Japanese military resisted the temptation to press on southward and eventually enter World War II, this boom should have lasted substantially longer than the seven years Ohkawa and Rosovsky allot to it.

CHAPTER XII

Cyclical Instability and Fiscal-Monetary Policy in Postwar Japan

HUGH T. PATRICK

ASSOCIATED with the rapid growth of the postwar Japanese economy have been rather wide swings of a cyclical nature in the growth of Gross National Product (GNP), industrial output, and other facets of the economy. The purpose of this paper is to analyze the properties of these cycles and the nature and effectiveness of the fiscal and monetary policies that have been taken to damp them. I shall not provide here either an analysis of the causes of rapid growth or a detailed description of each cycle and the policy steps taken, inasmuch as these have been treated elsewhere.[1]

The period under consideration is 1951 to 1962, since the earlier postwar years were a period of reconstruction in which policy was dominated by the Occupation authorities. I am concerned here with the short cycle of three to four years' duration; of these there have been three, with peaks reached in 1954, 1957, and 1961. Longer cycles, Juglar or Kuznets, are not treated because the postwar period has been too short to identify clearly even their existence, and because the short cycles have been a significant feature of postwar growth. In fact, it is difficult to separate the cycle from the

[1] See Japan, Economic Planning Agency (hereafter cited as EPA), *Economic Survey of Japan* annual issues; Hugh T. Patrick, *Monetary Policy and Central Banking in Contemporary Japan* (Bombay, 1962), especially Chapter X; Bank of Japan, Economic Research Department, *Financial Chronology of Japan, 1868-1960*, 1961; and two papers in this volume: W. W. Lockwood, "Japan's 'New Capitalism'" (Ch. X) and Martin Bronfenbrenner, "Economic Miracles and Japan's Income-Doubling Plan" (Ch. XI). The Lockwood essay links up well with my discussion; Bronfenbrenner's is less closely related because it concentrates on growth with only indirect consideration of cyclical fluctuation, and because it utilizes a different theoretical framework.

trend of rapid growth, since the causal factors of growth and concomitant rapid structural change influence the cycle. At the same time rapid growth makes the adjustment problems of cyclical fluctuation considerably easier than they would be under conditions of relatively slow growth and this mitigates criticism of government anti-cyclical policy.

The instability of an economy in terms of GNP and other variables may be measured in different ways: as changes in absolute levels; as changes in rates of increase; or as deviations from trends of growth. Changes in absolute levels are important in indicating the degree of the burden of cyclical swings, but where the growth trend is strong the downswing phase of the cycle appears abbreviated. Deviations from the trend line, on the other hand, usually relate to a single trend line over a considerable period of time, whereas in Japan the trend line of growth in output itself appears to have shifted. Nevertheless, by all these criteria the postwar Japanese economy has exhibited strong cyclical tendencies and with essentially the same periodization.[2] Absolute levels of real GNP (measured by seasonally adjusted quarterly data at annual rates) increased from trough to peak 31 percent between 1951-1954, 37 percent between 1954-1957, and about 60 percent between 1958-1961. They decreased from peak to trough 8 percent in 1954, 4 percent in 1957-1958, and an even milder decline in 1962. In terms of changes between peak and trough annual rates of growth of absolute levels of real gross expenditure, the differences were 10.7 percentage points between 1951 peak and 1954 trough growth rates, then a rise of 6.3 percentage points to 1956, a drop of 5.8 percentage points to

[2] For statistical data see EPA, *op. cit.*; EPA, *Kokumin shotoku hakusho 1960* [White Paper on National Income, 1960]; and Bank of Japan, Statistics Department, *Economic Statistics of Japan, 1962*—the basic statistical sources from which data for this paper are derived; EPA, Economic Research Institute, *Japanese Economy in the Fiscal Year 1959 Based on National Income Statistics* (Economic Bulletin No. 8; August 1961); and Bank of Japan, Statistics Department, *Waga kuni no keiki hendo shihyō* [Business Cycle Index of Japan], various issues. See also Shinohara Miyohei, *Growth and Cycles in the Japanese Economy* (Tokyo, 1962), Chapter 6.

1958, an increase of 14.8 percentage points to 1959, and a decline of about 13.5 percentage points to 1962. The industrial production index has had similar but even wider swings. The Bank of Japan and the Economic Planning Agency have developed diffusion indexes of the National Bureau of Economic Research type which demonstrate swings that are similar though of lesser amplitude because both seasonal and trend factors have been removed. Similarly, the growth rate of industrial production, which averaged 14.8 percent between 1951-1960, had a standard deviation from this trend of 5.9 percentage points; both the trend and the amplitude of variation were considerably larger than for West European countries and the United States.

Cyclical Fluctuations in Prewar Japan

While this essay concentrates on the postwar period, short-run cyclical fluctuations are not a new feature of the Japanese economy. Rather, as Allen has put it:[3] "Throughout the modern period Japan's development has been attended by frequent and severe fluctuations, and it is arguable that her progress was made possible, in part, by her vigorous pursuit of an expansionist policy, and at the same time by her readiness to apply checks ruthlessly whenever that policy provoked, as it frequently did, a crisis in her balance of payments." While no comprehensive analysis has been made of the inter-relationship of fiscal, monetary, foreign exchange, and commercial policies and their relationship to short-run cyclical fluctuation in the prewar Japanese economy, several general points may be noted.[4]

[3] G. C. Allen, *A Short Economic History of Japan,* revised edition, (New York, 1963), p. 166.

[4] For greater detail see, for example, Tsuru Shigeto, "Economic Fluctuations in Japan, 1868-1893," *Review of Economic Statistics,* XXIII, 4 (November 1941), pp. 176-89; H. Aoyama and T. Nishikawa, "Business Fluctuations in the Japanese Economy During the Inter-War Period," *Kyoto University Economic Review,* XXVIII, 7 (April 1959), pp. 14-39; K. Ohkawa and H. Rosovsky, "Economic Fluctuations in Prewar Japan: A Preliminary Analysis of Cycles and Long Savings," *Hitotsubashi Journal of Economics,* III, 1 (October 1962),

First, there have been substantial short-term (several-year) swings in the Japanese economy since the beginning of Meiji. They have not followed a simple, single pattern in terms of causality, length of cycle, or nature of response. In part this was because the government shifted its emphasis among major economic objectives from time to time. Exogenous forces, especially wars, have had particularly strong effects. By switching from a closed to an open economy Japan reduced the random effects of weather on total output but, while bene-fiting significantly from the gains from trade, made itself more susceptible at the same time to the forces of the interna-tional business cycle. Changes in the structure of the economy and in the development of institutions also influenced the nature of the cycle.

Second, expansionist fiscal and monetary policies most of the time provided aggregate demand pressures promoting rapid growth. The real miracle of Japanese growth, both in the long run and in the postwar period, has been the extraordi-nary responsiveness to demand of the factors of production and thereby of the supply of goods, and a willingness and an ability to engage in rapid transformation in the use of re-sources and in the composition of output. Domestic price stability seldom seems to have been a strong objective in itself —exceptions perhaps being the Matsukata Deflation in 1881-1886, the Katsuda period of fiscal restraint starting in 1908, and the Dodge plan reforms of 1949—although external price stability has been important for balance of payments reasons. While fiscal policy has been relatively more expansionist and monetary policy relatively more conservative, by and large they have tended historically to pursue complementary rather than conflicting objectives. Thus they have been quite well integrated. This has been partly because fiscal policy has always had a positive role to play, since economic growth was

---

pp. 10-33; Shinohara, *op. cit.*, Chs. 3-4; and Kang Moon Hyung, "The Monetary Aspect of the Economic Development in Japan with Special Reference to Monetary Policies: 1868-1935" (University of Nebraska, unpublished Ph.D. thesis, 1960).

an important objective and since the Bank of Japan has never been very independent of the Ministry of Finance. Both fiscal and monetary instruments have generally been utilized rather pragmatically to achieve desired goals, frequently in advance of the theoretical thinking of the times. Examples are the early use of fiduciary note issue even under a specie standard and the Takahashi fiscal and monetary policies from late 1931 to 1936, as well as the postwar application of "unorthodox" methods for controlling the availability of credit.

Third, the interplay between domestic growth and balance of payments difficulties has always been an important feature of cyclical movements of the economy. Growth-oriented fiscal and monetary policies, by generating high domestic demand and rapid growth, resulted in rising prices as well as rising output and also in increasing domestic absorption both of imports and of domestically produced goods which otherwise would have been exported. The relationship for a country between internal growth and external balance can pose major problems when the two become inconsistent. Japan has been no exception: periodically the constraint of external balance— the locus for which is the balance of payments—has impinged upon the maintenance of domestic growth. Yet at times external forces in the form of suddenly increased export opportunities have given a tremendous impetus to growth, not only by providing the extra necessary doses of aggregate demand but also by temporarily eliminating the very problems of paying for additional import needs emanating from the surge of growth. Japan's relationship with the economies of the rest of the world was particularly close between 1868 and 1931. The international environment and the rules of the game encouraged a stable international monetary mechanism and relatively free trade (in which Japan was forced to participate, if unwillingly, by the early unequal treaties). Thus the state of Japan's balance of payments has both influenced and been influenced by the growth and the cyclical features of the Japanese economy. The kinds of influences included: multiplier effects of the difference between exports and imports on domestic aggregate demand; the gold-standard fixed-exchange-rate specie-flow effect on the domestic money supply, promoting inflation when specie flowed in or when foreign exchange reserves increased as in World War I or deflation when they flowed out; and the effect on domestic production of the varying ability to finance imports of machinery, intermediate goods, and raw materials essential for the production process.

Like other nations, Japan substantially loosened the connection between internal and external stability after 1931, with world depression, the collapse of the international financial system, and the surge of nationalistic economic policies at the expense of internationalism. It was not that the underlying forces reflected in the balance of payments disappeared. Rather, new objectives and policy instruments developed. Thus the multiplier effects of foreign trade, while still important, could be supplanted by domestic fiscal and monetary policies even more than earlier. Similarly dependence of money supply on specie or foreign exchange reserves was reduced. And the new approach of direct controls over foreign exchange and imports provided an additional way to reduce the balance of payments impact. These new forces continued and were strengthened throughout the wartime and early postwar period, though the leeway they provided to reduce external impacts on the domestic economy was dissipated rather quickly during the war. The underlying forces have reasserted themselves strongly in the postwar period, and balance of payments problems have once again emerged.

Japanese policymakers have responded to periodic balance of payments crises in a variety of ways in the past century. The orthodox remedy of restrictive fiscal and especially monetary policies has frequently been used, especially for short spans, and also for two longer periods with unfortunate effects on the growth rate: the Matsukata Deflation and the deflation of 1927-1931. The strong Matsukata reform was a brutal and perhaps expensive way of putting the house in order after a period of rapid inflation; but given the general state of economic knowledge at the time there may have been no viable alternative. The 1927-1931 deflation was in retrospect a major error. Japan like England attempted to return to the gold standard at the pre-World War I par, an exchange rate clearly overvalued in terms of prices in Japan and abroad in the late 1920's. This necessitated a deflationary policy in order to adjust the domestic price level downward sufficiently, even at the expense of growth. Moreover, the timing was horrendous; Japan returned to the gold standard in January 1930, when the world depression was already under way.

In addition to restrictive fiscal and monetary measures aimed at balance of payments difficulties, a number of approaches directly related to the foreign sector have been used. Gold, silver, and foreign exchange reserves, always utilized as short-run buffers, were also run down over more extended periods on a sustained basis: from 1868 to 1881, after the Sino-Japanese War, and after World War I. Substantial foreign borrowing to extend the limits of the balance of payments constraint was of major importance between 1902-1910, and recently has again become significant. Use of a fluctuating (and depreciating) exchange rate has also been a major means to adjust the balance of payments, especially between 1868 and 1897, when Japan was on a *de facto* silver standard during a period of declining silver prices, and between 1931 and 1949. Finally, Japan shifted from the almost completely free, open economy of the latter half of the nineteenth century to increasingly severe restrictions on foreign exchange and imports. This trend, which began in 1931, reached its peak in World War II, continued in the early postwar period, and began to decline substantially only after 1959. These measures have succeeded in eliminating, or at least postponing and mitigating, the balance of payments constraint upon domestic growth.

In the postwar period the Japanese government has relied primarily upon fiscal and monetary policies to counter cyclical tendencies in the economy. No doubt this has been in part because the downswing phases of the cycle have been relatively mild. At any rate, it has firmly adhered to the International Monetary Fund system of fixed exchange rates and to the rate (360 yen equals one dollar) set in April 1949. At the same time, direct controls over imports, especially of machinery and manufactured consumer goods, have remained strong enough until recently so that there has been relatively little room for selective tightening of import controls over non-essentials on a cyclical basis and almost equal reluctance to ease them. Despite direct controls in the foreign sector and in some areas of production and investment, it should not be forgotten that government fiscal and monetary policy operates essentially within the framework of a free enterprise economy with decision-making quite decentralized on the whole and with prices quite responsive to demand and supply conditions in the market.

The following sections treat specifically the properties of postwar cycles and the fiscal and monetary policies which have been used to damp them. Empirical evidence on the three postwar cycles is analyzed in terms of a simple Hicksian-type theoretical framework. Whether the degree of cyclical fluctuation was good or bad and whether alternative approaches could have been effectively utilized are treated next. The following section is devoted to a more detailed discussion of fiscal and monetary policies and techniques. In conclusion some suggestions are made about the future possibilities of cyclical fluctuation in the Japanese economy and the attendant fiscal and monetary policies.

Causes of Cyclical Fluctuation: Theory and Fact

Although each of the three cycles since 1951 has had its own specific characteristics, in broad terms they have been quite similar not only in their effects and in the fiscal and monetary responses they engendered but also in their underlying causes. Thus we can generalize in theoretical terms about the causal forces at work. In order to have theory correspond fairly closely to the reality of events, the approach is rather eclectic. The crucial issues to be explained are: what causes the upswing, and particularly the upper turning point; and what causes the downswing, and particularly the lower turning point. In the following discussion, a theoretical skeleton is set up, to which is added the flesh of empirical evidence for the period.

THE ANALYTICAL FRAMEWORK

The analytical framework utilized is basically a variant of Hicks' theory of an explosive boom halted by resource limitations. Both exogenous and endogenous forces are at work to cause cyclical instability in the growth pattern, while growth itself brings about structural changes which influence the length of the upswing and downswing of the cycle. A common feature of all these forces is that they manifest themselves through changes in the balance of payments as the proximate cause of cyclical fluctuation. It is the balance of payments constraint that brings about the upper turning point, and the elimination of the constraint that results in the lower turning point.

Let us examine first the underlying pattern of instability and the major endogenous variables. We begin our analysis of the sequence of the cycle in the latter part of its upswing phase, when the economy is growing rapidly under the impetus of strong private demand, generated in part by accelerator-multiplier effects. The boom is forced to an end by a combination of specific bottlenecks, difficulties in restructuring production toward exports rapidly enough, and excessive aggregate domestic demand, which together cause unsustainably large deficits in the balance of payments.

As the boom progresses specific bottlenecks emerge when certain industries, especially in basic sectors, run up against short-run capacity constraints which make supply inelastic. The economy is not so synchronized that all industries reach the limits of capacity at the same time. These bottlenecks may be in the raw material producing sector or may show up in intermediate products or capital goods. The inability of such bottleneck industries to provide additional inputs necessary for the continued growth of industrial production means that demand for these goods spills over to imports. Even though the economy generally is flexible enough to engage in transformation rather rapidly in the longer run, the gestation period for new investment in bottleneck industries is sufficiently long so that this means of increasing supplies is not adequate in the interval between after the bottleneck appears and before the balance of payments crisis becomes acute.

A related problem of transformation is the inability to restructure exports rapidly enough in the short run to pay for the sharply increasing imports. There are two aspects to such restructuring. In an aggregative sense, because the proportion of imports to GNP is rising the proportion of total exports in total output must also rise. Moreover, this is likely to require a change in the composition of exports in response to foreign market prospects. In a micro sense this restructuring is also difficult in the short run, not because of Japan's particular inability to transform, but because of the high degree of restructuring required by the very large increases in imports in boom periods. Such transformation is also hampered in boom periods when resources are more fully employed and hence less readily shifted.

The pressure of strong domestic aggregate demand on both exports and imports during a boom contributes significantly to the balance of payments deficit. Exports are retarded by a combination of domestic absorption and price effects. Goods which otherwise would have been available for export go to meet rapidly expanding demand at home. In part this is a reflection of the tendency for desired investment to exceed saving. High aggregate demand generates domestic price increases which spill over to export industries and make them less competitive in world markets. Strong aggregate demand also raises import demands, even though such potential demand by consumers may be constricted by controls. In part this merely reflects the requirement of imports as a fixed proportion of inputs in the production process when industrial output is growing. In addition, the composition of demand and of output shifts during the upswing, with rapid increases in plant and equipment and inventory investment relative to consumption. In the Japanese case, investment goods on the average have a larger import component than consumption goods, because of resource endowment and import controls.

Thus the combination of strong domestic aggregate demand and specific bottlenecks results in a shortage of domestic resource inputs for the production process—raw materials, intermediate products, and/or machinery—relative to demand. This spills over into increases in imports and retards increases in exports that otherwise might appear. The growing deficit in the current account of the balance of payments is financed by drawing down foreign exchange reserves. Eventually reserves reach such a low level that this imbalance cannot continue. At this point the government steps in with restrictive fiscal and monetary policies which halt the boom and induce the downswing of the cycle. It should be noted that the boom is not brought to an end by endogenous forces such as accelerator effects or tighter money, nor by a general shortage of labor. Similarly, investment demand does not dry up; rather in aggregative terms it continues to outstrip domestic saving. In other words, the growth of the economy has become explosively (or at least excessively) rapid; the balance of payments cannot support such a growth rate on a sustained basis, and this constraint begins to operate.

In such an analytical framework, in terms of maintaining the growth trend, ideally the downswing phase of the cycle is based primarily on a sharp inventory adjustment. This is brought about by a combination of downward accelerator effects once the boom is halted, of restricted availability of funds to finance inventories, and of pessimistic short-run price expectations. Total plant and equipment investment may also decline with available funds restricted and some reduction in expectations, but less rapidly and drastically. The strength of autonomous investment demand underlying the basic growth trend prevents such induced downward effects from producing a sizable decline. Moreover, fixed investment in specific bottleneck sectors continues to be encouraged by relative prices and/or selective monetary and fiscal policy to eliminate shortages. An important element of the adjustment is the decline in domestic and export prices, which ideally respond flexibly in the recession in order to minimize the required reduction in real output.

Reduced domestic aggregate demand, lower prices, and gradual elimination of specific bottlenecks combine both to lower the demand for imports and to provide renewed incentives to restructure production and sales toward export markets. The result is a movement from a deficit to a surplus in the balance of payments. As soon as it appears that external equilibrium is being restored, the government first eases its restrictive measures, then shifts soon to an expansive fiscal and monetary policy in order to end the downswing. This anti-recession action, plus the strong autonomous growth forces at work, result in a rather mild and short-lived recession, a shallow trough, and then a new upswing. Both upper and lower turning points, then, are a direct consequence of government policy measures.

The upswing becomes strong and a new boom phase gets under way as vigorous private demand factors once again assert themselves. Initially inventory investment is large; depleted inventories are replenished and, as short-term expectations become more favorable, businessmen tend to speculate in inventories. The increase in exports relative to imports, reflected in the improvement in the balance of payments at the end of the recession and in the early stages of the boom, also strengthens demand. Later in the boom there is a major surge in plant and equipment investment, both because capacity limits are being reached and because highly optimistic expectations are generated. Not only are strong multiplier effects derived from the increases in exports and inventory and plant and equipment investment but also accelerator forces operate to reinforce demand in the upswing as well as contracting it in the downswing. Once again an explosive boom develops, only to be halted by domestic resource limits which become reflected in the balance of payments constraint.

EXOGENOUS FORCES AND STRUCTURAL CHANGE

While this model of cyclical fluctuation is consistent with actual events in postwar Japan, as is discussed in some detail below, the major importance of exogenous events both for growth and for cyclical fluctuation must be emphasized. Exogenous forces as well as structural changes have raised and lowered the balance-of-payments ceiling on growth. There has been no single growth rate over time for the dynamic Japanese economy for which the balance of payments would be in equilibrium. Rather, this equilibrium growth rate has shifted about as it has been buffeted by these influences.

Exogenous forces have been both foreign and domestic, both random and regular. Even random exogenous shocks can set off cyclical fluctuation in an economy.[5] The Korean War and the Suez crisis were major random foreign events. The former provided strong external demand for Japan's goods and services which financed large increases in imports, and set off a boom that lasted until 1953. The Suez crisis not only increased sharply the landed price of Japan's imports but touched off a certain amount of inventory speculation in imported raw materials.

A more regular foreign influence of extreme importance has been the world business cycle, more particularly the world foreign trade cycle, since Japan is closely linked via its balance of payments with fluctuations in world trade. This is especially true for exports. The Japanese economy is rather more closely linked to the United States business cycle than are the industrial European countries.[6] Japan is the second largest trading partner of the United States, and the United States is Japan's largest customer, purchasing 20-30 percent of its exports. Moreover, these exports have been quite elastic relative both to total Japanese exports and to increases in American imports during upswings in the American economy.

Domestic exogenous influences have not been negligible.

[5] For a discussion of the cyclical properties of random shocks on an economy see Lawrence R. Klein, *An Introduction to Econometrics* (Englewood Cliffs, N.J., 1962), Ch. 6.

[6] On a quarterly basis the turning points of the Japanese cycle are frequently close to those in the American cycle, but a clear-cut pattern of Japanese lags does not exist. For example, in 1957 the Japanese economy turned down before the American economy; the U.S. cycle turned downward in 1960 and upward in 1961, while the boom in Japan continued through 1960 until the end of 1961 before a downward swing developed. See EPA, *Economic Survey of Japan 1961-62*, p. 211.

The random forces of weather, for example a poor rice crop in 1953 and a bumper crop in 1955, were reflected in the balance of payments. A more persistent influence has been the government, which intervenes with restrictive measures only when the balance of payments gets into serious trouble, and with expansionary measures otherwise, especially in recessions. This helps set the tone of continued business optimism. Another strong, favorable influence on expectations has been the series of five-year or ten-year projections by the government. They have not only provided bench marks for individual firms but also inspired business confidence in an optimistic image of the future of the economy.[7] It may be only coincidental that the last three plans have been published either in recessions or in early phases of the upswing, but the subsequent overwhelming surge of private plant and equipment investment has been no coincidence. Though these plans have been formulated presumably to foster growth rather than to combat cyclical fluctuation, their effect has been so to stimulate private fixed investment as to increase cyclical instability.[8] Private investment is carried out much more rapidly and vigorously than projected in the plan.

Structural change within the Japanese economy and abroad has also affected the longer-run level of the balance of payments constraint upon growth. On the import side, the changing structure of industrial production has necessitated smaller raw material inputs and also made possible import substitution. Technological change has economized raw ma-

[7] A similar situation seems to exist in France and Sweden. Cf. Pierre Masse, "French Methods of Planning," *Journal of Industrial Economics*, XI, 1 (November 1962), 1-17; and Ingvar Svennilson, and Rune Beckman, "Long-Term Planning in Sweden," Skandinaviska Banken *Quarterly Review*, XLIII, 3 (1962), 71-80.

[8] It is on this point that the interrelationship between cyclical fluctuation and growth becomes especially difficult to untangle. If the surge of private fixed investment demand between 1955-62 is regarded as upward shifts in autonomous investment demand which raised the trend growth rate, at the same time these shifts have promoted booms which have brought about the cyclical pattern being analyzed. See the quotations from Shinohara and the related discussion by Bronfenbrenner, above, pp. 532-33.

terials (e.g., substantial reductions in the amount of coal and iron ore required per ton of steel) and made possible domestic substitutes for imported raw materials (e.g., synthetic fibers for cotton and wool). However, domestic raw material resources are limited and are becoming increasingly costly; the substitution of cheap foreign petroleum for domestic coal is the most notable example. Moreover, there has been a definite trend toward trade liberalization in the world, although Japan herself has moved relatively slowly. This has had some impact and will presumably have a greater impact in the future. The net effect over-all has been for the average propensity to import goods and services in real terms to rise substantially in the postwar period, from 8.0 percent in 1950 to 15.6 percent in 1960. This has been partially offset in value terms by the decline in world prices of raw materials, so that Japan's price (unit value) index for imports decreased by about 20 percent between 1953 and 1962. On the export side, Japan has increased domestic capacities so that it can supply much larger quantities of export goods and has rapidly become competitive in new products as the economy has continued to diversify. At the same time the tremendous rise in labor productivity has meant a reduction of unit labor costs, part of which has been reflected in reduced prices of export goods. Thus Japan has been increasingly competitive in world markets.[9]

Another structural change not only important for its long-run effect on the balance of payments constraint but with strong cyclical implications has been Japan's recently developed ability to borrow foreign funds.[10] In the main this

[9] For example, two-thirds of Japan's increase in exports between 1953-59 can be attributed to improved price and quality competitiveness, and only one-third to general growth in world trade. Cf. Kawashima Yoko, *Productivity, Efficiency Wage Cost and Price Competitiveness of Japanese Exports in the 1950's,* Keio University, Institute of Management and Labour Studies, English Series No. 7 (Tokyo, June 1963). The price (unit value) index of exports declined by about 9% between 1953 and 1962.

[10] The point here relates to foreign portfolio capital, not direct investment. Japan has restricted the latter quite severely; see Lockwood, above, pp. 470-71; 488-91. The proposed American tax legislation on

has been a matter of establishing Japan's credit-worthiness with foreign suppliers of funds; it has also reflected a higher level of interest rates in Japan (which is desirable), and a growth of her trade. Her ability to borrow long-term was first revived after the war with a series of loans from the International Bank for Reconstruction and Development, beginning in the mid-1950's. She became the second largest borrower from the World Bank, though now this source is drying up as she progresses and develops alternative sources of long-term portfolio capital. These have been the long-term private capital markets in New York and in Europe, especially Switzerland and Germany, where she has turned with increasing success since 1959.

Japan has been an even larger borrower of short-term funds, especially since 1960. These have been mainly short-term trade credits from American banks to finance her imports, but she has also been a major borrower of "Eurodollars" and recipient of substantial inflows of convertible bank deposits from abroad, primarily from the United States. Her short-term borrowings from United States non-governmental sources amounted to $1.8 billion in March 1962. This represented an increase of $1.4 billion since the beginning of 1960, 45 percent of total recorded United States short-term capital outflows in this period.[11] The net effect of this massive short-term capital inflow was to postpone the decline in foreign exchange reserves arising from current-account deficits in the balance of payments in late 1960 and early 1961. It thus lengthened the boom by postponing the time when restrictive monetary and fiscal policies had to be put into effect. Since much short-term borrowing is tied to the level of imports, its availability will probably continue to lengthen the boom phase of the cycle. This may well be true of other forms

---

foreign securities purchased by Americans has slowed down the flow of American portfolio capital to Japan considerably since July 1963, but has been offset somewhat by increased American bank loans and enhanced Japanese borrowing in European capital markets.

[11] Hal B. Lary, *Problems of the United States as World Trader and Banker* (New York, 1963), Table 5, p. 38.

of short-term borrowing as well, when tight money market conditions in Japan make it profitable to borrow from abroad.

EMPIRICAL EVIDENCE AND THE ANALYTICAL FRAMEWORK

The three cycles between 1951 and 1962 have indeed displayed the general pattern outlined in our analytical framework, though of course not nearly as smoothly as the model suggests. In aggregative terms, as presented in Table 1, the upswings have been vigorous, the downswings mild.

Investment demand has been of increasing importance from one cycle to the next, and particularly plant and equipment investment. Moreover, the upswing phase of the cycle has tended to lengthen, mainly because of shifts in the balance of payments constraint brought about by foreign capital inflows and structural change. The main adjustment in the downswing has been the decline in inventory investment, larger than the decrease in GNP itself. The data in Table 1 on the decline in plant and equipment investment are somewhat misleading, since the trough in plant and equipment investment was reached only after five quarters from the 1954 peak, as compared with three quarters in 1957-1958. The data for the 1962 decline, while preliminary, reflect the mild decline. Actually the seasonally adjusted quarterly data for 1962 provide a zigzag picture, with a rise in the second quarter and a smaller decline in the third quarter before the upward trend is renewed. The importance of inventories in the cyclical pattern and the relative downward inflexibility of fixed investment are ably treated by Professor Shinohara in his recent book.[12] At the same time strong private consumption as well as government expenditures have been a basic support on the demand side, providing a rather stable growth of demand in recession as well as boom periods.[13]

Not only are multiplier effects derived from increases in inventory and plant and equipment investment but also accelerator forces are at work to keep private demand strong

[12] *Op. cit.*, Chs. 6-8.
[13] Cf. Gleason, "Economic Growth and Consumption in Japan," above, especially Table 1 and pp. 424-27.

TABLE 1

PERCENTAGE COMPOSITION OF CHANGE IN GNP IN POSTWAR CYCLES—TROUGH
TO PEAK AND PEAK TO TROUGH IN CURRENT PRICES

(minus indicates decline)

	Rise Oct.-Dec. 1951- Apr.-June 1954 (10 quarters) %	*Decline* Apr.-June 1954 July-Sept. 1954 (1 quarter) %	*Rise* July-Sept. 1954- Apr.-June 1957 (11 quarters) %	*Decline* Apr.-June 1957- Apr.-June 1958 (4 quarters) %	*Rise* Apr.-June 1958- Oct.-Dec. 1961 (14 quarters) %	*Declin* Oct.-De 1961 Jan.-Ma 1962 (1 quart %
GNP	100	—100	100	—100	100	—100
Consumption	66.6	10.2	34.8	48.5	36.5	0.6
Govt. Exp.	19.9	21.0	6.8	6.2	18.7	8.5
Housing	2.9	—1.2	2.8	—1.3	2.2	3.6
Inventories	12.5	—155.7	43.9	—210.7	18.2	—103.9
Plant & Equip.	8.8	—6.0	28.7	—22.3	32.9	—71.7
Net Trade Balance	—10.6	31.8	—16.9	79.6	—8.5	62.9
Exports	—0.7	3.9	12.1	—6.1	7.4	10.8
Imports	9.9	—27.8	29.0	—85.7	15.8	—52.1
Change in real GNP	+31%	—8%	+37%	—4%	+60%	—3

SOURCE: Derived from EPA, Economic Research Institute, *Japanese Economy*
the Fiscal Year 1959, Economic Bulletin No. 8, Table 39, and *National Incom*
Statistics and National Income Statistics Quarterly (January-March, 1962), Ec
nomic Bulletin No. 11, Reference Table 1.

NOTE: Seasonally adjusted quarterly data at annual rates. Data are somewh
less reliable than annual GNP estimates. The estimate for the 1962 decline is bas
on preliminary data, but is not significantly different from later data except th
the real decline was even smaller.

in the upswing and to contract demand in the downswing.
These are not the only forces in operation. Businessmen, who
generally have quite optimistic expectations, in the short run
overestimate sales and inventories in recessions and underestimate them in booms, but always overestimate plant and

equipment investment.[14] This optimism prevents recessions from becoming severe, while pro-cyclical swings in expectations tend both to make the downswing adjustment more rapid and the upswing more vigorous.

Of great benefit to the adjustment process has been the flexibility of prices in the downswing phase of the cycle. This is especially true for export prices; the major improvements in Japan's export competitiveness have come in recession periods. In 1953 a major problem was the failure of Japanese prices to decline as rapidly as they had in the rest of the world with the end of the Korean boom; they actually rose slightly in 1953. Wholesale prices did fall 6.2 percent and export prices 5 percent in 1954 under the impetus of the restrictive fiscal and monetary policies taken. Wholesale prices increased by about 8 percent in 1956 and export prices by 3 percent, but they declined from their early 1957 peaks over the course of the subsequent recession by 9.4 percent and 14 percent, respectively. Between the fall of 1960 and 1961 the wholesale price index went up 6 percent and the export price index 2 percent; by the fall of 1962 they had decreased respectively by about 4 percent and 3 percent.

As suggested in the analytical framework, disequilibrium in the balance of payments has been the proximate cause of cyclical fluctuation. Changes in official foreign exchange reserves sensitively reflect this disequilibrium. The peak in foreign exchange reserves was reached in each cycle about six months before the peak in GNP. Thereafter reserves declined sharply, and a restrictive policy was adopted with about a six-month lag. The current account of the balance of payments probably turned to a deficit about three months in advance of the peak in reserves. The data for the 1953-1954 period are less reliable, but a peak in reserves was reached in November 1953 (though there had been some decline over

[14] Cf. EPA, Economic Research Institute, *Business Cycles and Entrepreneurial Expectations* (Economic Bulletin No. 4; June 1960), and K. Asakura and T. Shimamura, "An Analytical Exposition of the Banks of Japan's Short-Term Economic Survey of Principal Enterprises," Bank of Japan, Statistics Department, June 1962 (mimeographed, 61 pp.).

the summer from the spring peak of $913 million), and there-
after declined by $215 million in six months. The next peak
was in December 1956 at $941 million; in the following six
months the current account of the balance of payments ran a
deficit of $667 million, and foreign exchange reserves dropped
by $430 million even though $125 million was borrowed from
the International Monetary Fund. The next peak in foreign
exchange reserves was $2,035 million in March 1961. The
current account deficit in the following six months totaled
$664 million, and reserves went down by $529 million, despite continued short-term capital inflows. In all these periods
current account deficits and foreign exchange reserve losses
continued beyond these six-month periods, and at the time
when restrictive measures were undertaken there was no
prospect that the balance of payments would automatically
right itself without such action.

The main component of these swings in the balance of payments has been the wide fluctuations in imports. Imports had
a standard deviation from the trend line of growth of 15.5
percent for the period 1952-1961, more than double the deviation of mining and manufacturing production. Moreover, the
fluctuation of imports is greater than that of exports, as is
indicated in Table 2.[15]

The nature of the import cycle is incisively described and
analyzed in the EPA's White Paper for the 1961-1962 fiscal
year.[16] In summary, there are two phases in the increase in
imports in the upswing of the cycle. While imports increase
fairly rapidly in the first phase, the rate of increase approximately doubles in the second phase. "Raw materials, processed materials and machinery are all typical examples of
this pattern."[17] The elastic responsiveness of imports rela-

[15] Note that Lockwood, above, pp. 476-77 appears more sanguine
than I about the constraint of imports. We do not disagree basically
however; he is referring to imports relative to the trend of growth
while I am concerned about imports in boom periods of exceptionally
rapid growth.

[16] EPA, *Economic Survey of Japan, 1961-1962*, pp. 213-20.

[17] *Ibid.*, p. 214.

TABLE 2

<small>Annual Rate of Increase in Value of Imports and Exports of Goods and Services, and in World Imports (IMF Balance of Payments Basis) in %</small>

	Imports	Exports	World Imports
1952	1.0	2.5	—1.7
1953	20.8	0.0	—5.7
1954	1.4	8.2	4.2
1955	2.6	14.7	12.0
1956	33.7	21.5	10.5
1957	28.1	12.6	9.7
1958	—25.6	—1.2	—6.4
1959	20.8	16.1	5.7
1960	23.4	16.0	11.8
1961	28.3	4.8	4.5
1962	—3.3	14.9	6.1

Source: Bank of Japan, Statistics Department, *Historical Statistics of Japanese Economy* (Tokyo 1962), *Economic Statistics of Japan 1962* (Tokyo, 1962) ; IMF, *International Financial Statistics*, January 1960 and May 1963, and (for 1962) Nihon keizai shimbun, *Japan Economic Journal*, I, 21 (May 21, 1963), p. 5.

tive to mining and manufacturing production are indicated in Table 3; data on value of exports, imports, and the net trade balance for selected commodity groupings are provided in Table 4. The relationship of the rate of increase of imports relative to increases in industrial production thus is not linear over the course of the upswing; instead the elasticity increases as the boom develops and become prolonged. Imported raw materials used in the production process are responsive to changes in production. Surprisingly enough, given domestic supply inelasticities, this is less so in the later phase of the upswing, and the elasticity value has been declining from cycle to cycle. Evidently this reflects the strong development of import-substituting raw materials, such as synthetic fibers, of raw material-saving technological improvements, and of changes in the composition of industrial production. Fluctuations in import prices are also significant in affecting these elasticity estimates.

TABLE 3

ELASTICITY OF IMPORTS TO MINING AND MANUFACTURING PRODUCTION

	(1)	(2)	(3)
1952-54 Cycle			
Upswing			
First Phase	1.32	1.04	0.98
Second Phase	1.29	0.64	1.49
Downswing	2.87	0.65	6.71
1955-58 Cycle			
Upswing			
First Phase	1.19	1.67	1.13
Second Phase	1.07	1.15	2.27
Downswing	6.09	1.25	8.37
1959-61 Cycle			
Upswing			
First Phase	0.86	1.09	0.90
Second Phase	0.84	0.98	1.58

Column 1: The rate of change of imported raw material inputs divided by the rate of change of the index of mining and manufacturing production.

Column 2: The rate of change of raw material imports divided by the rate of change of total imports.

Column 3: The rate of change of total imports divided by the rate of change of the index of mining and manufacturing production.

SOURCE: EPA, *Economic Survey of Japan 1961-1962* (Tokyo, 1962), Tables 1-5, p. 219.

The wide fluctuations in imports are attributable both to domestic aggregate demand and to bottlenecks. The rapid growth of aggregate demand in boom periods alone accounts for a substantial increase in imports; other things equal, this would explain a proportional increase in imports. Changes in the composition of aggregate demand make for a greater than unitary elasticity response of imports. This is manifested in several forms. Over the cycle the swings in the production of industries which rely heavily on raw materials imports are larger than the swings in total industrial production. Those components of aggregate demand which increase most in a boom, and fall most in a recession, have higher than average import inputs. Thus, while for 1960 in value terms total import of goods was 9.2 percent of total demand (GNP plus imports), the specific import component was 14.1 percent of exports, 12.6 percent of inventories, and 11.8 percent of private plant and equipment investment, but only 7.6 percent of private consumption and 4.4 percent of government consumption.[18] In addition, there tends to be some inventory investment in imported raw materials in the late upswing of the cycle: less than $100 million in 1953, $250-300 million in late 1956-early 1957, and $200 million in 1961. In the main these were normal rises related to increases in sales and production, though there was considerable speculation in imported raw materials inventories, especially petroleum, at the time of the Suez crisis.

Inventory speculation derives both from expectations that the landed price of raw materials imports will rise and from fears that the system of direct import controls will be utilized to restrict future imports and hence domestic production which requires these imports. The data on actual imported raw material inventories are not very accurate. The importance of raw material imports for inventory purposes can be seen in the various elasticity figures for the 1954-1958 cycle; particularly in the second phase of the upswing, import increases in raw materials were large relative to the rate of increase in total imports. While total imports were quite elastic relative to the rate of increase in industrial production, imported raw material inputs for production were not nearly so elastic.[19] This implies that raw material imports were being stockpiled.

Most of the greater-than-proportional responsiveness of imports to changes in industrial production is attributable to specific bottlenecks. Bottleneck sectors have changed from one cycle to another. Indirect evidence for this appears in

[18] Based on the MITI 1960 input and output table, and cited in M. Fujioka, "Appraisal of Japan's Plan to Double Income," International Monetary Fund, *Staff Papers*, X, 1 (March 1963), 150-83.

[19] Shinohara derives higher elasticities of raw material imports relative to industrial production in the upswing of the cycle. *Op. cit.*, pp. 179-87.

Columns 1 and 3 of Table 3, while more direct evidence appears in Table 4. In 1953-1954 raw materials were relatively more important, becoming less so in the latter two cycles, when certain intermediate products and capital goods were the bottleneck areas. Fluctuation in import of processed materials—iron and steel, chemicals, petroleum products, etc.—has been wide, as domestic constraints have been reached. This was especially true in 1957 for iron and steel semi-manufactures, as they shifted from a net export to net import balance (see Table 4). Accordingly, the government channeled investment funds into these bottlenecks (and into transportation and electric power bottlenecks, for which imports

TABLE 4

Exports, Imports, and Net Trade Balance for Selected Commodity Group
(SITC classification; million dollars at current prices)

	Inedible Crude Materials			Coal & Petroleum			Iron & Steel Semi-Manufactures			Machinery[a]		
	X	M	X–M	X	M	X–M	X	M	X–M	X	M	X–
1951	30	1213	−1133	1	160	−159	206	8	198			
1952	84	964	− 880	9	234	−225	263	7	256			
1953	70	1151	−1084	8	289	−281	140	13	127	53	161	−1
1954	83	1126	−1043	5	267	−262	167	11	156	70	177	−1
1955	98	1226	−1128	5	289	−284	260	10	250	102	132	−
1956	95	1710	−1615	11	413	−402	223	61	162	143	161	−
1957	92	2010	−1918	5	680	−675	209	305	−96	174	288	−1
1958	76	1299	−1223	12	514	−502	245	24	221	175	341	−1
1959	109	1735	−1626	13	557	−544	253	47	206	221	352	−1
1960	123	2170	−2047	16	742	−726	388	88	300	320	403	−
1961	131	2749	−2618	20	932	−912	380	156	224	457	599	−1
1962	158	2362	−2204	19	1041	−1022	531	112	419	587	767	−1

[a] Excludes textile machinery, sewing machines, radio receivers, ships, and mot vehicles from exports. Not on SITC basis, since sufficiently disaggregated SIT data not available after 1960.

Notes: X = exports, M = imports, X–M = net trade balance.

Source: UN., *Yearbook of International Trade Statistics 1953, 1956, 1960*. Ba of Japan, *Economic Statistics of Japan 1962* (Tokyo, 1963) ; Office of Prime Min ter, Bureau of Statistics, *Monthly Statistics of Japan*, March 1963.

were not substitutable) so that the degree of fluctuation of processed goods imports has lessened over the course of the three cycles. This suggests there is better synchronization of the capacity levels for basic intermediate products with total output.

On the other hand, the fluctuation in imports of finished goods, notably machinery, has widened. This was particularly noticeable in the most recent cycle when capacity limits in the capital goods sector were a major bottleneck. The cycle has become more directly related to constraints in the producer goods sector, which even more than other sectors cannot both increase its capacity and its net sales to other sectors.

In the downswing phase of the cycle the highly elastic response of the use of imported raw materials and of total imports relative to industrial production is striking. This supports the view that these imports are to alleviate domestic bottlenecks; once the growth of the economy slows down, domestic production can better meet domestic demand and at more competitive prices, so that imports of many such commodities are no longer necessary. The large downswing in raw materials imports reflects both inventory disinvestment and reduced reliance on imported, instead of domestic, raw materials for industrial production. It is not necessary that such reduction in raw materials inventories be a working off of stocks acquired through speculation; as has been discussed by Shinohara, this represents to a considerable extent simply the working of an inventory accelerator in a downward direction.

While exports have displayed a trend of rapid growth, they too have been subject to cyclical forces (see Tables 2 and 4). Foreign demand for the sorts of goods Japan might export is exogenously determined, independent of Japan's actions, by world demand and other market conditions. Nonetheless, how Japan responds to opportunities in the world market lies very much within her own domain. That her exports have grown rapidly relative to world trade suggests both how successful she has been in her export orientation and competitiveness and how protective measures abroad have not been a major deterrent to the growth of her exports. Granted that foreign restrictions against goods in which Japan may have its greatest competitive advantage have somewhat reduced the potential increase in exports, it has been rapid growth and high domestic demand which have limited exports of such goods as iron and steel products and machinery, rather than lack of foreign market opportunities. Evidence of this is the way in which exports of such commodities increase substantially when demand within Japan slackens. Note also (Table 2) the contrast in the relative rates of expansion of Japan's exports and world imports in periods—1957 and 1960-1961—when aggregate demand is high in Japan, with periods—1954, 1959, 1962—when demand is less strong.

In other words, strong domestic aggregate demand siphons off potential exports into domestic use. This is especially relevant in the case of bottleneck industries. As discussed earlier, a symptom of changes in domestic demand for export-type goods is the pro-cyclical change in export prices. The trend of declining export prices has been reversed in boom periods and reinforced in recessions. The restructuring of output toward export markets has been very rapid in periods of slack domestic demand and underutilized domestic resources, such as 1955-1956 and 1959-1960. However, as the boom progressed, the rate of increase of imports became even more rapid (1956-1957, 1960-1961) than even the most rapid rate of growth of exports.

While all three postwar cycles have been discussed as a group with similar underlying characteristics, each cycle has had its own special features. In part this has been due to random exogenous events. The 1951-1954 cycle involved adjustments to the ending of the Korean War boom, to a poor rice crop in 1953, and to regional trade imbalance at a time when sterling was not fully convertible externally. The cycle was also influenced both by a boom in consumption and by a large change in the use of imported industrial raw materials. The 1954-1958 cycle got under way not only with inventory investment but mainly with an export boom which then shifted to a boom in plant and equipment investment. Price fluctuations, especially those attendant upon the Suez crisis and its aftermath, had widespread effects on Japan's international price competitiveness and on inventory speculation. Bottlenecks in certain intermediate goods and in transportation were an important feature of the cycle. The 1958-1962 cycle featured a substantial and sustained increase in plant and equipment investment, with previous bottlenecks less constraining but with new bottlenecks, especially in machinery, emerging. A new reliance on major increases in short-term and long-term borrowing postponed the balance of payments crisis but did not prevent its development.

In summary, the empirical evidence for 1951-1962 supports the analytical framework utilized very well. Probably this model is applicable to any period in which rapid growth, as reflected in government maintenance of high levels (rapid rates of growth) of total domestic aggregate demand, is the dominant economic goal. Thus one would expect it to be useful for analysis of many cyclical fluctuations before World War II. Moreover, with only slight reservation, one may predict that it will be verified by the future course of the Japanese economy.[20]

Cyclical Instability and Approaches to Damping

GROWTH AND INSTABILITY

Before analyzing specific fiscal and monetary instruments of policy and their utilization, two questions should be asked:

[20] This prediction is based on my assumptions that growth will continue to be the dominant economic objective of the government and that the government will successfully take sufficient steps to maintain aggregate demand. In the Conference discussion, Professor Ohkawa pointed out that the continued rise in the consumer price level may force the government to adjust objectives toward more explicit concern for price stability at the consumer level. How seriously such a shift would affect my model depends on whether the policy steps taken to achieve price stability act to reduce aggregate demand or to increase supplies of those consumer goods for which prices have risen most rapidly. For example, a policy of importing selected, relatively cheap foodstuffs would reinforce the applicability of my analytical approach. Indeed, the course of the economy in 1963 and early 1964 bear out the continuing validity of this framework.

Has cyclical fluctuation been good or bad for the Japanese economy? Were there alternatives to a general restrictive policy by which the short-run balance of payments constraint at the peak of the cycle could have been more effectively met?

Evaluation of the beneficial and harmful effects of cyclical fluctuation depends on what objectives are considered important and on knowledge of the actual effects of stability or instability. It depends also on the framework of evaluation. Comparing the past experience of Japan and other countries historically, one finds it difficult to be very critical. Japan's recent growth has been so rapid, and the recession phase of the cycle has been so mild and short-lived, that large burdens of wasted or misallocated resources or of decreased welfare of specific groups have not been imposed.

It is always easier to be critical in terms of a narrower, policy-oriented viewpoint which emphasizes optimal solutions. If the economy could maintain the same longer-run trend of rapid growth independent of cyclical fluctuations, it clearly would be preferable to avoid fluctuations. For the recession phase of the cycle imposes certain burdens, while resources may be misallocated in the late stages of the boom.[21] In Japan the burden of recessions is mainly in its impact on welfare and less in completely unused resources.[22] Certain industries—in 1962 cotton textiles, iron and steel, and some chemicals—do cut back output and have idle machinery. Restrictive policies

[21] Cf. Lockwood, above, p. 466: "The frantic pace of industrial capital formation during 1958-64 suggested a good deal of hasty calculation and waste."

[22] I disagree strongly with Bronfenbrenner on this point (above, pp. 540-41). The empirical evidence does not suggest there has been substantial "piling up of capacity in advance of demand." Certainly there has been no increase from one recession to the next in the proportion of excess to idle capacity. On the other hand, certain industries which over-expand in the boom do have idle capacity for relatively brief periods in the recession; this is a sectoral rather than a general characteristic of industry. Bronfenbrenner may really be proposing such "pyramid-building" as a necessary policy alternative in the future, rather than a characteristic of the recent past; it seems to me that the Japanese economy has clearly displayed much more flexibility than the rigidities of the Harrod-Domar model.

fall mainly on non-essential (consumer goods) industries and on small businesses, the latter being numerically large and also bearing much of the impact of the recession.

The increase in overt unemployment is quite small in recessions. This is due to the mildness of the recession, the system of retaining regular employees (though this is less important since it affects a relatively small proportion of the labor force), and a flexibility of wages and the economic system such that new entrants and discharged workers are absorbed into smaller manufacturing enterprises, services, and to some extent in agriculture. The main impact of the recession on the labor force is on new entrants, more of whom have to accept lower wage and lower productivity jobs. They bear the burden throughout their lifetime since, due to the nature of the hiring system by the larger firms, they remain with lower-paying firms with restricted opportunity to move upwards. The combination of the cycle and the imperfection of the labor market thus also make for a less efficient allocation of labor by quality than otherwise would be the case. Cyclical fluctuations in the domestic price level—rising and then falling back to the same level—impose a burden on fixed income recipients, to the benefit of producers.

The crucial question is whether such fluctuations enhance or retard the secular growth rate, assuming that aggregate demand could be made to grow smoothly at the appropriate rate. Unfortunately there is no easy empirical answer. Criteria to be considered include: the degree of waste of resources; the investment level; and the effect on long-run expectations. The cycle probably involves a greater waste of resources than would rapid but steady growth. In the height of the boom, investment and labor are misallocated, and probably resources generally are wastefully used because discipline is weakened in business under conditions of rapidly expanding profits. In the recession, on the other hand, capital and labor resources are not fully utilized, and incremental labor resources are misallocated. If it could be shown that the recession causes sufficient cost-reducing innovations, rationalization, economies in the use of resources, etc., all together benefitting the economy more than the costs of cyclical fluctuation, such a pattern would then be beneficial. This seems unlikely when underlying growth forces are strong. The postwar recessions have probably been too mild to have net beneficial effects on the growth rate in this respect. One aspect does have a beneficial effect on resource allocation and indirectly on the balance-of-payments constraint: the late stages of the boom make painfully clear where the specific production bottlenecks in the economy are, impelling a sense of urgency to eliminate them. However, in a sophisticated economy (and one in which the hand of government is strong) such as Japan's, it is possible to predict fairly well where bottlenecks will develop when growth is rapid, and steps can be taken in advance to alleviate these conditions without having to rely on the late warning of an acute bottleneck.

Inasmuch as long-run growth depends substantially upon the proportion of fixed plant and equipment investment in total output, it is important to determine whether the cycle increases this proportion beyond what it would have been otherwise, or whether the amount of extra real plant and equipment investment above the trend at the height of the boom is more than offset by the decline in fixed investment below the trend in the downswing. This is particularly hard to estimate because of the difficulty in determining the trend either of growth or of investment. Even if the former is given, the incremental capital-output ratio shifts over a period of time due to changes in technology, in the composition of demand, and in the supply of other productive inputs. Has the cycle had an asymmetric effect on balance, increasing both the incentive to invest and the amount of saving beyond what they would otherwise have been? Probably so. Saving has been increased because business has additional incentives to retain earnings for investment in boom periods, and because temporary inflation produces some forced saving. The explosive nature of the boom—demand always outstripping supply—has provided profit incentives for increased investment. The past three cycles appear to have had an upward ratchet effect on the proportion of private fixed plant and equipment investment in total output.

This may have been due partly to a favorable effect of the cycle on long-run expectations. One would expect that cyclical fluctuation would increase uncertainty and risk, and thereby reduce the investment rate. Yet the very pattern of large upswings in output and rapid growth, coupled with only mild recessions and government support of aggregate demand, may have induced more optimistic business expectations about long-run growth prospects than otherwise would have been the case. Nothing succeeds like success, especially when experience demonstrates that the government is able and anxious to maintain the high growth pattern. The problem is that in any recession it is difficult to estimate the degree to which the underlying autonomous growth forces remain unabated. Many people were concerned both in the 1957 and 1962 recessions whether private plant and equipment investment demand would continue, or whether conditions had changed in some fundamental way. Thus far optimism has been justified. In some future cyclical swing, however, it may be necessary to slow down the economy sufficiently to cause a serious reduction in longer-run optimistic expectations.

Thus, it is not clear whether the sum of various effects of the cycle in themselves have had a net beneficial effect on the growth rate of the economy. Whether or not elimination of the domestic forces enhancing cyclical instability would be desirable, certainly some instability is inevitable, given the impact of random shocks and of exogenous cyclical forces such as the world business cycle. And certainly it is desirable to take advantage of newly developing export opportunities, even if they do manifest themselves in irregular or cyclical patterns, since this provides a way to raise the ceiling of the balance of payments constraint on growth.

While rapid growth may possibly be enhanced by a *pattern* of cyclical instability, it can be argued that the *degree* of instability has been excessive. This apparently is the government view, as expressed not only in annual economic White

Papers but explicitly in the 1961-1970 income-doubling plan. Here it is recognized that the Japanese economy will continue to be susceptible to short-run fluctuations caused by changes in economic conditions abroad; but it is also stated that the period and scale of such fluctuations should be deliberately minimized.[23] I concur that the upswing phase of the cycle has been somewhat excessive, on the basis both of growth and welfare criteria, and should have been damped somewhat. The misallocation of resources and increases in the price level become cumulative as the boom continues until a balance-of-payments crisis becomes acute; moreover they tend to worsen more rapidly the longer the boom lasts. Retrenchment policy and adjustments in the economy must therefore be all the more severe. Partly it is a question of the responsiveness of domestic and export prices to downward adjustment; for both economic and political reasons they become progressively harder to push down the more they have already declined. Also, while in the past the tempering of optimistic business expectations has not been too difficult a problem, there is the danger of inducing a rather more pessimistic set of expectations if the downward adjustment has to be stringent at a time in the future when exogenous forces are posing balance of payments problems. In addition, pressures on the consumer price level become particularly strong in the later stages of a prolonged boom, as was the case in 1961 and early 1962. This makes for a possible price-wage spiral; it is noteworthy that only in the most recent boom did the increases in wages outstrip increases in labor productivity.

To mitigate these problems of adjustment and to lessen the burden on small business and on new entrants into the labor force, it probably would have been better to damp cyclical fluctuation somewhat by anticipating the balance of payments crisis and by applying the brakes sooner and perhaps more gradually. Specifically, a restrictive monetary and fiscal policy might perhaps have been undertaken about six months earlier than was actually done in the last two cycles. It is difficult to

[23] EPA, *New Long-Range Economic Plan of Japan* (*1961-1970*) (Tokyo, 1961), pp. *27*, *63*.

judge just when the balance of payments ceiling is being reached, but there are indicators which give earlier warning than large monthly decreases in foreign exchange reserves. Such indicators include seasonally adjusted exports, imports, and balance on current account; projected stable short-term and long-term foreign capital borrowing; wholesale and export price indexes; and evidences of capacity constraints in specific basic industries, such as percentage of capacity in operation, number of months backlog of orders, and delays in loading and shipment.

APPROACHES TO THE BALANCE-OF-PAYMENTS CONSTRAINT

This leads directly to the second question: were there alternative ways to meet the short-run balance of payments constraint at the peak of the cycle? Either of two divergent approaches might have been used instead of the orthodox measures of restrictive fiscal and monetary policy under a system of fixed exchange rates. One would have been a flexible exchange rate system, not just for the peak phase but for the whole period. Devaluation of the fixed rate at the peak and appreciation in the trough would have been inefficient. A once-and-for-all depreciation at the peak might have helped, but likely would have been subject to retaliatory restrictions by other countries, given Japan's rapid increase in exports. The flexible exchange rate would have allowed Japan to maintain its price competitiveness even in a boom, but at the price of possibly great deterioration in the terms of trade. At the same time a flexible system would provide the government more leeway in its adjustment policies. At the height of the boom, with specific bottlenecks and *ex ante* investment outstripping saving, the same kind of domestic absorption problem emerges under fixed or flexible exchange rates. In order to have intermediate goods and machinery as inputs for the production process, their prices would have to rise relative to consumer goods, which then would be exported instead of intermediate goods; but this would imply forced saving. The depreciating exchange rate and shifts in relative prices under these circumstances would probably bring the boom to a halt, or else result in runaway inflation. Flexible exchange rates would also imply a considerably more open economy with greater possibilities of capital flows, some of which might have been disequilibrating. At any rate, it is unlikely that the government seriously considered shifting to a flexible exchange rate, especially since it was not the practice of other industrialized countries.

The other alternative would have been to strengthen import controls, to be more restrictive about the imports admitted, and to allow moderate price increases in order to achieve continued rapid real growth. This approach is more in line with the thinking among important segments of Japanese policy-makers and deserves serious attention. It was a major policy issue in the fall of 1956, when the import of raw materials increased so rapidly. Shimomura Osamu argued that it represented primarily inventory speculation, and all that was necessary was to outwait the speculators, or at worst temporarily to tighten direct controls on raw material imports. Goto Yonosuke argued that, while there was some inventory speculation, the increased raw material imports mainly were being used up in the industrial process as the economy grew rapidly. The basic data were poor, and at the time Shimomura's views prevailed since a restrictive monetary policy was postponed. Subsequent data indicate that the increase in imported raw material inventory investment was within the range Goto suggested.[24]

To support substantially increased trade controls when the balance of payments is running into difficulties implies one or more of three assumptions. Endogenous forces will make the economy turn down eventually anyway, and this would be preferable to halting the boom earlier through fiscal and monetary policy; or further import restrictions would encourage sufficient import substitution so that the balance of payments constraint could be mitigated; or further import restrictions would at least postpone the balance of payments

[24] See EPA, *Economic Survey of Japan 1961-1962* (Tokyo, 1962), Annex 17, p. 396, and p. 215. For a discussion and analysis of the Shimomura-Goto "inventory controversy" see Shinohara, *op. cit.*, Ch. 5.

crisis, and this would be desirable. The Japanese case suggests that more severe import controls have not been justified on any of these grounds.

First, while it is possible that there are endogenous forces within the economy which would make the upswing reach a peak and turn down automatically, this has never happened in the period we are considering. Evidence suggests instead that the boom was indeed explosive. The 1961 case is particularly relevant. The upswing lasted longer than it had in earlier cycles, mainly because short-term capital inflows raised the balance of payments ceiling. Plant and equipment investment and the rate of growth accordingly surged considerably ahead of what had been predicted for 1961. There certainly was no indication that there were sufficiently strong endogenous forces in the economy to force a downturn in the boom.

Similarly, more restrictive import controls to encourage import substitution would have had only limited effects. It should be remembered that the economy has been vigorously engaging in import substitution over the entire postwar period, particularly in those sectors in which technology has a large role relative to natural resources in determining price competitiveness.[25] A point is reached, however, where the benefits of import-substituting domestic production in raising the balance of payments ceiling on growth are offset by the loss of growth from the inefficient allocation of resources. It is reached relatively soon in an economy such as Japan's where resources are quite mobile, transformation is rather easy, and there is a strong export orientation. Although Japan may still engage profitably in import substitution in some sectors, in many others it has probably gone beyond the limit, so less import substitution would be profitable. This is true for parts of agriculture, some machinery, and even for certain manufactured consumer goods. Particularly if world trade conditions continue to become more liberalized, to specialize more in export production and rely less on inefficient import substitution would be to Japan's advantage.

[25] Cf. Chenery, Shishido, and Watanabe, "The Pattern of Japanese Growth, 1914-1954," *Econometrica*, XXX, 1 (January 1962), 98-139.

At the height of the boom it is unlikely that more severe import restrictions would substantially increase import-substituting domestic investment in the short run, or that such transformation could be carried out rapidly enough to solve the immediate balance of payments difficulties. We are after all concerned with a period when the Japanese economy is growing exceptionally rapidly and specific domestic bottlenecks have already become significant. These industries certainly need no further encouragement to investment. The problem is rather one of the gestation period; to eliminate bottlenecks in basic sectors by investment which increases output takes more time than the rapid growth at the height of the boom and the onrushing balance of payments crisis will tolerate.

The third justification for more restrictive import controls—to postpone the balance of payments crisis—is related to that of import-substitution. Just as import-substitution has been quite fully pursued in the postwar economy, so too have the possibilities of rigid import controls. The leeway in the balance of payments that import controls provide is in the reduction of non-essentials. These are usually thought of either as luxury consumer goods or as items for which relatively close domestic substitutes are available with elastic supplies at prices fairly close to the landed (freight and import duties) prices of imports. Such non-essential imports are a negligible proportion of Japan's imports; virtually all imports are basic foodstuffs, industrial fuels and raw materials, intermediate goods, and machinery. Moreover, the specific bottleneck problems of rapid growth imply that domestic supplies of import-competing goods are highly inelastic in the short run. An administrative decision at the height of the boom to restrict certain imports for the production process, with attendant cut-backs in output of specific industries due to lack of imported raw materials or intermediate products, would very likely be less efficient in terms of meeting the preferences of those who represent final demand (both domestic and foreign) than would the restrictions in output brought about by fiscal and monetary policy through the marketplace. This holds especially where the imports are of basic industrial inputs which will be processed many times before emerging as final demand. Administrators do not know enough about inter-sectoral demands, technological constraints, or possibilities of substitution to make satisfactory decisions.

Postponing the balance of payments crisis by adding quantitative import controls would likely make the inevitable adjustment only that much more difficult. Even fiscal and monetary restraints have probably not been imposed as quickly as they should have been, as noted earlier. Moreover, further restrictions of imports would be at the expense of a greater increase in the domestic price level. This, together with the reallocation of resources away from export industries (possibly even those that can readily sell abroad), would reduce export earnings; the balance of payments ceiling would not have been raised after all.

The trend among the industrialized countries has been away from trade and foreign exchange controls and toward greater liberalization of trade and payments. Aside from the political aspects, it is important economically for Japan to obtain the benefits of trade liberalization, given its balance of payments constraint on growth and given the relative efficiency of its incremental resources in export instead of import-substituting production. She can so benefit only by participating herself in liberalization. This she has been doing, especially since 1959, though somewhat slowly and from an initially high degree of restriction. Liberalization does allow greater latitude in applying contra-cyclical trade controls in the future. However, so long as Japan continues to benefit from more liberalized world trade conditions, it would be unwise to impose further trade restrictions of her own that would invite retaliatory action abroad.

Fiscal-Monetary Instruments and Policies

Since the government has not used changes in the exchange rate or in direct trade controls as major instruments of contra-cyclical policy in the period under consideration,[26] it has relied

[26] This is not to imply that trade controls have had *no* contra-cyclical

mainly on fiscal and monetary measures. Fiscal measures—government taxes and expenditures—change aggregate demand directly in altering private income and expenditure streams, while monetary measures affect aggregate demand (mainly investment) indirectly by altering prices (interest rates) and the relative and absolute supplies of different kinds of financial assets (mainly money). In Japan these price and asset effects have direct and strong influences on investment, primarily through the availability of funds.

While the central bank normally implements monetary policy, in Japan monetary policy is somewhat complicated by the existence of such government financial institutions as postal savings and life insurance, the Trust Fund Bureau, and institutions which lend to the private sector. Not only do these agencies influence the composition of investment through their lending activities, they may at times change the total supply of funds in the money market by such actions as Trust Fund Bureau purchase or sale of securities from private financial institutions. Such actions are not always merely for portfolio purposes, but are sometimes instruments of general monetary policy. They may reinforce central bank action, or where they partially offset it there is also a reduction in the psychological effectiveness of central bank policy. This is not a major problem, however, because overt changes in Bank of Japan policy in fact require government (Ministry of Finance) acquiescence as a minimum. Although Bank of Japan officials may disagree with government fiscal and monetary policies and may try to influence these policies by intra-governmental negotiation, the Bank in practice cannot pursue a policy at all different from or independent of that of the government. In this sense fiscal and monetary policy are well integrated. The most recent attempt of the Bank of Japan

role. They were used somewhat in 1953-54, especially for the import of raw cotton, and less so in 1957. Techniques utilized have included a slowdown of the administrative processing of import licenses and required advance deposits for certain imports.

to achieve independence, in part by defining price stability as its primary objective, ended in failure in 1960.[27]

As in many countries there is an asymmetry in the way in which fiscal and monetary instruments are applied respectively over the course of the cycle. Monetary techniques are used as the major restrictive device when a balance of payments crisis ends the boom, and fiscal steps supplement and reinforce the monetary restriction. In the recession, on the other hand, expansive tax and especially expenditure measures are relied upon, while an easier monetary policy plays a facilitating role. Consequently there tends to be the bias of a relatively easy discretionary fiscal policy and a relatively tight monetary policy, rather than a balance of both, over the full course of the cycle. Sound political and economic reasons exist for this division of labor. It is politically difficult for an elected government to increase tax rates and/or lower its expenditures in a boom; the direct effects on personal incomes hurt. The indirect and perhaps more mysterious measures of a central bank, whose decision-makers consist of appointed officers, are more palatable to the average citizen. Thus monetary measures can be much more rapidly and flexibly administered than fiscal ones when a restrictive policy is to be pursued. It is politically popular in Japan for the government to cut tax rates and to increase expenditures in a recession.

A tight money policy is more effective in a boom than is an easy money policy in a recession. This is partly because in the boom it strikes directly at investment, the most volatile component of aggregate demand and the one that presumably can be restricted most readily and with the least burden on welfare. In addition, monetary policy in Japan operates by controlling the availability of funds, an extremely important determinant of investment in boom periods. In the recession

[27] See Patrick, *op. cit.*, pp. 33-40; Shionoya, T., *Problems Surrounding the Revision of the Bank of Japan Law* (Nagoya, 1962) ; and Frank C. Langdon, "Big Business Lobbying in Japan: The Case of Central Bank Reform," *American Political Science Review*, LV, 3 (September 1961), 527-38.

increased availability of funds seems to have a moderately expansive effect on investment, but not as strong as the restrictive effect in the boom. Because the central bank is more conservative, it presses for restrictive action sooner and is slower to relax its tight money measures. As a result the government is more likely to acquiesce in restrictive monetary policies before it will undertake restrictive fiscal measures, while in the recession it moves with alacrity to expansionary policies.

This asymmetry in monetary and fiscal policy is the opposite of what is sometimes said to be desirable for rapid long-run growth. For other industrial countries it has been recommended that a tight fiscal policy which restricts consumption and an easy money policy which encourages investment is the most desirable mix. In Japan, however, it is not the lack of investment demand that has held back the rate of growth of the economy. Here the asymmetry adopted has probably been preferable partly because both sets of instruments are used directly and vigorously to promote growth. The relatively easy fiscal policy produces favorable long-range expectations in business and keeps private investment demand high. Tighter money policy, by keeping Japanese interest rates above the level in foreign capital markets, encourages inflows of long-term and short-term portfolio capital which raise the balance of payments ceiling.[28] At the same time monetary policy over-all has been expansive enough to make funds available for new investment quite readily, especially in the early and middle stages of the boom.

FISCAL POLICY

Considering fiscal policy in more detail, we should remember that it has objectives in addition to damping cyclical fluctuation in the economy. It controls the provision of public goods and services through its expenditures, redistribution

[28] See, for instance, Robert A. Mundell, "The Appropriate Use of Monetary and Fiscal Policy for Internal and External Stability," International Monetary Fund, *Staff Papers*, IX, 1 (March 1962), 70-77.

of income via taxes, transfers of income and wealth into socially more desirable patterns, and maintenance of a high rate of economic growth. This final objective has on the whole been dominant.[29] No doubt the great emphasis that the political leadership, and especially Prime Minister Ikeda, has placed on growth of the economy and on using whatever policy measures are appropriate to this end has established an environment which is highly conducive to the growth of private demand, especially investment demand. This attitude, however, has probably increased cyclical instability, since the government, psychologically and politically committed to its growth program, has been unwilling to slow down the "overheated" economy, preferring to temporize in the hope that the balance of payments danger signals will prove false, or that the high growth rate will be sustained by a sufficient upward shift in foreign demand. Thus far Japan has not been rescued from periodic balance of payments crises by such a dilatory approach.

Contra-cyclical fiscal policy is bounded by some general constraints. Legally, the general account of the national budget must be balanced or in surplus, with one-half of any surplus being used to reduce government debt in the second succeeding fiscal year.[30] There is strong political pressure to utilize budgetary surpluses in this general account to reduce tax rates and increase government expenditures. The government cannot increase its net long-term debt without special legislation for specific investment uses; in fact it has not borrowed from the domestic private sector or the central bank by issuing its long-term securities since 1949. What might appear to be a serious limitation has not been so in fact, mainly

[29] This government emphasis on growth among its objectives can be interpreted in a variety of ways: recognition and acceptance of the social responsibility to achieve rapid, sustained growth; a means of buying off the electorate, especially that part which is not particularly enchanted by other aspects of government policy; or a way to reward those who support the Liberal-Democrat Party, especially big business.

[30] Public Finance Law (Law 34, March 31, 1947), reproduced in English in Ministry of Finance, Budget Bureau, *Japanese-English Budget Dictionary* (Tokyo: 1949).

because the strong private demand, especially for investment, has required a cash surplus budget over the course of the full cycle in order to restrain inflationary pressures. Thus, when I refer to an easy fiscal policy, this is not in terms of a surplus or a deficit budget, but relative to the level of private aggregate demand; government fiscal policy has been relatively easy in that it has kept total aggregate demand almost bursting against the seams of aggregate supply.

The legal balanced budget constraint can be and has been evaded to some extent. First, the government can so juggle its complex bookkeeping system that it can actually run cash deficits in recessions, and indeed has done so, as is indicated in Table 5. Second, the government has access to private savings through postal savings and life insurance programs and through long-term bonds issued by government-owned activities such as Japan National Railways, Japan Housing Corporation, and Japan Highway Public Corporation. To the extent that net inflows of funds from postal savings and life insurance are a regular item, they may be taken as a leakage of aggregate demand similar to tax revenues. Thus aggregate demand is reduced unless the government either spends these funds or lends them to the private sector which then spends them. In this way also the government can influence the total level of aggregate demand. Its borrowing of private funds through debenture issue of government-affiliated agencies results mainly in a restructuring of final demand rather than a net change since these funds alternatively would likely have flowed directly into private spending.

A second constraint has been a policy commitment to limit total government tax revenues to about 20 percent of national income.[31] Since Japan has a progressive tax rate structure, this policy implies annual tax cuts as the economy grows. In practice this ratio has not been rigid, increasing when growth was faster than the rate expected when the budget was formulated. However, this constraint has a pro-cyclical bias and reduces the flexibility of contra-cyclical policy.

[31] Ministry of Finance, Tax Bureau, *An Outline of Japanese Tax, 1962*, p. 14.

TABLE 5

National Government Tax Cuts, Increases in Expenditure, and Cash Budget

(amounts in billion yen)

	Tax Cuts		Purchases of Goods & Services		General Acc't		Gov't Inv. & Loan Program		Consolidated Cash Budget Net Balance
Fiscal Year	Amount	% of increased revenue	Amount increase	% increase	Amount increase	% increase	Amount increase	% increase	Amount
)51	74.3	100.1	338.2	54.0	116.5	18.4	97.3	72.7	96.9
)52	75.9	28.2	191.0	19.8	124.1	16.6	41.3	17.9	15.5
)53	105.2	58.3	255.1	22.1	143.3	16.4	27.2	10.0	−30.9
)54	13.0	26.6	27.8	2.0	23.6	2.3	−48.2	−16.1	−134.1
)55	39.5	92.9	41.6	3.9	−49.3	−0.8	−12.0	−4.8	−98.1
)56	0	0.0	72.0	2.9	43.4	4.4	−8.1	−3.4	102.5
)57	72.0	37.5	177.0	6.1	102.6	9.9	103.0	44.5	147.8
)58	26.1	24.8	231.0	6.6	174.6	15.3	60.9	18.2	−56.3
)59	13.3	12.2	202.0	8.7	107.1	8.2	42.9	10.9	17.7
)60	−5.8	−2.8	343.0	8.5	148.7	10.6	43.8	10.0	243.5
)61	64.8	16.5	415.0	11.9	383.1	24.4	119.7	24.8	717.4
)62	98.7	20.5	620.0	14.5	474.0	24.3	109.8[a]	18.3[a]	−34.9

[a] Original appropriation.

Note: Columns 1-6 based on original budgetary estimates for the fiscal year from)55; columns 7-9 based on actual results.

Source: EPA, *Economic Survey of Japan 1961-62* (Tokyo, 1962), pp. 276, 278; Bank of Japan, *Economic Statistics of Japan 1956, 1960, 1962* (Tokyo, 1957, 1961, 1963), and *Economic Statistics Monthly* (March 1963).

A third constraint is that once the fiscal budget is passed by the Diet—in March or so, for the year beginning April 1— it is politically and administratively difficult to make restrictive adjustments during the year. Expenditures which have already been committed are hard to cut back. Moreover, politically it is virtually impossible to increase tax rates even for long-term growth purposes, much less as a contra-cyclical measure, since the populace has become accustomed instead to reductions in tax rates, or at the worst, no change. It is easier to increase expenditures through supplementary budgets, and indeed this is done virtually every year; restriction can be effected by making the supplementary budget small.

Government tax and expenditure policy can affect the level of private spending both directly and indirectly. In addition to the direct multiplier effect on total aggregate demand, the indirect effect in Japan on private, and especially business, expectations is also quite strong. Changes in the amount of tax cuts, government general account expenditures, and the government investment and loan program are the three main indicators to which business expectations respond. Changes in the investment and loan program are the most volatile. The effect of budgetary changes on expectations is not perverse: large increases in tax cuts, general account expenditures, and/or the investment and loan program promote optimism, while small increases or decreases have a restraining impact.

Several automatic stabilizers with a definite contra-cyclical impact have been built into the fiscal system. The main automatic stabilizer is a consequence of the elastic nature of the tax system. In addition there are such measures as unemployment insurance and support to the price of rice. Quantitatively these are not very important: unemployment is rather limited, so the total payments of unemployment insurance are not large; the official price of rice has not been above the equilibrium price, given import policy (which in itself helps stabilize agricultural prices, at least in a downward direction), until the past few years, and even now the difference does not appear to be large.

Between 1951-1960 the elasticity of tax revenue to national income was 1.71 for direct (essentially corporate and personal income) taxes, and 1.24 for indirect (excise) taxes excluding revenues of the tobacco monopoly, which are quite inelastic.[32] This elasticity results from the increasing proportion

[32] *Ibid.*, p. 145. These estimates were evidently computed on the

of profits in national income as the boom progresses, the progressive structure of personal income tax rates, and the relatively high taxes on luxury durable consumer goods. In a boom the very large increase in governmental tax revenues reduces the level of private aggregate demand from what it would be otherwise, and especially consumer demand (as is desirable in order to facilitate the shift of composition of output in favor of investment).

However, the government has substantially offset the advantages of the contra-cyclical features of the tax system with a discretionary policy which is pro-cyclical, particularly in reinforcing the boom phase. As is indicated in Table 5, the government has cut taxes and increased its expenditures substantially at the height of the boom. Not only are the absolute changes relatively large but there are rises in the rates of increase of government expenditures and of tax cuts relative to projected additional tax revenue. These steps, in opposition to those desirable to counteract the cycle, are a consequence of the constraints of having a balanced general account budget and taxes 20 percent of national income.

The strength of the pro-cyclical impact of such an expansionary fiscal program at the height of the boom depends inversely on the interval between the time when the budget goes into effect (April 1) and the point at which the balance of payments problem becomes acute. In 1953 the balance of payments problem began to emerge only some six months after the fiscal 1953 budget was passed. This was late enough so that the fiscal 1953 budget had less of an impact, and early enough so that the fiscal 1954 budget could be one of restraint. In 1957, in contrast, the balance of payments problem developed just at a time when a highly expansionary budget was being passed (see data for the 1957 fiscal budget in Table 5). This made matters worse. A very restrictive monetary policy had to be put into effect in May, barely two months after the 1957 budget went into effect. In 1961 the timing was almost

---

basis of changes in tax revenues that would have occurred in the absence of changes in tax rates.

as bad. The 1961 budget was quite expansionary. The current account of the balance of payments started running a deficit from January 1961 ; the short-term capital inflow masked the approaching difficulties for a while, but by late spring these difficulties were quite evident, again only a few months after the budget went into effect.

Fiscal policy has played a rather mixed role in supplementing the restrictive monetary policies at the height of the boom. Its contribution was strongest in 1954, particularly in its psychological effects. The timing made a retrenchment budget appropriate. There was some attempt, not very successful, to reduce expenditures in the 1957 budget. The adjustment in the balance of payments was sufficiently well along by early 1958 so that a mildly expansive rather than restrictive budget was in order. In the most recent case, inasmuch as the tight money policy was inaugurated only in September 1961, the adjustment process could have been facilitated in 1962 by a restrictive fiscal policy. Surprisingly enough, however, the 1962 budget was somewhat expansionary, rather than restrictive, in tone. While this reflected in part a reaction to the rapid growth of the economy and of tax revenues (the balanced budget and 20 percent of GNP constraints continuing to be important), it also represented the basic unwillingness of Prime Minister Ikeda to do much of even a short-term nature to slow the economy down.

The combination of automatic stabilizers and discretionary policy has been rather more effective in the recession phase of the cycle. There has been little hesitation to use an expansionary fiscal policy, and even to increase expenditures further via supplementary budgets, once the balance of payments constraint has been lifted. In 1955 the original projection of government purchases of goods and services was for an increase of only 3.9 percent, while the actual increase realized was 11.5 percent; similarly in 1958 the respective figures were 6.6 percent and 9.9 percent. The government is less constrained by the balanced budget concept and tax revenue limit of 20 percent of national income in recessions, which makes good political sense.

MONETARY POLICY

Monetary controls, as previously noted, accordingly bear the main responsibility for ending the boom and bringing about an appropriate adjustment by slowing down the rate of growth of the "overheated" economy. The function of monetary policy is considered to be rather more limited than that of fiscal policy; the Bank of Japan's prime emphasis has been on price stability and on damping cyclical fluctuation in the economy as requisites for rapid growth. To this end it attempts to control the general level of aggregate demand by controlling the level of expenditures on investment. At the same time, the Bank of Japan encourages saving, the transmission of saving to investors, and the appropriate allocation of investment funds as determined by the market.

The Japanese economy tends to be highly illiquid, depending directly for its liquidity on Bank of Japan credit. There are a number of interrelated reasons for this.[33] Since 1949 the private sector (private financial institutions, businesses, and households) has held a very small amount of negotiable short-term or long-term government debt. The early postwar inflation in effect virtually wiped out the government debt. The subsequent tendency for the government to run a cash surplus and to retire debt has further reduced the absolute amount of negotiable government debt held privately.[34] Because of this, as well as the relatively low pegged interest rate on Treasury bills, the private sector does not hold claims on the government which it can readily monetize. There is some net supply of domestic liquidity from the increase in

[33] For greater detail on this and on business reliance on bank loans for investment financing, see Patrick, *op. cit.*, especially Ch. 4; EPA, Economic Research Institute, *An Analysis of Deposits, Loans and Liquidity of Japanese Banks*, Economic Bulletin No. 10 (July 1962); and Mizuno M., "Funds, Investment and Multiplier," *Weltwirtschaftliches Archiv*, Band 88, Heft 2 (1962), pp. 259-84.

[34] Most debt retirement has been that held by government financial accounts and by the Bank of Japan. Nevertheless, the private sector holdings of negotiable short- and long-term government securities in March 1961 was only 0.4% of fiscal 1960 GNP. Cf. Patrick, *op. cit.*, p. 97.

foreign exchange reserves over time (to finance growing imports), as foreign exchange is purchased by the government or the Bank of Japan. This, however, is insufficient to compensate both for the government cash surplus and the large increases in currency in circulation demanded for transactions purposes in a rapidly growing economy.[35] Accordingly the Bank of Japan has to inject liquidity into the economy in order to prevent strong deflationary pressures from developing. Under these circumstances, by controlling the availability of its credit the Bank of Japan directly determines the degree of liquidity of the economy. The mechanism by which the central bank provides credit is essentially loans to the large banks.

Coupled with this is the high degree of corporate business reliance on external funds to finance investment—a natural consequence of rapid economic growth—which is manifested most strongly in the boom phase of the cycle. Given its extremely high investment demand and its price-cost-profit structure, corporate business cannot finance such large increments in investment from internal sources, despite fairly high rates of depreciation and of retention of profits. Net worth for corporate enterprise is only about one-third of total liabilities. Large business, which carries out a sizable proportion of total corporate investment, relies substantially on large banks as an external source of funds. This is due to the nature of the financial system.

While a number of specialized financial institutions exist for specific purposes (such as financing agriculture and small business), the commercial banks are the core of the financial system. "All banks" are classified into four categories: city banks, local banks, trust banks, and long-term credit banks. The thirteen city banks, which operate branches on a national basis, dominate in terms of deposits, loans, and other indica-

---

[35] This suggests that sizable changes in the private sector's preference for holding currency would have very large impacts on the ability of banks to lend. In fact, the proportion of currency held by individuals and the non-financial corporate sector to GNP is not particularly high, and has been quite stable (between 7.5-8% for the period 1954-1962).

tors of banking activity. Aggressively competitive, they are
the main borrowers of call market and Bank of Japan funds,
as well as the main lenders to large business.

The enterprise seeking external funds to finance fixed investment has several potential alternative sources. It can issue
debentures or new equity stock, borrow long-term funds from
long-term credit banks, city banks, or government lending
institutions, or short-term funds from city (or local) banks.
Government lending, though significant for certain industries,
is not dominant. It is not directly influenced by monetary
policy, and so is excluded from this discussion. The capital
market for industrial debentures is limited, too, owing to
market imperfections and interest rates pegged at relatively
low levels. In effect, a certain volume of industrial bond issue
is allowed by the government and the Bank of Japan each
month, the issue being purchased in substantial part by that
city bank which is the prime lender to the company. City
banks hold approximately one-quarter of all industrial debentures outstanding. The stock market offers better opportunities for raising funds through new stock issue, especially
in a boom. However, this form of financing is particularly
costly, because profits are subject to corporate tax while
interest payments are not, and because it is the custom to
issue new stock at par, normally far below market value. It
has been estimated that the real interest cost of equity issue
for large companies is about 25 percent, more than double the
costs of borrowing in alternative ways.[36]

This encourages large business borrowers to seek long-term
loans from long-term credit banks, which provide about two-
thirds of all bank long-term loans, or from city banks, which
provide about one-quarter. However, the long-term credit
banks in themselves are really only intermediaries between
business and other financial institutions, since they derive
their loanable funds primarily from their own bank debenture
issue. One-third of long-term credit bank bonds are held by
city banks.

[36] EPA, Economic Research Institute, *Capital Structure by Firm
Size*, Economic Bulletin No. 6 (February 1961), p. 38.

Thus, directly and indirectly city banks are major providers of long-term loans. In addition, they are the major source of short-term loans, much of which is rolled over and, in effect, finances fixed investment. The city banks, in their attempt to develop and maintain a select group of large preferred customers (for ex-*zaibatsu* banks their old *zaibatsu* firms), are almost invariably willing to lend to big business, although they may not always be able to do as much as they would like because of limitations on the availability to them of additional loanable funds. Several points should be noted. City banks are not as anxious to lend to small business; in recessions, loans to small business rise when banks have excess loanable funds but are reduced when supplies become tighter. City banks are quite willing to borrow short-term funds heavily in the call market (from local banks and other financial institutions which tend to be surplus collectors of deposits relative to their customers' demands for funds) or from the Bank of Japan. In the late stages of the boom and early stages of the downswing, city bank borrowings from the Bank of Japan have been as high as 10-11 percent of their own loans and investments. This is not just a postwar phenomenon; the larger banks also were substantially in debt to the Bank of Japan from the late 1880's until 1910. From then until about 1948 either the general liquidity of the economy was such that the commercial banks did not need to rely on borrowing directly from the Bank of Japan or a deflationary policy was being pursued. Moreover, the city banks borrow short-term funds at high rates of interest when credit is tight, while charging lower rates to large corporate borrowers at a net marginal loss. These banks apparently think in terms of long-term rather than short-term profit maximization; in addition it is clear that such non-profit objectives as bank size (measured by deposits) and close affiliation with selected large business firms enter importantly in their decision-making.

This interrelationship of substantial business reliance on banks (especially city banks) to finance additional investment particularly in the boom, and of substantial city bank reliance on loans from the Bank of Japan provides the central bank with a strong and direct linkage between the availability of its credit and realized business investment. It also has made for some problems in implementing monetary policy. This is in large part because the Bank of Japan has the orthodox view that it should use general instruments of monetary control which rely on changes in interest rates and in the degree of liquidity through adjustments of a price-competitive nature in the money market rather than on direct controls over the availability of central bank credit. Nonetheless, the Bank of Japan does respond in a healthily pragmatic way to the exigencies of the particular economic and institutional conditions which exist in Japan.

One of these conditions is an interest rate structure distorted by a variety of restrictions setting upper limits on interest rates on deposits, bank loans, government debt, and local government, industrial, and bank debentures. This is achieved both by legal means and by government (and central bank) suasion. In tight money periods especially, interest rates run up against these ceilings (and beyond them where evasion is possible). The rate structure is such that short-term lending rates of commercial banks are equal to or higher than long-term rates on any category of bonds; bonds are bought mainly because of government pressure. The general range within which official or stated interest rates can vary is fairly small, although the entire structure may move one or two percentage points over the course of the cycle in response to changes in the Bank of Japan discount rates (to which commercial bank lending rates are, in effect, tied). Because the call market interest rate is the freest in the structure, it is a good indicator of the degree of tightness of credit. It has tended to be above the long-term rates over much of the cycle, especially so in the late stages of the boom and the early part of the downswing. When the Bank of Japan has imposed its restrictive policy in the last two booms, the real call rate has risen to peaks of more than 20 percent before it was arbitrarily reduced by official pressure.

The Bank of Japan would prefer to have a more flexible,

market-determined structure of interest rates, which would tend to raise rates to a higher level in tight money periods than has been true in the past. The Bank bases its position on the criteria of increasing real saving through the interest stimulus and of effective allocation of investment funds among alternative uses on the basis of competition in the market. The government, however, has insisted upon a policy of relatively low interest rates. Its main justification has been to increase Japan's export competitiveness by reducing the interest cost of producing exports; it evidently neglects the role of low interest rates in accelerating increases in aggregate demand and in pushing up the domestic and export price levels. Another reason that apparently has become important recently is that the government would like to develop the long-term capital market, especially for government bonds and for bonds of government-affiliated agencies. This could be done by allowing an increase in the long-term interest rate on debentures, but the government may feel that as a matter of international prestige it should not borrow at a rate more than its current 6.5-7.0 percent. The alternative is to reduce short-term rates sufficiently so that the appropriate relationship between short-term and long-term rates can be achieved. There was a substantial move in this direction between October 1962 and the summer of 1963, as the basic discount rate of the Bank of Japan was reduced four times from a level of 7.3 percent to 5.84 percent, the lowest effective rate in the postwar period. This was a potentially dangerous course, not only in increasing domestic demand but also in tending to discourage inflows of foreign portfolio capital. Subsequent events proved how misguided it was; balance of payments problems again emerged in 1963 and a progressively tighter monetary policy had to be imposed from early autumn.

Because it has been constrained from using large changes in interest rates to control the level of investment demand (it is not certain how strong this influence would be anyway) and because changes in the availability of its credit have such a strong influence, the Bank of Japan has relied substantially upon credit rationing as the instrument whereby monetary policy is implemented. In effect, this approach utilizes and strengthens the credit market's imperfections by raising obstacles to credit transfers through rationing and priorities. This makes it impossible for firms in various situations to obtain credit, or as much credit as they would like. Such an approach is not unique to Japan; it is also used in various European countries, including France and Sweden.[37]

Western tools of open market operations, changes in reserve requirements, and discount policy have been adapted to the requirements of Japanese institutions and conditions of the Japanese economy.[38] The Bank of Japan does not have selective credit controls in its arsenal of techniques, since consumer and mortgage credit are quite limited. The Ministry of Finance determines stock market margins. MITI, under advice from the Ministry of Finance and the Bank of Japan, sets import advance deposit requirements; these have been a useful supplementary device of restriction but have not been of major importance.

While open market operations are considered the main instrument of monetary policy in the United States, they have been unimportant in the postwar Japanese context until very recently. No impersonal capital market exists; Bank of Japan securities transactions have to be done on a face-to-face basis with individual city banks and other private financial institutions, usually under terms of a repurchase agreement. More important, the general trend has been for the Bank of Japan to supply credit, but there has not been a large stock of negotiable securities held privately which the Bank has deemed eligible for open market operations. This is especially true of government debt. Since the fall of 1962 the Bank of Japan has shifted its policy somewhat by widening the definition of securities eligible for purchase to include bank and

---

[37] See, for example, Erik Lundberg, "Economic Stability and Monetary Policy," *Skandinaviska Banken Quarterly Review*, XLIII, 1 (1962), 9-18.

[38] For an extended discussion of the techniques of monetary control, see Patrick, *op. cit.*, especially Chs. 5-9.

selected local government and public enterprise debentures and by engaging in fairly substantial purchases.

Reserve requirements against deposits have also not been utilized as a major technique of monetary control. There were no legal provisions for reserve requirements until 1957, and they were not put into effect until 1959. Reserve requirements were increased as one of the September 1961 measures of restraint, but then the maximum rate was only 3 percent, and that only for current deposits of city banks. Since the city banks were already large borrowers from the Bank of Japan, increased reserve requirements have not been operationally significant.

The main burden for implementing restrictive monetary policy, accordingly, rests with changes in the discount rate and in the availability of funds from the discount window. The Bank of Japan has a complex discount rate structure, based both on the quality of eligible collateral and on the amount of borrowing by the individual bank. The former structure of rates is predicated upon risk differentials for different types of collateral as reflected in the commercial bank lending rates, except for export paper which is given preferentially low rates. The latter component of the structure is really a device to encourage some city bank borrowing in order to offset deflationary pressures in the economy, but to discourage it beyond a certain point by imposing higher (penalty) rates on discounts and loans above a ceiling stipulated for each bank. The highest effective penalty rate has been 1.1-2 percentage points above the basic discount rate structure. In implementing a tight money policy, both the basic discount rate (structure) and the penalty rate are raised and the ceiling at which banks can borrow at the basic discount rate is lowered, so that the penalty rate applies to a higher proportion of bank borrowing from the central bank. However, the penalty rate has not thus far been sufficiently high to choke off additional city bank applications for Bank of Japan credit in a period of strong restriction. The Bank of Japan did increase its penalty rate to a differential of 3.65 percentage points in the fall of 1962, once it was no longer applicable, presumably to make this technique more effective the next time it is needed. Aside from cost effects, the increase in the basic discount rate and the structure has a significant psychological impact, since it heralds a policy of restriction. While an important indicator, it alone certainly will not bring an end to the boom.

In 1954 therefore, and especially in 1957 and 1961-1962, the Bank of Japan had to resort to direct credit rationing.[39] This is done by setting limits monthly above which the loans and investments of each city bank and long-term bank should not expand. Since each bank's expansion of loans in a tight money period has to rely to a considerable extent on additional borrowing from the central bank, the Bank of Japan can keep a fairly accurate check on the behavior of individual banks relative to their stipulated loan ceilings. No explicit, formal penalties exist for non-compliance, but there always lurks the threat of such penalties if the bankers do not behave in a gentlemanly manner. In addition, the number of banks involved is small, so that direct face-to-face negotiations, together with the use of the shame sanction, can be used. This informal rationing system has been quite effective, especially once it is clear that the Bank of Japan and the government mean to enforce a restrictive policy one way or another. An indicator of central bank credit rationing is the interest rate in the call market; while the tight money policy is in force, the effective call rate has been considerably above the Bank of Japan highest penalty rate on its loans and discounts to banks.

[39] The term for this is *madoguchi shidō*. The Bank of Japan does not like to have this technique called credit rationing, referring to it instead as "window operation," a more literal translation. Cf. Bank of Japan, Economic Research Department, " 'Window Operation'—Its Nature and Function in Bank of Japan Monetary Policy," *Monthly Economic Review* (September 1961). The city banks very clearly recognize this as direct control over the availability of credit. Cf. "Banking in Modern Japan," *Fuji Bank Bulletin*, XI, 4 (December 1961, special issue), p. 236. In May 1963 the Bank of Japan announced that it would no longer use *madoguchi shidō*. I suspect that this technique will be re-instituted the next time a restrictive monetary policy is being implemented. (In fact, *madoguchi shidō* was again applied, with minor changes, from January 1964.)

The use of specific instruments of monetary policy has evolved over the course of the three cycles. In the 1951-1954 boom, the tight money policy was begun in September 1953 and reinforced in the early months of 1954. The main technique was to end the system of preferential treatment for a variety of types of discountable paper, especially that financing imports, and to increase the penalty discount rate. Direct control over commercial bank lending was tried out as a supplementary technique of control. As noted earlier, major emphasis was also placed on the austerity 1954 budget to bring about the adjustment process. The tight money policy undertaken in May 1957 differed from the previous one in that it was implemented rapidly and rigorously, essentially by raising the discount rate and penalty rate and by imposing strict credit rationing. The same techniques were applied in September 1961, and in addition reserve requirements were increased. The main weapon in practice continued to be credit rationing. The 1961-1962 adjustment was slower and milder than in 1957-1958. Monetary policy was less strong, partly because the government offset somewhat the pressures on small business by making funds available specifically to them. Fiscal policy was not restrictive. Structurally, it was somewhat more difficult to cut back rapidly, inasmuch as the increase in aggregate demand had been relatively more in fixed investment and consumption, and relatively less in inventories. However, since exports rose sharply and imports declined somewhat during 1962 (as indicated in Table 2), the balance of payments problem could be handled much more readily than in 1957-1958, when world trade conditions were not as propitious. Monetary policy was eased from the fall of 1962 as the balance of payments turned surplus during the summer. This easing may have been premature, for the current account of the balance of payments registered a deficit for the first three months of 1963 at a seasonally adjusted annual rate of about $370 million.[40]

[40] Board of Governors of the Federal Reserve System, Division of International Finance, Far Eastern Section, *Asian Economic Developments (Financial Supplement)* 63, 4 (May 8, 1963), p. 4. (As

While Bank of Japan monetary policy has been highly effective in ending the boom and in bringing about the necessary adjustment in the balance of payments, once it has been implemented, it cannot be judged an unqualified success by its own standards. Its most important defect has not been the inefficacy of its techniques, but its slowness in forcing a decision to restrict aggregate demand. This lag in the making of policy is not entirely the Bank's fault, subject as it is to the views of the government. Nonetheless, it has not taken as strong a stand as it might have done in support of its position that a restrictive policy should be inaugurated more quickly; taking such a stand is not an easy thing to do. In addition, the Bank at times has made mistakes in estimating the economic situation. It allowed easy access to its credit facilities longer than was necessary in the early fall of 1956. It should not have lowered the discount rate in January of 1961. On the whole, however, these mishaps have been relatively minor.

Conclusion

Japan has been very successful in maintaining a high rate of growth of aggregate demand, particularly of private investment and exports, and strong incentives to produce. Her problem of maintaining sustained growth has therefore been that of the neo-classical world, in which changes in technology and in the supply of factors are the determinants of growth. It has been the responsiveness of the Japanese economy on the supply side that has produced the exceptionally rapid rate of growth in the past decade. A quite natural result of this and of the high level of private aggregate demand has been a set of conditions which make Japan appear a topsy-turvy world to Western eyes, especially those used to viewing the American economy: It includes such features as surplus government budgets, tax rate cuts, retirement of government debt, an extremely high rate of growth of private investment in plant and equipment, extensive business borrowing from banks,

---

indicated elsewhere, balance of payments difficulties did increase during 1963, and a restrictive policy had to be reimposed).

absolutely high effective interest rates, and large-scale city bank borrowing from the central bank.

Concomitant with rapid growth, the Japanese economy has been subject to rather wide cyclical fluctuation. For all the three post-war cycles there have been basic similarities in the immediate and underlying causes of the cycle, in the methods with which the cycle has been damped (to the extent that it has been), and the effectiveness of these fiscal and monetary measures. Sustained growth, explosive in nature, runs up against a domestic resource constraint in terms of raw materials and specific bottlenecks in intermediate products and producers goods. The locus of this constraint is the balance of payments, which turns strongly deficit at the height of the boom. A restrictive monetary policy is implemented to eliminate the immediate balance of payments difficulty by reducing aggregate demand and the price level. As soon as this is corrected, an expansionary fiscal policy is renewed in order to end the induced recession and to stimulate the economy on to new heights.

Looking to the next decade, cyclical fluctuation and fiscal and monetary policy appear inextricably intertwined with the question whether and in what degree long-run growth will continue to be explosive, at least relative to the balance of payments constraint. Framed somewhat differently, will the high rate of increase in private aggregate demand continue unabated? A key component is private plant and equipment investment. Is the Japanese economy shifting from excess demand to general productive over-capacity and excess supply? I do not think so, although there may be excess capacity in selected industries, and no doubt the amazingly high rate of plant and equipment investment of 1959-1961 cannot be maintained. Certainly there will be some adjustments in the industrial composition of investment reflecting changes in the structure of final demand, but no reason exists for thinking that ample investment opportunities and longer-run optimistic expectations will not continue.[41]

[41] My optimism about continued rapid growth was properly subjected to criticism at the Estes Park Conference where the papers of

While high aggregate demand will continue to be a pre-eminent characteristic of the Japanese economy, there are two potential sources of compensation if private plant and equipment investment should decline drastically: private housing demand and government fiscal policy to increase aggregate demand. There exists a strong demand for housing in Japan because of wartime destruction, population and income growth, and the low rate of new housing investment in the postwar period; so far this demand has been substantially pent up by lack of credit facilities to finance it. Reduced business investment demand would free saving to be channeled into increased housing investment.

The government could also increase aggregate demand by tax and expenditure measures. A quite large adjustment could be accomplished within the present balanced account budget constraint by increasing the proportion of government expenditure in GNP. Such expenditure would likely be public investment, as outlined in the income-doubling plan for 1961-1970. It could readily be financed, within fairly wide limits, by reallocating government funds which are currently lent to finance private investment, and by increased issue of debentures of government-affiliated agencies. If, on the other hand, private aggregate demand does remain high, and if it is felt desirable to raise the ratio of government investment to total output, this could be financed without generating excess aggregate demand by retaining a higher proportion of the increased tax revenues, reducing tax cuts.

---

this volume were discussed. In essence, my view is that there will be no problem on the demand side. I do expect the supply side to be somewhat less responsive in the future, because labor will be relatively less available, the investment proportion in GNP will decline, the cream of foreign technology has been skimmed, and the increased proportion of government investment will result in a higher capital-output ratio (in part since some of the resulting services will not be adequately measured in national income). Nonetheless, I expect the growth rate to remain substantially above the prewar historical rate. The major issue really is whether the government will alter its policy of rapid growth to emphasize other goals, such as consumer price stability. See n. 20 above.

The balance of payments will remain the major operative constraint upon growth, continuing to generate cyclical fluctuations. This ceiling, relative to the growth rate, is not fixed over time, but will shift about in response to exogenous forces, changes in the structure of the Japanese economy, and adjustments in Japanese policy. Tentative projections can be made for some of these influences on the balance of payments.

The average propensity to import will rise somewhat above its present level, with limited supplies of domestic raw materials at competitive prices, and trade liberalization more than offsetting import-substitution; technological improvement economizing on raw material resources; and changed structure of final demand. It is difficult to know whether speculation in imported raw materials inventories will become damped or not. The ending of import controls reduces incentives to hoard such goods, but allows speculative demand to assert itself without restraint. The main factor is whether there will be a strong shift in business expectations regarding rises in the landed price of imports. A random exogenous shock, such as the Korean War or the Suez incident, could generate such expectations. To the extent that the country has or can obtain sufficient foreign exchange reserves, it could follow a policy of waiting the speculators out.

Japan's exports will continue to grow rapidly. Stable unit labor costs will allow stable export prices, while prices in competitor nations will probably rise slowly. The composition of exports will shift as Japan becomes increasingly able to supply at competitive prices certain chemicals, types of machinery, and other heavy goods, as well as electronics and selected durable consumer goods. Further liberalization of world trade would be helpful in providing Japan with increased access to foreign markets. The rate of growth of world income, as manifested in the growth of world trade, will be an important determinant of the absolute rate of increase of Japan's exports, while in the shorter run the world trade cycle will continue to influence the export level. No doubt unexpected and random events elsewhere in the world, too, will have repercussions both on Japanese growth and on cyclical fluctuations.

Japan probably cannot expect its terms of trade to continue to improve as much as they have over the past decade. This will lower the balance of payments ceiling. However, increased inflows of long-term and short-term portfolio capital and perhaps direct investment will raise the ceiling, and also provide a short-term cushion for the adjustment process at the height of the boom. Greater liberalization of capital and trade flows may also enhance the short-run instability of the economy to the extent that it results in disequilibrating speculation, since the government's direct control over the balance of payments will be reduced.

Just what policy measures the government will use to meet these problems remains to be seen. Hopefully, balance of payments difficulties will continue to be minor relative to the rapid average growth of the economy, and the same general fiscal and monetary approach will be appropriate and adequate. If Japan should find herself with really serious, long-run problems in the balance of payments which limit the economy to a slow growth rate, very likely either the exchange rate would be depreciated or strict trade controls would be re-imposed. So long as the world tendency is toward trade liberalization and Japan benefits thereby, direct trade controls will probably not be used. There are, nonetheless, considerable pressures in Japan to apply direct controls in the domestic economy as well as in the foreign trade sector, either in the form of legislation or of social controls via consultation, administrative guidance, and the like. With government acceptance of responsibility for maintenance of rapid growth goes a desire to minimize uncertainty and to have a stable economic system. Many policy-makers in Japan apparently feel that this can be best achieved by direct controls to reduce the sudden swings that market forces sometimes bring. It is not always recognized that controls may also result in rigidities, reduced ability to transform, inefficient allocation of resources, slower growth, and a lesser degree of satisfaction of consumer preferences.

It seems probable on balance that fiscal and monetary measures will continue to be major techniques of economic policy. Fundamentally this is determined, as noted above, by the strength of private aggregate demand. The rapid rate of growth has made necessary only marginal fiscal adjustments, and a certain degree of flexibility relatively easy. The fiscal system retains sufficient flexibility to meet the aggregate demand problems with which Japan is likely to be faced in the foreseeable future. If changed conditions should necessitate a large shift in fiscal policy, the system does have major areas of inflexibility: the balanced general account budget and constraint on long-term government debt; the decision to limit central plus local government tax revenues to 20 percent of national income; and the development of the expectation by the electorate that tax rates will be reduced virtually every year. None of these is immutable. Expenditures are being increased by the enlarged government investment program. If private aggregate demand should drop so substantially that government deficit spending would be needed over a sustained period, I am confident that the government would change laws, institutions, and its behavior patterns enough to enable it to keep total aggregate demand sufficiently high for rapid growth.

Major issues in the future development of monetary policy and monetary techniques of control relate to the general level of interest rates, and to the use of rate changes as the major means to affect the liquidity of the economy. It is likely that some reduction of the general level of interest rates is possible, especially in the recession phase, without overstimulating aggregate demand and without a loss in the incentives or opportunities to borrow foreign capital. The problem is whether in attempting to correct the distorted interest rate structure by forcing the short-term rates down, the general level of interest rates will not be pushed too low. If flexible changes in the level of the interest rate structure, rather than direct control over the availability of credit, does become the basic mechanism for adjusting liquidity and effective aggregate demand (by altering costs as well as general availability), a changed emphasis in the utilization of specific instruments of monetary policy will be required.[42] The test regarding the appropriate level of the interest rate structure and the flexible use of interest rates to influence liquidity, will come when another boom sets in with rising prices and an emerging balance of payments crisis. In such a boom the credit market tends to tighten and interest rates to rise. Moreover, interest rates rise even further once the Bank of Japan imposes its tight money policy to meet the onrushing balance of payments crisis. In a free market presumably the entire structure of rates would move up sharply, beyond the level rates have been in the past two tight money periods. Would the government allow interest rates, and especially long-term rates, to rise to the degree that market forces would dictate? I suspect not. In a restrictive period arbitrary ceilings would again be imposed on interest rates. Therefore the Bank of Japan would have to continue to resort to informal credit rationing as its main technique of monetary policy, rather than open market sales of debentures (whose rates would be pegged too low to attract prospective buyers); or its penalty discount rate (which would also be set too low relative to commercial bank demand for funds).[43]

In conclusion, basic changes in the pattern of growth and cyclical fluctuation are unlikely in the foreseeable future. Stimulated by high aggregate demand, growth will be explosive and cyclical instability will result, as inadequate domestic resource supplies and specific bottlenecks are manifested in increasing balance of payments deficits. It is doubtful that the government, in its pursuit of growth, has learned

[42] For a more detailed discussion, see Patrick, *op. cit.*, pp. 204-08.

[43] I may be too pessimistic; the recent developments in monetary policy may provide a sufficient cost squeeze to control city bank borrowing from the central bank. Nonetheless, it appears that in late 1963 and early 1964 the Bank of Japan has been forced once again to rely increasingly on its informal credit rationing more than on market forces to implement its new restrictive monetary policy.

from the past three cycles to make the decision to restrict the boom more quickly in order to mitigate the cycle and ease the adjustment process. Rather, one expects Japan to go careening successfully along from one balance of payments crisis to another every few years, with generally the same type and degree of cyclical fluctuation in the economy. Specific techniques of fiscal and monetary control and the asymmetry in their use will probably not change in any major way. Ministry of Finance officials will continue to be expansive, central bankers cautious, credit will be rationed and informal sanctions applied when necessary, and things will all work out pretty well in the end.

CHAPTER XIII

Regional Planning in Japan Today

SABURO ŌKITA

WHEN World War II ended, Japan was left with the four main islands—a total land area of 143,000 square miles—and a population beginning to approach 100 million. The former overseas territories of Sakhalin, Korea, and Taiwan were lost to her; the foreign trade so vital to her economy was almost at a standstill. National recovery demanded a realistic assessment of natural and industrial resources, of population trends and needs, and of aid required in specific areas to revive and develop the economy.

For this purpose a comprehensive plan for regional development of natural resources was clearly indicated. Coordinated reconstruction of river basins was needed to meet urgent demands for flood-control, irrigation to increase agricultural production, and generation of electric power for industry. Something had to be done, too, about the growing congestion in metropolitan areas, the relative backwardness of rural areas, and consequent disparity of income and opportunity. Extensive public works of all sorts were required to facilitate and spread the expansion of industry, thereby increasing employment opportunities for a rapidly growing labor force.

In postwar years these emerging problems generated an overlapping succession of public and private development programs, both regional and national. As they multiplied, the growing necessity to coordinate such programs physically and financially eventually led to measures of control by the national government. The legislative development of this process between 1950 and 1963 is the subject of this study.

Postwar Regional Development Acts

The comprehensive Land Development Act, approved by the Japanese Diet in May 1950, provided the first basic legislation for regional planning. It authorized action on four levels: prefectural and local plans to be formulated by local authorities, and national and specific area plans to be prepared by the government. Such was the pressure for development of specific areas, however, that early action was confined to particular regions. Twenty-two regions, comprising about one-third of the country were singled out for public works—chiefly in flood-control, irrigation, and power generation. Special legislation followed to meet the needs of individual areas: Hokkaidō (1950), Tōhoku (1957), Kyūshū (1959), Shikoku and Hokuriku (1960), and Chūgoku (1961). A national plan finally materialized late in 1962.

Other laws for rural and metropolitan development were also drawn up and implemented on an ad hoc basis. For example, the Act for Development of Special Soil Areas (1952) provided for government subsidized improvement of unfertile soil by removing volcanic ash and gravel. A large part of Kagoshima prefecture is covered by this special soil; in some areas agricultural output has been increased as much as 50 percent by its improvement. Another such ad hoc measure is the Special Act for Heavy Snow Areas (1962) designed to relieve the predicament of persons living in snow-bound districts of Hokkaidō, Tōhoku and Hokuriku.

Still another regional problem is the relative backwardness of outlying islands equipped with inadequate communications with the main islands. A ten-year development program for such islands was prepared in 1953, to be followed by another a decade later. Altogether there are about 3,000 such outlying islands, of which 424 are inhabited; some 292 were designated for assistance under the act. A public works budget for the entire program was appropriated to the Economic Planning Agency (EPA), and then distributed to individual islands through the ministries and prefectural governments. This ususual case of regional budgeting has effectively coordinated spending on various types of public works, and total allocations to these remote islands rose from 0.8 percent of Japan's total public works budget to 1.4 percent in 1962. Living standards among their communities have risen as a result, though they still do not measure up to those in more prosperous parts of the country.

Overcrowded metropolitan areas were also the object of legislative relief from 1956 on. Under the Capital Region Development Act of that year, a ten-year plan of redevelopment for the Tokyo area was adopted in 1958. It called for construction and improvement of ten radial roads and seven loop roads in and around Tokyo; new buildings within congested areas were to be restricted; and some thirty satellite cities were proposed to absorb industrial expansion in the environs. A similar concern for the cities of Osaka, Kobe, and Kyoto led to the passage of the Kinki Region Development Act in 1963. This left without regional development legislation only the Tōkai district, with its rapidly growing industrial city of Nagoya.

With so much legislation and so many agencies operating more or less independently in response to pressure for special bills coming from local interests, it is no wonder that confusion and some overlapping with the provisions of the comprehensive Land Development Act has resulted. For example the Hokkaidō Development Agency, the National Capital Development Commission, and the Kinki Regional Development Bureau are independent organs within the Prime Minister's Office. Other functions of regional planning and coordination are assigned, however, to the Development Bureau of the EPA.

Possible reorganization of the whole machinery of Japanese government, including the administration of regional planning, was under study in 1963 by the Temporary Commission for the Reorganization of Government Administration. One of its committees suggested a new single agency to take over the various organs now in existence and plan and coordinate the whole on a national basis.

Regional Development under the Income Doubling Plan

Renewed attention to imbalances and congestion in regional development as a result of Japan's postwar industrial boom is found in the government's Income Doubling Plan of 1960.[1] Here the need for large investments in social overhead capital was emphasized as essential to the doubling of income during the decade 1961-1970. The "belt areas" along the Pacific Coast and Inland Sea, connecting Tokyo, Nagoya, Osaka, and northern Kyūshū, were considered the most important for new industrial development, and they require for the purpose new public facilities such as road, water supply, and port installations. Special efforts were proposed to disperse factories away from existing industrial concentrations to new centers in these belt areas and other more remote areas. While private enterprise should be permitted free choice of location, the plan argued, decisions should be guided by public assistance and should be made with due regard to the need to strengthen Japan's competitive position.

If it took almost two months for the Cabinet to adopt the Income Doubling Plan, after the proposed draft was submitted to the Prime Minister; one of the main reasons for the delay was controversy within the government party over its provisions for regional development. There were complaints that the document failed to give adequate consideration to improving conditions in underdeveloped areas. By way of compromise a government statement was attached to the draft plan and contained the following passage:

"Promotion of Development of Backward Areas: A comprehensive national development plan will be mapped out to promote development of such backward areas as southern and western Kyūshū, Sannin, and Southern Shikoku areas and to rectify the existing income disparity between advanced areas and underdeveloped areas. Specific measures on taxation, financing and subsidy rate for public works will be taken in connection with the development of backward areas. Necessary legislative measures will be studied to materialize desired geographical distribution of industries with a view to pro-

[1] Japanese Government, *Economic Planning Agency, New Long-Range Economic Plan of Japan (1961-1970)* (Tokyo, 1961), Ch. 2.

moting the public welfare of local residents and to eliminate the backwardness of the respective areas."

Fulfillment of this pledge for "the development of backward areas" called for some clarification of basic national policy in regional development. It finally led to long-delayed action to prepare a nationwide regional development plan as prescribed in the comprehensive Land Development Act of 1950. Accordingly, the EPA set to work upon a draft, and released it to the public in July 1961 under the name of the National Over-all Development Plan. After a year of comment and criticism it was approved by the National Development Council in 1962 and by the Cabinet itself in October of that year.

Basic to the new plan were three objectives: (a) to curb excessive congestion and to redevelop existing big cities; (b) to narrow income gaps among different regions of the country; and (c) to develop new industrial sites in areas adequately furnished with land, water, and labor to accommodate growing industries. To assist in reaching these objectives, regions were classified by the type of development policy needed. Core areas were envisioned as nuclei for development within various regions. Targets for nine regions of the country were specified in the form of shares of national industrial production.

The classification by development policy need was threefold, in turn: (a) overcongested areas; (2) adjustment areas; and (3) development areas.

Overcongested areas include Tokyo, Nagoya, Osaka, and their environs along with the industrial section of northern Kyūshū. For these areas the goal is to discourage further increases of population and industry, and through various incentives to set in motion widespread dispersion to other sections of the nation. Simultaneously, measures are to be taken to improve living conditions and urban functions in the big cities.

Adjustment areas cover the central part of Honshū Island, including the Kantō, Tōkai, Kinki, and Hokuriku districts (excluding overcongested areas). Under the plan, the adjustment hinterland for the big three centers of Tokyo, Nagoya,

623

and Osaka will be prepared with public facilities to accommodate hard-pressed industries in an orderly manner so as to forestall acute congestion. Meanwhile transportation facilities, especially roads, are to be improved within the adjustment area and connect it with neighboring cities and the three major metropolitan centers.

Development areas comprise the remainder of Japan. This includes Hokkaidō, Tōhoku, Chūgoku, Shikoku, and Kyūshū, all of which are relatively remote from metropolitan sections. Here government action is especially necessary to plan, finance, and construct basic public facilities; otherwise few industries are likely to be attracted to these regions. Incentives to industrial development were increased in 1961 by legislation for reduction of real estate acquisition and corporate taxes and accelerated depreciation of fixed assets for a specified number of years. Additional inducement was offered through low interest loans available from the Japan Development Bank and the Hokkaidō-Tōhoku Development Bank.

The designation of an area confers considerable status as well as economic value. Selection is made on the basis of applications from the prefectures. Often accompanied by political pressures, the choice necessarily gives rise to controversy. The final decision may well represent political compromise. Under the Act of 1961 for Industrial Development of Underdeveloped Areas some 96 areas have been officially designated. Similarly, under a 1962 Act for the Establishment of New Industrial Centers, 13 new industrial areas have been selected from 44 applications. In addition, six more were designated as Special Areas for the Improvement of Facilities for Industrial Location. The former are all in the development area, save one in Nagano Prefecture; the latter are all in the belt area from Tokyo west to Kyūshū. Although the government lays down guidelines for development of new industrial centers, detailed planning is left to local authorities.

Concentration or Deconcentration?

The target shares of industrial production for the nine regions for 1970, as specified in the National Over-all Development Plan, are given in Table 1. The plan envisages a reduction in the existing shares of the Kantō and Kinki districts, and a considerable increase in Tōkohu, Tōkai, and Chūgoku.

TABLE 1

REGIONAL SHARES OF INDUSTRIAL PRODUCTION

Regions	1950	1955	Base Year of Plan 1958	1960	Target Year 1970
Whole country	100.0	100.0	100.0	100.0	100.0
Billion yen	(2,140)	(6,220)	(9,380)	(14,800)	(43,000)
Hokkaidō	3.5	3.1	2.9	2.6	3
Tōhoku	5.8	5.4	4.9	4.6	6
Kantō	26.4	29.5	31.8	33.1	29
Tōkai	14.8	16.1	15.8	16.1	19
Hokuriku	3.7	2.7	2.3	2.2	3
Kinki	25.4	24.8	25.2	25.2	20
Chūgoku	7.1	6.7	6.9	6.9	9
Shikoku	4.0	3.0	2.5	2.4	3
Kyūshū	9.2	8.6	7.7	6.9	8

SOURCE: For the years 1950, 1955, 1958 and 1960 figures are computed from the Census of Manufactures; Ministry of International Trade and Industry; figures for 1970 are included in the National Over-all Development Plan.

The actual drift of industrial location, however, has been rather different. Industry has continued to concentrate in the central part of Honshū, i.e. Kantō, Tōkai, and Kinki regions. The share of the above three highly developed regions, out of total Japanese industrial production, rose from 67 percent in 1950 to 74 percent in 1960. During the same period the share of the remainder of the country fell from 33 to 26 percent. In spite of increasing concentration, over-all production has increased in almost every region because of rapid industrial growth. In monetary terms, over-all national industrial production climbed from 2,140 billion yen in 1950 to 14,480 billion yen in 1960 as measured by current prices. The industrial production index (1955 = 100) jumped from 47 in 1950 to 217 a decade later.

It should be noted that industrial production in the Kantō

region has been expanding with exceptional speed, increasing from one-fourth to one-third of the national total between 1950 and 1960. The location of new industry in overcongested areas, especially Tokyo, is beginning to slow down; but the build-up in the neighboring areas of Kanagawa, Chiba, and Saitama prefectures is very heavy. Thus Table 1 indicates production trends are running somewhat counter to the objectives of the plan. Stronger measures may be essential if the aims of deconcentration are to be met.

Regional Differentials and Inter-regional Mobility

The regional and urban-rural differentials that have motivated these first steps to regional development planning remain a conspicuous feature of Japanese society. Also visible, however, are the basic mechanisms that work slowly to correct them through large inter-regional movements of labor and business enterprise in search of opportunity. The spread of education and mass media of communications, along with efficient transport, all add to the new geographic and social mobility of postwar Japan. So rapid has been Japan's industrial growth since 1950, to be sure, that the differentials among regions remain large. There is evidence, nevertheless, that they are being narrowed, especially now that greater equalization is the avowed aim of government policy, as outlined above.

These tendencies will be apparent from the statistics of income differentials and population movements. Although the disparity of income among Japanese prefectures has become a major political issue, Table 2 indicates that in 1961 only five prefectures had a per capita income that was less than 70 percent of the national average. This compares with 10 in 1951 and 35 in 1935. The prefecture with the lowest per capita income was Kagoshima which was 55 percent under the national average; Tokyo with 184 percent was the highest. (This ratio of approximately three to one is, incidentally, almost equal to the income disparity among American states.) The disparity among Japanese prefectures is likely to persist as a political issue because of growing public awareness of

TABLE 2

INCOME DISPARITY BY PREFECTURES

Percentage of National Average	*Number of Prefectures*		
	1935	1951	1961
over 130	3	3	4
100–130	3	4	4
90–100	2	3	7
80–90	1	11	13
70–80	2	9	13
below 70	35	10	5
Total	46	40	46

SOURCE: The 1935 estimate was made by the Research Institute of National Economy; those for 1951 and 1960 were prepared by the EPA.

NOTE: In 1951 six prefectures did not publish income statistics.

the problem. Such awareness can be traced to greater mobility of the population, the introduction of television into virtually all sections of the country, and the stronger voice of the average citizen in the political process.[2]

Population statistics, too, reflect the unequal pull of opportunity. Between 1955 and 1960, 26 of the nation's 46 prefectures lost population, while eight registered increases (Table 3). The eight gainers were Tokyo, Kanagawa, Saitama, Chi-

TABLE 3

SPREAD OF INDUSTRIAL PRODUCTION INTO NEIGHBORING PREFECTURES OF TOKYO

	Industrial Production, Share of Prefectures		Ratio of Production
	1952	1960	1960/1952
Tokyo	14.53%	15.95%	3.95
Kanagawa	6.99	9.22	4.33
Chiba	0.98	1.35	4.49
Saitama	1.98	2.29	3.78
Whole nation	100	100	3.28

SOURCE: Ministry of International Trade and Industry, Figures are computed from the Census of Manufactures.

[2] Additional data on regional differentials in consumption standards are given by Lockwood, above p. 453, Table 4, while Gleason discusses urban-regional differentials at some length in Ch. IX.

ba, Aichi, Osaka, Hyōgo, and Hokkaidō—all prefectures with big industrial cities except Hokkaidō. The decline occurred mostly in the more rural regions, of course, where agricultural labor has been decreasing absolutely since 1955 (Table 4).

TABLE 4

NUMBER OF PREFECTURES CLASSIFIED BY ABSOLUTE AND
RELATIVE CHANGE IN POPULATION

	Prefectures with Absolute Decrease in Population	Prefectures with Relative Decrease in Population	Prefectures with Relative Increase in Population	Rate of Increase of Total Population during Five Years
1930–35	3	31	12	7.5
1935–40	13	25	8	5.6
1945–50	3	11	32	15.6
1950–55	7	31	8	7.3
1955–60	26	12	8	4.6

SOURCE: Isomura Eiichi, *Gendai toshi mondai* [Modern Urban Problems], 1962.

The rate of population growth has been much greater, too, in the larger cities than in towns and villages (Table 5). Most of the migrants are young; for example, 62 percent of the males and 56 percent of the females who migrated to Tokyo in 1960 ranged in age from fifteen to twenty-four. In the predominantly agricultural prefecture of Kagoshima, far to the southwest, 90 percent of the male and 97 percent of the female graduates from junior high school migrated in search of jobs. In the Iwate Prefecture far to the north, the corresponding percentages were 70 percent for males and 76 percent for females.

A factor that may tend eventually to counter migration from the countryside, but equally to narrow income differentials, is the movement of industry into rural areas. It is induced by city-wide shortages of labor, water supply, and land for expansion. Such industrial dispersion is being furthered in a very practical way by the rapid improvement of Japanese highway

TABLE 5

CHANGES IN POPULATION BY SIZE OF COMMUNITIES (1955-60)

Communities by Size of Population	Number of Communities 1960	Population 1960 (million)	Rate of Change of Population 1960/1955 (%)
over 500,000	9	18.49	+18.3
300–500,000	12	4.26	+13.3
100–300,000	92	15.05	+ 9.0
50–100,000	160	10.72	+ 4.6
10–50,000	1,791	35.19	— 1.3
less than 10,000	1,447	9.70	— 4.8
Total	3,511	93.42	+ 4.6

SOURCE: Economic Planning Agency, *Kokumin seikatsu hakusho* [White Paper on National Life] (Tokyo, 1962), p. 161.

facilities, and the day may come when highways reaching into rural Japan will be dotted on each side with industrial plants. A ready supply of labor has so far been available in what is generally regarded as the most mobile group of the rural population: the *jisannan* (second and third sons who have no expectation of succeeding to the occupation of their father). Such a source of mobile labor is now gradually diminishing as the result of heavy outflow from rural areas; and the employment of underutilized but immobile labor such as family heads and eldest sons remaining in the rural district has become necessary. On the other hand, industrial enterprises are now moving into rural sections seeking a labor supply. The resultant increase in cash income for rural families has the added advantage of reducing the differences between urban and rural ways of life. Already in 1962 over half of total income of farm households was derived from non-agricultural sources.

Administrative Investment

Under the plan for doubling the national income, strengthening of "social overhead investment" ranked first among objectives. Expenditures for roads, port development, flood-control, public housing, improvement of sewage facilities have increased rapidly within recent years. As a percentage of GNP, government capital formation was up from 7.1 percent in 1956 to 11.4 percent in 1962. For example, the total outlay by central and local governments for highway construction rose from 61 billion yen in 1955 to 393 billion yen in 1962, and estimates anticipate 511 billion yen in 1963.

It is noteworthy that the emphasis in such administrative investment has been shifting gradually from underdeveloped areas to the development and redevelopment of central Honshu (Kanto, Tokai, and Kinki regions). In fact the share spent for these regions increased from 46.1 percent in the period 1951-1954 to 54.7 percent in 1958-1960. Their share for highway construction outlays rose from 46.3 to 53.3 percent during the same period.[3] The apportionment between the highly developed central area and the underdeveloped areas is shown in Table 6, along with population and industrial

TABLE 6

REGIONAL DISTRIBUTION OF POPULATION, INDUSTRIAL PRODUCTION AND ADMINISTRATIVE INVESTMENT

	Population (1960)	Industrial Production (1960)	Public Works Expenditure by Central and Local Government (1958-60 average)
Central regions (Kantō, Tōkai, Kinki)	53.4%	74.4%	54.7%
Other regions	46.6	25.6	45.3
Whole nation	100.0	100.0	100.0

production percentages. Allocation of public expenditures is indeed a constant source of controversy. On the one hand,

[3] Data compiled from Japanese Government, Economic Planning Agency, *Chihōbetsu gyōsei toshi jisseki* [Breakdown of Administrative Investment by Regions] (Tokyo, 1963).

heavier financial outlay for improvements in the highly developed areas are justified in the name of industrial need and
efficiency; on the other, the long-range objectives of reducing
congestion, maximizing land-use, controlling migration of
population and stimulating the development of new industrial
centers have also fundamental importance.

No simple formula can be found for meeting these divergent
claims upon the resources of the Japanese nation. But the
history of regional planning, from the early ad hoc legislation
to the more systematic efforts at coordinated development in
recent years, indicates the path that must be followed.
Greater systematization is needed, with the help of more
analytical studies of regional development. In recent years
interest in the problems of regional development such as
effective acquisition of land for public use, prevention of
public nuisances, and strengthening of regional and local
planning has been very much stimulated in government,
business and academic circles. One move was the establishment of the Research Committee for Regional Economic
Problems within the Economic Planning Agency. With members from universities, business, and banking institutions, the
committee has gone to work on basic lines of regional development. Another move is the establishment of a non-governmental institution, the Japan Center for Area Development
Research financed by the leading business firms, with plans
to assist research activities in the field of regional science and
planning. This way lies progress.

CHAPTER XIV

Labor Markets and Collective Bargaining in Japan[*]

SOLOMON B. LEVINE

THIS PAPER may appropriately begin with a quotation from a recent book by John Dunlop:[1] "It might more conventionally be said that industrialization requires the creation of a labor market, or that economic development creates a labor market. But such a statement tends to neglect the elaborate system of rules which are erected in the labor market of any industrial relations system. Labor markets are arranged in different ways, and it will be seen that different industrializing elites have different strategies for organizing the labor market. In any one country, the labor market may in fact be structured or subject to quite different rules on recruitment, training, and redundancy at different periods in the course of economic development." The analysis that follows explores the elaboration of labor market arrangements that have been peculiar to Japan in the course of her industrialization. The objective is to compare the major features of Japanese labor market organization with its counterpart in the industrialized West and to assess the likelihood of growing convergence or divergence. In particular, the focus is upon the nature of wage relationships as one of the principal facets of what Dunlop calls the system of labor market rules; for studies of industrialized Western economies have especially examined the evolution of wage differentials and structures for evidence of the modernization process. Also of special concern is the impact of trade unionism and col-

[*] I am indebted to Dr. Tsuda Masumi for his assistance in preparing this paper.
[1] John T. Dunlop, *Industrial Relations Systems* (New York, 1958), p. 355.

lective bargaining upon the wage hierarchy, since these institutions—unlike the experience in most of the industrialized West—came to Japan in appreciable proportions only after the elaboration of the labor market rule system had been well underway for several decades. Before proceeding to the Japanese case, however, it will be useful to begin with a brief summary of Western labor market development.

The Western Labor Market Model in Economic Development

Western labor economists tend to supplement economic analysis of labor markets with insights derived from the other social sciences. This approach is based on the notion that labor market behavior, perhaps more so than any other branch of economics, resists the analytical precision of economic theory and therefore should be treated differently from commodity markets. Within this context, the general model of wage structure evolution in the course of economic development usually follows the pattern described below.

The earlier stages of economic growth may be expected to bring forth sharp wage rate differentials. In the attempt to attract scarce skills into the emerging industrial sectors, wide occupational and geographical wage differences develop. In addition, wage rates at the outset are likely to diverge as the result of differentiations in personal factors such as age, sex, tribe, nationality, and race—usually carry-overs of cultural and social distinctions that existed in the preindustrial society. However, as industrialization proceeds, all of these grounds for wage relationships begin to weaken. Technological and production "imperatives" lead to the creation of more and more definable job classes and occupations and, in turn, to an increasing specification of job or occupational wage rates (including both direct and indirect wage components). At the same time, labor markets gradually open and set into motion a competitive process on both the supply and demand sides that serves to standardize job wage rates and, hence narrows occupational, geographical, and personal

634

wage differentials. This process is hastened by the steady spread of educational opportunities and an accompanying diffusion of political power produced in the wake of industrialization and multiplication of group interests. Wage uniformity begins to appear first among firms in the "same or closely allied product markets in a locality" and then to move outward to "more distant localities in the same product grouping."[2] Complete uniformity may never be achieved, since the various industrial sectors continually expand and contract in the transformation to industrialism, but there is a tendency even for industrial wage differentials to narrow as the other types of differentials are eradicated.

The entrance of trade unionism and collective bargaining does not seem to upset this model of wage structure evolution. In perhaps the most exhaustive comparative study of the question for the industrialized West, Reynolds and Taft in fact conclude that these institutions impel, rather than impede, a movement of the wage structure in the direction of the equilibrium conditions of market competition. They find, moreover, that, while the union impact is substantial in narrowing personal differentials within firms and interfirm differentials within competing product markets, unions produce only slight effects upon geographical, occupational, and interindustry differentials (although the effects seem greater in Europe than in the U.S.). The latter give way primarily as the result of the glacial competitiveness in the markets. Hence, they conclude that "the development of union organization and collective bargaining does not transform the labor market as drastically as sometimes supposed"[3] and, if there is an influence at all it is "in the same general direction as the economic forces."[4]

In comparing the Japanese experience to this Western model, it will be seen first that industrial wage structures in Japan have singularly resisted following the prescription

[2] *Ibid.*, p. 365.

[3] Lloyd G. Reynolds. and Cynthia H. Taft, *The Evolution of Wage Structure* (New Haven, 1956), p. 373.

[4] *Ibid.*, p. 366.

offered and, second, that Japanese trade unionism and collective bargaining so far may have contributed even less pressure for change than what little Reynolds and Taft claim is their role in affecting the long-run movement of wage structures.

This may be understood with greater clarity if we return to the Dunlop statement quoted above and view wage rates as one of an elaborate series of interconnected rules, which taken altogether comprise the industrial relations system of a nation. Thus, the alteration of wage relationships is likely to occur only if compatible with changes in other parts of the total system; that is, wage differentials must correspond to a wide range of labor market practices and, in all likelihood, not merely to supply and demand factors grossly conceived. In this view industrial relations are a definable subsystem of the society, which, while overlapping the economic subsystem, has its own distinctive components and determinants. An industrial relations system is conditioned by the combination of technological, market, social, and political factors, and the rules of the system are determined concretely by separate or joint decisions of "actor" groups (usually government agencies, employers, and worker organizations), each of which consciously or unconsciously formulates its own goals and ideology.[5]

Such a view of industrial relations admits the possibility of a number of models of wage relationships during the process of economic and industrial development. If this is the case, it raises the question not only of whether the Western model of labor market evolution aptly fits the experience of a country such as Japan but also, should there be significant differences among the models, whether any are more or less congenial to the economic growth process itself.

The remainder of the paper will undertake (1) a brief review of the long- and short-run behavior of Japanese wage relationships since industrialization began, for purposes of comparison with the Western model; (2) a sketch of labor

[5] Dunlop, especially Chapter I.

market arrangements that characterized or accompanied Japanese economic development up to the end of World War II; and (3) an analysis of the impact of trade unionism and collective bargaining upon these arrangements in the postwar period. The concluding sections take up the prospects for change in labor market organization, especially wage relationships, within the broad context suggested by Dunlop; and touch upon the problem of whether the wage structure imposes a constraint for the future growth of Japan's economy.

Evolution of Japanese Wage Differentials

Various investigations have analyzed the evolution of the Japanese wage structure on a national scale since the early Meiji period. Taira's recent detailed study admirably summarizes most of these analyses and develops the findings for both long-run and short-run behavior.[6] Accepting the accuracy of his data, this section draws heavily upon this work.

In contrast to Western experience outlined above, the behavior of the Japanese wage structure over the long-run has been rather nonconformist. For the entire period 1881-1959, Taira concludes: "Some differentials are clearly subject to a trend of secular narrowing, while others show one of secular

---

[6] See Taira Koji, "The Dynamics of Japanese Wage Differentials, 1881-1959" (unpublished Ph.D. Dissertation, Stanford University, 1961). In addition, cf. Hotani Rokurō and Hayashi Takashi, "The Evolution of Wage Structure in Japan," *Industrial and Labor Relations Review*, XV, 1 (October 1961), 52-66. Other basic references include the following: Nakayama Ichirō, ed., *Chingin kihon chōsa* [Basic Investigation of Wages] (Tokyo, 1956); Ōkochi Kazuo, *Chingin no kakudo kara mita rōdō undō* [The Labor Movement Seen from the Angle of Wages] (Tokyo, 1959); Shinohara Miyōhei. *Shotoku bumpai to chingin kōzō* [Income Distribution and Wage Structure] (Tokyo, 1953); Shinohara Miyōhei, *Sangyō kōzō* [Industrial Structure] (Tokyo, 1959); Shinohara Miyōhei and Funahashi Naomichi, eds., *Nihongata chingin kōzō no kenkyū* [Research on Japanese-Type Wage Structures] (Tokyo, 1962); Takahashi Chōtarō, *Dynamic Changes of Income and Its Distribution in Japan* (Tokyo, 1959); and Tsuru Shigeto and Ohkawa Kazushi, eds., *Nihon keizai to bunseki* [Analysis of the Japanese Economy] (Tokyo, 1957).

widening,"[7] and "it is difficult to establish an unequivocal trend either for narrowing or widening in regards to the Japanese wage differentials as a whole."[8] He finds that those that have tended to converge over the long-run include the interindustry, clerical-manual, male-female, and geographical differentials, but only the very last is especially pronounced, while the others are open to serious reservations. For example, the differential between agriculture and industry, a subcategory of the interindustry classification, appears ambiguous depending on the statistical method used. Those that have shown almost no signs of long-run compression, and actually have widened, include skilled-unskilled and interfirm differentials by firm size of employment[9]—those expected to be among the earliest to compress. Thus, the long-run pull of the "imperatives" of Western industrialization seem to have been exceptionally weak for most relationships in the Japanese case.

Numerous explanations have been set forth for this seeming perversity of Japan's long-run wage structure behavior. It has been attributed to tenacious Japanese cultural traditions that stress non-economic distinctions based on age, sex, hierarchical status, loyalty, personal obligations, and the like— that is, the remarkable persistence of preindustrial value systems which overpower concepts of labor market competition. It has been laid at the door of the monopolization of political and economic power in the hands of a small ruling oligarchy that led to the structuring of monopsonistic labor markets and the arbitrary prolongation of wage differentials. It has also been accounted for by the "imbalanced" or "dual" nature of economic development—a modern economy coexisting with a traditional economy—in the face of heavy population growth and labor oversupply, so that wide differentials may be expected to persist under these conditions. Related to this is the idea that Japan's industrialization, after almost 100

[7] Taira, p. 95. The above quotation summarizes a careful analysis of year-by-year statistical series that are far too lengthy to permit inclusion here. Taira follows the Reynolds and Taft classification of wage differentials with certain modifications.

[8] *Ibid.*, p. 217.

[9] *Ibid.*, pp. 95-97.

years, is still at an early stage despite spurts of rapid growth. (Taira, for example, concludes that even as late as the 1950's the Japanese economy was at about the stage of the U.S. development in the 1890's.)[10] No doubt, there is some validity to each of these explanations; but the problem, as will be explored later, is to judge their relative importance and inter-relationship in the process of rule-making for the labor market.

One may gain additional insight into the long-run per-versity of Japanese wage relationships by examining their short-run cyclical movement. For the years up to World War II, Taira observes: "The distinct characteristics of wage differentials in Japan . . . is their variations in systematic swings over time."[11] He finds that virtually all the differen-tials studied coincide in the direction of their cyclical move-ment, and do so in fairly common rhythm (in general, as in the West, wage differentials widen in depression and defla-tion, and narrow in prosperity and inflation). In this respect then, the behavior of Japanese differentials differs little from Western experience. The major difference, however, is the greater degree to which the Japanese structure apparently re-turns to previous relationships. Thus, while the structure has been pliable, its short-run variability, at least so far, has not fundamentally affected its persistent "stickiness."

The problem is seen to be especially complex when the national wage structure since 1945 is examined. A narrowing of most differentials took place in the immediate postwar years of very low economic activity and extreme inflation (1945-1948), followed by a widening in the late 1940's and early 1950's, when economic reconstruction became brisk and prices stabilized. Since then there has been an almost imperceptible narrowing, at least until very recently when the compression accelerated, accompanying Japan's greatest period of economic

[10] *Ibid.*, p. 217.

[11] Taira Koji, "The Dynamics of Wage Differentials in Japanese Economic Development," *Proc. of the 35th Annual Conference of the Western Economic Association,* 1960, p. 22. See also Taira, "Wage Differentials, 1881-1959," pp. 97-100.

boom and price stability. This sequence of developments is not readily explained merely in terms of employment levels and price movements. Such wage structure behavior poses the analytical problem, perhaps more acutely for Japan than the West, of depicting the mechanics and institutions for organizing labor markets, with the likelihood of having to account more specifically for the role of non-economic elements. The need to undertake this analysis does not necessarily abandon the use of economics in favor of a sociological explanation, but calls for a judicious blending of the two.

I am dubious that the external characteristics of wage structure behavior sufficiently explains the interrelationship among the forces at work. A stress on the external behavior tends to focus primarily on labor supply factors, such as the relationship between the "labor reserve" and volume of employment—an approach that appears to be the essence of the Taira analysis.[12] However, this type of emphasis, while contributing significantly to an understanding of the contour of wage structure and its evolution, is not likely to pay enough attention to the way in which demand factors are channeled and affect the actual labor market rules around which wage rates tend to cluster.

The latter perspective calls for an equally penetrating analysis of wage structure *internal* to the firm.[13] Forces playing upon the external and internal structures may vary significantly from one another and may be related only at certain select points in each. In all probability, non-market considerations will loom with greater prominence in the internal structure, while the economic may more readily explain the ex-

---

[12] Drawing on Reder's concept of shifting hiring standards, Taira says: "The inter-industry wage differentials tend to narrow (or widen) when labor reserve dwindles (or is replenished) under the impact of good (or poor) economic conditions." (Taira, "Wage Differentials, 1881-1959," p. 153.) See also, M. W. Reder, "The Theory of Occupational Wage Differentials," *American Economic Review*, XLV, 5 (December 1955).

[13] See especially E. Robert Livernash, "The Internal Wage Structure," in George W. Taylor, and Frank C. Pierson, eds., *New Concepts in Wage Determination* (New York, 1957), pp. 140-72.

ternal. An integration, or at least a juxtaposition, of the two perspectives would make clear why the Japanese wage structure, while outwardly exhibiting Western cyclical characteristics, seems to have been less amenable to the expectations for the secular trends. Since the external structure has already been rather fully treated by Taira and other scholars, this study will next be concerned principally with the evolution of institutions that have linked internal wage relationships with external labor market organization and then will attempt to clarify the impact of postwar unionism and collective bargaining upon these institutions.

Labor Market Institutions in Japan's Industrialization

Like other phases of Japanese economic development, labor market history up through the Second World War may be roughly divided into two distinct periods with regard to the relative roles of internal and external factors determining wages. The dividing line between the two is approximately World War I. Until that time, wage structures were subject more to mechanisms external to the firm; later on internal mechanisms gain in importance.

FROM EARLY MEIJI TO WORLD WAR I[14]

The workings of the labor market during the Meiji period are familiar to most economic historians of Japan. It is fairly well established that, from the 1880's to the World War I period, the flow of industrial labor in Japan had three primary

[14] The themes in this and the following section are drawn from the following works: Ōkochi Kazuo, *Labor in Modern Japan* (Tokyo, 1958); Ōkochi Kazuo. *Shakai seisaku no keizai riron* [Economic Theory of Social Policy] (Tokyo, 1952); Sumiya Mikio, *Nihon chinrōdō shi ron* [History of Japanese Wage Labor] (Tokyo, 1956); and Ōkochi Kazuo and Ujihara Seijirō, eds., *Rōdō shijō no kenkyū* [Labor Market Research] (Tokyo, 1955).

Now in preparation is a 10-volume *Nihon rōdō undō shiryō* [Documentary Labor History of Japan] under the auspices of the Japan Labor Documentary History Group chaired by Professor Okochi, which is expected to provide far more documentation than has been previously available.

characteristics: (1) a major portion of the industrial work force was composed of young unmarried females who were not expected to remain permanently (and, indeed, did not) in industrial work; (2) of the males engaged in industrial work, only a small proportion remained regularly in a given work place, while most of them either floated back and forth between farm and factory (so-called *dekasegi*) or moved around from one workshop to another; and (3) independent labor contractors or master workmen (*oyakata*) for the main part provided labor for and withdrew it from the industrial work places under agreements with employers. During much of this period, large wage differentials of various types existed and were structured in a haphazard pattern.[15] Only within the government bureaucracy and the few large-scale enterprises did internal wage systems become systematically established. Turnover rates remained at unusually high levels and systematic wage scales were as temporary as most workers. These conditions, of course, arose in a context of relatively limited industrialization predominantly characterized by many small and often unstable enterprises.

In many instances, wage determination fell largely in the hands of the *oyakata* middle-men, who developed highly particularized and personalized methods for setting rates, usually without direct employer participation. It was common for employers in need of workers outside his own family to make lump-sum production contracts with *oyakata*, whose responsibility it then became to find the labor, determine methods of work, supervise operations, provide payment to the workers, and meet the production deadlines. To accomplish this, most *oyakata* built up bands of followers (*kokata*) and added and subtracted other recruits as necessary. *Oyakata* nurtured their own personalized sources of labor supply—principally through personal connections among families and *kokata* and other sub-contractors in the rural villages. To secure a place in an *oyakata*'s retinue (*batsu*), young workers had to find where these connections existed and to devise an entrée into them.

[15] See Hotani and Hayashi, pp. 53-58.

In some instances of severe labor shortages, *oyakata* are known to have offered special bonuses to parents, engaged in labor piracy among themselves, and in a few famous cases actually resorted to kidnapping. But, by and large, the personalized interconnections they developed served to channelize much of the labor flow.

Oyakata control apparently was extensive among the cadres of skilled workmen. By regulating the use of such key skilled *kokata*, *oyakata* no doubt could also manipulate the unskilled. Wage structures thus hinged critically upon the *oyakata-kokata* system. Like most master-apprentice guilds, strong personal ties existed between *oyakata* and *kokata*. To become an apprentice, a youngster had to rely upon intimate personal connections of family, friends, or home community. Psychological forces such as *on* and *giri* (both are types of obligation) served to bind the *oyakata* and his *kokata* for life. Within the *batsu* of an *oyakata*, there developed a status hierarchy based more on the time length of *oyakata-kokata* attachment and less precisely on the value of tasks performed.

This very attachment, paradoxically, permitted apprentices considerable freedom to move from one workshop to another. As industrialization spread, it became more and more apparent that *oyakata* were incapable of transmitting the necessary knowledge and skills required for increased production, complex machinery (usually imported from abroad), diverse products, and new types of raw materials. An individual *oyakata* could pass on only his own limited trade "secrets," and therefore had to turn to other *oyakata* to train his own *kokata*. Yet for many years the exchange of *kokata* remained largely under the close control of *oyakata*. Exchanges tended to be selective, usually within the orbit of personal connections the *oyakata* developed among themselves. Moreover, although a *kokata* might work at a number of shops in the course of his training career, usually he returned sooner or later to his original master, or, when he became qualified to become a master himself, remained a member of the original master's expanding *batsu*.

Such collaboration between *oyakata* and *kokata* and between *oyakata* and sub-*oyakata* kept control of wage structures out of the hands of employers to a significant degree. Despite the apparently high degree of labor turnover, the *oyakata* mechanism could hardly equate it with open market competition (and, in this sense, the relatively high turnover figures of the Meiji period are somewhat deceptive). Instead, the institution operated for the most part within the preexisting social structure and based most of its compensation rules on the preindustrial value system. Wages followed the *oyakata-kokata* status hierarchy. The *kokata* who moved about could not necessarily expect to progress in his wages even though he was continually accumulating new skills; with each new master, he was likely to receive fairly low status in the hierarchy (especially since in no one shop was he apt to utilize all of his skills) and had to wait until he returned to the original master for any substantial advancement. Wages, highly personalized as they were, perhaps in many cases did not deserve the label of wages at all. They seldom provided for all of the worker's needs and were supplemented by various benefits provided by the paternalistic *oyakata*, in much the same way that farm households had traditionally operated. Wage payments were often irregular and sometimes merely symbolized membership in an *oyakata*'s entourage. Erratic wages, moreover, frequently accompanied erratic working conditions—irregular, long stretches of work, ad hoc rewards and penalties, variable task assignments, and so forth.

Substantial efforts to dissolve *oyakata* control in the labor market did not appear until the closing years of Meiji. A brief flurry of trade unionism around the turn of the century represented an attempt to systematize employment relationships, but Japan's first experience with labor organization met a quick demise not only because of employer and government suppression but also because of the inability to survive the buffeting of high degrees of labor mobility, temporary employment practices, and the personalized *oyakata-kokata* attachments. An attack on the problem came in the government's enactment of mining legislation in 1905 and in the passage of the first factory act in 1911, but more than a decade was to pass before these acts had a serious impact on labor market arrangements. Also, by the early 1900's vocational secondary schools were beginning to multiply; but this new source of skilled labor supplies was not to come into its own for some years. In the meantime, employers mounted a direct onslaught upon *oyakata* controls.

FROM WORLD WAR I THROUGH WORLD WAR II

Following the Russo-Japanese War, the organization of industrial labor markets in Japan began to experience radical changes—a transformation well underway by the end of the First World War. It was this period, of course, which witnessed Japan's first great spurt into industrialization and with it a growing number of large establishments using advanced Western technology, importing vast quantities of raw materials, and developing sizable production capacities. By the end of World War I, Japan had crossed the barrier from a predominantly agricultural to a predominantly industrial nation, although it should be constantly borne in mind that "traditional" industry, mainly in the form of small family-centered shops, expanded apace with the development of modern industry.

The emergence of "dualism" produced a new amalgam of institutions in Japanese labor markets. In the expanding traditional sectors, most of the labor and wage practices retained the characteristics of the Meiji period described above, especially since many *oyakata* themselves became small business operators; but a number of sharp departures were developed in the modern industrial sectors. The technology and scale of the latter could no longer tolerate high rates of turnover and made it economically and administratively feasible to fix workers in a single work place, to employ males rather than females, and to modify the haphazard and personalized methods of *oyakata* for recruiting, selecting, training, and assigning workers.

These changes came rapidly—but not by resorting to open labor market operations. Rather, the main strategy of the modern employers, public and private, was to take over the functions of the *oyakata* without obliterating their status. This cooptation process had the effect of fusing the preexisting system of wage relationships with the new technological and product requirements for skilled labor. As a result, in the modern sectors, labor markets became increasingly, not less, compartmentalized, although internal wage structures became more systematized and wage levels in modern industry rose distinctly above the agricultural average.

Management's rivalry with the *oyakata* was a sizable struggle that at times evoked considerable hostility. *Oyakata* resisted the threat to their control over labor (especially as companies expanded their white-collar staffs) and refused to pass their knowledge of skill to "strangers" directly recruited by employers. As the latter moved more and more into the labor market, *oyakata* responded by forming "unions"—relatively easy to establish because of strong *kokata* support and the network of relations among the *oyakata* themselves. The first real growth of trade unionism in Japan appeared in this period following the establishment of the *Yūaikai* in 1912, and no doubt was due in large measure to *oyakata* leadership. It is notable that the Japanese labor movement during the World War I period reflected the characteristics of American "business unionism" in its "control of job territories" rather than ideological or political drives. Although after the war, the *Sōdōmei* (the successor of the *Yūaikai*) was rent with ideological schisms, there remained a substantial conservative trade union wing throughout the interwar period that had its origins in *oyakata* resistance to management's take-over.

The decline of *oyakata* control over wage rates came in two major ways. First, modern industry placed increasing pressure upon the government to widen the multi-track secondary school system so that it would directly provide a steady and reliable supply of young workers capable of learning new skills and supervising workers. In addition, most large firms established a network of in-plant training programs to make certain that the new school graduates would apply their knowledge to techniques directly utilizable in an enterprise's specific production processes. The huge step-up of direct recruiting and training activities required organization of staff specialists employed on behalf of the company, rather than continued reliance upon personalized *oyakata* connections that at times ended in chaotic disruption of the flow of labor supplies. The well-known arangement among the major spinning companies to divide up the labor supply on a geographical basis was a major example of the work of these directly employed professionals.[16]

Such steps alone, however, were not sufficient to displace the control of the *oyakata*, especially over existing supplies of skills. Still another tack was required to dislodge knowledge and secrets from *oyakata* and their retinues that could be economically applied to the new technology and expanded production and transmitted to the new school recruits. With skills still highly personalized, management was at a serious disadvantage in its lack of expertise on technical production problems (most officials were university graduates without practical shop experience). Thus, it was not feasible merely to cast the *oyakata* aside. Their cooperation was needed. To gain this, employers offered a variety of inducements to the *oyakata*, including status as full-time employees, guarantees of life-long attachment to the enterprise, regularized salaries and salary progression, management recognition of *oyakata*-led unions or establishment of company unions, and in some cases managerial or supervisory titles. Typically, work remained organized around these key workmen. Such lures of status and financial reward not only won over many *oyakata* but also brought along their *batsu* of *kokata* and sub-*oyakata*, who were slotted into wage positions in line with the preexisting status hierarchy and were guaranteed tenure. They permitted *oyakata* to retain the personalized relationships earlier developed and to command a continuing influence in recruiting, selecting, and training the new school graduates. What had changed was that the *oyakata* collectivities were now brought under a single enterprise roof (shifting the former interfirm mobility to intrafirm movement, incidentally). Such

[16] Shindō Takejiro, *Labor in the Japanese Cotton Industry* (Tokyo, 1961), pp. 46-47.

organizational complexes, perhaps as much as the threat of radical trade unionism, impelled employers in the 1920's to seek means of achieving cohesion, such as employer representation systems and similar activities promoted by the *Kyōchōkai*.

Out of these organizational rearrangements grew the now well-known *nenkō joretsu* (length of service and experience) wage system among modern industrial enterprises. Once established within a firm, *oyakata* usually received the highest wages and benefits, and their followers, as mentioned, were scaled down according to length of attachment to the *oyakata*. New school graduates had to take their place at the bottom of this hierarchy. Progression up the scale depended on demonstration of faithful devotion to work and respect for the status system. Such internal wage structures, therefore, accentuated differentials and also isolated the differentiations from the impact of market competition. In all likelihood, the institutional arrangements that arose in this period—reflecting management's need to compromise with preexisting mechanisms in order to secure appropriate enterprise work forces— had much to do with the long-run persistence of wage differentials.

Within this context, *nenkō joretsu* was not necessarily a non-economic or "irrational" system.[17] Managers of the new modern enterprises probably were well aware of the methods of Western scientific management (many had studied industrial practices in the U.S. and Europe), and no doubt recognized the value of piece and job rates for wages, based on skills and other productivity-related factors. In fact, from the beginning of the widespread utilization of the *nenkō* system, incentive payments had also been widely adopted. Certainly, too, the new managers could see the virtues of open labor markets as a means for achieving the optimum allocation of the labor force. Their problem was how to structure demand to ensure control over the flow and allocation of labor skills. *Nenkō* was probably a small price to pay to

[17] For a contrary view, see James N. Abegglen, *The Japanese Factory* (Glencoe, 1958).

overcome the resistance of the established *oyakata* system, to maximize for production use the social cohesion of *oyakata-kokata* relationships, and to solve the technical problem of measuring unknown skills and variable skill requirements.

Moreover, *nenkō* attracted into modern industry high-grade young recruits who were willing to discount present earnings for future advancement and security—powerful attractions in view of the large mass of underemployed, growing population, and bare subsistence earnings in the traditional sectors and among the small enterprises. *Nenkō* assured work force stability, particularly in the skilled category, for an enterprise at a time when stability was crucial for carrying out expansion plans.

Nenkō internally was not a strict non-economic system of wage payment, for the status ladder forced workers to compete vigorously among themselves *within* the firm, thus allowing management (by preserving the *oyakata*'s position) to keep down the rate of wage progression and to substitute non-monetary rewards and benefits for wages. To enter the system always remained considerably more difficult for the factory worker than for the white-collar employee. New workers had to pass through severe probationary periods, and were tested not only for ability but also character and family background or connections. Loyalty and subservience, let alone satisfactory performance, had to be demonstrated. Management was continually wary of overstaffing its permanent work force, especially because of the ups and downs of Japanese business activity and regularly weeded out the doubtful candidates. The threat of discharge continually bore down upon the younger worker or the older worker without connections; and large numbers of new school graduates were readily available to take the places of those who failed to show all the "desirable" qualities. Managements hedged the permanent employment system with layers of temporary workers at skilled and unskilled levels of work. These practices no doubt served to permit the operation of *nenkō* and *shūshin koyō* (lifetime employment)—but only for a select section of the labor force.[18] Job or piece rates probably would not have afforded management as great a measure of control over the work force and labor costs.

Emergence of the *nenkō* system on a wide scale, at least in the modern sectors, meant that internal wage structures became highly particularized. The wage structures of modern enterprises were isolated not only from those in the traditional sectors but also from one another. Firms differed in their *batsu* composition and continued to differentiate themselves in this respect as their distinctive technologies and product mixes developed. With opportunities for workers to move from one enterprise to another sharply reduced, the isolation of the internal structures persisted. Essentially what had occurred was that wage clusters which earlier developed around the independent *oyakata* and were interconnected by an apprentice exchange system had now lost their external contacts, except at the point of entry for new young workers. Wage contours[19] extending from company to company and across industries and regions weakened in the modern industrial sectors. The large differentials of various types which could be expected in the earlier stages of industrialization achieved an institutional underpinning which permitted them to persist into the advanced stages.

The second great spurt of Japanese industrialization, following the Manchurian Incident and lasting to the Second World War, saw an intensification of these wage patterns. Expansion of heavy and military industry during the 1930's might appear to have threatened the compartmentalization of the modern industrial labor force; and indeed there was

[18] The use of devices such as *nenkō joretsu* and *shūshin koyō* probably helps to explain Taira's observation that in Japan "the group which gains (or loses) most in wages gains (or loses) least in employment, whether we substitute for 'group' industry, occupation, firm, region, sex, or any category of workers classified by some characteristic for the purpose of inter-group comparison of wages." (See Taira, "Wage Differentials, 1881-1959," pp. 218-19.)

[19] For the concept of wage contours, see John T. Dunlop, "The Task of Contemporary Wage Theory," in Taylor and Pierson, pp. 117-39.

considerable drawing upon the traditional sectors for skills in short supply. Nonetheless, the system did not give way. For example, skilled workers, lured from the traditional sectors and now dubbed "half-way employees" (*chutō saiyō sha*— signifying that they had begun and pursued their careers in more than one given enterprise in the modern sector) very typically were not employed at a level of wages and benefits to which their regular worker counterparts had become entitled under the *nenkō* system. Rather, they were slotted in at an experience discount within the existing status hierarchy— a practice that was to become even more widespread in the immediate post-World War II period. Certainly, the higher wages and benefits had pulled these workers from the lower-paid small enterprises, but the particularized internal structures also continued to determine the position they came to occupy on the internal wage scale.

When labor mobility further threatened to disrupt plans for military production at the outbreak of the Pacific War, the government sanctioned direct labor controls and instituted patriotic labor associations (*sampō*), one of whose prime objectives it was to fasten workers to their enterprises and freeze their wages. Using the rhetoric of patriotism and an appeal to "tradition," simple administrative devices such as *nenkō* were bound to remain. By this time, the last traces of prewar unionism—which might have challenged the wage system—had been obliterated, and in the modern enterprise sector the *nenkō* system was firmly anchored.

Postwar Unionism and Collective Bargaining

Labor reform under the Occupation aimed not only to develop trade unionism as a countervailing force against the reemergence of the former ruling oligarchy but also to equalize income opportunities for the wage earning class. The economic objectives, then, were to achieve both an increased labor share and income redistribution. To implement this, labor was guaranteed the right to organize, bargain, and strike; universal labor standards were enacted; social security systems launched; and public employment exchanges greatly expanded, while labor contracting agents were outlawed or subject to strict supervision. It was anticipated that a large network of collective bargaining would become the chief mechanism for wage determination, assisted by an elaborate machinery of tripartite committees to handle conciliation, mediation, arbitration, and unfair labor practice charges. An onslaught against the existing wage structure appeared to be in the making.

GROWTH AND STRUCTURE OF UNIONISM

We now need only to review briefly the development of trade unionism and collective bargaining since 1945.[20] The spectacular response of industrial workers to the call for unionism is well known. By 1947 more than 5.6 million workers, over 45 percent of the total wage and salary earners, had joined. More than 23,000 basic organization units, conforming to the legal registration requirements, had been established. This mushroom growth continued for another two years. By 1949, union membership stood close to seven million, totaling at least 55 percent of the wage and salary labor force. The number of union units approached 35,000. Labor agreements spread rapidly, covering almost 80 percent of the organized workers in 1948.[21] These, then, formed a widespread network of bargaining mechanisms for launching an onslaught on the established rules for wage relationships.

In these formative four years, the present characteristics of the Japanese labor movement and collective bargaining took shape; and since about 1949, relatively little has been added to the basic pattern of Japanese industrial relations. Certain

[20] In addition to the chapter in this volume by Robert Scalapino, see the following for details of postwar trade unionism in Japan: The Institute of Social Science, University of Tokyo, *Sengō rōdō kumiai no jittai* [The Actual Condition of Postwar Labor Unions] (Tokyo, 1950); Okochi Kazuo, Ujihara Seijirō and Fujita Wakao, eds., *Rōdō kumiai no kōzō to kinō* [The Structure and Functions of Labor Unions] (Tokyo, 1959); and Solomon B. Levine, *Industrial Relations in Postwar Japan* (Urbana, 1958).

[21] *Japan Labor Bulletin*, Japan Institute of Labor, New Series, Vol. 2, No. 3 (March 1963), pp. 4, 7.

significant readjustments, however, occurred in the interim. For example, from 1949-1951—on the heels of changes in Occupation policy toward the Japanese economy, political reform, and the labor movement itself—trade unionism and collective bargaining suffered a sharp decline. Membership fell almost one million; 7,000 union units were eliminated; a "no-contract" bargaining era set in, with coverage falling to less than 60 percent.[22] The early political alignments of the trade unions were reshaped; Sanbetsu precipitously disappeared, Sōdōmei fell apart, and Sōhyō emerged as the principal new central labor federation, to be rivaled later by the present Dōmei.

On the other hand, with the boom produced by the Korean War, trade unionism and collective bargaining resumed their growth—although they continually, until 1962, lost out in proportion to the total organizable labor force. (The rate of organization fell gradually to 34 percent by 1961, but went up to 36 percent in 1962.)[23] Each year membership figures climbed at a steady pace of 300,000 net additions, and on the average 2,000 organizational units were added. In 1962, total trade union membership reached close to nine million, and the number of basic union organizations was more than 47,000.[24] (At present, the Japanese labor movement is the third or fourth largest in the free world.)

Despite this remarkable growth, trade unionism and collective bargaining have as yet to be accompanied by the "revolution" in labor market organization and wage determination institutions that may have been hoped for. Except in a few notable instances, labor market arrangements have continued to exhibit characteristics established earlier. Reasons for the limited impact of the labor movement may be seen in the very nature of the trade unions themselves.

First, it should be stressed that unionization took place almost exclusively in the modern sectors (public and private). Unions have penetrated only to a minor degree into the great mass of small and medium enterprises that still employ the

[22] *Ibid.*   [23] *Ibid.*   [24] *Ibid.*

majority of the non-agricultural work force. Two-thirds of the total union membership are concentrated in fewer than five percent of the basic union units (each with 1,000 or more members).[25] Because the unions have been concentrated mainly among enterprises that expand rapidly under conditions of growth and enjoy the highest levels of productivity and capital investment per worker, collective bargaining has dealt almost exclusively with the highest wage groups and has failed to come to grips directly with the problem of eradicating the sizable external wage differences between large- and small-scale enterprise.

Second, the very structure of trade unionism that emerged was prejudicial to a solution of the internal wage differential problem. Unions, for understandable reasons at the time they were formed, were for the most part enterprise-based. Very few were organized along craft or occupational lines, and general unions have also been uncommon. Attempts to amalgamate the enterprise unions into strongly coordinated, highly unified industrial organizations generally failed. Thus, collective bargaining proceeded on an enterprise-by-enterprise basis in most cases, and perforce primarily focused upon needs of exclusive concern to the work force of a given enterprise rather than of an industry, region, or wage earner group as a whole. Only recently, in fact, has there again begun to be important breaks in this pattern (in coal, private railways, small machinery shops, branches of the textile industries, synthetic chemicals, and maritime trades), but there have also been reversions to the enterprise level even among these.

Third, although the majority of enterprise unions affiliated along industrial lines with national union organizations (a substantial number, however, have remained completely unaffiliated), and in turn most of the latter with national trade union centers, the inherent nature of the enterprise unions is such as to permit but a weak role for national unions in collective bargaining. The national organizations espouse

[25] Japan Ministry of Labor, *Rōdō kumiai kihon chōsa hōkoku* [Report of the Basic Survey of Labor Unions] (1960), p. 33.

egalitarian wage structures, seek to coordinate enterprise union bargaining demands, and exert pressure upon their affiliates to insist upon "equal pay for equal work"; but they hesitate to push too far in these directions for fear of alienating their enterprise-union constituents or causing them to split over ideological issues. Accordingly, national labor organizations have turned largely to political action to achieve their economic objectives. Political "struggle" has become their chief preoccupation—removing the national organization even further from the plant level problems. (See "Labor and Politics in Postwar Japan," by Robert A. Scalapino, below, Ch. XV.)

Fourth, in organizing unions on an enterprise basis, membership tended to comprise all the blue-collar and white-collar employees regularly employed by the firm. Although egalitarianism was an initial objective of these "combined" units, actually at work were a number of other motivations having to do with the leadership provided by the white-collar intellectuals in the initial stages, the common identification of both groups with the enterprise in a time of great stress, the heritage of the *sampō* influence, and the traditional *oyakata-kokata* cohesion. For collective bargaining purposes, however, the very combination of these diverse elements within the enterprise union made it difficult to undertake serious attempts to alter the basic wage relationships even within the enterprise. Rather, in order to retain unity, collective bargaining has had to be concerned mainly with broad common issues—such as across-the-board "base-ups" and over-all bonus payments—that left the basic wage structure unaltered.

Fifth, enterprise unions typically have limited their membership only to the regular workers, excluding temporary employees, subcontract labor, casuals, etc. By permitting management to use the latter groups as buffers against the ups and downs of employment, enterprise unions have become all the more exclusively concerned with their own particularized situations. Further, the demarcation of the regular group from "outside" workers—expressed in union recognition, union shop, and dues checkoff clauses in labor agreements—did little to dispel the criterion of employment status for wage rate determination within the regular employee group itself (except perhaps to break down some of the sharp preexisting status barriers between blue-collar and white-collar regulars).

The net effect of these characteristics is that for most of the industrial wage earners during much of the postwar period, collective bargaining has had a relatively small direct impact upon the external wage structure and not much more upon internal wage structures.

Nonetheless, there have been certain accomplishments in achieving equity for workers. Union pressure no doubt has led to a greater systematization of *nenkō joretsu* by requiring managements to make more exact specifications of the incremental pay increases a permanent worker can expect as he goes up the career ladder in his enterprise. Also, it has eliminated arbitrary treatment of union members in the distribution of base wage increases and bonus payments and in dispensing of non-money welfare benefits. Through such agreements, however, unionism probably has strengthened the attachment of the unionized worker to his particular enterprise.

POSTWAR WAGE STRUCTURE: NENKŌ AND ENTERPRISE BARGAINING

Only during the period immediately following the surrender did it appear that the wage structure would be fundamentally altered. From 1945 through 1946, a notable compression of wage rates of all types apparently took place[26]—despite the low levels to which economic activity had fallen. A rampant inflation and chaotic economy no doubt produced a wide consensus throughout Japan—assisted by the egalitarian preachings of the Occupation and radical groups—for eliminating income differences. This movement, however, was not merely the product of trade union pressure. The sweep of trade unionism in itself reflected the egalitarian tide that engulfed Japan at the time. Unions were not merely protest movements against employers, for in many cases members in

[26] Hotani and Hayashi, p. 64.

high reaches of management itself helped form the unions and company officials often became union members themselves. Workers and managers, often together, supported the general upsurge for reform. In addition to the attitude of management, the Occupation and the government itself favored achievement of greater equalization. Wholesale unemployment and underemployment, repatriation, demilitarization, overstaffing of enterprises, a flight back to the farms, and so forth made it imperative for all to share alike in salvaging what the nation could from the great destruction and chaos wrought by the war. Soon to be added was the spectre of rapid population growth. Furthermore, there was little prospect at the time that Japan would be permitted to resume a high level of economic development; and in fact, shorn of her overseas possessions, the likelihood of reverting to a stage of economic underdevelopment and bare subsistence was exceedingly strong. A principal concern was how to ward off mass starvation. Per capita income had fallen to barely half the previous level, real wages to less than one-third. Major government and Occupation measures dealt with rationing and sharing, requiring compressed wage rates and limits to wage increases in the face of the price spiral. Under these conditions skills could not become important differentiations among workers.

Although the new unions, especially those organized among the government employees, were constantly dissatisfied with the levels set for their wages and led a series of demonstrations and strikes in the latter part of 1946 (culminating in the abortive call for a general strike on February 1, 1947), in general they sought a formula for wage egalitarianism that would set a pattern for the nation as a whole. Perhaps the major contribution of the union movement at that time was the so-called *densangata* wage proposal (which took its name from demands of the electric power workers union in 1946). Since the electric power industry was then unified under government ownership, the plan had the potential of becoming a model for the whole industrial economy. An extremely simple idea, *densañgata* called for a basic "livelihood" wage for all industrial workers regardless of position, status, or occupation, with allowable upward adjustments based on age, number of dependents, and differences in living costs from area to area. While the unions insisted on guaranteeing *shūshin koyō* for all workers in an enterprise, the plan ruled out length-of-service in a given enterprise as the major wage criterion and essentially (through collective bargaining) would have set a universal minimum wage level.

In its search for an egalitarian formula, the government did accept this plan for the electric power industry, and it was widely copied throughout the economy. As a result, Japan appeared to be on the brink of launching an entirely new historical phase in the development of wage relationships. Wage rates within and among enterprises would become highly comparable and interdependent, wage determination would become considerably centralized, and components of compensation would be universally geared to specific economic needs—all factors, as Dunlop and Rothbaum have pointed out, that would serve to keep a national wage structure relatively compressed despite variations in the level of general economic activity.[27]

In all likelihood, the narrowing of wage differentials in the immediate postwar years may be attributed in great measure to the wide consensus produced by the disastrous consequences of the war itself, rather than merely to trade union pressure. This consensus, however, was short-lived once the Japanese economy was permitted to redevelop. The shift in Occupation policy that came with the outbreak of the cold war led to the reemergence of wage differentials of all types. The egalitarian approach was soft-pedalled. Conservatives took control of the government. Employers found their prestige restored. Trade unionism began to retreat. Collective bargaining entered a "no-contract" era, and the *densangata* proposal fell by the wayside as managers refused to renew or conclude

[27] See John T. Dunlop, and Melvin Rothbaum, "International Comparisons of Wage Structures," *Int. Lab. Rev.*, lxxi, 4 (April 1955), for an analysis of these variables in Western European countries and the U.S.

agreements. The characteristics of the labor unions, earlier described, began to assert themselves clearly.

With the recovery that began after 1948, internal wage structures elongated; once again length of service, status, sex, age, and level of education became the important determinants of a worker's position in a large enterprise's wage hierarchy. The government's earlier flirtation with a universal minimum wage system and with centralized wage determination was virtually abandoned and had to wait a decade or more before even feeble gestures were again made in these directions. As the major enterprises retrenched and rationalized their work forces, internal wage structures once more were cut off from contact with labor markets. Average differentials by size of firm widened as the large enterprises leaped ahead in productivity.

In the transition back to the *nenkō* system among the large enterprises, it is not likely that trade unions played a critical role. Given the nature of the Japanese labor movement, unions seemed to follow the leadership of management in resurrecting the length-of-service criterion. With internal wage structures unhinged from the general labor market, management returned to *nenkō* for many of the same reasons that it was initially adopted. Rapid redevelopment of industry could be more readily achieved by catering to particularized political and social pressures exerted through *batsu* structures at the enterprise level. Although the national union organizations continued to call for a *densangata* wage system, enterprise unions now had to defend their membership against rationalization and reductions of force so that their attention was diverted from wage structure problems. Concerted union efforts largely centered on assuring places for the regular workers in the enterprise and limiting wage demands to across-the-board "base-ups" and seasonal bonuses. Gains were won on these demands but at the expense of relinquishing to management the control over the structuring of internal wage hierarchies. By about 1952 the process was virtually complete. The principle of "equal pay for equal work" was further relegated to the background when the national trade union movement itself split, with the establishment in 1954 of the *Zenrō kaigi* federation in rivalry with *Sōhyō*. Unions at the enterprise level largely contented themselves with working *within* the *nenkō* system.

Thus, the concerted attempts to achieve wage uniformity on a national scale had been extremely brief. Rather than promoting a system of centralized wage determination, the government now supported policies to confine bargaining to the enterprise level. New legislation restricted public employees in their rights to organize, bargain collectively, and strike. The labor relations commissions virtually abandoned the notion of extending contract settlements beyond the individual enterprise (which the law permitted them to do). Wage increases for government workers, for the most part, tended to follow the patterns of private industry rather than to set the pace. The key electric power industry—where the *densangata* plan had originated—was broken up and returned to private ownership. A last-gasp strike of the then unified electric power workers union led to its demise in 1952. Electric power employees (along with coal miners, whose principal union also suffered a stunning defeat in that year as it was to do again nearly a decade later at Miike) were subjected to a special law limiting their dispute activities.

Enterprise bargaining, with only a few important exceptions, has since prevailed. The reestablishment of the *nenkō* wage structure and the emergence of enterprise unionism as the dominant feature of the Japanese trade union movement may be said to be the products of the same set of forces, and they are inseparable features of the Japanese industrial relations system. As long as these institutions are entrenched, the likelihood of rapid alteration of wage hierarchies through collective bargaining remains seriously impeded.

CURRENT PRESSURES ON THE WAGE STRUCTURE

The reemergence of the *nenkō* system is alleged to saddle modern Japanese enterprise with cost rigidities and mobility barriers that handicap her drive for rapid economic growth. In various circles, there is a growing impatience with its continuation. The problem of "labor constraint" probably has been exaggerated, however, despite the "lifetime commitment" that *nenkō* implies for many industrial workers. There have been a number of economic escape hatches which are likely to remain open for some time to come.[28] These illustrate the role of market pressures alongside the non-market forces.

First, it should be stressed that *nenkō* is not a universal system. It applies only to the employees in the largest firms and government agencies, probably to no more than one-third of the workers in the medium size firm category, and in all likelihood not at all, or in very rare cases, in small companies with fewer than 100 workers. A rough estimate places the ratio of non-agricultural wage earners at work under *nenkō* systems at less than 45 percent.[29] The very existence of the non-*nenkō* sectors, as developed below, probably has sustained the use of *nenkō* where it applies.

Second, throughout most of the 1950's, at least until two or three years ago, the firms using *nenkō* added relatively small proportions of young workers to their permanent employee rolls. Despite the retrenchments after 1948, most major enterprises were overstaffed when Japan entered its period of rapid technological change and growing productivity in the modern industrial sectors. This factor, coupled with early retirement, permitted managements of such firms to maintain

[28] Further, in light of the growth potential of Japan that, as Ohkawa and Rosovsky (above, pp. 84-85) point out, lies in the "movement from lower to higher productivity occupations," the barriers to mobility represented by *nenkō* and lifetime commitment do not appear to be significant compared to factors such as investment and foreign trade.

[29] As of 1960, of approximately 22 million wage earners in Japan, there were 15.8 million "regular" workers in all private non-agricultural establishments and close to 3.5 million government employees. About 3.5 million workers were employed in private establishments in the size category of 100 to 499 employees, while less than 3.1 million workers were in the category of more than 500 employees. (See Japan Ministry of Labor, *Yearbook of Labor Statistics, 1960*, pp. 21-24, and 164.) Probably far less than the 7 to 9 million working under *nenkō* wage systems actually have received "lifetime commitments" from their enterprises.

a "balanced" labor force of regular workers based on length of service—a condition under which *nenkō* may be most easily administered. Since the *nenkō* structure permitted a deferment of wages, it provided advantages of capital accumulation for the large companies. At base, of course, was the factor of plentiful supplies of new school graduates coming onto the labor market when the demand for such workers by the large enterprises was relatively low. It is this factor, however, which is now changing rapidly (see below).

Third, expansion of enterprise work forces could depend to a large extent, temporarily and in some cases rather permanently, upon hiring workers not subject to *nenkō*. Thus, there was a steady increase in the decade in the numbers employed as temporary or "outside" workers. No precise estimate of these workers exists, but on the average it is believed to be about 10 percent of the non-agricultural work force and in some industries, such as shipbuilding, steel, and machinery, considerably higher. By employing such buffer groups at lower wage rates and without welfare benefits, management has thus been able to maintain the *nenkō* system for its regular workers.

Fourth, the very structure of Japanese industry has sustained the *nenkō* systems. Most major enterprises are surrounded with a welter of subcontracting and other types of dependent firms—often provided with capital, materials, and management resources by the parent companies. Since most of these enterprises are small, their technological levels low, and work forces young and unorganized, subcontracting has permitted the large firms to avoid some *nenkō* commitments. In many respects, this structure provides a substitute for open labor market mobility.

Fifth, the enterprise union system, as mentioned, rests considerably on the preservation of the *nenkō* hierarchy. In turn, bargaining issues between union and management have given the organized major companies a considerable amount of wage flexibility. Wage increases are distributed as a rule on the basis of *nenkō* rates, thus helping to preserve in many instances the deferred wage principle. Bonus settlements and incentive payments are likely to be variable, depending upon a company's past profit position—not an insignificant amount when it is considered that bonuses alone have often amounted to one-third of the total wage bill of an enterprise. Furthermore, "base-up" and bonus demands are likely to be closely interrelated. If one adds to these the usual built-in plant-wide incentive systems and periodic wage increments, both of which are essentially based on *nenkō* rates, it may be seen that management has countered the "fixed" commitments of the *nenkō* system with considerable opportunity for controlling wage costs.[30]

These various escape hatches, however, may now be in the process of changing. Tightening up of labor supplies, need for new labor skills, and growing strength of the national union movement (with noises in the direction of unification) are pressures that may be weakening management's freedom and flexibility in administering the *nenkō* systems.

As a result, major Japanese industry is now beginning to see attempts to abandon *nenkō* by transforming internal wage

[30] Thus far, therefore, Japanese trade unions, perhaps even more so than their Western counterparts, have had relatively little effect upon reducing wage differentials within firms, let alone between firms, in closely related product markets. (See n. 4 above.) This does not mean that union pressure has not contributed to a rise in the general wage level (although it may be implied that union wage demands have been of minor importance in this respect), nor that unions have been ineffective in politics and social relations—matters not discussed particularly in this paper. But with regard to wage structure, the lack of impact of the Japanese unions appears to be an especially apt illustration of (1) declining motivation of workers and their organizations to affect wage rates the more remote they are from the immediate work place, and (2) declining power of unions as the area of wage determination grows. See Clark Kerr, "Wage Relationships— the Comparative Impact of Market and Power Forces," in John Dunlop, ed., *The Theory of Wage Determination* (London, 1957), pp. 173-93. On the other hand, in view of the enterprise structure widely found in Japanese industry—with parent and dependent enterprises forming closely related product, technological, capital, managerial, and employment clusters—it may be more meaningful to analyze internal wage relationships in terms of such entities than by the conventional unit of the firm. Unfortunately, little data are available to undertake such an analysis.

structures into a base of job classification and job evaluation. However, it remains uncertain that the transformation will go very far. Since about 1959, hiring competition for the new school graduates has become especially intense—perhaps for the first time in Japan's industrializing experience. Some small firms in fact are offering higher wages to these workers than are the large firms. In part, this reflects the low birth rate of the war years (and thus soon may be relieved by large numbers of new workers seeking work in the mid-1960's and the steady exodus of the rural population to urban areas), the greater length of time young people remain in school, and the greater ease with which it is believed young workers may be trained for the new skills required by technological change. The low deferred wage set for the new graduate under the *nenkō* system also, of course, prompts firms to seek out these workers first. As a result, in the last two or three years, there has been a noticeable closing of the gap between average wage levels among large and small enterprises. In addition, the increased flow of young workers into the modern establishments has exercised pressure through their unions to compress the internal wage structures.

However, the closing of the size of firm wage differential may be somewhat deceptive. While the smaller firms have hired young workers, they have also been disgorging themselves of older workers ("older" usually means above the age of thirty). Increasing proportions of young workers in both large and small companies, hiring in at about the same rate, tend to bring their averages closer together. But an examination of the internal wage structures by age distribution indicates that marked differentials have remained.[31] Whether the size-of-firm differences narrows will depend critically upon the age distributions that emerge in both groups.

The likelihood that both large and small enterprises will be faced with growing bulges of older workers as the result of the recent young graduate competition between them will

[31] See Sumiya Mikio, "Chūshō kigyō rōdō mondai no honshitsu" [The Nature of Labor Problems in Minor Industries], *Nihon rōdō*

depend upon their relative production expansion, the types of technologies each develops, and the spread of enterprise unionism. No doubt small firms will generally resist keeping workers on as they get older, while the large will tend to avoid hiring so many young entrants as to disrupt internal work force relationships previously built on *batsu* structures. It is a strong probability, however, that the new labor market pressures cannot be wholly resisted. Small firms are likely to develop *nenkō* structures of their own as young workers stay on (and organize unions increasingly), and large firms are likely to shift over to job rates or some combination of job classification and *nenkō*.[32] Although in this process average wage differentials by size of firm may decline, other differentials based on length of service, age, sex, and status may well persist for some time to come. Internal wage structures are

---

kyōkai zasshi, Vol. 3, No. 9 (September 1961), pp. 43-61. The following table illustrates the same point:

Average Monthly Contract Cash Earnings in Yen for Male Workers in Non-Agricultural Industry, by Size of Firm and Age Group, 1961

Firm Size (no. of workers)	Age Group								
	Less than 18	18-19	20-24	25-29	30-34	35-39	40-49	50-59	60 and over
10-29	9,237	11,987	15,461	18,495	19,607	21,189	21,219	19,080	16,060
30-99	9,266	12,678	16,516	20,485	22,595	24,695	24,705	22,647	19,157
100-499	8,611	12,516	16,457	21,383	24,801	27,474	28,792	26,216	19,926
500-999	8,294	12,147	16,097	21,448	26,932	30,565	33,445	31,233	19,818
1000 & over	8,369	12,680	16,385	22,602	29,943	34,741	39,396	40,038	21,074

Source: Japan Ministry of Labor, *Yearbook of Labor Statistics, 1961*, pp. 192-95.

[32] Actually, the substitution of job evaluation systems may not prove as formidable a change as it appears. In the absence of many market-determined rates, job evaluation rates could be highly arbitrary in weighing relative skills and still leave plenty of room for age, education levels, and length-of-service factors with a minimum of violence to the basic *nenkō* structure. Hence, most new job evaluation plans have combined productivity and length-of-service elements, the latter often still receiving the greatest weights. For some examples, see Nihon rōdō kyōkai, *Shokumukyū to rōdō kumiai* [Job Classification and Labor Unions] (Tokyo, 1961).

likely to remain somewhat isolated from one another and permit widespread retention of *nenkō* systems.

Conclusion: Japanese Experience and Western Models

Whatever the outcome, a struggle over the transformation of the industrial wage structure is well on its way. At stake is whether labor market compartmentalization will give way to increased worker mobility or remain as a major feature of allocating workers in the industrialization of Japan. Certainly as indicated, economic considerations played an important role in leading to this labor market arrangement. But, at the same time, it also represented an accommodation to political, social, and technological forces. The mixture of these factors apparently has remained exceedingly stable, at least until recently. A new combination threatened to supplant this established blend only for a brief period in the immediate postwar period, but the threat has subsided at least for a decade. The new institutions of trade unionism and collective bargaining have also failed to alter the situation and in fact appear to accommodate to it. As a result Japan has yet to experience a rapid change in the structure of its labor markets and wage relationships despite mounting economic and technological pressures.

If we return for a moment to Dunlop's framework for analyzing industrial relations systems, the Japanese experience with wage structure behavior becomes clear. Historically, wage relationships, as part of the total "web of rule," may be traced to the particular confluence of changes in economic markets, technological development, political power distribution, and cultural values embodied in the industrial relations "actors." Further changes in all of these factors are now in process, and, no doubt, will produce alterations in a wage system that has held fairly steady for almost half a century. One can be sure that another generation or two will see a marked transformation, probably in the direction of lessening differentials.

But at present there is little wholehearted commitment to

any precipitous change in labor market rules among the principal institutions in positions to bring pressure for change. Government resists the development of a centralized wage determination mechanism that would link wage structures on the basis of universal criteria. Management is divided within itself between those elements that have developed entrenched positions in the existing personalized compensation system and those that would gain advantage if the reward structure increasingly stressed impersonal elements. The trade unions similarly face a series of organizational and ideological dilemmas[33] which threaten to tear the movement apart if there is a precipitous attempt to alter the wage hierarchy.

The lack of consensus within and among the chief actors concerning the desirability of rapid change probably favors only a gradual move toward change under the pressure of economic forces. This should result at most in a continual but almost imperceptible blending of new and established ingredients rather than sharp departures in the system of labor market rules. Provided that economic growth continues, wage relationships and labor market structures will probably continue to represent still another facet of the talent of Japan to combine both old and new in its evolution toward a "modern" society. Despite mounting pressures for economic growth, technological change, and shifting political power, Japanese wage relationships under these circumstances are likely to continue to fail to meet the expectations of Western economic model builders.

[33] Bernard Karsh, and Solomon B. Levine, "Present Dilemmas of the Japanese Labor Movement," *Proceedings of the Spring Meeting of the Industrial Relations Research Association*, Philadelphia, May 8-9, 1962, pp. 541-48.

CHAPTER XV

Labor and Politics in Postwar Japan

ROBERT A. SCALAPINO

THE STRONG political orientation of the Japanese labor movement should occasion no surprise. Everywhere in the modern world, organized labor has gravitated toward politics, and in most of the so-called "late developing" societies the labor movement has issued out of the political revolution. Only in those states where bans or special controls have been imposed upon labor have its natural proclivities for politics in this age been thwarted or canalized. Thus the central question is less why did Japanese labor develop extensive political commitments, and more what constitutes the particular content and expression of those commitments and what political trends lie ahead?

The labor movement of contemporary Japan is the product of many factors: the history and culture of its society; the special timing of Japanese modernization; the structure of Japanese industry together with the type and quality of industrial resources; and the nature of various external stimuli. Before exploring some of the ways in which these factors have shaped the character of labor politics in Japan, let us set forth briefly the most salient feature of Japanese trade unionism today. (They are discussed in greater detail in Solomon B. Levine's "Collective Bargaining and Labor Markets in Japan," above, Ch. XIV.)

As of May 1964, the total labor force in Japan was recorded as 48,570,000 of whom 25,380,000 individuals were listed as non-agricultural-forestry employees. Figures of the Labor Ministry covering 1963 indicated that there were 49,796 unions in Japan containing 9,357,179 members on 36.1 percent of the current labor force.[1] Nearly one-half of organized

[1] These figures are from the Division of Statistics and Research, Ministry of Labor, *Basic Survey Report on Trade Unions, 1963*.

labor, including all of the major government employee unions, belonged to Sōhyō, the General Council of Trade Unions of Japan. Sōhyō membership totalled 4,192,000. The newly formed Domei Kaigi, Japanese Confederation of Labor, had 1,348,000 members. Three federations made up the bulk of Domei Kaigi membership: Zenrō, the Japanese Trade Union Congress with 911,000 members; Sōdōmei, the General Federation of Trade Unions with 430,000 members; and Zenkanko, the National and Local Government Workers Council, with 72,000 members. In addition to Sōhyō and Domei Kaigi, two other organized federations exist: Churitsu Roren, the Federation of Independent Unions, with 895,000 members, and Shin Sanbetsu, the National Federation of Industrial Organizations, with 49,000 members. Moreover, trade unions totaling some 2,954,000 members exist outside all of these federations.

In the post-1945 era, the Japanese labor movement has revolved mainly around large-scale industry. In 1960 69.1 percent of the total number of employees in enterprises having 500 or more permanent workers were unionized; 38.5 percent were in enterprises with 100-499 workers; 8.9 percent were in enterprises with 29 or less workers.[2] The unionization of large-scale industry was practically completed by 1948, and in recent years, particularly since 1956, special attention has been given to the organization of the small- and medium-scale industrial work force. Progress has been slow, however, and the overwhelming number of union members continues to come from large-scale industry.

It is well known that the typical Japanese union today is the so-called "enterprise" union. It is organized on the basis of a single plant or enterprise. Membership comprises all permanent workers of the plant, white collar as well as manual workers, but "temporary" workers and those affiliated via the sub-contracting system are excluded.[3] When the primary unit

[2] *Ibid.*

[3] For a discussion in English of the Japanese factory system, see James C. Abegglen, *The Japanese Factory—Aspects of Its Social Organization* (Glencoe, Illinois, 1958).

is the plant, a federation of all unions connected with the same enterprise is normally established. The next level of organization is either a regional or prefectural grouping, or direct affiliation on an industrial basis with a national union. These national unions in turn are generally members of one of the national federations, although as noted above, more than two and one-half million union members remain apart from such federations.

The organizational pattern of Japanese unionism has been characterized by three pronounced tendencies: "enterprise consciousness" among Japanese unionists remains strong despite the inroads of modernization, and many central economic functions of unionism continue to be executed at the plant or enterprise level; the autonomy of locals, regional councils, and separate national unions remains high, and the struggle on the part of national federation officials to enlarge their power and functions has been exceedingly difficult; finally, a certain natural specialization of function or division of labor has developed, with national federation leadership concentrating upon politics, particularly in Sōhyō, while collective bargaining and other aspects of economic unionism have occupied the attention of sub-federation union leaders. With respect to all of these tendencies, and particularly the last, there are signs of growing complexity and change. The national federations, including Sōhyō, are increasingly involving themselves in economic unionism; local and national unions, on the other hand, now run their own candidates for public office and in a variety of other ways participate in politics at the grass-roots level.

The Past and Its Image Today

To probe the politics of Japanese labor, however, it is not sufficient to concentrate only upon the present. The political attitudes and actions of organized labor in Japan are shaped partly by the past, and particularly by labor's image of the past. The militarist era remains a vivid memory, along with the hectic decade of strife that preceded it. The living traditions of the Japanese labor movement are those of desperation and struggle, a movement operating against overwhelming odds and in the face of imminent disaster. Whatever the elements of exaggeration or distortion in this picture, it continues to have a substantial influence upon the labor movement of the present. The political proclivities of Japanese labor are shaped in considerable measure by a deeply engrained psychology of "under-dogism" and pessimism that permeates the ranks of leadership.

The history of the Japanese labor movement has indeed been replete with tragedy and failure, with weakness and human error. Could more have been expected from a movement that in certain respects was totally foreign to Japanese tradition and that has had a history of only fifty or sixty years? In broad terms, the prewar labor movement may be divided into three eras. The first era began at the very close of the nineteenth century, when modern Japanese industry was still in its infancy, when the feudal flavor was strong, and the traditional guild system still existed. In such a period, there could be a curious interaction between medievalism and modernity. Out of the West came the idea of labor unions, and, more or less simultaneously, the gospel of Christian socialism. As might have been expected, this first era of the labor movement was dominated by the concept of "social settlement" service to the downtrodden, rendered by Western-oriented Christian humanists such as Katayama Sen and Takano Fusatarō.[4]

From its beginnings, the Japanese labor movement suffered from a problem which we may define as "teleological insight." The intellectuals who led labor looked into the future and assumed that they saw the evolution of their movement reflected in the contemporary West. They knew—or thought they knew—what lay ahead and this tended to produce a

[4] For the earliest period of the Japanese labor movement, such primary sources as Katayama's newspaper, *Rōdō sekai* [Labor World] should be consulted. This has been reprinted by the Committee on Labor Movement Historical Materials (*Rōdō undō shi shiryō iinkai*), 1960. See also Okochi Kazuo, *Reimeiki no nihon rōdō undō* [The Dawning of the Japanese Labor Movement], Tokyo, 1952.

furious impatience with the gap between idea and reality, between desire and capacity.

The frustrations involved in the non-fulfillment of an anticipated evolution have had a powerful effect in inducing intellectual radicalism throughout the non-Western world, and Japan is an excellent illustration of this fact. Repeatedly, the Japanese labor movement gravitated from moderation to radicalism, and thence, after devastating failure, wearily back toward moderation. This pendulum-like movement also reflected a shift from relatively close attunement to indigenous conditions to a growing infatuation with non-indigenous models, a sweep from "realism" to "utopianism."[5]

The first swing of the pendulum took place in the opening years of this century. In the decade between 1897 and 1907, the infant labor movement of Japan shifted from being essentially moderate and reformist in character and became heavily influenced by the doctrines of anarcho-syndicalism, at that time the most *avant-garde* form of Western radicalism. Consequently, within a few years, the first Japanese labor movement had gone down to oblivion in the midst of bitter struggles among a handful of intellectuals over ideological differences, a mounting interaction between radicalism and governmental repression, and a widening gap between labor leaders and the rank-and-file workers. Various factors contributed to the decline of this first labor movement: administrative inexperience and grave financial problems were of at least equal importance with governmental policies. In the most fundamental sense, the necessary conditions for a successful labor movement on the Western model were not present, and, consequently, the temptation on the part of Westernized intellectuals to engage in a progressively aberrant political movement was great.

Thus, when a new labor movement was launched by Suzuki

[5] The concept of the pendulum-like swings of the Japanese labor movement has been advanced by Professor Ōkochi in a number of his writings. See, for example, his article, "Those Who Shoulder the Trade Union Movement," in *Nihon rōdō kyōkai zasshi* [Japan Institute of Labor Journal] (hereafter cited as *NRKZ*), II, No. 4 (April 1960), 4-12.

Bunji in 1912, a dark legacy had to be overcome. After the so-called Great Treason Case of 1910, which resulted in the execution of Kōtoku Shūsui and his associates on charges of plotting the assassination of the Emperor Meiji, the labor movement and socialism were coupled in official eyes as subversive. Moreover, few workers, even among those previously involved, could be persuaded to participate in activities so dangerous and so remote from their understanding or immediate interests.

Another cycle began. Once more, social settlement operations were commenced by a few Christian humanists, aided by the small but influential German Social Policy school of Japanese intellectuals and a couple of enlightened industrialists such as Shibusawa Eiichi.[6] The initial political overtones were moderate and democratic. The central themes were in tune with Japanese society in considerable degree, but they also reflected the influence of Wilsonian democracy, which was now making its impact felt among the Japanese intelligentsia. Harmony was to be the basis of managerial-labor relations, the establishment of a just and equitable balance between the rights of the worker and the entrepreneur.

While the doctrine of harmony drew some of its meaning from the new egalitarianism, it also bore a close relationship to the familial values so intimately connected with Japanese culture in all of its phases. Thus, the managers were exhorted to be kind, thoughtful, and to treat their workers as fellow human beings. Workers were urged to acquire the traits of sobriety, promptness and efficiency—and at the same time to develop the quality of self-respect. The word of the hour was "self-consciousness"—being aware of one's talents and potentials. On the broader front, support was given to universal

[6] A large amount of material is available pertaining to the emergence of the Yūaikai and the development of the labor movement during the Taishō era. See Suzuki Bunji, *Rōdō undō ni-jū nen* [Twenty Years in the Labor Movement] (Tokyo, 1931); and Nishio Suehiro, *Taishū to tomo ni—watakushi no hansei no kiroku* [With the Masses—The Record of Half My Life] (Tokyo, 1951), for two significant autobiographies, and *Yūai shimpō, Rōdō oyobi sangyō,* and *Rōdō,* the official journal of the Yūaikai-Sōdōmei for this era.

suffrage, party government, and the movement away from "clan clique" politics. It was in this period, about the time of the First World War, that Japanese labor had its rendezvous with classical liberalism of the Western type.

As the war came to a close, however, new and more radical political currents were beginning to flow. A fresh generation of young intellectuals was moving out of the universities and into union headquarters, most of them deeply committed to contemporary socialist thought. It was natural for them to scan the Western horizons, to become intrigued with such events as the Russian Revolution. Political disputation mounted within the labor movement and once again, politics became of commanding importance. Initially, the doctrines of anarcho-syndicalism made a strong impact, partly because of earlier roots that had not been obliterated, and partly because anarchism seemed to have a continuing vitality in Europe, particularly in Italy and France. But European anarchism suffered a series of defeats shortly after World War I, and soon the Bolshevik Revolution was the center of attraction.

In this setting rival ideologies within the Japanese labor movement confronted each other, with 1923-1925 representing an era of increasing sound and fury. First, the anarcho-syndicalists were forced to retreat, defeated in a critical struggle that had its climax in the fall of 1922.[7] With anarchism vanquished, a series of new battles were fought between Social Democrats and Communists, and by 1925 the strife-torn labor movement was openly split into two nearly equal parts.

In the decade that followed, Japanese labor assumed its "mature" political form, albeit in miniature, and it was also in this decade that the "classic" political problems for Japanese labor were first posed. Hence, this era is of particular interest because of the links which it provides to the future. By understanding this era, one is enabled in considerable measure to separate the basic and continuing political factors involved

---

[7] See *Rōdō* No. 135, November 1922 for details of the Eleventh Annual Meeting of the Sōdōmei, which witnessed the climactic battle.

in the Japanese labor movement from those that can be designated trivial or ephemeral.

After 1925, three major political divisions emerged within Japanese labor. The moderates or "Right," whose basic creed was social democracy, strongly espoused parliamentarism and advocated a separation between unionism and the type of political activities that should be the responsibility of a political party. The "Center," more or less influenced by and committed to Marxism but having no connection with the international Communist movement, supported the use of parliament without feeling bound to pursue only parliamentary tactics and felt that politics had to play a major role in unionism. Finally the "Left," itself not completely united, composed of orthodox and unorthodox Communists, but dominated by the former, was committed generally to the tactics and strategy of Marx-Leninism, advocating the use and abuse of parliamentarism and insisting upon political supremacy within the union movement.

Already we have suggested some of the basic political issues that were developed during this era. First, there was the broad ideological division itself: the moderates who tended toward Fabian socialism, the Center who represented Marxist revisionism, and the Left who held one or another of the Marx-Leninist positions. Under these conditions, one burning question was that of the "United Front." The moderates came to a position of absolute opposition to any cooperation with the Communists; the Center insisted upon the total integration of all "proletarian" forces; and the Left, not without some wavering, ultimately espoused a position of uniting with the "progressives," but not with the "reactionaries" within the labor-proletarian party movements.

The second fundamental issue was that of party-union relations. To what extent should the union dominate the so-called "proletarian parties," and how much weight should be given to purely political activities? No segment of the Japanese labor movement favored pure "economic unionism." All recognized that the role of the government and the nature of Japanese society required political involvement. At issue was the proper balance between political and economic emphasis and the most suitable tactics for political action. The moderates took the position that the primary object of labor unionism was the struggle for an improved livelihood on behalf of the workers and that concentration upon "rice and fish unionism" was essential. Men such as Matsuoka and Nishio advocated a strict separation in function between union and party despite the fact that they participated in both movements. The Center and the Left in varying degrees preached and practiced the doctrines of political supremacy. Arguing that even the economic achievements of the labor movement depended upon the seizure of political control, their slogan was "On with the Revolution," their orientation heavily political. The Left, especially the orthodox Left, insisted that the unions were an important arm of the Communist Party, that union policies had to be in conformity with and subordinate to party directives.

Coupled with this issue was that of international ties. Initially, the attitude toward the International Labor Organization was complicated by a fierce struggle between government and organized labor over the issue of delegate selection. After 1925, however, the moderates supported the ILO and participated in it, thus associating themselves with the main stream of the Western labor movement. Beginning in this period, moreover, Suzuki and other Sōdōmei leaders sought to establish an Asian Labor Conference which would bring together the non-Communist labor movements of the Far East, particularly those of Japan, India, and China. This effort was largely frustrated by the deep political cleavages that existed throughout the Asian labor movement and by the general trend toward the Left.

Meanwhile, the Left fought the ILO bitterly, denouncing it as a tool of Western imperialism and a "harmonist" organization dedicated to capital-labor peace rather than to the class struggle. Its own affiliations were with the Profintern, the Communist international labor movement, and in Asia it belonged to the Communist-sponsored Pan-Pacific Trade Union Conference. The Center generally eschewed international affiliations, maintaining a neutralist stance, although some Center unions did become involved in ILO activities.

In this era, all elements of organized labor generally found themselves on the defensive, hampered in their growth by the socio-economic nature of Japanese society, confronted with an implacably conservative government, and buffeted by conditions of economic instability. Once again, the pendulum moved strongly to the left, and the historic interaction between extremism and suppression was a prominent feature of the era. However, after the Left had been thoroughly smashed by an efficient police-state (and its demise greatly aided by its own foolish, hopelessly unrealistic actions) the moderates remained to pick up the pieces. As the era ended, the only truly viable unions, such as the Seamen's Union, were firmly under moderate control; and the so-called "Right" dominated about 75 percent of the labor movement.

The basic issues set forth above were not resolved in this era, and hence they were bequeathed to the period after 1945. No true ideological unity was attained. The Japanese labor movement remained fundamentally divided. As Marx-Leninism retreated, National Socialism advanced. Social Democrats were under continuous fire from a variety of quarters. Marxism, moreover, could not be liquidated despite the strongly adverse trends affecting it during this period. The seeds had been firmly implanted. Under more favorable conditions, they could sprout again.

No United Front was possible under these circumstances, however. Frequently, labor leaders proclaimed that the choice was between unity and impotence or even destruction. Unity talks were scheduled. Amalgamation conferences were held. Literature urging a United Front abounded. But the political cleavages were too pronounced and too significant. Abetting these, moreover, were deep personal rifts, feuds among a small group of leaders who had known each other too long and too well.

This was the era that firmly established the politicization of the Japanese labor movement. Under any conditions of freedom, the extensive political involvement of organized labor in Japan would continue to expand. Even the moderates were heavily involved in proletarian party leadership and were able to maintain a theory of separation of functions only with great difficulty. There were strong indications also that the parties of the Left were likely to be dominated by organized labor—however weak the latter force in the total context of Japanese society. Organized labor and organized socialism were born at roughly the same time in Japan. Both were the progeny of a small group of intellectuals, and it might be argued that the two movements were born organically connected, in the manner of Siamese twins. Even after the transition in leadership from the intellectual to the skilled worker began, the organic tie remained firm.

These facts were all reflected in the international sphere. The Right affiliated itself with the Western trade union movement and took many of its guidelines from British unionism. The Left received its instructions from the Profintern. The Center sought to maintain a neutral position, with access to all elements. Both Right and Left attempted to forward a Pan-Asian movement that would advance their own principles.

The final prewar era was dominated by the "patriotic labor movement," commonly known as Sampō, an abbreviation for Greater Japan Patriotic Industrial Association.[8] The immediate antecedents of Sampō go back to June 1933, when the Industrial Labor Club was established, with its theme "industrial patriotism." By 1936, a rightist "United Front" had been formed, the National Association of Patriotic Unions. Finally, on July 30, 1938, the Patriotic Industrial Association was established with the purpose of "organically combining capital, management, and labor." By 1940, all independent labor unions had "voluntarily" dissolved, and there remained only Sampō.

From the beginning, the Sampō movement was guided by the Ministry of Welfare, and was closely connected with purposes of state. The aim was to attain maximum harmony at

---

[8] Among the many materials on the Sampō movement, see Labor Bureau, Ministry of Welfare, *Sangyō hōkoku undō gaikyō* [A General Survey of the Patriotic Labor Movement] (Tokyo; December 1940).

the workshop level—and, hence, maximum productivity. The individual plant or enterprise served as the initial unit of organization, with all employees enrolled and with the president of the company serving as head. At the meetings, discussions centered on a variety of topics: patriotism—support for the Greater Japan; methods of increasing production; and improvements in working conditions and facilities.

What was the significance of Sampō in terms of subsequent Japanese labor history? Ironically, perhaps, this era was one of considerable progress for the industrial worker of Japan. Conscious of the need for maximum production and confronted with an increasingly acute labor shortage as involvement in war grew, the government initiated a series of welfare measures that had been rejected or ignored in the "liberal" era.

Moreover, it was only in this period that the Japanese worker had experience with mass organization. By September 1940, nearly all enterprises had Sampō units: some 70,679 associations existed with 4,183,050 members. At its height, the prewar union movement had less than 500,000 members. For the first time, the worker was enrolled en masse in a labor organization, albeit one that was strongly statist and corporate in character. The form of that association, however, was most significant. Sampō was based upon the individual plant or enterprise, the most natural unit of organization given the nature of the broader Japanese social and economic organizational patterns. The pattern for postwar enterprise unionism, however, was now fully established.

Sampō did not work to the complete satisfaction of any group. Labor naturally chose to emphasize its "reformist" aspects, seeking improvements in working conditions and welfare measures. Management sought to use Sampō to achieve worker loyalty to the plant. The government served sometimes as arbiter between these conflicting interests, but with its eye mainly upon maximum productivity and heightened national patriotism. Thus, "spiritual training" was given increased emphasis, along with vocational training and improved workshop facilities. But in the broadest sense, the

Japanese labor movement continued to be highly political in the Sampō era. A mass labor organization was indoctrinated in the values and purposes of state on a scale unprecedented for modern Japan.

Major Phases of the Postwar Era

UNIONIZATION AND LABOR POLITICS, 1945-1947

The history of the Japanese labor movement after 1945 can conveniently be divided into four general phases, each with its characteristic political tone.[9] The first phase began with the reemergence of independent labor unions under SCAP guidance and came to its climax with the abortive general strike of February 1, 1947. This initial period was strongly dominated by two massive forces: the American Occupation and the critical economic conditions that followed total defeat. SCAP—both through its policies and through the attitudes it succeeded in communicating—had an enormous impact upon all aspects of the postwar labor movement in its formative period, including its political coloration. That movement was also greatly affected by the chaotic conditions in which it operated: a society that was close to economic collapse, and one in which old political values and leaders were being deeply questioned for the first time since the early Meiji era.

The premium placed upon rapid unionization tended to reenforce the established patterns of organization, namely, the use of the individual plant or enterprise as the primary unit. Only certain changes in personnel were necessary, and even these were not uniformly made in the initial period. Employers, for example, continued in many cases to "aid" in the establishment of unions in the months after surrender. Many unions were scarcely different from the old Sampō units.

[9] For the earlier general surveys of the postwar labor movement in English, see Solomon B. Levine, *Industrial Relations in Postwar Japan* (Urbana, 1958), and Robert A. Scalapino, "Japan," in Walter Galenson (ed.), *Labor and Economic Development* (New York, 1959). In Japanese, see Yamazaki Goro, *Nihon rōdō undō shi* (Tokyo, 1957), and the very valuable *Shiryō—rōdō undō shi* [Source Materials on the History of the Labor Movement], published annually by the Ministry of Labor.

Considering the rapid pace at which unionization was being attempted, trends could not have been otherwise. On October 11, 1945, a SCAP directive on democratization was issued to Prime Minister Shidehara. The appeal to encourage unionization was prominent among its exhortations. On December 22, the Trade Union Law, a Magna Carta for Japanese labor patterned in considerable measure after the Wagner Act, was enacted. And SCAP in a variety of ways was lending full support to organizational efforts. Thus, even in the short and chaotic period between surrender and the end of 1945, some 380,000 individuals had been enlisted in unions, a figure nearly equal to the prewar high of 420,000 reached in 1936. By the end of 1946, government statistics indicated that there were 17,266 unions with 4,925,598 members. At the end of the "reform" era, by June 1948, there were 33,900 unions with 6,533,954 members.[10]

Labor politics in this first period were characterized by three central tendencies. First, the degree and the nature of political involvement of the locals varied greatly, but there was a certain tendency for the balance between economic and political activities to vary with the level of union organization. A rough separation of functions tended to develop. At the local level, primary emphasis was placed upon main-stream economic functions—collective bargaining and the settlement of plant working conditions. Political activities assumed a progressively important role at the level of the national unions, and especially within the national federations. Second, in a relatively short time, the same basic political divisions and many of the same basic political issues characteristic of the prewar era reemerged in the Japanese labor movement. Finally, once again, a pendulum-like swing began to operate, a movement toward the left, which reached its climax with the abortive general strike.

Prior to some further analysis of these three basic tendencies, let us look briefly at the key events of this initial period. SCAP set the opening tone with its strong emphasis upon

[10] Yamazaki, *op. cit.*, pp. 223-24.

"democratization." This was the era of punishment and reform—a period when "war criminals" were to be rooted out of Japanese life and a radically new, democratic society was to be created. In considerable measure, the revitalized labor movement took its political cues from these themes. At the same time, SCAP adopted a "hands off" policy in connection with the Japanese economy, taking the position that the Japanese government itself would have to solve problems that came as a result of its ill-fated militarist adventures. The economic crisis steadily deepened.

The first labor organization to establish itself on a national basis was the old Sōdōmei. The Sōdōmei began reorganizational efforts as early as October 1945, and it held its first national convention on August 1, 1946. Some 1,000 delegates claimed to represent 850,000 Sōdōmei members. The Action Policy adopted at this convention placed a strong emphasis upon the immediate problems of the Japanese workers, headed up by the dramatic problem of sheer survival. At the same time, however, Sōdōmei policy proclaimed the absolute necessity of involvement in politics. The federation pledged itself to an anti-Fascist, anti-bourgeois, pro-socialist position, with its central affiliation directed toward the Socialist Party. Officially, however, Sōdōmei members were free to join the political party of their choice, thereby leaving open the possibility of a "United Front" within the labor movement.

Meanwhile, a rival federation had emerged, the Sanbetsu Kaigi, the Industrial Congress. From February 1946, plans for a Left-dominated federation had been developed. When the first Sanbetsu Kaigi convention opened on August 19, 1946, some 1,094 delegates claimed to represent 1,631,500 members, giving Sanbetsu Kaigi nearly twice the strength of Sōdōmei. By this point, moreover, Sanbetsu Kaigi was largely under Communist control. The central political themes expressed at the convention were completely in line with current Communist policies: the creation of a "People's Democratic Front," via an alliance of the workers, peasants, and national bourgeoisie, led by the proletariat; opposition to the "sabotage of bureaucrats and capitalists," and directing every effort to shifting the democratic revolution into the hands of the working class.

Soon, a third loosely-knit national federation was created, the Nihon Rōdō Kumiai Kaigi (Japan Labor Union Congress). With a Socialist-Communist split reflected in both party and union activities by mid-1946, a third force led by Yamakawa Hitoshi organized the "neutral" unions so that this group could have representation on the Central Labor Committee. The Kumiai Kaigi essentially represented elements that were committed to the political views characteristic of the prewar Center, with the *rōnō* (farmer-labor) brand of Marxist revisionism representing their basic political creed.

By the middle of 1946, therefore, the major political divisions of the prewar period had been reestablished at the national level. The trend, moreover, was to the left. From August 1946 to February 1947, the influence of the Japanese Communist Party upon the labor movement as a whole steadily increased. There were many reasons for this. The old political order had been thoroughly discredited, and a quasi-revolutionary atmosphere prevailed, a susceptibility to radical change. This was particularly true within the government itself, contributing to the militancy of the government employee unions, most of which were affiliated with Sanbetsu Kaigi. Economic conditions, moreover, were bad and growing worse. According to the statistics of the Bank of Japan, the Price Index, with September 1945 fixed at 100, reached 305 in March 1947. Over 60 percent of the average worker's expenditures was now going for food, as compared with 30 percent in the prewar era.

SCAP policy also contributed to Communist strength in certain important respects. The primary objective of SCAP in this era, as noted earlier, was punishment and reform—the eradication of all individuals and institutions that had contributed to "the old, militarist Japan," and the inauguration of a radically new order based upon the principles of egalitarianism, welfare, and democracy. SCAP viewed with suspicion most of the older moderate labor leaders because it regarded them as collaborators with the old order. Only the

Communists, after all, had a perfect anti-imperialist, anti-militarist, anti-chauvinist record. Thus, the Communists were accepted by SCAP as a part of the democratic front. Men such as Tokuda Kyuichi were moved directly from prison to such high offices as the Central Labor Relations Board.

In this era, moreover, the Communists contributed to their own strength by pursuing a policy that was essentially moderate and tactically sound. They urged support for the Occupation, proclaiming its central policies to be progressive and democratic. They dedicated themselves to making the party "lovable" and insisted that a peaceful advance toward socialism could occur under prevailing conditions. They strongly championed a United Front with "all progressive elements," thereby placing the moderates in an uncomfortable, defensive position.

These were the circumstances under which the labor movement gravitated toward the left. The leftward trend was especially evident in the issues and tactics of labor disputes. In several spectacular cases, such as the *Yomiuri shimbun* (*Yomiuri News*) dispute, the Left insisted upon making democratization or the removal of "war criminals" from management a central issue. Production control, moreover, gained favor as a dispute tactic. Ousting management, workers took over the operation of plants in the course of a dispute—"in order not to deprive the Japanese people of vital goods and services." Was this a promising route to permanent worker control?

By the fall of 1946, leftist leadership was preparing massive labor offensives that would combine political and economic objectives. The earlier May Day slogans had suggested the key desires: Overthrow the Cabinet! Establish a Democratic People's Front! Popular Control of Food! Exclude War Criminals![11] Already certain labor leaders were voicing the cry, "To the streets! The revolution has begun!" The October Offensive was the first major attempt to force sweeping political changes. The general strike was now viewed as a prime weapon on behalf of revolution. Anarcho-syndicalism,

[11] *Shiryō—Rōdō undō shi* (1945-46), pp. 937-38.

once so prominent in Japanese circles, appeared to be making a comeback, this time under Communist aegis.

As noted earlier, the abortive February 1 strike represented the climax to this era.[12] The February 1 movement was led largely by the government workers' unions affiliated with Sanbetsu Kaigi. Such unions as the Railway Workers and the All-Communications Workers served as the spearhead. In many cases, it should be noted, the wages and working conditions of government workers were lower than those of workers in private enterprise. The old bureaucratic structure of authority operating in public enterprise had broken down, moreover, and nothing had taken its place. In addition, many of the government-enterprise unions had a sizable quotient of intellectuals, especially in the leadership ranks, and this contributed to the ideological, militant position of such unions— along with the fact that confrontation with the government represented an economic necessity for public employees as well as a political temptation.

The plans of 2,600,000 workers to strike on February 1, 1947, were prevented only by an eleventh hour SCAP directive prohibiting such action. Prior to that time, however, moderate and some centrist elements within labor had begun to oppose the Left. While Sōdōmei did participate in the United Struggle Front that planned the strike, it became increasingly passive and in the end, opposed action. Its spokesmen began to speak out against the "small, extremist group" which was leading the labor movement into "suicidal policies" in its drive to foment revolution and seize power.

Before any further analysis of this era, let us examine one additional factor—the initial labor leadership of the postwar period. Fortunately, an interesting survey on this subject was conducted by a Tokyo University research team.[13] In mid-1947, some 397 unions and 1,757 individuals prominently connected with union organizational activities were studied. The basic findings were as follows: In general, postwar labor

[12] *Ibid.* (1947), pp. 5-195.
[13] Tokyo University, Social Research Group, *Sengo rōdō kumiai no jittai* [The True Condition of Postwar Labor Unions] (Tokyo, 1949).

leaders were relatively young men, having no connection with the prewar labor movement. Nearly 50 percent were between the ages of 31 and 40. *Shokuin,* or white collar workers played an important leadership role, especially in the Sanbetsu Kaigi. In broad terms, labor leadership came from middle-level *shokuin* and skilled *koin* (blue collar workers) who had a continuous work experience in their plant of from 5 to 10 years and possessed at least upper level primary schooling. However, the importance of upper educated and "intellectual" elements should not be underestimated, particularly in Sanbetsu Kaigi. Of its leaders 33 percent had had some higher school, college or university training. The comparable figure for the Sōdōmei was 11 percent.

The Tokyo survey indicated that the direct influence of external forces such as the political parties upon the formation of the postwar unions was relatively low. Only about 20 percent of the 397 unions studied were classified as "politically inspired," and, of the 1,757 individuals prominently connected with organizational activities, only 13.4 percent were found to have clear party affiliations. Most local unions were found to be a "natural" development from within a given enterprise or plant, stimulated either by the broad policies of SCAP or because of felt economic needs. Political involvement was found to have a close correlation with the level of unionism, with involvement being lowest at the local level.

About 10 percent of the labor leaders of this period identified themselves with the Socialist Party, approximately 4 percent with the Communist Party. In Sanbetsu Kaigi, about 15 percent of the leaders were party-affiliated, with 8.8 percent being members of the Communist Party, 5 percent Socialist Party members, and the remainder affiliated with other parties. About 20 percent of the Sōdōmei leaders had party affiliations, 18.1 percent with the Socialist Party and the remainder with other parties, the Communist Party having no representation. Approximately 10 percent of the Center (Nihon Rōdō Kumiai Kaigi) had party affiliations.

These statistics, of course, do not tell the whole story, and in certain respects, they can be misleading. The survey was undertaken at a time when the postwar parties were still in their embryonic stage. It probably underestimates the degree of political influence and commitment. Nevertheless, the broad conclusions are undoubtedly correct: Sanbetsu Kaigi, with a substantial proportion of its leaders drawn from intellectual or quasi-intellectual ranks, had more Communist Party than Socialist Party members at the leadership level. And while the former numbered less than 10 percent of total leaders, this was sufficient to direct union policy, especially when many of these were at headquarters level and held key posts. The Sōdōmei, on the other hand, was strongly committed to the Socialist Party, and contained no Communist leaders. It was in this union, moreover, that prewar leadership had its strongest representation.

Returning to the three basic trends noted earlier, we are now in a position to make more positive statements. All evidence suggests that while the politicization of the union movement advanced rapidly in this period, the commitment to politics was most clearly articulated at the national and federation levels. Local unions were deeply involved in the struggle to survive and only where that struggle coincided with politics (as in the case of government worker unions) was there a natural proclivity for political action. Elsewhere, a certain resistance to "politics first," and hence a resistance to Communist leadership, began to be felt at the local level. A gap existed or was created between headquarters and local, and this gap provided a natural ceiling for Communist expansion.

While Communist tactics in the labor movement contained fundamental defects that would ultimately be telling, Communist gains up to the spring of 1947 were continuous and substantial. The Communists dominated Sanbetsu Kaigi, which in numbers was the leading national federation, and they had almost complete control over such unions as the Metal Workers and Miners. Their opposition, moreover, was divided, and with a few exceptions weak. Top Sōdōmei leaders for the most part were from an older generation, lacking in the type of dynamism necessary to compete with the vigorous young leftist elements whom they sought to oppose.

International affiliations were scarcely an issue in this period, since Japan was still largely isolated from the world, and under the complete control of the American Occupation. The other political issues that had absorbed the prewar labor movement, however, had all reemerged. The broad ideological divisions between social democracy, Marxist revisionism, and Marx-Leninism were again present. The issue of a United Front was of critical importance once more. The questions of union-party relations, and political versus economic primacy within the labor movement were again being hotly debated, with the tide of battle indicating the relative strength of Left, Right and Center.

"DEMOCRATIZATION"—A NEW PHASE, 1947-1950

The second phase of the labor movement in postwar Japan began in the spring of 1947 after the failure of the general strike and culminated with the formation of Sōhyō in 1950. In this phase, a new political climate existed, product of many factors. SCAP policy underwent a dramatic change, primarily as a result of the growing intensity of the cold war. The transplanted New Deal era in Japan abruptly ended, replaced by a much more conservative program on the part of Occupation authorities. It could be argued, of course, that punishment and reform had gone far enough—perhaps too far. In any case, the new SCAP objective was stabilization—and, gradually, an alliance with the Japanese conservatives.

These trends in turn aided the industrial-commercial world of Japan in regaining its strength. There were many who insisted that organized labor had grown complacent or arrogant because it had first been handed all of its gains on a silver platter without having to fight for them, and it had then won most of its struggles in an atmosphere of acute business insecurity and weakness. To the extent that this had been true, it ceased to be so in this era. Gone was the time when labor could successfully threaten a cowed, timid, and uncertain business world. Now victories were less frequent and the costs were higher. The balance of power was tipping once again toward management.

Economic conditions greatly abetted this trend. The problem of inflation had finally been tackled. Under SCAP urging, the Nine-Point Stabilization Program was put into effect, and a period of economic tightness ensued. Japan was threatened with a serious economic recession, a threat ultimately averted as a result of the Korean War. But the new stabilization policies helped to push labor onto the defensive.

These various developments encouraged a growing cleavage in socialist ranks. The Katayama-Ashida coalition governments failed in succession, and, in their failures, produced mounting bitterness between the moderates and the radicals within the Socialist Party. Meanwhile, major changes were taking place in Communist policy. In three short years, the Communist Party moved from being an exemplary Occupation collaborator to becoming a most bitter opponent. When this period ended, indeed, the Communist Party was only a semi-legal organization, and its top leaders were all underground.

The politics of Japanese labor during this period should be viewed against the background sketched above. Three trends stand out: the failure of unification efforts, the sharp decline of Communist power in the labor movement, and the increasing involvement of Japanese labor in the political scene. Each deserves brief attention.

Attempts to unify the labor movement continued after the February 1 fiasco. On March 10, 1947, Zenkoku rōdō kumiai renraku kyōgikai, the National Labor Union Liaison Council (Zenrōren) was created, with all major unions participating. From the beginning, however, Sōdōmei took a skeptical attitude toward unity prospects and insisted upon maximum autonomy for council members. An exchange of views concerning unification between Sōdōmei and Sanbetsu Kaigi in May 1947 illustrates well the wide political separation between the two federations. Sōdōmei urged that in tackling the economic crisis, the unions make fullest use of their economic powers, and concentrate upon improving the workers' livelihood. It called for a rejection of strike "extremism," and insisted that the democratic operation of labor unions be realized. It advocated neutrality with respect to political parties, but argued that the Socialist Party should be supported since it was currently coming to power.

The response of Sanbetsu Kaigi was an appeal for the unification of the labor front through a "common struggle for common objectives." It urged that participation in the World Federation of Trade Unions be used as a mechanism for unification, along with the positive utilization of Zenrōren and advocated an unconditional union of all labor organizations without concern for differences of policy or principle. Receiving this response, Sōdōmei decided to work only for unification of the Right. All attempts at total unity on its part were abandoned. In June 1948, it left Zenrōren. Unification remained a dream, primarily because there was no way in which to bridge the significant political differences between the two major federations.

Meanwhile, a democratization movement had taken root within the labor movement. After the February 1 failure, reflection and self-criticism had emanated from certain quarters. Much of this self-criticism was directed against "extremists" who sought to use the labor movement for their own political ends, the small clique of radicals who were secretly conspiring to seize full power. By the fall of 1947, this democratization movement had been launched within most of the Sanbetsu Kaigi unions. Its objectives were to ensure democratic procedures and administration in labor unions: fair elections, wider participation in decision-making, fuller membership control over policies. The struggle against Communist domination was underway.

The battle was a complex and difficult one. Communist influence remained extensive in many unions during the 1947-1948 period. However, there were some notable defections from Communist ranks, with men like Hosoya Matsuta breaking away and leading the fight to destroy the old relationship whereby unions served merely as an arm of the Communist Party. By the spring of 1948, the democratization movement had made deep penetrations into almost all of the Sanbetsu Kaigi unions. The tide was now running strongly against the Left.

Changes in SCAP policy were one major factor contributing to the new trend, as has been suggested earlier. SCAP cooperation or involvement with Communist leaders totally ceased, and trenchant criticisms of Communism as "false democracy" began to be voiced regularly by Occupation officials. In addition, SCAP now pushed a labor education campaign that emphasized many of the key objectives of the democratization movement: democratic union procedures; collective bargaining and labor contracts; independent, dignified labor-management relations. Beginning in 1948, moreover, revisions in labor legislation were made, with substantial curbs being applied to the activities of government employees. In this fashion, one primary center of leftist strength was challenged.

By the end of 1948, Sanbetsu Kaigi was openly split, with the so-called *mindō*, "democratization," elements walking out of the 3rd National Convention in November after a resolution excluding them had been passed. Ruptures occurred almost continuously in 1949. Zenrōren, which had once represented nearly 5,000,000 workers, was down to about 2,000,000 by early 1949. Sanbetsu Kaigi, with a membership of approximately 1,250,000, was its main element. By November 1949, however, Sanbetsu Kaigi itself was rapidly dwindling, with its membership down to 760,000. Several additional factors were now abetting Communist decline. Emboldened by the new SCAP policies, Japanese management and government began to take tough measures against Communist workers and Communist-led unions. The Red Purge commenced in 1949, reaching its zenith shortly after the outbreak of the Korean War in June 1950. A large number of Communist leaders were dismissed from their jobs, thereby weakening their hold over various unions. This tactic was especially effective in certain public worker unions. In addition, the split of the WFTU and the formation of the International Confederation of Free Trade Unions (ICFTU) in July 1949 was an important stimulus to those breaking away from Communist control.

Thus, on March 11, 1950, some 17 unions representing 3,000,000 workers held a national convention to form the Nihon rōdō kumiai sōhyōgikai, General Council of Trade Unions of Japan, popularly known as Sōhyō. The formal inaugural convention was held on July 11-12, at which time Sōhyō claimed 19 unions and about 3,500,000 members. Representatives from the American CIO, the British TUC, and the ICFTU were present at this convention. These foreign delegations reflected the alignments of the new federation.

In its initial policy statements, Sōhyō defined itself as a free, democratic labor organization designed to promote the political, economic, and social status of the Japanese workers and to expedite the construction of a socialist society. It pledged full support of the ICFTU. It further asserted that it would enforce a separation between union and party functions, but would engage in political activities, cooperating with social democratic parties. Both Yoshida "reactionarism" and Communism would be fought. On the burning issue of the hour, the Korean War, Sōhyō denounced North Korean aggression, but opposed any Japanese involvement in the war. It is not surprising that the Communists bitterly denounced Sōhyō as "a tool of international imperialism."

Meanwhile, from the time of the House of Representatives elections of 1947, organized labor had been actively involved in party politics at all levels. In the elections of April 25, 1947, Sōdōmei gave full support to the Socialist Party, while Sanbetsu Kaigi aided Socialists, Communists, and other Left elements, urging always a United Front. The results were a substantial victory for the Socialists and defeat for the Communists. The Socialists polled 7,175,939 votes (26.2 percent of the total) and obtained 143 Diet seats, making them the leading party in the House, although the Liberal Party got 131 seats and the Democrats 121 seats. The Communists, on the other hand, polled only 1,002,903 votes (3.7 percent of the total) and obtained only 4 seats.[14] Understandably, the Socialists saw no need for a United Front with the Communists.

Labor participated actively in the Katayama and Ashida Cabinets, which followed the 1947 elections. For the first time in their history, the Socialists shared in power, and labor leaders such as Nishio Suehiro and Katō Kanju held Cabinet posts and other high offices. Unfortunately, however, the Katayama-Ashida era was not very successful. The reasons need not concern us here. It is sufficient to note the results. By 1948, both the Socialist Party and its union components were deeply divided over policy issues. The moderate-radical cleavage was threatening to split both the party and some of the major unions. Naturally, the Communists made every effort to exploit this cleavage.

Thus in the elections of January 23, 1949, that followed the fall of the Socialist-Democratic coalition, the Socialists suffered a major reverse, obtaining only 4,129,794 votes (13.5 percent) and 48 Diet seats. On the other hand, the Communists scored substantial gains, polling 2,984,780 votes (9.7 percent) and obtaining 35 Diet seats. A Left-Socialist splinter group, the Labor-Farmer Party, got 606,840 votes (2.0 percent) and 7 Diet seats. As is well known, this election was to mark the high tide of Communist electoral strength. Its effect, however, was minimized because it came at a time when Communist influence in the labor movement was already declining. Moreover, the Communist Party was shortly to be thrown into inner turmoil by the Cominform criticism, the resulting policy shift, and the Korean War. In any case, Communist gains in the 1949 elections were probably less a tribute to the party and more the product of a popular reaction against the Socialist Party, a protest vote that sought new channels. It is also true, however, that the policy of seeking to make the party "lovable"—a policy soon to be abandoned under Cominform orders—had very real advantages in the open political arena.

[14] For materials on postwar Japanese elections, and trends in connection with the socialist and labor movements, see Robert A. Scalapino and Junnosuke Masumi, *Parties and Politics in Contemporary Japan* (Berkeley, 1962).

In summary, at the beginning of 1950, the Japanese labor movement remained deeply divided. The moderates or Right, now represented by Sōhyō, were in the ascendancy. More than one-half of all Japanese unionists belonged to this federation. The official Center was represented by Shin Sanbetsu, a federation numbering not more than 60,000 members. Shin Sanbetsu was to join Sōhyō temporarily in November 1950 but split off again in 1952. The Left was now represented by Zenrōren, into which Sanbetsu Kaigi had been absorbed, but the Left now had official control over fewer than 700,000 union members.

The primary causes for the Left decline have already been suggested. A natural reaction had taken place against Communist "commandism" within the major unions, and also against the costly failures of Communist tactics. Once again, the doctrines of "separation between union and party functions" and "the importance of economic unionism" had a strong appeal. Also, this era witnessed a restructuring of the socio-political pressures operating in the Japanese scene. Economic recession and the resurgence of the business community pushed organized labor onto the defensive, tending to make it more cautious, or at least, weaker. The reorientation of SCAP policy and reflections of this in the policies and attitudes of the Japanese government were additional factors contributing to these ends. Finally, the international scene was conducive to political reflection, the establishment of sharper distinctions, and the isolation of the Communists. The split of the WFTU and the emergence of the ICFTU, together with the coming of the Korean War, had sharp repercussions in Japan.

In certain respects, however, the aura of moderation that surrounded this period was misleading. No fundamental changes had yet taken place in the basic position or nature of the Japanese labor movement to sustain moderation. Organized labor remained essentially a protest movement, strongly dissatisfied with the status quo. Labor leadership retained its deep suspicions of management, and these suspicions were reciprocated. The relatively backward system of managerial-labor relations that existed did not alleviate such suspicions. Antagonism between labor leaders and the conservative parties was equally powerful, and once again the existing communications system was primitive. The very structure of Japanese unionism, moreover, lent itself to extensive politicization at the top, especially in a federation such as Sōhyō.

In sum, the grievances—real and fancied—were numerous. Direct access to power was blocked. And the channels of communication that might relate labor constructively to those in power were either nonexistent or ineffective. Under such circumstances, moderation was not likely to prevail for long.

TREND TO THE LEFT, 1950-1960

The postwar Japanese labor movement entered its third phase in 1950, and remained in that phase until 1960. In the initial years, organized labor again moved sharply to the left. Then, with minor adjustments, it maintained that left position until the end of the period, with the climax coming in the titanic struggle over the revision of the U.S.-Japan Security Treaty.

What produced the new leftward trend? We have already suggested some of the most basic causes. In an immediate sense, however, the movement to the left was a natural reaction to the emerging alliance between SCAP and the Japanese conservatives. That alliance appeared to threaten the unions in a variety of ways. An "anti-socialist" bloc had been formed. Legislation regarded by labor as anti-liberal and anti-labor was drafted. A separate peace treaty excluding the Communist nations was signed. Japan moved toward military alliance with the United States and began rearmament.

These actions, encompassing both domestic and foreign policy, represented a direct affront to Sōhyō-Socialist Party views. But there were also psychological considerations. Wooed ardently by SCAP only a few years earlier, organized labor now felt threatened with abandonment unless it was willing to serve the American anti-Communist cause fully. Thus, certain proclivities of Japanese labor, implicit in its background, quickly reasserted themselves: Marxism, pacifism, and a penchant for affinity with Asia. In some respects, each of these forces was able to ride a rising nationalist tide, the natural reaction to seven years of foreign occupation.

The trend to the left began immediately after the formation of Sōhyō, and by 1953 a completely new position had been established. These years were dominated by Takano Minoru and his "peace faction."[15] The Takano line came to be that of "peace and democracy." On the international front, Sōhyō championed "positive neutrality." In theory, this meant "an active campaign for peace, establishing full and equal relations with both world camps." In practice, Sōhyō was either forced or voluntarily moved into a progressively anti-American, pro-Communist position. As an organization, Sōhyō now took a negative attitude toward the ICFTU, although some individual unions and leaders retained their affiliations. The ICFTU was condemned for supporting the separate Peace Treaty and American military bases in Japan. The Takano group strongly pushed the idea of an All-Asian Union Conference that would include both Communist and non-Communist Unions. Ultimately, Peking's active cooperation and support for such a conference was obtained, but almost all non-Communist unions remained cool. Meanwhile, Sōhyō was opening "cultural relations" with the Communist world on an ever-expanding scale. In a period when relations with the American labor movement were sharply contracting, Sōhyō delegations trooped to Peking, Moscow, and various East European centers, as well as establishing contact with certain Communist-controlled unions of the Western world.

The anti-American tone of Sōhyō pronouncements grew ever sharper. The July 1953 Convention policy statement contained this sentence, "Monopoly capital at home and abroad supported by the United States is planning to throw the

[15] For an insight into Takano Minoru, see his book, *Rōdō kumiai unei ron* [Theories on Labor Union Operation] (Tokyo, 1952). For this and subsequent periods, one vital primary source is the Sōhyō central organ, *Sōhyō*, a newspaper now available in a reduced-size edition for the first 500 issues, edited by Komori Masao, published May 1, 1960, Tokyo.

peoples of the entire world into the crucible of war."[16] A great distance had been traversed since the spring of 1950! Despite various caveats, and considerable internal opposition or ambivalence, Sōhyō "positive neutrality" in this period leaned toward the Communists.

Trends in the domestic arena paralleled those in the international scene. Sōhyō was securely in Marxist hands. Support for the parliamentary system and opposition to Communism were still proclaimed. Moderates, however, began to have doubts. Once again, the politicization of the union movement advanced sharply. Huge demonstrations and political strikes were mounted against "reactionary" legislation. Sōhyō took an ever more active role in national elections and in the Left Socialist Party. Many Sōhyō leaders, moreover, demanded a popular front with all "progressives" on behalf of "the peace movement."

The leftward swing naturally provoked opposition from within the new federation, an opposition that could not unite and hence took two courses of action. The most moderate elements—the old Sōdōmei, together with the Textile Workers, the Seamen, and the Motion Picture Workers—formed an inside group, Minrōren, and formally broke away from Sōhyō in the spring of 1954 to form Nihon rōdō kumiai zenrō kaigi, the Japanese Trade Union Congress, commonly known as Zenrō.[17] Thus after a brief period of unity (the Communist Zenrōren had been outlawed in August 1950), the Japanese labor movement was again split. Zenrō claimed some 860,000 members, almost all of them workers in private industry. Sōhyō remained the dominant labor force with about 3,000,000 members, two-thirds of whom were civil servants or employees of public corporations.

As in the prewar era, party and union cleavages were closely interrelated. Zenrō announced its full support for the Right Socialist Party, allowing Sōhyō to have a monopoly on the Left Socialists. The Zenrō policy keynoted the word

[16] *Sōhyō*, Nos. 150-151, July 17, 1953, p. 1.

[17] For primary source materials on Zenrō, see the bimonthly organ, *Zenrō*, the first issue of which was published on February 15, 1954.

"realism." It insisted that the primary function of trade unions had to be the elevation of the working man's livelihood and proclaimed the integrity and freedom of the labor movement against *all* forces—government, capitalists, or political parties. It denounced as "undemocratic and suicidal" the tendency of such unions as Sōhyō "to act as a political party."

At the same time, however, Zenrō insisted that the struggle for a democratic socialist society had to be carried on in both the political and economic arenas—"through peaceful, democratic, constitutional, legal and orderly means." This meant full support to parliamentarism and total opposition to any popular front with Communists or proto-Communists.

The Sōhyō "peace struggle" was attacked by Zenrō leaders as a part of the Communist "peace movement," and many other Sōhyō policies were declared to be pro-Communist or favorable to the Communists. Zenrō announced its support for the United Nations and the ICFTU. At the same time, it attacked militarism, McCarthyism, and imperialism. It criticized American nuclear testing in the Pacific, but was even more critical of the Communists who "want peace-by-conspiracy or peace-built-on-enslavement."

Once again, labor was divided on the historic issues: social democracy versus Marxian revisionism; union-party separation versus politics-first; parliamentarism versus parliamentarism-plus; principle before unity versus a United Front; an alliance with all non-Communist "progressive" forces versus "positive neutralism"—a policy of the open door to both camps, a popular front for peace, and pan-Asianism of a leftist type.

Meanwhile, opposition to the Takano group had been developing from within the Left Socialist camp itself. Finally, at the General Convention of 1955, the Ōta-Iwai "third force faction" won a very narrow victory over the Takano "peace faction." By a vote of 128 to 123, Iwai Akira defeated Takano for the post of Secretary-General. There was almost no immediate change in Sōhyō policies other than a stabilization of the line, but this shift in leadership was to have significance when viewed in the longer perspective. The ideological-political differences between the Takano and Ōta factions, while they might seem minuscule to the non-Marxist, revealed much about the political orientation of the two groups.

The Takano group had the full support of the Communist faction within Sōhyō. It upheld the principle of a national front, a unity among all "Left" elements, and defined Japan as an American colony, giving priority to the national emancipation of the nation as a whole from American control. There was little if any discernible difference between its basic position and that of the Communists. The Ōta group had as its chief ideological mentors such old *rōnō* Marxists as Yamakawa Hitoshi and Sakisaka Itsurō, "revisionists" dubbed Kautsky-ites by their Communist opponents. While supporting an "open door" policy internationally, championing the widest possible contacts, the Ōta group rejected any full-fledged popular front with the Communists either at home or abroad. While talking about cooperation with all renovationist forces, it threw its weight strongly behind the Left Socialist Party. Ōta and his supporters described Japan as a dependency of the United States, argued that full independence and socialism could be achieved through peaceful means, and insisted that the Hatoyama government rather than the United States had to be made the central target.[18]

These subtle but important differences did not produce any immediate changes in basic Sōhyō policy, as noted earlier. The defection of Zenrō undoubtedly strengthened the Left within Sōhyō. The Ōta-Iwai line was faced with opposition only from the Left within the organization, and, initially, the new leaders had a precarious margin. The American policies and attitudes of this period, moreover, did not provide many openings for a switch in Sōhyō policy. On the contrary, the Dulles-Robertson line tended to lead to confrontation and rigidity on

[18] The Ōta-Iwai line is effectively set forth in many places. See for example Iwai Akira, Wada Haruo, Hosoya Matsuta, and Ebata Kiyoshi, *Rōdōsha* [The Worker], The Japan Institute of Labor (Tokyo, 1959). Also, "Forum on Labor: The Significance and Issues of Trade Unionism," *NRKZ*, III, No. 2 (February 1961), 64-75.

both sides. It had its logical culmination in the Security Treaty fight.

Thus, the Sōhyō leaders continued to insist that the ideological struggle was as important as the economic struggle and to place themselves solidly in the camp of Marxist revisionism. They proclaimed themselves in full support of a class rather than a national party, maintained an ambivalent attitude toward parliamentarism, and sought to shape the socialist movement in their own image. Political involvement on the part of the main stream of Japanese labor reached new heights. To Zenrō critics, moreover, Sōhyō tactics continued to skirt the narrow edge of legality; actions of an extra-parliamentary nature involved a more or less continuous guerrilla warfare against constituted authority.

Extensive ties with the Communist world were maintained, and little progress was made in establishing a series of counterpart connections in the West. And by 1959 Ōta was asserting that the greatest problem facing Japan was that of Security Treaty revision. Within a few months, Sōhyō was deeply involved in the campaign to block the proposed revision and topple the Kishi government, a part of a heterogeneous, loosely-knit front that brought Japan to the verge of political chaos by May-June 1960.

In the decade that began in 1950, the main stream of the Japanese labor movement again moved to the Left. At home, Marxist revisionism established itself as the dominant ideology of Sōhyō leaders, and this was reflected in their attitudes and policies. Theirs was an unbending opposition to "reactionary monopoly capitalism" as illustrated by the successive conservative governments and their American allies. And in considerable measure, theirs was a philosophy of gloom and doom that always saw militarism, Fascism, and depression standing in the wings. Left Socialist Party pronouncements faithfully echoed these themes.

In the fifties, Sōhyō established itself as the leading patron and mentor of the Left Socialists. Assessing from each member a political contribution, Sōhyō leaders acquired sizable campaign chests. Funds were then distributed both to party headquarters and to individual candidates, both to Sōhyō headquarters and to individual unions. The bulk of Sōhyō support went to the Left Socialists, but some aid was given to the Right Socialists and the Labor-Farmer Party. Sōhyō patronage, however, was the primary reason for the gradual supremacy of the Left over the Right within the socialist movement. By the end of this decade, the Left Socialist Party was essentially the party of Sōhyō, a fact strongly criticized by Zenrō and by some within Sōhyō as well.

Abroad, "positive neutrality" continued to be the central theme, but in practice Sōhyō leaned decidedly to the Left, even after the advent of the Ōta-Iwai era. Between 1953 and 1960, some 1,200 labor leaders went to Communist countries and 180 trade union meetings were held between Sōhyō representatives and unions affiliated with the WFTU. One hundred and fifty WFTU representatives visited Japan and some 35 "friendship treaties" between Sōhyō and WFTU unions were signed.[19] In contrast, relations with the ICFTU were cool, and those with most non-Communist Western unions were minimal. The dream of a great Afro-Asian labor federation continued to be actively promoted, but, under prevailing conditions, it could not possibly be realized.

TURN TOWARD POLITICAL REALISM, 1960-

By the fall of 1960, a fourth phase of the postwar labor movement had begun to unfold. Indications multiplied that Sōhyō was seeking through slow and cautious steps to move away from the militantly radical position it had held for ten years, establishing a position that could more easily be defined as Center. Certain Sōhyō leaders had desired such a readjustment for some years. Now, however, conditions made it possible—indeed, demanded it. A new administration existed in Japan—and in the United States. Of the Kennedy administration particularly, Sōhyō leaders had hopes. At the same time, moreover, various weaknesses in the Communist world had been exposed: Tibet, Hungary, de-Stalinization, the Sino-

[19] "Symposium on Sōhyō's International Route," NRKZ, II, No. 10 (October 1960), 48-60.

Soviet dispute, and other events cast a long shadow over the Communist image among many of the Japanese intellectuals who directly or indirectly influenced Sōhyō politics. Finally, some cognizance had to be paid to the realities of the Japanese scene: unprecedented prosperity coupled with the problems of a dual economy, an antiquated labor relations system, and such trends as automation; the gap between leadership and the labor rank-and-file, and the precarious image of labor unions in the Japanese public mind; the weakness of the Socialist Party; and trends in world socialism, particularly in the "advanced West."

The first clear evidence of a shift came immediately after the American presidential elections of 1960, although all of the above factors played some role in the timing. Iwai had just completed an extensive tour of China, the USSR, and various East and West European centers. A joint communiqué signed by Sōhyō and the Soviet Central Council of Trade Unions had just been issued. But in preparation for the November 20 Diet elections, Sōhyō issued a number of statements sharply critical of the Japanese Communist Party, placing extensive emphasis upon economic issues and making clear its primary support for the Japanese Socialist Party.[20]

During 1961 and 1962, the trend toward realism continued, with both domestic and international repercussions. The attack upon the Communists was broadened. Sōhyō continued to speak in the Marxian vernacular on most occasions, but it took every opportunity now to differentiate its objectives from those of the Communist Party. Thus, in July 1961, it stated that, while the political struggle against monopoly capitalism had to be strengthened, the "peace struggle" or the "struggle against U.S. imperialism" should not be made the center of Sōhyō activities, and armed struggle should be resolutely opposed.

Events taking place at the 1962 Hiroshima Anti-A Bomb Convention widened the rift between Sōhyō and the Left. Angered by the Communist insistence upon a defense of

[20] See *Sōhyō*, No. 528, November 11, 1960, p. 1.

renewed Soviet nuclear tests, Sōhyō and its Socialist affiliates withdrew from the conventions. Iwai subsequently asserted that the Japanese peace movement had to be based upon the Japanese people's demands and their conditions, not dictated by minority militants. Increasingly, Sōhyō leaders talked about the necessity of protecting their organization from Communist infiltration and control, and drawing a clearer line between union and party functions. At least in theory, Sōhyō was beginning to approach the historic moderate position. Moreover, a new "democratization" movement had emerged, both inside and outside Sōhyō. Even within Sōhyō, an important group called for a "Japanist labor movement" that would cast off useless foreign accretions, and adjust more adequately to the character of Japanese society.

Meanwhile, a serious attempt was being made to achieve a truer neutralism on the international scene. Sōhyō's four peace principles—first enunciated in 1951—continued to be supported: a complete ban on nuclear weapons; no nuclear armaments in Japan; abolition of such unequal treaties as the U.S.-Japan Security Treaty; and no amendment of the Peace Constitution. Moreover, extensive contacts with the Communist bloc and WFTU-affiliated unions continued. Relations with the ICFTU, however, greatly improved despite continued Sōhyō objections to certain ICFTU positions. Moreover, Sōhyō delegations began to go to the West, and especially the United States, in increasing numbers. Symbolic of the new era was the visit of Walter Reuther, the American trade union leader, to Japan in the fall of 1962. "Positive neutrality" remained the keynote to Sōhyō foreign policy, but the content or operation of this neutrality was undergoing important changes.

By early 1963, Sōhyō, with its 4,100,000 members, held the following basic political views :[21]

1. Trade unions exist primarily to maintain and improve

[21] See the English-language pamphlet, *This Is Sōhyō—Its Principles and Activities—1963*, published by The General Council of Trade Unions of Japan (Tokyo, 1963).

the common interests of the working class, and, as such, they are "entirely different" in function and character from political parties. Of necessity, labor activities must extend to the political sphere, but a trade union "must repulse whatever control or interference may be attempted from the outside." It must not be so mixed up with a political party that it becomes merely an action group for acquiring political power. Union-party relations must be based upon a thorough recognition of the different function of each, and a mutual respect for independence.

2. The interests of the working class and those of the capitalist class are fundamentally opposed, and, for the liberation of the working class, it is extremely important that political power be secured by the workers. This must be done by constitutional means, however, and unions should align themselves only with those parties that are dedicated to achieving a socialist Japan through peaceful and democratic means. Totalitarianism either from the Right or the Left must be prevented.

3. The unification of the labor movement must be made a cardinal objective, and this should be possible even if full agreement on all issues cannot be immediately attained.

4. The key to world peace is international solidarity. Positive neutrality can enable Japan to play an important role in maintaining the peace, and the Japanese labor movement should foster an organization of African, Asian, and Latin American unions to tackle the problems common to the non-Western world.

These principles indicate clearly the current views of Sōhyō leaders on the historic issues that have confronted the labor movement of Japan. Today, Sōhyō puts increasing emphasis upon economic priorities for trade unions, without depreciating the political role that unions must play. It calls for a clearer separation of union and party, based upon the principles of mutual respect and independence. Sōhyō ideology remains deeply influenced by Marxism, but now it is a Marxism that must be considered strongly revisionist. The commitment to parliamentarism and constitutional processes has grown in the recent past, even if some of the influence in this respect comes from the Italian Communists and their doctrine of structural reform. And in the international sphere, Sōhyō seeks to combine neutralism with the idea of a "third force," a loosely-knit organization reflecting the interests and problems of the non-Western world, without the same formal structure as the ICFTU or the WFTU, but serving in some senses as a pressure group upon both.

To what extent do these Sōhyō policies accord with the contemporary position of the Right? As noted earlier, Zenrō, Sōdōmei, and Zenkanko combined to form Dōmei Kaigi in April 1962. With a membership of some 1,200,000, Dōmei Kaigi is currently the primary exponent of the moderate position. Its political position can be summarized as follows:[22]

1. The trade union is essentially an economic organization dedicated to improving the workers' livelihood. Primary attention must be given to developing union organization and administration so that unions are truly democratic and so that they can conduct successful negotiations with management. There must be a complete separation between union and party, and the latter must be liberated from such dependence upon the former as now exists in relations between the Japan Socialist Party and Sōhyō.

2. The absolute theory of class struggle must be abandoned. Conflict between labor and management is a relative matter; some interests are shared in common, hence struggle is not the only means of settling problems and some mutual cooperation is possible. The workers must not be sacrificed upon the altar of ideology or mass political struggles.

3. Unification of the labor front is most desirable but the basic political differences existing within the Japanese labor movement cannot be ignored or brushed aside. There must be no "unconditional unification." Rather, unity should be based upon the acceptance of such principles as economic

[22] The position of Dōmei Kaigi is fully set forth in recent issues of *Zenrō*, also in Iwai, et al., *op. cit.*, pp. 74-114.

706

unionism, support for the ICFTU, and complete opposition to cooperation in any form with the Communists.

4. The Japanese labor movement must commit itself internationally to close cooperation with free and democratic trade unions, as represented by the ICFTU.

Dōmei Kaigi represents a position different in degree, if not in kind, from that of Sōhyō. It preaches—and practices—an economic unionism that keeps political involvement relatively low. Moreover, in practice as well as in theory, it insists upon a high degree of separation between union and party. Its ideological commitments are squarely to democratic socialism rather than to Marxism, and it supports the Democratic Socialist Party. In contrast to Sōhyō's support for parliamentarism-plus, Dōmei Kaigi argues that respect for constitutional limits as well as rights is essential. Its views upon unification of the labor front are colored by the conviction that only those holding similar political positions can and should stand together. It is totally opposed to any popular front with the Communists, and its continues to have doubts about various policies of Sōhyō. Its international commitments are clearly with the ICFTU, but it also claims in some degree to espouse neutralism, rather than any full alliance with the West.

Finally, what are the current views of the Center, as represented by Chūritsu Rōren (800,000) and Shin Sanbetsu (57,000)?[23]

1. The trade union is a voluntary organization of workers which must make its primary concern the problems of the workshop. Unions must be independent from the power of the government, the guidance of political parties, and the management of capitalists. There must be a clear division of functions between union and party and cooperation on the basis of mutual respect and independence.

2. As long as capitalism exists, a confrontation between labor and management is inevitable. Japanese trade unions

[23] For the Shin Sanbetsu position, see *ibid.*, pp. 120-60.

will naturally seek the realization of socialism. But the ideology of trade unions should not be imposed from without; it must develop naturally, from within. The mechanical struggles of the Left must be avoided. To develop the wage struggle artificially into the class struggle is irresponsible.

3. Unification of the labor movement should take place by working out joint struggles, and rejecting the Communist unions. The Socialist Party and the trade union movement should cooperate closely. It is meaningless to debate whether the Socialist Party is a class or a national party. It is a party organized by various strata of progressive, democratic people centering on the objectives of the working class. It is and must be a party which makes the parliamentary struggle its center.

4. The postwar world has been dominated by Soviet-American conflict. This conflict is one between two different types of imperialism. Staunch adherence to neutralism is essential for Japan as the only path to peace and independence.

On most critical issues, the Center currently takes a position that leans rather more toward Sōhyō than toward Dōmei Kaigi. Still, it has some claim to the role of an intermediate. Supporting in practice a considerable political involvement for the unions, the Center ascribes to the principle that a rigid party or ideological position must not be allowed to dictate union activities. While showing varying degrees of Marxian influence, it is firmly committed to parliamentarism and hostile to any popular front with the Communists. Its approach to unification is a pragmatic one, and it displays its own type of neutralism with respect to international affiliations.

POLITICAL ATTITUDES OF UNION LEADERS

Before attempting any further analysis of labor politics in Japan, let us set forth briefly some extremely interesting data pertaining to contemporary labor leaders. Between September 1959 and February 1960, a questionnaire survey was conducted, involving some 4,132 labor leaders at local, regional, and national levels.[24] This survey covered the leaders of all the major federations, and in ratio to their strength. To our knowledge, there has been no complete tabulation of the results, but with the extensive assistance of Mikio Higa, I undertook this task. A fuller discussion of these results will be given elsewhere, but the most essential facts can be indicated here.

Let us first note factors of age, education, and birthplace. The average age of Sōhyō leaders as of January 1, 1960 was 38.7 years. We have divided the educational listings into three categories: lower (education not beyond prewar primary school, postwar junior high school, elementary vocational school, or youth school); middle (attendance at prewar middle school or postwar high school); higher (attendance at Normal School [for teachers], prewar higher school, college or university). 40.3 percent of Sōhyō leaders are in the "lower" category, 33.0 percent in the "middle," and 26.1 percent in the "higher," of whom 18.9 percent have attended a college or university. Slightly more than 25 percent of all Sōhyō leaders were born in four areas: Hokkaidō, Osaka-Hyōgo, Tokyo, and Fukuoka.

The average age of Zenrō leaders as of January 1, 1960 was 39.1. Zenrō leaders had the following educational background: 32.5 percent were in the "lower" category; 44.1 percent in the "middle"; 23.4 percent in the "higher," with 21.8 percent having attended a college or university. Nearly 30 percent of all Zenrō leaders come from Osaka-Hyōgo, Hiroshima, Tokyo, Nagano, and Fukushima.

Shin Sanbetsu and Chūritsu Rōren leaders averaged 39.7 years in age as of January 1, 1960. 40.7 percent were in the "lower" educational category; 31.0 percent in the "middle"; 28.2 percent in the "higher," with 26 percent having attended a college or university. Nearly 27 percent of the Center leaders came from Tokyo, Kanagawa, Kyoto, Niigata, and Hokkaidō.

---

[24] This survey has been published in raw-data form as *Rōdō jinji meikan*, 2nd edition [Labor Personnel Directory], compiled under the direction of Kitazawa Shinjirō, Ōkochi Kazuo, and Fujibayashi Keizō, Tokyo, 1960.

From the above facts, it is to be noted that the average trade union leader in Japan today, irrespective of the federation to which he is connected, is young—barely in his forties at present—and has had no prewar experience as a labor leader or politician. (A fair number, however, have held some political office—local, prefectural assembly, or national Diet—since the war.) Most leaders, as would be expected, come from the key industrial areas. It is interesting to note, however, that Sōhyō has a strong "northern" complexion—reflective of the mining industries of Hokkaidō and the sizable concentration of public as well as private employees in the Kantō area. Zenrō has a more "southern" orientation, being particularly well represented in Ōsaka-Hyōgo. In part, this reflects the area of historic Sōdōmei strength. It is not unimportant that Ōsaka-Hyōgo have traditionally been regarded as the stronghold of "free enterprise," whereas the Kantō region has been considered the region of government industry and the "political merchant." The constituent union members of Sōhyō and Zenrō, the geographic areas of greatest strength, and the political coloration of the two federations are interrelated factors. Shin Sanbetsu and the neutral unions, as might be suspected, have a relatively balanced north-south orientation.

The "average" trade union leader today is a white collar or skilled worker with what might be called "upper" lower or "lower" middle education. In all of the federations, however, the quotient of "intellectual" leaders is significant, averaging between 20-25 percent.

One question in the survey sheds some light upon political attitudes. Respondents were asked, "What individual do you respect most?" Only about one-fourth of the respondents answered this question, but the results are truly interesting. We have divided the answers into six broad categories of individuals: Japanese socialist leaders and intellectuals; famous foreign figures; Japanese national heroes and conservatives; Japanese liberal leaders and intellectuals; Japanese Communists and Anarchists, and Unknown. The latter category includes many so-called "cultural men," especially prominent literary figures, and it is also used for purely local personalities or unionists having no political significance, even if their identity is known.

The leading category among Sōhyō leaders was Japanese socialists, representing 38.7 percent of the total names mentioned. The leading figures of this category were Suzuki Mosaburō (mentioned 64 times), followed by Oyama Ikuo (21), Takano Minoru (20), Yamakawa Hitoshi (19), Kawakami Jōtarō (16), Asanuma Inejirō (15), and Sakisaka Itsurō (11). It is to be noted that Left Socialists strongly dominate this list. The second category in terms of strength was that of famous foreign figures, with 29.8 percent of the total. The leading foreign figures mentioned in order of frequency were Mao Tse-tung (73), Nehru (37), Lenin (22), Marx (14), and Lincoln (13). The next highest individual was Chou En-lai (5). If foreign Communists were added together, they came to 60.2 percent of the "foreign figure" category. About 22 percent could be labeled "neutralists," Western socialists, or Afro-Asian nationalists. Neither the USSR nor the USA did well. No contemporary political leaders from either society received any votes.

The next category was that of Japanese liberal leaders and intellectuals with 10.3 percent of the total. Here Fukuzawa Yukichi was the dominant figure. Following this category came the Japanese national heroes and conservatives, who accounted for 10.2 percent of the total. The famous Saigō Takamori, with 27.8 percent of votes in this category, far outdistanced others. The Emperor, incidentally, was listed only once along with such men as Hara Kei, Yoshida Shigeru, and Ōkawa Shūmei. The great bulk of individuals in this category were late Tokugawa-Meiji Restoration leaders, not contemporaries.

Representing the fifth category in size, 6.06 percent of Sōhyō responses have been labeled as "unknown." Lastly, Japanese Communists and Anarchists accounted for only 5.1 percent of the total, counting Kawakami Hajime and Yamamoto Senji who led the list. Postwar Communist leaders did very badly. The late Tokuda Kyuichi was mentioned six times and Nosaka Sanzō only once.

Perhaps there are four important conclusions to be drawn from this particular part of the survey:

1. Japanese Socialists, and more particularly Left Socialists, are the overwhelming favorites among the contemporary political alternatives available to Sōhyō leaders. They received more than one-third of the total vote. It might be argued, of course, that no one Socialist commanded great respect. Suzuki did not get as many votes as Mao, suggesting that Sōhyō leaders have not been very well satisfied with current Socialist leadership.

2. Conservatives and liberals have relatively little support among the contemporary generation of Sōhyō leaders. The votes in these categories totaled only 20.5 percent, and were cast almost entirely for historic figures.

3. Contemporary Japanese Communists obtained practically no support. There is certainly no indication that Sōhyō leaders are enthusiastic about Nosaka or other Communist Party leaders, or that a popular front with the Communists will be a demand voiced by local or prefectural leaders.

4. Support for international Communists, on the other hand, is surprisingly high, and falls mainly into two categories: votes for Marx, Lenin, and Engels, the great historic trinity (but no votes for Stalin); and votes for the contemporary leaders of Communist China, led by Mao. (It is possible that the left socialist enthusiasm for Mao diminished after the clash at the Anti A-Bomb Conference and the subsequent coolness between Peking and Sōhyō main stream leaders.) It is clear that the Chinese Communist revolution has struck a responsive chord among Sōhyō leaders. While Sōhyō is not "pro-Communist" at home, it has a certain leaning toward the Communists abroad.

5. Another factor of interest with respect to the international scene is a Sōhyō image of the world that is largely Afro-Asian in its orientation, or perhaps one should merely say, largely Asian, although there are few African leaders from whom to choose. Undoubtedly it is natural for Asians to think primarily in terms of Asian leaders and heroes. Still,

it is significant that outside of Lincoln, no American political leader is mentioned. Nor do the Russians fare better. If one excepts Lenin, no Soviet political leader is listed. (It should be noted that this survey was conducted before the Kennedy era, and also before the Sino-Soviet dispute had become a matter of public knowledge. Hence, issues of "peaceful coexistence" like the test ban treaty which undoubtedly benefited the images of both Khrushchev and Kennedy—particularly the former—could not be measured in this poll.)

Let us now look at results among Zenrō leaders. Once again, Japanese Socialist leaders and intellectuals are the first category by a significant margin, with 44.9 percent of the total vote. In contrast to Sōhyō, however, Zenrō leaders favored mainly the moderate or Right Socialists. The front runner was Kawakami Jōtarō (19) followed by Abe Isoo (16), Nishio Suehiro (9), and Takida Minoru (9). The Left Socialists got a sprinkling of votes but they were a distinct minority.

Famous foreign figures were the second highest category, with 18.4 percent of the total. Essentially the same leaders were involved as were present in the Sōhyō poll, except that the order was different. Lincoln was most frequently mentioned (10), followed by Nehru (8) and Mao Tse-tung (6). The only other persons to receive more than 2 votes were Lenin (5) and Bertrand Russell (3). Foreign Communists received 24.1 percent of the total foreign vote, with Afro-Asian nationalists, Western socialists, and neutralists receiving 35.8 percent of the total. Once again, there were no votes for Western political leaders outside of the above categories, and no votes for contemporary U.S. or USSR leaders.

The third highest category was that of Japanese national heroes and conservative leaders, with 15.3 percent. As in the case of Sōhyō, the leader in this category was Saigō Takamori, with nearly 25 percent of the vote, followed by Yoshida Shōin (5), and no other individual receiving more than 3 votes. Again, late Tokugawa-Meiji figures dominated the category. The category that followed was that of Japanese liberal leaders and intellectuals (11.9 percent). Fukuzawa Yukichi

713

had more than one-third of the votes in this category. We have designated as "Unknown" 7.1 percent of the total. The Japanese Communist and Anarchist category was last, with only 2.4 percent of the vote. Moreover, these votes were divided between Kawakami Hajime (4), Kobayashi Takiji (1), and two famous anarchist leaders of the past, Kōtoku Shūsui (1) and Ōsugi Sakae (1).

What can be drawn from Zenrō results?

1. As in the case of Sōhyō, Zenrō find their primary heroes or respected men in the ranks of Japanese Socialists. Indeed, the percentage of Zenrō votes cast for this category (44.9 percent) is significantly higher than that of Sōhyō. Moreover, the bulk of the vote was for Right Socialists. The extent to which personal predilections simply mirror current political divisions between Sōhyō and Zenrō, and the extent to which they are a primary factor in producing such divisions, of course, cannot be ascertained through the data. It can only be said that the personal preferences of Sōhyō and Zenrō leaders reflect accurately the political separation that currently exists between them. But once again, the Zenrō vote does not indicate any overwhelming favorite. Indeed, the second-highest figure, Abe Isoo, has been dead for a number of years. Only Kawakami Jōtarō, fifth in the Sōhyō poll and first in the Zenrō poll, appears to bridge in some measure the two camps.

2. Contemporary conservatives and liberals get scarcely more support from Zenrō than they got from Sōhyō. The appeal of these elements lies mainly in the past—unless we define democratic socialism as modern liberalism.

3. There was no support for Japanese Communists in Zenrō leadership ranks. The votes in this category were all for "historic intellectuals."

4. Once again, however, support for international Communists was surprising, although not nearly so great as among Sōhyō leaders. Nevertheless, Communists represented nearly 25 percent of the "famous foreign figures" category, and Mao Tse-tung was third, after Lincoln and Nehru. Moreover, as in the case of Sōhyō, it was the Chinese, not the Russian,

Communists who showed strength, along with classic Communist founders.

5. The Zenrō poll also followed the Sōhyō poll in showing a decided preference for Asian as against Western political leaders. No contemporary American or Soviet leaders were mentioned.

Finally, let us look at the results among Shin Sanbetsu and neutral leaders. The leading category again was that of Japanese socialist leaders and intellectuals, with 34.8 percent of the total, and the preference was generally Left. Leaders were Hosoya Matsuta (11), Suzuki Mosaburō (9), Asanuma Inejirō (9), Oyama Ikuo (6), and Takano Minoru (6). Very few moderates among the Japanese Socialists are mentioned.

The second category in terms of size was that of famous foreign figures, with 23.4 percent of the total. Mao got 11 votes, more than twice as many as his nearest competitor. He was followed by Marx (6) and Lincoln (5). Foreign Communists polled 49.0 percent of the total foreign vote. Again, the next highest category was that of Afro-Asian nationalists.

National heroes and conservatives accounted for 17.6 percent of the total, and again, Saigō (11) and Yoshida Shōin (5) led this category, with no other figure getting more than 2 votes. The "Unknown" category represented 10.1 percent of the total, with the Japan liberal category having precisely the same percentage (primarily Fukuzawa). The Japanese Communist and Anarchist category was last, with 4.0 percent. Once again, most of these votes went to historic intellectual figures. Nosaka was the only contemporary mentioned, and he got only 1 vote.

Almost every generalization drawn earlier with reference to Sōhyō could be applied to Shin Sanbetsu and the neutral unions, allowing for some reduction in emphasis. Again, it is clear that in terms of "figure preferences" the Center is closer to Sōhyō than to Zenrō.

As against this survey of union leaders, is there any data pertaining to rank-and-file union members? Unfortunately, we do not have the type of survey tabulated above. Several

surveys do exist which have sought to measure worker attitude toward employers, and degree of loyalty to union versus
management. As might be expected, the general results suggest that the rank-and-file are more conservative and more
apolitical than their leaders, although they are voting "regular" with much greater frequency in recent years.[25]

A Summing Up: Toward Social Democracy

There is no one central explanation for the particular forms
which labor politics have taken in modern Japan. Rather, one
is confronted with a mosaic, an intricate pattern of causes,
each of which has interacted and contributed something to
the whole.

In Japan, the modern labor movement was not government-
sponsored; indeed, it was not legitimized until 1945, and then
by a foreign occupation force. Nor have labor leaders been a
part of the establishment, even in the postwar period. Thus
organized labor has not identified itself with the Japanese
modernization process. Rather, it has functioned as a protest
movement. Psychologically, union leaders have been primarily conditioned to the role of critics, perpetually con-
demning the "crimes," "sins," and "errors" of those in power.
Marxism has served as an excellent tool of social criticism,
and thus it is only slowly and with reluctance that the main
stream of the labor movement reexamines its Marxian assumptions as these relate to capitalism, socialism, democracy,
class, war, and revolution.

Modern Japan emerged against a background of rigid hierarchy, a feudal tradition in which respect for the official was
extremely high. This fact alone made an orientation toward
State, and hence, toward politics, logical on the part of individuals and organizations in Japanese society. But it was not
merely a question of tradition. The State played an enormously
important role in the modernization process, and no Japanese
element involved ever lost sight of that fact. Through its legislative, police, and financial powers and through its foreign

[25] Concerning worker attitudes the writings of Odaka Kunio are of
particular interest.

policy, the State established the basic conditions that governed labor and management alike.

But the politicization of the Japanese labor movement and more especially, its specific ideological and policy content, was also implicit in the timing of that movement. The emergence of Japan into the world stream was such that the labor movement was born at the very end of the nineteenth century, got a second start on the eve of World War I, and reached a certain political ripeness in the decade after 1920, before it was caught in the tide of rising militarism. The basic political issues with which the movement still wrestles were all developed—at least in embryonic form—by 1930.

Even at the outset, in the period of its birth, the Japanese labor movement confronted a world in which much of organized labor had been made radical by a combination of men and events. Bakunin, Kropotkin, Marx, Lassalle, and many others vied for labor's attention. First anarchism, and then Marxism swept through the international labor movement, and Japanese labor leaders—themselves mainly intellectuals—strove to master all that was *avant-garde*. Deeply conscious of their "backwardness," they were determined to catch up. Only when their excesses led to failure and isolation did the pendulum swing back toward an adjustment to what was indigenous rather than what was foreign.

Thus, the labor and Socialist movements were born together in Japan and from the beginning were closely intertwined. They shared a common leadership, common stimuli, and, it might be added, a common fate, at least until recently. Earlier, we noted that fascinating problem of teleological insight—a capacity to see the future of one's own society by projecting it along the lines of other, more advanced societies. But this capacity can be overvalued—since there is no guarantee of identical development and the odds are against it. Moreover, it can be misused, producing an uncontrollable impatience, an insensitivity to facts unless they square with theory, and an unwillingness to move in logical sequences. All of these tendencies plagued the modern Japanese intellectual, and, via him, were transmitted into the labor movement.

The relatively primitive conditions of management-labor relations into the postwar era were also conducive to the politicization of the Japanese labor movement. In a familial atmosphere where the favor of paternalism was still strong, the choices were often between "obedience" and "dishonor," "loyalty" and "treachery." And although this paternal pattern had long been breaking down, especially in large-scale industry, the particular type of political climate connected with paternalism often lingered on: relative docility with occasional great upsurges of violence, eruptions of pent-up emotions. This so-called anarchist strain in the Japanese labor movement is in goodly measure a product of workshop conditions. The basic political position of organized labor will always bear some relation to the general pattern of industrial relations under which it operates.

Closely connected with the problem of industrial relations was that of the industrial structure itself. The Japanese industrial revolution was relatively rapid and relatively successful partially because all resources available in the society were utilized, with little waste. The modernizing oligarchy that governed Japan in the Meiji era harnessed tradition to the task of modernization wherever possible. They encouraged various forms of private enterprise, moreover, with the result that a myriad of small and medium enterprises underwrote large-scale industry and greatly abetted economic development. All of this is well known. But what was the impact of this structure upon labor unions? As noted earlier, the particular forms of the Japanese industrial structure undoubtedly played a major role in creating the enterprise union, and this in turn had an impact upon the politics of Japanese labor. At the local levels, the tasks of economic unionism were carried out; at the level of the federation, having little else to do, leaders engaged in the safe work of issuing political philippics.

In the past decade, great socio-economic changes have taken place in Japan, and now, in response to these, the labor movement is entering a new phase. Certain old changes are being accelerated and new ones initiated. The movement is away from intellectual leadership and toward skilled worker

leadership; away from impotence and toward mass organization and power; away from either paternalism or harmonism
of the older type, and toward rationalized labor-management
relations; away from highly differentiated functions depending upon the level and type of union and toward multifunctional unions at all levels; away from decentralized unionism
and toward centralized unionism.

The Japanese labor movement has begun to reckon with
certain facts that can no longer be ignored. Prosperity is real,
and the basic struggle must be one to share more fully in it,
and also to tackle some of the problems of modernization like
automation. Japan is a post-Marxist society. The primary
political issues of the future relate not to the seizure of power
by one class (as if a class could ever seize power), but the
achievement by labor of a greater degree of influence and
power. This means extensive involvement in politics: running
one's own candidates, supporting one's own party, and seeking to woo elements not in one's camp so that that party will
be victorious. Today, the Japanese labor unions—even at the
local level—are sponsoring and electing candidates. Unions
constitute the backbone of the two socialist parties, and they
are in politics to stay.

What are likely to be the political trends of the future?
Barring depression or major international upheaval, the present trend toward political realism on the part of the major
federations should continue, because it fully conforms to the
socio-economic trends of the times. No doubt, the progression
will not be in a straight line. The pendulum will continue to
swing, but it will never return to the same spot, any more
than it has in the past. Slowly, the main stream of the Japanese labor movement will gravitate away from Marxism and
establish itself as an exponent of social democracy. Gradually,
it will accept parliamentarism in deed as well as in word, and
acknowledge also that conservatives sufficiently enlightened
to support a welfare state cannot be banished to the shadows
with words like "militarists" and "Fascists," however haughty
and condescending their leaders may be in private. Labor will
remain deeply involved in Japanese politics, and in the So-

cialist Party—united or divided. It will, however, constantly increase its economic functions, and the growing interaction between economic and political functions will abet the trend toward realism.

Any broadly gauged popular front with the Communists will be ruled out. The Japanese Communists are not now, nor will they be in the foreseeable future, a significant force. At this stage, the Japanese labor movement has no reason to want a popular front with so impotent and so unpopular an element. On the international front, labor will continue to espouse neutralism, but a neutralism that leans geographically toward the Afro-Asian world and almost exempts that world from political categorization; a neutralism that leans ideologically toward the Socialist (and possibly certain moderate elements of the Communist) world; a neutralism that continues to mirror the curious mixture of pacifism, nationalism, racial sensitivity, and commitment to international participation that are all hallmarks of the Japanese labor movement. In brief, barring some unsuspected disaster, organized labor in Japan is likely to take on those forms of political expression and behavior that can be classified as symbolic of the "mature" labor movement of an "advanced" society.

LIST OF CONTRIBUTORS

MARTIN BRONFENBRENNER is Professor of Economics at the Graduate School of Industrial Administration, Carnegie Institute of Technology. He has also served on the faculties of Wisconsin and Minnesota Universities, and held appointments in the U.S. Treasury and Federal Reserve System. He is the author of *Academic Encounter*, a study of relations between universities in the United States, Japan and Korea, as well as numerous articles on the Japanese economy, and has studied and lectured at several Japanese universities.

E. SYDNEY CRAWCOUR is a Fellow in Far Eastern History in the Institute of Advanced Studies, Australian National University. He is the author of a number of articles on Japanese economic history, including "Some Observations on Merchants: A Translation of Mitsui Takafusa's *Chōnin koken roku*, with an Introduction and Notes," *Transactions of the Asiatic Society of Japan*, 8 (1962), 9-139. His hobby is classical Chinese grammar, and he once wrote a textbook on one of its more outlandish aspects. He was educated at the Universities of Melbourne and Cambridge.

ALAN H. GLEASON is Professor of Economics at International Christian University in Tokyo. His research has centered on the measurement of consumption levels in Japan, and their comparison with other countries as in his "Postwar Housing in Japan and the United States," in *Studies on Economic Life in Japan*, University of Michigan, 1964. Before coming to Japan in 1956, he was on the faculty of the University of Rochester. He received his education at Princeton University, the University of Rochester, and the Massachusetts Institute of Technology.

JOHANNES HIRSCHMEIER, S.V.D., is Associate Professor of Economics at Nanzan University, Nagoya. He is author of *Origins of Entrepreneurship in Meiji Japan* and several articles published in Japanese. He studied theology in Germany and economics at Catholic University of America and Harvard University.

YASUZŌ HORIE is Professor of Economic History, Kyoto University and the librarian of the University. He is the author of *The Economic History of Japan* (in Japanese), *Meiji Restoration and Economic Modernization* (in Japanese), and several books on special problems of Japanese economic development. He has also published many articles in English on Tokugawa and early Meiji Japan in the *Kyoto University Economic Review* since 1937. Professor Horie was educated at Kyoto University, under the guidance of the celebrated economic historian, Professor Honjō Eijirō.

DAVID S. LANDES is Professor of History at Harvard University. He is well known for his work in European economic history, especially *Bankers and Pashas: International Finance and Economic Imperialism in Egypt* (Heinemann, 1958), and "Technological Change and Industrial Development in Western Europe, 1750-1914," *Cambridge Economic History*, Vol. VI. Before coming to Harvard in 1964, he taught for some years at the University of California (Berkeley). He is President of the Council on Research and Economic History and a Trustee of the Economic History Association. In 1963-1964 he was Ellen McArthur Lecturer at Cambridge University.

SOLOMON B. LEVINE is Professor of Labor and Industrial Relations and Director of the Asian Studies Center at the University of Illinois. He is author of *Industrial Relations in Postwar Japan* and of a number of articles dealing with Japanese labor affairs. In Japan he has served as a Fulbright research scholar and visiting professor, a Ford Foundation research fellow, and consultant to the Ford and Asia Foundations. Educated at Harvard and Massachusetts Institute of Technology, he has taught at MIT, Pennsylvania State University, and Keio University, in addition to the University of Illinois, where he has been a faculty member of the Institute of Labor and Industrial Relations since 1949.

WILLIAM W. LOCKWOOD is Professor of Politics and International Affairs at Princeton University. He is the author of

The Economic Development of Japan and various articles and reports on Far Eastern affairs. Long active in the development of such studies in the United States, he was President of the Association for Asian Studies in 1963-1964. Earlier he served on the staff of the American Institute of Pacific Relations, of the wartime Office of Strategic Services, and of the Department of State. Born in China he was educated at DePauw and Harvard Universities.

JAMES I. NAKAMURA is Assistant Professor of Economics at Columbia University. He is the author of a volume soon to be published on *The Place of Agricultural Production in Japan's Economic Development*. He is also the author of a study of "The Role of Meiji Land Reform" in the forthcoming *Proceedings of the Conference on Land and Tax Reform in Underdeveloped Countries*. He was educated at Columbia University, and has also engaged in research at the Institute of Economic Research of Hitotsubashi University.

KAZUSHI OHKAWA is Professor of Economics at Hitotsubashi University, Tokyo. He also serves as chief of the section on Japanese Economy of the Hitotsubashi's Institute of Economic Research and adviser to the Economic Planning Agency, Japanese Government. He is the author (in association with others) of *The Growth Rate of the Japanese Economy since 1878* and of several other volumes on the Japanese economy and agriculture (in Japanese). Educated at Tokyo University as an agricultural economist, he now occupies himself with the wider fields of growth and development economics. He is the co-author with Professor Henry Rosovsky of a forthcoming volume on Japan's *Century of Growth*.

SABURO ŌKITA is Executive Director of the Japan Economic Research Center, Tokyo, and Special Assistant to the Minister for Economic Planning. Formerly Head of the Economic Planning Agency's Development Bureau (1962-1963) and its Planning Bureau (1956-1962), he is widely known both at home and abroad for his pioneering work in this field. His writings include *Aiji keizai no hatten* [Development of Asian

Economy], *Nippon keizai no shōrai* [Outlook for the Japanese Economy], *Nippon no keizai seisaku* [Japan's Economic Policy], *Keizai keikaku* [Economic Planning], and *Asu no nihon keisai* [Japan's Economy Tomorrow]. Born in Dairen, Dr. Ōkita was educated at Tokyo University.

HARRY T. OSHIMA is Professor of Economics at the University of Hawaii. He has contributed numerous articles on national income and economic development to professional journals. He was educated at the University of Hawaii and Columbia University. Before going to the University of Hawaii, he taught at Stanford and the University of Washington and worked for the Statistical Office of the United Nations and the National Bureau of Economic Research. On a grant from the Ford Foundation, he carried on research at Hitotsubashi University in Tokyo from 1959 to 1961.

HUGH T. PATRICK is associate professor of Far Eastern Economics at Yale University and formerly assistant director of Yale's Economic Growth Center. He is the author of *Monetary Policy and Central Banking in Contemporary Japan* and has contributed articles on the Japanese economy to various professional journals. He was educated at Yale and the University of Michigan, and held a teaching appointment at the University of Michigan before going to his present post. He also taught at the University of Bombay in 1961-62. In 1964 he was appointed Treasurer of the Association for Asian Studies.

HENRY ROSOVSKY is Professor of Economics and History and Chairman of the Center for Japanese and Korean Studies at the University of California, Berkeley, and a member of the Board of Directors of the Association for Asian Studies. He is a former editor of *Explorations in Entrepreneurial History* and Associate Editor of the *Journal of Economic History*. He has been a visiting faculty member at Hitotsubashi University and at Tokyo University in Japan. His writings on Japan include *Capital Formation in Japan, 1868-1940* and a forthcoming volume (with Kazushi Ohkawa) entitled *A Century of Growth*.

Shūjirō Sawada is Professor of Agricultural Economics at Kyushu University and a member of the special committee of Japan's National Research Institute of Agriculture. He is the author of *The Feed and Livestock Economy of Japan* (in Japanese). Other writings include *Economic Analysis on Technological Development in Japanese Agriculture, Dynamic Aspects of Regional Competition in Agriculture*, and numerous other symposia contributions and articles mainly in the fields of technological development and marketing. He received his education at Tokyo University, and was a visiting fellow at Cornell University in 1962-1963.

Robert A. Scalapino is Professor of Political Science at the University of California, Berkeley; Editor of the *Asian Survey*; and member of the Executive Board of the Institute of International Studies. He has served as consultant to the Ford and Rockefeller Foundations and to the RAND Corporation. His writings on Japan include *Democracy and the Party Movement in Pre-War Japan, Parties and Politics in Contemporary Japan* (with Masumi Junnosuke), and numerous other symposia contributions and articles. Professor Scalapino has lectured in many Japanese universities as well as in other institutions in the Far East.

INDEX

Aachen, 153

Abe Isoo, 713-14

Abegglen, James C., 648n, 670

Abraham, Karl, 156n

accounting, Tokugawa era, 35-36

advertising, 454

Africa, trade with, 480, 484

agrarian reform, compared with Germany's, 158-71, 178

Agricultural Association Law of 1899, 343

agriculture, associations, 340, 344, 422, 515; consumption levels, 414, 421-22; cooperatives, 422; depression of 1920's and 1930's, 419-21, 433; diversification, 345; equipment, 329, 333, 336-37, 455; experimental stations, 343f; farm size, 284-85, 339; fiscal policy, 353-89; France, 168-69; from 1906 to 1930, 77ff; Germany, 158-71, 178; Great Britain, 166f; income, 364, 410-19 *passim*, 449-50, labor's share, 347-48; information dissemination, 340-44;

innovations from 1880 to 1935, 8-9, 259, 325-51: agricultural production coefficients, 326-30, land and labor, 326-28, capital, 328-30; technological developments and their economic implications, 331-39, land, 331-35, labor, 335-37, capital, 337-39; incentives and leadership, 339-49, Meiji era, 339-44, interwar years, 344-49

investment, 411-15, 432; labor force, 73; land use, 331-34, 336; market economy and, 57, 73, 336-42

measurement of growth from 1875 to 1920, 249-324: concealment of arable land, 249-61

passim, 261-73; undermeasurement of arable land, 249-61 *passim*, 274-77; underreporting of yield, 249-61 *passim*, 277-309; index of production, 309-15;

Meiji era: government policies, 9, 198; growth statistics, 249-324 *passim*; fiscal policy, 353-89; agrarian distress, 364-66; productivity, 163, 354-55;

modernization, *see* agriculture, innovations; organization of, 67, 72-73ff; pest control, 333; postwar period, 74, 449-50, government aid, 550; prices, 419-21;

productivity: 9, 37, 57, 69n-70n, 90-92, 277-309, 326, 331, 334f, 394n, 410-11, 426, 432; Meiji era, 163, 354-55; postwar, 461; France, 168; Germany, 162-63; and soil improvement, 620;

role in national development, 71-76; technology, 60, 67, 72-74, 291, 294-95, 325-51 *passim*, in Germany, 164ff; terms of trade, 416-17;

Tokugawa era: 32-33, 37-42; production and income, 21-23, 25, 28; restrictions, 43

agriculture-industry wage differentials, 638

Aichi prefecture, 271; population gain, 628

airlines, ownership, 493

Akasaka Keiko, 393n, 398n, 412, 414, 420n, 437-38, 444

Alcock, Sir Rutherford, 26, 31

All-Asia Union Conference, 697

All-Communications Workers, 686

Allen, G. C., 94, 97n, 401n, 402, 409n, 418n, 420n, 421, 423n, 493n, 557

727

legislation, 620; regional planning, 624-25

Churitsu Roren, 670f, 707-09ff

civil liberties, 521

civil service, and politics, 513-16

Clark, Colin, 400n

class conflict, 144-45

coal industry, 496, 504-05; German, 158

Cobb-Douglas function, 546-47

Cockerill, 98, 106n

Cole, A. H., 205-06

Cole, W. A., 167n

collective bargaining, and wage structure, 635; post-World War II, 650-60ff. *See also* labor markets; trade unions

Cologne, 153

Cominform, 694

commercial bills, 221-22

Commonwealth, trade with, 482

communications, 60, 302, 339-40, 354, 367-71, 380n, 388. *See also* government expenditures

Communist Party, 517-18, 684-95, 703ff. *See also* labor movement, Communist role in

competition, *see* market behavior; capitalism

Confucianism, 206-07; and the entrepreneur, 242-46; and leadership traits, 196-97

consumer goods, 427, 454; distribution, 391-97 *passim*, 403-19 *passim*; imports, 562, 564; industry, 582-83; prices, 543-45, 550-51, 581n, 613n

consumption,

and economic growth: 9-10, 391-444; expansion from 1887 to 1925, 397-419, 432-33ff; consumption lag from 1925 to 1945, 419-24, 433ff; expansion of postwar period, 424-31, 433-34ff, 449;

food, 258f, 296-97, 300-03, 354, 361-62, 400-03, 453; market

economy, 465-66, 474; patterns, 4, 41-42, 51, 117-18, 261, 451-54; postwar cycles, 571-81 *passim*; rates from 1879 to 1960, 90, 92; rural, 410-19; Tokugawa era, 29-33 *passim*

contract labor, *see* kokata

Conze, Werner, 162n

cooperatives, 422, 492

corporate finance, use of external funds, 602-04ff, 611. *See also* stockholding; banks and banking

cost of living, 421

cost rigidities, and *nenkō joretsu*, 660-67 *passim*

costs, in competitive world markets, 482

cotton cultivation, 340

cotton spinning, 183-86, 202, 225-29, 501

Craig, Albert M., 137n, 140n, 149n

Crawcour, E. Sydney, 93n, 113, 114, 286n

credit, consumer, 454, 536n; controls, 473-74, 559, 606-07, 609-10, 617; expansion, 492, 537; mortgage, 536n; cyclical changes and balance of payments, 568-71. *See also* banks and banking; inflation; depression; cyclical instability; fiscal-monetary policy

Crédit Foncier, 101n

Crisp, Olga, 97n

cropping, multiple, 267-69, 323-33f

crops, commercial, 286, 340; grain, 337; measurement, 249-52ff, 277-309 *passim*; principal types, 270; restrictions, 43, 339; production, *see* agriculture, productivity. *See also* land surveys

currency, from 1868 to 1885, 61-66 *passim*; depreciation, 421, 432-33f; expansion, 545. *See also* money; credit; banks and banking

POLITICAL SCIENCE

Studies in the Modernization of Japan

This book is one in a series of volumes published by Princeton University Press for The Conference on Modern Japan of the Association for Asian Studies. The other volumes in the series are:

CHANGING JAPANESE ATTITUDES TOWARD MODERNIZATION, Edited by Marius B. Jansen*

ASPECTS OF SOCIAL CHANGE IN MODERN JAPAN, Edited by R. P. Dore*

POLITICAL DEVELOPMENT IN MODERN JAPAN, Edited by Robert E. Ward*

TRADITION AND MODERNIZATION IN JAPANESE CULTURE, Edited by Donald H. Shively

DILEMMAS OF GROWTH IN PREWAR JAPAN, Edited by James W. Morley*

Also available in Princeton Paperbacks

PRINCETON UNIVERSITY PRESS